T0260892

Mastering
AutoCAD®
Civil 3D® 2016

Mastering

AutoCAD®
Civil 3D® 2016

Cyndy Davenport

Ishka Voiculescu

AUTODESK.
Official Press

SYBEX
A Wiley Brand

SeniorAcquisitions Editor: Stephanie McComb

Development Editor: Tom Cirtin

Technical Editor: Tom Richardson

Production Editor: Rebecca Anderson

Copy Editor: Kim Wimpsett

Editorial Manager: Mary Beth Wakefild

Production Manager: Kathleen Wisor

Associate Publisher: Jim Minatel

Book Designer: Maureen Forys, Happenstance Type-O-Rama; Judy Fung

Proofreader: Nancy Carrasco

Indexer: Robert Swanson

Project Coordinator, Cover: Brent Savage

Cover Designer: Wiley

Cover Image: ©Simon Bradfild/iStockphoto

Copyright © 2015 by John Wiley & Sons, Inc., Indianapolis, Indiana
Published simultaneously in Canada

ISBN: 978-1-119-05974-5
ISBN: 978-1-119-05947-9 (ebk.)
ISBN: 978-1-119-05973-8 (ebk.)

No part of this publication may be reproduced, stored in a retrieval system or transmitted in any form or by any means, electronic, mechanical, photocopying, recording, scanning or otherwise, except as permitted under Sections 107 or 108 of the 1976 United States Copyright Act, without either the prior written permission of the Publisher, or authorization through payment of the appropriate per-copy fee to the Copyright Clearance Center, 222 Rosewood Drive, Danvers, MA 01923, (978) 750-8400, fax (978) 646-8600. Requests to the Publisher for permission should be addressed to the Permissions Department, John Wiley & Sons, Inc., 111 River Street, Hoboken, NJ 07030, (201) 748-6011, fax (201) 748-6008, or online at http://www.wiley.com/go/permissions.

Limit of Liability/Disclaimer of Warranty: The publisher and the author make no representations or warranties with respect to the accuracy or completeness of the contents of this work and specifially disclaim all warranties, including without Imitation warranties of fitness for a particular purpose. No warranty may be created or extended by sales or promotional materials. The advice and strategies contained herein may not be suitable for every situation. This work is sold with the understanding that the publisher is not engaged in rendering legal, accounting, or other professional services. If professional assistance is required, the services of a competent professional person should be sought. Neither the publisher nor the author shall be liable for damages arising herefrom. The fact that an organization or Web site is referred to in this work as a citation and/or a potential source of further information does not mean that the author or the publisher endorses the information the organization or Web site may provide or recommendations it may make. Further, readers should be aware that Internet Web sites listed in this work may have changed or disappeared between when this work was written and when it is read.

For general information on our other products and services or to obtain technical support, please contact our Customer Care Department within the U.S. at (877) 762-2974, outside the U.S. at (317) 572-3993 or fax (317) 572-4002.

Wiley publishes in a variety of print and electronic formats and by print-on-demand. Some material included with standard print versions of this book may not be included in e-books or in print-on-demand. If this book refers to media such as a CD or DVD that is not included in the version you purchased, you may download this material at http://booksupport.wiley.com. For more information about Wiley products, visit www.wiley.com.

Library of Congress Control Number: 2015946146

TRADEMARKS: Wiley, the Wiley logo, and the Sybex logo are trademarks or registered trademarks of John Wiley & Sons, Inc. and/or its affiliates, in the United States and other countries, and may not be used without written permission. AutoCAD and Civil 3D are registered trademarks of Autodesk, Inc. All other trademarks are the property of their respective owners. John Wiley & Sons, Inc. is not associated with any product or vendor mentioned in this book.

Printed and bound by CPI Group (UK) Ltd, Croydon, CR0 4YY

C9781119059745_040324

It has been a difficult year, and taking on a project such as this was a tremendous effort. So, I would like to dedicate my work to my son, Zachary, whose life was cut short suddenly and tragically last year. Rest in peace, Zac. You'll always be in my heart.

—*Cyndy Davenport*

Acknowledgments

Thanks to all of you who continually encourage and support me to achieve my dreams. Without you, this just wouldn't be fun anymore.

Thanks again to Ish for agreeing to do this again. Co-authoring a book such as this is no easy task, so I appreciate you hanging in there.

My thanks to Tom and Tom for keeping me busy with edits. Really, thanks. I couldn't believe how quickly they kept coming. And I can't believe how Richardson always finds something new to pick on after it has been edited three times! It's all good, though.

Thanks, Wiley Publishing, for inviting me back to do this. Third time's a charm!

—*Cyndy Davenport*

I'd like to thank Wiley and their editorial crew for allowing me to collaborate with Cyndy for a second year on this wonderful project. I also have to thank our editors whose orange highlighters steered this project into a good direction right from the start.

On a personal level, I thank God for another year of blessings. Being alive and healthy to embark on such an adventure is a gift and blessing from Him. Also, I thank my amazing wife and kids, who were there for me all the time. Without their support, everything would have been so much harder. I would also love to send my thanks to all my extended family here in the United States—the Breeton and in Romania—the Voiculescu and the Polocoser. I love you all!

On a professional level, I am thankful for the awesome crew at Northern Engineering & Consulting Inc. (NECI) up in the frozen Bemidji, Minnesota, who brought me into this civil engineering world and helped me grow. Thanks are in order for Tom Groll from Tom Groll Engineering, PC in Austin, Texas, an outstanding boss, who through his dedication to work inspired me to give my best in all that I do. Last, I am thankful for all the people I get to share my workday with, from the Engineering Services Division of the City of Austin Public Works Department to all the geeks of Austin's Civil 3D User Group.

Finally, I want to thank to everyone who helps and supports me on this journey through the civil engineering wonderland.

—*Ishka Voiculescu*

About the Authors

Cyndy Davenport has been working in the land development industry for 29 years in the capacity of design and the management, implementation, training, and support of land development technology. She's earned Civil 3D, Map, and AutoCAD certifications in the areas of implementation, support, and training. Cyndy has spoken several times at Autodesk University teaching classes such as "Building the Perfect Template: Making All Your Civil 3D Dreams Come True," "Diary of a Mad CAD Manager," and "Join the Part Builder Skull and Bones Society."

Occasionally, she contributes workflow solutions on her blog to the Civil 3D community (http://c3dcougar.typepad.com). She currently works for Dewberry as a visual design mentor and support specialist.

Ishka Voiculescu (Austin, Texas) is an engineer at the City of Austin Public Works with extensive experience using the Autodesk Suite products for planning, design, and visualization. He is a member of various engineering groups, an active forum contributor, and blogs at http://civildigest.com. He got his AutoCAD Civil 3D Associate certification in 2012 and is a long-time member of Autodesk User Group International.

Contents at a Glance

Contents

Introduction

The AutoCAD® Civil 3D® program was introduced in 2004 as preview software. Over the past 12 years, the AutoCAD Civil 3D series has matured from a not so functional concept to a platform used worldwide to handle the most complex dynamic engineering designs. Even though Civil 3D has assumed a strong presence in the land development and transportation markets, there are companies, teams, and individuals who must transition from other software products to the Civil BIM solution offered by Civil 3D.

We hope this book will help you in this journey. As the user base grows and users get beyond the absolute basics, more materials are needed, offering a multitude of learning opportunities. This book thoroughly covers the basics and will give you the insight needed to proceed onto complex workflows. We would love to hear suggestions from you, so feel free to contact us. Please refer to the "How to Contact the Authors" section for details.

Designed to help you get past the steepest part of the learning curve and teach you some cool tricks along the way, *Mastering AutoCAD Civil 3D 2016* is the ideal addition to any AutoCAD Civil 3D user's bookshelf.

Who Should Read This Book

Mastering AutoCAD Civil 3D 2016 was designed with specific users in mind. We expect you'll have a solid knowledge of AutoCAD in general and some basic engineering knowledge as well. A basic understanding of AutoCAD Civil 3D will not be necessary, and if you are new to Civil 3D, it is strongly suggested that you start with Chapter 1. Those who do have some fundamental knowledge can jump straight to the sections that interest them. We expect this book will appeal to a large number of AutoCAD Civil 3D users, but we envision a few primary users.

Beginning Users Looking to Make the Move to Using AutoCAD Civil 3D   These people understand AutoCAD and some basics of engineering, but they are looking to learn AutoCAD Civil 3D on their own, broadening their skill set to make themselves more valuable in their firms and in the market.

AutoCAD Civil 3D Users Looking for a Desktop Reference   With the digitization of the official help files, many users still long for a book they can flip open and keep beside them as they work. These people should be able to jump to the information they need for the task at hand, such as further information about a confusing dialog or troublesome design issue.

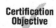
Certification Objective

Users Looking to Prepare for the Autodesk Certification Exams   This book focuses on the fundamental elements you need to pass the Professional exam with flying colors and includes margin icons to note topics of interest. Just look for the icon.

Classroom Instructors Looking for Better Materials This book was written with real data from real design firms. We've worked hard to make many of the examples match the real-world problems we have run into as engineers. This book also goes into greater depth than any other available text, allowing short classes to review the basics (and leave the in-depth material for self-discovery) and longer classes to cover the full material presented.

This book can be used front to back as a self-teaching or instructor-based instruction manual. Each chapter has a number of exercises, and most (but not all) build on the previous exercise. You can also skip to almost any exercise in any chapter and jump right in. We've created a large number of drawing files that you can download from www.sybex.com/go/masteringcivil3d2016 to make choosing your exercises a simple task.

What You Will Learn

Although this book was written to teach you how to use just about all of the tools Civil 3D has to offer, working with a good Civil 3D mentor will be invaluable. There are ways you can combine tools and develop workflows in various design scenarios that may not be obvious to you.

This book teaches you to use the tools Civil 3D has to offer, presents you with a number of options and real-world scenarios, and introduces you to the new features in the current version. If you work through the entire book, you should be able to look at any design task you run across, consider a number of ways to approach it, and have some idea of how to accomplish the task.

What You Need

Before you begin learning AutoCAD Civil 3D, you should make sure your hardware is Civil 3D capable. Visit the Autodesk website, www.autodesk.com, and view the hardware requirements, certified and recommended graphic requirements, and so on. One of the most frustrating things that can happen is to be ready to learn only to be stymied by hardware-related hang-ups and crashes. AutoCAD Civil 3D is a hardware-intensive program, testing the limits of every computer on which it runs. You'll also want to download any service packs available.

We also strongly recommend using a dual-monitor setup. The number of dialogs, palettes, and so on, makes AutoCAD Civil 3D a real estate hog. By having the extra space to spread out, you'll be able to see more of your design along with the feedback provided by the program itself.

You need to visit www.sybex.com/go/masteringcivil3d2016 to download all the data and sample files. We recommend you save these files locally on your computer in C:\Mastering\Ch# unless told otherwise.

FREE AUTODESK SOFTWARE FOR STUDENTS AND EDUCATORS

The Autodesk Education Community is an online resource with more than five million members that enables educators and students to download—for free (see website for terms and conditions)—the same software used by professionals worldwide. You can also access additional tools and materials to help you design, visualize, and simulate ideas. Connect with other learners to stay current with the latest industry trends and get the most out of your designs. Get started today at www.autodesk.com/education/free-software/all.

The Mastering Series

The Mastering series from Sybex provides outstanding instruction for readers with intermediate and advanced skills in the form of top-notch training and development for those already working in their field and clear, serious education for those aspiring to become pros. Every Mastering book includes the following features:

- Real-world scenarios ranging from case studies to interviews that show how the tool, technique, or knowledge presented is applied in actual practice

- Skill-based instruction, with chapters organized around real tasks rather than abstract concepts or subjects

- A self-review section called "The Bottom Line" so you can be certain you're equipped to do the job right

What Is Covered in This Book

This book contains 19 chapters and two appendixes:

- Chapter 1, "The Basics," introduces you to the interface and many of the common dialogs in AutoCAD Civil 3D. This chapter discusses navigating the interface and customizing your drawing's settings. You will also explore various tools for creating linework.

- Chapter 2, "Survey," examines the Survey tab of Toolspace and the unique toolset it contains for handling field surveying and for field book data handling. You will also look at various surveying relationships and analysis tools available on the Survey tab of the ribbon.

- Chapter 3, "Points," introduces AutoCAD Civil 3D points and the various methods of creating them. You will also spend some time exploring the control of AutoCAD Civil 3D points with description keys and groups.

- Chapter 4, "Surfaces," introduces the various methods of creating surfaces, using free and low-cost data to perform preliminary surface creation. Then you will investigate the various surface editing and analysis methods. The chapter also discusses point clouds and their use.

- Chapter 5, "Parcels," examines the best practices for keeping your parcel topology tight and your labeling neat. It examines the various editing methods for achieving the desired results for the most complicated plats.

- Chapter 6, "Alignments," introduces the basic horizontal layout element. This chapter also examines using layout tools that maintain the relationships between the tangents, curves, and spiral elements that create alignments.

- Chapter 7, "Profiles and Profile Views," examines the vertical aspect of road design from the establishment of the existing profile to the design and editing of the proposed profile. In addition, you will explore how profile views can be customized to meet the required format for your design and plans.

◆ Chapter 8, "Assemblies and Subassemblies," introduces the building blocks of AutoCAD Civil 3D cross-sectional design. You will look at the many subassemblies available in the Tool Palettes and look at how to build full design sections for use in any design environment.

◆ Chapter 9, "Basic Corridors," introduces the basics of corridors—building full designs from horizontal, vertical, and cross-sectional design elements. You will look at the various components to understand how corridors work before moving to a more complex design set.

◆ Chapter 10, "Advanced Corridors, Intersections, and Roundabouts," further examines using corridors in more complex situations. You will learn about building surfaces, intersections, and other areas of corridors that make them powerful in any design situation.

◆ Chapter 11, "Superelevation," takes a close look at the tools used to add superelevation to roadways and railways. This functionality has changed greatly in the last few years, and you will have a chance to use the axis of rotation (AOR) subassemblies that can pivot from several design points.

◆ Chapter 12, "Cross Sections and Mass Haul," looks at slicing sections from surfaces, corridors, and pipe networks using alignments and the mysterious sample line group. Working with the wizards and tools, you will see how to make your sections to order. You will explore mass haul functionality to demonstrate the power of AutoCAD Civil 3D for creation of the mass haul diagrams.

◆ Chapter 13, "Pipe Networks," gets into the building blocks of the pipe network tools. You will look at modifying an existing part to add new sizes and then building parts lists for various design situations. You will then work with the creation tools for creating pipe networks and plan and profile views to get your plans looking like they should.

◆ Chapter 14, "Grading," examines both feature lines and grading objects. You will look at creating feature lines to describe critical areas and then using grading objects to describe mass grading.

◆ Chapter 15, "Plan Production," walks you through the basics of creating view frame groups, sheets, and templates used to automate the plan and profile drawing sheet process. In addition, you will look at creating section views and section sheets.

◆ Chapter 16, "Advanced Workflows," looks at the various ways of sharing and receiving data. We describe the data-shortcut mechanism for sharing data between AutoCAD Civil 3D users. We also consider other methods of importing and exporting, such as XML and the new Export Civil 3D Drawing tool.

◆ Chapter 17, "Quantity Takeoff," shows you the ins and outs of assigning pay items to corridor codes, blocks, areas, and pipes. You learn how to set up new pay items and generate quantity takeoff reports.

◆ Chapter 18, "Label Styles," is devoted to editing and creating label styles. You learn to navigate the Text Component Editor and how to master label style conundrums you may come across.

◆ Chapter 19, "Object Styles," examines editing and creating object styles. You will learn how to create styles for surfaces, profile views, and other objects to match your company standards.

◆ Appendix A, "The Bottom Line," gathers together all the "Master It" problems from the chapters and provides a solution for each.

◆ Appendix B, "Certification," points you to the chapters in this book that will help you master the objectives for the Certified Professional Exam.

How to Contact the Authors

We welcome feedback from you about this book or about books you'd like to see from us in the future. Feel free to connect with us on LinkedIn:

◆ www.linkedin.com/pub/cyndy-davenport/13/61b/1a9

◆ www.linkedin.com/pub/istvan-voiculescu/2b/834/949/

You can also keep up with Cyndy on Twitter (C3DCougar) and Ishka Voiculescu (C3DIsh).

Sybex strives to keep you supplied with the latest tools and information you need for your work. Please check its website at www.sybex.com/go/masteringcivil3d2016, where we'll post additional content and updates that supplement this book if the need arises.

Thanks for purchasing *Mastering AutoCAD Civil 3D 2016*. We appreciate it and look forward to exploring AutoCAD Civil 3D with you!

Mastering
AutoCAD®
Civil 3D® 2016

Chapter 1

The Basics

If you want to be a master in anything, you have to start with the basics. Since the Autodesk® AutoCAD® Civil 3D® platform has evolved so much over the years, now more than ever you need to have a good grip on the basics. Like with every new release of the product, many features have been enhanced, while other new ones have been added.

To get familiar with the software, you will need to go through many dialogs, ribbons, tabs, menus, and icons. Some of them may be familiar, while others will be new. This chapter will help you get used to both the familiar and the new. When you learn the interface of the Civil 3D environment and understand the terminology used in the book, everything becomes easier to use. So, please arm yourself with patience and take the time to understand every part of the workflow.

Let's start learning about the interface and Civil 3D–specific terminology. Toward the end of the chapter, you'll dive into the use of the Lines and Curves commands that, coupled with the use of transparent commands, offer multiple ways of drawing accurate lines and curves.

In this chapter, you will learn to:

◆ Find any Civil 3D object with just a few clicks.

◆ Modify the drawing scale and default object layers.

◆ Navigate the ribbon's contextual tabs.

◆ Create a curve tangent to the end of a line.

◆ Label lines and curves.

The Interface

If you are new to Civil 3D, this part of the chapter is especially for you, since this section will introduce you to the terminology used throughout this book. This release introduces a new startup interface that streamlines the design process. In previous versions, on startup Civil 3D created a new drawing based on a default template; with the 2015 release, you were presented with a Start tab. Now, 2016 does both: offers the Startup tab as well as creates a drawing based on the default template. Within the Start tab, four options are present: Learn, Get Started, Recent Documents, and Connect, as shown in Figure 1.1.

FIGURE 1.1
The Startup tab
provides a quick
way to get your
design going.

Learn   The Learn option will take you to a dashboard containing videos that will familiarize you with new features and "Getting Started" basics. There will also be links to Learning Tips and Online Resources. To go back to the startup dashboard, click the Create option on the right.

Get Started   The Get Started section allows you to start a new drawing from a template that can be selected from the drop-down list or gives you the opportunity to open an existing file from a location, open a sheet set, find more industry-standard templates on the online repository, or open sample drawings that are provided through the software's installation.

Recent Documents   Recent Documents is pretty straightforward; it allows you to select and open a drawing from a list of most recently worked-on documents.

Connect   The Connect section deals with the Autodesk online experience for AutoCAD-based products. While using the software, you can sign in with your Autodesk account to take advantage of the cloud-enabled features within AutoCAD products. This section also provides a means to deliver software feedback to the development team.

The 2014 version introduced a new feature within the interface: tab-based access to all the files opened in the same working session. If you haven't experienced this feature in AutoCAD, you might be familiar with it in the latest browsers that use a tab-based display of open web pages, allowing quick access to any open web page, all in the same window. In the case of AutoCAD, this display shows the opened files. Using this feature, you can switch between the opened drawings just by clicking the desired file in the tab list. You can also switch between the opened drawings by using the old Ctrl+Tab key combination, but the tab-based file option lets you choose any drawing from the list of opened drawings without going through the whole list in the order in which the files were opened. On hovering over one of the file tabs, you will be presented with the option to switch between the Model and Layout tabs for that file. Figure 1.2 shows the new tab-based file feature. Other options related to the management of that drawing are available when you right-click the tab.

FIGURE 1.2
The tabbed file
option allows easy
switching between
multiple open files
and the Model and
Layout tabs for the
opened files.

Before we jump into the definition of the Civil 3D–specific interface items, we need to note that the overall organization of the tools and tool palettes is managed through workspaces. Once you create or open a drawing, the current workspace will be indicated on the toolbar in the top left of the application, as shown in Figure 1.3. Out of the box, the default workspace is set to Civil 3D.

FIGURE 1.3
The workspace selection lets you organize the tools of the interface to suit your needs.

The *workspace* defines the display of the available tools based on a preset understanding of which tools are necessary for the specific tasks. The Civil 3D workspace interface is tailored to display the most common tools used for civil design, while the Planning And Analysis workspace is tailored for use with geographic information system (GIS) and mapping-industry data. Two other workspaces are available that focus on the use of basic AutoCAD tools, stripping out the Civil 3D environment and leaving in place only the core AutoCAD tools. In other words, the last two available workspaces convert your environment from a civil design–based environment to a basic drafting one. Activating any of the workspaces will result in a reorganization of the tools based on the workspace's customization. You can also save the changes you make to the current workspace or customize the whole interface based on your company's preferred layout.

Civil 3D uses a ribbon-based interface consisting of tabs and panels that organize the civil design tools based on their use in workflows. If you're used to the menu-based interface of older versions of AutoCAD verticals, you can switch to it by changing the AutoCAD MENUBAR variable from the default 0 to 1. However, the use of that menu is discouraged since ribbon management of the tools is now standard in the Civil 3D environment and the menu layout may not include all the latest tools. Therefore, in this book, we will talk about the ribbon-based interface.

On the ribbon, each of the tabs and panels is associated with one or more of the major tasks in the design process. When working on the Civil 3D 2016 ribbon, the top level in the organizational chart is represented by the tabs. The default tab, which you will see upon opening any drawing and where you will spend the majority of your time, is the Home tab, shown in Figure 1.4.

FIGURE 1.4
The Home tab of the ribbon and the default configuration of the ribbon for drawings with no coordinate systems assigned (top) and with them assigned (bottom)

Don't hesitate to look at the other tabs to see the many tools available, noticing that the name of each tab is assigned based on the general function of the subset of tools available under it. Furthermore, each of the tabs will provide both Civil 3D environment-specific tools and basic AutoCAD tools, reinforcing the fact that Civil 3D is a vertical product that relies on AutoCAD as its engine. The following is a description of each tab and its purpose:

Home Tab   Contains the tools you use most often in Civil 3D, including the Civil 3D object-creation tools

Insert Tab   Provides the tools for both import and insertion of data into the current drawing. Here you will find the tools to link to outside databases, manage external references, and even manage point clouds, among others.

Annotate Tab   Provides the tools to annotate both AutoCAD and Civil 3D objects within the drawing. Also in this area, the drawing-specific settings for the core AutoCAD annotative tools can be managed along with the annotative scales. You will learn more about Civil 3D annotation tools in Chapter 18, "Label Styles."

Modify Tab   Provides the modification and editing tools for both AutoCAD and Civil 3D objects; in addition, provides access to opening the contextual ribbon tabs for Civil 3D objects

Analyze Tab   Provides the tools for performing various analyses and inquiries on the existing object data. Here you will find the tools to perform, for example, hydraulic area analysis, road design analysis, surface volumes, and estimation of quantities by means of quantity takeoffs. Also in this area is the startup for various side packages that come with Civil 3D such as the Hydraflow tools.

View Tab   Provides the tools that allow you to change the way things are displayed on the screen. Here you can define multiple viewports and customize the way objects are displayed, for example.

Manage Tab   Provides the tools for referencing data across multiple drawings via data shortcuts. Also included in this area you will find the tools to define macros, customize the user interface file, load custom runtime files, and enforce CAD standards as well as the means to import Civil 3D styles and even purge unneeded styles from the current drawing. New in 2016 will be the data shortcut manager found in this tab.

Output Tab   Provides for the production of plan sets, management of plotting, and export of data from Civil 3D to other Autodesk-based and third-party software platforms

Survey Tab   Provides the tools to manage Civil 3D survey databases. You will learn all about using and managing them in Chapter 2, "Survey."

Autodesk 360 Tab   Provides access to the cloud services managed by the Autodesk 360 platform

Help Tab   Provides access to help tools using multiple resources

Express Tools Tab   Provides access to lots of useful AutoCAD sets of tools that have been part of the AutoCAD platform for many years

BIM 360 Tab   Provides access project collaboration tools in the BIM 360 Glue cloud

Performance Tab   Provides tools for sending performance-based reports to the AutoCAD engineering team that include detailed information about what is occurring when problems are encountered

Geolocation Tab Provides access to the geolocation tools that were introduced in the 2014 release of the software. This is a contextual tab that is added to the list of tabs whenever a coordinate system is assigned to the drawing file.

When a Civil 3D object is selected, you will see a *contextual tab* appearing in the ribbon as an extension to the default group of tabs.

While these are the default tabs found in Civil 3D, their number and description can vary based on the installed add-ons and/or the user interface customization.

Please note that you can enlarge the screen area by setting the ribbon to one of its minimization states. You can access these states from the drop-down options menu located at the top-right end of the ribbon tabs, as indicated by Figure 1.5.

FIGURE 1.5
Overview of a Civil 3D environment. Toolspace is docked to the left, and the Tool Palettes panel floats over the drawing window. The ribbon is at the top of the workspace with the Quick Access toolbar above it.

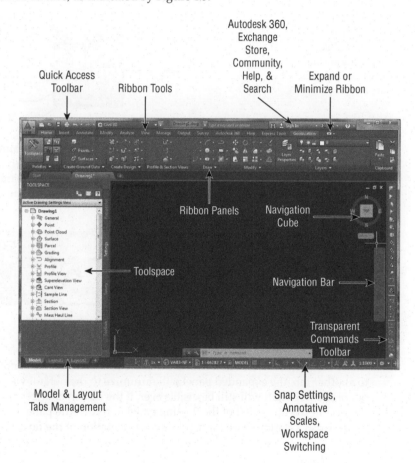

Figure 1.5 shows the typical Civil 3D work environment. Besides the ribbon, you see the Quick Access toolbar, Toolspace, the Tool Palettes panel, and the Transparent Commands toolbar, among others.

On a side note, the Quick Access toolbar highlighted in Figure 1.5 gives you access to often-used tools. By default, it includes the QNew command, which creates new drawings from the default template set in Options; it also includes the Open, QSave, Print, Undo, and Redo commands. On the Quick Access toolbar, you'll also find the workspaces drop-down menu. You can add commands to this menu by clicking the drop-down to the right of the toolbar and selecting the desired command. You can also right-click an icon on the ribbon and choose Add To Quick Access Toolbar.

The ribbon is organized by tabs. Each tab is organized by panels delineated by vertical lines to the right and the left and the panel name in the bottom area. The Palettes panel on the Home tab (shown in Figure 1.6) is where you can toggle on or off different palettes. A palette is active or visible when its corresponding icon is highlighted in blue. Some of these icons enable the display of Toolspace palette tabs, while others enable the display of specific palettes.

FIGURE 1.6
Palettes panel of
the Home tab.
The icons are blue
when the palettes
are active.

Some panels can be expanded to show additional tools. For example, in Figure 1.7, notice that on the Home tab, the Create Design panel has a drop-down arrow; if you click it, the panel will expand, and additional tools are displayed. Also, when the panels are expanded, you have the option to lock the expansion in place by toggling the pin on the bottom-left side of the expanded panel.

FIGURE 1.7
Some panels have
additional tools
that can be dis-
played by expand-
ing the panel.

This expanded view will be locked as long as the ribbon tab is not switched. On switching to another tab, the expanded panel will minimize to the default view. You can also drag a panel out of the ribbon. It will still be visible even if the ribbon changes. You can then hover and click the icon in the upper left of the floating panel to return the panel to the original ribbon tab. There's also a button there for toggling the orientation of the floating panel.

Toolspace

Toolspace defines a set of palettes that is specific to Civil 3D. We recommend that you have this set visible anytime you are working in the Civil 3D environment. If you do not see it, click the Toolspace button on the Palettes panel of the Home tab of the ribbon.

Toolspace has four tabs to manage drawing and user data, as follows:

◆ Prospector

◆ Settings

◆ Survey

◆ Toolbox

You can turn these tabs on or off by toggling the corresponding button on the Palettes panel, but it is perfectly fine to have all four displayed at all times.

Although each tab has a unique role to play in working with Civil 3D, the Prospector and Settings tabs will be your most frequently used tabs. Survey and Toolbox serve their specific purposes, which we will examine in the following sections.

PROSPECTOR

Prospector allows you to explore your drawing file for Civil 3D objects, which makes assessing object data contained in a drawing a lot easier. Any objects will be listed under their corresponding object branch. When an object branch is expanded by clicking the plus sign to its left, Civil 3D named objects of that type are listed within the branch. Some branches, such as alignments, display object type branches when expanded. You can then expand the type branch to display the named objects of that type.

The Points branch is actually referred to as a *collection*. It does not expand, but it contains objects that can be displayed in Panorama. We will discuss Panorama later in this chapter. At the top of Prospector, you will see a pull-down menu giving you the following options: Active Drawing View and Master View.

Active Drawing View displays the following branches:

◆ The current drawing

◆ Data Shortcuts

Master View displays the following branches:

◆ All Open Drawings

◆ Data Shortcuts

◆ Drawing Templates

Master View displays every drawing you have open in the active session. The name of the active drawing you are working with appears at the top of the list in bold. To make another open drawing current, just right-click its name in Prospector and select Switch To.

In Master View, the Drawing Templates branch will contain templates saved in the path defined in Options ➤ Files tab ➤ Template Settings ➤ Drawing Template File Location. You may open a template or create a new drawing with a template by right-clicking it and choosing either option from the right-click menu.

Besides the two view options, Prospector has a series of icons across the top that toggle various settings on and off. Let's take a closer look at those icons:

Item Preview Toggle This icon enables an object's graphic preview at the bottom of Prospector when Show Preview is enabled for the object category.

Refresh Icon When Master view is enabled, the Refresh icon will display. The Refresh icon is operational only when in the Autodesk Vault Environment. Clicking it will refresh the status icons for the Vault project.

Preview Area Display Toggle This icon will be active only when Toolspace is undocked. This button moves the preview area from the bottom of the tree view to the right of the tree view area.

Panorama Display Toggle This icon provides one of several ways to turn on and off the display of the Panorama window. The icon will be grayed out if there are no active warnings or if you have not yet viewed data in the Panorama window.

You can always return to the Panorama window, regardless of your warning status, by clicking the Event Viewer button from the Home tab ➤ Palettes panel.

Help Don't underestimate how helpful Help can be!

HELP USING HELP

At any time during your use of Civil 3D, you can use the F1 key to bring up the help file relevant to the dialog you are working in.

Even for seasoned users, Help provides a comprehensive reference to objects and options. The most difficult part of using Help is knowing what terminology is used to describe the task you are trying to perform. Luckily, you have this book to assist you with that!

The Data Shortcuts branch provides access to shared Civil 3D objects across the project, which are objects that can be referenced into the current drawing and updated dynamically from their source (you will learn about data shortcuts and how to work with and manage them in Chapter 16, "Advanced Workflows"). Each main grouping under the drawing name is referred to as a *branch*. If you expand a branch by clicking the plus sign next to its name, you will see the contents of that branch. Also, you will notice that some of the branches are subcategorized based on their functional class. For example, by expanding the Alignments group, you will notice the functional subdivision based on the purpose for that object. In the case of the alignments, this categorization is assigned on object creation but can be changed at any time in the Alignment Properties dialog. You will learn about this in Chapter 6, "Alignments."

Because all Civil 3D data is dynamically linked, you will see object dependencies as well. You can learn details about an individual object by expanding its group type collection and selecting the object (Figure 1.8).

FIGURE 1.8
A look at the Alignments group branch of the Prospector tab. Profiles and Profile Views are linked to alignments; therefore, they appear under Alignments.

When an object branch is selected, the bottom of Prospector displays the Item View. Clicking the plus sign next to the object branch also provides you with the list of the objects created under that object type. Using the Item View, you can edit the object's name, description, and style without having to open the Civil 3D Properties dialog. Right-clicking the object type gives you access to a number of commands that apply to all the members of that collection. For example, right-clicking the Point Groups branch brings up the menu shown in Figure 1.9 (left).

In addition, right-clicking the individual object offers many commands unique to Civil 3D, such as Zoom To and Pan To, shown in Figure 1.9 (right). By using these commands, you can find any parcel, point, cross section, or other Civil 3D object in your drawing almost instantly.

FIGURE 1.9
Context-sensitive menus in Prospector for creating new objects (left) and zooming to a specific object (right)

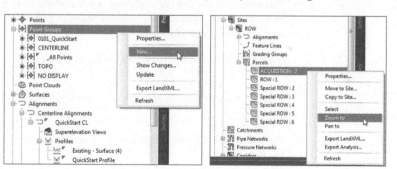

For example, if you are interested in locating a parcel named ACQUISITION : 7 using the Zoom To command, locate the Sites branch on the Prospector tab of Toolspace. Expand Proposed Site and highlight Parcels. Select the Parcel object either from the Item View or from the expanded Parcels collection, right-click, and select Zoom To. Civil 3D will locate the object and zoom to its whereabouts.

Also, note that by using the Properties option shown under the context menu for the object (see Figure 1.10, left), you can access its settings. Within the dialog that opens, you can modify the object's name, select its Civil 3D display style, and change its description, among other tasks (see Figure 1.10, right).

FIGURE 1.10
The Civil 3D object Properties dialog allows you to define the object's name, style, and definition and perform specific tasks in some cases.

As you navigate the tabs of Toolspace, you will encounter many symbols to help you along the way. Table 1.1 shows you a few that you should familiarize yourself with.

TABLE 1.1:   Common Toolspace symbols and meanings

SYMBOL	MEANING
	This represents the object or style is in use. It also appears when there is a dependency to the object or if the style has child styles. For example, you will see this icon on a surface when a profile has been created from it.
	Clicking this will expand the object branch of Toolspace.
	Clicking this will collapse the object branch of Toolspace.
	This indicates a collection. Data resides in a collection, and more information will be listed in the Item View.
	The object needs to be rebuilt or updated. This can also indicate a broken data reference.
	Civil 3D may still be processing the object, or the collection of Prospector needs to be refreshed.
	This symbol next to an object indicates that the object is data referenced from another drawing. A larger version of this icon is shown next to the Data Shortcuts branch of the Prospector tab.

HIT THE ROAD RUNNING: QUICK-START PROJECT

This exercise will give you a chance to work through a basic project. Unless otherwise specified, don't change the dialog box default options.

1. Open the drawing `0101_QuickStart.dwg` (`0101_QuickStart_METRIC.dwg`). You can download this and all other files related to this book from this book's web page, `www.sybex.com/go/masteringcivil3d2016`.

2. From the Home tab ➤ Create Ground Data panel, click the Import Survey Data.

   To learn more about survey data and workflow, see Chapter 2.

3. Click Create New Survey Database.

4. In the New Local Survey Database dialog, name the new database **QuickStart** and click OK.

5. Click Next.

   Where is this survey data stored? Find out in Chapter 2 in the section "Understanding the Survey Database."

Continues

Continued

6. In the Import Survey Data – Specify Data Source dialog, follow these steps:

   a. Set Data Source Type to Point File.

   b. Click the plus sign to the right of the Selected Files box.

   c. Set your Files Of Type option to Text/Template/Extract File (*.txt), browse for 0101_ QuickStart.txt (0101_QuickStart_METRIC.txt), and click OK.

   d. Verify that Specify Point File Format is set to PNEZD (Comma Delimited).

   e. Click Next.

7. In the Import Survey Data – Specify Network dialog, click Next.

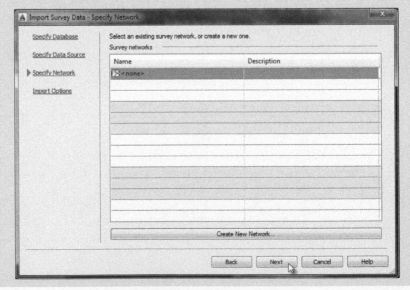

8. In the Import Survey Data – Import Options dialog, follow these steps:

a. Fill in the check box for Process Linework During Import.

b. Fill in the check box for Insert Network Object.

c. Fill in the check box for Insert Figure Objects.

d. Fill in the check box for Insert Survey Points.

e. Leave all other options at the default settings and click Finish.

See the sections "The Figure Prefix Database" and "The Linework Code Set Database" in Chapter 2 for more information on creating figures and importing survey data.

The first thing you will notice is that when the import process is complete, Civil 3D zooms to the area of the processed data. Also, did you notice that shots with the description TOPO look different from other survey points in the drawing? Find out why in Chapter 2 in the section "Configuring Description Keys for Point Import."

9. Expand the Point Groups branch on Prospector and notice that the TOPO point group that you will be incorporating in the existing surface shows an exclamation mark.

This indicates that the point group needs to be updated. To have all the point groups updated, right-click the Point Groups collection and select the Update option, as shown on the left of the following figure. After updating, the list of point groups will appear, as shown on the right side of the following figure.

Continues

Continued

Table 1.1 describes the Toolspace symbols.

10. From the Home tab of the ribbon, find the Create Ground Data panel and choose Surfaces ➤ Create Surface.

11. In the Create Surface dialog, change the name to **Existing** and click OK.

12. In the Prospector tab of Toolspace, expand Surfaces ➤ Existing ➤ Definition.

Chapter 4, "Surfaces," contains the section "Creating Surfaces," which describes the different types of data that can be used to define elevations in a surface model.

13. Right-click Point Groups and select Add.

For an in-depth look at the importance of point groups, be sure to read the section "Point Groups: Don't Skip This Section!" in Chapter 3, "Points."

14. Select TOPO and click OK.

At this point you should see contours and the surface border. See Chapter 4 for more information on creating, editing, and displaying surfaces.

15. On the Survey tab of Toolspace, right-click Figures and select Create Breaklines.

In the Create Breaklines dialog, note that you are adding breaklines to the surface you created earlier.

16. Click the Check All option and click OK.

17. In the Add Breaklines dialog, click OK.

You might get a Panorama error. You can dismiss it by clicking the check mark on the top-right of the Panorama window. See the section in Chapter 4 called "Adding Breaklines" for a detailed explanation.

Continues

Continued

18. Save the drawing.

19. From the Home tab of the ribbon, in the Create Design panel, click Alignment ➤ Create Best Fit Alignment.

You can find the many methods for creating and editing alignments in Chapter 6.

20. In the Create Best Fit Alignment dialog, do the following:

   a. Change Input Type to COGO Points.

   b. Change Path 1 Point Group to CENTERLINE.

   c. Change Alignment Name to **QuickStart CL**.

   d. Clear the check box for Show Report.

   e. Click OK.

21. Select the new alignment (the green line).

Want to know why the alignment appears green? See the section "Linear Object Styles" in Chapter 19, "Object Styles," for more information.

22. From the Alignment contextual tab ➢ Launch Pad panel, click Surface Profile.

23. In the Create Profile From Surface dialog, click Add.

24. Click Draw In Profile View.

25. In the Create Profile View – General dialog, change Profile View Name to **QuickStart Profile View** and then click Create Profile View.

Continues

Continued

26. Click anywhere to the north of the site, outside the surface area, to select the origin point for the profile view.

27. Save the drawing.

You should now see the profile in the profile view. Chapter 7, "Profiles and Profile Views," will take you through the details of these objects.

28. From the Home tab of the ribbon, in the Create Design panel, click Profile ➤ Create Best Fit Profile.

29. When prompted to select a profile view, click the grid of the profile view you created in the previous steps.

30. In the Create Best Fit Profile dialog, follow these steps:

a. Set the input type to Surface Profile (the surface profile will automatically go to Existing – Surface (4)). If the name for your surface profile is not the same for any reason, don't worry about it since there is just a single surface profile available for selection.

b. Change the profile name to **QuickStart Profile**.

c. Change the profile style to Design Profile.

d. Clear the check box for Show Report.

e. Click OK.

31. From the Home tab of the ribbon, in the Create Design panel, click Corridor.

32. In the Create Corridor dialog, do the following:

a. Set the name of the corridor to **QuickStart Corridor**.

b. Verify that the alignment is set to QuickStart CL.

c. Set Profile to QuickStart Profile.

d. Set Assembly to Shoulder Widening.

e. Set Target Surface to Existing.

f. Clear the check box for Set Baseline And Region Parameters.

g. Click OK.

Continues

Continued

33. If you receive any Event Viewer warnings, dismiss the Panorama window by clicking the green check mark in the upper-right corner of the Panorama window.

34. Save the drawing.

You can explore the objects you created by expanding the specific object collections. You can compare your drawing against the finished drawing for this exercise found on the book's web page, `0101_QuickStart_FINISHED.dwg` (`0101_QuickStart_METRIC_FINISHED.dwg`).

You will learn all about assemblies and their role in the development of corridors in Chapter 8, "Assemblies and Subassemblies." To learn about corridor creation and the meanings of various warnings associated with their creation, you will need to read Chapter 9, "Basic Corridors," and to get deep into corridor modeling, you will need to visit Chapter 10, "Advanced Corridors, Intersections, and Roundabouts."

Now that you've had your first taste of the power behind Civil 3D, you should be ready to buckle down and get more in depth with the details. This is just a sampling of the functionality of Civil 3D. You may want to learn about parcels (Chapter 5), pipe networks (Chapter 13), grading (Chapter 14), plan production (Chapter 15), or quantity takeoff (Chapter 17).

SETTINGS

The Settings tab of Toolspace provides the tools to manage the way Civil 3D objects display in the drawing and define the default behavior of the commands associated with the creation of these objects. Any annotation or text that is placed by Civil 3D is controlled by *Label styles*. *Object styles* control the way the features of the Civil 3D objects are displayed within the drawing. So if you take, for example, an alignment, the dynamic annotation of the stationing, offsets, and the like is controlled by its Label styles, while its graphic representation is controlled by the Object styles.

These settings and styles are defined and contained within the drawing itself; therefore, the need for a good template that defines these items before you begin working is obvious. When you have a standard defined for your Civil 3D drawings, these settings and styles will already be set so that you can go ahead and start your design. Chapters 18 and 19 are dedicated to the management and definition of these styles. Later in this chapter, you will learn more about templates.

Drawing Settings

As with the Prospector tab, at the top of the Settings tab you will see the name of the drawing. When using Civil 3D, it is a common startup practice to make sure that your drawing settings match the requirements of the project. To access the overall settings for the current drawing, from the Toolspace Settings tab, right-click its name and select Edit Drawing Settings from the displayed list, as shown in Figure 1.11, to access the Drawing Settings dialog.

FIGURE 1.11
Accessing the Drawing Settings dialog

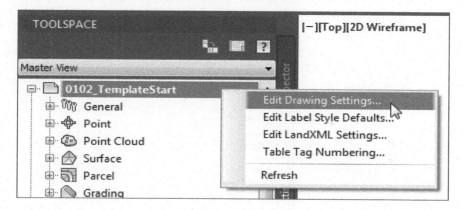

Each tab in this dialog focuses on the management of specific settings for the drawing. If the settings for the Object Layers, Abbreviations, and Ambient Settings tabs are usually the same over all your projects, you can define them from a company-wide template. Because that does not usually apply for the drawing scale and coordinate information settings, which are project specific based on the desired output or its geographic location, you are likely to visit this tab at least once for each design file.

The Units And Zone Tab

On the Units And Zone tab, you have the option to define the default measurement system by selecting the default drawing units from the drop-down menu. In the same place you also have the option to define how the Imperial-to-metric conversion is handled. For the base template that ships with Civil 3D, by default the conversion takes the International Foot. If no coordinate system is assigned to the drawing, as in the case of the stock template, then by default your drawing will have assigned a No Datum, No Projection coordinate system. As soon as a coordinate system is selected from the Zone portion of the dialog, the Imperial To Metric Conversion option becomes grayed out. This happens because by assigning a coordinate system to the drawing, the coordinate system will take care of the conversion for you.

This tab also includes the options Scale Objects Inserted From Other Drawings and Set AutoCAD Variables To Match. The Set AutoCAD Variables To Match option sets the base AutoCAD angular units, linear units, block insertion units, hatch pattern, and linetype units to match the values set in this dialog. As shown in Figure 1.12, even though these settings are enabled in the figure, the base template has them disabled in order to avoid issues that might arise based on work environments. So, feel free to experiment with them and see how they affect your data.

FIGURE 1.12
Before placing any project-specific information in a drawing, set the coordinate system in the Units And Zone tab of the Drawing Settings dialog.

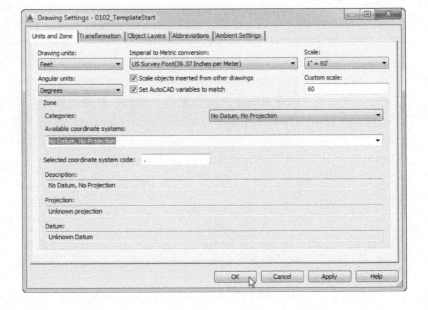

The scale that you see on the right side of the Units And Zone tab is the same as your *annotation scale*. You can change it here, or you can change it by selecting the desired scale from the annotation scale list in the bottom-right corner of the drawing window. Note that this scale is available only in modelspace.

In the Zone area of the Units And Zone dialog, if you choose to work with the default No Datum, No Projection option, then you will work using an assumed coordinate system. However, since most projects today are developed within a spatial reference, it is advisable to set the coordinate system to the one that is local to the area of your project. If your drawing file does not require the use and management of space-referenced data, then you can leave the coordinate system set to No Datum, No Projection.

Civil 3D has an extensive database of coordinate systems that can be assigned. This database is common to and shared across multiple Autodesk products. The first step in assigning the coordinate system is to select the category that your coordinate system resides in. The categories are based on geographic location. Since Civil 3D is used worldwide, its coordinate system's database contains most of the standard coordinate systems (including the obsolete ones). Once the category is selected, the collection of coordinate systems that are available within that category will be listed in the Available Coordinate Systems drop-down.

As soon as a coordinate system is selected, you will notice that the Selected Coordinate System Code, Description, Projection, and Datum areas will be filled with the specific data that defines that coordinate system. If you use a coordinate system often, a quick way to select that system is by inputting its code in the Selected Coordinate System Code section of the dialog.

Try the following quick exercise to practice setting a drawing coordinate system:

1. Open the drawing `0102_TemplateStart.dwg` (`0102_TemplateStart_METRIC.dwg`).

   You can download this and all other files related to this book from this book's web page, `www.sybex.com/go/masteringcivil3d2016`.

2. Switch from Toolspace's Prospector tab to the Settings tab.

3. Right-click the filename and select Edit Drawing Settings.

4. Switch to the Units And Zone tab to display the options shown previously in Figure 1.12.

5. Select USA, Texas from the Categories drop-down menu on the Units And Zone tab.

6. Select NAD83 Texas State Planes, Central Zone, US Foot (NAD83 Texas State Planes, Central, Meter) from the Available Coordinate Systems drop-down menu.

   You could have also typed **TX83-CF** (**TX83-C**) in the Selected Coordinate System Code box.

7. Click OK and save the drawing for use in an upcoming exercise.

Notice that once you have set the coordinate system, the Geolocation tab becomes active in the ribbon, and you can use the tools that are available under this tab.

By default, the `mapstatusbar` variable is now set to Show, which displays the name of the coordinate system on the status bar. If you do not want the coordinate system name displayed in the bottom bar, run the `mapstatusbar` command and change its status from the default of Show to Hide.

The Transformation Tab

Most survey-grade global positioning system (GPS) equipment takes care of the transformation to local grid coordinates for you. In the United States, state plane coordinate systems already have regional projections taken into account. In the rare case that surveyors need to manually transform local observations from geoid to ellipsoid and ellipsoid to grid, the Transformation tab enables access to enter transformation factors.

With a base coordinate system selected, you can do any further refinement you'd like using the Transformation tab, shown in Figure 1.13. The coordinate systems on the Units And Zone tab can be refined to meet local ordinances, tie in with historical data, complete a grid-to-ground transformation, or account for minor changes in coordinate system methodology.

FIGURE 1.13
The Transformation tab

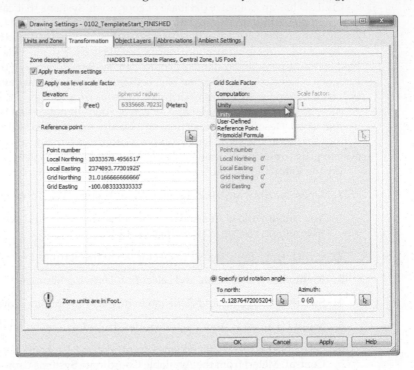

These changes can be made with the following options:

Apply Sea Level Scale Factor   This value is known in some circles as *elevation factor* or *orthometric height scale*. The sea level scale factor takes into account the mean elevation of the site and the spheroid radius that is currently being applied as a function of the selected zone ellipsoid.

Grid Scale Factor   At any given point on a projected map, there is a distortion between the "flat" measurement and the measurement on the ellipsoid. In the Grid Scale Factor area, you are presented with four options. When your selection is set to Unity, the grid factor is assumed to be 1, which basically disables the grid scale factor. In the case of User-Defined, which is the most-used option, you will provide a scale factor.

When you use this option, the Civil 3D Northing and Easting values define the localized or project coordinates, while the Grid Northing and Grid Easting values define an approximation of the grid coordinates for the point. If you choose Reference Point, Civil 3D will determine a scale factor that is based on a selected reference point. The last option is Prismoidal Formula, where Civil 3D defines a different grid scale factor for each point in the drawing.

Reference Point   To apply the grid scale factor and the sea level factor correctly, you need to tell Civil 3D where you are on Earth. You can use Reference Point to set a transformation value for a singular point in the drawing field via the pick button or the Point Number. The pick button and point number options both populate the Local Northing and Local Easting values. The Grid Northing and Grid Easting values must be entered manually.

Rotation Point Rotation Point can be used to set the reference point for rotation via the same methods as for the reference point. The pick button and point number options both populate the Local Northing and Local Easting values. The Grid Northing and Grid Easting values must be entered manually.

Specify Grid Rotation Angle Some people may know this as the *convergence angle*. This is the angle between Grid North and True North. Enter an amount or set a line to north by picking an angle or deflection in the drawing. You can use this same method to set the azimuth if desired. You can assign a rotation point or a grid rotation angle, but not both at the same time.

It should be noted that this is not the place to transform assumed coordinates to a predefined coordinate system. See Chapter 2 to learn how to translate a survey.

The Object Layers Tab

When you think about AutoCAD, you imagine lines, polylines, circles, and so on. Civil 3D adds its own specific entities, including points, surfaces, alignments, corridors, and others. All Civil 3D objects at the basic level comprise basic-level AutoCAD entities, but Civil 3D objects are dynamic elements.

Civil 3D is built on top of AutoCAD; therefore, all the objects reside on layers. When you define a basic AutoCAD object, you know the object will be created and placed in the current layer. When Civil 3D objects are created, they are placed on a predetermined object layer set up in your Civil 3D template.

Layers are found in several areas of the Civil 3D template. The first location you will examine is the Drawing Settings dialog ➤ Object Layer tab. The layers listed here represent overall layers where the objects will be created. For those of you who are familiar with AutoCAD blocks, it is useful to think of these layers in the same way as a block's insertion layer.

In the Object Layers tab, every Civil 3D object must have a layer set, as shown in Figure 1.14. It is a common practice to not have any of the object layers set to 0. An optional modifier can be added to the beginning (prefix) or end (suffix) of the layer name to further separate items of the same type.

FIGURE 1.14
For each Civil 3D object type in the list, a placement layer is defined for the new objects.

A common practice is to add wildcard suffixes to corridor, surface, pipe, and structure layers to make it easier to manipulate them separately. For example, if the layer for a corridor is specified to be C-ROAD-CORR and a suffix of -* (dash asterisk) is added as the modifier value, a new layer will automatically be created when a new corridor is created. The resulting layer will take on the name of the corridor in place of the asterisk. If the corridor is called Congress Ave, the new layer name will be C-ROAD-CORR-Congress Ave. This new layer is created once and is not dynamically linked to the object name. In other words, if you find out that you got the name of the street wrong and need to change it, you can't just change the name of the Civil 3D object.

If the layer name that you chose to use for an object does not exist in the drawing, you can create it as you work through the Object Layers dialog. To access the mentioned dialog and be able to create a new layer if needed, double-click the layer name assigned to the object within the Layer column, and if the layer is not within the list, click the New button and set up the layer as needed, including color, lineweight, linetype, and so forth, as shown in Figure 1.15.

FIGURE 1.15
After you click New, you can set up a new layer.

Make sure you have the Immediate And Independent Layer On/Off Control Of Display Components setting checked. As mentioned earlier, the layers listed here are the ones the objects will reside on. However, even though the objects reside in those layers, their display components can be configured to other layers as defined by the Object styles, which you will learn about in Chapter 19. Having this option selected means that when you turn off the layer in which an object resides, its graphic display of its components will act independently of the object. When this option is cleared, by turning off the layer the object layer resides on, all its components will be turned off, with no regard to what layer they reside on.

In the following exercise, you will set object layers in a template:

1. Continue working in the drawing that you saved in the previous exercise, 0102_TemplateStart.dwg (0102_TemplateStart_METRIC.dwg).

2. From the Settings tab of Toolspace, right-click the name of the drawing and select Edit Drawing Settings.

3. Switch to the Object Layers tab.

4. Double-click the Layer field next to Alignment and click New to create a new layer in the Layer Selection dialog box (see Figure 1.15).

5. Create a new layer called **C-ROAD-ALIN**. Leave other layer settings at the defaults. Click OK.

6. Select the newly created layer as the layer for the Alignment object in the Layer Selection dialog and click OK.

7. Set the layer for Building Site to A-BLDG-SITE. Since the layer is already present in the drawing, you can just select it from the Layer Selection dialog's Layers list.

8. Set the layer for Catchment-Labeling to C-HYDR-CTCH-TEXT.

9. For the Corridor layer, keep the main layer as C-ROAD-CORR.

   ◆ Set the modifier to Suffix by clicking the Modifier field and selecting Suffix from the drop-down list.

   ◆ Set the modifier value to -* by clicking and typing it in the Value column field for the object.

   The asterisk acts as a wildcard that will add the corridor name as part of a unique layer for each corridor, as previously described.

10. Scroll down to locate the Pipe in the Object list.

11. Create several new layers and add suffix information.

    ◆ For Pipe, create a layer called **C-NTWK-PIPE** with a modifier of Suffix and a value of -*.

    ◆ For Pipe-Labeling, create a new layer called **C-NTWK-PIPE-TEXT**.

    ◆ For Pipe And Structure Table, set the layer to **C-NTWK-PIPE-TABL**.

    ◆ For Pipe Network Section, create a new layer called **C-NTWK-SECT**.

    ◆ For Pipe Or Structure Profile, create a new layer called **C-NTWK-PROF**.

12. Scroll down a bit further and create a new layer for Structure called **C-NTWK-STRC**.

13. Add a modifier of Suffix and a value of -*.

14. For Structure-Labeling, create a new layer called **C-NTWK-STRC-TEXT**.

15. Add a modifier of Suffix to the Tin Surface object layer and a value of -*.

Your layers and suffixes should now resemble Figure 1.16.

FIGURE 1.16
Examples of the
completed layer
names in the
Object Layers
tab

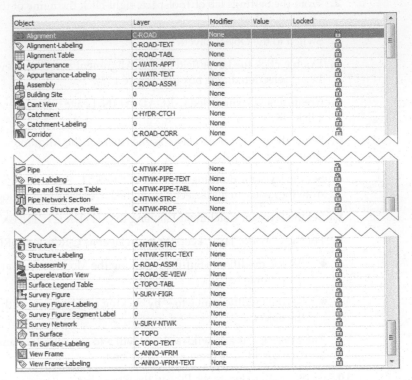

Object	Layer	Modifier	Value	Locked
Alignment	C-ROAD	None		🔒
Alignment-Labeling	C-ROAD-TEXT	None		🔒
Alignment Table	C-ROAD-TABL	None		🔒
Appurtenance	C-WATR-APPT	None		🔒
Appurtenance-Labeling	C-WATR-TEXT	None		🔒
Assembly	C-ROAD-ASSM	None		🔒
Building Site	0	None		🔒
Cant View	0	None		🔒
Catchment	C-HYDR-CTCH	None		🔒
Catchment-Labeling	0	None		🔒
Corridor	C-ROAD-CORR	None		🔒
Pipe	C-NTWK-PIPE	None		🔒
Pipe-Labeling	C-NTWK-PIPE-TEXT	None		🔒
Pipe and Structure Table	C-NTWK-PIPE-TABL	None		🔒
Pipe Network Section	C-NTWK-STRC	None		🔒
Pipe or Structure Profile	C-NTWK-PROF	None		🔒
Structure	C-NTWK-STRC	None		🔒
Structure-Labeling	C-NTWK-STRC-TEXT	None		🔒
Subassembly	C-ROAD-ASSM	None		🔒
Superelevation View	C-ROAD-SE-VIEW	None		🔒
Surface Legend Table	C-TOPO-TABL	None		🔒
Survey Figure	V-SURV-FIGR	None		🔒
Survey Figure-Labeling	0	None		🔒
Survey Figure Segment Label	0	None		🔒
Survey Network	V-SURV-NTWK	None		🔒
Tin Surface	C-TOPO	None		🔒
Tin Surface-Labeling	C-TOPO-TEXT	None		🔒
View Frame	C-ANNO-VFRM	None		🔒
View Frame-Labeling	C-ANNO-VFRM-TEXT	None		🔒

16. Click to place a check mark next to Immediate And Independent Layer On/Off Control Of Display Components.

As described previously, this setting will allow you to use the On/Off toggle in the layer manager to work with Civil 3D objects.

17. Click Apply and then OK.

18. Save the drawings.

You can check your finished drawings against the completed file that can be downloaded from the book's web page. The file you will be looking for is `0102_TemplateStart_FINISHED.dwg` (`0102_TemplateStart_METRIC_FINISHED.dwg`).

The Abbreviations Tab

When you add labels to certain objects, Civil 3D automatically uses the abbreviations assigned in this tab to indicate geometry features. For example, left is L, and right is R. Figure 1.17 shows a sampling of customizable abbreviations.

FIGURE 1.17
Features are
customizable
down to the
letter on the
Abbreviations
tab.

Civil 3D uses industry-standard abbreviations wherever they are found. If necessary, you can easily change VPI to PVI for Point of Vertical Intersection. In most cases, changing an abbreviation is as simple as clicking in the Value field and typing a new one. You might notice that most of the abbreviations are simply defined, but some of them are defined by using macros, as in the case of the Alignment Geometry Point Entity Data. You will find that these macros are widely used in the naming conventions for the Civil 3D objects.

The Ambient Settings Tab

Examine the settings in the Ambient Settings tab to see what can be set here. The main options you'll want to adjust are in the General category, and the display precision settings are in the subsequent categories. You will also want to visit the Angle and Direction categories to verify the format of the angles.

The level of precision that you see in this dialog does not change the precision in labels. What you see here is the number of decimal places reported to you in various dialog boxes.

Becoming familiar with the way this tab works will help you further down the line because almost every other settings dialog box in the program works like the one shown in Figure 1.18.

FIGURE 1.18
Ambient
Settings at the
main drawing
level

You can set the following options in the General category:

Plotted Unit Display Type   Civil 3D knows you want to plot at the end of the day. In this case, it's asking how you would like your plotted units measured. For example, would you like that bit of text to have a height of 0.25" or ¼"? In the civil engineering world there is mostly a consensus on the use of decimal units. For example, many people who used Land Desktop before Civil 3D are comfortable with the Leroy method of text heights (L80, L100, L140, and so on), so the decimal option is an obvious choice.

Set AutoCAD Units   This option specifies whether Civil 3D should attempt to match AutoCAD drawing units, as specified on the Units And Zone tab. This setting is specified on the Units And Zone tab but is displayed here for reference so you can lock it if desired.

Save Command Changes To Settings   Set this to Yes. This setting is incredibly powerful but a secret to almost everyone. By setting it to Yes, you ensure that your changes to commands will be remembered from use to use. This means if you make changes to a command during use, the next time you call that Civil 3D command, you won't have to make the same changes. By setting it to Yes, you will save yourself the frustration of setting it over and over again.

Show Event Viewer   Event Viewer is the main Civil 3D feedback mechanism, especially when things go wrong. Event Viewer uses the Panorama interface to display warnings such as when a surface contains crossing breaklines. Event Viewer will pop up with informational messages as well. If you have multiple monitors, it is a good idea to leave Panorama on but set aside for review.

Show Tooltips   One of the cool features that people remark on when they first use Civil 3D is the small pop-up that displays relevant design information when the cursor is paused on the screen. If the cursor is paused over an object, it will display some basic properties about that object. If it is paused in a blank space on the screen, depending on the Civil 3D objects present in the drawing, it can provide horizontal and/or vertical data of the position of the cursor relative to those objects or within the definition area of the object. For example, for alignments it can provide name, station, and offsets of the cursor relative to all the alignments in the drawing as long as the cursor position from the alignments is perpendicular; for a surface, it can provide the name and the elevation of the point the cursor is placed over.

Once a drawing gets complex, the amount of data displayed in the tooltip can be overwhelming; therefore, Civil 3D offers the option to turn off these tooltips universally with this setting. If you want to micromanage these tooltips, then you have the option to toggle the tooltip display for each Civil 3D object individually by accessing the toggle found in the Information tab of the Properties dialog for those objects.

Imperial To Metric Conversion   This setting displays the conversion method specified on the Units And Zone tab. The two options are US Survey Foot and International Foot. This setting is specified on the Units And Zone tab but is displayed here for reference so you can lock it if desired.

New Entity Tooltip State   This setting controls whether the tooltip is turned on at the object level for new Civil 3D objects. If you change this setting to Off partway through a project, the tooltip will not be displayed for any Civil 3D objects created after the change. Of course, you can go back to each of the objects and enable the tooltip if necessary.

Driving Direction   This specifies the side of the road that forward-moving vehicles use for travel. This setting is important in terms of curb returns and intersection design.

Drawing Unit, Drawing Scale, and Scale Inserted Objects   These settings are specified on the Units And Zone tab but are displayed here for reference and so that you can lock them if desired.

Independent Layer On   This is the same control that is set on the Object Layers tab. Yes is the recommended setting, as described previously.

Moving down to the Direction category, you have the following choices:

Unit   Degree, Radian, and Grad

Precision   0 through 8 decimal places

Rounding Round Normal, Round Up, and Truncate

Format Decimal, DD°MM' SS.SS", DD°MM'SS.SS" (Spaced) and DD.MMSSSS (decimal dms)

In most cases, people want to display DD°MM'SS.SS". Also, this setting controls how directions are entered at the command line.

Direction Short Name (spaced or unspaced) and Long Name (spaced or unspaced)

Capitalization You can preserve case or force uppercase, lowercase, or title caps.

Sign Gives you a choice of how negative numbers are displayed. You can use a minus sign to denote negative numbers only, use a set of parentheses to denote a negative, or use a sign regardless of value. The latter option will show a plus for positive values and a minus for negative values.

Measurement Type Bearings, North Azimuth, and South Azimuth

Bearing Quadrant This should be left at the industry standard: 1 – NE, 2 – SE, 3 – SW, 4 – NW.

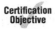
Certification
Objective
When you're using the Bearing Distance transparent command, for example, these settings control how you input your quadrant, your bearing, and the number of decimal places in your distance.

Besides the Direction category, you can explore the other categories, such as Angle, Lat Long, and Coordinate, and customize the settings to how you work.

At the bottom of the Ambient Settings tab is a Transparent Commands category. These settings control how (or if) you're prompted for the following information:

Prompt For 3D Points Controls whether you're asked to provide a z elevation after x and y have been located

Prompt For Y Before X For transparent commands that require x and y values, this setting controls whether you're prompted for the y-coordinate before the x-coordinate. Most users prefer this value set to False so they're prompted for an x-coordinate and then a y-coordinate.

Prompt For Easting Then Northing For transparent commands that require Northing and Easting values, this setting controls whether you're prompted for Easting first and Northing second. Most users prefer this value set to False so they're prompted for Northing first and then Easting.

Prompt For Longitude Then Latitude For transparent commands that require Longitude and Latitude values, this setting controls whether you're prompted for Longitude first and Latitude second. Most users prefer this value set to False so they're prompted for Latitude and then Longitude.

The settings that are applied here can be changed both at the drawing level and at the object level. For example, you may typically want elevation to be shown to two decimal places, but when looking at surface elevations, you might want just one. The Override and Child Override columns give you feedback about these types of changes (see Figure 1.19).

FIGURE 1.19
The Child Override indicator in the Time, Distance, and Elevation values

Property	Value	Override	Child Override	Lock
⊞ General				
⊞ Degree of Curvature				
⊞ Labeling				
⊟ Time				
Unit	min			🔓
Precision	3		⬇	🔓
Rounding	round normal			🔓
⊞ Unitless				
⊟ Distance				
Unit	meter			🔓
Precision	3		⬇	🔓
Rounding	round normal			🔓
Sign	sign negative '-'			🔓
⊞ Dimension				
⊞ Coordinate				
⊞ Grid Coordinate				
⊟ Elevation				
Unit	meter			🔓
Precision	3		⬇	🔓
Rounding	round normal			🔓
Sign	sign negative '-'			🔓

The Override column shows whether the current setting is overriding something higher up. Because you're at the Drawing Settings level, these are clear. However, the Child Override column displays a down arrow, indicating that one of the objects in the drawing has overridden this setting. You can check child overrides by accessing the Feature Settings of an object such as a surface (see Figure 1.20, left) and looking for a filled Override check box (see Figure 1.20, right).

FIGURE 1.20
The Surface Edit Feature Settings and the Override indicator

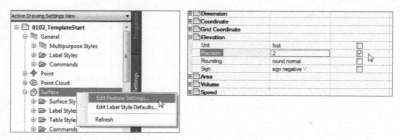

Notice that in this dialog, the box for the Precision setting is checked in the Override column. This indicates that you're overriding the settings mentioned earlier, and it's a good alert that things have changed from the general drawing settings to this object-level setting.

But what if you don't want to allow those changes? Each settings dialog includes one more column: Lock. At any level, you can lock a setting, graying it out for lower levels. This can be handy for keeping users from changing settings at the lower level that perhaps should be changed at a drawing level, such as sign or rounding methods.

SURVEY

The Survey tab of Toolspace is where survey settings, equipment settings, linework code sets, and figure prefix database settings are controlled. You can toggle this tab off and on by using the corresponding button under the ribbon's Home tab ➤ Palettes panel. Surveying is an essential part of land-development projects. Because of the complex nature of this tab, all of Chapter 2 is devoted to it.

TOOLBOX

The Toolbox tab of Toolspace is a launching point for add-ons and reporting functions. To display the Toolbox, from the Home tab of the ribbon, under the Palettes panel you can find the Toolbox icon to enable/disable the tab. The location of this icon was shown previously in Figure 1.6. Out of the box, the Toolbox contains reporting tools created by Autodesk, but you can expand its functionality to include your own macros or reports. The buttons on the top of the Toolbox, shown in Figure 1.21, allow you to customize the report settings and add new content. If you are an Autodesk® Subscription customer, here is where you will find lots of the add-ons released for subscription customers only.

FIGURE 1.21
The Toolbox
with the
Edit Toolbox
Content icon
highlighted

Panorama

The Panorama window is the Civil 3D feedback and tabular editing mechanism. It's designed to be a common interface for a number of different Civil 3D–related tasks, and you can use it, for example, to provide input in the creation of profile views, to edit pipe or structure information, or to run basic volume analysis between two surfaces. For an example of Panorama in action, open it by going to the Home tab ➤ Palettes panel flyout and clicking the Event Viewer icon. You'll explore and use Panorama more during this book's discussion of specific objects and tasks.

Contextual Ribbon Tab

As with AutoCAD, the ribbon is the primary interface for accessing Civil 3D commands and features. When you select an AutoCAD Civil 3D object, the ribbon displays commands and features related to that object in a *contextual tab*. If several object types are selected, the Multiple contextual tab is displayed. Use the following procedure to familiarize yourself with the contextual tab of the ribbon:

1. Open 0103_Example.dwg (0103_Example_METRIC.dwg), which you will find at www .sybex.com/go/masteringcivil3d2016.

2. Select the parcel label reading Acquisition : 7.

   Notice in the Parcel contextual tab that the Labels & Tables, General Tools, Modify, and Launch Pad panels are displayed, as shown in Figure 1.22.

FIGURE 1.22
The Parcels
contextual
tab within the
ribbon

3. With the Parcel still selected, click a parcel line and notice the display of the Multiple contextual tab (Figure 1.23).

FIGURE 1.23
When more
than one object
is selected,
the Multiple
contextual tab
appears.

4. Use the Esc key to cancel all selections.

5. Reselect a parcel by clicking one of the numeric labels.

6. Select the down arrow next to the Modify panel name.

7. Click the pin at the bottom-left corner of the panel to keep it open.

8. Select the Properties command in the General Tools panel to open the AutoCAD Properties palette.

   Notice that the Modify panel remains open and pinned until the current selection set changes.

> **STYLES AND MORE STYLES**
>
> Civil 3D uses *styles* to define the graphic display of its objects and labels. Styles control every-thing from which layer your surface contours will be displayed on to the number of decimal places displayed in a label.
>
> Civil 3D has an extensive number of options when it comes to how you want your design elements to look. It is easy to get bogged down in the intricacies of object and label style creation. For this reason, within this book the management and definition of styles have their own chapters. Before getting deep into style management, it is desirable to learn and understand the functionality of the Civil 3D environment. Once you have an understanding of how the tools operate, you can then define how your designs are represented graphically.
>
> In this chapter and throughout the book, you will be using styles that have already been created for you. For an in-depth look at styles, refer to Chapter 18 and Chapter 19.

Civil 3D Templates

Styles and settings should be defined within your template. Some people manage to have all the settings and styles defined within a single file, while others take the approach of separating the templates based on the type of projects they deal with. Therefore, we assume your template will have all the styles you need for the type of project you are working on. If you find you are constantly changing style settings, you should reexamine your workflow.

When starting a project or continuing a project from an outside source, it is important to start with a Civil 3D template file. You will find all the information you need on customizing the template to have the desired styles for both objects and annotations in Chapters 18 and 19.

Right after installing the software, you will see two usable Civil 3D–specific templates (Figure 1.24).

FIGURE 1.24
Selecting a Civil 3D template by going through the Application menu ➤ New ➤ Drawing

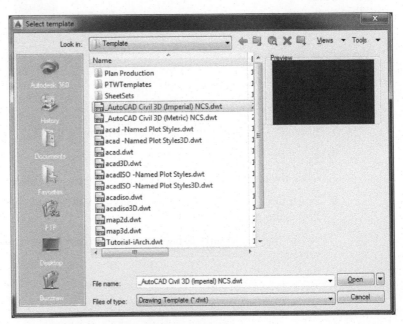

TEMPLATES USED IN THIS BOOK

By default, when Civil 3D is installed either in an Imperial or metric work environment, every new file created will use a stock template, whose location and file are defined within the configuration portion of the software that can be accessed by using either the `Config` or `Options` command. In the same way, since you use the default configuration of Civil 3D, all the way through the book the CAD files that are supplied for your instruction will use the same templates.

These template files may not necessarily reflect the standards for design of your company, but they represent a good startup file for the definition of your company's templates. Listed here are the stock templates that Civil 3D uses based on your unit work environment:

◆ `_AutoCAD Civil 3D (Imperial) NCS.dwt`

◆ `_AutoCAD Civil 3D (Metric) NCS.dwt`

Starting New Projects

When you start a project with the correct template file (defined by a `.dwt` file extension), the repetitive task of defining the basic framework for your drawing is already completed. Since Civil 3D runs on top of AutoCAD, the template will have two parts. The first part of the Civil 3D template is the AutoCAD side of the template, and it will contain the following:

◆ Unit type (architectural or decimal) and insertion scale (meters or feet)

◆ Layers and their respective linetypes, colors, and other properties

◆ Text, dimension, tables, and multileader styles

◆ Layouts and plot setups

◆ Block definitions

The second part is represented by the specific Civil 3D side. Therefore, in addition to the items just listed, you will encounter the following:

◆ More specific unit information (international feet, survey feet, or meters), together with the coordinate systems defined within the Drawing Settings dialog that you've learned about.

◆ Civil object layers, defined with the object layers. (You've learned about this one, as well.)

◆ Ambient settings. (Try to remember, did you see this one somewhere already?)

◆ Label styles and formulas (expressions). (There is an awesome chapter on this: Chapter 18.)

◆ Object styles. (Chapter 19 will give you all you need to know about them.)

◆ Command settings of which you'll learn more in this chapter. (The customization takes a new level when these are defined.)

◆ Object-naming templates defined by macros within command settings. (Your typing life will be so much easier when these are defined.)

◆ Report settings that can be found within the Toolbox tab of Toolspace.

◆ Description key sets. (You will learn how these can streamline your survey processing in Chapter 2.)

Now that you've learned what makes up the Civil 3D template, make sure to start your design adventure using the proper template. Many times you will receive files from people who don't use Civil 3D as their design platform. When these files are opened for the first time in Civil 3D, the template will create standard settings and styles. For this reason, opening a file within Civil 3D, when accessing the Settings tab of Toolspace, you will see that for each of the objects a Standard style is defined (Figure 1.25). This style is created for both object and labels and defines all of its properties using Layer 0.

FIGURE 1.25
A non–Civil
3D DWG will
list all styles
as Standard,
which is the
Civil 3D equiva-
lent to drawing
on Layer 0.

Also, there will be no specific object layers defined since all of them will be set to Layer 0, so any Civil 3D object you create will be placed by default in that layer. You will learn in this section about a feature that allows you to import the settings and styles from a template, taking away all the hassle of redefining that data for every drawing.

Real World Scenario

BEST PRACTICES FOR RECEIVING A NON–CIVIL 3D DRAWING

Say someone sends you a drawing that was not done in Civil 3D. Perhaps it was exported from a non-AutoCAD-based product or created in an outdated civil drafting program. You now have the task of creating Civil 3D objects, but making this task even more difficult is that there are no Civil 3D styles present. Perhaps the drawing was created in Civil 3D but your organization's styles look completely different.

The best course of action to take when receiving an outside drawing is to insert it into a blank file that you started using your Civil 3D template. When you insert a drawing, Civil 3D does several things to help you:

◆ The Insert command detects the units of the incoming drawing and scales it to match your drawing.

◆ If both drawings have a coordinate system defined, Civil 3D places the incoming drawing by geographic data.

◆ All of your styles and settings remain intact.

The following exercise walks you through what you need to do in this situation:

1. Start by choosing Application ➢ New ➢ Drawing. Select either _AutoCAD Civil 3D (Imperial) NCS.dwt or _AutoCAD Civil 3D (Metric) NCS.dwt and click Open.

2. Click the Save icon from the Quick Access toolbar.

3. Save the drawing with the rest of your Mastering Civil 3D files as **0104_Project.dwg (0104_Project_METRIC.dwg)**.

4. Go to the Insert tab of the ribbon. From the Block panel, click Insert ➢ More Options.

5. In the Insert dialog, click Browse and locate the file 0104_MysteryFile.dwg (0104_MysteryFile_METRIC.dwg), which is part of the dataset for this chapter. Click Open.

6. Be sure that the Insertion Point, Scale, and Rotation check boxes are clear.

7. Select the Explode check box. Your Insert dialog should look like this:

Notice that AutoCAD has picked up the units of the 0104_MysteryFile.dwg (0104_MysteryFile_METRIC.dwg) file and is automatically scaling them as needed. If you used the English units template, you will see the conversion scale factor as 0.0833. If you used the metric template drawing, you will see the scale factor as 0.025.

8. Click OK. Using the Zoom command, expand the view to extents to see the result. You can check the resulting file against the completed file that can be found on the book's web page under the name 0104_Project_FINISHED.dwg (0104_Project_METRIC_FINISHED.dwg).

Continues

Continued

A quick measurement of the north wall of the conservatory building should reveal that it is 200′ (61 m) in length.

At this point you can now work on the drawing in Civil 3D without re-creating any established standards. Everything from the outside source has come in, including blocks, layers, and dimension styles, but they will not override any of your blocks, layers, or styles if they happen to have the same name. If the inserted drawing contains dimensions with the same name as one in your drawing (such as Standard) but different definition in your drawing, you might get undesired results. This is a strong reason for not redefining or using any style named Standard in your template.

Note that if the drawings are in different coordinate systems, the previously mentioned workflow will not deliver the desired result. For those cases the workflow is different and involves the use of AutoCAD Map tools.

Importing Styles

Now let's imagine that you are working in your drawing and your company's template was updated to include one or more object and label styles. There has also been a change to one of the properties of a style you commonly use, and you need to integrate that change within your drawing. How would you incorporate those changes within your drawing? Looking at the original styles and trying to re-create them within your drawing would be tedious work and prone to errors. That's where the recently introduced Import Styles tool comes into action.

This tool allows you to import one or more object and label styles from a source drawing. You can also import from the source drawing its Table styles, Quantity Takeoff criteria, Alignment Design Check sets, Drawing Ambient settings, Feature settings, Command settings, and other user-defined settings such as expressions, property classifications, and page layouts. The last three can be imported as long as they are referenced by any of the imported label or table styles. However, using this tool does not allow you to import description key sets and point file formats (see Chapter 3 for their definition), all the settings defined within the Drawing Settings dialog (except for the ambient settings mentioned previously), and the user-defined settings mentioned that are not referenced by a style. As shown in Figure 1.26, you can find this tool on the Manage tab ➤ Styles panel. In the same panel, there is also an option to purge styles. But for now we will explain the basics of importing styles.

FIGURE 1.26
Import and Purge found on the Styles panel give you access to tools to import Object and Label styles from your drawing of choice into the current drawing.

Before importing styles, you must save the file. In case you forget, Civil 3D will be kind enough to prompt you to save the drawing before you can proceed with the import. The import workflow begins when you click the Import button of the Styles panel. First you will be asked to select your source drawing for import of styles. This drawing can be either a DWG file or a template file, which is defined by the .dwt extension.

Once you select the file whose styles you will import, a dialog box similar to the one in Figure 1.27 appears.

FIGURE 1.27
Import Civil 3D Styles dialog

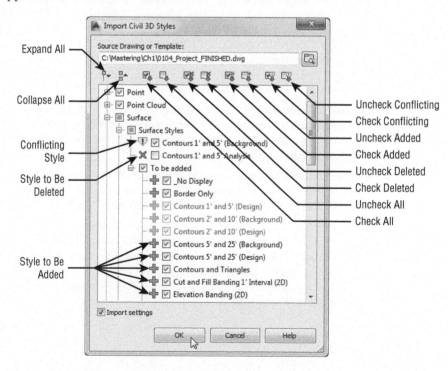

The Import Civil 3D Styles dialog has the following options:

Import Settings   The Import Settings option is located at the bottom of the dialog. This option is turned on by default. If you want to import the styles with disregard to the drawing settings, then you can uncheck Import Settings. However, if you want to match your drawing in all aspects to the source drawing, you should leave the option checked, which is the default setting. As you look through the list of styles to be imported, you will notice that some items are grayed out and can't be modified.

The grayed-out styles represent items that are referenced by the command settings to be imported. As mentioned, the only time those styles would not be grayed out and available would be when the Import Settings box is not checked. You will learn about command settings toward the end of this section. Also note that you can either import all the styles from the source drawing or select which styles you want to import.

When importing styles, Civil 3D will do the following:

1. If the style is not within your drawing, the style will be added.

2. If the style already exists in your drawing, presenting the same style name, Civil 3D will recognize it as a conflict of styles and will check its settings against its equivalent in the source file; if the settings are different, they will be overwritten.

3. If a style is present in the drawing but not present in the source file, that style will be deleted, as long as it is not used (referenced) by an object in the drawing.

For each of the actions listed here, there is a way to toggle off one or more actions. Following, you can see what happens when you use the toggles:

Uncheck/Check Conflicting   You will also notice items with a warning symbol (see the surface style Contours 1′ and 5′ (Background) in Figure 1.27). The warning symbol indicates that there is a style in the current drawing with the same name as a style in the batch to be imported. Use the Uncheck Conflicting button if you do not want styles in your drawing to be overwritten by the style from the source file. As mentioned, if you leave these items selected, the incoming styles "win." If you are not sure whether there is a difference between the styles, pause your cursor over the style name, and a tooltip will tell you what (if any) difference exists.

Uncheck/Check Added   Use the Uncheck Added button if you want only those styles with the same name to come in. Wherever possible, Civil 3D will release items in the To Be Added categories. In cases where a style is used by a setting, you will not be able to uncheck it unless you do not import settings.

Uncheck/Check Deleted   A style in the current drawing will be deleted if the source drawing does not contain a style with the same name and the style is not in use. Use the Uncheck Deleted button to prevent the style from being deleted.

The Import Styles command does not replace the best practice of starting with a proper template. Again, note that some critical items will not get transferred with this tool. As we mentioned, description key sets, unused expressions, point file settings, and predefined point groups will not import. Drawing settings and Label style defaults do not update. In addition, precision and units set in the Feature Settings dialog do not get transferred. The AutoCAD drawing units will remain unchanged, also.

To bring the items that cannot be imported, such as description keys, unused expressions, point file settings, and predefined point groups into your drawing, use the following steps:

1. Open the drawing containing the settings or styles you want to import.

2. In the same session, open the drawing needing these settings.

3. Switch your Toolspace tab to Settings. Make sure your view is set to Master View so that you can see both drawings at the same time.

4. Verify that the drawing needing the settings is active.

5. On the Settings tab, browse the source drawing for the style or setting you want to import, select the style or setting, and then drag and release it over the drawing area.

Command Settings

We have mentioned command settings many times in this chapter; now you'll learn what they are and their intended purpose. When you create a Civil 3D object, you define its properties, set design parameters, set default styles for objects, and so on. A Civil 3D object is defined through a command. To speed up the standardization of the creation process, the command settings take care of the default values used when a Civil 3D object is created. So, for example, in Figure 1.28 you can see that most of the default settings that the CreateAlignmentLayout tool uses are defined within the command settings. The fact that most of the settings are defined at the drawing level can be seen by the small number of check marks in the Override column.

FIGURE 1.28
Command settings for Create Alignment Layout define the defaults when this tool is used.

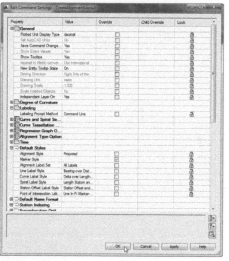

You have the option to customize the defaults for the tool so that every time the tool is launched you don't have to type in the same values. Even though the values will be prepopulated in the specific fields, the user still has the option to overwrite those choices within the creation dialog box. Note, however, that only part of the predefined defaults are available to the user within the dialog box. For most of the defaults, the specific command setting dialog is the only place where those values can be defined.

Most of the settings within the command settings are defined on a global level for the drawing within the Ambient Settings tab. Going from a global level to the object level, the same settings can be found and overridden at the object level through the Edit Feature Settings for that type of object. From the object level, you can move to the tool level, where within the command settings for the tool they can again be overridden to achieve the desired settings when using that tool.

IMPORTING OBJECT LAYERS

You know that Object, Table, and Label styles can be imported using the Import Styles tool, but what about the object layers?

At this time, Civil 3D does not have a built-in tool to do that, so if you are provided with a drawing that does not have any object layers defined or doesn't have your company's object layers, you have two options: Define or redefine the object layers for the drawing or use the workflow presented previously in this section. But what happens if you want to keep the current file as is and just define its object layers without too much hassle? Fortunately, there is a workflow that will take care of that. Follow these steps:

1. Open 0105_Blank_Object_Layers.dwg (0105_Blank_Object_Layers_METRIC.dwg) from this chapter's folder.

2. From the same folder, open 0105_Defined_Object_Layers.dwg (0105_Defined_Object_Layers_METRIC.dwg).

3. Examine the object layers of the first drawing and notice that they are all set to 0, while the object layers for the second drawing are defined. You will transfer the object layers from the second drawing to the first.

4. Set your Toolspace to the Settings tab. Make sure that the view is set to Master View since you will want to have both drawings visible.

5. Make sure that the active drawing is set to 0105_Blank_Object_Layers. You will know it is the active one if it is at the top of the list and its name is bold. If it is not active, switch to the Prospector tab, right-click its name, and use the Switch To option to make it active or select it using the file tabs.

6. With drawing 0105_Blank_Object_Layers active in the Toolspace, right-click 0105_Defined_Object_Layers and select Edit Drawing Settings from the list. See the following figure for the layout:

7. In the dialog, do not change any settings and click OK. If you check now, you will notice that the object layers of your source drawing (0105_Defined_Object_Layers) have been transferred to the desired drawing. If you want to check the result of the transfer, you can download the finished file, named 0105_Blank_Object_Layers_FINISHED.dwg (0105_Blank_Object_Layers_METRIC_FINISHED.dwg).

Note that while this will populate the layer list, the actual layers will not be created until their objects are created. The layers will be created, their color set to white, and their linetype set to continuous. To import the layers with the desired properties, use the Design Center to bring in the layers, then perform the above procedure.

Creating Lines

If you have used AutoCAD for a while, you will be familiar with the way you draw lines. Whether you use the command line or the ribbon, the same tools will be available in both Civil 3D and AutoCAD. However, Civil 3D takes it up a notch by providing multiple methods of defining these entities, though the end result will be the same—a line. The tools to draw lines are found in the Draw panel within the Home tab of the ribbon. Figure 1.29 displays the available line commands.

FIGURE 1.29
Line-creation tools

Later in this chapter you will take a look at *transparent commands*. Transparent commands provide extra help in the definition of the elements by expanding a user's options of data input within a command.

COGO Line Commands

The next few commands help you create a line using Civil 3D points and/or coordinate inputs. Each command requires you to specify a Civil 3D point, a location in space, or a typed coordinate input. These line tools are useful when your drawing includes Civil 3D points that will serve as a foundation for linework, such as the edge of pavement shots, wetlands lines, or any other points you'd like to connect with a line.

CREATE LINE COMMAND

The Create Line command on the Draw panel of the Home tab of the ribbon issues the standard AutoCAD Line command. It's equivalent to typing **line** on the command line or clicking the Line tool on the Draw toolbar.

Certification
Objective

CREATE LINE BY POINT # RANGE COMMAND

The Create Line By Point # Range command prompts you for a point number. You can type in an individual point number, press ↵, and then type in another point number. A line is drawn connecting those two points. You can also type in a range of points, such as **601-607**. Civil 3D draws a line that connects those points in numerical order from 601 to 607 and so on (see Figure 1.30). The line that is created by this method connects point to point regardless of the description or type of point. Since a line is an element that allows each of its end vertices to hold different elevations, in this case each endpoint will inherit the elevation of the COGO point used for its definition unless the AutoCAD OSNAPZ variable is set to 1.

FIGURE 1.30
Lines created using 601-607 as input

Alternatively, you can enter a list of points such as **600, 603, 610, 605** (Figure 1.31). Civil 3D draws a line that connects the point numbers in the order of input. This approach is useful when your points were taken in a zigzag pattern (as is commonly the case when cross-sectioning pavement) or when your points appear so far apart in the AutoCAD display that they can't be readily identified.

FIGURE 1.31
Lines created
using 600, 603,
610, 605 as input

CREATE LINE BY POINT OBJECT COMMAND

The Create Line By Point Object command prompts you to select a point object. To select a point object, locate the desired start point and click any part of the point. This tool is similar to using the regular Line command and a Node object snap (also known as an *Osnap*); however, it will work on only Civil 3D points. Each endpoint will inherit the elevation of the point to which it is created unless the AutoCAD OSNAPZ variable is set to 1.

CREATE LINE BY POINT NAME COMMAND

The Create Line By Point Name command prompts you for a point name. A *point name* is a field in point properties, not unlike the point number or description. The difference between a point name and a *point description* is that a point name must be unique, just as point numbers are. It is important to note that some survey instruments name points rather than number points as is the norm.

To use this command, enter the names of the points you want to connect with linework. Each endpoint will inherit the elevation of the point used for its definition unless the AutoCAD OSNAPZ variable is set to 1.

CREATE LINE BY NORTHING/EASTING AND CREATE LINE BY GRID NORTHING /GRID EASTING COMMANDS

The Create Line By Northing/Easting command lets you input northing (y) and easting (x) coordinates as endpoints for your linework.

The Create Line By Grid Northing/Grid Easting command also lets you input grid northing (y) and grid easting (x) coordinates as endpoints for your linework but requires that the drawing have an assigned coordinate system; otherwise, the command resumes to be used as a simple line command.

CREATE LINE BY LATITUDE/LONGITUDE COMMAND

The Create Line By Latitude/Longitude command prompts you for geographic coordinates to use as endpoints for your linework. This command also requires that the drawing have an assigned coordinate system. Enter the latitude and longitude as separate entries at the command line using degrees, minutes, and seconds.

> **IMPORTANT NOTES ON ENTERING DATA INTO CIVIL 3D**
>
> In this chapter, you will get your first taste of entering data at the command line. Always keep an eye out for what is on your command line (or your tooltip, if dynamic input is on). Sometimes you are asked to confirm an option; other times you are asked for input.
>
> As stated previously, most people prefer to enter angles by degrees, minutes, and seconds rather than decimal degrees. The ambient setting format will affect exactly how Civil 3D displays this information but is more flexible when it comes to your data entry. To enter angles into Civil 3D, you can use a *DD.MMSS* format. To input 15°21'35", you can use **15.2135**. Any numbers beyond four decimal places will be considered decimal seconds. To input 6°5'2", enter **6.0502**. You could also enter **6d5'2"** at the command line, but most people find it faster to use the former method.
>
> When entering station values into Civil 3D, it is not necessary to use station notation. In English units, if you are asked to enter station 3+25, you can simply enter **325**. In metric, a station of 0+110 can be entered as **110**. Similarly, a metric station of 2+450 can be entered as **2450**.

Direction-Based Line Commands

The next few commands help you define a line and its direction. Each of these commands requires you to choose a start point for your line before you can specify the line direction. You can specify your start point by physically choosing a location, using an Osnap, or using one of the point-related line commands discussed earlier.

Many of these line commands require a line or arc and will not work with a polyline. Those commands include Create Line By Sideshot, Create Line By Extension, Create Line From End Of Object, Create Line Tangent From Point, and Create Line Perpendicular From Point.

CREATE LINE BY BEARING COMMAND

Certification Objective

The Create Line By Bearing command is one of the most commonly used line-creation commands.

This command prompts you for a start point, followed by prompts to input the Quadrant, Bearing, and Distance values. You can enter values on the command line for each input, or you can graphically choose inputs by picking them onscreen. The glyphs at each stage of input guide you in any graphical selections. After creating one line, you can continue drawing lines by bearing, or you can switch to any other method by clicking one of the other Line By commands on the Draw panel (see Figure 1.32).

FIGURE 1.32
The tooltips for a quadrant (top), a bearing (middle), and a distance (bottom)

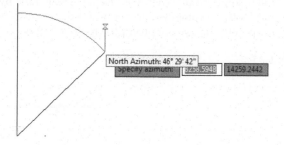

CREATE LINE BY AZIMUTH COMMAND

The Create Line By Azimuth command prompts you for a start point, followed by a north azimuth and then a distance (Figure 1.33).

FIGURE 1.33
The tooltip for the Create Line By Azimuth command

CREATE LINE BY ANGLE COMMAND

The Create Line By Angle command prompts you for a start point, an ending point to establish a backsight direction, a turned angle, and then a distance (Figure 1.34). By default, this command assumes the angle-right surveying convention (clockwise from starting direction). However, an option to turn counterclockwise is offered at the command line if needed.

FIGURE 1.34
The tooltips for a turned angle (top) and a distance (bottom) for the Create Line By Angle command

CREATE LINE BY DEFLECTION COMMAND

By definition, a *deflection angle* is the amount of angular deviation (usually measured clockwise) from a backsight direction. In other words, 180 added to a given deflection angle would be an equivalent angle-right. When you use the Create Line By Deflection command, the command line and tooltips prompt you to define a direction to deflect the angle off of by selecting or clicking two points; then you're prompted for a deflection angle followed by a distance (Figure 1.35).

FIGURE 1.35
The tooltip for the Create Line By Deflection command

CREATE LINE BY STATION/OFFSET COMMAND

To use the Create Line By Station/Offset command, you must have a Civil 3D Alignment object in your drawing. The line created from this command allows you to start and end a line on the basis of a station and offset from an alignment.

You're prompted to choose the alignment and then input a station and offset value. The line *begins* at the station and offset value. You will not see a line form until at least two points are specified.

When prompted for the station, you're given a tooltip that tracks your position along the alignment, as shown in Figure 1.36. You can graphically choose a station location by clicking it in the drawing. Alternatively, you can enter a station value on the command line.

FIGURE 1.36
The Create Line By Station/Offset command provides a tooltip for you to track stationing along the alignment.

Once you've selected the station, you're given a tooltip that is locked on that particular station and tracks your offset from the alignment (see Figure 1.37). You can graphically choose an offset by clicking the station in the drawing, or you can type an offset value on the command line. A negative value for offset indicates an offset on the left side of the alignment.

FIGURE 1.37
The Create Line By Station/Offset command provides a tooltip that helps you track the offset from the alignment.

CREATE LINE BY SIDE SHOT COMMAND

The Create Line By Side Shot command starts by asking you to select a line (or two points) that will be the backsight for creating a new line and subsequent lines while in the command. After you select the first line, you will see a yellow glyph indicating your occupied point (see Figure 1.38). By default, Civil 3D is looking for an angle-right and distance to establish the first point of the new line. However, you can follow the command prompts to change the angle entry to bearing, deflection, or azimuth, if needed. You can also use the command-line options to change to counterclockwise.

FIGURE 1.38
The tooltip for the Create Line By Side Shot command tracks the angle, bearing, deflection, or azimuth of the side shot.

Once you have entered data for the first point, you will be asked a second time for an angle and a distance to place the second point of the new line.

CREATE LINE BY EXTENSION COMMAND

The Create Line By Extension command is similar to the AutoCAD Lengthen command. This command allows you to add length to a line or specify a desired total length of the line. Figure 1.39 shows the summary report that will pop up indicating the changes made to the line.

FIGURE 1.39
The Create Line By Extension command provides a summary of the changes to the line.

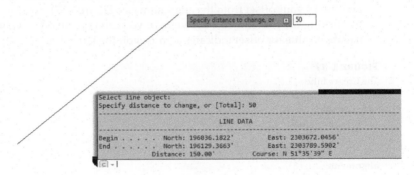

The advantage of the Create Line By Extension command over simply using the Lengthen command is the summary report that appears at the command line. The summary report shown in Figure 1.40 shows the same beginning coordinate as in Figure 1.39 but a different end coordinate, resulting in a total length of 100′ (30.5 m).

FIGURE 1.40
The summary report on a line where the command specified a total distance

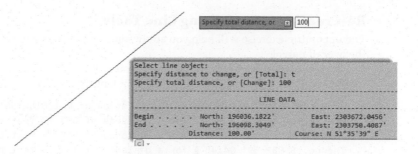

CREATE LINE FROM END OF OBJECT COMMAND

The Create Line From End Of Object command lets you draw a line tangent to the end of a line or arc (but not polyline) of your choosing, as shown in Figure 1.41.

FIGURE 1.41
The Create Line From End Of Object command lets you add a tangent line to the end of an arc.

CREATE LINE TANGENT FROM POINT COMMAND

Certification
Objective

The Create Line Tangent From Point command is similar to the Create Line From End Of Object command, but Create Line Tangent From Point allows you to choose a point of tangency that isn't the endpoint of the line or arc. Use the Nearest or Midpoint Osnap to pick a point on the line. If you pick an endpoint, the command behaves the same as Create Line From End Of Object.

CREATE LINE PERPENDICULAR FROM POINT COMMAND

Using the Create Line Perpendicular From Point command, you can specify that you'd like a line drawn perpendicular to any point of your choosing along a line or arc. In the example shown in Figure 1.42, a line is drawn perpendicular to the endpoint of the arc.

FIGURE 1.42
A perpendicular line is drawn from the endpoint of an arc using the Create Line Perpendicular From Point command.

Re-Creating a Deed Using Line Tools

The upcoming exercise will help you apply some of the tools you've learned so far to reconstruct the overall parcel.

When you open the file for the exercise, you will see a legal description with the following information (the metric file will have different lengths, of course):

```
From the POINT OF BEGINNING at a location of N 186156.65', E 2305474.07'
Thence, S 11° 45' 41.4" E for a distance of 693.77 feet to a point on a line.
Thence, S 73° 10' 54.4" W for a distance of 265.45 feet to a point on a line.
Thence, S 05° 59' 04.4" E for a distance of 185.89 feet to a point on a line.
Thence, S 45° 55' 02.4" W for a distance of 68.73 feet to a point on a line.
Thence, N 06° 04' 37.0" W for a distance of 217.80 feet to a point on a line.
Thence, N 73° 21' 22.5" E for a distance of 4.22 feet to a point on a line.
Thence, N 06° 04' 51.6" W for a distance of 200.14 feet to a point on a line.
Thence, S 87° 32' 10.4" W for a distance of 121.22 feet to a point on a line.
Thence, N 02° 25' 32.2" W for a distance of 168.91 feet to a point on a line.
Thence, N 15° 38' 57.5" E for a distance of 283.16 feet to a point on a line.
Thence, N 06° 19' 22.4" W for a distance of 79.64 feet to a point on a line.
N 76° 55' 49.8" E a distance of 250.00 feet Returning to the POINT OF BEGINNING;
Containing 5.58 acres (more or less)
```

Follow these steps (note that the legal description for metric users is located in the DWG file as text):

1. Open the 0106_Legal.dwg (0106_Legal_METRIC.dwg) file, which you can download from this book's web page at www.sybex.com/go/masteringcivil3d2016.

2. Turn off dynamic input by pressing F12 if it is enabled.

3. From the Draw panel on the Home tab of the ribbon, select the Line drop-down and choose the Create Line By Bearing command.

4. At the Select first point: prompt, use endpoint object snap to snap to the arrow head of the note indicating POB.

5. At the >>Specify quadrant (1-4): prompt, enter **2** to specify the SE quadrant and then press ↵.

6. At the >>Specify bearing: prompt, enter **11.45414** and press ↵.

7. At the >>Specify distance: prompt, enter **693.77'** (**211.4615** m) and press ↵.

8. Repeat steps 5 through 7 for the rest of the courses and distances.

9. Press Esc twice to exit the creation workflow and exit the Create Line By Bearing command.

The finished linework should look like Figure 1.43.

FIGURE 1.43
The finished
linework

10. Save your drawing. You'll need it for the next exercise.

Creating Curves

Curves are an important part of surveying and engineering geometry. The curves you create in this chapter are no different from AutoCAD arcs. What makes the curve commands unique from the basic AutoCAD commands isn't the resulting arc entity but the inputs used to draw the arc. Civil 3D wants you to provide directions to the arc commands using land surveying terminology rather than with generic Cartesian parameters. Figure 1.44 shows the Create Curves menu options.

FIGURE 1.44
Create Curves
commands

Standard Curves

When re-creating legal descriptions for roads, easements, and properties, users such as engineers, surveyors, and mappers often encounter a variety of curves. Although standard AutoCAD arc commands could draw these arcs, the AutoCAD arc inputs are designed to be generic to all industries. The following curve commands have been designed to provide an interface that more closely matches land surveying, mapping, and engineering language.

CREATING A CURVE BETWEEN TWO LINES

The Create Curve Between Two Lines command is similar to the AutoCAD Fillet command, except that by using this tool you also have other options to define a curve besides using the radius. The command draws a curve that is tangent to two lines of your choosing. This command also trims or extends the original tangents so their endpoints coincide with the curve endpoints. The lines are trimmed or extended to the resulting PC (point of curve, which is the beginning of a curve) and PT (point of tangency, which is the end of a curve). You may find this command most useful when you're creating foundation geometry for road alignments, parcel boundary curves, and similar situations.

The command prompts you to choose the first tangent and then the second tangent. The command line gives the following prompt:

```
Select entry [Tangent External Degree Chord Length Mid-ordinate
miN-dist Radius]<Radius>:
```

Pressing ↵ at this prompt lets you input your desired radius. As with standard AutoCAD commands, pressing T changes the input parameter to Tangent, pressing C changes the input parameter to Chord, and so on.

As with the Fillet command, your inputs must be geometrically possible. For example, your two lines must allow for a curve of your specifications to be drawn while remaining tangent to both. Figure 1.45 shows two lines with a 25′ (7.6 m) radius curve drawn between them. Note that the tangents have been trimmed so their endpoints coincide with the endpoints of the curve.

If either line is too short to meet the endpoint of the curve, then the software returns a no solution result, and you will need to adjust the length of the line.

FIGURE 1.45
Two lines using the Create Curve Between Two Lines command

CREATING A CURVE ON TWO LINES

Certification Objective

The Create Curve On Two Lines command is identical to the Create Curve Between Two Lines command, except that in this case the tangents are not trimmed on curve creation.

Figure 1.46, for example, shows two lines with a 25' (7.6 m) radius curve drawn on them. The tangents haven't been trimmed and instead remain exactly as they were drawn before the Create Curve On Two Lines command was executed.

FIGURE 1.46
The original lines stay the same after you execute the Create Curve On Two Lines command.

CREATING A CURVE-THROUGH POINT

The Create Curve Through Point command lets you choose two tangents for your curve followed by a pass-through point. This tool is most useful when you don't know the radius, length, or other curve parameters but you have two tangents and a target location. It isn't necessary that the pass-through location be a true point object; it can be any location of your choosing.

This command also trims or extends the original tangents so their endpoints coincide with the curve endpoints. The lines are trimmed or extended to the resulting PC and PT of the curve.

Figure 1.47, for example, shows two lines and a desired pass-through point. Using the Create Curve Through Point command allows you to draw a curve that is tangent to both lines and that passes through the desired point. In this case, the tangents have been trimmed to the PC and PT of the curve.

FIGURE 1.47
The first image shows two lines with a desired pass-through point. In the second image, the Create Curve Through Point command draws a curve that is tangent to both lines and passes through the chosen point.

CREATING MULTIPLE CURVES

The Create Multiple Curves command lets you create several curves that are tangentially connected. The resulting curves have an effect similar to an alignment spiral section. This command can be useful when you are re-creating railway track geometry based on field-survey data.

The command prompts you for the two tangents. Then, the command line prompts you as follows:

```
Enter Number of Curves:
```

The command allows for up to 10 curves between tangents.

One of your curves must have a flexible length that's determined on the basis of the lengths, radii, and geometric constraints of the other curves. Curves are counted clockwise, so enter the number of your flexible curve, as shown here:

```
Enter Floating Curve #:
Enter curve 1 Radius:
Enter curve 2 Radius:
Enter curve 2 Length:
```

The floating curve number will prompt you for a radius but not a length.

As with all other curve commands, the specified geometry must be possible. If the command can't find a solution on the basis of your length and radius inputs, it returns no solution (see Figure 1.48).

FIGURE 1.48
Two curves were specified with the #2 curve designated as the floating curve.

CREATING A CURVE FROM THE END OF AN OBJECT

The Create Curve From End Of Object command enables you to draw a curve tangent to the end of your chosen line or arc.

The command prompts you to choose an object to serve as the beginning of your curve. You can then specify a radius or a point for the way the curve will be defined. If a point is selected, then the curve will automatically be drawn ending at the selected point in the drawing. If a radius is selected, then you have the option to specify the radius or let the software determine the radius based on the arc's degree or the chord's degree. Finally, you can define its length by using an additional parameter (such as Delta or Length) (see Figure 1.49).

FIGURE 1.49
A curve, with a 25' (7.6 m) radius and a 30' (9.1 m) length, drawn from the end of a line

CREATING A REVERSE OR COMPOUND CURVE

The Create Reverse Or Compound Curve command allows you to add curves to the end of an existing curve. Reverse curves are drawn in the opposite direction (that is, a curve to the right tangent to a curve to the left) from the original curve to form an *S* shape. In contrast, compound curves are drawn in the same direction as the original curve (see Figure 1.50). This tool can be useful when you are re-creating a legal description of a road alignment that contains reverse and/or compound curves.

FIGURE 1.50
A tangent and curve before adding a compound curve (left); a reverse curve drawn from the end of the original curve (right)

USING THE CURVE CALCULATOR

Certification
Objective

Sometimes you may not have enough information to draw a curve properly. Although many of the curve-creation tools assist you in calculating the curve parameters, you may find an occasion where the deed you're working with is incomplete.

The Curve Calculator found in the Curves drop-down on the Draw panel helps you calculate a full collection of curve parameters on the basis of your known values and constraints. It can also be found as part of the Transparent Commands toolbar that is discussed later in this chapter.

The Curve Calculator can remain open on your screen while you're working through commands. You can send any value in the Calculator to the command line by clicking the button next to that value (see Figure 1.51).

FIGURE 1.51
The Curve
Calculator

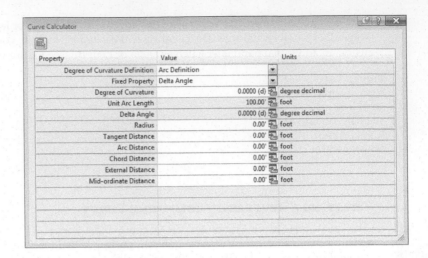

The button at the upper left of the Curve Calculator allows you to pick an existing arc in the drawing, and the drop-down menu in the Degree Of Curvature Definition selection field allows you to choose whether to calculate parameters for an arc or a chord definition.

The drop-down menu in the Fixed Property selection field also gives you the choice of fixing your radius or delta angle when calculating the values for an arc or a chord, respectively. The parameter chosen as the fixed value is held constant as additional parameters are calculated.

To send any value in the Curve Calculator to the command line, use the button next to that value. This ability is most useful while you're active in a curve command and would like to use a certain parameter value to complete the command.

To test your new line and curve knowledge, follow these steps (you do not need to have completed the previous exercises to complete this one):

1. Continue working in the file 0106_Legal.dwg (0106_Legal_METRIC.dwg).

2. Start the Line By Northing/Easting command.

3. For Northing, enter **184898.42** (**56357.038** for metric users) and press ↵.

4. For Easting, enter **2305136.46** (**702605.593** for metric users) and press ↵.

   You will not see any graphic indication that the line has been started. You will not see the segment until after you complete step 5.

   You will again be prompted for Northing and Easting.

5. Using the same procedure you used in step 2, type in the endpoint of the line at Northing = **185059.94** (**56406.270** for metric users), Easting = **2305413.52** (**702690.041** for metric users).

6. Press Esc once to end the Northing and Easting entries.

7. Press Esc again to exit the line command.

To look at everything you have drawn until now, you can zoom to extents.

8. Start the Create Curve From End Of Object command.

You are then prompted to select the Line or Arc object.

9. Pan to the left and click the east end of the line you created in steps 2–5.

You will then be prompted to select the entry.

10. Press ↵ to select the default Radius option.

11. Enter a Radius value of **550′** (**167.6** m) and press ↵.

Next you will see the Select entry [Tangent/Chord/Delta/Length/External/Mid-ordinate] <Length>: prompt.

12. Enter **D** (for Delta) and press ↵.

13. Enter a delta angle of **40** and press ↵. (Note: The degree symbol is not needed in angular entry.)

You should now have an arc tangent to the first segment.

14. Return to the Curves menu and select Create Reverse Or Compound Curve.

15. Select the east end of the arc you created in the previous steps.

16. When prompted with Select [Compound/Reverse] <Compound>:, press **R** and then ↵ to specify a reverse curve.

17. Enter a radius of **630′** (**192.0** m) and press ↵.

18. When you see the prompt Select entry [Tangent/Chord/Delta/Length/External/Mid-ordinate] <Length>:, press ↵ to accept the default.

19. Enter a length of curve value of **400′** (**121.9** m) and press ↵.

20. For the last tangent segment, return to the Lines menu and select Create Line From End Of Object.

21. Select the east end of the second arc you created in this exercise.

22. At the Specify Distance: prompt, enter **150′** (**45.7** m) and press ↵.

Your completed lines and arcs will look like Figure 1.52, and they will be located just south of the property you entered in the previous exercise. You can check the result against the completed exercise as found on the book's web page; it's named 0106_Legal_FINISHED.dwg (0106_Legal_METRIC_FINISHED.dwg).

FIGURE 1.52
Lines and arcs
of the completed
exercise

FIGURE 1.52
Lines and arcs
of the completed
exercise

Best-Fit Entities

AutoCAD Civil 3D provides many tools for relating surveyed information to a graphic. Best-fit tools like the ones in the following sections perform analysis on different types of irregular geometry to create uniform shapes (see Figure 1.53). Similar tools are available for alignment creation, as discussed in Chapter 6.

FIGURE 1.53
The Create Best Fit
menu options

CREATING A BEST-FIT LINE

The Create Best Fit Line command under the Best Fit drop-down on the Draw panel takes a series of Civil 3D points, AutoCAD points, entities, or drawing locations and draws a single best-fit line segment on the selected input. In Figure 1.54, the Create Best Fit Line command draws a best-fit line through a series of points that aren't quite collinear. The best-fit line will adjust as more points are selected.

FIGURE 1.54
A preview line
drawn through
points that are not
collinear

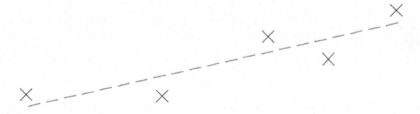

After you press Enter to complete the selection, a Panorama window appears with a regression data chart showing information about each point in the selection, as shown in Figure 1.55.

FIGURE 1.55
The Panorama window lets you optimize your best fit.

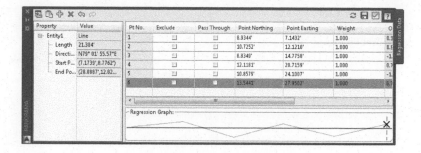

This interface allows you to optimize your best-fit element by adding more points, excluding points, selecting the check box in the Pass Through column to force one of your points on the line, or adjusting the value under the Weight column based on how important each point position should be in the definition of the element relative to the other points.

CREATING A BEST-FIT ARC

The Create Best Fit Arc command on the Best Fit drop-down works the same as the Create Best Fit Line command, including the Panorama adjustment window, except that the resulting entity is a single arc segment as opposed to a single line segment (see Figure 1.56).

FIGURE 1.56
Preview of the curve created by best fit

CREATING A BEST-FIT PARABOLA

The Create Best Fit Parabola command on the Best Fit drop-down is similar to the line and arc commands in how it works. After you select this command, the Parabola By Best Fit dialog appears (see Figure 1.57).

FIGURE 1.57
The Parabola By
Best Fit dialog

You can select inputs from entities (such as lines, arcs, polylines, or profile objects) or by clicking onscreen. The command then draws a best-fit parabola on the basis of this information. In Figure 1.58, the shots were represented by AutoCAD points; more points were added by selecting the By Clicking On The Screen option and using the Node Osnap to pick each point.

FIGURE 1.58
The best-fit preview line updates as more points are picked.

Once you've selected your points, a Panorama window (shown in Figure 1.59) appears, showing information about each point you chose. Also note the information in the left pane regarding the K value, curve length, grades, and so forth. You can optimize your K value, length, and other values by adding more points, selecting one or more check boxes in the Pass Through column to force one of your points on the line, or adjusting the values in the Weight column.

FIGURE 1.59
The Panorama window lets you make adjustments to your best-fit parabola.

Attaching Multiple Entities

The Attach Multiple Entities command that can be called out in the command line as `attachmultiple` is a combination of the Line From End Of Object command and the Curve From End Of Object command. Using CUI, you can bring this command into the ribbon if desired. Each entity created with this tool is tangent to the previous segment. Using this command saves you time because you don't have to switch between the Line From End Of Object command and the Curve From End Of Object command (see Figure 1.60).

FIGURE 1.60
The Attach Multiple Entities command draws a series of lines and arcs so that each segment is tangent to the previous one.

Adding Line and Curve Labels

Certification
Objective

In Civil 3D the dynamic and intelligent labeling is not limited to Civil 3D objects alone. You can add dynamic linked labels to basic AutoCAD elements like lines and curves. These labels share the most common properties of the labels used for other Civil 3D objects such as parcels and alignments.

This exercise leads you through labeling the deed you entered earlier in this chapter:

1. Open the file `0107_Legal_Labels.dwg` (`0107_Legal_Labels_METRIC.dwg`), which can be downloaded from the book's web page.

2. On the Annotate tab of the ribbon, choose Labels And Tables Panel ➤ Add Labels.

   The Add Labels dialog appears.

3. Choose Line And Curve from the Feature drop-down menu.

   Your Add Labels dialog will look similar to Figure 1.61.

FIGURE 1.61
The Add Labels dialog, with Label Type set to Multiple Segment

4. Choose Multiple Segment from the Label Type drop-down menu.

The Multiple Segment option places the label at the midpoint of each selected line or arc.

5. Confirm that Line Label Style is set to Bearing Over Distance and that Curve Label Style is set to Distance-Radius And Delta (as shown in Figure 1.61).

6. Click the Add button.

7. At the Select Entity: prompt, select each line from the deed and the lines and arcs that you drew in the previous exercises.

A label appears on each entity at its midpoint, as shown in Figure 1.62.

FIGURE 1.62
The labeled
linework

8. Save the drawing and close it.

You can check the result of your drawing against the completed file found on the web page for the book; it's named 0107_Legal_Labels_FINISHED.dwg (0107_Legal_Labels_METRIC_FINISHED.dwg).

The use of these labels does not stop at lines and curves; they can be used on polylines as well. Based on the selection of a single segment or multiple segments, Civil 3D can apply the labels to a single segment on the polyline or all segments of the polyline, assigning the specific label to lines and curves that define the polyline.

Using Transparent Commands

You might be surprised to know that you have already been using a form of the transparent commands if you tried to use, for example, the Line By Point # Range command or the Line By

Bearing command. That's because each of those commands is a variation of the line command with a transparent command already built in.

Transparent commands are "helper" commands that make base AutoCAD input more surveyor- and civil designer–friendly. Transparent commands can be used only when another command is in progress. They are "commands within commands" that allow you to choose your input based on the available data you have to provide.

For example, you may have a plat whose information you are trying to input into AutoCAD. You may need to insert a block at a specific northing and easting. While the Line command has a built-in option for Northing Easting, the Insert command does not, and a transparent command will help you. In this case, you would start the Insert command with the Specify On Screen option checked. Before you click to place the block in the graphic, click the Northing Easting transparent command. The command line will then walk you through placing the block at your desired location.

While a transparent command is active, you can press Esc once to leave transparent mode but stay active in your current command. You can then choose another transparent command if you'd like. For example, you can start a line using the Endpoint Osnap, activate the Angle Distance transparent command, draw a line-by-angle distance, and then press Esc, which takes you out of angle-distance mode but keeps you in the line command. You can then draw a few more segments using the Point Object transparent command, press Esc, and finish your line with a Perpendicular Osnap.

You can activate the transparent commands using keyboard shortcuts or the Transparent Commands toolbar. Be sure you include the Transparent Commands toolbar (shown in Figure 1.63) in all your Civil 3D and survey-oriented workspaces.

FIGURE 1.63
The Transparent Commands toolbar

The seven profile-related transparent commands will be covered in Chapter 7.

Standard Transparent Commands

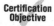Certification Objective

The transparent commands shown in Table 1.2 can be called out within any AutoCAD or Civil 3D draw command, such as a line, polyline, alignment, parcel segment, feature line, or pipe-creation command.

TABLE 1.2: The transparent commands used in plan view

TOOL ICON	MENU COMMAND	KEY-IN	TOOL ICON	MENU COMMAND	KEY-IN
	Angle Distance	'AD		Latitude Longitude	'LL
	Bearing Distance	'BD		Point Number	'PN
	Azimuth Distance	'ZD		Point Name	'PA
	Deflection Distance	'DD		Point Object	'PO
	Northing Easting	'NE		Zoom To Point	'ZTP
	Grid Northing Grid Easting	'GN		Side Shot	'SS
	Station Offset	'SO			

Matching Transparent Commands

You may have construction or other geometry in your drawing that you'd like to match with new lines, arcs, circles, alignments, parcel segments, or other entities.

While actively drawing an object that has a radius parameter, such as a circle, an arc, an alignment curve, or a similar object, you can choose the Match Radius transparent command and then select an object in your drawing that has your desired radius. Civil 3D draws the resulting entity with a radius identical to that of the object you chose during the command.

The Match Length transparent command works the same as the Match Radius transparent command except that it matches the length parameter of your chosen object.

Some people find working with transparent commands awkward at first. It feels strange to move your mouse away from the drawing area and click an icon while another command is in progress. If you prefer, each transparent command has a corresponding command-line entry.

Try a few transparent commands to get the feel for how they operate.

1. Open the drawing 0108_Transparent_Commands.dwg (0108_Transparent_Commands_METRIC.dwg).

2. On the Home tab of the ribbon, click the Draw flyout ➤ 3D Polyline.

3. From the Transparent Commands toolbar, click the Point Number Transparent command.

4. At the Enter Point Number prompt, type **100-112** and press ↵.

The 3D polyline will connect the points in the drawing.

5. Press Esc once.

Notice that you are now back in the 3D polyline command with no transparent commands active.

6. Press Esc a second time.

This will exit the 3D polyline command.

7. On the Insert tab ➤ Block panel ➤ Insert flyout ➤ More Options.

8. From the Name pull-down, select the block Fire Hydrant 01.

You do not need to browse because this block is already defined in this example drawing.

9. Check the Specify On-Screen option for Insertion Point.

10. Uncheck the Explode option.

11. Verify that your settings match what is shown in Figure 1.64 and click OK.

FIGURE 1.64
Using the Insert command to place a block

12. At the Specify insertion point: prompt, select the Station Offset transparent command.

You are then prompted to select an alignment.

13. Click the alignment to the south of the site. (Hint: Be sure to click the green line rather than the labels.)

14. At the Specify station along alignment: prompt, enter **450′ (175** m) and press ↵.

15. At the Specify station offset: prompt, enter **–30′ (–10** m) and press ↵.

You should now see the fire hydrant symbol at the specified station, on the left of the alignment. You can go ahead and save the drawing, and you can compare the final result against the completed file as found on the web page for the book under the name

0108_Transparent_Commands_FINISHED.dwg (0108_Transparent_Commands_METRIC_FINISHED.dwg).

The Bottom Line

Find any Civil 3D object with just a few clicks.   By using Prospector to view object data collections, you can minimize the panning and zooming that are part of working in a CAD program. When common subdivisions can have hundreds of parcels or a complex corridor can have dozens of alignments, jumping to the desired one nearly instantly shaves time off everyday tasks.

Master It   Open 0103_Example.dwg (0103_Example_METRIC.dwg) from www.sybex
.com/go/masteringcivil3d2016 and find parcel number 6 without using any AutoCAD commands or scrolling around on the drawing screen.

Modify the drawing scale and default object layers.   Civil 3D understands that the end goal of most drawings is to create hard-copy construction documents. When you set a drawing scale, Civil 3D removes a lot of the mental gymnastics that other programs require when you're sizing text and symbols. When you set object layers for the entire drawing, Civil 3D makes uniformity of drawing files easier than ever to accomplish.

Master It   Continue working in the file 0103_Example.dwg (0103_Example_METRIC
.dwg). It is not necessary to have completed the previous exercise to continue. Zoom to extents and change the Annotation scale in the Model tab from the 50-scale drawing to a 100-scale drawing. (For metric users, change the scale from 1:250 to 1:1000.)

Navigate the ribbon's contextual tabs.   As with AutoCAD, the ribbon is the primary interface for accessing Civil 3D commands and features. When you select an AutoCAD Civil 3D object, the ribbon displays commands and features related to that object. If several object types are selected, the Multiple contextual tab is displayed.

Master It   Continue working in the file 0103_Example.dwg (0103_Example_METRIC
.dwg). It is not necessary to have completed the previous exercise to continue. Using the ribbon interface, access the Alignment properties for QuickStart Alignment and rename it Existing CL.

Create a curve tangent to the end of a line.   It's rare that a property stands alone. Often, you must create adjacent properties, easements, or alignments from their legal descriptions.

Master It   Open the drawing MasterIt_0101.dwg (MasterIt_0101_METRIC.dwg). Create a curve tangent to the east end of the line labeled in the drawing. The curve should meet the following specifications:

◆   Radius: **200.00′ (60 m)**

◆   Arc Length: **66.58′ (20 m)**

Label lines and curves.   Although converting linework to parcels or alignments offers you the most robust labeling and analysis options, basic line- and curve-labeling tools are available when conversion isn't appropriate.

Master It   Add line and curve labels to each entity created in `MasterIt_0101.dwg` or `MasterIt_0101_METRIC.dwg`. It is recommended that you complete the previous exercise so you will have a curve to work with. Choose a label that specifies the bearing and distance for your lines and length, radius, and delta of your curve. Check your final result against the completed file found on the book's web page named `MasterIt_0101_FINISHED.dwg` (`MasterIt_0101_METRIC_FINISHED.dwg`).

Chapter 2

Survey

The Autodesk® AutoCAD® Civil 3D® software supports a collaborative workflow in many aspects of the design process but especially in the survey realm. Accurate data starts outdoors. A survey that has been consistently and correctly coded in the field can save hours of drafting time. Surveyors can collect line information for such things as swales, curbs, or even pavement markings and communicate this digitally to data collectors.

Civil 3D can often eliminate the need for third-party survey software because it can download and process survey data directly from a data collector. To enter data in a manner that is easily digested by Civil 3D, your survey process should incorporate the information from this chapter.

In this chapter, you will learn to:

◆ Properly collect field data and import it into Civil 3D.

◆ Set up description key and figure databases.

◆ Translate surveys from assumed coordinates to known coordinates.

◆ Perform traverse analysis.

Setting Up the Databases

Before any project-specific data is imported, you should do a bit of initial setup to improve the translation between the field and the office. For this chapter you will need to see your Survey tab in Toolspace. If you do not see this tab, click the Survey button on the Home tab ➤ Palettes panel.

Your survey database defaults, equipment database, linework code set, and the figure prefix database should be in place before you import your first survey. You can find the location of these files by going to Toolspace ➤ Survey tab and clicking the Survey User Settings button in the upper-left corner of the palette. The dialog shown in Figure 2.1 opens.

FIGURE 2.1
Survey User
Settings dialog

The survey database settings path points to the locations of the equipment database, figure prefix database, and linework code sets. Note that these files are separate from the Civil 3D template. These databases are separate files that reside in `C:\ProgramData\Autodesk\C3D 2016\enu\Survey\` by default. It is common practice to place these files on a network server so your organization can share them. You can set these paths while installing the software. Otherwise, change the paths in the Survey User Settings dialog on each individual computer, and they will "stick" regardless of which drawing you have open.

Survey Database Defaults

Every survey database that is created for a project has settings that you will need to examine and verify. To create a new survey database for a project, click the Import Survey Data button from the Home tab of the ribbon or right-click Survey Databases from Toolspace ➢ Survey tab and select New Local Survey Database.

Once the new database is created, you will be able to edit its properties, as outlined in the upcoming exercise. The Survey Database Settings dialog contains these settings:

Units Most likely, the Units setting is the only one you will ever need to modify in the Survey Database Settings dialog. Pay close attention to the units (Imperial vs. US Foot) if you choose not to select a master coordinate zone. This section is where you set your master coordinate zone for the database.

Potentially, your drawing and your incoming survey data may have different coordinate systems. If you insert any information stored in the database into a drawing with a different coordinate zone, the program will automatically translate that data to the drawing coordinate zone (upon initial import only). Your coordinate zone units will lock in the distance units in the Units section. Although usually not necessary, you can also set the angle, direction, temperature, and pressure specific to the survey database here.

Precision This section is where you define and store the precision information of angles, distance, elevation, coordinates, and latitude and longitude specific to the database. Note that this affects display precision for the survey interface and is independent from label precision and drawing precision set in the Drawing Settings dialog discussed in Chapter 1, "The Basics."

Measurement Type Defaults This section lets you tell Civil 3D what type of information to expect when importing survey data from a file. The information can be measurement types, such as angle type, distance type, vertical type, and target type.

Measurement Corrections This section is used to define the methods (if any) for correcting measurements. You will probably not need to change anything in this section because most data collectors will have processed this for you.

Traverse Analysis Defaults This section is where you choose what types of traverse analysis you want to perform. You can control the method you want to use and required precision and tolerances for each. There are four types of 2D traverse analysis methods: Compass Rule, Transit Rule, Crandall Rule, and Least Squares Analysis.

There are three potential types of 3D traverse analyses: Length Weighted Distribution, Equal Distribution, and Least Squares Vertical. Vertical options for Least Squares will be available only if it is first set as the Horizontal Adjustment Method. Of course, you can always choose None to omit that calculation from the analysis.

Least Squares Analysis Defaults If you are performing a Least Squares analysis, you must specify 2-Dimensional or 3-Dimensional adjustment type. Use 3-Dimensional if you are performing both horizontal and vertical Least Squares adjustment.

Survey Command Window In the rare event that you'll need it, the Survey Command window is the interface for manual survey tasks and for running survey batch files. This section lets you define the default settings for this window.

Error Tolerance Set tolerances for the survey database in this section. If you perform an observation more than one time and the tolerances established here are not met, an error will appear in the Survey Command window, and you will be asked what action you want to take.

Extended Properties You may work with LandXML files that contain information beyond traditional "P,N,E,Z,D" data. If this is the case, you will want to turn both Extended Properties options to Yes. Create New Definitions Automatically will add extended properties to your survey database and populate the fields from the imported file. Display Warnings For Missing Required Fields will display the Panorama interface if there is missing information in the imported file.

Change Reporting It is a great idea to turn this option to Yes by setting Logging Enabled to Yes. This will create an audit trail of changes to the database that occur after import. The changes to the database are stored in a LOG file (*.log) located in the same directory as your survey database. At any time, you can access the contents of the log by right-clicking the name of the survey database and selecting Display Change Report.

When you first configure your survey database settings, it is a good idea to create a test database for setting the defaults. Because survey database settings are independent of which drawing you are in, you can perform these steps with any file open. To create the test database, follow these steps:

1. In the Toolspace ➤ Survey tab, right-click Survey Databases.

2. Select Set Working Folder.

   Civil 3D will create a working folder to contain your survey database. Ideally, this will be stored in a network location for your organization's projects. For examples in this book, this will be set to your local C drive.

3. Verify that the C:\Civil 3D Projects folder is highlighted and click OK.

4. In the Toolspace ➤ Survey tab, right-click Survey Databases and choose New Local Survey Database.

5. Name the new database **Test** and click OK to continue.

6. Right-click the new Test database and select Edit Survey Database Settings.

7. Set your desired defaults for units, precision, and other options, as shown in Figure 2.2.

FIGURE 2.2
Survey Database
Settings dialog

8. Click the Export Settings To A File button.

9. Save the settings to the folder specified in the Survey User Settings dialog (shown earlier in Figure 2.1) as MySettings.sdb_set and then click Save and then OK.

To delete your Test database, you will need to close the database from the Survey tab. To do so, locate the database in Toolspace ➤ Survey tab. Right-click it and select Close Survey Database. Using Windows Explorer, you can then browse to the working folder containing the database and delete it. There is no way to delete a survey database from within the software.

The Equipment Database

The equipment database is where you set up the various types of survey equipment that you are using in the field. Doing so allows you to apply the proper correction factors to your traverse analyses when it is time to balance your traverse. Civil 3D comes with a sample piece of equipment for you to inspect to see what information you will need when it comes time to create your equipment. The Equipment Database Manager dialog provides all the default settings for the sample equipment in the equipment database. On the Survey tab of Toolspace, expand Equipment Databases, right-click Sample, and click Manage Equipment Database to access this dialog, shown in Figure 2.3.

FIGURE 2.3
Use Equipment Database Manager.

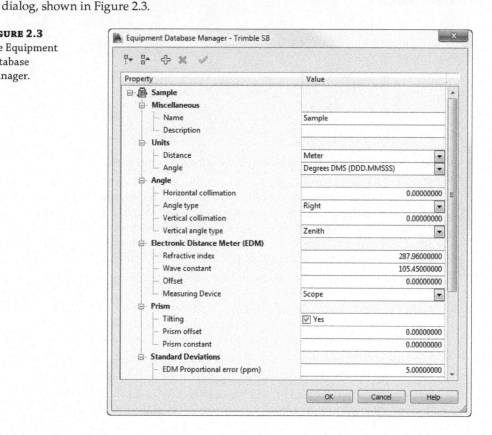

Figure 2.3 shows the settings for a specific model of total station—the Trimble S8. When you input this data to an equipment database, consult your instrument's datasheet for specifications. The specifics of total station equipment will vary by manufacturer and model.

You will want to create your own equipment entries and enter the specifications for your particular total station. Add a new piece of equipment to the database by clicking the plus sign at the top of the Equipment Database Manager window. If you are unsure of the settings to enter, refer to the user documentation that you received when you purchased your total station. Also be careful that you aren't applying a correction that hasn't already been applied in the gun itself such as prism offset.

The Figure Prefix Database

Certification Objective

The figure prefix database is used to translate descriptions in the field to lines in CAD. These survey-generated lines are called *figures*. If a description matches a listing in the figure prefix database, the figure is assigned the properties and style dictated by the database (see Figure 2.4).

FIGURE 2.4
The Figure Prefix Database Manager

The Figure Prefix Database Manager contains these columns:

Name The figure name is important because it must match the description used by the surveyor in the imported survey file. For example, if the surveyor collects points along the back of curb using the description BC, then there must be a figure name called BC in the figure prefix database in order to create linework or figures with those points using the properties specified in the database. If the figure name doesn't match up with a figure prefix, the linework will be drawn using default settings specified on the Settings tab.

Breakline Placing a check mark in this column will allow you to flag a figure as a breakline. The most powerful use of this setting is the Create Breaklines command on the context menu of the Figures collection located within the survey database on the Toolspace ➤ Survey tab. Figures with this setting on can be added to the definition of a surface model. Even if you don't flag a figure as a breakline, you can still add it to a surface model manually.

Lot Line This column specifies whether the figure should behave as a parcel segment. If a closed area is formed with figures of this kind, a parcel is formed automatically.

Layer This column specifies the insertion layer of the figure. If the layer already exists in the drawing, the figure will be placed on that layer. If the layer does not exist in the drawing, the layer will be created and the figure placed on the newly created layer. In the case of the latter, you may need to manually reset the layer properties so your figures display according to your standards. In the case where an incoming figure name doesn't match up with a figure prefix, the newly created figure will be placed on the layer specified for Survey Figure on the Object Layer tab of Drawing Settings. Drawing Settings were discussed in Chapter 1.

Style   This column specifies the style to be used for each figure. Figure styles will override color and linetype of the insertion layer if the style layer is set to something other than Layer 0. See the section on linear object styles in Chapter 19, "Object Styles," for more information on this type of style.

Site   This column specifies which site the figures should reside on when inserted into the drawing. As with previous settings, if the site exists in the drawing, the figure will be inserted into that site. If the site does not exist in the drawing, a site will be created with that name, and the figure will be inserted into the newly created site.

Remember that figure prefix databases are not drawing specific. The only reason a drawing is needed is to access the styles that the figures will use.

You'll explore these settings in a practical exercise:

1. Open the drawing `0201_SurveySetup.dwg` or `0201_SurveySetup_METRIC`
   `.dwg`, which you can download from this book's web page, `www.sybex.com/`
   `go/masteringcivil3d2016`.

   This file contains the survey figure styles needed to complete this exercise.

2. In Toolspace ➢ Survey tab, right-click Figure Prefix Databases and select New.

   The New Figure Prefix Database dialog opens.

3. Enter **Mastering Civil 3D** in the Name text box and click OK to dismiss the dialog.

   If you expand the Figure Prefix Database listing, you will see the Mastering Civil 3D entry.

4. Right-click the newly created Mastering Civil 3D figure prefix database and select Manage Figure Prefix Database.

   The Figure Prefix Database Manager will appear.

5. Select the white + symbol in the upper-left corner of the Figure Prefix Database Manager to create a new figure prefix.

6. Click the default name, Sample, and change the name of the figure prefix to **BB** (for Bottom of Bank).

7. Click the check box next to the word *No* in the Breakline column. This will turn into a Yes, indicating that it will contain the breakline property.

   Leave the box in the Lot Line column unchecked so that the figure will not be treated as a parcel segment.

8. In the Layer column, select V-SURV-FIGR.

9. In the Style column, select BB.

10. In the Site column, leave the name of the site set to Survey Site.

11. Complete the figure prefix database with the values shown in Table 2.1.

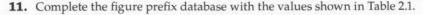

TABLE 2.1:   Figure settings

NAME	BREAKLINE	LOT LINE	LAYER	STYLE	SITE
BLDG	No	No	V-SURV-FIGR	BLDG	SURVEY SITE
CL	Yes	No	V-SURV-FIGR	CL	SURVEY SITE
DL	Yes	No	V-SURV-FIGR	DL	SURVEY SITE
DW	Yes	No	V-SURV-FIGR	DW	SURVEY SITE
EC	Yes	No	V-SURV-FIGR	EC	SURVEY SITE
EG	Yes	No	V-SURV-FIGR	EG	SURVEY SITE
EP	Yes	No	V-SURV-FIGR	EP	SURVEY SITE
PPE	No	No	V-SURV-FIGR	ELEC	SURVEY SITE
PROP	No	Yes	V-SURV-FIGR	PROP	SURVEY SITE
TB	No	No	V-SURV-FIGR	TB	SURVEY SITE

Hint: For figures with similar properties, select a figure definition already in the database and then use the Copy Figure Prefix button.

12. Click OK to dismiss the Figure Prefix Database Manager.

Keep this drawing open to use in the next portion of the exercise.

You can choose whether lines are automatically formed in the linework code set when they match one of these figure prefixes.

The Linework Code Set Database

The linework code set (Figure 2.5) lists what designators are used to start, stop, continue, or add segments to lines. For example, the B code that is typically used to begin a line can be replaced with an *S*, RT can be simplified to *R* for a right turn, and PC and PT can be used to begin and end curves. Linework code sets allow a survey crew to customize their data-collection techniques based on methods used by various types of software not related to Civil 3D.

FIGURE 2.5
The Edit Linework
Code Set dialog

LINEWORK OPTION: BEGIN ON FIGURE PREFIX MATCH

There is a setting in the linework code set called Automatic Begin On Figure Prefix Match (as you can see in Figure 2.5). If you select this option, lines will start when a shot description matches one of your figure prefixes (such as EP or CL in Figure 2.4), with no additional coding needed.

Depending on your survey department's method for picking up linework, Automatic Begin On Figure Prefix Match can be a good thing or a bad thing. If the survey crew has fastidiously collected each line with its own name, such as CL1, CL2, EP1, EP2, and so on, with no repeats, it can work well. If they use start and stop codes but reuse line names throughout the survey, it can produce figures that connect unintentionally.

Configuring Description Keys for Point Import

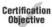
Certification
Objective

Description keys bridge the gap between the field and the office. Unlike the linework code set and figure prefix database, which are each external files, description keys should be created and saved in your Civil 3D template. *The description key set* is a listing of field descriptions and parameters that control how points look and behave once they are imported into or manually created in Civil 3D.

For example, a surveyor collects a point with the description FH to indicate a fire hydrant. When the file is imported into Civil 3D either through the survey database or by point import from a text file (as you will do in Chapter 3, "Points"), it will be checked against the description key set. If FH exists in the list, as it does in Figure 2.6, then the styles, format, layer, and several other parameters are applied to the point as it is placed in the drawing.

FIGURE 2.6
Description key set

To access your description key set, you will need to expand Toolspace ➤ Settings tab ➤ Point ➤ Description Key Sets.

Right-click the description key set and select Edit Keys; the Description Key Editor will open (using the Panorama interface) with the following columns for you to edit:

Code The code is the raw description or field code entered by the person collecting or creating the points. The code works as an identifier for matching the point with the correct description key. Click inside this field to activate it and then type your desired code. Wildcards are useful when more information is added to the shot in addition to the field code. Right-click an existing code to copy or create a new description key or delete an existing one.

Codes are case sensitive! The code fh is read differently from FH. A match to the description key set will not be made if the capitalization does not match perfectly.

Style Style refers to the point style that will be applied to points that meet the code criteria. Check the box and then click inside the field to activate a point style selection dialog. By default, styles set here will take precedence over styles set elsewhere (unless overridden in a point group, see Chapter 3). For more information on creating or modifying point styles, see Chapter 19.

Point Label Style   This is the point label style that will be applied to points that meet the code criteria. Check the box and then click inside the field to activate a style selection dialog. By default, styles set here will take precedence over styles set elsewhere (unless overridden in a point group). For more information on creating or modifying point label styles, see Chapter 18, "Label Styles."

Format   The Format column can convert a surveyor's shorthand into something that is more drafter friendly. In Civil 3D terms, the Format column converts the *raw description* to the *full description*. The default of $* means the raw description and full description will have the same value. You can also use $+, which means that information after the main description will appear as the full description. In Figure 2.6, Format will convert all codes starting with MB to a full description of MAILBOX.

If a survey crew is consistent in coding, even fancier formats can be used. The code should always come first, but the crew can use a space to indicate a *parameter*.

Consider this example raw description: TR 30 PINE ELIM. TR is the code, or $0. Parameter 1 is 30, or $1 in the Format field. PINE is the second bit of information after the code referred to as parameter 2, or $2. ELIM is the third item after the code, so it is $3. Based on the example description key set in Figure 2.6, this would translate to a full description of PINE 30. You can have up to nine parameters after the code if your survey crew is feeling verbose. Table 2.2 shows some example formats and the corresponding full description.

TABLE 2.2:   Format examples

RAW DESCRIPTION	FORMAT	FULL DESCRIPTION
TR 30 PINE ELIM	Tree	Tree
TR 30 PINE ELIM	$*	TR 30 PINE ELIM
TR 30 PINE ELIM	$0	TR
TR 30 PINE ELIM	$1"	30"
TR 30 PINE ELIM	$2	PINE
TR 30 PINE ELIM	$3	ELIM
TR 30 PINE ELIM	$2 $1	PINE 30
TR 30 PINE ELIM	$+	30 PINE ELIM

Layer   Points that match a description key will be inserted on the layer specified here. Click inside this field to activate a layer selection dialog. The layer set here will take precedence over layer defaults set in the point command settings or the point creation tools.

Scale Parameter   The Scale parameter is used to tell Civil 3D which bit of information after the code will be used to scale the symbol. By default, it is checked, but it won't do anything unless Apply To X-Y is also selected. Once you enable Apply To X-Y (or Apply To Z, which is less frequently used), you can change which parameter contains scale information.

In our example, TREE 30 PINE ELIM, 30 ($1) is the Scale parameter.

Fixed Scale Factor   Fixed Scale Factor is an additional scale multiplier that can be applied to the symbol size. A common use of Fixed Scale Factor is to convert a field measurement of inches to feet. If the 30 in our example represents a dripline measurement and is meant to be feet, no Fixed Scale Factor is needed. However, if the 30 represents inches (i.e., a trunk diameter), you would need to turn on Fixed Scale Factor and set the value to 0.0833.

Use Drawing Scale   In most cases, you will leave this option unchecked. By default, marker styles dictate that they will grow or shrink based on the annotative scale of the drawing. Generally, this setting is not needed unless you want to scale your point symbol based on a parameter in addition to the scale factor.

Apply To X-Y   If you want to scale symbols based on information in the field code, you need to turn this option on by placing a check mark in the box. This option works with the marker style and the Scale parameter to increase the size of an item to a scale indicated by the surveyor in the raw description.

Apply To Z   In most cases, you will leave this option unchecked. Most marker symbols are 2D blocks, so selecting this option will have no effect on the point. If your marker symbol consists of a 3D block, it will be stretched by the parameter value, which is rarely needed.

Marker Rotate Parameter, Marker Fixed Rotation, Label Rotate Parameter, Label Fixed Rotation, and Rotation Direction   These options are similar to the scale factor parameter except they dictate the rotation of a symbol or label. They are not widely used, however, because it is often more time effective to have the drafter rotate the points in CAD than to have the surveyor key in a rotation. If you would like to rotate the points for readability, the better method to rotate the text is in the point label style (discussed in Chapter 18).

Creating a Description Key Set

Description key sets appear on the Toolspace ➢ Settings tab, under the Point branch. You can create a new description key set as follows:

1. Right-click the Description Key Sets collection and choose New, as shown in Figure 2.7.

FIGURE 2.7
Creating a new
description key set
on the Settings tab
of Toolspace

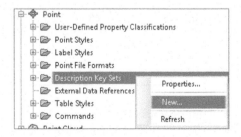

2. In the resulting Description Key Set dialog, give your description key set a meaningful name, such as your company name.

3. Click OK.

You'll create the actual description keys in another dialog.

Creating Description Keys

To enter the individual description key codes and parameters, expand Toolspace ➤ Settings tab ➤ Point ➤ Description Key Set. Right-click the description key set, as illustrated in Figure 2.8, and select Edit Keys. The DescKey Editor in the Panorama interface appears.

FIGURE 2.8
Editing a description key set

To enter new codes, right-click a row with an existing key in the DescKey Editor and choose New or Copy from the right-click menu, as shown in Figure 2.9.

FIGURE 2.9
Creating or copying a description key

USING WILDCARDS IN DESCRIPTION KEY SETS

Civil 3D can use several special characters to do more complex matching or exclusions in your Description Key Set Code field. You can use combinations of these wildcards to build intelligence into the translation between the field and Civil 3D.

◆ Most commonly, the asterisk (*) acts as a general wildcard and is recommended after most codes. An asterisk before or after your code will allow a surveyor to add more information to a shot without compromising the matching on the Civil 3D end.

◆ A hash mark or pound sign (#) signifies a single-digit numeric value 0 through 9.

◆ An "at" symbol (@) signifies any letter of the alphabet A through Z.

Continues

Continued

◆ A question mark (?) signifies any letter of the alphabet or a number.

◆ A period in a code signifies any character that is not alphanumeric, such as an ampersand (&) or a plus sign (+).

◆ A tilde (~) is an operator you can use to exclude characters or groups of characters. A tilde inside square brackets tells Civil 3D to not match characters inside the brackets.

◆ The use of square brackets is supported and allows for additional logic. Multiple characters inside brackets is like telling the description keys "Any of these will work." You can even use a range such as [1-9] or [A-N]. Add the tilde to the brackets to signify "None of these will work."

For the @ symbol, hash mark, question mark, and period, a character must be in place; blanks will not form the match.

The following table demonstrates how description key wildcards can be used:

CODE	EXAMPLE MATCHES	WILL NOT MATCH
G*	GR	g
	G	
	GAS	
CL#	CL1	CL
	CL2	cl1
	CL9	CLZ
1@	1A	12
	1z	1
A.	A+	A1
	A!	AB
	A<	A
F?	F7	F
	FZ	F+
~*ASB*	XINL	INL-ASB
	GR	ASB
	FL	ASBCL
T[+-]	T+	T
	T-	TR
[1-5]FL	1FL	FL
	4FL	6FL
[~XE]SMH	ASMH	XSMH
	1SMH	ESMH
	+SMH	SMH

Don't forget that description keys are case sensitive. Additionally, you can have multiple description key sets as discussed in the section "Activating a Description Key Set." With the knowledge you have gained so far in this chapter, you can create a powerful tool for managing survey points.

In the following exercise, you'll create and populate a description key set.

1. Continue working in your 0201_SurveySetup.dwg or 0201_SurveySetup_METRIC.dwg file. You must have completed the previous exercise.

2. From the Toolspace ➤ Settings tab, expand the Points branch, right-click Description Key Sets, and click New.

3. In the Description Key Set – New DescKey Set dialog, type **Mastering Civil 3D** in the Name field. Click OK to continue.

4. From the Toolspace ➤ Settings tab under the Points branch, expand Description Key Sets, right-click the Mastering Civil 3D description key set, and click Edit Keys.

   The DescKey Editor will open in Panorama.

5. Create the description keys in Table 2.3 by right-clicking a description key line in the list and clicking New or Copy.

TABLE 2.3:   New description keys

CODE	STYLE	POINT LABEL STYLE	FORMAT	LAYER
BB*	Elevation Marker	Elevation Only	$*	V-NODE-TOPO
BLDG*	Linework	No Display	$*	V-NODE-BLDG
CL*	Elevation Marker	Elevation Only	$*	V-NODE-TOPO
DL*	Elevation Marker	Elevation Only	$*	V-NODE-TOPO
DW*	Elevation Marker	Elevation Only	$*	V-NODE-DRIV
EC*	Elevation Marker	Elevation Only	$*	V-NODE-CONC
EG*	Elevation Marker	Elevation Only	$*	V-NODE-GRVL
EP*	Elevation Marker	Elevation Only	$*	V-NODE-PVMT
FH*	Hydrant (existing)	No Display	$*	V-NODE-WATR
GS*	Elevation Marker	Elevation Only	$*	V-NODE-TOPO
GUY*	Guy Wire	No Display	$*	V-NODE-POWR

TABLE 2.3: New description keys *(CONTINUED)*

CODE	STYLE	POINT LABEL STYLE	FORMAT	LAYER
IPF*	Iron Pin	Description Only	IRON PIN (F)	V-NODE-PROP
IRF*	Iron Pin	Description Only	IRON ROD (F)	V-NODE-PROP
MB*	Mailbox	Description Only	MAILBOX	V-NODE-SITE
PED*	Telephone Pedestal	Description Only	T PED	V-NODE-COMM
PP*	Power Pole	No Display	$*	V-NODE-POWR
PROP*	Linework	No Display	$*	V-NODE-PROP
TB*	Elevation Marker	Elevation Only	$*	V-NODE-TOPO
TREE*	Tree	Description Only	$1" $2	V-NODE-TREE
TRANS*	Transformer	Description Only	TRANS	V-NODE-POWR
WM*	Water Meter	Description Only	$*	V-NODE-WATR
WV*	Water Valve	Description Only	$*	V-NODE-WATR

You may have noticed an extra description key on the list called New DescKey, which was created by default when the description key set was made. This description key can be deleted by clicking it and selecting Delete from the context menu. Another option would be to edit the entry to represent a description key you need.

When this exercise is complete, you may close the drawing. A saved copy of this drawing (0201_SurveySetup_FINISHED.dwg or 0201_SurveySetup_METRIC_FINISHED.dwg) is available from the book's web page.

Activating a Description Key Set

Once you've created a description key set, you should verify the settings for your commands so that Civil 3D knows to match your newly created points with the appropriate key.

In Toolspace ➢ Settings tab, expand Point ➢ Commands and right-click CreatePoints. Select Edit Command Settings, as shown in Figure 2.10.

In the Edit Command Settings – CreatePoints dialog, expand the Points Creation category and ensure that Match On Description Parameters is set to True and that Disable Description Keys is set to False, as shown in Figure 2.11.

It is common to have multiple description key sets in your template. You can leverage description key sets for multiple clients or external survey firms that you work with. If you have multiple description key sets, they are all active, but if a set has a duplicate key, the first one

Civil 3D runs across will take precedence. For example, if one set uses FL for flowline but a second set uses FL for fence line, the second occurrence of the FL key gets ignored.

FIGURE 2.10
Right-click
CreatePoints
and choose
Edit Command
Settings.

FIGURE 2.11
Verify that Match
On Description
Parameter is set to
True, and Disable
Description Keys
is set to False.

You can control the search order from the Toolspace ➤ Settings tab ➤ Points branch by right-clicking Description Keys Sets and selecting Properties. Figure 2.12 shows the Description Key Sets Search Order dialog. Choose a description key set in the list and then use the arrows on the right side of the dialog to set the order. The set listed first takes first priority, then the second, and so on. Note that the listing in the Settings tab may not reflect the true listing in the properties.

FIGURE 2.12
The Description
Key Sets Search
Order dialog

Understanding the Survey Database

Now that you know how to get everything set up, you are probably eager to get some real, live data into your drawing.

First set your survey working folder to your desired survey storage location. The Civil 3D survey database is a set of external database files that reside in your survey working folder. By default, this folder is located in `C:\Civil 3d Projects\`. This is another item you will want to send to a network location in your own projects.

On the Toolspace ➤ Survey tab, right-click Survey Databases and select Set Working Folder, as shown in Figure 2.13.

FIGURE 2.13
Set the survey
working folder.

In the current version of Civil 3D, this is a different, independent setting from the working folder for data shortcuts (as discussed in Chapter 16, "Advanced Workflows"). Most folks want this on a network location, tucked neatly into the survey folder for the project.

To create a survey database, either you can right-click and select New Local Survey Database from Toolspace ➤ Survey tab as mentioned earlier, or you can select Import Survey Data from the Home tab's Create Ground Data panel.

The contents of a survey database are organized into the following categories:

Import Events   Import events provide a framework for viewing and editing specific survey data, and they are created each time you import data into a survey database. The default name for the import event is the same as the imported filename. The Import Event collection contains the networks, figures, and survey points that are referenced from a specific import event and provides an easy way to remove, reimport, and reprocess survey data in the current drawing.

Survey Queries   Survey queries allow users to search for specific information within a survey database. You can use a query to locate and group related survey points and figures.

For example, you may want all figures representing power lines in a query with survey points representing power poles. If you create a query containing your utilities, you can isolate specific figures and points to insert into another drawing.

A survey query can be used in conjunction with a surface. When a query containing points and figures is added to a surface model, the figures are automatically added as breaklines. Figure 2.14 shows an example query that might be used for generating surface data.

FIGURE 2.14
Survey database query

If the survey query you create is worthy of using in other databases, you can export it for use in other databases. Right-click Survey Queries and choose to export or import the query.

Networks   A survey network is a collection of related data that is collected in the field. The network consists of setups, control points, non-control points, directions, and traverses. A survey database can have multiple networks. For example, you can use different networks for different phases of a project.

Network Groups   Network groups are collections of various survey networks within a survey database. These groups can be created to facilitate inserting multiple networks into a drawing at once, simply by dragging and dropping.

Figures   Figures are the linework created by codes and commands entered into the raw data file during data collection. The figure names typically come from the descriptor or description of a point.

Figure Groups   Similar to network groups, figure groups are sets of individual figures. These groups can be created to facilitate quick insertion of multiple figures into a drawing.

Survey Points   One of the most basic components of a survey database, points form the basis for each and every survey. Survey points look just like regular Civil 3D point objects, and their visibility can be controlled just as easily. However, one major difference is that a survey point cannot be edited within a drawing. Survey points are locked by the survey database, and the only way of editing them is to edit the observation that collected the data for the points. This provides the surveyor with the confidence that points will not be accidentally erased or edited. Like figures, survey points can be inserted into a drawing either by dragging and dropping from the Toolspace ➤ Survey tab or by right-clicking Surveying Points and selecting the Points ➤ Insert Into Drawing option.

Survey Point Groups   Just like network groups and figure groups, survey point groups are sets of points that can be easily inserted into a drawing. When these survey point groups are inserted into the drawing, a Civil 3D point group is created with the same name as the survey point group. This point group can be used to control the visibility or display properties of each point in the group.

In the following exercise, you'll create an import event and import an ASCII file with survey data. The survey data includes linework.

1. Open the drawing 0202_ImportSurveyData.dwg or 0202_ImportSurveyData_METRIC.dwg.

   If you did not complete the previous exercise, copy the file Mastering Civil 3D.fdb_xdef from the dataset to C:\ProgramData\Autodesk\C3D 2016\enu\Survey. Note that this directory is hidden in Windows by default, so you will need to change the folder view options or type this path into the address bar of Windows Explorer.

2. From the Home tab ➤ Create Ground Data panel, click Import Survey Data to open the Import Survey Data Wizard.

3. Click Create New Survey Database.

4. Enter **Ditch Survey** as the name of the folder in which your new database will be stored. Click OK.

   Ditch Survey is now added to the list of survey databases.

5. With Ditch Survey highlighted, click Edit Survey Database Settings and verify that the Distance units are set to US Foot (or meter). Click OK to dismiss the dialog.

6. Click Next.

7. Set the Data Source Type pull-down to Point File.

8. Click the white plus sign on the right side of the Selected Files list to browse to the 0203_ImportPoints.txt or 0203_ImportPoints_METRIC.txt file, which you can download from this book's web page.

If necessary, change the File Of Type drop-down selection to Text/Template/Extract File (*.txt).

9. Select the file and then click Open, and the name will be listed in the dialog, as shown in Figure 2.15.

FIGURE 2.15
Select the correct source type, file, and format in the Import Survey Data Wizard.

10. Under Specify Point File Format, scroll through the list until you find PENZD (Comma Delimited).

11. Highlight the PENZD (Comma Delimited) format.

    The preview will show that the correct data type is selected, as shown at the bottom of Figure 2.15.

12. Click Next to continue.

13. Click Create New Network.

    Note that if you forget to create a network to place your points, you will not be able to manipulate this group apart from other points.

14. Enter **Ditch Survey 4-22-2015** as the name of the network and click OK.

15. Highlight the new network and click Next to continue.

16. Enter the following settings:

    a. Set Current Figure Prefix Database to Mastering Civil 3D.

    b. Set the Process Linework During Import option to Yes.

    Be sure Insert Survey Points is set to Yes.

17. When your import options match what is shown in Figure 2.16, click Finish.

FIGURE 2.16
The Import
Options page in
the Import Survey
Data Wizard

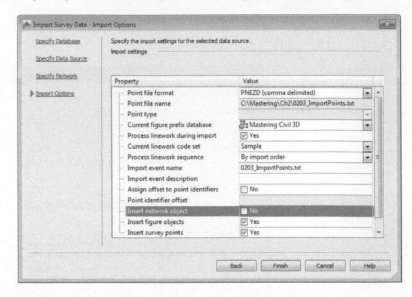

18. Save the file as **0203_DitchSurvey.dwg** to the same location as the rest of your downloaded example files. You will need it in the next exercise.

The data is imported and the linework is drawn; however, there are some mistakes in the
coding, which is producing erroneous linework. The following steps will resolve this issue:

1. Continue working in the drawing from the previous exercise. In the Toolspace ➤ Survey
tab, expand Survey Databases and then select Ditch Survey ➤ Networks ➤ Ditch Survey
4-22-2015 ➤ Non-Control Points.

2. Right-click Non-Control Points and select Edit to bring up the Non-Control Points Editor
in Panorama.

3. Scroll to point Number 1104, right-click, and click Zoom To.

The red line represents the flowline of the ditch. Notice in the drawing how the linework
crosses over the brown top of bank line to the flowline of another ditch. The points along
the ditches were collected simultaneously using the code DL for the left side and DL2
for the right side. Point 1104 representing the right side was obviously miscoded, and
correcting the description in the editor will allow you to reimport the corrected linework.

4. In Panorama, double-click the Description field.

5. Use the arrow keys on your keyboard to move your cursor to the end of the
description DL.

6. Add **2** ↵ to the end of the description, as shown in Figure 2.17.

FIGURE 2.17
Editing the import event to fix the linework representing the ditch flowline

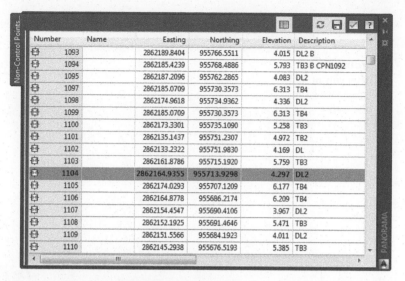

Number	Name	Easting	Northing	Elevation	Description
1093		2862189.8404	955766.5511	4.015	DL2 B
1094		2862185.4239	955768.4886	5.793	TB3 B CPN1092
1095		2862187.2096	955762.2865	4.083	DL2
1097		2862185.0709	955730.3573	6.313	TB4
1098		2862174.9618	955734.9362	4.336	DL2
1099		2862185.0709	955730.3573	6.313	TB4
1100		2862173.3301	955735.1090	5.258	TB3
1101		2862135.1437	955751.2307	4.972	TB2
1102		2862133.2322	955751.9830	4.169	DL
1103		2862161.8786	955715.1920	5.759	TB3
1104		2862164.9355	955713.9298	4.297	DL2
1105		2862174.0293	955707.1209	6.177	TB4
1106		2862164.8778	955686.2174	6.209	TB4
1107		2862154.4547	955690.4106	3.967	DL2
1108		2862152.1925	955691.4646	5.471	TB3
1109		2862151.5566	955684.1923	4.011	DL2
1110		2862145.2938	955676.5193	5.385	TB3

This will be corrected after reprocessing the linework.

The surveyor was simultaneously picking up points for two ditch lines coded DL and DL2. Miskeying codes is a common mistake when so much data is being collected.

7. Click the Save icon in the upper-right corner of Panorama and then click the green check mark in the upper right of the palette to apply changes and save your edits.

At this point you should see a yellow exclamation mark symbol next to the network name. This indicates that a change has been made to the survey database that has not yet been processed in the drawing. In the next steps, you will update the network to reflect the change graphically.

8. Click Yes if you are asked to apply your changes.

9. Right-click the network name (Ditch Survey 4-22-2015) and select Update Network.

10. Click Close to dismiss the Survey Network Updated dialog.

Updating the survey network has triggered a change in the figures as indicated by the exclamation mark symbol next to the Figures branch.

11. Right-click the Figures collection and select Update Figures.

12. Click the green check mark in the upper right of Panorama to dismiss the Event Viewer.

13. While still working in Survey Databases ➤ Ditch Survey, expand Import Events and select 0203_ImportPoints.txt (0202_ImportPoints_METRIC.txt).

14. Right-click the import event and select Process Linework to bring up the Process Linework dialog.

15. Click OK to reprocess the linework with your updated point description.

The ditch (DL2) figure line and your drawing should look something like Figure 2.18. Repeat steps 2–3 to zoom to the point again.

FIGURE 2.18
After editing and reprocessing the linework

16. Repeat steps 2–15 for the points in Table 2.4.

   For three of the points, you will be adding a Begin command (B) after the description separated by a space.

TABLE 2.4:   Corrections to non-control points

NUMBER	NEW DESCRIPTION
1134	DL2
1864	DL1
1925	DL
2217	BB1 B
3966	BB1 B
4058	BB2 B
4060	BB1 B

When this exercise is complete, you can close the drawing. A saved copy of this drawing (0203_DitchSurvey_FINISHED.dwg or 0203_DitchSurvey_METRIC_FINISHED.dwg) is available from the book's web page.

When you make modifications to survey data, only the Civil 3D database is changed. The original import file remains untouched. The survey database doesn't use the file unless you reimport the data.

If you edit raw data in the Survey tab, Civil 3D will recalculate all affected information. For example, if you modify an instrument height, all elevations that need to be updated will automatically adjust.

Keep in mind that if you edit the source file and reimport, the data in the Civil 3D database (and any edits you made) will be overwritten.

FINE-TUNING FIGURES

Survey figures are usually 3D lines (unless you have flattened them in the figure style). Figures can be edited with the same type of tools you use on feature lines, which you will learn about in Chapter 14, "Grading." You can find an editing tool unique to survey figures in the Figure contextual tab of the ribbon.

1. Select the figure you want to edit and select Survey Figure Properties.

   You will then see the details of the figure in tabular form.

Continues

Continued

2. Once you are in the Figure Properties dialog, fix any errors created by improper data collection or change fundamental qualities about the line, such as its name or breakline status.

3. Explore the tools in this dialog to locate ways to modify vertices; add or delete vertices; reverse figure direction; and break, trim, and join figures.

4. When you have completed editing your figures with this method, click Update Survey Data From Drawing on the Figure contextual tab of the ribbon to commit the change to the survey database.

Working with Survey Networks

Once you import survey data into a network, expand the branch to see how Civil 3D helps you make sense of it. In each network, data is organized by type, as shown in Figure 2.19.

FIGURE 2.19
A typical survey database network with data

 Control Points Control points are created when data from an FBK file is imported. Inside the FBK, control points are prefaced by NE, NEZ, or LAT LONG. You can force any point to be listed as a control point by right-clicking this collection and selecting New.

Non-Control Points   Keyed-in points, GPS-collected points, and any point brought in through an ASCII file will appear as non-control points. This is the default type if no other information is known about the point.

Directions   The direction from one point to another must be manually entered into the data collector for the direction to show up later in the survey network for editing. The direction can be as simple as a compass shot between two initial traverse points that serves as a rough basis of bearings for a survey job.

Setups   If you imported data that contains setups and observations, Setups is where the meat of the data is found. Every setup, as well as the points (side shots) located from that setup, can be found listed here. Setups will contain two components: the station (or occupied point) and the backsight. To see or edit the observations located from the setup, right-click Setups and select Edit Setups That Observe. Figure 2.20 shows the interface for editing setups. Backsight orientation and instrument heights can also be changed in this dialog.

FIGURE 2.20
Setups can be changed in the Setups Editor.

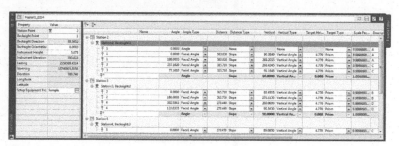

Traverses   The Traverses section is where new traverses are created or existing ones are edited. These traverses can come from your data collector, or they can be manually entered from field notes via the Traverse Editor, as shown in Figure 2.21. You can view or edit each setup in the Traverse Editor, as well as the traverse stations located from that setup.

FIGURE 2.21
The Traverse Editor

Once you have defined a traverse, you can adjust it by right-clicking its name and selecting Traverse Analysis. You can adjust the traverse either horizontally or vertically, using a variety of methods. The traverse analysis can be written to text files to be stored, and the entire network can be adjusted on the basis of the new values of the traverse.

In the following exercise, you will adjust a traverse:

1. Create a new drawing from the _AutoCAD Civil 3D (Imperial) NCS.dwt (_AutoCAD Civil 3D (Metric) NCS.dwt) template file.

2. Navigate to the Toolspace ➢ Survey tab.

3. Right-click Survey Databases and select New Local Survey Database.

   The New Local Survey Database dialog opens.

4. Enter **Traverse** as the name of the folder in which your new database will be stored.

5. Click OK to dismiss the dialog.

   The Traverse survey database is created as a branch under the Survey Databases branch.

6. Expand the Traverse branch, right-click Networks, and select New.

   The New Network dialog opens.

7. Expand the Network branch in the dialog if needed.

8. Name your new network **Traverse Practice** and click OK.

9. Right-click the Traverse Practice network and select Import ➤ Import Field Book.

10. Select the file 0204_Traverse.fbk (0204_Traverse_METRIC.fbk), which you can download from this book's web page, and click Open.

    The Import Field Book dialog opens.

11. Make sure you have checked the boxes shown in Figure 2.22.

FIGURE 2.22
The Import Field
Book dialog

There is no linework in this file because it is just traverse shots.

12. Click OK. Double-click your middle mouse wheel to zoom extents to get a look at the imported traverse.

The Traverse Practice network is now listed as a branch under Toolspace ➤ Prospector ➤ Survey ➤ Networks.

13. Save the drawing as `0204_Traverse.dwg` for the next exercise.

Looking back at the Toolspace ➤ Survey tab, expand the network you created earlier and inspect the data. You have one control point in the northwest corner that was manually entered into the data collector. There is one direction, and there are four setups. Each setup combines to form a closed polygonal shape that defines the traverse. Notice that there is no traverse definition. In the following exercise, you'll create that traverse definition for analysis.

Continue working in the drawing from the previous exercise:

1. Go to Toolspace ➤ Survey ➤ Survey Databases ➤ Traverse ➤ Networks ➤ Traverse Practice; then right-click Traverses and select New to open the New Traverse dialog.

2. Name the new traverse **Traverse 1**.

3. Type **2** as the Initial Station point number and press Enter.

The traverse will now pick up the rest of the stations in the traverse and enter them in the next box.

4. Verify that the points on the traverse match what is shown in Figure 2.23.

FIGURE 2.23
Defining a new traverse

5. Click OK.

6. Right-click Traverse 1 in the Item View of Toolspace. Select Traverse Analysis.

7. In the Traverse Analysis dialog, ensure that Yes is selected for Do Traverse Analysis and Do Angle Balance.

8. Select Least Squares for both Horizontal Adjustment Method and Vertical Adjustment Method.

9. Set both Horizontal Closure Limit 1:X and Vertical Closure Limit 1:X to **20,000**.

10. Leave Angle Error Per Set at the default.

11. Make sure the option Update Survey Database is set to Yes.

The Traverse Analysis dialog will look like Figure 2.24.

12. Click OK.

The analysis is performed, and four text files are opened that show the results of the adjustment. These files are automatically saved in the survey working folder under the same directory as the survey database (in this example, it should be `C:\Civil 3D Projects\Traverse\Traverse 1\`).

Note that if you look back at your survey network, all points are now control points because the analysis has upgraded all the points to control point status. Also, error ellipses are displayed in the drawing area at each station adjusted. The size of error ellipses are controlled by a scale factor set in the Survey Network style. If you are seeing extra-large ellipses, it is not an indication of an extra-large error. Styles will be discussed more in depth in Chapter 19.

FIGURE 2.24
Specify the adjustment method and closure limits in the Traverse Analysis dialog.

Figure 2.25 shows the `Traverse 1 Raw Closure.trv` and `Traverse 1 Vertical Adjustment.trv` files that are generated from the analysis. The raw closure file shows that your new precision is well within the tolerances set in step 8. The vertical adjustment file describes how the elevations have been affected by the procedure.

`Traverse 1.lso` is the output file displaying the adjustments of the traverse analysis. The first part of the file, shown in Figure 2.26, displays the various observations along with their initial measurements, standard deviations, adjusted values, and residuals. You can view other statistical data at the beginning of the file.

FIGURE 2.25
Horizontal and
vertical traverse
analysis results

```
Traverse 1 Raw Closure.trv - Notepad
File  Edit  Format  View  Help
Angular error          = 0-00-01
Angular error/set  = 0-00-00 Over
Elevation error : 0.0797
Error North      : 0.0163
Error East       : 0.0050
Absolute error   : 0.0170
Error Direction  : N 16-56-34 E
Perimeter        : 1618.7834
Precision        : 1 in 95281.9312
Number of sides  : 4
Area             : 149898.2 sq. ft. , 3.4412 Acres


Closure at other Traverse Points -----
Attention is called to maxima-minima separations
Point       Separation Distance
2               0.0170
3               0.0183
4               0.0199
1               0.0200
2               0.0170
Possible distance error in leg : 4 - 1
Angular error (if any) most probable at point 2
```

```
Traverse 1 Vertical Adjustment.trv - Notepad
File  Edit  Format  View  Help

                RAW        LEAST SQUARES RULE
Point       Elevation         Elevation          Delta
1           774.5994          774.6350           0.0356
2           780.7400          780.7400           0.0000
3           774.0201          774.0264           0.0063
4           769.7905          769.8017           0.0112
```

FIGURE 2.26
Statistical and
observation data
portion of text file

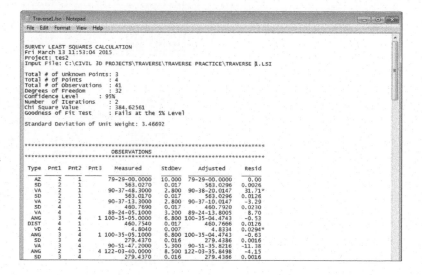

```
Traverse1.lso - Notepad
File  Edit  Format  View  Help

SURVEY LEAST SQUARES CALCULATION
Fri March 13 11:53:04 2015
Project: tes2
Input File: C:\CIVIL 3D PROJECTS\TRAVERSE\TRAVERSE PRACTICE\TRAVERSE 1.LSI

Total # of unknown Points : 3
Total # of Points         : 4
Total # of Observations   : 41
Degrees of Freedom        : 32
Confidence Level          : 95%
Number  of Iterations     : 2
Chi Square Value          : 384.62561
Goodness of Fit Test      : Fails at the 5% Level

Standard Deviation of Unit weight: 3.46692


********************************************************************
                         OBSERVATIONS
********************************************************************

Type  Pnt1  Pnt2  Pnt3   Measured       StdDev    Adjusted       Resid
 AZ     2     1          79-29-00.0000   10.000  79-29-00.0000     0.00
 SD     2     1             563.0270      0.017     563.0296      0.0026
 VA     2     1          90-37-48.3000    2.800  90-38-20.0147    31.71"
 SD     2     1             563.0170      0.017     563.0296      0.0126
 VA     2     1          90-37-13.3000    2.800  90-37-10.0147    -3.29
 SD     4     1             460.7690      0.017     460.7920      0.0230
 VA     4     1          89-24-05.1000    3.200  89-24-13.8005     8.70
 ANG    3     4      1 100-35-05.0000     6.800 100-35-04.4743    -0.53
 DIST   4     1             460.7540      0.017     460.7666      0.0126
 VD     4     1               4.8040      0.007       4.8334      0.0294*
 ANG    3     4      1 100-35-05.1000     6.800 100-35-04.4743    -0.63
 SD     3     4             279.4370      0.016     279.4386      0.0016
 VA     3     4          90-51-47.2000    5.300  90-51-35.8216   -11.38
 ANG    2     3      4 122-03-40.0000     8.500 122-03-35.8498    -4.15
 SD     3     4             279.4370      0.016     279.4386      0.0016
```

Figure 2.27 shows the second portion of this text file (you will need to scroll down to see it) and displays the adjusted coordinates, the standard deviation of the adjusted coordinates, and information related to error ellipses displayed in the drawing. If the deviations are too high for your acceptable tolerances, first check the instrument settings and tolerances in the equipment database. If everything is set correctly, you may need to redo the work or edit the field book.

Figure 2.28 displays the final portion of this text file—Blunder Detection/Analysis. Civil 3D will look for and analyze data in the network that is obviously wrong and choose to keep it or throw it out of the analysis if it doesn't meet your criteria. If a blunder (or bad shot) is detected, the program will not fix it. You will have to edit the data manually, whether by going out in the field and collecting the correct data or by editing the FBK file.

Traverse 1.lsi is the input file for displaying the station-to-station observations of the traverse analysis. This file can be edited and used to rerun the analysis based on the revised observations.

Other Methods of Manipulating Survey Data

Often, it is necessary to edit the entire survey network at one time. For example, rotating a network to a known bearing or azimuth from an assumed one happens quite frequently. To find this hidden gem of functionality, go to Toolspace ➤ Survey tab ➤ Survey Databases, right-click the name of the database you want to modify, and select Translate Survey Database, as shown in Figure 2.29.

FIGURE 2.27
Adjusted coordinate information portion of text file

FIGURE 2.28
Blunder analysis
portion of text file

FIGURE 2.29
The elusive yet
indispensable
Translate Survey
Database command

🌐 Real World Scenario

MANIPULATING THE NETWORK

Sometimes surveys performed in assumed coordinate systems need to be adjusted to match a known coordinate system. Along with changing coordinate systems, you will probably need to rotate the survey to the correct orientation. Additionally, networks may need to be adjusted from assumed elevations to a known datum.

In this example, the DWG you will be working with contains two known points from the desired coordinate system. The file you will import is initially in an assumed coordinate system. You will use the Translate command to move and rotate the network accordingly.

1. Open the file 0205_Translate.dwg (0205_Translate_METRIC.dwg).

2. In the Toolspace ➤ Survey tab, right-click Survey Databases and select New Local Survey Database.

   The New Local Survey Database dialog opens.

3. Enter **Translate** in the text box.

   This is the name of the folder for the new database.

4. Click OK, and the Translate database will now be listed under the Survey Databases branch.

5. Select Networks under the new Translate branch.

6. Right-click and select New to open the New Network dialog.

7. Enter **Translate** as the name of this new network.

8. Click OK to dismiss the dialog.

9. Right-click the Translate network and select Import ➤ Import Point File.

10. Navigate to the file 0205_Translate.txt (0205_Translate_METRIC.txt), which you can download from this book's web page, and click Open.

    The Import Point File dialog opens.

11. Verify that the point file format is PNEZD (Comma Delimited).

12. Verify that the Insert Survey Points option is set to Yes and click OK.

13. Zoom extents to view the points.

    Points 1 and 47 from the newly imported network correspond to 10000 and 10001 from the actual coordinate system. This is all the information needed to perform a translation.

14. Make sure you are able to locate these points for the next steps by panning and zooming with your mouse.

    It will also be helpful to turn on your Node object snap.

15. In the Toolspace ➤ Survey tab, right-click the name of the survey database and select Translate Survey Database, as shown earlier in Figure 2.29.

16. For Base Point Number, enter **1** and press ↵.

    Civil 3D will pick up the assumed coordinate of this point.

17. Click Next.

18. For the rotation angle, click the Pick In Drawing button in the bottom-left corner of the dialog.

    You will be prompted for an initial direction.

19. For Initial Direction, use the Node Osnap to pick point 1 and then point 47.

    You will then be prompted to specify a new direction.

20. Use the Node Osnap to pick points 10000 and 10001.

    The resulting rotation angle should be 45°.

21. Click Next.

22. In the Destination Point screen, click Pick In Drawing.

23. Use the Node Osnap to select point 10000.

24. Click Next.

25. Verify your translation setup on the Summary screen and then click Finish.

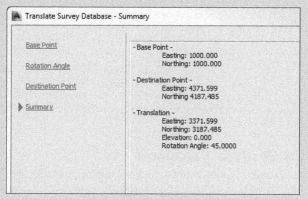

26. Save and close the drawing.

The changes were made directly to the database, and the network can be imported into any drawing.

Other Survey Features

Other components of the survey functionality included with Civil 3D 2016 are the Astronomic Direction Calculator, the Geodetic Calculator, Mapcheck reports, and the Coordinate Geometry Editor. All of these features are accessed from the ribbon under Survey tab ➤ Analyze panel.

The Astronomic Direction Calculator

The Astronomic Direction Calculator, shown in Figure 2.30, is used to calculate azimuths based on sun shots or star shots. Sun shots are based on solar observations by the hour-angle-method using the multiple foresight procedure. Star shots are based on star observations, usually of Polaris, by the hour-angle-method using the single foresight procedure.

Direct and reverse observations can be created by clicking the Create New Observation Set icon.

Direct and reverse observations can be deleted by clicking the Delete Selected Observation icon.

FIGURE 2.30
The Astronomic Direction Calculator

The Geodetic Calculator

The Geodetic Calculator is used to calculate and display the latitude and longitude of a selected point as well as its local and grid coordinates. It can also be used to calculate unknown points. If you know the grid coordinates, the local coordinates, or the latitude and longitude of a point, you can enter it in the Geodetic Calculator and create a point at that location. Note that the Geodetic Calculator works only if a coordinate system is assigned to the drawing in the Drawing Settings dialog. In addition, any transformation settings specified in this dialog will be reflected in the Geodetic Calculator, shown in Figure 2.31.

FIGURE 2.31
The Geodetic
Calculator

The Mapcheck Report

The Mapcheck report computes closure based on line, curve, or parcel segment labels, as you'll see in the following exercise:

1. Open the 0206_Mapcheck.dwg (0206_Mapcheck_METRIC.dwg) file, which you can download from this book's web page.

2. Change to the Survey tab of the ribbon, and select Mapcheck from the Analyze panel to display the Mapcheck Analysis palette.

3. Click the New Mapcheck button at the top of the menu bar.

4. At the Enter name of mapcheck: prompt, type **Record Deed** and press Enter.

5. At the Specify point of beginning (POB): prompt, choose the north endpoint of the line representing the east line of the parcel (the longest line in the file).

   A red glyph will appear to represent the POB.

6. Working clockwise, select each parcel label one at a time.

   Be sure not to skip the small segment in the southwest portion of the site.

   In the northwest portion of the site, you will encounter a label whose bearing is flipped. Before selecting the last segment, you will use the Mapcheck Reverse command to fix this in your Mapcheck report.

7. At the Select a label or [Clear/Flip/New/Reverse]: prompt, type **R** and then press ↵ to reverse direction.

   The Mapcheck glyph will now appear in the correct location along the segment, as shown in Figure 2.32.

FIGURE 2.32
The Mapcheck glyph
verifies that your
input is correct.

FIGURE 2.32
The Mapcheck glyph
verifies that your
input is correct.

8. Select the last line label along the north section of the parcel.

9. Press ↵ to complete the Mapcheck entry.

   The completed parcel should have 12 sides.

10. Select the output view as shown in Figure 2.33 to verify closure.

The Coordinate Geometry Editor

**Certification
Objective**

The Coordinate Geometry Editor (Figure 2.34) is a powerhouse tool that makes creating and evaluating 2D boundaries easier than before. The functionality introduced with this feature supplants entering parcel data one segment at a time using the Line By Bearing And Distance command. Traverse analysis can be performed on manually entered segments, polylines, or COGO point objects without needing to define them in a survey database.

Boundary data can be entered in the Coordinate Geometry Editor using a mix of methods. As shown in the first line of the traverse shown in Figure 2.34, you can use formulas to enter data. In the example shown, multiple segments with the same bearing have been consolidated into a single entry.

If a value is unknown, such as the distance in line 6 of Figure 2.34, you can enter a **U**. Civil 3D will calculate the unknown value when you generate the traverse report.

FIGURE 2.33
The completed deed in the Mapcheck Analysis palette

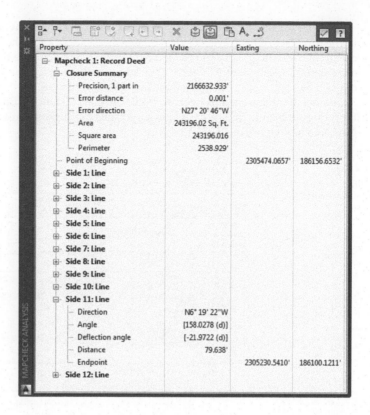

FIGURE 2.34
Your new best friend, the Coordinate Geometry Editor

To enter data using points, use the Pick COGO Points In Drawing button to select the points in the direction of the traverse side. You may need to click the chevron button in the upper-right corner of the dialog to expand the toolbar button selection. Note that the direction and distance are entered independently of each other, so you will need to repeat the selection for each column of the table. You can also copy and paste between columns.

If a line has been entered in error, the Coordinate Geometry Editor offers a variety of tools for fixing problems. To remove a line of the table, highlight the row, right-click, and select Delete Row, as shown in Figure 2.35.

FIGURE 2.35
Removing
unwanted traverse
data

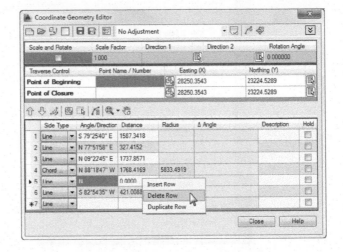

Similar to the glyphs you saw in the Mapcheck command, the Coordinate Geometry glyph will appear in the graphic showing the side directions and point of closure, as shown in Figure 2.36.

When you want to run a traverse report, set the report type you want to run from the top of the Coordinate Geometry Editor. If you have unknowns in your traverse, your only option will be to calculate the unknown values. Click the Display Report button to view the results of your entries. Depending on the type of adjustment you chose, your results should resemble Figure 2.37.

FIGURE 2.36
Temporary graph-
ics, or "glyphs," to
help you identify
your boundary

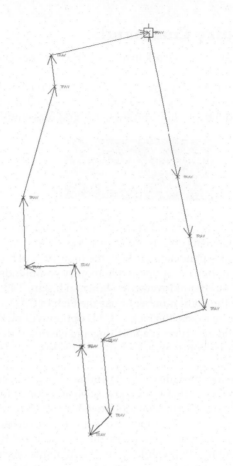

FIGURE 2.37
Traverse report
created by the
Coordinate
Geometry Editor

Traverse Report

Closure

Total Traverse Length	2538.928
Error in Closure	0.001
Closure is one part in	1866445.9895
Error in North(Y)	0.0013
Error in East(X)	0.0004
Direction of Error	N 19°00'01" E

Traverse Control

	Point Name	Northing	Easting
Point of Beginning	1001	186156.6532	2305474.0657
Point of Closure	1	186156.6532	2305474.0657

Input Data

Side	Angle/Direction	Distance	Radius	#Delta Angle	Description
1	S 11°45'41" E	365.2154			
2	13 TO 14	13 TO 14			
3	S 11°45'41" E	181.1671			
4	S 73°10'54" W	265.4503			
5	S 05°59'04" E	185.8889			
6	S 45°55'02" W	68.7261	-393.6557		
7	N 06°04'37" W	217.8016			

Using Inquiry Commands

A large part of a surveyor's work involves querying lines and curves for their length, direction, and other parameters.

The Inquiry commands panel (Figure 2.38) is on the Analyze tab of the ribbon, and it makes a valuable addition to your Civil 3D and survey-related workspaces. Remember, panels can be dragged away from the ribbon and set in the graphics environment much like a toolbar.

FIGURE 2.38

The Inquiry commands panel

The Inquiry Tool (shown in Figure 2.39) provides a diverse collection of commands that assist you in studying Civil 3D objects. You can access the Inquiry Tool by going to the Analyze tab of the ribbon ➤ Inquiry panel and clicking the Inquiry Tool button.

To use the Point Inverse option in the Inquiry commands, first set the Select An Inquiry Type pull-down to Point ➤ Point Inverse, as shown in Figure 2.40.

You can enter the point number or use the Pick In CAD icon to select the points you want to examine. If no point exists, the Pick In CAD option will pick up the northing and easting of the location. You could also type in a northing and easting if desired.

The other Inquiry commands that are specific to Civil 3D are also handy to the survey process.

The List Slope tool provides a short command-line report that lists the elevations and slope of an entity (or two points) that you choose, such as a line or feature line.

The Line And Arc Information tool provides a short report about the line or arc of your choosing (see Figure 2.41). This tool also works on parcel segments and alignment segments. Alternatively, you can type **P** and press Enter for points at the command line to get information about the apparent line that would connect two points onscreen.

FIGURE 2.39

Choosing an inquiry type from the Inquiry Tool palette

FIGURE 2.40
Point Inverse
results

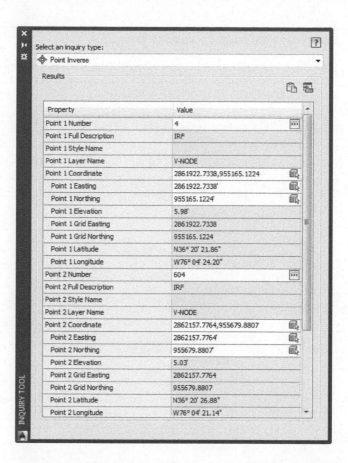

FIGURE 2.41
Command-line
results of a line
inquiry and arc
inquiry

```
Command: _AeccCgList
Select object or [Points]:
-------------------------------------------------------------------------
                          LINE DATA
-------------------------------------------------------------------------
Begin . . . . . X: 2436.10'          Y: 7438.46'
End . . . . . . X: 2444.96'          Y: 7449.10'
              Distance: 13.84'          Course: N39° 46' 32"E
Select object or [Points]:
-------------------------------------------------------------------------
                          ARC DATA
-------------------------------------------------------------------------
Begin . . . . . X: 2461.22'          Y: 7449.52'
Radial Point . . X: 2453.37'          Y: 7438.53'
End . . . . . . X: 2444.96'          Y: 7449.10'
PI . . . . . . X: 2452.93'          Y: 7455.44'
   Tangent: 10.19'      Chord: 16.27'      Course: S88° 30' 04"W
Arc Length: 17.46'      Radius: 13.51'      Delta: 74.0515 (d)
Select object or [Points]:
```

`[▼] Type a command`

Don't Get Burned by AutoCAD Angles

When looking for information about a line, use the Line And Arc tool rather than the base AutoCAD LIST command. The Civil 3D Line And Arc Information tool (CGLIST) works on more object types and is not affected by rotated coordinate systems.

When entering angles in base AutoCAD, the full N50d10'10"E is needed to denote a bearing. In Civil 3D commands, N50.1010E will denote the same thing and is much faster to type. However, as every surveyor knows, there is a huge difference between 50.1010° and 50°10'10".

A setting you will want to change in your Civil 3D template is the angular entry method for general angles, as shown here. This setting mainly affects the Angle Distance and Bearing Distance Transparent commands. Check back in Chapter 1 for more information on template settings and transparent commands.

The Angle Information tool lets you pick two lines (or a series of points on the screen). It provides information about the acute and obtuse angles between those two lines. Again, this also works for alignment segments and parcel segments.

The Continuous Distance tool provides a sum of distances between several points on your screen or one base point and several points.

The Add Distances tool is similar to the Continuous Distance command, except the points on your screen do not have to be continuous.

The Bottom Line

Properly collect field data and import it into Civil 3D. Once survey data has been collected, you will want to pull it into Civil 3D via the survey database. This will enable you to create lines and points that correctly reflect your field measurements.

Master It Open `MasterIt_0201.dwg`, create a new survey database, and import the `MasterIt_0201.txt` (or `MasterIt_0201_METRIC.txt`) point file into the drawing. The format of this specific file is PENZD (comma-delimited).

Set up description key and figure databases. Proper setup is key to working successfully with the Civil 3D survey functionality.

Master It Create a new description key set and the following description keys using the default styles. Make sure all description keys are going to layer V-NODE:

◆ CL*

◆ EOP*

◆ TREE*

◆ BM*

Change the description key search order so that the new description key set takes precedence over the default.

Create a figure prefix database called MasterIt containing the following codes:

◆ CL

◆ EOP

◆ BC

Test the new description key set and figure prefix database by importing the point file `MasterIt_CodeTest_0202.txt` (use the same file for both US and metric units). Note that this file is a comma-delimited PNEZD file.

Translate surveys from assumed coordinates to known coordinates. Understanding how to manipulate data once it is brought into Civil 3D is important to making your field measurements match your project's coordinate system.

Master It Create a new drawing based on the template of your choice and start a new survey database. Import `MasterIt_0203.fbk` (or `MasterIt_0203_METRIC.fbk`). When you import the file, turn on the Insert Network Object option. Translate the database based on the following settings:

◆ Base Point 1

◆ Rotation Angle of 10.3053°

Perform traverse analysis.   Traverse analysis is needed for boundary surveys to check for angular accuracy and closure. Civil 3D will generate the reports that you need to capture these results.

Master It   Use the survey database and network from the previous "Master It" exercise. Analyze and adjust the traverse using the following criteria:

◆ Use an Initial Station value of 2 and an Initial Backsight value of 1.

◆ Use the Compass Rule option for Horizontal Adjustment.

◆ Use the Length Weighted Distribution Method for Vertical Adjustment.

◆ Use a Horizontal Closure Limit value of 1:20,000.

◆ Use a Vertical Closure Limit value of 1:20,000.

Chapter 3

Points

In the previous chapter, "Survey," you looked at a specific method for bringing in points and figures by the means of survey databases. In this chapter, you will take a closer look at the multiple ways of creating, modifying, and managing Autodesk® AutoCAD® Civil 3D® points.

Most commonly, Civil 3D points are used to identify the location of existing features, such as trees and property corners; topography, such as ground shots; or stakeout information, such as road geometry points. However, their use is not limited to the data specified here. This chapter will both focus on traditional point uses and introduce ideas to apply the dynamic power of point editing, labeling, and grouping to other applications.

In this chapter, you will learn to:

◆ Import points from a text file using description key matching.

◆ Create a point group.

◆ Export points to LandXML and ASCII format.

◆ Create a point table.

Anatomy of a Point

Civil 3D *points* (see Figure 3.1) are intelligent objects that represent x, y, and z locations in space. Each point has a unique number and, optionally, a unique name that can be used for additional identification and labeling.

FIGURE 3.1
A typical point object showing a marker, a point number, an elevation, and a description

2627 ←— Point Number**

Marker* —→ +6.39 ←— Elevation**

GS ←— Description**

*Marker is part of the marker style
**Text components are part of the
point label style

Each Civil 3D point is represented graphically using two components: a marker and a label. Even though we will focus on the styles to display these components in Chapter 18, "Label Styles," and Chapter 19, "Object Styles," we will discuss the basics of these items here. Most of the users are familiar with the representation of the marker as a + and the label in the form of number, elevation, and description, as shown in Figure 3.1. The marker's representation is defined by an object marker style, while the label is defined by a label style. Note that even if the Civil 3D point object resides on a specified layer, its marker and label can reside on different layers based on the settings defined for those styles. Because of this, a well-defined set of styles in the definition of your template is vital to a functional and productive environment.

A QUICK WORD ON STYLES

Separating the point functionality discussed in this chapter from the styles that manage their graphical representation in the drawing is difficult. Since you won't get into the complexity of creating and manipulating label styles and point styles until Chapters 18 and 19, in this chapter you will work with styles that are already part of a drawing. This is true for points, labels, and tables.

COGO Points vs. Survey Points

In Chapter 2, "Survey," you imported survey data that contained points. Points brought in through the methods described in Chapter 2 are referred to as *survey points*. In this chapter, you will import points from a delimited text file and place them in the drawing using the point-creation tools. Points created in this manner are referred to as *COGO points*. Figure 3.2 shows the contextual tab differences between points brought in as COGO points (top) and points brought in through a survey database (bottom).

FIGURE 3.2
The context-sensitive ribbon reflects similarities and differences between COGO points (top) and survey points (bottom).

The differences between COGO points and survey points are subtle but important to note. The definition and graphical representation of a COGO point are stored in the drawing. For this reason, its definition can be easily altered at any time, either through its Properties palette or through the tabular view used in Panorama. On the other hand, a survey point has its definition stored within a survey database and its graphical representation stored in the drawing. To change its definition, you need to be able to access its survey database and have the rights to write changes to it. Because of these controls and the legal implications that arise from unwanted changes to the topographic data, the use of survey points and databases is becoming more prevalent in today's market. Since these points are managed by the survey database, the place to manage any changes to their definition is within the Survey tab of Toolspace. Regardless of their origin, both COGO points and survey points obey the principles outlined in this chapter.

Creating Basic Points

Certification
Objective
You can create points in many ways using the Points menu in the Create Ground Data panel on the Home tab of the ribbon. Points can also be imported from text files or external databases or converted from AutoCAD points or other legacy point types.

Point Settings

When we talk about point settings, we're actually referring to what is known as *command settings* for points. We provided a quick introduction to command settings in the first chapter, so you know that all the settings that define the creation of Civil 3D objects are available as command settings in the Settings tab of Toolspace. As we discuss the creation and management of Civil 3D points, it is recommended to have the previously mentioned settings readily available for on-the-fly modifications. Whether or not the changes you make on the fly are remembered the next time you create points depends on your template settings.

To make sure that the settings you change hold every time you create points, follow these steps:

1. On the Settings tab of Toolspace, locate the Point branch and click the plus sign to expand.

2. Click the plus sign to expand Commands.

3. As shown in the first screen in Figure 3.3, right-click the command CreatePoints and select Edit Command Settings.

FIGURE 3.3
In your Civil 3D template, make sure Save Command Changes To Settings is set to Yes for Points.

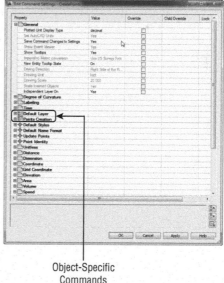

Object-Specific
Commands

4. Expand the General section and verify that Save Command Changes To Settings is set to Yes.

You will notice that this change affects only the CreatePoints command. If you want to save the settings at the Point collection level for all the commands related to point creation, you will do that from the Edit Feature Settings option that can be selected when you right-click the Point collection.

By setting the Save Command Changes To Settings option to Yes, you are ensuring that changes you make on the CreatePoints toolbar will be saved for the next time you use the command. If you explore the command settings further, you will see the options Default Layer and Points Creation. You will notice that these commands are represented with a different icon from the other settings. This is because these are object-specific command settings defined at the object level, while the others are defined as part of the overall drawing level within the Ambient Settings tab of the Drawing Settings. You will find a defined subset of the options available within the command settings in the Create Points toolbar.

To access the Create Points toolbar, follow these steps:

1. Go to the Home tab of the ribbon.

2. In the Create Ground Data panel, select Points ➢ Point Creation Tools.

3. Expand the toolbar by clicking the chevron icon on the far-right side (Figure 3.4).

FIGURE 3.4
Overview of the
Create Points
toolbar

Surface Tools

Alignment
Tools

Interpolation Tools

Intersection
Tools

Slope Tools

Expand/
Collapse Toolbar
Button

Miscellaneous
Tools

Import Point
Data

DEFAULT LAYER

For most Civil 3D objects, the object layer is established in the drawing settings. In the case of points, the layer depends on whether it matches a description key when a description key set is present in the drawing or the point's creation command settings when a default layer is defined. When a description key set is present and active in the drawing, the layer assignment set by the description key set takes precedence over the one defined as the default layer. In other words, when there is no description key set in the drawing or when the point's raw description does not match any of the keys, then the layer for the specific point will be the one set as default in the Default Layer section of the Create Points dialog (see Figure 3.5). Review Chapter 2 for more information about description key sets.

FIGURE 3.5
Verify the point object layer before creating points.

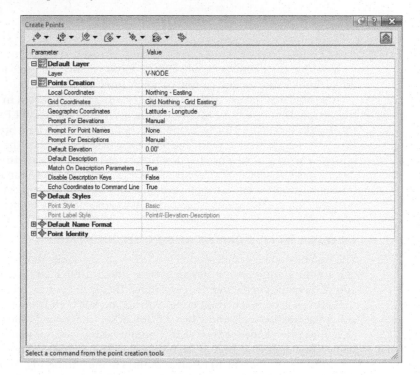

POINTS CREATION AND DEFAULT STYLES

When creating points in your drawing, you have the option of being prompted for elevations, point names, and descriptions (see Figure 3.5). This process can be changed to take advantage of the intelligent environment of Civil 3D in the case of creating points from alignment geometry, when you can choose to have points pick up descriptions using the Automatic – Object option. Initially, the Default Description options are blank. In many cases, you'll want to leave these options set to Manual. That way, the command line will ask you to assign an elevation and description for every point you create. Even though the point names option is available, it is best to avoid using them in general (as described later in this section); therefore, leave the Prompt For Point Names option set to None.

If you're creating a batch of points that have the same description or elevation, you can change the Prompt toggle from Manual to Automatic and then provide the description and elevation in the default cells. For example, if you're setting a series of test pits with variable elevations, you can establish settings as shown in Figure 3.6.

FIGURE 3.6
Default settings for placing tree points at an elevation of 10'

Points Creation	
Local Coordinates	Northing - Easting
Grid Coordinates	Grid Northing - Grid Easting
Geographic Coordinates	Latitude - Longitude
Prompt For Elevations	Manual
Prompt For Point Names	None
Prompt For Descriptions	Automatic
Default Elevation	0.00'
Default Description	TP
Match On Description Parameters ($1, $2, etc.)	True
Disable Description Keys	True
Echo Coordinates to Command Line	True

Note that these settings apply only to points created from this toolbar. The settings do not affect the elevation or description of points imported from a file.

Also note that the use of description key sets can be disabled in the creation of points, when the Disable Description Keys option is changed from the default False to True. The status of this toggle also defines the availability of options in the Default Styles section of the dialog. When the toggle is set to allow the use of key descriptors, then the Default Point and Label Style options are grayed out since the descriptors will define those settings. But when the use of key descriptors is disabled, the default styles for points and labels can be customized. However, the default styles used in the creation of points can be changed even with the description keys enabled. You will learn more about this in Chapter 18 and Chapter 19.

DEFAULT NAME FORMAT AND POINT IDENTITY

The Default Name Format section is where you can define the macros that manage the naming of the point groups and point names when these are created. You will learn about point groups and point names in the following sections. The Point Identity section is where you can define the settings used in the numbering of the point data both when it's created in the drawing by using the creation tools and when it is imported from outside sources. For example, here you have the option to define the starting number used, whether to use sequential numbering, and what offset should be used in the numbering. Also among these options you will find the settings that define the way to resolve conflicts in the numbering. You will usually run into these kinds of conflicts in the case of point data imported from outside sources that has point numbers that match existing points. In that case, you have the option to define how the software should proceed when one of these conflicts arises.

WHAT'S IN A NAME?

Users often confuse a point's *name* with its *description*. The name is a unique, alphanumeric sequence that some software programs use in lieu of a point number. The description refers to the all-important code given to a point out in the field. In Civil 3D terms this is referred to as the Raw Description property for the point. You learned about this and how it is used in the description key set in Chapter 2. Even though you could use point names as well, Civil 3D workflow favors the use of point numbers, so the Prompt For Point Names option is usually set to None. If you do have a point file that uses a name instead of a point number, you will need to create a custom point format, as described later in this chapter.

Importing Points from a Text File

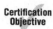
Certification
Objective

One of the most common means of creating points in your drawing is to import an external text file (see Figure 3.7). The Import Points tool can be accessed either from the Create Points toolbar or from the Import Panel of the Insert tab on the ribbon.

FIGURE 3.7
The Import Points and Point File Formats dialogs

To add a file to your Import Points dialog, click the white plus sign to browse. You can add multiple files at once if they are in the same point format—such as a comma-delimited point number, northing, easting, elevation, description (i.e., PNEZD). The import process supports most text formats as well as Microsoft Access database (MDB) files. Later in this chapter, you will experience adding your own text format.

When your file is listed in the top of the dialog, a green check mark indicates that Civil 3D can parse the information. Be careful, though, because Civil 3D does not know the difference between a northing and an easting or a point number and an elevation. You still need to select the correct file format. When the format of the imported data does not match any of the present formats, a red mark will be displayed, and you will not be able to proceed without defining a custom import format that matches the layout of the data, as shown in Figure 3.7.

The file format filter is available to help you. Civil 3D recognizes how the file is delimited (i.e., tab, comma, space) and shows you only the formats that apply. If you don't want the help, you can turn the filtering off by clicking the Filter icon. This will give you access to the full list of formats defined in the drawing.

CUSTOM POINT FILE FORMATS AND ADVANCED OPTIONS

If the file format you need is not available or you want to use the adjustment and transformation capabilities, you can do so by clicking the Manage Formats icon. Many types of data are available for adding to a point format, including LIDAR classification and various latitude-longitude types.

As you can see in Figure 3.7 (shown previously), advanced options are available at the bottom of the Import Points dialog.

◆ Do Elevation Adjustment If Possible.

◆ Do Coordinate Transformation If Possible.

◆ Do Coordinate Data Expansion If Possible.

These options will not affect your points unless the point file format has adjustment, transformation, or expansion built into it.

You can make an elevation adjustment if the point file contains additional columns for thickness, Z+ or Z–. To get Civil 3D to recognize these extra data columns, a new point file format is needed. You can perform a coordinate system transformation if a coordinate system has been assigned both to your drawing (under the drawing settings) and as part of a custom point format. In this case, the program can also do a coordinate data expansion, which calculates the latitude and longitude for each point.

 Real World Scenario

THE NAME GAME

A common use of importing points using point file formats is the case of a name-based point file. Since point file formats used for import are stored in the drawing, this is another item that you would want to have already set up in your Civil 3D template. In the following example, you will create a new file format to accommodate names (instead of point numbers):

1. Open the drawing 0301_PointFileFormat.dwg (0301_PointFileFormat_METRIC .dwg), which you can download from this book's web page at www.sybex.com/go/ masteringcivil3d2016.

2. Select the Settings tab of Toolspace and choose Point ➤ Point File Formats.

   You can also access this functionality on the fly from the Import Points dialog.

3. Right-click Point File Formats and select New.

4. Select User Point File and click OK.

5. Name the format **Name-NEZD (Comma Delimited)**.

6. Toggle on the Delimited By option and place a comma in the field.

7. Click the first <unused> column heading, select Name from the Column Name pull-down, and click OK.

8. Click the next <unused> column and select Northing from the Column Name pull-down.

9. Leave the Invalid Indicator and Precision fields at their defaults and click OK.

10. Repeat the process for Easting, Point Elevation, and Raw Description.

    Be sure to add the columns in the correct order or the format will not work with the example file. You may notice that as you use an item from the Column Name list, it is no longer available for use in another column.

11. To test the format, click Load, select the file 0301_TestFormat.txt (0301_TestFormat_METRIC.txt), and click Open.

12. Click Parse.

If the format has been created successfully, you will see the file preview, as shown here.

13. Click OK to complete the format.

After you learn how, revisit this drawing and import points. You will see that Civil 3D assigns point numbers in addition to using the names.

To compare your work with a completed example, see 0301_PointFileFormat_FINISHED.dwg (0301_PointFileFormat_METRIC_FINISHED.dwg).

IMPORTING A TEXT FILE OF POINTS

In this exercise, you'll learn how to import a TXT file of points into Civil 3D:

1. Open the 0302_PointImport.dwg (0302_PointImport_METRIC.dwg) file, which you can download from this book's web page.

2. On the Home tab ➢ Create Ground Data panel ➢ Points, select Point Creation Tools.

3. On the Create Points toolbar, click the Import Points icon.

4. Click the white + icon to the right of the Selected Files field and navigate to locate the 0302_Points.txt (0302_Points_METRIC.txt) file.

5. Select the file and click Open.

6. In the Specify Point File Format field, set the format to PNEZD (Comma Delimited).

7. Place a check mark in the box next to Add Points To Point Group and click the Create Point Group icon. Name the point group **Mastering Survey Data** and click OK.

8. Leave the boxes under Advanced Options unchecked.

9. Click OK.

   You may have to use Zoom Extents to see the imported points. (Hint: Double-click your middle mouse wheel for zooming extents.)

10. Save the drawing.

To compare your work with a completed example, see 0302_PointImport_FINISHED.dwg (0302_PointImport_METRIC_FINISHED.dwg).

Converting Points from Non–Civil 3D Sources

Base AutoCAD points, Land Desktop points, and Softdesk points are types of data that Civil 3D can readily convert from within a drawing. Other types of data that can be converted to Civil 3D points are represented by blocks. To convert, blocks must minimally be defined so that the insertion point's coordinates coincides with the coordinate values of the point and have an assigned z value that defines the elevation. If a block also has the number, description, and elevation as block attributes, it is even easier to convert them to Civil 3D points. Therefore, whenever possible, your best course of action would be to request the survey in text format or LandXML that can be easily imported into Civil 3D. However, if you need to migrate a drawing that contains legacy point data, tools are available to convert that data to Civil 3D point objects.

A Land Desktop point database (the Points.mdb file found in the COGO folder in a Land Desktop project) can be directly imported into Civil 3D in the same interface in which you'd import a text file.

Land Desktop point objects, which appear as AECC_POINTs in the AutoCAD Properties palette, can also be converted to Civil 3D points via the Convert Land Desktop Points option (see Figure 3.8). Upon their conversion, this tool gives you the opportunity to assign styles, create a point group, and more.

CONVERTING POINTS

In this exercise, you'll convert Land Desktop point objects into Civil 3D points and export the data to LandXML and ASCII format files:

1. Open the 0303_ConvertPoints.dwg (0303_ConvertPoints_METRIC.dwg) file, which you can download from this book's web page.

2. Use the List command or the AutoCAD Properties palette to confirm that most of the objects in this drawing are AECC_POINTs, which are points from Land Desktop.

3. On the Home tab ➤ Create Ground Data panel ➤ Points menu, select Convert Land Desktop Points.

   Note that the Convert Autodesk Land Desktop Points dialog allows you to choose point-creation settings and styles.

4. Place a check mark next to Add Points To Point Group.

FIGURE 3.8
Selecting the
Convert Land
Desktop Points
option (left)
opens the Convert
Autodesk Land
Desktop Points
dialog (right).

5. Click the Create A New Point Group icon.

6. Name the group **Converted From LDT**, as shown in Figure 3.8, and click OK.

7. Clear the Preserve Original Point Layers check box.

   This option will move the resulting points to the layer specified in the description key set if there is a match. If there is no match, the point will go to the default layer.

8. Click OK to complete the conversion process.

   Civil 3D scans the drawing looking for Land Desktop point objects.

9. Once Civil 3D has finished the conversion, zoom in on any of the former Land Desktop points.

   The points should now show as COGO points in the AutoCAD Properties palette, confirming that the conversion has taken place. The Land Desktop points have been replaced with Civil 3D points, and the original Land Desktop points are no longer in the drawing.

10. In Toolspace ➤ Prospector tab, expand the Point Groups category.

    Notice that there is a yellow exclamation shield symbol indicating that the Converted From LDT point group needs to be updated.

11. Right-click Point Groups and select Update.

12. On update, the points will display using the defined settings.

13. Select the Converted From LDT point group, right-click it, and select Export Points from the menu.

14. Now do the following:

    a. Set the export format to PNEZD (Comma Delimited).

    b. Define the destination file as a text file.

    c. Name it `0303_ConvertPoints.txt` (`0303_ConvertPoints_METRIC.txt`).

    d. Click Open.

By default the selection of points is limited to the selected group.

15. Clear the advanced options check marks if any are selected and click OK.

16. Select the Converted From LDT point group once more and right-click it.

17. From the context menu, select the Export LandXML option found toward the bottom of the menu.

In the dialog box, by default your point group is selected to be exported.

18. Just click OK.

You will be prompted to save the LandXML file, and the suggested name should be fine.

19. Save the file.

20. Once the export is done, save the drawing file.

To compare your work with a completed example, see `0303_ConvertPoints_FINISHED.dwg` (`0303_ConvertPOints_METRIC_FINISHED.dwg`).

Converting Blocks

In this exercise, you'll convert blocks with data that can be extracted into Civil 3D points:

1. Open the `0304_ConvertBlocks.dwg` (`0304_ConvertBlocks_METRIC.dwg`) file, which you can download from this book's web page.

Notice the point data in the form of blocks. You'll see that all of them are instances of the same block, their insertion point coincides with the origin of the field shot, they have a z value assigned to each that corresponds to the field elevation, and the attribute data assigned to each instance actually contains fields that you can use. This is the best scenario for conversion of blocks (see Figure 3.9).

To convert the data, you need to generate the text file that you can import back and create points.

2. Go to the Insert tab ➢ Linking & Extraction Panel and click the Extract Data icon.

3. In the Data Extraction – Begin (Page 1 Of 8) dialog, select Create A New Data Extraction. Click Next.

You will be prompted to save your data extraction as a new `.dxe` file.

4. Select the location and give it a proper name.

FIGURE 3.9
Block with data that
can be extracted to
a text file and reim-
ported as a Civil 3D
point

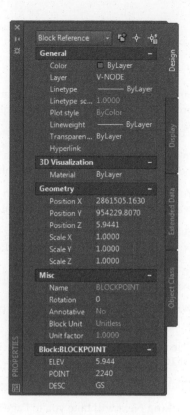

5. Click Save to go to the next step.

6. In the Data Extraction – Define Data Source (Page 2 Of 8) dialog, change the selection from the default to Select Objects In The Current Drawing.

7. Using the selection icon to the right of the option, select the point blocks in the drawing, press ↵, and then click Next.

8. In the Data Extraction – Select Objects (Page 3 Of 8) dialog in the Display Options section, clear all check boxes with the exception of Display Blocks With Attributes Only. The BLOCKPOINT object should be the only item displayed and selected in the object area. Click Next.

9. In the Data Extraction – Select Properties (Page 4 Of 8) dialog, in the Category Filter area, clear the selection for everything but the Attribute and Geometry filters.

   Once these two filters are selected, you will have options for which properties you want to extract.

10. To have a working PNEZD file, select and extract the following:

    ◆ POINT property for the Point Number

    ◆ Position Y for the northing

- ◆ Position X for the easting
- ◆ ELEV property for Elevation
- ◆ DESC property for Description

Since the block already has a z value assigned to it, you can swap, if needed, the ELEV property for the Position Z, but for this exercise you will just use the ELEV property.

11. Check the selection for the items listed here, clear the ones not in the list, and click Next.

12. In the Data Extraction – Refine Data (Page 5 Of 8) dialog, clear the selections for Show Count Column and Show Name Column.

You will be left with the five known columns for a PNEZD file, which you will need to rearrange to meet your point format requirement.

13. Select the column headers and drag them into this order from left to right: POINT, Position Y, Position X, ELEV, and DESC. Click Next.

14. In the Data Extraction – Choose Output (Page 6 Of 8) dialog, select to output data to an external file.

15. When you see the file path and file type the data will be saved into, click the ellipsis icon to select a new path.

16. Select where you want to save, select the name for the file, and choose .xls from the Files Of Type drop-down menu.

17. Click Save to exit the dialog and Next to advance to the next step.

Clicking Next will take you to Page 8. In this particular workflow, you will not see Page 7.

18. In the Data Extraction – Finish (Page 8 Of 8) dialog, click the Finish button to end the extraction process.

19. Open the file in Microsoft Excel and delete the first row, which contains the header cells.

20. Save the modified file as CSV (Comma Delimited) by doing the following:

   a. Browse to a location of your choice.

   b. Assign a name to the file.

   c. Click Yes in the Microsoft Excel dialog warning about the loss of functionality when saving to CSV.

The dialog box might provide you with different warnings based on what version of the Office suite you have. When closing the file, you will see the same Microsoft Excel warning again.

21. Click Yes to force the file to close.

22. In Civil 3D, using the Import Points option from the Creation Points toolbar, choose PNEZD (Comma Delimited) as the format for points, and select the created CSV file as the source for the data.

23. Add the points to a point group.

A point group called Mastering Survey Data is already in the drawing, so you can use that as the point group for the insertion of this data.

Once the import is complete, the points will be created in the drawing, and you can safely delete the source blocks or change their layer if you still want to keep them in the drawing.

The Extraction file (.dxe) can be used for future extractions that match the settings for your non–Civil 3D data.

24. Save the drawing.

To compare your work with a completed example, see 0304_ConvertBlocks_FINISHED.dwg (0304_ConvertBlocks_METRIC_FINISHED.dwg).

A Closer Look at the Create Points Toolbar

Certification Objective

In Civil 3D 2016, you can find point-creation tools directly under the Home tab ➤ Create Ground Data Panel ➤ Points drop-down as well as in the Create Points toolbar. The toolbar is *modeless*, which means it stays on your screen even when you switch between tasks. If you go back to Figure 3.4, you'll see the available point-creation methods.

As you place points using these tools, a few general rules apply to all of them. If you place a point on an object with elevation, the point will automatically inherit the elevation of the object. If you use the surface options, the point will automatically inherit the elevation of the surface you choose.

Miscellaneous Point-Creation Options   The options in the Miscellaneous category allow you to create a point by manually specifying its location onscreen or relative to existing basic objects in the drawing. Also within this category are the options to convert data from AutoCAD points or Softdesk point blocks (see Figure 3.10).

FIGURE 3.10
Miscellaneous
point-creation
options

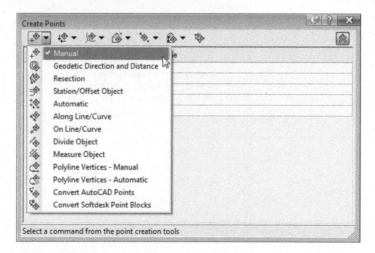

Intersection Point-Creation Options The options in this category allow you to place points based on the calculated intersection of specific items without defining construction lines. For example, if you needed a point at the intersection of two bearings, you could draw two construction lines using the Bearing Distance transparent command, manually place a point where they intersect, and then erase the construction lines. By using the tools within this category, you could use the Direction/Direction tool to accomplish the same without using construction lines (see Figure 3.11).

FIGURE 3.11
Intersection point-creation options

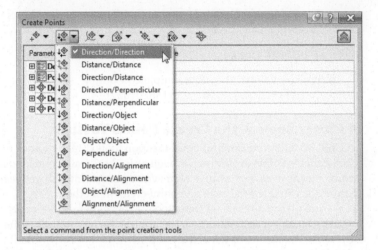

Alignment Point-Creation Options The options in the Alignment category are designed for creating stakeout points based on a road centerline or other alignments. You can also set profile geometry points along the alignment using a tool from this menu. See Figure 3.12.

FIGURE 3.12
Alignment point-creation options

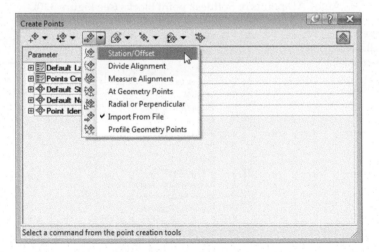

Surface Point-Creation Options The options in the Surface category let you set points that harvest their elevation data from a surface. Note that these are points, not labels, and therefore aren't dynamic to the surface. You can set points manually, along a contour or a polyline, or in a grid (see Figure 3.13).

FIGURE 3.13
Surface point-creation options

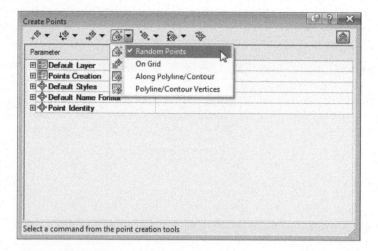

Interpolation Point-Creation Options The Interpolation category lets you fill in missing information from survey data or establish intermediate points for your design tasks. For example, suppose your survey crew picked up centerline road shots every 100′ (30 m) and you'd like to interpolate intermediate points every 25′ (8 m). Instead of doing a manual slope calculation, you could use the Incremental Distance tool to create additional points (see Figure 3.14).

FIGURE 3.14
The Interpolation point-creation options

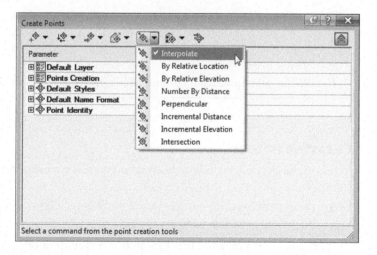

Another use would be to set intermediate points along a pipe stakeout. You could set points for the starting and ending inverts and then set intermediate points along the pipe to assist the field crew.

Slope Point-Creation Options   The Slope category allows you to set points between two known elevations by setting a slope or grade. Similar to the options in the Interpolation and Intersection categories, these tools save you time by eliminating construction geometry and hand calculations (see Figure 3.15).

FIGURE 3.15
Slope point-
creation options

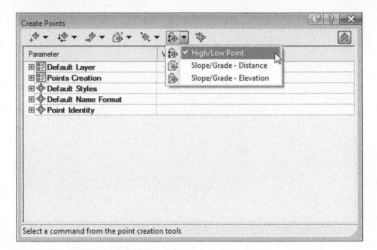

USING THE AUTOMATIC – OBJECT OPTION

The Description option in the point settings Automatic – Object can be used only when placing points along an alignment. For example, when you're placing points using the At Geometry Points option, the point will inherit the alignment's name, the station value of the point, and the type of geometry as its description.

For all other point-placement options, Automatic – Object will behave the same as Automatic.

CREATING POINTS

In this exercise, you'll learn how to create points along a parcel segment and along a surface contour:

1. Open 0305_PointCreation.dwg (0305_PointCreation_METRIC.dwg), which you can download from this book's web page.

   Note that the drawing includes alignments, a series of parcels, and an existing ground surface.

2. On the Home tab ➢ Create Ground Data panel ➢ Points menu, click Point Creation Tools.

3. If it is not already expanded, click the chevron icon on the right to expand the dialog.

4. Expand the Points Creation category.

5. Change the Prompt For Elevations value to None and the Prompt For Descriptions value to Automatic by clicking in the respective cell in the Value column, clicking the down arrow, and selecting the appropriate option.

6. Enter **LOT** for Default Description (see Figure 3.16).

FIGURE 3.16

Point-creation settings in the Create Points dialog

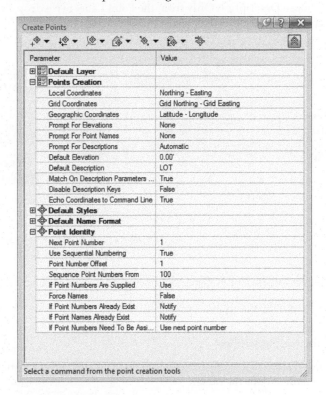

This will save you from having to enter a description and elevation each time. Because you're setting stakeout points for rear lot corners, you will disregard elevation for now.

7. Select the Automatic tool from the Miscellaneous flyout (the first icon flyout on the top left of the Create Points toolbar).

8. Focusing on the area at end of the cul-de-sac you will find the parcel named BCG_Lots : 1. Select that parcel by selecting one of its segments. Press ↵.

9. Press Esc to exit the command.

A point is placed at each property corner and at the endpoints of each curve. Even if the marker is visible, you will not see the point label. The reason is that since there is no description key within the set to manage the LOT key, the point's labeling is managed by the settings of the point group it belongs to. It belongs to the only point group defined in the drawing, the default _All Points, which has by default the labeling for its points set to <none>.

10. Right-click the _All Points group within the Point Groups collection in the Prospector tab of Toolspace and choose Properties, as shown in Figure 3.17.

11. Choose Description Only from the Point Label Style drop-down on the Information tab of the Points Group Properties – _All Points dialog.

12. Click OK to exit the dialog.

FIGURE 3.17
To assign a label style to the _All Points group, access its properties (left) and assign the desired style (right).

13. Select the Measure Object tool from the Miscellaneous flyout.

14. Click anywhere on the parcel boundary for BCG_Lots : 29.

    After you select the parcel boundary for BCG_Lots : 29, this tool prompts you for starting and ending stations.

15. Press ↵ twice to accept the default starting and ending stationing and again to accept the default of 0 for the offset.

16. At the Interval prompt, enter **25** if you are working in feet and **10** if you are working in metric units.

17. Press Enter to continue.

18. Press Esc to exit the command.

    A point is placed at 25′ (10 m) intervals along the property boundary.

    Next, you'll experiment with the Direction/Direction option from the Intersection Point flyout. Be sure your Endpoint Osnap is on for the next steps.

Let's focus now on BCG_Lots : 33.

19. Click the Direction/Direction icon and click the northwest endpoint of the parcel line that this property shares with BCG_Lots : 1.

20. Click the opposite endpoint of the segment that the two of them share to establish the direction of the line.

The yellow arrow that appears indicates the direction.

21. Press ↵ to specify the default of 0 for the offset.

22. Click the southeast corner of BCG_Lots : 33 on the property line that this property shares with BCG_Lots : 34 and then click the endpoint of the same property line to establish the second direction.

23. Press ↵ to specify a zero offset.

A point is generated where the two lines would intersect if they were to be extended. Press Esc to exit the command.

24. In the point-creation settings, change Prompt For Descriptions to Automatic – Object.

25. From the Alignments flyout, choose At Geometry Points.

26. When prompted for an alignment, select the green centerline alignment, ROAD G.

You are now prompted for a profile.

27. Select FG-ROAD G from the drop-down and click OK.

28. Press ↵ twice to confirm the starting and ending station values along the alignment.

29. Press Esc to exit the command.

You should now see points whose names are based on alignment information.

30. Return to the Point Settings category and change Prompt For Elevations to Manual and Default Description to **EG**.

The next round of points you'll set will be based on the existing ground elevation.

31. Select the Along Polyline/Contour tool in the Surface flyout.

32. When prompted with `Distance between points<10.0000>`, key in **9** for feet (3 for meters) and press Enter to continue.

33. Click the magenta polyline inside BCG_Lots : 1.

Notice that the points will be created, but their label style will not use the default of the _All Points group. You will know why if you look at the description key for the EG code.

34. Press Esc to exit the command, close the Create Points toolbar, save the drawing, and keep it open for the next exercise.

You can go ahead and experiment with the variety of point-creation tools available.

DOUBLE TROUBLES

Civil 3D does not allow two points to share the same point number or name. If a duplicate point number is detected, Civil 3D will warn you and ask you how you would like to handle it.

The Duplicate Point Number dialog allows you to take action. You have several options in the Resolution drop-down.

Add An Offset   This option allows you to add a value to all incoming points. Specifying an offset of 1000 would turn 1, 2, and 5 into 1001, 1002, and 1005.

Merge   If the existing point has a description but no elevation and the incoming point has an elevation and no description, Civil 3D will fill in the gaps with the incoming information. If there is no missing data and the coordinates are identical, the incoming point will be ignored. Be careful using Merge; it will behave similar to the Overwrite option if the coordinates don't match.

Overwrite   This option deletes the existing point and replaces it with the incoming point.

Sequence From   This option will restart the numbering at a higher value. Unlike with adding an offset, the original point number is ignored. Setting a sequence from 1000 would turn 1, 2, and 5 into 1001, 1002, and 1003.

Use Next Point Number   The default option in the Resolution drop-down, Use Next Point Number, finds the next-available point number and assigns it to the point on import.

Point numbers are assigned using the Point Identity settings in the Create Points dialog or the point file from which they originated. To list available point numbers, enter `ListAvailablePointNumbers` on the command line, or select any point to open the COGO Point contextual tab and choose COGO Point Tools ➤ List Available Point Numbers.

In the case of duplicate point names, options exist to ensure that you keep these unique as well.

The Duplicate Point Name dialog gives you options to resolve duplicates. In the Resolution drop-down you will find the following options:

Counter   This option takes the name and adds a numeric counter. For example, if you are attempting to import duplicate number V100, the new name will become V100(1).

Specify   This option lets you type in the name you want for the new point. Even though names are optional for points in general, this option requires you to key in a name before allowing you to proceed.

Use Name Template   This is the default option, which looks back at the point-creation command settings. The existing point name is ignored and overridden by the setting from the point name template.

Please note that for both of the options for dealing with duplicates a check box in the dialog box allows the selected resolution to be applied automatically to all the conflicts found. If you'd rather apply the same resolution to all the conflicts rather than select the resolution on a point-by-point basis, make sure to check that box.

Basic Point Editing

Despite your best efforts, the point data will often be placed in the wrong location or need additional editing to bring it to the desired status. For example, points may need to be rotated as a group to match a different horizontal datum or may need to be raised or lowered to match a different benchmark.

Graphic Point Edits

Points can be moved, copied, rotated, deleted, and more using standard AutoCAD commands and grip edits. When you pause your cursor over a grip, a special grip menu will appear with different options. Figure 3.18 (left) shows the grip menu options for the label. Figure 3.18 (right) shows the options available directly on the point. Using the options shown here, you can move the point and rotate it independently of the text and rotate the text label independently of the marker.

FIGURE 3.18
The top grip allows label modifications (left); the center grip allows marker modifications (right).

Panorama and Prospector Point Edits

You can access many point properties through the Point Editor in Panorama.

1. Continue working in the drawing from the previous exercise or open 0305_ PointCreation_FINISHED.dwg (0305_PointCreation_METRIC_FINISHED.dwg) and choose a point (or several points).

2. From the COGO Point contextual tab ➤ Modify panel, select Edit/List Points.

   Panorama brings up information for the selected points (see Figure 3.19).

FIGURE 3.19
Edit points in Panorama

You can access a similar interface on the Prospector tab of Toolspace in the Item View by following these steps:

1. Highlight the Points collection (see Figure 3.20).

2. In either location, right-click the point or points you want to examine and select Zoom To.

   Prospector works like a spreadsheet in many ways. You can sort by any column by clicking the heading of the column. Clicking the column a second time will sort the data in the opposite order. For example, if you'd like to list your points alphabetically by description, click the Description column heading.

3. Click the Raw Description column heading to re-sort the points.

4. You can close Panorama for editing the points and close the file.

It is up to you whether you want to save any modifications to the file.

Also note that the same interface is available for editing points when dealing with point groups.

FIGURE 3.20
Prospector lets you view your entire Points collection at once.

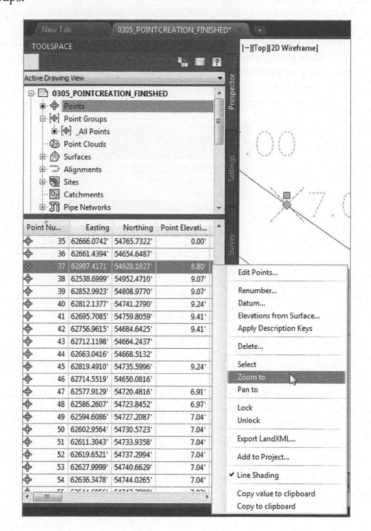

Point Groups: Don't Skip This Section!

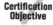

Certification Objective

Working with point groups is one of the most powerful techniques you will learn from this chapter. Do you want to select all your ground shots from within the survey? Make a point group! Want to move up last week's survey by the blown instrument height difference? Make a point group! Want to prevent invert shots from throwing off your surface model? You get it. Use a point group!

A *point group* is a collection of points that results when a criteria-based filter is applied to the point data in the drawing. For the filter criteria you can use any point property or combination of properties such as description, elevation, and point number, or you can select specific points in the drawing.

You will see that a point group is already created by default in any Civil 3D drawing: the _All Points group. This group contains all points in the drawing regardless of filter criteria. This group cannot be renamed or deleted, nor can it have its properties modified to exclude any points. Therefore, you should create point groups for collections of points you might want to separate from others, as shown in Figure 3.21.

FIGURE 3.21

An example of useful point groups in Prospector

Point groups can (and should!) be created upon import of a text file, as shown previously in Figure 3.7. It is a good practice to create a point group for any new survey data added to the drawing so that if a problem comes to light about that group of points (such as incorrect instrument height), they can be isolated and dealt with apart from other points. Create a new point group by right-clicking the main point group category and selecting New.

In this exercise, you'll learn how to use point groups to separate points into usable categories:

1. Open the drawing 0306_PointGroups.dwg (0306_PointGroups_METRIC.dwg), which you can download from this book's web page.

2. In Prospector, right-click Point Groups and select New.

3. On the Information tab, name the point group **Breaklines**.

4. Set Point Style to Basic Circle.

5. Set Point Label Style to Description Only.

6. Switch to the Include tab and place a check mark next to With Raw Descriptions Matching.

7. In the With Raw Descriptions Matching field, enter **BB*,TB***.

The asterisk acts as a wildcard to include points that may have additional information after the description. You are adding multiple descriptions by separating them with a comma, as shown in Figure 3.22.

FIGURE 3.22
The Include tab of the Breaklines point group properties

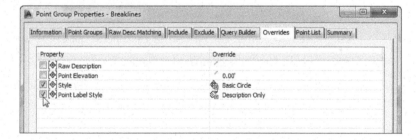

8. Switch to the Overrides tab.

9. Place check marks next to Style and Point Label Style, as shown in Figure 3.23.

FIGURE 3.23
Overrides force the display of the points to use styles assigned by the point group rather than the description key.

Doing so ensures that the point group, instead of the description keys, will control the styles.

10. Switch to the Point List tab and examine the points that have been picked up by the group.

   Only points beginning with BB and TB should appear in the list.

11. Click OK.

12. Again, right-click Point Groups and select New.

13. On the Information tab, name the group **No Display**, as shown in Figure 3.24.

FIGURE 3.24
Most drawings should contain a No Display point group with styles set to <none>.

14. Set both Point Style and Point Label Style to <none>.

15. Switch to the Include tab, and at the bottom of the dialog, put a check mark next to Include All Points.

16. Switch to the Overrides tab and place a check mark next to Style and Point Label Style.

17. Click OK.

All the points are hidden from view as a result of the point group.

18. Create another point group called **Topo**.

19. Set Point Style to Basic Cross and Point Label Style to Elevation and Description.

20. Switch to the Exclude tab and place a check mark next to With Elevations Matching.

21. Enter **<=0** in the accompanying field.

22. Place a check mark next to With Raw Descriptions Matching.

23. Type **PP*, TRANS*, WV*, WM*, FH*, MB*, PED*, GUY*** in the accompanying field, as shown in Figure 3.25, and click OK.

You may need to use the AutoCAD REGEN command to refresh the graphic and show your points again.

24. Save the drawing.

To compare your work with a completed example, see 0306_PointGroups_FINISHED.dwg (0306_PointGroups_METRIC_FINISHED.dwg).

Point groups will dictate point and label styles only if the description key set does not manage those properties. If a description key set manages the point and label styles for the point, then the only way to override it is to use the settings in the Overrides tab for the point group. For example, if you have a point group that encompasses all your ground shots and the description key set defines their marker as an *X*, you could change that representation to + for the point group on the Overrides tab by toggling the setting for Point Style and selecting the style that has the desired representation. So, in this case, these settings take control of the styles away from the description key and place it with the point group.

FIGURE 3.25
Use Exclude to create a Topo point group.

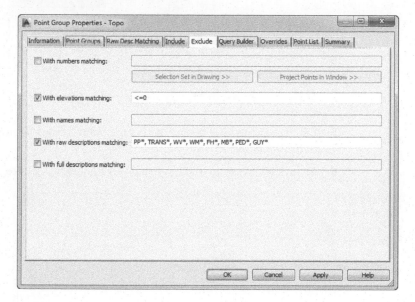

BEST PRACTICE: CONTROL POINT DISPLAY USING POINT GROUPS RATHER THAN LAYERS

Civil 3D drawings have many layers. It is much easier to switch the display of the point groups rather than create layer states for each point-visibility scenario.

A point can belong to more than one group at once. For instance, a water valve cover with elevation may be in a Topo group to be used in the definition of the surface, a Utilities group since it is part of the utilities point data, and the _All Points group since this is the default Civil 3D all-inclusive group. In these cases, the order in which the point groups are displayed in Prospector determines which point group controls the display of a specific point.

In this exercise, we will walk you through an example of how point group display order works:

1. Open the drawing 0307_PointDisplay.dwg (0307_PointDisplay_METRIC.dwg), which you can download from this book's web page.

2. In Prospector, right-click Point Groups and select Properties (see Figure 3.26).

FIGURE 3.26
Select Point Groups
➤ Properties to
change point group
display precedence.

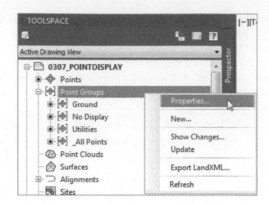

3. Using the arrows on the far right of the Point Groups listing, select Utilities and move it to the top of the list.

4. Move No Display so that it is listed directly below Utilities, as shown in Figure 3.27.

FIGURE 3.27
The order in
which the point
groups appear in
this list controls
precedence.

5. Click OK. If the displayed objects are not updated to reflect the change, run a regen command.

   Notice that only points defined by the Utilities group are visible.

6. Experiment with changing the order of the point groups using the properties.

7. Save the drawing.

To compare your work with a completed example, see 0307_PointDisplay_FINISHED.dwg (0307_PointDisplay_METRIC_FINISHED.dwg).

Changing Point Elevations

We've already discussed the idea that points placed on or along an object that has elevation will automatically inherit the object's elevation. For the same reason, points placed with tools in the Surface flyout will automatically inherit the elevation of a surface model. If you have chosen to place points with manual elevation entry and then press ↵ when prompted to specify an elevation, the elevation will be null (no elevation).

You are never stuck with a COGO point's elevation. It can be changed individually or as a group using the Panorama window. Additional tools are available for manipulating points (see Figure 3.28) in the COGO Points contextual tab that opens when you select a point object.

FIGURE 3.28
Point-editing commands in the ribbon

Elevations From Surface is an extremely handy tool for forcing points to a surface elevation (see Figure 3.29).

FIGURE 3.29
Hydrant Points as placed (top); hydrant points moved up to surface elevation (bottom)

0.00   0.00   0.00   0.00   0.00

6.31   6.33   6.34   6.36   6.37

In the event that you change the datum, you are most likely going to move a group of points' elevations.

1. Right-click the name of the point group in Prospector and select Edit Points.

   Panorama will appear for your point-editing delight.

2. Use Windows keyboard tricks to control which points are selected for modification.

   Pressing Ctrl+A will select all points in the Panorama listing, as shown in Figure 3.30.

FIGURE 3.30
Right-click to access point-modification tools from Panorama.

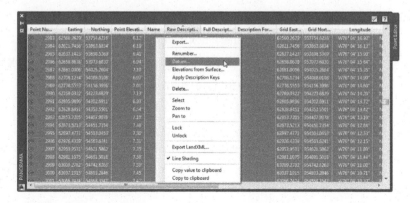

3. When you have finished selecting points, right-click and choose Datum.

   The command line will prompt you to specify the change in elevation you require.

Point Tables

You've seen some of the power of dynamic point editing; now let's look at how those dynamic edits can be used to your advantage in point tables.

Most commonly, you may need to create a point table for survey or stakeout data; it could be as simple as a list of point numbers, northing, easting, and elevation. These types of tables are easy to create using the standard point-table styles as a beginning reference. Follow these steps to create a point table:

1. Open the 0308_PointTable.dwg (0308_PointTable_METRIC.dwg) file, which you can download from this book's web page.

   This file will appear empty, but it isn't. First, you will review reordering point group properties to change the display of points. You don't need to see points to make a point table from a group, but this will help you see that the table reflects the specific group.

2. In Prospector, expand Point Groups.

   You will see that No Display is listed on the top, which means the styles set in its properties are taking over the other point groups.

3. Right-click Point Groups and select Properties.

4. In the listing, move the group Corners To Locate to the top by using the arrows on the right. Click OK.

5. Right-click the Corners To Locate point group and select the Zoom To option to focus on the desired points.

6. Switch to the Annotate ribbon tab and click Add Tables ➤ Add Point Table.

7. Verify that Table Style is set to Corner To Locate and click the Select Point Group icon next to the No Point Groups Selected label.

8. In the Point Groups dialog, select Corners To Locate and click OK.

9. Verify that the check box next to Split Table is clear.

10. When all your settings match those in Figure 3.31, click OK.

11. Click anywhere in the graphic to place the table.

12. Save the drawing.

To compare your work with a completed example, see 0308_PointTable_FINISHED.dwg (0308_PointTable_METRIC_FINISHED.dwg).

FIGURE 3.31
Point Table
Creation options

User-Defined Properties

Standard point properties include items such as number, easting, northing, elevation, name, description, and the other entries you see when examining points in Prospector or Panorama. Now, what if you'd like to assign extra information to a point object and the field data for that information is not among the standard fields that ship with the software? Civil 3D is versatile in this situation since it provides the means to add custom fields to suit your needs.

It's common to receive points from a soil scientist that list additional information, such as groundwater elevation or subsurface elevation. Surveyed manhole points often include invert elevations or flow data. Tree points may also contain information about species or caliber measurements. All this additional information can be added as user-defined properties to your point objects. By using user-defined properties, you will be able to parse the nonstandard information and attach it to the point data during the import process. You can then use user-defined properties in point labeling, analysis, point tables, and more.

Real World Scenario

HOW CAN CIVIL 3D WORK WITH SOIL BORING DATA?

There are several options for users who want to work with subsurface data in Civil 3D. One option is the Autodesk Geotechnical Module. This subscription-only tool allows users to import borehole data in several formats including AGS31, AGS4, and CSV and from a Keynetix HoleBASE database. The boreholes created with this tool are not point objects. For more information about the Autodesk Geotechnical Module, log into http://subscription.autodesk.com.

The option discussed here involves using user-defined properties on points to enter subsurface data. This option does not require any special downloads.

In the following example, you will add user-defined properties to some soil boring points and leverage point groups to work with the data. The skills you learn in this example can be applied to multiple soil boring values for the purposes of creating subsurface data.

1. Open the file 0309_SoilBorings.dwg (0309_SoilBorings_METRIC.dwg).

   This file contains an existing ground surface together with the property linework for the site using Civil 3D Parcels.

2. Import into the drawing the soil boring points that are provided to you in a LandXML file by using the LandXML tool that is on the Insert tab ➤ Import panel.

   The file that you will need is located in this chapter's data folder and is named 0309_SoilBorings.xml.

Take a moment to examine the soil boring points and the current elevation listing.

3. From the Settings tab of Toolspace, expand the Point collection, right-click User-Defined Property Classifications, and select New.

4. Name the new classification **Soil Borings** and click OK.

5. Expand the User-Defined Property Classifications category (if it is not already expanded), right-click Soil Borings, and select New.

6. Name the new property **Watertable Elevation**.

7. Set Property Field Type to Elevation, uncheck Default Value, and then click OK.

8. Jump back to the Toolspace ➢ Prospector tab and highlight the main Point Groups listing.

At the bottom of Toolspace you will see a listing of all the point groups, as shown here.

Continues

Continued

9. Set the classification as shown in the previous image.

10. Right-click the Soil Borings point group and select Edit Points.

11. Scroll over in Panorama until you locate the new classification column named Watertable Elevation.

    This is the information you added in the previous steps.

12. Add the Watertable Elevation entries in Panorama, as shown here. Dismiss Panorama when you've finished.

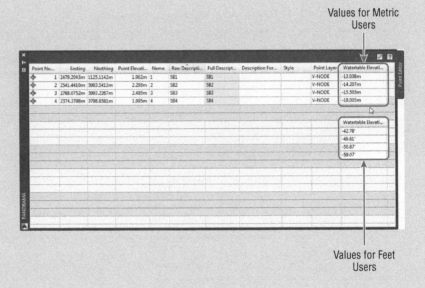

Values for Metric Users

Values for Feet Users

13. Right-click the Soil Borings group and select Properties. Switch to the Overrides tab, as shown here.

14. Place a check mark next to Point Elevation on the Overrides tab.

15. Click the tiny pencil icon twice or until it turns into the user-defined property icon. Initially the value will be <none>.

16. Click the field next to the icon to set the value to Watertable Elevation.

17. Click OK to dismiss the Point Group Properties dialog.

Notice that the elevation labels for the five points are listed as the water table elevations.

To compare your work with a completed example, see 0309_SoilBorings_FINISHED.dwg (0309_SoilBorings_METRIC_FINISHED.dwg).

The Bottom Line

Import points from a text file using description key matching. Most engineering offices receive text files containing point data at some time during a project. Description keys provide a way to automatically assign the appropriate styles, layers, and labels to newly imported points.

> **Master It** Open Masterit_0301.dwg (Masterit_0301_METRIC.dwg), which you can download from the book's web page. Revise the Civil 3D description key set to contain only the parameters listed next.

CODE	POINT STYLE	POINT LABEL STYLE	FORMAT	LAYER
GS*	Basic	Elevation Only	Ground Shot	V-NODE
EP*	Basic	Elevation and Description	Road Edge	V-NODE
HYD*	Hydrant (existing)	Elevation and Description	Hydrant	V-NODE-WATR
SW*	Basic	Elevation and Description	Sidewalk	V-NODE
TREE*	Tree	Elevation and Description	Tree	V-NODE-TREE

Import the PENZD (space delimited) file `MasterIt_0301.txt` (`MasterIt_0301_METRIC .txt`). Confirm that the description keys made the appropriate matches by looking at a handful of points of each type. Do the trees look like trees? Do the hydrants look like hydrants?

Save the resulting file for use in the remaining exercises.

Create a point group.   Building a surface using a point group is a common task. Among other criteria, you may want to filter out any points that tend to have erroneous elevations such as utilities or vegetation.

Master It   Create a new point group called Topo that includes all points *except* those with a descriptor code of TREE and HYD. Use the DWG created in the previous "Master It" exercise or start with `MasterIt_0301_FINISHED.dwg` (`MasterIt_0301_METRIC_ FINISHED.dwg`).

Export points to LandXML and ASCII format.   It's often necessary to export a LandXML or ASCII file of points for stakeout or data-sharing purposes. Unless you want to export every point from your drawing, it's best to create a point group that isolates the desired point collection.

Master It   Create a new point group that includes all the points with a raw description of SW. Export this point group via LandXML and a PENZD comma-delimited text file.

Use the DWG created in the previous "Master It" exercise or start with `MasterIt_0302_ FINISHED.dwg` (`MasterIt_0302_METRIC_FINISHED.dwg`).

Create a point table.   Point tables provide an opportunity to list and study point properties. In addition to basic point tables that list number, elevation, description, and similar options, you can customize point table formats to include user-defined property fields.

Master It   Use the DWG created in the previous "Master It" exercise or start with `MasterIt_0303_FINISHED.dwg` (`MasterIt_0303_METRIC_FINISHED.dwg`). Create a Centerline point group to include all the centerline points and create a point table for this point group using the PNEZD format table style.

Chapter 4

Surfaces

One of the most fundamental elements in a three-dimensional model of any design is the surface model. As you learned in the previous chapter, once survey information is gathered and points are set with elevations, you can proceed to turn some of that information into an intelligent surface model.

This chapter examines various methods of surface creation and editing. Then it moves into discussing ways to view, analyze, and label surfaces and explores how they interact with other parts of your project.

In this chapter, you will learn to:

◆ Create an existing ground surface using points.

◆ Modify and update a TIN surface.

◆ Prepare a slope analysis.

◆ Label surface contours and spot elevations.

◆ Import a point cloud into a drawing and create a surface model.

Understanding Surface Basics

A surface in the Autodesk® AutoCAD® Civil 3D® program is generated using the principle of triangulation. At the very simplest, a surface consists of points. The computer generates a triangular plane using a group of three points. Each triangular plane shares an edge with another, and a continuous surface is made. This methodology is referred to as a *triangulated irregular network (TIN)*, as shown in Figure 4.1.

FIGURE 4.1
A triangulated irregular network, or TIN

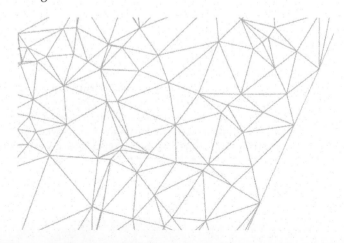

For any given (x,y) point, there can be only one unique z value within the surface (since slope is equal to rise over run, when the run is equal to 0, the result is "undefined"). What does this mean to you? It means surfaces created by Civil 3D have several rules:

No Thickness Modeled surfaces can be thought of as a sheet draped over a surface; they have no thickness in the vertical direction associated with them.

No Vertical Faces Vertical faces cannot exist in a TIN because two points on the surface cannot have the same (x,y) coordinate pair. Vertical walls or curb structures must have a slight offset of at least 0.001' (0.0001 m); otherwise, they will appear flattened.

No Caves or Tunnels The triangular planes that make up a TIN cannot overlap. If a design requires any tunnel-like structures, you will need to accomplish this with several surfaces instead.

UNDERSTANDING TRIANGULATION MATHEMATICS

TIN surface calculations are based on computational geometry known as Delaunay triangulation. Delaunay triangulation takes a set of points, isolates three in close proximity, and applies a circle intersecting those three points, producing a triangle. This algorithm is repeated for the remaining points, resulting in a collection of circles called *circumcircles*, which produce a network of triangles. Elevation interpolation occurs along those triangle lines, which determines where contours are drawn.

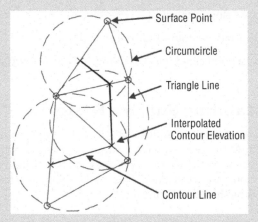

It's important that the points used in surface calculations be a good representation of surface elevations. This means that points representing fire hydrants, power poles, or trees, for example, should be excluded since those points more than likely were not collected at ground level.

Other information we provide to a surface definition influences how those triangles are drawn. Breaklines prevent triangle lines from being drawn through them but allow them to be drawn along them. Boundaries prevent interpolation from occurring inside or outside their extents depending on the type of boundary defined. Surface edits can override the Delaunay triangulation. Surface property settings can be used to apply a set of rules governing how the surface is created.

There are four types of surfaces in Civil 3D: TIN surfaces, grid surfaces, grid volume surfaces, and TIN volume surfaces. A TIN surface is based on a set of points using Delaunay triangulation. A grid surface is based on a Digital Elevation Model (DEM) file consisting of a set of data points arranged in a regularly spaced grid configuration. DEM files can be obtained from various mapping agencies. Volume surfaces are built by measuring vertical distances between two surfaces. Volume surfaces can be created from two grid or two TIN surfaces.

Creating Surfaces

Certification
Objective

When you first create a surface in Civil 3D, you give it a name and set its style. Initially, your surface will be empty, containing no data; your next step is to add data to the surface definition.

In Prospector, you can view the contents of the surface by expanding its branch and then further expanding the Definition area, as shown in Figure 4.2.

FIGURE 4.2
Create a new surface (left). Expand a surface's definition to add or modify elevation data (right).

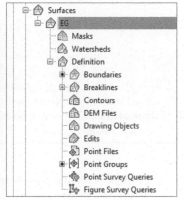

The following components can be used as part of a surface definition:

Boundaries   *Boundaries* are closed polylines that determine data inclusion and visibility for the surface. A boundary can be a 2D polyline, a 3D polyline, or even a feature line, but only the horizontal information will be used to generate the boundary—the elevation of the polyline is ignored. If the polyline that created the boundary is modified, the surface will become out of date.

Breaklines   *Breaklines* are used to create triangulation paths, thereby preventing triangle lines that could be generated off adjacent points from crossing these paths. Breaklines are mandatory for defining flow lines, curb lines, ditch lines, pavement edges, or any linear representation of ridges or valleys. Breaklines can be defined using lines, arcs, 2D polylines, 3D polylines, survey figures, parcels, or feature lines. Similar to boundaries, if a breakline is modified, the surface will become out of date, thus requiring a rebuild. Breaklines will be discussed in more detail later in this chapter.

THE YELLOW EXCLAMATION POINT FLAG

At some point you are bound to see a yellow exclamation point status icon in Prospector. This is a flag showing you that some elements are out of date and require rebuilding. In the image shown here, the EG surface needs to be rebuilt because the Point Groups branch is out of date.

No matter what type of definition in a surface is out of date, to rebuild the surface, right-click the surface's name (in this example that would be EG) and select Rebuild. You could also select Rebuild Automatic, which would result in the surface always rebuilding when required instead of you always having to manually select Rebuild.

Contours Polyline representations of surfaces can be used to create a Civil 3D surface. These polylines must be assigned the elevation of the contour they represent. Points will be placed along the contours to be used in the triangulation process. In addition, algorithms are run to ensure that the Civil 3D contours generated closely match the polyline contours used to define the surface. This process will be discussed in more detail later in this chapter in the section "Surfaces from Polylines." Similar to boundaries, if the polyline contour is modified, the surface will become out of date, thus requiring a rebuild. Adding contour data will be discussed further later in this chapter.

DEM Files *Digital Elevation Model (DEM)* files are the standard format files from governmental agencies and geographic information system (GIS) systems. These files are typically large in scale but can be great for planning purposes.

Drawing Objects These are AutoCAD objects that have an insertion point at an elevation (e.g., text, blocks, lines, AutoCAD points, 3D faces, or polyfaces) that can be used to populate a surface with elevation data. For text and blocks, the text insertion point z position is used as the elevation. Changes to these objects will not cause the surface to become out of date.

Edits Any manipulation after the surface is completed, such as adding or removing triangles or changing the datum, will be part of the edit history. These changes can be viewed in the surface properties, where edits can be toggled on and off individually to simplify reviewing and changing. They can also be reordered since edits are applied in the order in which they are added.

Point Files   Point files work well when you're working with large data sets where the points themselves don't necessarily contain extra information. Examples include laser scanning or aerial surveys. A drawing will stay referenced to a point file. If the point file is moved or deleted, the reference in the drawing will be broken unless a surface snapshot is taken. Snapshots will be discussed later in the chapter.

Point Groups   Civil 3D point groups or survey point groups can be created to isolate a set of points used to build a surface. The surface is linked to that point group. If points are added, removed, or modified in the point group, the surface will become out of date and must be rebuilt.

Point Survey Queries and Figure Survey Queries   Point survey queries and figure survey queries perform similar tasks. A saved survey query created on the Survey tab of Toolspace can be used similarly to a point group for populating surface elevation data.

If the query contains both points and figures, you can choose to use both types of data, only points, or only figures. Unlike a point group, data from the query can be added without the points or figures being inserted in the drawing. Prior to adding point survey queries or figure survey queries to surfaces, you must open the survey database containing those queries.

Creating a Surface with Point Groups

Usually, existing surfaces are created from data collected from topographic surveys. From that data, a set of relevant surface points can be isolated by defining a point group. This point group is a quick means of adding point data to a surface definition. Point groups are covered in Chapter 3, "Points."

In the exercise that follows, you'll build your first basic surface with a point group:

1. Open the file 0401_SurfaceFromPointGroup.dwg (0401_SurfaceFromPointGroup_METRIC.dwg), which you can download from this book's web page, www.sybex.com/go/masteringcivil3d2016.

2. On the Home tab of the ribbon ➤ Create Ground Data panel, select Surfaces ➤ Create Surface.

3. In the Create Surface dialog, shown in Figure 4.3, click in the Name field.

FIGURE 4.3
Creating your first new TIN surface

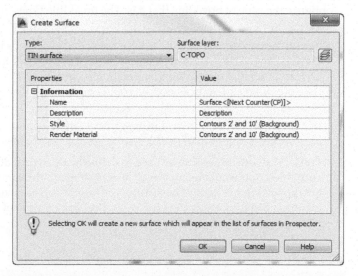

4. Remove the default text by highlighting it and replacing it with the name
   Existing Surface.

5. Set Style to Contours 1′ and 5′ (Background) or Contours 0.5 m and 2.5 m (Background)
   for metric users and click OK.

6. In Prospector, expand the Surfaces branch. You should now see your new surface in
   the listing.

7. Expand Existing Surface and then expand Definition by clicking the tiny plus sign to the
   left of the listing in Prospector.

8. Right-click Point Groups and select Add.

9. In the Point Groups dialog, highlight TOPO Shots and click OK. You should now see
   contours for your surface.

10. Save your drawing at the conclusion of the exercise. Compare your work with `0401_`
    `SurfaceFromPointGroup_FINISHED.dwg` or `0401_SurfaceFromPointGroup_METRIC_`
    `FINISHED.dwg` if desired.

Adding Breaklines

Breaklines change the triangulation of a surface by forcing triangle edges to follow along the
segments of the breakline. Breaklines represent linear features where a change in the slope of a
surface occurs. Examples of such features would be ridges, streams, ditches, curbs, and retaining walls, just to name a few.

There are several methods for adding breaklines to a surface. On the Prospector tab of
Toolspace, you can select the Breakline branch of the surface definition, right-click, and select
Add. Additionally, you can easily add survey figures by going to the Survey tab of Toolspace,
right-clicking the Figures branch, and selecting Create Breaklines. When feature lines are
selected, an Add To Surface As Breakline option is displayed in the contextual tab.

BREAKLINE TYPES

No matter which method you use to add breaklines to a surface's definition, you will need to
configure the type of breakline that it is. The breakline types are as follows:

Standard   Standard breaklines can be 2D or 3D polylines, arcs, lines, splines, feature lines,
figures, or parcels. These entities have the actual elevations for the surface assigned at their
vertices. The vertex elevations become surface points, TIN lines are drawn along the breakline, and then the remaining triangulation is calculated. Standard breaklines represent both
the horizontal and vertical locations of linear features of a surface.

Proximity   Proximity breaklines represent horizontal location only. In fact, if the entity used
to define the proximity breakline is 3D, the vertex elevation will be ignored. The elevation of
each vertex is determined from a nearby surface point already added to the surface.

Wall   Wall breaklines can be used to define near-vertical drops such as retaining walls or
curb lines. You would define a wall breakline much the same as you would define a standard
breakline. After selecting the feature, you would define a horizontal offset side and then an
elevation difference at each vertex or for the entire length of the feature.

From File   The From File option is needed only if you have an FLT text file containing breakline data. This file type is usually the result of output from another program and contains XYZ data on each vertex for the lines described in the file. Once the FLT file has been imported, the effect on the surface is identical to a standard breakline. File Link options can be dynamically linked to the file, or the link can be broken so the surface will no longer be dependent on the file.

Non-destructive   Non-destructive breaklines neither change elevation nor change grades of the surface model. Non-destructive breaklines simply control the horizontal orientation of triangle lines. You may find yourself needing a non-destructive breakline in anticipation of cleaning up triangle data, as discussed later in this chapter, in the section "Manual Surface Edits."

By far, standard is the most frequently used type of breakline, followed by proximity and wall breaklines.

WEEDING FACTORS

Turning on Weeding Factors in the Add Breaklines dialog allows you to omit extraneous data from your surface. You will want to consider weeding when your breaklines contain a lot of vertices very close together. Each vertex is added to your surface as a point, so when you weed, your aim is to exclude extraneous point data. This not only reduces the size of your surface but helps to eliminate the formation of skinny triangles, which can produce saw-toothed contours.

Weeding requires that a distance and angle be entered in the Add Breaklines dialog. With these settings, the program will examine each vertex as follows:

1. It measures the length of the segment leading into the vertex.

2. It measures the length of the segment leaving the vertex.

3. If the sum of both lengths is less than the entered distance value, it checks the delta angle.

4. If the delta angle is less than the entered angle value, it omits the vertex.

SUPPLEMENTING FACTORS

Turning on Supplementing Factors in the Add Breaklines dialog enables you to add additional surface points along your breaklines. Doing this helps to eliminate the generation of long triangle lines. It also allows you to define breaklines more precisely along curves.

The Distance setting works like the AutoCAD measure command. When breaklines are added to a surface, Civil 3D will add additional vertices based on this increment value.

The Mid-ordinate Distance setting is applied to arc segments in your breaklines. If this setting were absent, the program would create a single breakline segment from the PC to the PT of the arc. With this setting in place, the program creates shorter segments along the arc. With each segment considered to be tiny chords, the Mid-ordinate Distance value is the resulting measurement from the midpoint of each chord to the midpoint of each segmented arc.

In this example, you'll add some breaklines that describe road and ditch features:

1. Open the `0402_SurfaceFromBreaklines.dwg` file or the `0402_SurfaceFromBreaklines_METRIC.dwg` file.

This drawing is similar to the drawing used in the first exercise. It contains a surface created with a point group. It also contains 3D survey figures. Without the survey database, you'll have to add the figures conventionally, meaning through the Breakline branch of the surface.

2. Inspect the drawing by panning and zooming along the linework.

Notice that the TIN lines are not drawn along the figures representing the edge of pavement, centerline of roads, flowline of ditches, and top of banks.

3. Select and then right-click one of the brown figures representing the top of bank, and choose the Select Similar option.

The tooltip will indicate a figure prefix style of TB.

All the brown figures representing the tops of banks are now highlighted.

4. In Prospector, expand the Surfaces ➢ Existing Surface ➢ Definition branches.

5. Right-click Breaklines and select the Add option.

The Add Breaklines dialog appears.

6. Enter the description **Top of Bank** and leave all other settings at their default, as shown in Figure 4.4.

FIGURE 4.4
Entering a description in the Add Breaklines dialog

7. Click OK to accept the settings and close the dialog.

You can dismiss Panorama if it appears.

8. Repeat steps 3–7 for figures DL (Flowline of Ditch), BB (Bottom of Bank), CL (Centerline of Road), and EP (Edge of Pavement).

9. Zoom extents and notice that the TIN lines are now running along the survey figures now acting as breaklines.

As shown in Figure 4.5, by adding the breaklines, you force the TIN lines to align with them, thus cleaning up the contours and making them follow the ridgelines of the road centerline, gutter lines, and shoulders as well as the changes in grade around the small detention area.

FIGURE 4.5
Existing surface with contours displayed before breaklines are added (left) and after (right)

When this exercise is complete, you can close the drawing. A completed version of this drawing is available from the book's web page with the filename `0402_SurfaceFromBreaklines_FINISHED.dwg` or `0402_SurfaceFromBreaklines_METRIC_FINISHED.dwg`.

CROSSING BREAKLINES

Eventually, you will see Panorama pop up with a message about crossing breaklines. In general, Civil 3D does not like breaklines that cross themselves. The Resolve Crossing Breaklines tool will let you examine those situations. To use the Resolve Crossing Breaklines tool, do the following:

1. Click a surface with breaklines.

2. From the TIN Surface contextual tab ➤ Analyze panel, choose Resolve Crossing Breaklines.

3. At the `Please specify the types of breakline you want to find or [surveyDatabase Figure Surface]:` prompt, enter **S ↵** to select the surface option.

The Crossing Breaklines tab on Panorama lists the crossing breaklines. You can decide how you want to resolve them using Use Higher Elevation, Use Lower Elevation, Use Average Elevation, or Specify Elevation, as shown here.

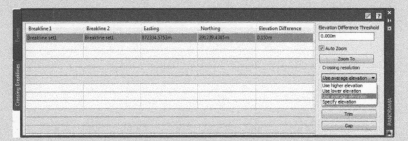

4. Select each breakline and click the Resolve button, which is located underneath the drop-down list shown in the preceding image; the conflict disappears from the Crossing Breaklines conflict list.

Adding Boundaries

Use boundaries when you want to restrict the area where triangles are being generated. Many object types can be used as surface boundaries, such as survey figures, feature lines, 2D polylines, and 3D polylines. Whatever type of line you choose as your boundary, it must be closed and cannot cross itself (i.e., no "loop-the-loops"). Elevations of the boundaries are ignored. There are four types of surface boundaries:

Outer Outer boundaries are used to conceal surface components (triangles, contours, or points) occurring outside the boundary extents.

Hide Hide boundaries are used to conceal surface components inside the boundary extents. For example, consider a hide boundary to hide any interpolation occurring inside a building perimeter.

Show Show boundaries are used to reveal surface components inside a hide boundary. If a hide boundary was used around a building perimeter, a show boundary can be applied to reveal contours in the building's courtyard for landscape purposes. Show boundaries can also be used to show surface areas outside an outer boundary.

Data Clip A data clip is a type of boundary drawn around the extents of a site. It is used to prevent surface calculations from occurring beyond its extents. The data clip boundary should be the first component added to the surface definition. For example, if a DEM file representing the surface of an entire county will be used to create a surface, a data clip boundary can be applied first to exclude the grid information outside the construction site. Using a data clip boundary will result in smaller surfaces (fewer surface points), which will impact your file size.

DESTRUCTIVE VS. NON-DESTRUCTIVE BOUNDARIES

The boundary types outer, show, and hide all have the option to be destructive (i.e., the Non-destructive Breakline check box is cleared) or non-destructive (i.e., the Non-destructive Breakline option is checked). What Civil 3D is "destroying" are the triangles that underlie the boundary.

The following image shows a schematic of a surface model before a boundary is added. For illustration purposes, triangle vertices have been highlighted with different shapes. The stars represent surface data points inside the boundary, and the circles represent points outside of the boundary.

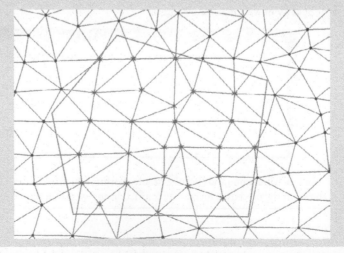

Use the Non-destructive Breakline option when the data you are working with is valid right up to the boundary edge. A boundary added as a non-destructive breakline will retriangulate the surface and create triangles up to the boundary, as shown in the following image. The squares show locations where Civil 3D has interpolated a surface data point at the boundary. The portion of the surface that would be hidden by adding a boundary is being shown in light gray for illustration purposes.

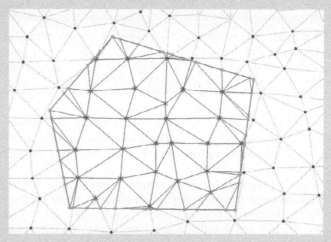

Use a destructive boundary if the line you are adding as a boundary is an approximation of the area you want to rein in. A boundary added as destructive will remove any triangle lines it crosses. The following image shows the illustration surface with the same boundary as before but added as destructive. The portion of the surface that would be hidden by adding a boundary is being shown in gray for illustration purposes. Notice how the outermost triangle legs of the surface are all inside the boundary.

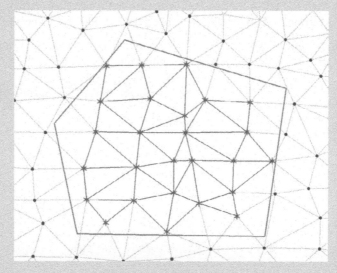

Consider a surface that needs an outer boundary, for example. If you create a rough polyline that encloses the points you want to include as your surface model, add the polyline to the surface as an outer boundary with the non-destructive option cleared.

Continues

Continued

If you deliberately created the polyline by snapping each vertex of the boundary to a surveyed point, for example, you could add it as a non-destructive breakline.

You will need to use your professional judgment to know when to use the Non-destructive Breakline option and when to use the Destructive Breakline option, but a good rule of thumb is that outer boundaries are usually destructive. Hide and show boundaries are usually non-destructive.

With the exception of data clip boundaries, you'll want to have your boundaries among the last operations in your surface-building process. Therefore, as future edits are made, you may want to move the Add Boundary build operation back to the bottom of the Data Operations list on the Definition tab in the Surface Properties dialog, which will be discussed later in this chapter.

The addition of every boundary is considered a separate part of the building operations. This means that the order in which the boundaries are applied controls their final appearance. For example, a show boundary listed before a hide boundary created in the same area will be overridden by that hide operation.

One way to start defining more accurate boundaries is to first extract the boundary defining the extents of the surface to a polyline and then edit the polyline to the optimum shape. The Extract Objects From Surface utility allows you to re-create any displayed surface element (contours, border, and the like) as an independent AutoCAD entity. It is important to note that only the objects that are currently visible in the surface style can be extracted. In this exercise, you'll extract the existing surface boundary as a starting point for creating a more refined boundary that will limit triangulation:

1. Open the 0403_SurfaceBoundary.dwg or 0403_SurfaceBoundary_METRIC.dwg file.

2. Select the surface.

3. From the TIN Surface contextual tab ➤ Surface Tools panel, choose Extract From Surface ➤ Extract Objects to open the Extract Objects From Surface dialog.

4. Leave the Border object selected and deselect the Major Contour, Minor Contour, and Points options, as shown in Figure 4.6.

FIGURE 4.6
Extracting the border from the surface object

5. Click OK to finish the process. Press Esc to deselect the surface.

A 3D polyline has been created from the surface border.

6. Pick the border 3D polyline.

This polyline will form the basis for your outer surface boundary. By extracting the border polyline from the existing surface, you save a lot of time playing connect the dots along the points that are valid. Next, you'll add this polyline into the surface as a boundary.

7. In Prospector, expand the Surfaces ➤ Existing Surface ➤ Definition branches.

8. Right-click Boundaries and select the Add option.

The Add Boundaries dialog opens (Figure 4.7).

FIGURE 4.7
Add Boundaries
dialog

9. Enter the name **Outer**, leave Type set to Outer, and keep the check mark next to the Non-destructive Breakline option; then click OK.

10. Pick the 3D polyline border that you previously extracted.

11. Working your way around the site clockwise, grip-edit the polyline you created in step 6 to exclude some of the area at the northwest area of the site around the ditch where there are no points. Use the Add Vertex option from the grip menu, as shown in Figure 4.8.

FIGURE 4.8
Using the grips to
adjust the border

Note that this process does not require you to use object snaps. This boundary only needs to be approximate. You will see the surface dynamically update with each grip edit since the surface is set to Rebuild Automatic.

12. If time permits, edit the entire boundary.

On a large site, you can see that this is a time-consuming process but worth the effort to clean up the site nicely (Figure 4.9). Thankfully, there are other methods you can use to clean up the surface border; we will discuss these methods in later exercises.

FIGURE 4.9
A non-destructive outer boundary in action

13. Save the drawing and keep it open for the next portion of the exercise.

Notice in some areas along the outer boundary how the edge of the triangulation includes points shown as a square with a + symbol; these are the additional points created along the boundary line where it intersects with the triangles it crosses. The points you attempted to exclude from the surface are still being included in the calculation of elevations for this point; they are just excluded from the display and calculations. This isn't the result you were after, so let's fix it now.

14. In Prospector, expand the Surfaces ➤ Existing Surface ➤ Definition branches and select Boundaries.

A listing of the boundaries appears in the preview area of Toolspace.

15. Right-click the boundary you just created and select the Delete option.

16. Click OK in the warning dialog that tells you the selected definition items will be permanently removed from the surface.

You can dismiss Panorama if it appears.

17. In Prospector, right-click Boundaries and select the Add option again.

The Add Boundaries dialog appears.

18. Enter the name **Outer**, leave Type set to Outer, and leave the check box unchecked next to the Non-destructive Breakline option; then click OK.

19. Pick the revised 3D polyline again.

Notice that no triangles intersect your boundary now where it does not connect points, as shown in Figure 4.10.

FIGURE 4.10
A destructive outer boundary in action

Next, you will add a hide boundary to the surface.

20. In Prospector, right-click Boundaries and select the Add option again.

21. Name the boundary **Buildings** and change Type to Hide. Make sure that Non-destructive Breakline is checked, as shown in Figure 4.11, and click OK.

FIGURE 4.11
Adding build-ings as non-destructive, hide boundaries

22. Select the outer outline of the cyan building in the northwest portion of the site. Press Enter.

You should now have a void in your surface where the building exists.

23. Right-click Boundaries and select the Add option one last time.

24. Name the boundary **Courtyard**, set the type to Show, and verify that Non-destructive Breakline is checked.

25. Click OK; then click the closed polyline inside the building outline and press Enter.

You should now see an island of surface data inside the previously hidden location.

When this exercise is complete, you can close the drawing. A finished copy of this drawing is available from the book's web page with the filename 0403_SurfaceBoundary_FINISHED.dwg or 0403_SurfaceBoundary_METRIC_FINISHED.dwg.

WORKING WITH LARGE SURFACES

A surface has a limit to the number of points it can contain before caching its definition to an external file. The only way to prevent this is to reduce the amount of data in the surface definition. If this is not an option, the cache file will be created in the same folder where the drawing file has been saved. This file must remain in the folder with the drawing file for the surface definition to remain in the drawing. If the cache file is deleted, moved, or renamed, the surface will no longer appear in the Prospector or function in the drawing. What will remain in the drawing will be a proxy entity.

The cache file will bear the name of the drawing file along with its AutoCAD object handle (<drawing_name>_<surface object handle>). For grid surfaces, the limit for the number of points is about 1 million, and the file extension of the cache file will be .grs. For TIN surfaces, the limit is about 2 million, and the file extension of the cache file will be .mms.

There are several options for working with large surfaces depending on the situation:

Data Clip Boundaries   As discussed earlier, a data clip boundary is a type of boundary that can be added before any elevation data is added. This is the best option to use if you have information covering a large geographic area but are working only in a smaller area.

Cropped Surface   The Create Cropped Surface command can be found in the contextual tab of your surface, hidden in the Surface Tools panel flyout. This command will break off a piece of a surface model and allow you to send the smaller piece to a new drawing. This is a fast way to create a new drawing containing the desired surface data. The major disadvantage to the cropped surface tool is that there is no connection between the original surface and its spawn. In other words, if the original surface is changed, the new surface will not be affected.

Data Shortcuts   The best of both worlds, data shortcuts allow you to work in a new file but remain connected to the surface's source data. Another major advantage of using data shortcuts is that multiple users can access the surface data without duplicating it. Data shortcuts are discussed at length in Chapter 16, "Advanced Workflows."

Here are some other hints that will be helpful in increasing performance when working with large surfaces:

◆ Turn on the Level Of Detail option in the Views panel of the View tab.

◆ Do not use the Rebuild-Automatic option.

◆ Turn off the selection preview on the Selection tab of the Options dialog.

◆ Clear the Show Tooltips option in the Surface Properties dialog.

Additional Surface Creation Methods

Many forms of data can be processed by Civil 3D to create a surface. The data types discussed in the following sections are common when working with organizations that are not using Civil 3D.

File types like TIN and LandXML are often best for moving data from other civil design software programs into Civil 3D. DEM files can be used to create surfaces for preliminary drainage analysis.

TIN Files A TIN file represents a surface that was generated by AutoCAD Land Desktop. The corresponding PNT file from the Land Desktop surface folder must be present in the same folder as well. These files contain the baseline TIN information from the original surface and can be used to regenerate it easily.

LandXML Files LandXML files can be exported from most land development software applications for use in another land development software application. LandXML has become a common means of migrating data in the land development industry. LandXML files contain the point elevations along with the associated 3D face definitions resulting from the creation and surface edits performed in the originating software application.

Digital Elevation Models Digital Elevation Model files are used by the U.S. Department of the Interior's United States Geological Survey (USGS) and are commonly produced by government organizations for their GIS systems. The DEM format can be read directly by Civil 3D, but the USGS typically distributes the data in a complex format called Spatial Data Transfer Standard (SDTS). The files can be converted using a freely available program named sdts2dem. This DOS-based program converts the files from the SDTS format to the DEM format you need. Once you are in possession of a DEM file, creating a surface from it is relatively simple.

Surface from LandXML Files

Oftentimes, the engineering and survey tasks for a land development project are performed by separate companies. If you are tasked with the engineering design and are receiving a DWG file representing the existing site with contours from another firm, you should ask for a LandXML export of the existing surface. It is much more precise than using the contours to build your existing surface. It will also save time as compared with building the surface from scratch with points and breaklines.

1. Create a new drawing using the _AutoCAD Civil 3D (Imperial) NCS template. Metric users should use the _AutoCAD Civil 3D (Metric) NCS template.

2. Switch to the Settings tab of Toolspace, right-click the drawing name, and select Edit Drawing Settings.

   The Drawing Settings dialog appears.

3. Imperial users should set the zone category to USA, North Carolina, and set the coordinate system to NAD83 North Carolina State Planes, US Foot (NC83F) via the Units And Zone tab of the Drawing Settings dialog. Metric users should set the zone category to USA, North Carolina, and set the coordinate system to NAD83 North Carolina State Planes, Meter (NC83).

4. Click OK.

5. From the Insert tab ➤ Import panel, choose LandXML.

The Import LandXML dialog appears.

6. Select 0404_SurfaceFromFile.XML and click Open to continue.

The Import LandXML dialog changes, as shown in Figure 4.12.

FIGURE 4.12
Understanding the Import LandXML dialog

7. In the Import LandXML dialog, expand the Surfaces collection.

Notice the check boxes. A LandXML file can contain many forms of design data such as alignments, profiles, parcels, points, and pipe networks as well as surfaces. If you receive a file with multiple forms of design data, here in this dialog is where you would uncheck what you do not want to import into the immediate drawing. It isn't possible to uncheck Units, Project Name, or Application Description. These lines are in there for informational purposes only, giving a history of the file: originating units, originating drawing name, originating application. In this example, the originating application was Civil 3D. Sometimes firms make it a policy of not sharing their object data (in this case, the existing surface) when performing file exchanges. This is so they can retain ownership of the model and keep their styles in house. We'll discuss more about styles in Chapter 19.

8. Click Edit LandXML Settings.

The LandXML Settings dialog appears.

9. Expand the Surface Import Settings collection and configure these settings to match Figure 4.13.

FIGURE 4.13
Configuring
Surface Import
Settings

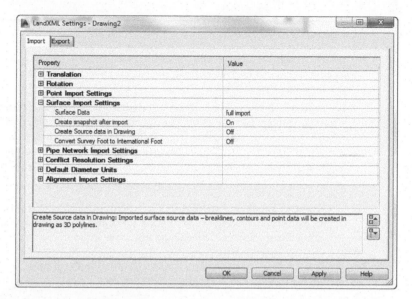

10. Click OK to continue and OK again to close the Import LandXML dialog.

    After the surface imports, Civil 3D will zoom extents.

11. In Prospector, expand the Surfaces ➤ Existing From LandXML ➤ Definition collection and click Definition.

    Notice in the list view that no data is being used in the surface definition. The definition of this surface is coming directly from the LandXML file. As a matter of fact, if this LandXML file were moved or deleted, the surface definition would be lost if it weren't for the automatic creation of a snapshot.

12. Right-click the Existing From LandXML Surface and click Surface Properties.

13. On the Definition tab, notice the Data Operations list on the bottom half of the dialog.

    The first item on the list is the Import XML File operation. Notice the Browse button next to the path to the file. This button can be used to redefine the path to the LandXML file if the location must change or the file gets renamed. The next line contains the Create Snapshot operation, which preserves the surface definition in case the XML file is lost. Either line can be deleted from the surface definition. Since a snapshot ignores any previous surface operations, if a new XML file is sent to you containing an updated surface definition, you would need to delete and then re-create the snapshot based on the new definition.

14. Click OK to close the Surface Properties dialog.

    A completed version of this drawing is available from the book's web page (0404_SurfaceFromFile_FINISHED.dwg or 0404_SurfaceFromFile_METRIC_FINISHED.dwg).

SURFACE SNAPSHOTS

A *surface snapshot* captures the state of the surface at the time it was created. If there is a snapshot in a surface, a surface's rebuild will start at the snapshot since the snapshot summarizes all of the previous build operations.

As mentioned previously, a drawing will stay referenced to any external data used to create it, most commonly a point file, LandXML file, or breakline file. If the external data is moved or deleted, the reference in the drawing will be broken. To prevent this from affecting the surface, you can create a snapshot of the surface while the surface is still working as intended. Then if anything happens to the external data, the surface will remain intact if a snapshot exists.

If you right-click a surface's name in Prospector, you will see three options related to snapshots:

Create Snapshot By creating a snapshot, you add a build operation that captures the surface information in the current state. Once a snapshot is created, the icon next to Definition in the Prospector tree will change to a camera icon.

Remove Snapshot This option will remove the snapshot from the build operation. After a snapshot is removed, the surface will behave as if the snapshot was never there.

Rebuild Snapshot If the operations prior to the snapshot become outdated, you will see a yellow status icon next to its node in the Prospector tree. If you rebuild the snapshot, a new snapshot is created, incorporating all changes to the surface model from the point of its initial creation. In many cases, you will want to leave the snapshot in place if you do not want the changes to affect the surface.

Surface from DEM Files

In the following exercise, you will be creating a surface from a DEM file:

1. Start a new drawing from the _AutoCAD Civil 3D (Imperial) NCS template that ships with Civil 3D. Metric users should use the _AutoCAD Civil 3D (Metric) NCS template.

2. Switch to the Settings tab of Toolspace, right-click the drawing name, and select Edit Drawing Settings.

   The Drawing Settings dialog appears.

3. Imperial users should set the zone category to USA, North Carolina, and set the coordinate system to NAD83 North Carolina State Planes, US Foot (NC83F) via the Units And Zone tab of the Drawing Settings dialog. Metric users should set the zone category to USA, North Carolina, and set the coordinate system to NAD83 North Carolina State Planes, Meter (NC83).

4. Click OK.

The coordinate system of the DEM file that you will import will be adjusted to the coordinate system of the drawing.

5. From the Home tab ➤ Create Ground Data panel, choose Surfaces ➤ Create Surface.

   The Create Surface dialog appears. If a coordinate system transformation wasn't necessary, Create Surface From DEM would be a quicker method for creating this surface. However, Create Surface From DEM produces a grid surface, which cannot be adjusted.

6. Accept the options in the dialog, and click OK to create the surface.

   This surface is added as Surface1 to the Surfaces collection in Prospector.

7. In Prospector, expand the Surfaces ➤ Surface1 ➤ Definition branches.

8. Right-click DEM Files and select the Add option (see Figure 4.14).

FIGURE 4.14
Adding DEM data
to a surface

The Add DEM File dialog appears.

9. Use the button to the right of the DEM File Name area to navigate to the 0405_Camden_NC.DEM file and click Open.

   Remember, you can download all data and drawing files for this book from www.sybex.com/go/masteringcivil3d2016. The DEM file information will populate in the Add DEM File dialog, showing that the DEM file you are using is UTM Zone 18, NAD27 Datum, Meters.

10. In the Add DEM File dialog, click in the Value column next to CS Code to display the ellipsis button; click that button to display the Select Coordinate Zone dialog.

11. Both Imperial and metric users, set the coordinate system code (CS code) to match the DEM file by selecting UTM With NAD27 Datum, Zone 18, Meter; Central Meridian 75d W (UTM27-18), as shown in Figure 4.15, and click OK.

    Note that you can find the coordinate system information for this DEM by reviewing the DEM file information section of the Add DEM File dialog.

FIGURE 4.15
Setting the 0405_
Camden_NC.DEM
coordinate zone

This information is necessary to properly translate the DEM's coordinate system to the drawing's coordinate system.

The Add DEM File dialog should now match the one shown in Figure 4.16.

FIGURE 4.16
Setting the 0405_
Camden_NC.DEM
file properties

12. Click OK in the Add DEM File dialog.

You may receive a message regarding the level of detail, which is discussed later in this chapter. If a Level Of Detail dialog appears, click the Keep The Current Display Mode option.

13. In Prospector, right-click Surface1 and select Zoom To to bring the surface into view.

14. Select the surface. From the Surface contextual tab of the ribbon ➤ Modify panel, click the Surface Properties icon.

The Surface Properties dialog appears. Earlier, in the Create Surface dialog, you allowed the default surface name to be used, which created the name of Surface1. Since the default name does not provide much information, you will now revise the default name to something that offers more information to the user.

15. On the Information tab, change the Name field entry to **Camden Point NC**.

16. Change the Surface Style drop-down list to Contours And Triangles and then click OK to accept the settings in the Surface Properties dialog.

Once you have the DEM data imported, you can pause over any portion of the surface and see that feedback showing the surface elevation is provided through a tooltip. This surface can be used for preliminary analysis but isn't accurate enough for construction purposes.

The main drawback to DEM data is the sheer bulk of the surface size and point count. The `0405_Camden_NC.DEM` file you just imported contains 173,185 points and covers more than 60 square miles. This much data can be overwhelming, and it covers an area much larger than the typical site. If you try zooming in and out on the surface, you may notice performance lag. To ease the processing and activate the Level Of Detail display, do the following:

1. Switch to the View tab on the ribbon.

2. Expand the bottom of the Views panel.

3. Select Level Of Detail. A Level Of Detail Display warning message may appear. If so, click Close.

 After these steps are complete, you will notice that a new icon appears in the upper-left corner of your model space, showing you that Level Of Detail is activated. To turn off Level Of Detail, follow the same steps.

Turning on the Level Of Detail display does not change the data in the surface but simply changes what is viewable at the different zoom levels. Figure 4.17 shows the same area of the surface before turning on Level Of Detail (left) and after (right). The left version of the surface appears shaded because that is how dense the triangles are. You'll look at some data reduction methods later in this chapter.

FIGURE 4.17
DEM surface:
shown without
Level Of Detail
(left), zoomed
out with Level Of
Detail (right)

With Level Of Detail turned on, save your drawing at the conclusion of the exercise. Compare your work with `0405_SurfaceFromDEM_FINISHED.dwg` or `0405_SurfaceFromDEM_METRIC_FINISHED.dwg` if desired.

Surface from GIS Data

Whether the source is internal or from an outside firm, elevation data from geographic information systems is becoming increasingly common. Civil 3D understands GIS and can work with the data given. In this section, we'll show you how to import GIS data pertaining to surfaces:

1. Start a new drawing by using the `_AutoCAD Civil 3D (Imperial) NCS` template and set the coordinate system to NAD83 Virginia State Planes, North Zone, US Foot (VA83-NF). Metric users should use the `_AutoCAD Civil 3D (Metric) NCS` template and set the coordinate system to NAD83, Virginia State Planes, North Zone, Meter (VA83-N).

2. From the Home tab ➤ Create Ground Data panel, choose Surfaces ➤ Create Surface From GIS Data.

   The Create Surface From GIS Data – Object Options page appears.

3. Set Name to **GIS Data**, change Description to **Import from GIS Data**, and set the style to Contours 5′ and 25′ (Background) or Contours 2 m and 10 m (Background) for metric users, as shown in Figure 4.18; then click the Next button.

FIGURE 4.18
The Create Surface
From GIS Data –
Object Options
page

The Create Surface From GIS Data – Connect To Data page appears.

4. You are importing a SHP file, so change Data Source Type to SHP.

5. Click the ellipsis next to SHP Path. Locate the `0406_Contours.shp` file (which you'll find at www.sybex.com/go/masteringcivil3d2016). Then click Open.

The path is now populated with the location of the SHP file, as shown in Figure 4.19.

FIGURE 4.19
The Create Surface
From GIS Data –
Connect To Data
page

6. Click the Login button.

You won't need a username or password to log in.

The Create Surface From GIS Data – Schema And Coordinates page now appears (Figure 4.20).

FIGURE 4.20
The Create Surface From GIS Data – Schema And Coordinates page

You will notice that the name of the file appears as well as the coordinate system in which the SHP was created. If you are an Imperial user, the NAD83 Virginia State Planes, North Zone, US Foot system matches what you set the drawing up with. For metric users, the coordinate system of the SHP file is different from the drawing coordinate system.

7. Verify that the 0406_Contours check box is checked under Feature Class and click Next.

8. On the Create Surface From GIS Data – Geospatial Query page, look at the settings for future reference, but do not make any changes (Figure 4.21). Click Next.

FIGURE 4.21
The Create Surface From GIS Data – Geospatial Query page

9. On the Create Surface From GIS Data – Data Mapping page, click the drop-down list next to FLABEL in the GIS Field column and select Elevation, as shown in Figure 4.22.

FIGURE 4.22

The Create Surface From GIS Data – Data Mapping page

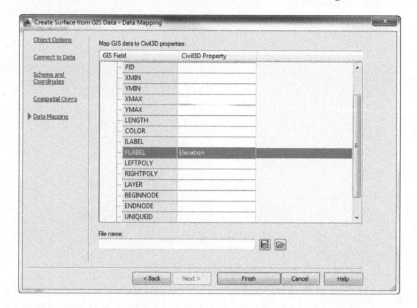

Many dialogs throughout the software use tables such as those shown on this page for you to input data. If at any time the column is not wide enough for you to view all of the contents, you may modify the column width by clicking between the column headings.

At the bottom of the Create Surface From GIS Data – Data Mapping page you will notice a File Name field as well as Save and Open icons. That means you can save the current data mapping information that you've set for future use.

10. Click the Finish button.

11. Dismiss Panorama and zoom extents to see the surface based on the SHP file (Figure 4.23). If the Level Of Detail Display setting is still on from the previous exercise, turn it off (View tab ➤ Views panel expanded ➤ Level Of Detail).

When this exercise is complete, you can close the drawing. A finished copy of this drawing is available from the book's web page with the filename 0406_SurfaceFromGIS_FINISHED.dwg or 0406_SurfaceFromGIS_METRIC_FINISHED.dwg.

This is just another avenue for getting data from other sources into Civil 3D.

FIGURE 4.23
The finished
imported GIS
contours

Surfaces from Polylines

The quality of the data you receive if you are working with contours varies greatly. The contour interval and smoothing factors will affect the result when imported to Civil 3D. The resulting surface may not accurately reflect the original survey data. This is because elevation information is provided along the contour lines but not in between the contour lines, causing the interpolation between the contours to lack accuracy. Civil 3D includes a series of surface algorithms that work well at matching the resulting surface to the original contour data by providing additional derived data points. You'll look at those surface edits in this series of exercises:

1. Open the `0407_SurfaceFromPolylines.dwg` file (or the `0407_SurfaceFromPolylines_ METRIC.dwg` file).

   Note that the contours in this file are composed of polylines with elevation values.

2. In Prospector, right-click the Surfaces branch and select the Create Surface option.

   The Create Surface dialog appears.

3. Leave the Type field set to TIN Surface, but change the Name value to **EG-Polylines**.

4. Change Description to **Surface From Polylines**.

5. Click in the Value column next to Style to display the ellipsis button; once it's visible, click the ellipsis button to display the Select Surface Style dialog.

6. From the drop-down list, select Contours 5' And 25' (Background) or Contours 2m And 10m (Background) for metric users; click OK to close the Select Surface Style dialog.

7. Click OK to close the Create Surface dialog.

8. In Prospector, expand the Surfaces ➢ EG-Polylines ➢ Definition branches.

9. Right-click Contours and select the Add option.

   The Add Contour Data dialog appears.

10. Set Description to **Polylines**. Under Weeding Factors, set:

    ◆ Distance to **15** (or **5** for metric users)

    ◆ Angle to **4** degrees.

    Under Supplementing Factors, set:

    ◆ Distance to **100** (or **30** for metric users)

    ◆ Mid-Ordinate Distance to **1** (or **0.3** for metric users).

11. Verify that no check boxes are checked, as shown in Figure 4.24, and click OK.

FIGURE 4.24
The Add Contour
Data dialog

In this example it is okay to leave all the Minimize Flat Areas By options unchecked. You will return to the Minimize Flat Areas By options in a bit.

12. At the Select contours: prompt, enter **ALL** ↵ to select all the entities in the drawing and press ↵ again to end the command.

    You can dismiss Panorama if it appears by clicking the green check mark. Save the drawing and keep it open for the next portion of the exercise.

    The contour data has some tight curves and flat spots where the basic contouring algorithms simply fail. Zoom into any portion of the site, and you can see these areas by looking for the blue and cyan original contours not matching the new Civil 3D–generated contour, as shown in Figure 4.25.

FIGURE 4.25
Contour surface without minimizing flat areas

You'll fix that now.

13. In Prospector, expand the Definition branch of the EG-Polylines surface if it's not already open from the previous exercise and right-click Edits.

14. Select the Minimize Flat Areas option to open the Minimize Flat Areas dialog.

Note that the dialog has the same options found in that portion of your original Add Contour Data dialog.

15. Click OK to accept the defaults.

16. Save the drawing and keep it open for the next portion of the exercise.

Now the contours displayed more closely match the original contour information, as shown in Figure 4.26. There might be a few instances where gaps exist between old and new contour lines, but in a cursory analysis, none was off by more than 0.4′ in the horizontal direction—not bad when you're dealing with almost a square mile of contour information.

FIGURE 4.26
Contour surface with minimizing flat areas

17. Zoom into an area with a dense contour spacing and select the surface to make the contextual tab associated with the TIN Surface: EG-Polylines appear.

18. From the TIN Surface contextual tab ➤ Modify panel, choose the Surface Properties icon to display the Surface Properties dialog.

19. On the Information tab, set Surface Style to Contours And Points, and click OK to see a drawing similar to Figure 4.27. Press the Esc key to deselect the surface.

FIGURE 4.27
Surface data points and derived data points

In Figure 4.27, you're seeing the points the TIN is derived from, with some styling applied to help you understand the creation source of the points. Although you can't see the colors in the printed figure, on the screen the points are shown in color to help you differentiate them:

◆ Each point shown as a red + symbol is a point picked up from the contour data itself.

◆ The magenta points shown with a circle symbol circumscribed over a + symbol are all added data on the basis of the Minimize Flat Areas edits.

These points make it possible for the Civil 3D surface to match almost exactly the input contour data.

At this time, the original polylines are still present in the drawing, and you may find yourself tempted to delete them. Before doing so, you will want to change the surface property Copy Deleted Dependent Objects, as discussed in the section "Surface Build Options" later in this chapter.

When this exercise is complete, you can close the drawing. A completed version of this drawing is available from the book's web page with the filename 0407_SurfaceFromPolylines_FINISHED .dwg or 0407_SurfaceFromPolylines_METRIC_FINISHED.dwg.

Now that you have learned how to add several types of data to a surface definition, you will need to fine-tune your surface models for better accuracy.

Refining and Editing Surfaces

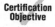
Certification Objective

Once a basic surface is built, and in some cases even before it is built, you can do some cleanup and modification to the TIN construction that make it much more usable and realistic. Some of these edits include limiting the input data, tweaking the triangulation, adding breakline information, and hiding areas from view. In the following sections, you'll explore a number of ways of refining surfaces to end up with the best possible model from which to build.

Surface Properties

The most basic steps you can perform in making a better model are right in the Surface Properties dialog. The surface object contains information about the build and edit operations, along with some values used in surface calculations.

Surface Build Options

There are two main places you can set surface build options:

Settings Tab The first location is on the Settings tab of Toolspace under Surfaces ➤ Commands ➤ Create Surface. If you right-click Create Surface, you will find an option to edit command settings. You can set these at the beginning of a project to automatically set the options for all surfaces as they are created. It is a great idea to configure the command settings in your template so your preferred triangulation defaults will be set on all projects.

Surface Properties The second place you will see the build options for a surface is in Surface Properties on the Definition tab. Changing the settings under Surface Properties will affect only the individual surface you are working with.

The basic options are listed here:

Copy Deleted Dependent Objects When you select Yes and an object (such as a surface boundary or breakline) that is part of the surface definition is deleted, the information derived from that object is copied into the surface definition. If this option is set to No for the surface, when elevation source objects (such as polylines added as contours) are deleted, they will be removed from the surface definition when the surface is rebuilt.

Exclude Elevations Less Than Setting Exclude Elevations Less Than to Yes allows you to set a surface's lowest valid elevation in the Elevation < field. Note that Elevation < is a "less than" operation, not "less than or equal to," so to rectify the problem caused by items at 0, you will need to set this to 1, for example.

Exclude Elevations Greater Than Setting this to Yes will allow you to set the Elevation > field. This option allows you to set a highest valid elevation value.

Use Maximum Angle Setting this option to Yes will allow you to set a value for Maximum Angle Between Adjacent TIN Lines. This setting will omit long "sliver" triangles that typically get generated along the exterior of the TIN.

Use Maximum Triangle Length Setting this option to Yes will allow you to set a value for Maximum Triangle Length. If a triangle leg is excessively long, it is often an indicator that valid elevation data for triangulation is sparse, as often occurs near the edges of a site. If you are using this option to minimize long triangle lines, double-check your TIN to make sure the length you specified isn't creating interior holes.

Convert Proximity Breaklines To Standard Toggling this option to Yes will create standard breaklines out of the entities used as proximity breaklines. The surface will no longer be dependent on the proximity entities. The standard breakline will be created internal to the surface but can be drawn by right-clicking the breakline in the surface definition and selecting Insert Into Drawing.

Allow Crossing Breaklines   Setting this option to Yes allows you to set the Elevation To Use option. These options specify what Civil 3D should do if two breaklines in a surface definition intersect in the X,Y plane with different elevations at the intersection. Leaving this option set to No will cause the surface to totally throw out both offending breaklines.

In this exercise, you'll go through a couple of the basic surface-building controls that are available. You'll use them one at a time in order to observe their effects on the final surface display.

1. Open the 0408_SurfaceProperties.dwg file (or the 0408_SurfaceProperties_METRIC .dwg file).

2. Locate the portion of the surface that contains poor elevation data inside the magenta circle. Use your mouse to pan and zoom in the drawing.

   You will know you have found the correct location when you zoom into the portion of the surface that resembles Figure 4.28. This blob is a batch of densely packed contours where the surface is incorrectly picking up elevations at zero.

FIGURE 4.28
EG surface show-
ing a batch of
densely packed
contours, indicat-
ing bad elevations

3. Select the surface by clicking any part of it in the graphic.

4. From the TIN Surface: EG contextual tab, click the Surface Properties icon.

   The Surface Properties dialog appears.

5. Select the Definition tab.

6. Under Definition Options at the top of the dialog (Figure 4.29), expand the Build branch by clicking the + symbol.

FIGURE 4.29
Surface Properties
Definition
Options

7. Verify that the Exclude Elevations Less Than value is Yes.

8. Set the value to **200** (**60** for metric users) and click OK to accept the settings in the dialog.

   A warning message will appear. Civil 3D is warning you that your surface definition has changed.

9. Click Rebuild The Surface to rebuild the surface.

10. You may see a message appear in Panorama indicating that three points were ignored because they are below the given limit. If this is the case, close the Panorama window by clicking the green check mark.

11. Zoom extents to view the full surface by double-clicking your middle mouse wheel.

    When this step is complete, the surface will look similar to Figure 4.30. Save the drawing and keep it open for the next portion of the exercise.

    Although this surface is improving, there are still large areas being contoured that shouldn't be. By changing the style to review the surface, you can see where you still have some issues.

12. Open the Surface Properties dialog again and switch to the Information tab.

13. Change the Surface Style field to Contours And Triangles.

14. Click Apply. Doing so makes the changes without exiting the dialog.

15. Drag the dialog to the side so you can see the site.

    On the outer edges of the site, you can see some long triangles formed in areas where there was no survey taken but the surface decided to connect the triangles anyway (Figure 4.31, left).

FIGURE 4.30
EG surface after
ignoring low
elevations

FIGURE 4.31
EG surface before
Use Maximum
Triangle Length
was applied (left)
and after (right).
Note that the
Level Of Detail
display option is
on in these figures.

16. In the Surface Properties dialog, switch to the Definition tab.

17. Expand the Build category by clicking the + symbol.

18. Set the Use Maximum Triangle Length value to Yes.

19. In the Maximum Triangle Length value field, enter **300** (or for metric, **70**).

20. Click OK to apply the settings and close the dialog.

21. Click Rebuild The Surface to update and dismiss the warning message to see the revised surface (Figure 4.31, right).

When this exercise is complete, you can close the drawing. A completed version of this drawing is available from the book's web page with the filename 0408_SurfaceProperties_FINISHED.dwg or 0408_SurfaceProperties_METRIC_FINISHED.dwg.

 Real World Scenario

REORDERING BUILD OPERATIONS

The order in which you add data to a surface impacts how the surface is formed. Ideally, an existing surface is created with surveyed data, so the order of operations would be to first add a point group containing surveyed points and then add breaklines delineating triangle edges such as pavement edges, ridges, and ravines. Lastly, boundaries are added to delineate the outer limits of the survey edges of ponds or buildings.

If existing surfaces are to be a blend of GIS contours and surveyed data, the GIS contours are added first. The surveyed data is compiled into a separate surface as described earlier and then pasted into the surface containing the GIS contours. Then boundaries are added.

Proposed surfaces are usually composed in this order: pasted roadway and pond surfaces, proposed breaklines, hand-drawn contours, and then boundaries.

In the following example, you will fix surface problems simply by changing the order in which elevation data is processed. The Operation Type listing is displayed at the bottom of the Definition tab in the Surface Properties dialog.

1. Open the file 0409_SurfaceBuildOrder.dwg or 0409_SurfaceBuildOrder_METRIC.dwg.

This is the surface you put together in the beginning of this chapter, but the order of operations has been altered. You will be placing the operations in the proper order.

2. Select the surface by clicking any part of it in the graphic.

3. From the TIN Surface: Existing contextual tab, click the Surface Properties icon.

4. Switch to the Definition tab.

   The Operation Type listing at the bottom of the dialog shows the order in which Civil 3D is using surface elevation information. Items in the list are processed from the top down. In this example, the boundaries are at the top of the list when they should be at the bottom.

5. Hold down the Ctrl key, highlight the listings for the three Add Boundary entries, and use the bottommost arrow on the left side of the dialog to move it to the bottom of the Operation Type list.

Continues

Continued

You'll see the warning symbol appear to the left of all the data types whose place in the Operation Type order is affected by the change.

6. Click OK and then click Rebuild The Surface when prompted to do so.

Examine the surface again by zooming and panning around the drawing. The contours have reformed in the drawing using the boundary information correctly, but the contours are not forming the ditches.

7. Return to Surface Properties by clicking the surface and clicking the Surface Properties icon from the TIN Surface: Existing contextual tab.

8. Fill in the check boxes next to the Add Breakline entries.

9. Click OK and then click Rebuild The Surface when prompted to do so.

The surface with completed edits will look like the following image.

A completed version of the file is available on the book's web page called `0409_SurfaceBuildOrder_FINISHED.dwg` or `0409_SurfaceBuildOrder_METRIC_FINISHED.dwg`.

You will need to use your professional judgment and a little common sense to determine the best order of operations for different surface data scenarios. If you would like to see what the surface would look like without a particular operation, you can clear the check box next to its listing in the Definition tab. You can completely remove operations from the list by right-clicking the item in the list and selecting Remove From Definition.

Manual Surface Edits

Manual edits allow further surface refinement by changing the surface at its core—the triangles. A number of manual edits can be performed on a surface. These edit options become part of the definition of the surface and include the following:

Add Line   Connects two points where a triangle did not exist before. This option essentially adds a breakline to the surface, so adding a breakline would generally be a better solution. This option is not available on grid surfaces.

Delete Line   Removes the connection between two points. In addition to using outer boundaries, this option is used frequently to clean up the edge of a surface or to remove internal data where a surface should have no triangulation at all. This can be an area such as a building pad or water surface, although hide boundaries are recommended in these scenarios.

Swap Edge   Changes the direction of the triangulation methodology. For any four points, there are two solutions to the internal triangulation, and the Swap Edge option alternates from one solution to the other. The necessity of numerous swap edge operations can be limited by the use of appropriate breaklines. This option is not available on grid surfaces.

Add Point   Allows for the manual addition of surface data. This function is often used to add a peak to a digitized set of contours that might have a flat spot at the top of a hill.

Delete Point   Allows for the manual removal of a data point from the surface definition. Generally, it's better to fix the source of the bad data, but this option can be a fix if the original data is not editable (in the case of a LandXML file, for example).

Modify Point   Allows for changing the elevation of a surface point. Only the TIN point is modified, not the original data input.

Move Point   Is limited to horizontal movement. Like Modify Point, only the TIN point is modified, not the original data input. This option is not available on grid surfaces.

Minimize Flat Areas   Performs the edits you saw earlier in this chapter to add supplemental information to the TIN and to create a more accurate surface, forcing triangulation to work in the z direction instead of creating flat planes. This option is not available on grid surfaces.

Raise/Lower Surface   A simple arithmetic operation that moves the entire surface in the positive or negative z direction. This option is useful for testing rough grading schemes for balancing dirt or for adjusting entire surfaces after a new benchmark has been observed.

Smooth Surface   Presents a pair of methods for supplementing the surface TIN data (note that this option is not available on grid surfaces). Both smoothing methods work by extrapolating more information from the current TIN data, but they are distinctly different in their methodology:

Natural Neighbor Interpolation (NNI)   Adds points to a surface on the basis of the weighted average of nearby points. This data generally works well to refine contouring that is sharply angular because of limited information or long TIN connections. NNI works only within the bounds of a surface; it cannot extend beyond the original data.

Kriging   Adds points to a surface based on one of five distinct algorithms to predict the elevations at additional surface points. These algorithms create a trending for the surface beyond the known information and can therefore be used to extend a surface beyond even the available data.

Kriging is volatile, and you should understand the full methodology before applying this information to your surface. Kriging is frequently used in subsurface exploration industries such as mining, where surface (or strata) information is difficult to come by and the distance between points can be higher than desired.

Paste Surface   Pulls in the TIN information from the selected surface and replaces the TIN information in the host surface with this new information while keeping the dynamic relationship to the original surface. This option is helpful in creating composite surfaces that reflect both the original ground and the design intent. This option is not available on grid surfaces. We'll look at pasting in Chapter 14, "Grading."

Simplify Surface   Allows you to reduce the amount of TIN data being processed while maintaining the accuracy of the surface. This is done using one of two methods: Edge Contraction, wherein Civil 3D tries to collapse two points connected by a line to one point, or Point Removal, which removes selected surface points based on algorithms designed to reduce data points that are similar. This option is not available on grid surfaces.

Manual editing should always be the last step in updating a surface. Fixing the surface is a poor substitution for fixing the underlying data the TIN is built from, but in some cases, it is the quickest and easiest way to make a more accurate surface.

TRIANGLE EDITING

In this section, you'll remove triangles manually and then finish your surface by swapping triangle edges.

1. Open the 0410_SurfaceEdits.dwg file (or the 0410_SurfaceEdits_METRIC.dwg file). Confirm that the EG surface style is set to Contours And Triangles.

   Note that if you have Level Of Detail turned on, you will want to turn it off by going to the View tab ➤ Views panel flyout. If the Level Of Detail button appears blue, that means it is on. Click the Level Of Detail button to turn it off.

2. Select the surface model by clicking it.

3. From the TIN Surface: Existing Surface contextual tab ➤ Modify panel, click Edit Surface ➤ Delete Line.

4. At the Select edges: prompt, enter **F** ↵ to use the Fence selection mode.

   In Fence selection mode you will draw a multisegment selection line, and any objects that cross the line will be selected.

5. Pick close to the center of the circle labeled A at the northwest corner of the site, as shown in Figure 4.32. Move to the left as shown, pick toward the center of the circle labeled B, and press ↵ twice.

FIGURE 4.32
Using a Fence
selection

Note that only triangles visible onscreen will be removed. In other words, if you zoom or pan such that some of the triangles you selected are not visible in your drawing area, they will not be removed from the surface definition. Be sure to zoom out so that points A and B are visible before proceeding to the next step.

6. Press ↵ to finish the selection set.

7. Repeat this process, for the following segments, removing triangles until your site resembles the image on the right in Figure 4.33:

   a. C–D.

   b. E–F.

   c. G–H.

   d. I–J.

   e. K–L.

   f. M–N.

   g. O–P.

   h. Use your best judgment to remove remaining extraneous triangles.

FIGURE 4.33
Surface before removal of extraneous triangles (left) and after (right)

8. Zoom to the green box in the southwest area of the site, and you'll notice a collection of contours that should be representing the shape of a ditch.

   Four red circles were placed on some triangle edges that are causing these contours to be pulled either away or toward the ditch line. Using the Swap Edge routine will redraw the triangle edges to available vertices nearby.

9. Select the surface. From the Tin Surface: Existing Surface contextual tab, click Edit Surface ➢ Swap Edge.

10. Zoom in on the area very closely.

11. Place the pick box inside each circle and select the triangle edges; notice the immediate change in the contouring.

12. Press ↵ when you have finished selecting edges to complete the command. The resulting contours should resemble the right side of Figure 4.34.

FIGURE 4.34
Surface before triangle swap (left) and after (right)

13. You may pan around and experiment with this command even further. Remember that any edit surface operations can be removed on the Definition tab in Surface Properties.

   When this exercise is complete, you may save the drawing and keep it open to continue to the next exercise.

SURFACE SMOOTHING

If you examine a surface when a style showing both contours and triangles is active, you could follow a contour and trace its path. What you would see is that contours are always a straight line across a triangle face. Civil 3D generates contours triangle by triangle.

If your goal is to create more flowing, natural-looking contours, the best thing to do would be to create a surface style for which contour smoothing is turned on in the Contours tab.

If your goal is to change the surface and change the physical characteristics of the surface, the Smooth Surface tool is the way to go. Surface smoothing will interpolate additional points on the surface, forming more triangles and giving the contours a less-angular appearance. Surface smoothing is often a first step before running a watershed analysis on the site because smoothing will blunt sharp ridges and create a more undulating form.

Use surface smoothing mindfully, however. Surface smoothing will smoosh breakline locations, making a retaining wall look more like a mudslide. Additionally, since this tool adds points, you are making the surface bigger from a data perspective. Similar to when applying boundaries, surface smoothing should be at/near the bottom of the list in the Definition tab of a surface. If additional changes are made to a surface, the order should be updated.

In this exercise, you'll use the NNI smoothing algorithm to reduce surface anomalies and create a more visually pleasing contour set:

1. Continue working in the 0410_SurfaceEdits.dwg file (or the 0410_SurfaceEdits_METRIC.dwg file).

2. Select the surface.

3. From the Tin Surface: Existing Surface contextual tab, click Edit Surface ➤ Smooth Surface.

4. Expand the Smoothing Methods branch and verify that Natural Neighbor Interpolation is the Select Method value.

5. Expand the Point Interpolation/Extrapolation branch and click in the Select Output Region value field.

6. Click the ellipsis button.

7. At the Select region or [rEctangle pOlygon Surface]: prompt, pick the large magenta rectangle located on the surface for smoothing, and then press ↵ to return to the Smooth Surface dialog.

8. Enter **10** for the Grid X-Spacing and Grid Y-Spacing values (metric users should enter **3** for both values).

   Note that Civil 3D will tell you how many points you are adding to the surface immediately below this input area by the value given in the Number Of Output Points field, as shown in Figure 4.35. It's grayed out, but it does change on the basis of your input values.

FIGURE 4.35
Smooth Surface
dialog

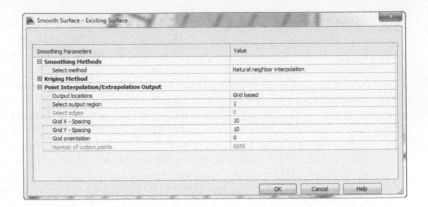

9. Click OK and the surface will be smoothed, similar to what is shown on the right in Figure 4.36.

FIGURE 4.36
Surface before
NNI smoothing
(left) and after
(right)

A completed version of this drawing is available from the book's web page with the filename 0410_SurfaceEdits_FINISHED.dwg or 0410_SurfaceEdits_METRIC_FINISHED.dwg. Zoom in and examine the ditches. Notice how the ditch shape is retained, thus respecting the breaklines used to define the flow lines and embankments.

When this exercise is complete, you can close the drawing.

SURFACE SIMPLIFYING

Because of the increasing use in land development projects of GIS and other data-heavy inputs, it's critical that Civil 3D users know how to simplify the surfaces produced from these sources. In this exercise, you'll simplify the surface created from a drawing earlier in this chapter.

1. Open the 0411_SurfaceSimplify.dwg file (or the 0411_SurfaceSimplify_METRIC.dwg file). For reference, Figure 4.37 shows the surface statistics of the GIS Data surface.

FIGURE 4.37
GIS Data surface
statistics before
simplification

2. Select the surface by clicking anywhere on it in the graphic.

3. From the Tin Surface: GIS Data contextual tab, click Edit Surface ➢ Simplify Surface.

4. Select the Point Removal radio button, as shown in Figure 4.38, and click Next to move to the Region Options page.

FIGURE 4.38
The Simplify
Surface – Simplify
Methods page

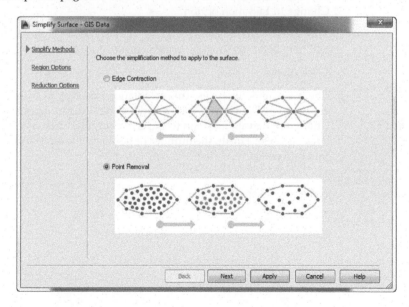

5. Accept the Region Options defaults, as shown in Figure 4.39, and click Next to move to the Reduction Options page.

FIGURE 4.39
The Simplify Surface – Region Options page

6. Set Percentage Of Points To Remove to 20 percent and then deselect the Maximum Change In Elevation option.

This value is the maximum change allowed between the surface elevation at any point before or after the simplify process has run.

7. Click Apply.

The program will process this calculation and display a Total Points Removed number, as shown in Figure 4.40. You can adjust the slider or place a check mark in the Maximum Change In Elevation option to experiment with different values. Note that every time you click Apply or Finish, the number of points in the simplified surface decreases again by that percentage.

FIGURE 4.40
The Simplify
Surface –
Reduction Options
page

FIGURE 4.40
The Simplify
Surface –
Reduction Options
page

8. Click Finish to close the wizard and process the Simplify command again.

A WORD ABOUT THE SIMPLIFY BUILD OPERATION

Notice that the Simplify build operation is listed twice in the preview area of Prospector under Edits. This is because the command was run once when you clicked Apply and a second time when you clicked Finish. If you want to run the Simplify Surface command only once, you should click Apply and then click Cancel or just click Finish without clicking Apply first.

When this exercise is complete, you can close the drawing. A finished copy of this drawing is available from the book's web page with the filename 0411_SurfaceSimplify_FINISHED.dwg or 0411_SurfaceSimplify_METRIC_FINISHED.dwg.

A quick visit to the Surface Properties Statistics tab shows that the number of points has been reduced, as shown in Figure 4.41. On something like an aerial topography or DEM, reducing the point count probably will not reduce the usability of the surface, but this simple point reduction will decrease the file size. Remember, you can always delete the edit or unselect the operation on the Definition tab of the Surface Properties dialog to "unsimplify" the surface.

FIGURE 4.41
EG-GIS surface statistics after simplification

The creation of a surface is merely the starting point. Once you have a TIN to work with, you have a number of ways to view the data using analysis tools and varying styles.

Surface Analysis

Certification Objective

Once a surface is created, you can display information in a number of ways. The most common so far has been contours and triangles, but those are the basics. By using various styles, you can show a large amount of data with one single surface. Surface styles are discussed further in Chapter 19, "Object Styles." While some of the styles are used for generating plans (such as contours), others lend themselves to analyzing the surface during creation.

For a surface object in plan view, Points, Triangles, Border, Major Contour, Minor Contour, User Contours, and Gridded are standard components and are controlled like any other object component. Directions, Elevations, Slopes, Slope Arrows, and Watershed components are unique in that their display is controlled elsewhere in the surface style.

Note that the Layer, Color, and Linetype fields are grayed out for these components. Each of these components has its own special coloring scheme, which we'll cover later in the section "Comparing Surfaces."

In the following sections, you will explore the elevation and slope analysis styles.

Elevation Banding

Displaying surface information as bands of color is one of the most common display methods for engineers looking to make a high-impact view of the site. Elevations are a critical part of the site design process, and understanding how a site varies in terms of elevation is an important part of making the best design. Elevation analysis typically falls into two categories:

- Showing bands of information on the basis of pure distribution of linear scales

- Displaying a lesser number of bands to show some critical information about the site

In this first exercise, you'll use a standard style to illustrate elevation distribution along with a prebuilt color scheme that works well for presentations:

1. Open the 0412_SurfaceAnalysis.dwg file (or the 0412_SurfaceAnalysis_METRIC.dwg file).

2. Select the surface in the graphic to activate the contextual tab.

3. From the Existing Surface contextual tab ➤ Modify panel, choose the Surface Properties icon.

4. On the Information tab, change the Surface Style field to Elevation Banding (3D).

5. Switch to the Analysis tab for the Elevations analysis type.

6. Set Create Ranges By Number Of Ranges to **6**. Then click the Run Analysis arrow in the middle of the dialog to populate the Range Details area.

7. Click OK to close the Surface Properties dialog.

   Notice that only the border is currently showing because the surface is being shown in plan view.

[-][TOP][2D WIREFRAME]

You may have noticed three pieces of text in the upper-left corner of your modelspace. If you click any of these viewport controls, you will find that they are drop-down lists that you can use to change what you are looking at.

The first set of bracketed text will either be [-] (denoting that one viewport is being displayed) or [+] (if two viewports are being displayed).

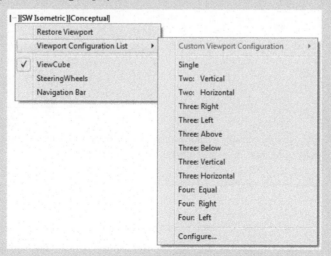

The second set of bracketed text is the View Control and will list the current view within the brackets.

Continues

Continued

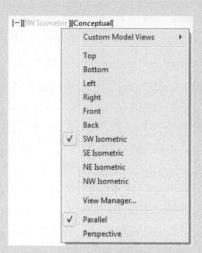

The third set of bracketed text is the Visual Style Control and will list the current visual style within the brackets.

All of these commands can also be changed from the View tab. If Level Of Detail is currently active, an additional small icon will appear below this line of text.

These three pieces of text provide valuable information for easy reference while you work.

8. From the View Control, select SW Isometric.

9. Zoom in if necessary to get a better view of the surface.

10. From the Visual Style Control, select the Conceptual option to see a semirendered view that should look something like Figure 4.42.

    Save and keep the drawing open for the next portion of the exercise.

FIGURE 4.42
Conceptual view of the site with the Elevation Banding style

AutoCAD Visual Styles

When you see triangles on a surface in the Object Viewer, they are visible because of the view style and can be modified via the Visual Styles Manager. Turning the Edge mode off will leave you with a nicely gradated view of your site. You can edit the visual style by clicking the Visual Style Control at the upper left of your drawing screen. You can also access the Visual Styles Manager on the View tab ➤ Visual Styles panel by clicking the small arrow in the lower-right corner of the panel. The Visual Styles Manager is shown here.

Continues

> *Continued*
>
> The Realistic visual style will allow you to see the render material applied to your surface—with some conditions. You must have triangles turned on in the Surface Style dialog, and you must have a render material specified in the Surface Properties dialog.

You'll use a 2D elevation to clearly analyze the lower elevations of the site. Next, you'll manually tweak the maximum elevation value to further understand how the site drains.

11. Click the View Control and select Top.

12. Click the Visual Style Control and select 2D Wireframe. Zoom extents if necessary.

13. Select the surface by clicking on the border. Right-click and choose the Surface Properties option.

The Surface Properties dialog appears.

14. On the Information tab, change the Surface Style field to Elevation Banding (2D).

15. On the Analysis tab, change Number Of Ranges to **1** and click the Run Analysis button.

16. Change Maximum Elevation for ID 1 to **5** (or **1** for metric users), as shown in Figure 4.43.

FIGURE 4.43
The Surface
Properties dialog
after manual
editing

17. Click Apply to apply the settings in the Surface Properties dialog and the surface.

18. Drag the Surface Properties dialog to the side. Notice the red solid fill in the ditch areas indicating elevations equal to or less than the maximum elevation entered.

19. Back on the Analysis tab in the Surface Properties dialog, change the Maximum Elevation value to **6** (**1.5** for metric users) and click Apply.

20. Review the drawing area for the expansion of the red fill indicating elevations equal to or less than 6 (or 1.5 for metric users).

21. Repeat steps 19 and 20 for a maximum elevation of **7** (or **2** for metric users).

22. Click OK to close the Surface Properties dialog.

23. Save the drawing for use in the next exercise.

Understanding surfaces from a vertical direction is helpful, but many times the slopes are just as important. In the next section, you'll take a look at using the slope analysis tools in Civil 3D.

Slopes and Slope Arrows

Beyond the bands of color that show elevation differences in your models, you also have tools that display slope information about your surfaces. This analysis can be useful in checking for drainage concerns, meeting accessibility requirements, or adhering to zoning constraints. Slope is typically shown as areas of color similar to the elevation banding or as colored arrows that indicate the downhill direction and slope. In this exercise, you'll look at the existing surface and run the two slope analysis tools:

1. Continue working in the 0412_SurfaceAnalysis.dwg file (or the 0412_ SurfaceAnalysis_METRIC.dwg file).

2. Select the surface on your screen to activate the contextual tab.

3. From the Existing Surface contextual tab ➤ Modify panel, click the Surface Properties icon.

4. On the Information tab, change the Surface Style field to Slope Banding (2D).

5. Switch to the Analysis tab of the Surface Properties dialog.

6. Choose Slopes from the Analysis Type drop-down list.

7. Set the Number field in the Ranges area to **6** and click the Run Analysis arrow in the middle of the dialog to populate the Range Details area.

   The Range Details area will populate. You could change the minimum and maximum values as you did in the previous exercise, but this time you'll keep the defaults.

8. Click OK to close the dialog.

   The colors are nice to look at, but they don't mean much, and slopes don't have any inherent information that can be portrayed by color association. To make more sense of this analysis, you'll add a legend table.

9. Select the surface again, and on the Existing Surface contextual tab ➤ Labels & Tables panel, choose Add Legend.

10. At the Enter table type [Directions Elevations Slopes slopeArrows Contours Usercontours Watersheds]: prompt, enter **S** ↵ to select Slopes.

11. At the Behavior [Dynamic Static]: <Dynamic> prompt, press ↵ again to accept the default value of a Dynamic legend.

12. At the Select upper left corner: prompt, pick a point onscreen to draw the legend, which is shown in Figure 4.44.

FIGURE 4.44
The slopes legend table

		Slopes Table		
Number	Minimum Slope	Maximum Slope	Area	Color
1	0.00%	0.37%	1822051.41	■
2	0.37%	0.84%	1667289.03	■
3	0.84%	3.07%	776911.42	■
4	3.07%	20.09%	286508.15	■
5	20.09%	54.91%	104714.53	■
6	54.91%	1497.70%	106016.32	■

By including a legend, you can make sense of the information presented in this view. Because you know what the slopes are, you can also see which way they go.

13. Select the surface, and on the Existing Surface contextual tab ➢ Modify panel, choose the Surface Properties icon.

    The Surface Properties dialog appears.

14. On the Information tab, change the Surface Style field to Slope Arrows.

15. Switch to the Analysis tab of the Surface Properties dialog.

16. Choose Slope Arrows from the Analysis Type drop-down list.

17. Verify that the Number field in the Ranges area is set to **6**, and click the Run Analysis arrow in the middle of the dialog to populate the Range Details area.

18. Click OK to close the dialog.

The benefit of arrows is in looking for "birdbath" areas that will collect water. These arrows can also verify that inlets are in the right location, as shown in Figure 4.45. Look for arrows pointing to the proposed drainage locations and you'll have a simple design-verification tool.

FIGURE 4.45
Slope arrows
pointing to a
proposed inlet
location

When this exercise is complete, you can close the drawing. A finished copy of this drawing is available from the book's web page with the filename 0412_SurfaceAnalysis_FINISHED.dwg or 0412_Surface Analysis_METRIC_FINISHED.dwg.

With these simple analysis tools, you can show a client the areas of their site that meet their constraints. Visually compelling and simple to produce, this is the kind of information that a 3D model makes available. Beyond the basic information that can be represented in a single surface, Civil 3D also contains a number of tools for comparing surfaces. You'll compare this existing ground surface to a proposed grading plan in the next section.

Visibility Checker

The Zone Of Visual Influence tool allows you to explore what-if scenarios. In this example, a 40′ (12 m) tower has been proposed for the site. A concerned neighbor wants to make sure that it won't obstruct their scenic view. You want to check it from the proposed surface:

1. Open 0413_VisibilityCheck.dwg or 0413_VisibilityCheck_METRIC.dwg.

2. In Prospector, expand the Surfaces branch, right-click the FG surface, and choose the Select option.

3. On the TIN Surface contextual tab ➤ Analyze panel, choose Visibility Check ➤ Zone Of Visual Influence.

4. At the Specify location of object: prompt, use the Intersection Osnap to select the center of the proposed tower located on the southern portion of the site (denoted by a large white square with an *X* inside).

5. At the Specify height of object: prompt, enter **40** ↵ to set the tower height to 40′ (metric users, enter **12** ↵).

6. At the Specify the radius of vision extent: prompt, pan to and select the endpoint at the upper-right corner of the cyan-colored house located at the northeastern corner of the site.

Save the drawing and keep it open for the next portion of the exercise.

The drawing now has bands of color:

◆ Green near the tower location indicates that the object is completely visible.

◆ Yellow indicates that the object is partially visible.

◆ Red indicates that the object is not visible.

So in our example, the homeowner on the upper right will be happy to know that the proposed 40′ tower will not appear in their view.

In the next portion of this exercise, you will use the Point To Point tool.

7. Using the same drawing, zoom to the intersection of Syrah Way and Cabernet Court, where you will see a car driving on the right side of the road.

You want to check the sight distance.

8. If it is not already selected, select the FG surface.

9. On the TIN Surface contextual tab ➢ Analyze panel, choose Visibility Check ➢ Point To Point.

10. At the Specify height of eye: prompt, enter **3.5** ↵ (metric users enter **1** ↵).

This sets the height of the eye of a driver sitting in a typical car.

11. At the Specify location of eye: prompt, click where the driver would normally be seated in the vehicle.

12. At the Specify height of target: prompt, enter **6** ↵ (metric users enter **1.8** ↵).

A rubber-banding sightline ray appears.

13. Click along the path where oncoming cars would be seen.

A sightline arrow is drawn on the screen:

◆ If the arrow is green, it means that the view is unobstructed, and the command line will tell you the distance from the eye.

◆ If any portion of the arrow is red, it indicates that the view is obstructed, and the command line will tell you the distance at which the obstruction occurs.

When this exercise is complete, you can close the drawing. A finished copy of this drawing is available from the book's web page with the filename `0413_SurfaceVisibility_FINISHED.dwg` or `0413_SurfaceVisibility_METRIC_FINISHED.dwg`.

Unfortunately, these visual tools are not dynamic; if you change the surface, you will need to rerun the visual tools.

Comparing Surfaces

Civil 3D contains a number of surface analysis tools designed to calculate earthwork quantities, and you'll look at them in the following sections. First a simple comparison provides feedback about the volumetric difference, and then a more detailed approach enables you to perform an analysis on this difference.

For years, civil engineers have performed earthwork using a section methodology. Sections were taken at some interval, and a plot was made of both the original surface and the proposed surface. Comparing adjacent sections and multiplying by the distance between them yields an end-area method of volumes that is generally considered acceptable. The main problem with this methodology is that it ignores the surfaces in the areas between sections. These areas could include areas of major change, introducing some level of error. In spite of this limitation, this method worked well with hand calculations, trading some accuracy for ease and speed.

With the advent of full-surface modeling, more precise methods became available. By analyzing both the existing and proposed surfaces, a volume calculation can be performed. Keep in mind that the quality of the result is highly dependent on the quality of the input surfaces. At every TIN vertex in both surfaces, a distance is measured vertically to the other surface. These delta amounts can then be used to create a third dynamic surface called a *volume surface*, which represents the difference between the two original surfaces.

TIN Volume Surface

Using the volume utility for initial design checking is helpful, but quite often contractors and other outside users want to see more information about the grading and earthwork for their own uses. This requirement typically falls into two categories: a cut-fill analysis showing colors or contours or a grid of cut-fill tick marks.

Color cut-fill maps are helpful when reviewing your site for the locations of movement. Some sites have areas of better material or can have areas where the cost of cut is prohibitive (such as rock). In this exercise, you'll use two of the surface analysis methods to look at the areas for cut-fill on your site:

1. Open the `0414_VolumeSurface.dwg` or `0414_VolumeSurface_METRIC.dwg` file.

2. From the Analyze tab ➢ Volumes And Materials panel, choose the Volumes Dashboard icon to display the Volumes Dashboard in Panorama.

3. Click the Create New Volume Surface button to display the Create Surface dialog.

   Notice that Type is already set to TIN Volume Surface. You also have the option to select Grid Volume Surface.

4. Change the name to **Pond Volume** and set the style to Elevation Banding (2D).

5. Click the <Base Surface> field next to Base Surface to display the ellipsis button.

6. Click the ellipsis to select the Existing Surface and then click OK.

7. Click the <Comparison Surface> next to Comparison Surface to display the ellipsis button.

8. Click the ellipsis to select the Pond surface and click OK.

The Create Surface dialog should now look similar to Figure 4.46.

FIGURE 4.46
Creating a volume surface

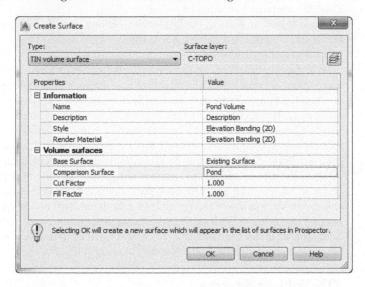

9. Click OK to accept the settings in the Create Surface dialog.

Civil 3D will calculate the volume (Figure 4.47). If the Event Viewer opens, click the green check mark in the upper-right corner of the dialog.

FIGURE 4.47
Composite volume calculated

Note that you can scroll right and left in Panorama to display additional information, including the ability to apply a cut or fill factor by typing directly into the cells for these values.

This new volume surface appears in Prospector's Surfaces collection, but notice that the icon is slightly different, showing two surfaces stacked on each other.

10. Leave Panorama open, and in Toolspace ➤ Prospector, expand Surfaces, right-click Pond Volume, and select Surface Properties.

11. On the Analysis tab, change Number Of Ranges to **2** and click the Run Analysis button.

12. Change Maximum Elevation to **0** for ID 1 and Minimum Elevation to **0** for ID 2.

According to the color scheme, the cut will now be displayed in red, and the fill will be displayed as purple.

13. Click OK to close the Surface Properties dialog.

14. In Prospector, expand the Surfaces ➤ Pond ➤ Definition branches.

15. Right-click Edits and select the Raise/Lower Surface option.

16. Enter **-0.25** at the command line to drop the pond 3″ (metric users enter **-0.075**).

Notice that a yellow exclamation point status flag has appeared next to the volume surface in Panorama as well as in Prospector. Panorama no longer lists the volumes and instead states "Out of date."

17. Right-click the Pond Volume surface in Panorama and select the Rebuild option.

18. Right-click the Pond Volume surface again and select Surface Properties.

19. On the Analysis tab, click the Run Analysis button to rerun the analysis.

Notice the minimum and maximum elevations update.

20. Change Maximum Elevation for ID 1 and Minimum Elevation for ID 2 to **0** and click OK to update the color mapping.

21. In Prospector under the Definition branch of the Pond surface, click Edits, right-click the Raise/Lower edit in the preview area, and select Delete.

A dialog will appear warning you that the selected definition item will be permanently removed from the surface.

22. Click OK.

23. Return to Panorama, right-click the Pond Volume surface, and select Rebuild All to return the original volume calculation.

24. Close Panorama when complete.

25. In Prospector, right-click Pond Volume in the Surfaces branch and select the Surface Properties option.

The Surface Properties dialog appears.

26. In the Surface Properties dialog, switch to the Statistics tab and expand the Volume branch.

The value shown for Net Volume (Unadjusted) is the same as that shown in Panorama in the first part of this exercise.

27. In the Surface Properties dialog, switch to the Analysis tab for the Elevations analysis type.

28. Verify that Create Ranges By is set to Number Of Ranges and that the value is set to **3**; then click the Run Analysis button to populate the Range Of Details area.

29. Change Maximum Elevation for ID 2 and Minimum Elevation for ID 3 to **0.25** (or **0.08** for metric users).

30. Change Maximum Elevation for ID 1 and Minimum Elevation for ID 2 to **-0.25** (or **-0.08** for metric users).

31. Modify your color scheme by double-clicking the color to be modified.

The recommended colors are red, yellow, and green, where red indicates the worst-case cut, green represents the worst-case fill, and yellow represents a balance.

Figure 4.48 shows the completed elevation analysis settings.

FIGURE 4.48
Elevation analysis settings for earthworks

32. Click OK to close the Surface Properties dialog.

Save the drawing and keep it open for the next portion of the exercise.

The volume surface now indicates areas of cut, areas of fill, and areas that are nearly balanced, similar to Figure 4.49.

FIGURE 4.49
Completed elevation analysis

To show where large amounts of cut or fill could incur additional cost (such as compaction or excavation protection), you would simply modify the analysis range as required.

The Elevation Banding surface is great for onscreen analysis, but the color fills are too dense for most plotting purposes and can slow down the performance of the drawing. In the next steps, you use the Contour Analysis tool to prepare cut-fill contours in these same colors.

33. In Prospector, right-click Pond Volume in the Surfaces branch and select the Surface Properties option to display the Surface Properties dialog again.

34. On the Analysis tab, choose Contours from the Analysis Type drop-down list.

35. Verify that the Number field in the Ranges area is set to **3** and click the Run Analysis arrow in the middle of the dialog to populate the Range Details area.

36. Change the ranges to match those you entered in the previous portion of the exercise (as shown in Figure 4.48).

37. In the Major and Minor Contour columns, click the small button to the far right of each to display the AutoCAD Select Color dialog, and set a color for each ID.

Typical contour colors are as follows:

- Shades of red for cut
- A yellow for the balance line
- Shades of green for fill

38. Switch to the Information tab on the Surface Properties dialog and change the Surface Style to Contours 1′ and 5′ (Design) or Contours 0.5m and 2.5m (Design).

39. Click the down arrow next to the Style field and select the Copy Current Selection option.

The Surface Style Editor appears.

40. On the Information tab, change the Name field to **Contours 0.25′ and 1.25′ (Earthworks)** or **Contours 0.15m and 0.75m (Earthworks)**.

41. On the Contours tab, expand the Contour Ranges branch.

42. Change the value of the Use Color Scheme property to True.

It's okay to ignore the range values here because you already set them in the surface properties.

43. Expand the Contour Intervals branch and change Minor Interval to **0.25** (or **0.15** for metric users).

The Major Interval setting will automatically update to 5× the Minor Interval value.

44. Click OK to close the Surface Style Editor and click OK again to close the Surface Properties dialog.

When this exercise is complete, you can close the drawing. A finished copy of this drawing is available from the book's web page with the filename 0414_VolumeSurface_FINISHED.dwg or 0414_VolumeSurface_METRIC_FINISHED.dwg.

The volume surface can now be analyzed on a lot-by-lot basis or labeled using the surface-labeling functions to show the depths of cut and fill, which you'll look at in the next sections.

Labeling the Surface

Certification Objective

Once the three-dimensional surface model has been created, it is time to communicate the model's information in various formats. This includes labeling contours, creating legends for the analysis you've created, adding spot labels, or labeling the slope. These exercises work through these main labeling requirements and building styles for each.

Contour Labeling

The most common requirement is to place labels on surface-generated contours. In Land Desktop, this was one of the last steps because a change to a surface required erasing and replacing all the labels. Once labels have been placed, their styles can be modified.

Contour labels in Civil 3D are created by special lines that understand their relationship with the surface. Everywhere one of these lines crosses a contour line, a label is placed. This label's appearance is based on the style applied and can be a major, minor, or user-defined contour label. Each label can have styles selected independently, so using some AutoCAD selection techniques can be crucial to maintaining uniformity across a surface.

In this exercise, you'll add labels to your surface and explore the interaction of contour label lines and the labels themselves:

1. Open the 0415_SurfaceLabeling.dwg or 0415_SurfaceLabeling_METRIC.dwg file.

2. Select the EG surface in the graphic to display the TIN Surface contextual tab.

3. From the TIN Surface contextual tab ➤ Labels & Tables panel, choose Add Labels ➤ Contour – Single.

4. Pick any spot on a major contour to add a label.

5. Press ↵ when complete and press Esc to deselect the surface.

6. From the Annotate tab ➤ Labels & Tables panel, choose Add Labels ➤ Surface ➤ Contour – Multiple.

7. Pick a point to the west of the site and then a second point to the south of the site, crossing a number of contours in the process.

8. Press ↵ to end the picking.

9. From the Annotate tab ➤ Labels & Tables panel, add Surface Labels to display the Add Labels dialog.

10. Verify that Feature is set to Surface and Label Type to Contour – Multiple At Interval.

11. Click the Add button.

12. Pick a point to the west of the site and then a second point to the north of the site.

13. At the `Interval along contour <100.00>` prompt, enter **200** (for metric **60**) at the command line for an interval value.

Save the drawing and keep it open for the next portion of the exercise.

You've now labeled your site in three ways to get contour labels in a number of different locations. You will need additional labels in the northeast and southwest to complete the labeling because you did not cross these contour objects with your contour label line.

The contour label line is a handy tool. It has grips you can use to stretch it over other contours, which produces additional labels. You can also stretch it for the purpose of relocating labels. You can also copy the label line to other locations. Using the Properties dialog, you can turn it off, or you can turn it off by default on the Settings tab ➤ Surface branch in Feature Settings. However, if a contour label is selected, the grips will reveal, and you can still use them to manipulate the position of the label.

Next, you'll fill in the labeling to the northeast.

14. Zoom to the northeast portion of the site, and notice that some of the contours are labeled only along the boundary or not at all, as shown in Figure 4.50.

FIGURE 4.50
Contour labels
applied

15. Zoom in to any contour label placed using the Contour – Multiple At Interval button and pick the text.

Three grips will appear. The original contour label lines are quite apparent, but in reality, every label has a label line beneath it.

16. Grab the northernmost grip and drag across an adjacent contour northeast of the original label, as shown in Figure 4.51.

FIGURE 4.51
Grip-editing a
contour label line

New labels will appear everywhere your dragged line now crosses a contour.

17. Drop the grip somewhere to create labels as desired. Be sure to press Esc a few times when you have finished labeling the contours to end the command.

Save the drawing and keep it open for the next portion of the exercise.

By using the created label lines instead of adding new ones, you'll find it easier to manage the layout of your labels.

Additional Surface Label Types

With Civil 3D's surface modeling, spot labels are dynamic and react to changes in the underlying surface. By using surface labels instead of points or text callouts, you can generate a grading plan early on in the design process and begin the process of creating sheets. In the following sections, you'll label surface slopes in a couple of ways, create a single spot label for critical information, and conclude by creating a grid of labels similar to the labels in many estimation software packages.

Labeling Slopes

Beyond the specific grade at any single point, most grading plans use slope labels to indicate some level of trend across a site or drainage area. Civil 3D can generate the following two slope labels:

One-Point Slope Labels One-point slope labels indicate the slope of an underlying surface triangle. These work well when the surface has large triangles, typically in pad or mass grading areas.

Two-Point Slope Labels Two-point slope labels indicate the slope trend on the basis of two points selected and their locations on the surface. A two-point slope label works by dividing the surface elevation difference between the points by the planar distance between the pick points. This works well in existing ground surface models to indicate a general slope direction but can be deceiving in that it does not consider the terrain between the points.
In this next exercise, you'll apply both types of slope labels:

1. Continue working in `0415_SurfaceLabeling.dwg` or `0415_Surface Labeling_METRIC` `.dwg`. It is not necessary to have completed the previous exercise before proceeding.

2. Select the surface to display the TIN Surface contextual tab.

3. From the TIN Surface contextual tab ➤ Labels & Tables panel, choose Add Labels ➤ Slope.

   Alternatively, you can go to the Annotate tab ➤ Labels & Tables panel and choose Add Labels ➤ Surface ➤ Slope.

4. At the `Create Slope Labels or [One-point Two-point]: <One-point>` prompt, press ↵ to select the default one-point label style.

5. Zoom in on the circle drawn on the western portion of the site and use a Center Osnap to place a label at its center, similar to that shown in Figure 4.52.

FIGURE 4.52
A one-point slope label

6. Press Esc or ↵ to exit the command.

7. From the TIN Surface contextual tab ➤ Labels & Tables panel, choose Add Labels ➤ Slope.

8. At the `Create Slope Labels or [One-point Two-point]: <One-point>` prompt, enter **T** ↵ to switch to a two-point label style.

9. Pan to the central portion of the site and use an Endpoint Osnap to pick the left end of the line.

10. Use an Endpoint Osnap to select the right end of the line to complete the label.

11. Press Esc or ↵ to exit the command and view the label, shown in Figure 4.53.

FIGURE 4.53
A two-point slope
label

This second label indicates the average slope of the property. By using a two-point label, you get a better understanding of the trend as opposed to a specific point. Please note when using the two-point label command, the arrow in the label points in the direction of the second point picked.

When this exercise is complete, you can close the drawing. A finished copy of this drawing is available from the book's web page with the filename 0415_SurfaceLabeling_FINISHED.dwg or 0415_SurfaceLabeling_METRIC_FINISHED.dwg.

SURFACE GRID LABELS

Multiple labels placed in a grid pattern on the plan can be a huge help for grading contractors and estimators. In this exercise, you'll use the volume surface you generated earlier in this chapter to create a set of surface labels on a volume surface that reflect depth of cut and fill:

1. Open the 0416_GridSurfaceLabels.dwg file (or the 0416_GridSurfaceLabels_METRIC .dwg file).

2. From the Annotate tab ➤ Labels & Tables panel, choose Add Labels ➤ Surface ➤ Spot Elevations On Grid.

3. At the Select a surface <or press enter key to select from list>: prompt, select one of the surface triangles and click OK.

4. At the Specify a grid basepoint: prompt, pick a point southwest of the Pond Volume surface to set a base point for the grid.

5. At the Grid rotation: prompt, pick a point to the right that defines a line relatively parallel to the surface.

6. At the Grid X spacing: prompt, enter **25** ↵ (**7** ↵ for metric users).

7. At the Grid Y spacing: prompt, enter **25** ↵ (**7** ↵ for metric users).

8. At the Specify the upper right location for the grid: prompt, pick a point northeast of the Pond Volume surface to set the area for the labels.

9. Verify that the preview window encompasses the Pond Volume surface, and press ↵ at the command line to continue.

   Back at step 4, a triangle edge from Existing Surface was selected. Therefore, the resulting labels are displaying elevations of this surface instead of depth labels of the Pond Volume surface. Beginning with Civil 3D 2015, you can now change the object a label is referencing.

10. Click a label, right-click, and choose Select Similar.

11. Type **PR** ↵ to open the Properties palette.

12. On the Properties palette under the second General section, double-click the value field next to Surface to change the surface being referenced by the labels to the Pond Volume surface.

13. Press Esc to deselect the elevation labels.

Your drawing should look similar to Figure 4.54. Incidentally, any labels placed over Existing Surface that do not coincide with Pond Volume will appear as question marks. These can be deleted.

FIGURE 4.54
Volume surface
with grid labels

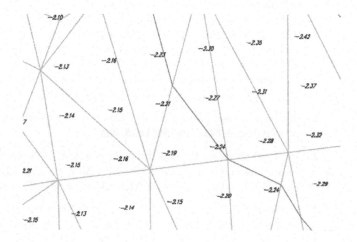

When this exercise is complete, you can close the drawing. A finished copy of this drawing is available from the book's web page with the filename 0416_SurfaceGridLabels_FINISHED.dwg or 0416_SurfaceGridLabels_METRIC_FINISHED.dwg.

Point Cloud Surfaces

A point cloud is a huge bunch of 3D points, usually collected by laser scanner or *Light Detection and Ranging (LiDAR)*. In a geographic information system, point clouds are often used as a source for a Digital Elevation Model. The technology has gotten less expensive and more accurate over the last few years, allowing LiDAR to quickly take over from traditional methods of collecting photogrammetry data.

Point clouds in many formats can be imported to Civil 3D. The most common format is the Log ASCII Standard (LAS) file. This binary format is a public format and at minimum contains x, y, and z data. LAS format can also include color, classification, and other information. For more information on the LAS standard, visit www.asprs.org.

Civil 3D can import a point cloud and use it in several ways. For instance, a laser scan of a bridge can be imported and placed for reference when you're designing a road through an existing abutment. In the example that follows, you will convert LiDAR data into a Civil 3D surface. It is important to note that point clouds often contain millions of points and may require a high-performance computer (and a little patience on your part) to process.

Importing a Point Cloud

A typical point cloud contains millions of points. These large files are kept external to Civil 3D in a point cloud database. After the LAS has been imported, the data is passed to three files: PRMD, IATI, and ISD. The ISD file contains the points themselves and is the only file needed by CAD if the point cloud would need to be re-created or used in base AutoCAD. By default, these files get created in the same directory as the DWG, but the location can be changed when importing the information.

If the point cloud you are working with contains coordinate system information (as all the examples in this book do), the software will automatically convert the point cloud to the units and coordinate system of the drawing. For the exercises in this chapter, it does not matter whether you choose the Metric or the Imperial template.

Civil 3D may take a long time to process these files, and you must ensure that you have sufficient disk space to store them, as you will find in the following exercise. It is also a good idea to close the software and then reopen it to help clear some memory before starting memory-intensive tasks such as working with point clouds.

The following exercise will show you how to import and work with a point cloud:

1. Start a new file by using the default Civil 3D template of your choice. Save the file before proceeding as **0417_PointCloud.dwg**.

2. Imperial users, set the coordinate system to UTM with NAD83 datum, Zone 17, US Foot; Central Meridian 81d W (UTM83-17F). Metric users, set the coordinate system to UTM with NAD83 datum, Zone 17, Meter; Central Meridian 81d W (UTM83-17).

3. In Prospector, right-click the Point Clouds branch and select the Create Point Cloud option to display the Create Point Cloud Wizard, shown in Figure 4.55.

FIGURE 4.55
The Create
Point Cloud –
Information page

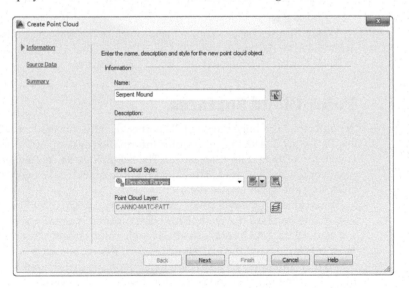

4. Set the name of the point cloud to **Serpent Mound**.

5. Set Point Cloud Style to Elevation Ranges, as shown in Figure 4.55, and click the Next button.

The Source Data page is displayed, as shown in Figure 4.56.

FIGURE 4.56
The Create Point
Cloud – Source
Data page

6. Using the white plus sign, browse to the `0417_Serpent Mound.las` file, select it, and click Open (both Imperial and metric users can use this file).

   Remember, you can download all data and drawing files for this book from `www.sybex .com/go/masteringcivil3d2016`.

   This is a large (90 MB) file containing roughly 1.4 million points and may require a minute or two to process.

7. Once the file appears in the Source Data page of the wizard, click the Next button to display the Summary page, shown in Figure 4.57.

FIGURE 4.57
The Create Point
Cloud – Summary
page

8. Accept the defaults, as shown in Figure 4.57, and click Finish to process the point cloud.

9. If the New Point Cloud Database – Processing In Background dialog appears, click Close to dismiss it.

   The components of the point cloud are being processed, including the graphic that will display in the lower-right corner of the application.

10. Once the point cloud and surface is created, the Panorama will open displaying several warnings about duplicate points being ignored. Click the green check to close the Panorama.

When the exercise is complete, a portion of a bounding box outlining a portion of the point cloud is displayed in the center of the screen. Save the drawing, but leave it open to complete the next exercise. A finished drawing will not be provided because of the large file size.

AUTODESK RECAP SOFTWARE AND NEW CREATE SURFACE FROM POINT CLOUD FEATURE

Included with your installation of Civil 3D 2016 is the Autodesk product called ReCap. ReCap allows you to look at laser-scanned data in a zippy environment outside of Civil 3D.

Using ReCap, you can consolidate, measure, crop, and visualize your scanned data before bringing it into Civil 3D. Recap produces an RCP file that can be loaded into Civil 3D through the External References palette.

You can find the new Create Surface from Point Cloud command in Civil 3D on the Home tab ➤ Create Ground Data panel ➤ Surfaces flyout. This will bring up the Create TIN Surface From Point Cloud wizard where you can choose from three filtering methods to create more precise point cloud surfaces.

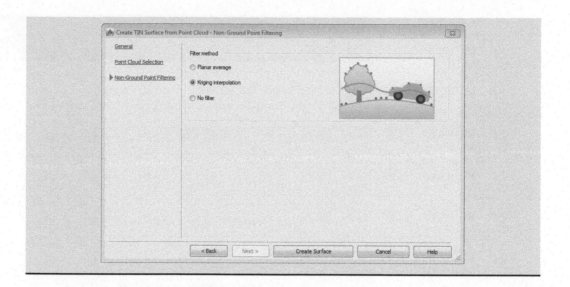

Working with Point Clouds

Once the point cloud is visible in your drawing, you'll want to follow a few rules of thumb to prevent performance problems. The key-in POINTCLOUDDENSITY value controls what percentage of the full point cloud displays on the screen at once. You can also access this value using a slider bar in the Point Cloud contextual tab. However, it is easier to hit the percentage you want on the first try if you use the key-in value. The lower this value, the fewer the points that are visible; hence, the easier it will be to navigate your drawing. The POINTCLOUDDENSITY value does not have any effect on the number of points used when generating a surface model (this is similar to the Level Of Detail value used to aid surface processing).

When you are changing view directions on a point cloud, we recommend you use preset views and named views to flip around the object. The orbit commands should not be used because they are a surefire way to max out your computer's RAM. If you used the default template, your surface will be located on the V-SITE-SCAN layer. We suggest you freeze the layer if you do not need to see the point cloud. Use Freeze instead of Off for layer management so the point cloud is not accounted for during pan, zoom, and regen operations (this is true for all AutoCAD objects, but it makes a huge difference when working with point clouds).

Creating a Point Cloud Surface

By specifying either an entire point cloud or a small region of a point cloud, you can create a new TIN surface in your drawing. Any changes to the point cloud object will render the surface definition out of date. In the following exercise, a new TIN surface is created from the point cloud previously imported:

1. Continue using the 0417_PointCloud.dwg file you created in the previous exercise.

2. Select the bounding box representing the point cloud to display the Point Cloud: Serpent Mound contextual tab, shown in Figure 4.58.

FIGURE 4.58
The Point Cloud
contextual tab

3. From the Point Cloud contextual tab ➢ Point Cloud Tools panel, choose Add Points To Surface to display the Add Points To Surface Wizard, shown in Figure 4.59.

FIGURE 4.59
The Add Points To
Surface – Surface
Options page

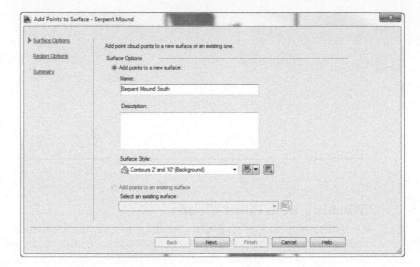

4. Name the surface **Serpent Mound South**. Leave the style set to the default.

5. Click Next and the Region Options page is displayed (Figure 4.60).

FIGURE 4.60
The Add Points To
Surface – Region
Options page

6. Choose the Window radio button and click Define Region In Drawing.

7. Define the region by creating a window around the southern half of the point cloud.

8. Click Next to see the Summary page, shown in Figure 4.61, and click the Finish button.

   Note that your number of points to be added will differ depending on the size of the window you created in the previous step.

FIGURE 4.61
The Add Points
To Surface –
Summary page

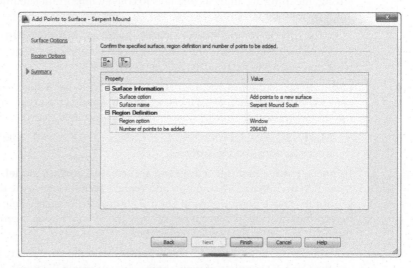

When this exercise is complete, you can close the drawing. Because of the large file size, a finished state of this drawing is not available for download.

Surfaces created from point clouds behave in the same way as any other Civil 3D surface. You will see the point cloud source information in the Definition tab of Surface Properties. By default, the surface's existence depends on the point cloud. Because point clouds are so large, you may want to delete the point cloud from the drawing after the Civil 3D surface is created. If you choose to do this, be sure to set the Copy Deleted Dependent Objects option to Yes in the surface Definition tab. That way, once the point cloud has been removed, the surface will retain the point information.

The Bottom Line

Create an existing ground surface using points. The most common way to create a surface model is by adding point data to the definition of a surface.

   Master It Open the MasterIt0401.dwg or the MasterIt0401_METRIC.dwg file. Create a new surface called **Existing**. Add the point group Topo to its definition. Leave the default styles.

Modify and update a TIN surface. TIN surface creation is mathematically precise, but sometimes the assumptions behind the equations leave something to be desired. By using the editing tools built into Civil 3D, you can create a more realistic surface model.

Master It   Continue working in the file from the previous exercise or open the `MasterIt0402.dwg` or the `MasterIt0402_METRIC.dwg` file. Use the irregular-shaped polyline and apply it to the surface as an outer boundary of the surface. Make the boundary a destructive breakline.

Prepare a slope analysis.   Surface analysis tools allow users to view more than contours and triangles in Civil 3D. Engineers working with nontechnical team members can create strong, meaningful, analysis displays to convey important site information using the built-in analysis methods in Civil 3D.

Master It   Open the `MasterIt0403.dwg` or the `MasterIt0403_METRIC.dwg` file. Create a slope banding analysis showing slopes under and over 10 percent and insert a dynamic slope legend to help clarify the result of the analysis.

Label surface contours and spot elevations.   Showing a stack of contours is useless without context. Using the automated labeling tools in Civil 3D, you can create dynamic labels that update and reflect changes to your surface as your design evolves.

Master It   Open the `MasterIt0404.dwg` or the `MasterIt0404_METRIC.dwg` file. Label the major contours on the surface.

Import a point cloud into a drawing and create a surface model.   As laser scan data collection becomes more common and replaces other large-scale data-collection methods, the ability to use point clouds in Civil 3D is critical. Intensity helps postprocessing software determine the ground cover type. While Civil 3D can't do postprocessing, you can see the intensity as part of the point cloud style.

Master It   Import an LAS format point cloud file (`MasterIt0405_Denver.las`) into the Civil 3D template of your choice. As you create the point cloud file, set the style to Elevation Ranges. Use a portion of the file to create a Civil 3D surface model. No coordinate system needs to be set for this example.

Chapter 5

Parcels

Land development projects often involve the subdivision of large pieces of land into smaller lots. Even if your projects don't directly involve subdivisions, you're often required to show the legal boundaries of your site and the adjoining sites.

Autodesk® AutoCAD® Civil 3D® parcels give you a dynamic way to create, edit, manage, and annotate these legal land divisions. If you edit a parcel object geometry to increase or decrease its size, all of the labels related to the object will reflect the update—including areas, bearings, distances, curve information, and table information.

In this chapter, you will learn to:

◆ Create parcels from objects.

◆ Create a right-of-way parcel using the right-of-way tool.

◆ Create subdivision lots automatically by layout.

◆ Add multiple-parcel segment labels.

Introduction to Sites

Before we dig into parcel objects, we have to talk first about the place these are stored, the sites. In Civil 3D, a *site* represents a collection of parcels, alignments, grading objects, and feature lines that share a common topology. In other words, Civil 3D objects that are in the same site are related to, as well as interact with, one another. The objects that react to one another are called *site geometry* objects.

Among the objects just listed, the following objects can be placed only in a site:

◆ Feature lines

◆ Grading groups

◆ Parcels

Feature lines and grading groups are discussed in depth in Chapter 14, "Grading." Alignments, discussed in Chapter 6, can be placed in a site or outside of a site.

Think Outside of the Lot

The reason for using sites is to separate objects of the same type from interacting with each other. For example, you may have a set of parcels that represent impervious areas for drainage calculations. In the same location, you may have an overlay of parcels representing property boundaries. By keeping these items on separate sites, you will be able to keep area information separate.

Dynamic area labels are useful for delineating and analyzing soil boundaries; paving, open space, and wetlands areas; and any other region enclosed with a boundary.

Like all Civil 3D objects, parcels utilize styles. With parcel styles, you can assign different layers, colors, hatch patterns, and other graphical properties to the parcel objects to differentiate between parcel types.

Certification
Objective

The default styles for the parcels and its labeling are defined within the Site Parcel Properties dialog that you can access by right-clicking the Parcels branch of the selected site in Prospector and then selecting the Properties option. On the Composition tab shown in Figure 5.1, besides the default styles, you can also define the order the styles are graphically displayed and the default user-defined property classification.

FIGURE 5.1
Site Parcel
Properties dialog
Composition tab

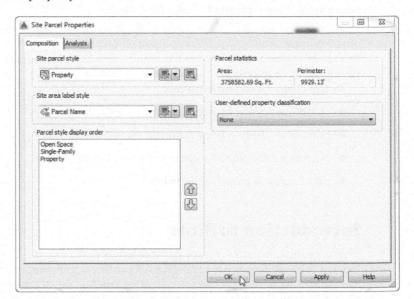

The styles can be assigned individually for each of the parcels using their properties dialog that you can access by right-clicking the name of the desired parcel and selecting Properties.

Information Tab   The Information tab of the dialog shown in Figure 5.2 allows you to assign a specific style to the parcel. Pay attention to the option Use Name Template In Parcel Style because once this is checked, the naming template of the parcel is set to use the style and a custom sequencing that is managed within the Settings tab of Toolspace.

FIGURE 5.2
Parcel Properties
dialog for a parcel

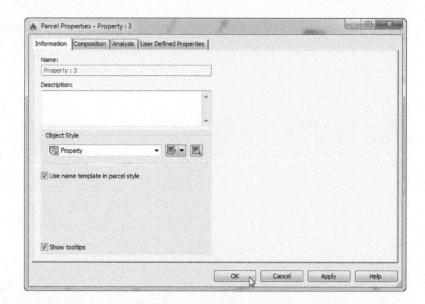

Composition Tab   The Composition tab allows you to assign an area label style to the parcel, as well as look at the data defined within the Parcel Statistics section.

Analysis Tab   The Analysis tab displays the selected analysis that was performed on the parcel, and within the Calculation settings the Point Of Beginning setting for this analysis is predefined. You can change the Point Of Beginning setting by using the selection box, and you can even define whether the processing should be done in a reverse order.

User Defined Properties Tab   The User Defined Properties tab allows you to assign values to the parcel for stock-defined properties or custom ones defined for parcels within the Settings tab of Toolspace.

Next, it's important to understand how site geometry objects react to one another. Figure 5.3 shows a typical parcel that might represent a property boundary.

FIGURE 5.3
A typical property
boundary

When an alignment is drawn and placed in the same site as the property boundary, the parcel splits into two parcels, as shown in Figure 5.4.

FIGURE 5.4
An alignment that crosses a parcel divides the parcel in two if the alignment and parcel exist in the same site.

You must plan ahead to create meaningful sites based on interactions between the desired objects. For example, if you want a road centerline, a road right-of-way (ROW) parcel, and the lots in a subdivision to react to one another, they need to be in the same site (see Figure 5.5).

FIGURE 5.5
ROW parcels, open-space parcels, and subdivision lots react to one another when drawn on the same site.

The alignment (or road centerline), ROW parcel, and lots all relate to one another. A change in the centerline of the road should prompt a change in the ROW parcel and the subdivision lots.

If you'd like to avoid the interaction between site geometry objects, place them in different sites. Figure 5.6 shows an alignment that has been placed in a different site from the boundary parcel. Notice that the alignment doesn't split the boundary parcel.

It's important that only objects that are intended to react to each other be placed in the same site. For example, in Figure 5.7 you can see parcels representing both subdivision lots and soil boundaries. Because it wouldn't be meaningful for a soil boundary parcel segment to interrupt the area or react to a subdivision lot parcel, the subdivision lot parcels have been placed in a Subdivision Lots site, and the soil boundaries have been placed in a Soil Boundaries site.

FIGURE 5.6
An alignment that crosses a parcel won't interact with the parcel if the alignment and parcel exist in different sites.

FIGURE 5.7
Parcels can be used for subdivision lots and soil boundaries as long as they're kept in separate sites.

If you didn't realize the importance of site topology, you might create both your subdivision lot parcels and your soil boundary parcels in the same site and find that your drawing looks similar to Figure 5.8. This figure shows the soil boundary segments dividing and interacting with subdivision lot parcel segments, producing unintended modifications to those parcels.

FIGURE 5.8
Subdivision lots and soil boundaries react inappropriately when placed in the same site.

Another way to avoid site geometry problems is to do site-specific tasks in different drawings and use a combination of external references and data references to share information. For example, you could place soil boundaries in one drawing file and subdivision lots in another drawing file and then use external references to show both drawings together.

You should always consider keeping your legal site plan in its own drawing. Because of the interactive and dynamic nature of Civil 3D parcel objects, it can be easy to accidentally modify a parcel segment when you meant to modify a manhole and unintentionally edit a portion of your plat.

You'll see additional examples and drawing divisions later in this chapter, as well as in Chapter 16, "Advanced Workflows."

If you decide to have sites in the same drawing, here are some sites you may want to create. These suggestions are meant to be used as a starting point. Use them to help find a combination of sites that works for your projects.

Roads and Lots This site could contain road centerlines, ROWs, platted subdivision lots, open space, adjoining parcels, utility lots, and other aspects of the final legal site plan.

Grading Feature lines and grading objects are considered part of site geometry. If you're using these tools, you could look into making at least one site for them. You may even find it useful to have several grading sites.

Easements If you'd like to use parcels to manage, analyze, and annotate your easements, you may consider creating a separate site for easements.

Impervious Areas If you'd like to use parcels to manage, analyze, and annotate paved areas, a separate site will be useful. Drainage areas can be tracked using a separate object called a *catchment*, so there is no need to create a site for drainage areas. You can read more about catchments in the bonus chapter, "Storm and Sewer Analysis," found on this book's web page, www.sybex.com/go/masteringcivil3d2016.

Soils   Many projects require knowledge of the different soil types present on the site. You will want soils in a separate site so that their boundaries don't interact with other objects in the drawing.

As you learn new ways to take advantage of alignments, parcels, and grading objects, you may find additional sites that you'd like to create at the beginning of a new project.

WHAT ABOUT THE "SITELESS" ALIGNMENT?

As mentioned earlier in this chapter, you have a choice whether to place your alignments in a site. There are many situations where having the alignment independent from other objects is desirable, and therefore the <none> site can be used.

However, you can still create alignments in traditional sites, if you desire, and they will react to other site geometry objects. For example, if you want to use the Create Right Of Way tool, the alignment you are working with must be on the same site as the main parcel.

You'll likely find that best practices for most alignments are to place them in the <none> site. For example, if road centerlines, road transition alignments, swale centerlines, and pipe network alignments are placed in the <none> site, you'll save yourself quite a bit of site geometry management.

If you decide you'd like to move the alignment to a site or to <none>, you can do so at any time. Click the alignment you want to reassign. On the Alignment contextual tab ➢ Modify panel flyout, click Move To Site. See Chapter 6 for more information about alignments.

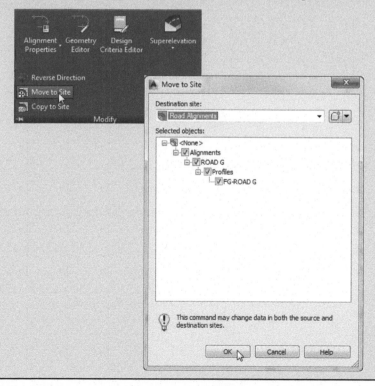

Creating a New Site

You can create a new site in Prospector. You'll find the process easier if you define the needed sites at the beginning of your project and create those sites right away—or, better yet, have them defined as part of your Civil 3D template. You can always add or delete sites later in the project, if needed.

You can access the Sites collection in Prospector, along with the other Civil 3D objects in your drawing.

The following exercise will lead you through creating a new site that you can use for creating subdivision lots:

1. Open the 0501_CreateSite.dwg (0501_CreateSite_METRIC.dwg) file, which you can download from this book's web page at www.sybex.com/go/masteringcivil3d2016.

   Note that the drawing contains alignments and the boundary for a future parcel, as shown in Figure 5.9.

FIGURE 5.9
The Create Site drawing contains alignments and a boundary parcel.

2. On the Prospector tab of Toolspace, go to Sites.

3. Right-click the Sites collection and select New to open the Site Properties dialog.

4. On the Information tab of the Site Properties dialog, enter **Subdivision Lots** for the name of your site.

5. Confirm that the settings on the 3D Geometry tab match what is shown in Figure 5.10.

   As you create parcels, Civil 3D will automatically number them for you. The values in the Numbering tab are the starting point. Note that there is a Site Display Mode property that you can use either to have the parcel data drawn at the elevation or to have all the data drawn at the elevation specified in the Site Elevation box.

FIGURE 5.10
Confirm the settings on the 3D Geometry tab.

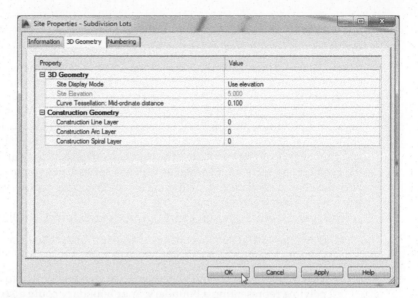

6. Confirm that both values on the Numbering tab are set to **1**. Click OK.

7. Expand the Sites collection on the Prospector tab of Toolspace, and note that your Subdivision Lots site appears on the list, as shown in Figure 5.11.

   You can repeat the process for all the sites you anticipate needing over the course of the project.

FIGURE 5.11
Your new site is listed in Prospector.

Please note that you also have the option of creating a new site when a parcel-creation command is issued within the Parcel Layout Tools toolbar or when parcels are created from objects.

8. Save and close the drawing.

If you would like to see what the drawing should look like at this point, you can open 0501_CreateSite_FINISHED.dwg (0501_CreateSite_METRIC_FINISHED.dwg), available from the book's website.

Creating a Boundary Parcel

The Create Parcel From Objects tool allows you to create parcels by choosing AutoCAD entities in your drawing or in a referenced drawing. In a typical workflow, it's common to encounter a boundary created by AutoCAD entities, such as polylines, lines, and arcs.

When you're using AutoCAD geometry to create parcels, it's important that the geometry is created carefully and that it meets certain requirements. The AutoCAD geometry must be lines, arcs, polylines, 3D polylines, or polygons. It can't include blocks, ellipses, circles, or other entities. Civil 3D may allow you to pick objects with an elevation other than zero, but you'll find you get better results if you flatten the objects so all objects have an elevation of zero. Sometimes the geometry appears sound when elevation is applied, but you may notice this isn't the case once the objects are flattened. Flattening all objects before creating parcels can help you prevent frustration when creating parcels.

This exercise will teach you how to create a parcel from Civil 3D objects:

1. Open the 0502_CreateBoundary.dwg (0502_CreateBoundary_METRIC.dwg) file, which you can download from this book's web page.

   This drawing has several alignments, which were created to use no site, and one closed polyline representing a boundary. Your boundary could also be composed of multiple lines and arcs, but for this example we have already defined the boundary as polyline.

2. On the Home tab ➤ Create Design panel, select Parcel ➤ Create Parcel From Objects.

3. At the Select lines, arcs, or polylines to convert into parcels or [Xref]: prompt, pick the polyline that represents the site boundary and press ↵.

   The Create Parcels – From Objects dialog appears.

4. From the drop-down menus, select Subdivision Lots, Property, and Name Square Foot & Acres (or Name Square Meter & Hectares if you are working in metric units) in the Site, Parcel Style, and Area Label Style selection boxes, respectively.

   Leave everything else set to the defaults, as shown in Figure 5.12. Check to make sure that the Erase Existing Entities box is selected. This means that the polyline you selected as a boundary will be deleted upon parcel creation.

5. Click OK to dismiss the dialog. You will notice that a parcel for the boundary has been created.

6. Go back to Prospector and expand the Alignments collection.

   You will notice that all the alignments in the drawing are grouped under the Centerline Alignments category.

7. Right-click that category and select the Move To Site option.

   Since you have only one site in the drawing, you will be presented with only one option.

8. Leave the selection of alignments as displayed and click OK.

   On a side note, you can also select them in Prospector individually or on the screen, and then from the context menu select the Move To Site option.

You will notice that on transferring the alignment objects to the site that has the parcels, these objects interact with the parcel objects, further dividing the initial parcel into a total of six parcels.

FIGURE 5.12
Site and style settings for your new boundary parcel

9. Save and close the drawing.

If you want to see what the drawing should look like at this point, you can open 0502_CreateBoundary_FINISHED.dwg (0502_CreateBoundary_METRIC_FINISHED.dwg), available from the book's website.

The boundary polyline forms parcel segments that react with the alignments. Area labels are placed within the newly created parcels, as shown in Figure 5.13.

FIGURE 5.13
The boundary parcel segments, alignments, and area labels

Using Parcel Creation Tools

When you don't have existing lines to work with, the best option is to draw parcel segments using the tools in the Parcel Layout Tools toolbar. Figure 5.14 shows the many commands available to you.

FIGURE 5.14

Selecting parcel creation tools

Although you may never have thought of things such as wetland areas or easements as parcels in the past, you can take advantage of the parcel tools to assist in labeling, stylizing, and analyzing these features for your plans.

This exercise will teach you how to create a parcel representing wetlands using the transparent commands that you got used to in previous chapters and the Draw Tangent-Tangent With No Curves tool from the Parcel Layout Tools toolbox:

1. Open the 0503_WetlandsParcel.dwg (0503_WetlandsParcel_METRIC.dwg) file, which you can download from this book's web page.

    Note that this drawing has several alignments and parcels. For the wetland point data, you will import them from a LandXML file using the tools you learned in Chapter 2, "Survey."

2. Go to the Insert tab and from the Import panel select the LandXML import option.

3. Browse and select to import the file 0503_WetlandParcelData.xml.

4. Click Open, accept the defaults, and click OK.

    The point data should be imported and ready to be used for parcel definition.

5. Right-click the Sites branch of Prospector, create a new site called Wetlands, and click OK to go to the next step.

6. On the Home tab ➢ Create Design panel, choose Parcel ➢ Parcel Creation Tools.

    The Parcel Layout Tools toolbar appears.

7. Click the Draw Tangent-Tangent With No Curves tool on the Parcel Layout Tools toolbar.

    The Create Parcels – Layout dialog appears.

8. From the drop-down menus, select Wetlands, Wetland, and Name Square Foot & Acres (or Name Square Meter Hectares) in the Site, Parcel Style, and Area Label Style selection boxes, respectively.

   Keep the default settings for all other options.

9. Click OK.

10. At the `Specify start point:` prompt, click the Point Number Transparent command available in the Transparent Commands Toolbar (or type **'PN** ↵ at the command prompt).

11. At the `Enter Point Number:` prompt, enter **1-11,1** ↵.

    You will see a line form through the wetland boundary points in the northwest corner of the project and immediately form the parcel.

12. Press Esc once to exit the transparent command and press Esc a second time to complete the parcel.

13. Press Enter to start a new lot line. Then repeat steps 10 through 12 for the other wetland points using points 12 through 22, entering **12-22,12** for the transparent point input.

14. Press Esc three times to exit the command.

    Your drawing should look similar to Figure 5.15.

FIGURE 5.15
The wetlands
defined on the site

To illustrate how to change the styles that are in use on a parcel, you will next change the parcel style and the area selection label style.

15. Select the northern wetland parcel's area label. From the Parcel contextual tab ➤ Modify panel, click the Parcel Properties icon.

The Parcel Properties dialog appears.

16. On the Information tab, select Mitigated Wetland from the drop-down menu in the Object Style selection box and then click Apply to observe the change.

Remain in the Parcel Properties dialog. The parcel hatch pattern will change from a full hatch to one that follows the inside of the parcel perimeter.

17. To change the parcel area label style, switch to the Composition tab in the Parcel Properties dialog.

18. From the Area Selection Label Style pull-down, select Name Area & Perimeter, and click OK. Press Esc to deselect the parcel.

19. Select the south wetland parcel by clicking its area label. From the Parcel contextual tab ➤ Modify panel, click Parcel Properties, as you did in step 15.

20. In the Composition tab, change the Area Selection Label Style setting to Parcel Name and click OK.

21. Save and close the drawing.

If you want to see what the drawing should look like at this point, you can open 0503_ WetlandsParcel_FINISHED.dwg (0503_WetlandsParcel_METRIC_FINISHED.dwg), available from the book's website.

Your parcels will look like Figure 5.16.

FIGURE 5.16
The wetlands parcels with the appropriate parcel styles and label styles applied

Creating a Right-of-Way Parcel

The Create ROW tool creates ROW parcels on either side of an alignment based on your specifications. The Create ROW tool can be used only when alignments are placed on the same site as the boundary parcel. The resulting ROW parcel will look similar to Figure 5.17.

FIGURE 5.17
The resulting parcels after applying the Create ROW tool

The Create ROW tool includes the following options:

- Offset distance from alignment

- Fillet or chamfer cleanup at parcel boundaries

- Alignment intersections

Figure 5.18 shows an example of chamfered cleanup at alignment intersections.

FIGURE 5.18
A ROW with chamfer cleanup at alignment intersections

Once the ROW parcel is created, it's no different from any other parcel. It should be noted that the ROW parcel doesn't maintain a dynamic relationship with the alignment that created it. A change to the alignment will require the ROW parcel to be edited or, more likely, re-created.

This exercise teaches you how to use the Create ROW tool to automatically place a ROW parcel for each alignment on your site:

1. Open the `0504_CreateROWParcel.dwg` (`0504_CreateROWParcel_METRIC.dwg`) file, which you can download from this book's web page.

   Note that this drawing has some alignments on the same site as the boundary parcel, resulting in several smaller parcels between the alignments and boundary.

2. On the Home tab ➤ Create Design panel, choose Parcel ➤ Create Right Of Way.

3. At the `Select parcels:` prompt, pick all existing parcels by selecting each of their area labels.

   On selection, feedback is provided through a change in the way the selected parcels display.

4. Press ↵ to stop picking parcels.

   The Create Right Of Way dialog appears.

5. Expand the Create Parcel Right Of Way branch, and enter **22.5'** (7 m) as the value for Offset From Alignment.

6. Expand the Cleanup At Parcel Boundaries branch.

7. Change the Cleanup Method setting to None.

8. Expand the Cleanup At Alignment Intersections branch.

9. Enter **25'** (8 m) as the value for Fillet Radius At Alignment Intersections.

10. Select Fillet from the drop-down menu in the Cleanup Method selection box.

11. Verify that the Create Right Of Way dialog matches Figure 5.19.

FIGURE 5.19
The Create Right Of Way dialog

12. Click OK to dismiss the dialog and create the ROW parcels. Exit the command by pressing Esc.

13. Save the drawing, but keep it open for the next exercise.

If you want to see what the drawing should look like at this point, you can open 0504_CreateROWParcel_FINISHED.dwg (0504_CreateROWParcel_METRIC_FINISHED.dwg), available from the book's website.

Your drawing should look similar to Figure 5.20.

FIGURE 5.20
The completed
ROW parcels

Adding a Cul-de-Sac Parcel

In this section you will add a cul-de-sac at the end of ROAD G and one at the end of the ROAD H alignment layout. Although drawing the cul-de-sac requires only basic drafting techniques, there are numerous steps. To save time, a block will be provided so that you don't have to draw it yourself. After inserting this block, you will convert its components into a parcel. This exercise also introduces some editing tools.

You will need to have completed the previous exercise before continuing or open the finished version of the drawing.

1. Continue working in the drawing from the previous exercise or open 0504_CreateROWParcel_FINISHED.dwg (0504_CreateROWParcel_METRIC_FINISHED.dwg), available on the book's website.

2. Locate 0504_CulDeSac.dwg (0504_CulDeSac_METRIC.dwg) in the chapter's directory and insert the file using the settings shown in Figure 5.21.

FIGURE 5.21
Inserting the cul-
de-sac block

3. From the Home tab ➤ Create Design panel, expand Parcel ➤ Create Parcel From Objects.

4. At the Select lines, arcs, or polylines to convert into parcels or [Xref]: prompt, select the two polylines that represent the outside of the cul-de-sac and press ↵.

5. In the Create Parcels – From Objects dialog, verify the following settings:

- ◆ Site is set to Subdivision Lots.

- ◆ Parcel Style is set to Property.

- ◆ Area Label Style is set to Name Square Foot & Acres (Name Square Meter & Hectares).

- ◆ Erase Existing Entities is checked.

6. Click OK.

Your drawing should look similar to Figure 5.22.

FIGURE 5.22
The cul-de-sac
turned into a
parcel

Both cul-de-sacs are now defined as parcels, but there are some extra lines that need to be taken care of. Let's see how to clean this up a bit.

7. Change the drawing scale to 1″ = 20′ (1:250).

This will cause the parcel area labels to scale down, making the next few steps easier.

8. From the Home tab ➢ Create Design panel, expand Parcel ➢ Parcel Creation Tools.

The Parcel Layout Tools toolbar opens.

9. Select the Delete Sub-Entity tool.

10. At the `Select subentity to remove:` prompt, select the right of way that interferes with the cul-de-sac, as shown in Figure 5.23. Apply the selected edits to both cul-de-sacs.

FIGURE 5.23
Delete these parcel segments.

11. Press Esc twice to exit the command.

12. Save and close the drawing.

If you want to see what the drawing should look like at this point, you can open 0504_ CreateROWParcelsCDS_FINISHED.dwg (0504_CreateROWParcelsCDS_METRIC_FINISHED.dwg), available from the book's website.

Your cul-de-sacs are complete, as shown in Figure 5.24.

FIGURE 5.24
The finished cul-de-sacs

Creating Subdivision Lot Parcels Using Precise Sizing Tools

The precise sizing tools allow you to create parcels to your exact specifications. You'll find these tools most useful when you have your roadways established and understand your lot-depth requirements. These tools provide automatic, semiautomatic, and freeform ways to control the parcel sizing using frontage, parcel area, and segment direction.

Attached Parcel Segments

Before learning about the parcel sizing tools themselves, let's discuss attached parcel segments. Parcel segments created with the precise sizing tools are called *attached segments*. Attached parcel segments have a start point that is attached to a frontage segment and an endpoint that is defined by the next parcel segment they encounter. Attached segments can be identified by their distinctive diamond-shaped grip at their start point and no grip at their endpoint (see Figure 5.25).

FIGURE 5.25
A series of attached parcel segments, with their endpoints at the front lot line and side lot lines

In other words, you establish their start point and their direction, but they seek another parcel segment to establish their endpoint. Figure 5.25 shows a series of attached parcel segments. You can tell the difference between their start points and endpoints because the start points have the diamond-shaped grips.

You can drag the diamond-shaped grip along the frontage to a new location, and the parcel segment will maintain its angle from the frontage. If the rear lot line is moved or erased, the attached parcel segments find a new endpoint (see Figure 5.26) at the next available parcel segment.

FIGURE 5.26
The endpoints of attached parcel segments extend to the next available parcel segment if the initial parcel segment is erased.

Parcel Sizing Settings

Before using the precise parcel sizing tools, you should understand that a number of settings affect the behavior of these tools. You can find these settings by expanding the Parcel Layout Tools toolbar, as shown in Figure 5.27. Each of these settings is discussed in detail in the following sections.

FIGURE 5.27
Automated sizing options on the expanded Parcel Layout Tools toolbar

PARCEL SIZING

Certification
Objective

When you create new parcels, the tools respect your default area and minimum frontage (measured from either a ROW or a building setback line). The program always uses these numbers as a minimum; it bases the actual lot size on a combination of the geometry constraints (lot depth, frontage curves, and so on) and the additional settings that follow.

Keep in mind that the numbers you establish under the Parcel Sizing option must make geometric sense. For example, if you'd like a series of 7,500-square-foot (700-square-meter) lots that have 100′ (30 m) of frontage, you must make sure that your rear parcel segment allows for at least 75′ (23 m) of depth; otherwise, you may wind up with much larger frontage values than you desire or a situation where the software can't return a meaningful result.

AUTOMATIC LAYOUT

Automatic Layout has two parameters when the list is expanded: Automatic Mode and Remainder Distribution. The Automatic Mode parameter can have the following values:

On   Automatically follows your settings and puts in all the parcels, without prompting you to confirm each one.

Off   Allows you to confirm each parcel as it's created. In other words, this option provides you with a way to semi-automatically create parcels.

The Remainder Distribution parameter tells Civil 3D how you'd like "extra" land handled. This parameter has the following options:

Create Parcel From Remainder   Makes a last parcel with "the leftovers" once the tool has made as many parcels as it can based on the settings in this dialog. This parcel is usually smaller than the other parcels.

Place Remainder In Last Parcel   Adds the leftover area to the last parcel once the tool has made as many parcels as it can based on the settings in this dialog.

Redistribute Remainder   Takes the leftover area and distributes it across all the default-sized parcels once the tool has made as many parcels as it can based on the settings in this dialog. The resulting lots aren't always evenly sized because of differences in geometry around curves and other variables, but the leftover area is absorbed.

There aren't any rules per se in a typical subdivision workflow. Usually the goal is to create as many parcels as possible within the limits of available land. To that end, you'll use a combination of AutoCAD tools and Civil 3D tools to divide and conquer the particular tract of land with which you are working.

Parcel Sizing Tools

The precise sizing tools consist of the Slide Line, Swing Line, and Free Form Create tools (see Figure 5.28).

FIGURE 5.28
The precise parcel
sizing tools

SLIDE LINE – CREATE TOOL

The Slide Line – Create tool creates an attached parcel segment based on an angle from frontage. You may find this tool most useful when your jurisdiction requires a uniform lot-line angle from the right of way.

This exercise will lead you through using the Slide Line – Create tool to create a series of subdivision lots:

1. Open the 0505_CreateSlide.dwg (0505_CreateSlide_METRIC.dwg) file, which you can download from this book's web page.

   Note that this drawing has several alignments on the same site as the boundary parcel, resulting in several smaller parcels between the alignments and boundary.

2. From the Home tab ➤ Create Design panel, expand Parcel ➤ Parcel Creation Tools.

   The Parcel Layout Tools toolbar appears.

3. Expand the toolbar by clicking the expansion chevron located at the end of the toolbar.

4. In the Parcel Sizing section, change the value of the following parameters by clicking in the Value column and entering the new values if they aren't already set. Notice how the preview window changes to accommodate your preferences:

   ◆ Minimum Area: **10890.00** sq. ft. (**1,012** m²)

   ◆ Minimum Frontage: **180.000'** (**54.75** m)

   ◆ Use Minimum Frontage At Offset: No

   ◆ Minimum Width: **75.000'** (**25** m)

   ◆ Minimum Depth: **50.000'** (**15** m)

   ◆ Use Maximum Depth: No

   ◆ Maximum Depth: (leave default value since this will not be used)

   ◆ Multiple Solution Preference: Use Shortest Frontage

5. In the Automatic Layout section, change the following parameters by clicking in the Value column and selecting the appropriate option from the drop-down menu, if it isn't already set:

   ◆ Automatic Mode: On

   ◆ Remainder Distribution: Redistribute Remainder

6. Click the Slide Line – Create tool. The Create Parcels – Layout dialog appears.

7. From the drop-down menus, select Subdivision Lots, Property, and Name Square Foot & Acres (Name Square Meter & Hectares) in the Site, Parcel Style, and Area Label Style selection boxes, respectively.

   Leave the rest of the options set to their defaults.

8. Click OK to dismiss the dialog.

9. At the Select parcel to be subdivided or [Pick]: prompt, click the PROPERTY : 1 area label.

10. At the Select start point on frontage: prompt, use your Endpoint Osnap to pick the point of curvature along the ROW parcel segment for Property : 1 (see Figure 5.29). The point will show with the Osnap marker over it.

FIGURE 5.29
Pick the point of curvature along the ROW parcel segment high-lighted by the Osnap marker.

The parcel jig appears.

11. Move your mouse slowly along the ROW parcel segment, and notice that the parcel jig follows the parcel segment.

12. At the Select end point on frontage: prompt, use your Endpoint Osnap to pick the point of curvature along the ROW parcel segment for Property : 1 (see Figure 5.30).

FIGURE 5.30
Allow the parcel-creation jig to follow the parcel segment and then pick the point of curvature along the ROW parcel segment highlighted by the Osnap marker.

13. At the Specify angle or [Bearing/aZimuth]: prompt, enter **90** ↵.

Notice the preview (see Figure 5.31).

FIGURE 5.31
A preview of the results of the automatic parcel layout

14. At the `Accept result? [Yes/No] <Yes>:` prompt, press ↵ to accept the default, Yes.

15. At the `Select parcel to be subdivided or [Pick]:` prompt, press ↵.

16. Click the X to close the Parcel Layout Tools toolbar.

Your drawing should look similar to Figure 5.32.

FIGURE 5.32
The automatically
created lots

17. Save and close the drawing.

If you want to see what the drawing should look like at this point, you can open 0505_
CreateSlide_FINISHED.dwg (0505_CreateSlide_METRIC_FINISHED.dwg), available from the
book's website.

CURVES AND THE FRONTAGE OFFSET

In most cases, the frontage along a building setback is graphically represented as a straight line
behind the setback. When you specify a minimum width along a frontage offset (the building setback line) in the Parcel Layout Tools dialog and when the lot frontage is curved, the distance you
enter is measured along the curve, as shown by the dashed line here.

In most cases, this result may be insignificant, but in a large development, the error could be the defining factor in your decision to add or subtract a parcel from the development.

SWING LINE – CREATE TOOL

The Swing Line – Create tool creates a "backward" attached parcel segment where the diamond-shaped grip appears not at the frontage but at a different location that you specify. The tool respects your minimum frontage, and it adjusts the frontage so it is larger, if necessary, to respect your default area. The Swing Line – Create tool is semiautomatic because it requires your input for the swing point location.

You may find this tool most useful around a cul-de-sac or in odd-shaped corners where you must hold frontage but have a lot of flexibility in the rear of the lot.

This exercise will lead you through using the Swing Line – Create tool to create lots:

1. Open the 0506_CreateSwing.dwg (0506_CreateSwing_METRIC.dwg) file, which you can download from this book's web page.

2. From the Home tab ➤ Create Design panel, expand Parcel ➤ Parcel Creation Tools.

   The Parcel Layout Tools toolbar appears.

3. If not already done, expand the toolbar by clicking the expansion chevron located at the end of the toolbar.

4. In the Parcel Sizing section, change the value of the following parameters by clicking in the Value column and entering the new values if they aren't already set. Notice how the preview window changes to accommodate your preferences:

   ◆ Minimum Area: **10890.00** sq. ft. (**1,012 m²**)

   ◆ Minimum Frontage: **180.000'** (**54.75 m**)

   ◆ Use Minimum Frontage At Offset: No

   ◆ Minimum Width: **75.000'** (**25 m**)

   ◆ Minimum Depth: **50.000'** (**15 m**)

   ◆ Use Maximum Depth: No

   ◆ Maximum Depth: (leave default value since this will not be used)

   ◆ Multiple Solution Preference: Use Shortest Frontage

5. In the Automatic Layout section, change the following parameters by clicking in the Value column and selecting the appropriate option from the drop-down menu, if it isn't already set:

   ◆ Automatic Mode: On

   ◆ Remainder Distribution: Redistribute Remainder

6. Click the Swing Line – Create tool. The Create Parcels – Layout dialog appears.

7. From the drop-down menus, select Subdivision Lots, Property, and Name Square Foot & Acres (Name Square Meter & Hectares) in the Site, Parcel Style, and Area Label Style selection boxes, respectively.

Leave the rest of the options set to their defaults.

8. Click OK to dismiss the dialog.

9. At the `Select parcel to be subdivided or [Pick]:` prompt, click the Property : 22 area label.

10. At the `Select start point on frontage:` prompt, use your Endpoint Osnap to pick the point on the curve along the ROW parcel segment for Property : 22 on its southeast corner (see Figure 5.33). The point will show with the Osnap marker over it.

FIGURE 5.33
Pick the point on the curve on the parcel's southeast corner, as highlighted by the Osnap marker along the ROW parcel segment.

The parcel jig appears.

11. Move your mouse slowly along the ROW parcel segment, and notice that the parcel jig follows the parcel segment.

12. At the `Select end point on frontage:` prompt, use your Endpoint Osnap to pick the end point along the ROW parcel segment for Property : 22 on its northwest corner (see Figure 5.34).

FIGURE 5.34
Allow the parcel-creation jig to follow the parcel segment and then pick the end point as highlighted by the Osnap marker on the ROW parcel segment.

13. At the `Specify swing point` prompt, select the interior corner of the parcel, as shown in Figure 5.35 and highlighted by the Osnap marker.

FIGURE 5.35
Swing point
selection

14. At the `Accept result? [Yes/No] <Yes>:` prompt, press ↵ to accept the default, Yes.

15. At the `Select parcel to be subdivided or [Pick]:` prompt, press ↵.

16. Click the X to close the Parcel Layout Tools toolbar.

Your drawing should look similar to Figure 5.36.

FIGURE 5.36
The automatically
created lots

17. Save and close the drawing.

If you want to see what the drawing should look like at this point, you can open 0506_CreateSwing_FINISHED.dwg (0506_CreateSwing_METRIC_FINISHED.dwg), available from the book's website.

FREE FORM CREATE TOOL

A site plan is more than just single-family lots. Areas are usually dedicated for open space, stormwater-management facilities, parks, and public utility lots. The Free Form Create tool can be useful when you're creating these types of parcels. This tool, like the precise sizing tools, creates an attached parcel segment with the special diamond-shaped grips.

A NOTE ON LOT NUMBERS

The lot numbers were designed by the authors for the exercises. Your lot numbers may vary from those shown in the exercises.

In the following exercise, you'll use the Free Form Create tool to create a new parcel:

1. Open the 0507_CreateFreeForm.dwg (0507_CreateFreeForm_METRIC.dwg) file.

Note that this drawing contains a series of subdivision lots.

2. Zoom to Property : 18.

3. Use the AutoCAD Erase command to delete the parcel lines highlighted in Figure 5.37.

FIGURE 5.37
Delete the high-
lighted parcel
lines.

Because the order in which the parcel segments are erased will determine the parcel numbers, your parcel numbers may vary from those created by the authors.

The parcels readjust, but the resulting lot is now much larger than needed. Let's add a line using the Free Form Create tool. You will explore deleting parcel lines in more depth later in this chapter.

4. From the Home tab ➤ Create Design panel, select Parcel ➤ Parcel Creation Tools.

5. On the Parcel Layout Tools toolbar, select the Free Form Create tool.

The Create Parcels – Layout dialog appears.

6. Select Subdivision Lots, Property, and Name Square Foot & Acres (Name Square Meter & Hectares) from the drop-down menus in the Site, Parcel Style, and Area Label Style selection boxes, respectively.

Keep the default values for the remaining options.

7. Click OK to dismiss the dialog.

8. Slide the Free Form Create attachment point along the frontage of the Property : 18 area.

9. At the `Select attachment point:` prompt, pick near the point shown in Figure 5.38.

FIGURE 5.38
Use the Free Form Create tool to select an attachment point.

10. At the `Specify lot line direction:(ENTER for perpendicular) or [Bearing/aZimuth]:` prompt, press ↵ to specify a perpendicular lot line direction.

A new parcel segment is created perpendicular to the ROW parcel segment, as shown in Figure 5.39 (your resulting lot numbers may differ). Note that a new lot parcel has formed.

FIGURE 5.39
A new parcel cre-
ated using the Free
Form Create tool

Although most parcel lines are created perpendicular to the right-of-way line, please note that you can use the Free Form Create tool to attach a new parcel segment to any parcel segment in the drawing.

11. Press ↵ to exit the Free Form Create command.

12. Click the X or press Esc to exit the Parcel Layout Tools toolbar.

13. Pick the new parcel segment so that you see its diamond-shaped grip.

14. Grab the grip and slide the segment along the ROW parcel segment (see Figure 5.40).

FIGURE 5.40
Sliding an
attached parcel
segment

Notice that when you place the parcel segment at a new location, the segment endpoint snaps back to the rear parcel segment. This is typical behavior for an attached parcel segment.

15. Save and close the drawing.

If you want to see what the drawing should look like at this point, you can open 0507_CreateFreeForm_FINISHED.dwg (0507_CreateFreeForm_METRIC_FINISHED.dwg), available from the book's website.

Editing Parcels by Deleting Parcel Segments

One of the most powerful aspects of Civil 3D parcels is the ability to perform many iterations of a site plan design. Typically, this design process involves creating a series of parcels and then deleting them to make room for iterations with different parameters or deleting certain segments to make room for easements, public utility lots, and more.

You can delete parcel segments using the AutoCAD Erase tool as shown in the previous exercise, or you can use the Delete Sub-Entity tool on the Parcel Layout Tools toolbar, a tool you used in the cleanup of the cul-de-sac exercise.

It's important to understand the difference between these two methods. The AutoCAD Erase tool behaves as follows:

- If a series of parcel segments was originally created from a polyline (or similar parcel layout tools, such as the Tangent-Tangent With No Curves tool), the AutoCAD Erase tool erases the entire series of segments (see Figure 5.41).

FIGURE 5.41
The highlighted segments will be erased after using the AutoCAD Erase tool.

- If a series of parcel segments was originally created using lines or arcs (or similar parcel layout tools, such as the precise sizing tools), then AutoCAD Erase erases each segment individually (see Figure 5.42).

FIGURE 5.42
The highlighted segment will be erased.

The Delete Sub-Entity tool acts more like the AutoCAD Trim tool. The Delete Sub-Entity tool erases only the parcel segments between parcel vertices. For example, if Parcel #69, as shown in Figure 5.43, must be absorbed into Parcel #23 based on the fact that the parcel changes ownership, you'd want to erase only the segment on the east of Parcel #23 and not the entire segment.

FIGURE 5.43
Using the Delete Sub-Entity tool to erase the east parcel segment for Parcel #23

If you look at Parcel #23, you will notice that it consists of a series of segments. If you had tried to use the AutoCAD Erase command, then the whole series would have been deleted, but since you want only the east segment, then the Delete Sub-Entity tool will accomplish that.

As an alternative to launching the Parcel Creation tools by choosing the Home tab ➤ Create Ground Data panel ➤ Parcel ➤ Parcel Creation Tools, you can access them by selecting the area label of a parcel and then, from the Parcel contextual tab ➤ Modify panel, selecting Parcel Layout Tools. Figure 5.44 shows the result of this deletion.

FIGURE 5.44
The east lot line
for Parcel #23 was
erased using the
Delete Sub-Entity
tool, thus enlarg-
ing this parcel
with the new
addition.

Best Practices for Parcel Creation

Now that you have an understanding of how objects in a site interact and you've had some practice creating and editing parcels in a variety of ways, you'll take a deeper look at how parcels must be constructed to achieve topology stability, predictable labeling, and desired parcel interaction.

Forming Parcels from Segments

Earlier in this chapter, you saw that parcels are created only when parcel segments form a closed area (see Figure 5.45).

Parcels must always close. Whether you draw AutoCAD lines and use the Create Parcel From Objects menu command or use the parcel segment creation tools, a parcel won't form until there is an enclosed polygon. Figure 5.46 shows four parcel segments that don't close; therefore, no parcel has been formed.

FIGURE 5.45
A parcel is created when parcel segments form a closed area.

Property : 1

FIGURE 5.46
No parcel will be formed if parcel segments don't completely enclose an area.

There are times in surveying and engineering when parcels of land don't necessarily close when created from legal descriptions. In this case, you must work with your surveyor to perform an adjustment or find some other solution to create a closed polygon.

You also saw that even though parcels can't be erased, if you erase the appropriate parcel segments, the area contained within a parcel is assimilated into neighboring parcels. Remember that you can delete parcels if you move them to a new site and delete that site. This is an easy way to delete those parcels that are not needed in the drawing.

Parcels Reacting to Site Objects

Parcels require only one parcel segment to divide them from their neighbor (see Figure 5.47). This behavior eliminates the need for duplicate segments between parcels, and duplicate segments must be avoided.

FIGURE 5.47
Two parcels, with one parcel segment between them

PROPERTY : 1
2061.37 SQ FT
0.05 ACRES

PROPERTY : 2
1979.60 SQ FT
0.05 ACRES

As you saw in the section on site interaction, parcels understand their relationships to one another. When you create a single parcel segment between two subdivision lots, you have the ability to move one line and affect two parcels. Figure 5.48 shows the moved parcel segment from Figure 5.47 once the parcel segment between them has been shifted to the right. Note that both areas change in response.

FIGURE 5.48
Moving one parcel segment affects the area of two parcels.

A mistake that many people new to Civil 3D make is to create parcels from closed polylines, which results in a duplicate segment between parcels. Figure 5.49 shows two parcels created from two closed polylines. These two parcels may appear identical to the two shown in the previous example because they were both created from a closed polyline rectangle; however, the segment between them is actually two segments. You can notice that in the figure when the Selection Cycling toggle (Ctrl+W) is enabled.

FIGURE 5.49
Adjacent parcels created from closed polylines create overlapping or duplicate segments.

The duplicate segment becomes apparent when you attempt to grip-edit the parcel segments. Moving one vertex from the common lot line, as shown in Figure 5.50, reveals the second segment. Also note that a sliver parcel is formed. Duplicate site geometry objects and sliver parcels make it difficult for Civil 3D to solve the site topology and can cause unexpected parcel behavior.

FIGURE 5.50
Duplicate segments become apparent when they're grip-edited and a sliver parcel is formed.

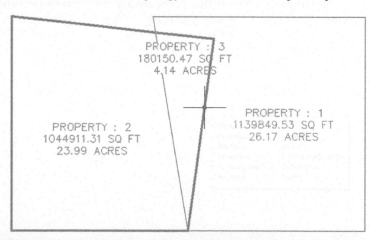

Creating a subdivision plat of parcels this way almost guarantees that your labeling won't perform properly and could lead to inaccurate data.

PARCELS AND LANDXML

The best method for importing lot data from other programs such as Land Desktop is LandXML. Parcels imported from LandXML will automatically clean up duplicate lines to prevent some of the pitfalls mentioned in this section. However, through this import, the data for right-of-way lines might not fit the desired intent on using the tool since they will be segmented at every place where it intersects a property line. This makes labeling more difficult and may require additional edits to the data to fit your design intent.

Parcels form to fill the space contained by the original outer boundary. You should always begin a parcel-division project with an outer boundary of some sort (see Figure 5.51).

FIGURE 5.51
An outer boundary
parcel with align-
ments that are not
part of any site

You can then move road centerline alignments to the site, which divides the outer boundary parcel, as shown in Figure 5.52.

It's important to note that the boundary parcel no longer exists intact. As you subdivide this site, Parcel 1 is continually reallocated with every division. As road ROW and subdivision lots are formed from parcel segments, more parcels are created. Every bit of space that was contained in the original outer boundary is accounted for in the mesh of newly formed parcels (see Figure 5.53).

FIGURE 5.52
Alignments moved to the same site as the boundary parcel divide the boundary parcel.

FIGURE 5.53
The total area of parcels contained within the original boundary is equal to the original boundary area.

From now on, you'll consider ROW, wetlands, parkland, and open space areas as parcels, even if you didn't before. You can make custom label styles to annotate these parcels however you like, including a "no show" or none area label.

Real World Scenario

OVERKILL IS JUST RIGHT FOR PARCELS

Frequently, parcel data comes from geographic information system (GIS) sources or from existing plats. The quality of this data can vary, making a direct conversion to Civil 3D parcels difficult.

An excellent tool for ensuring that the conversion of these lines, arcs, and polylines goes smoothly is the Overkill command. Overkill is an AutoCAD command that will clean up drawings based on the options and tolerance that you choose.

You can find the Overkill command on the Home tab ➤ Modify panel flyout.

Once you have selected the objects you want the Overkill command to analyze, you are prompted to choose options that determine how extensive the cleanup will be. The default settings, shown here, are rather conservative.

The Tolerance setting determines how close two lines can be before they are considered to be duplicates. The higher this value, the more overlap and duplicates the command will find.

The check boxes indicate properties Overkill will disregard when performing its edits. With all the check boxes clear, the objects are not considered duplicates unless all of the listed properties match.

Before you run the Overkill command, a selected batch of lines slated to become parcels shows many extraneous vertices. The plus signs next to the grips indicate where multiple grips overlap.

Before Overkill Command

After you run the Overkill command, the selection shows fewer visible grips and no indication that there are overlapping objects.

After Overkill Command

As you can see, the Overkill command can save you valuable time cleaning up drawings. Note that there are still multiple vertices that would require further cleanup; you'll learn more about this in the next section.

Constructing Parcel Segments with the Appropriate Vertices

Parcel segments should have natural vertices only where necessary and should have split-created vertices at all other intersections. A natural vertex, or point of intersection (PI), can be identified by picking a line, polyline, or parcel segment and noting the location of the grips (see Figure 5.54).

FIGURE 5.54
Natural verti-
ces on a parcel
segment

FIGURE 5.54
Natural verti-
ces on a parcel
segment

A split-created vertex occurs when two parcel segments touch or cross each other. Note that in Figure 5.55 the parcel segment doesn't show a grip even where each individual lot line touches the ROW parcel.

FIGURE 5.55
Split-created
vertices on a
parcel segment

It's desirable to have as few natural vertices as possible. In the example shown in Figure 5.55, the ROW frontage line can be expressed as a single bearing and length from the end of the arc through the beginning of the next arc, as opposed to having several smaller line segments.

If the foundation geometry is drawn with a natural vertex at each lot line intersection, the resulting parcel segment won't label properly and may cause complications with editing and other functions. This subject will be discussed in more detail in the section "Labeling Spanning Segments" later in this chapter.

Parcel segments must not overhang. Spanning labels are designed to overlook the location of intersection-formed (or T-shaped) split-created vertices. However, these labels won't span a crossing-formed (X- or + [plus]-shaped) split-created vertex. Even a very small parcel segment overhang will prevent a spanning label from working and may even affect the area computation for adjacent parcels. The overhanging segment in Figure 5.56 would prevent a label from returning the full spanning length of the ROW segment it crosses.

FIGURE 5.56
Overhanging
segment

Labeling Parcel Areas

A parcel area label is placed at the parcel centroid by default, and it refers to the parcel in its entirety. It doesn't necessarily have to include the actual area of the parcel. When asked to pick a parcel, you pick the area label; however, this behavior is valid only for Civil 3D commands. For example, if you pick a parcel area label and invoke the AutoCAD Erase command, the parcel will not be erased.

You can customize area labels to suit your needs. Figure 5.57 shows a variety of customized area labels.

FIGURE 5.57
Sample area labels

Certification
Objective

Area labels often include the parcel name or number, and often the names and numbers need to be changed after the parcels are placed in the drawing. To accomplish this, you can select a parcel and then on the Parcel contextual tab ➤ Modify panel choose Renumber/Rename.

The following exercise will teach you how to renumber a series of parcels:

1. Open 0508_RenumberParcels.dwg (0508_RenumberParcels_METRIC.dwg). Note that this drawing already contains some subdivision lot parcels.

2. Near the southeast corner of the project, select Property : 13. On the Parcel contextual tab ➤ Modify panel, select Renumber/Rename. The Renumber/Rename Parcels dialog appears.

3. In the Renumber/Rename Parcels dialog, make sure Subdivision Lots is selected from the drop-down menu in the Site selection box and that the Renumber radio button is selected.

4. Change the value of the Starting Number selection box to **100**. Click OK.

5. At the Specify start point or [Polylines/Site]: prompt, pick a point on the screen anywhere inside the Property : 13 parcel, which will become your new Property: 100 parcel at the end of the command.

6. At the End point or [Undo]: prompt, pick a point on the screen anywhere inside the Property : 18 parcel, almost as if you were drawing a line; then pick a point inside Property : 22 and end by picking a point inside the Property : 27.

7. Press ↵ to complete choosing parcels. Press ↵ again to end the command.

   Note that your parcels have been renumbered from 100 through 114.

8. Save the drawing, but keep it open for the next exercise.

If you would like to see what the drawing should look like at this point, you can open 0508_RenumberParcels_FINISHED.dwg (0508_RenumberParcels_METRIC_FINISHED.dwg), available from the book's website.

The next exercise will lead you through one method of changing an area label using the Edit Parcel Properties dialog:

1. Continue working in the 0508_RenumberParcels.dwg (0508_RenumberParcels_METRIC.dwg) file, or you can open 0508_RenumberParcels_FINISHED.dwg (0508_RenumberParcels_METRIC_FINISHED.dwg), available from the book's website.

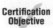

2. Select Property : 100; then on the Parcel contextual tab ➤ Modify panel, select Multiple Parcel Properties.

3. At the Specify start point or [Polylines/All/Site]: prompt, pick a point on the screen inside of Property : 100 close to the middle of the parcel.

4. At the End point or [Undo]: prompt, pick a point on the screen inside Property : 107 close to the middle of this parcel; then end by clicking inside Property: 108 close to the middle of this parcel using the same technique you used in steps 5 and 6 of the previous exercise. This line should cross sequentially only parcels 100–108.

5. Press ↵ to complete parcel selection and press ↵ again to open the Edit Parcel Properties dialog.

6. In the Area Selection Label Style portion of the Edit Parcel Properties dialog, use the drop-down menu to select the Parcel Number area label style, as shown in Figure 5.58.

FIGURE 5.58
The Edit Parcel
Properties dialog

7. Click the Apply To All Parcels button to the right of the Parcel Number setting under Area Selection Label Style.

8. Click Yes in the dialog displaying the question "Apply the area selection label style to the 9 selected parcels?"

9. Click OK to exit the Edit Parcel Properties dialog.

   The nine parcels now have parcel area labels that call out numbers only. Note that you could also use this interface to add a second area label to certain parcels by clicking the plus sign in the Area Label Styles section of the Edit Parcel Properties dialog.

10. Save the drawing, but keep it open for the next exercise.

If you want to see what the drawing should look like at this point, you can open 0508_ ChangeMultipleLabels_FINISHED.dwg (0508_ChangeMultipleLabels_METRIC_FINISHED .dwg), available from the book's website.

This section's final exercise will show you how to use Prospector to change a group of parcel area labels at the same time:

1. Continue working in the previous file or open the 0508_ChangeMultipleLabels_ FINISHED.dwg (0508_ChangeMultipleLabels_METRIC_FINISHED.dwg) file, available on the book's website.

2. In Prospector, expand Sites ➤ Subdivision Lots and select the Parcels collection.

3. In the expanded listing hold down the Ctrl key, and select all of the lots from Property : 109 to Property : 114.

4. Release the Ctrl key, and your parcels should remain selected.

5. Scroll to the Area Label Style column, right-click the column header, and select Edit (see Figure 5.59).

FIGURE 5.59
Right-click the
Area Label Style
column header and
select Edit.

6. In the Select Label Style dialog, select Parcel Name from the drop-down menu in the Label Style selection box.

7. Click OK to dismiss the dialog.

The drawing will process for a moment.

8. Once the processing is finished, minimize Prospector and inspect your parcels.

All the selected parcels should now have the Parcel Name area label style.

9. Save and close the drawing.

If you want to see what the drawing should look like at this point, you can open 0508_ChangeAreaLabel_FINISHED.dwg (0508_ChangeAreaLabel_METRIC_FINISHED.dwg), available from the book's website.

 Real World Scenario

WHAT IF THE AREA LABEL NEEDS TO BE SPLIT ONTO TWO LAYERS?

You may have a few different types of plans that show parcels. Because it would be awkward to have to change the parcel area label style before you plot each sheet, it would be best to find a way to make a second label on a second layer so that you can freeze the area component in sheets or viewports when it isn't needed. Here's an example where the square footage has been placed on a different layer so it can be frozen in certain viewports:

You can accomplish this by creating a second parcel area label that calls out the area only.

1. In any drawing containing parcels, change to the Annotate tab.

2. From the Labels & Tables panel, select Add Labels ➤ Parcel ➤ Add Parcel Labels.

3. Select Area from the drop-down menu in the Label Type selection box and then select an area style label that will be the second area label.

4. Click Add and then pick your parcel onscreen.

You'll find a second parcel area label to be a little more automatic when you place it (it already knows what parcel to reference).

You can also use the Edit Parcel Properties dialog, shown earlier in Figure 5.58 in the section "Labeling Parcel Areas," to add a second label.

Labeling Parcel Segments

Although parcels are used for much more than just subdivision lots, most parcels you create will probably be used for concept plans, record plats, and other legal subdivision plans. These plans, such as the one shown in Figure 5.60, almost always require segment labels for bearing, distance, direction, crow's feet, and more.

FIGURE 5.60
A fully labeled site
plan

FIGURE 5.60
A fully labeled site
plan

Labeling Multiple-Parcel Segments

The following exercise will teach you how to add labels to multiple-parcel segments:

1. Open the 0509_SegmentLabels.dwg (0509_SegmentLabels_METRIC.dwg) file, which you can download from this book's web page.

   Note that this drawing contains many subdivision lot parcels.

2. On the Annotate tab ➤ Labels & Tables panel, click the Add Labels icon.

3. From the drop-down menus in the Add Labels dialog, select Parcel, Multiple Segment, Bearing Over Distance (from the Parcel Line Label Style section), and Delta Over Length And Radius in the Feature, Label Type, Line Label Style, and Curve Label Style selection boxes, respectively, as shown in Figure 5.61.

FIGURE 5.61
The Add Labels
dialog

4. Click Add.

5. At the `Select parcel to be labeled by clicking on area label:` prompt, pick the area label for Property : 100.

6. At the `Label direction [CLockwise/COunterclockwise]<CLockwise>:` prompt, press ↵ to accept the default and again to exit the command.

Each parcel segment for Property : 100 should now be labeled.

7. Continue picking Property : 101 through 105 in the same manner.

Note that segments are never given a duplicate label, even along shared lot lines.

8. Press ↵ to exit the command. Close the Add Labels dialog.

9. Save the drawing, but keep it open for the next exercise.

If you want to see what the drawing should look like at this point, you can open `0509_SegmentLabels_FINISHED.dwg` (`0509_SegmentLabels_METRIC_FINISHED.dwg`), available from the book's website.

The following exercise will show you how to edit and delete parcel segment labels:

1. Continue working in the `0509_SegmentLabels.dwg` (`0509_SegmentLabels_METRIC .dwg`) file, or you can open `0509_SegmentLabels_FINISHED.dwg`. (`0509_SegmentLabels_ METRIC_FINISHED.dwg`), available from the book's website.

2. Zoom in on the label along the frontage of Property : 102.

3. Select the segment label.

You'll know your label has been picked when you see a diamond-shaped grip at the label midpoint (see Figure 5.62).

FIGURE 5.62
A diamond-shaped grip appears when the label has been picked.

4. On the Labels – Parcel Segment Label contextual tab ➤ Modify panel, click Flip Label, as shown in Figure 5.63.

FIGURE 5.63
The Parcel
Segment Label
contextual tab

The label flips so that the bearing component is outside the parcel and the distance component is inside.

5. On the Labels – Parcel Segment Label contextual tab ➤ Modify panel, click Reverse Label. Press Esc to clear your selection.

The label reverses so that the bearing now reads SW instead of NE.

6. Repeat steps 3 through 5 for several other segment labels, and note their reactions.

7. Select one of the labels along the back lot lines of parcels 100–105.

8. Once the label is picked, execute the AutoCAD Erase tool or press the Delete key.

You will notice that the label disappears, since even though it is dynamically linked to the segment object, it acts independently as an annotation object that can be managed in the same way as other Civil 3D objects.

9. Save and close the drawing.

If you want to see what the drawing should look like at this point, you can open 0509_EditSegmentLabels_FINISHED.dwg (0509_EditSegmentLabels_METRIC_FINISHED.dwg), available from the book's website.

Labeling Spanning Segments

Spanning labels are used where you need a label that spans the overall length of an outside segment, such as the example in Figure 5.64.

FIGURE 5.64
A spanning label

Spanning labels require that you use the appropriate vertices, as discussed in detail in the earlier section "Constructing Parcel Segments with the Appropriate Vertices." Spanning labels have the following requirements:

- Spanning labels can span only split-created vertices. Natural vertices will interrupt a spanning length.

- Spanning label styles must be composed to span the outside segment.

- Spanning label styles must be composed to attach the desired spanning components (such as length and direction arrow) on the outside segment (as shown previously in Figure 5.64), with perhaps a small offset.

Once you've confirmed that your geometry is sound and your label is properly composed, you're set to span. The following exercise will teach you how to add spanning labels to single-parcel segments:

1. Open 0510_SpanningLabels.dwg (0510_SpanningLabels_METRIC.dwg), available from the book's website.

2. Zoom in on the inner right-of-way parcel segment that runs from Parcel 100 through Parcel 105.

3. Change to the Annotate tab and select Add Labels ➢ Parcel ➢ Add Parcel Labels from the Labels & Tables panel.

4. From the drop-down menus in the Add Labels dialog, select Single Segment, (Span) Bearing And Distance With Crows Feet, and Delta Over Length And Radius in the Label Type, Line Label Style, and Curve Label Style selection boxes, respectively.

5. Click Add.

6. At the Select point on entity: prompt, pick somewhere near the middle of the outer parcel segment that runs from Parcel 100 through Parcel 105.

   A label that spans the full length between natural vertices appears (see Figure 5.64).

7. As time permits, create other span labels along the other inner lot lines in the project.

8. Save and close the drawing.

If you want to see what the drawing should look like at this point, you can open 0510_SpanningLabels_FINISHED.dwg (0510_SpanningLabels_METRIC_FINISHED.dwg), available from the book's website.

FLIP IT, REVERSE IT

If your spanning label doesn't seem to work on your first try and you've followed all the spanning label guidelines, try flipping your label to the other side of the parcel segment, reversing the label, or using a combination of both flipping and reversing.

Adding Curve Tags to Prepare for Table Creation

To keep plans tidy, it is common to show labels that reference a table for curves and lines. Civil 3D parcels provide tools for creating dynamic line and curve tables. You can keep lines and curves together or create separate tables for each.

Parcel segments must be labeled before they can be used to create a table. They can be labeled with any type of label, but you'll likely find it to be best practice to create a tag-only style for segments that will be placed in a table.

The following exercise will show you how to replace curve and line labels with tag-only labels:

1. Open 0511_TagLabels.dwg (0511_TagLabels_METRIC.dwg), available from the book's website.

   Note that usually the labels along tight curves, such as the cul-de-sac, would be better represented as curve tags.

2. Change to the Annotate tab ➢ Labels & Tables panel and select Add Labels ➢ Parcel ➢ Add Parcel Labels.

3. From the drop-down menus in the Add Labels dialog, select Replace Multiple Segment; for Line Label Style, use Line Tag Only, and for Curve Label Style use Curve Tag Only.

4. Click Add. At the Select parcel to be labeled by clicking on area label: prompt, pick the area label for Parcel 5.

   Note that the line and curve labels for Parcel 5 are replaced by tag labels.

5. Repeat step 4 for Parcels 107 through 114.

6. Press ↵ to exit the command.

7. Save the drawing, but keep it open for the next exercise.

If you want to see what the drawing should look like at this point, you can open 0511_TagLabels_FINISHED.dwg (0511_TagLabels_METRIC_FINISHED.dwg), available from the book's website.

Now that each curve and line label has been replaced with a tag, it's desirable to have the tag numbers be sequential. The following exercise will show you how to renumber tags:

1. Continue working in the previous drawing or you can open 0511_TagLabels_FINISHED .dwg (0511_TagLabels_METRIC_FINISHED.dwg), available from the book's website.

2. Zoom to the curve on the northwest corner of Parcel 5 (see Figure 5.65).

FIGURE 5.65
Curve tags on
Parcel 5 and the
northwest corner
curve

Your curve may have a different number than the one in the figure.

3. Click one of the parcel area labels. Then from the Parcel contextual tab ➤ Labels & Tables panel, select Renumber Tags.

4. At the Select label to renumber tag or [Settings]: prompt, type **S** and then press ↵.

The Table Tag Numbering dialog appears (see Figure 5.66).

FIGURE 5.66
The Table Tag
Numbering dialog

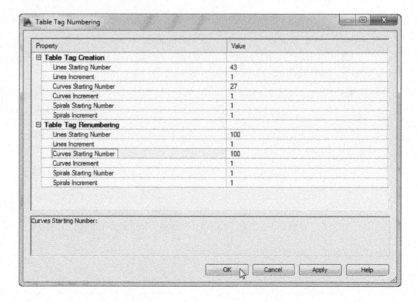

5. Within the Table Tag Renumbering branch, change the value in the Line Starting Number and Curves Starting Number selection boxes to **100** and click OK.

6. At the `Select label to renumber tag or [Settings]:` prompt, click the curve tag label at the northwest corner of Parcel 5.

   The command line may say `Current tag number is being used, press return to skip to next available or [Create duplicate]`, in which case you should type **C** ↵ to create a duplicate.

7. Continue clicking curve tag labels working east and then south.

   As you do so, you'll eventually resolve all of the duplicates and end up with a sequential set of curve tag numbers increasing as you move east and then south along the lot frontages.

8. When you're finished, press ↵ to exit the command.

9. Save and close the drawing.

If you want to see what the drawing should look like at this point, you can open `0511_TagLabelsRenumbered_FINISHED.dwg` (`0511_TagLabelsRenumbered_METRIC_FINISHED.dwg`), available from the book's website.

Creating a Table for Parcel Segments

The following exercise demonstrates how to create a table from line and curve tags:

1. Open `0512_SegmentTable.dwg` (`0512_SegmentTable_METRIC.dwg`), available from the book's website.

2. Select a parcel area label. From the Parcel contextual tab ➤ Labels & Tables panel, select Add Tables ➤ Add Segments.

3. In the Table Creation dialog, use the one and only option from the drop-down menu in the Table Style selection box.

4. In the Select By Label Or Style area of the dialog, click the Apply check box for the Parcel Curve: Curve Tag Only and Line Tag Only entry under Label Style Name.

   You might have to make the style name column wider to make it easier to pick up the name for the previously mentioned styles.

5. For both label styles, change the Selection Rule to Add Existing And New.

   The Add Existing And New option will ensure that the table updates as more labels fitting this criteria are added to the drawing. Keep the default values for the remaining options. The dialog should look like Figure 5.67.

FIGURE 5.67
The Table Creation dialog

6. Click OK.

7. At the Select upper left corner: prompt, pick a location in your drawing for the table. If the parcel area label is still selected, press Esc to deselect it.

   A segment table appears, shown in Figure 5.68. You will notice that the elements are not sorted in the table. You can enable sorting within the Data Properties tab of the Table Style dialog, which you can access by selecting the table, right-clicking, and choosing the Edit Table Style option from the context menu.

FIGURE 5.68
A segment table

Parcel Line and Curve Table			
Line #/Curve #	Length	Bearing/Delta	Radius
C102	16.09	115.21	8.00
L102	146.64	N65° 27′ 37.29″W	
L103	135.30	N65° 27′ 37.29″W	
C103	12.57	90.00	8.00
L104	120.71	N24° 32′ 22.71″E	
C100	10.83	77.58	8.00
L100	207.62	S77° 53′ 01.86″E	
C101	10.78	77.21	8.00
L101	182.84	30° 40′ 17.03″E	

8. Save and close the drawing.

   If you want to see what the drawing should look like at this point, you can open 0512_SegmentTable_FINISHED.dwg (0512_SegmentTable_METRIC_FINISHED.dwg), available from the book's website.

The Bottom Line

Create parcels from objects. The first step in any parceling project is to create an outer boundary for the site together with all the known linework.

> **Master It** Open the Masterit_0501.dwg (Masterit_0501_METRIC.dwg) file, which you can download from www.sybex.com/go/masteringcivil3d2016. Convert the polyline segments to parcels and place them in a new site named Subdivision Lots.

Create a right-of-way parcel using the right-of-way tool. For many projects, the ROW parcel serves as frontage for subdivision parcels. For straightforward sites, the automatic Create ROW tool provides a quick way to create this parcel.

> **Master It** Continue working in the Masterit_0501.dwg (Masterit_0501_METRIC.dwg) file or you can open Masterit_0501_FINISHED.dwg (Masterit_0501_METRIC_FINISHED .dwg), available from the book's website. Create a ROW parcel that is offset by 30′ (10 m) on either side of the road centerline with no fillets at boundary ends. Then clean up the ROW parcel area on each side of the alignment at the ends. Note: The south side parcel represents the existing main road ROW.

Create subdivision lots automatically by layout. The biggest challenge when creating a subdivision plan is optimizing the number of lots. The precise sizing parcel tools provide a means to automate this process.

> **Master It** Continue working in the previous drawing or open Masterit_0502_ FINISHED.dwg (Masterit_0502_METRIC_FINISHED.dwg), available from the book's website. Create a series of lots with a minimum of 10,890 sq. ft. (1,012 m^2) and 90′ (30 m) frontage on each side of the ROW beginning at the existing ROW and ending at the ROW intersection with the southeast segments of the two north parcels. Set the Use Minimum Frontage At Offset option to No and redistribute the remainder; then set the Minimum Depth and Width values to 50′ (15 m). Leave all other options at their defaults.

Add multiple-parcel segment labels. Every subdivision plat must be appropriately labeled. You can quickly label parcels with their bearings, distances, direction, and more using the segment labeling tools.

> **Master It** Continue working in the previous drawing or open Masterit_0503_ FINISHED.dwg (Masterit_0503_METRIC_FINISHED.dwg), available from the book's website. Place Bearing Over Distance labels on every parcel line segment and Delta Over Length And Radius labels on every parcel curve segment using the Multiple Segment Labeling tool.

Chapter 6

Alignments

When working on a linear project, whether it be the renovation of an old New England cow path or a network of new subdivision roads, you will need to convey the horizontal layout information to the contractor. This horizontal layout is called an *alignment* and drives much of the design. This chapter teaches you how to create alignments, how they interact with the rest of the design, how to edit and analyze them, and finally how they work with the overall project.

In this chapter, you will learn to:

- ◆ Create an alignment from an object.

- ◆ Create a reverse curve that never loses tangency.

- ◆ Replace a component of an alignment with another component type.

- ◆ Create alignment tables.

Alignment Concepts

Before you can efficiently work with alignments, you must understand two major concepts: the interaction of alignments and sites and the idea of geometry that is fixed, floating, or free.

Alignments and Sites

Prior to the Autodesk® AutoCAD® Civil 3D® 2008 release, alignments were always part of a site and interacted with the topology contained in that site. Civil 3D now has two ways of handling alignments in terms of sites: they can be contained in a site as before or they can be independent of a site (*siteless*).

There is no difference between the alignments contained in a site and those independent of a site since both can be used to cut profiles or control corridors, but only the alignments contained in a site will react with and create parcels as members of a site topology.

Unless you have good reason for them to interact, it makes sense to create alignments outside of any Site object. They can be moved later to a site if necessary. For the purpose of the exercises in this chapter, you won't place any alignments in a site. For more information about sites, check out the section "Introduction to Sites" in Chapter 5, "Parcels."

Alignment Entities

Civil 3D recognizes five types of alignments: centerline alignments, offset alignments, curb return alignments, rail alignments, and miscellaneous alignments. Each alignment type can consist of three types of entities, or *segments*: lines, arcs, and spirals. These segments control the horizontal alignment of your design. Their relationship to one another is described by the following terminology:

Fixed Segments Fixed segments are fixed in space (see Figure 6.1). They're defined by connecting points in the coordinate plane and are independent of the segments that occur either before or after them in the alignment. Fixed segments can be created as tangent to other components, but their independence from those objects lets you move them out of tangency during editing operations. An alignment that is defined from lines and arcs will have its segments fixed. If the lines on both sides of the arcs are tangents, they will be defined as free segments.

FIGURE 6.1
Alignment fixed
segments

Floating Segments Floating segments float in space but are attached to a point in the drawing and to a single segment to which they maintain tangency (see Figure 6.2). Floating segments work well in situations where you have a critical point but the other points of the horizontal alignment are flexible.

FIGURE 6.2
Alignment floating
segments

Free Segments Free segments are dependent upon the entities that come both before and after them in the alignment structure (see Figure 6.3). Unlike fixed or floating segments, a free segment must have segments that come before and after it. Free segments maintain tangency to the segments that come before and after them and move as required to make that happen. Although some geometry constraints can be put in place, these constraints can be edited and are user dependent. As a note, the alignment that is created from a polyline will be defined by free segments only if the segments before and after an Arc object are tangents; otherwise, the segments will be fixed, as mentioned previously.

FIGURE 6.3
Alignment free
segments

During the exercises in this chapter, you'll use a mix of these entity types to understand them better.

Creating an Alignment

You can create alignments using the following methods:

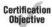

Certification Objective

From Objects   You will likely use this method to convert an existing centerline made out of arcs and lines or polylines to an Alignment object. With this method, you can also pull these types of entities from an attached external reference.

By Layout   The tools available under this method allow you to both define an alignment using dynamic line and curve elements and edit alignments created using all the other methods.

Best Fit   This method is used to define an alignment using as input data a selection of AutoCAD blocks, entities, points, COGO points, or feature lines. Based on specific constraints, a best-fitted Alignment object is created.

Offsets   These alignments define offset alignments that use a common centerline alignment as the source to which they are dynamically linked.

Widening   Widening alignments are based on either centerline or offset alignments and are dynamic linked to them. They are used in the definition of a road widening in a road corridor model.

From Corridor   This method allows a user to create an alignment using a corridor feature line.

From Network Parts   This method allows the creation of an alignment using the selection of a series of pipes and structures that belong to a Civil 3D pipe network.

From Pressure Network   This method allows the creation of an alignment using a selection of pipes, fittings, and appurtenances that belong to a Civil 3D pressure pipe network.

Using Existing Alignment   This method allows the creation of an alignment using a previously defined alignment object as source.

This section looks at the first four methods to create an alignment, outlining some of the advantages and disadvantages of each. The remaining methods are straightforward, and once you master the methods used in this section, you should not have any issues in mastering them as well. The exercise will use the street layout shown in Figure 6.4 as well as the different methods to achieve your designs.

FIGURE 6.4
Proposed street layout

Creating from a Line, Arc, or Polyline

Most designers have used either polylines or lines and arcs to generate the horizontal control of their projects. It's common for surveyors to generate polylines to describe the center of a right-of-way or for an environmental engineer to draw a polyline to show where a new channel should be constructed. These team members may or may not have Civil 3D software, so they use their familiar tools—the line, arc, and polyline—to describe their design intent.

Although these objects are good at showing where something should go, they don't have much data behind them. To make full use of these objects, you should convert them to Civil 3D alignments that can then be shared and used for myriad purposes. Once an alignment has been created from a polyline, offsets can be created to represent rights-of-way, building lines, and so on. In the following exercise, you'll convert a polyline to an alignment and create offset alignments:

1. Open the 0601_AlignmentFromObjects.dwg (0601_AlignmentFromObjects_METRIC .dwg) file.

   You can download this file from the book's web page at www.sybex.com/go/ masteringcivil3d2015. You will see a polyline that represents the centerline of a proposed road together with the parcels that you got familiar with in Chapter 5.

2. From the Home tab ➤ Create Design panel, choose Alignment ➤ Create Alignment From Objects.

3. When prompted to select the first line, pick the polyline that defines the centerline near its north end, and press ↵.

4. At the Press enter to accept alignment direction or [Reverse]: prompt, press ↵ once you confirm that the displayed arrow outlining the direction points from north to south.

The Create Alignment From Objects dialog appears.

5. Change the Name field to **ROAD D**, and set the Type field to Centerline from the drop-down list.

6. Verify that Alignment Style is set to Proposed, and Alignment Label Set is set to Major And Minor Only.

7. Within Conversion Options, make sure that the Add Curves Between Tangents option is unchecked, and the Erase Existing Entities box is checked.

The Create Alignment From Objects dialog should match Figure 6.5.

FIGURE 6.5
The settings used to create the ROAD D alignment

8. Accept the other settings and click OK.

When this exercise is complete, you may save the drawing, but keep it open for the following exercise. A finished copy of this drawing at this stage is available from the book's web page with the filename 0601_AlignmentFromObjects_A.dwg (0601_AlignmentFromObjects_A_METRIC.dwg).

A WORD ABOUT CONSTRAINTS

Prior to the 2014 release, creating from objects held no constraints (everything was fixed). In current versions, Civil 3D tries to find tangency where a curve is between two lines and establish that tangency as a constraint. Lines will always be set to Not Constrained (Fixed), but if the curve is tangent, it will be set to Constrained On Both Sides (Free). You will learn about changing those constraints later in this chapter.

 Real World Scenario

THE CREATE ALIGNMENT FROM OBJECTS DIALOG

In the Create Alignment From Objects dialog (shown in Figure 6.5), there are many settings that you can adjust when creating an alignment:

Name This is the alignment name. No alignment name can be duplicated in a drawing. When an alignment name is found to be a duplicate, a modifier is added to its name to show that difference.

Type The alignment types can be thought of as places for objects that are alike. The objects can react differently depending on which type is selected.

Centerline Used mainly for centers of roads, streams, or swales. Civil 3D places this type of alignment in the Alignments ➤ Centerline Alignments branch.

Offset Used for offset alignments. The difference between this and the centerline alignment is that you have the option in the Alignment Properties dialog to set Offset parameters, such as naming a parent alignment and offset values. Offset alignments are dynamically linked to their parent alignments and will update automatically when the parent alignment changes. Civil 3D places this type of alignment in the Alignments ➤ Offset Alignments branch.

Curb Return Used for curb returns, which are the radii at intersections. The difference between this and the offset alignment is that instead of Offset parameters, you have the option in the Alignment Properties dialog to set Curb Return parameters, such as setting two parent alignments and offsets. Curb return alignments are also dynamically linked to their parent alignments. Civil 3D places this type of alignment in the Alignments ➤ Curb Return Alignments branch.

Rail Used for rail design. The difference between this and the other alignments is that this alignment is set using typical rail geometry such as degree of curvature and cant. In addition, a unique tab is added to the Alignment Properties dialog called Rail Parameters, where you can specify the track width. Civil 3D places this alignment type in the Alignments ➤ Rail Alignments branch.

Miscellaneous This is a stripped-down alignment type that contains only Information, Stationing, Masking, Point Of Intersection, and Constraint Editing tabs. Civil 3D places this alignment type in the Alignments ➢ Miscellaneous Alignments branch.

Description This is an optional field where you can place the description of what your alignment represents.

Starting Station This value, either positive or negative, will be the starting stationing for the alignment. This is handy if you need to start your alignment to coincide with existing stationing or if you want to have your 0+00 stationing at an intersection of a road. If you forget to set this value here, you can change it later in the Alignment Properties dialog.

The General tab contains the following options:

Site This is a place to keep Civil 3D objects that you want to interact with each other. As previously mentioned, all of your alignments in these exercises will be put on the <None> site.

Alignment Style You can set different styles to visually show your alignment. For more on styles, refer to Chapter 19, "Object Styles."

Alignment Layer This setting overrides the layer that is specified in the drawing settings for the alignment that you create.

Alignment Label Set As with the Alignment Style, you can choose how your alignment will be labeled. For more on label styles, refer to Chapter 18, "Label Styles."

Conversion Options Depending on your selections, these will add curves and/or erase the original entities, or neither.

The Design Criteria tab contains these options:

Starting Design Speed Use this option to specify the design speed of the alignment for the starting station. If no additional design speeds are applied to a different section of the alignment, this speed will be used for the entire alignment. Design speed is used to calculate superelevation and to establish design criteria.

Use Criteria-Based Design When this check box is selected, the Use Design Criteria File and Use Design Check Set options are available. These options enable the software to keep track of certain design standards that you would like your alignment to meet and notify you when those standards are not met.

Use Design Criteria File Here you can define the design criteria, as it is defined in the design manual *A Policy on Geometric Design of Highways and Streets, 2011* from the American Association of State Highway and Transportation Officials (AASHTO).

Use Design Check Set Here you can set rules or expressions for lines, curves, spirals, and tangent intersections.

Many of these settings will be discussed further throughout this chapter.

You've created your first alignment and attached stationing and major and minor labels. It is common to create offset alignments from a centerline alignment to begin to model rights-of-way. In the following exercise, you'll create offset alignments and mask them where you don't want them to be seen:

1. Continue working on the previous file, or if you want to begin from the previous step, you can open the 0601_AlignmentFromObjects_A.dwg (0601_AlignmentFromObjects_A_METRIC.dwg) file.

2. From the Home tab ➤ Create Design panel, choose Alignment ➤ Create Offset Alignment option.

3. When prompted to select an alignment, pick the ROAD D alignment to open the Create Offset Alignments dialog shown in Figure 6.6.

FIGURE 6.6
The Create Offset Alignments dialog

4. With No. Of Offsets On Left set to **1**, change Incremental Offset On Left to **30** (metric users, **10**).

5. With No. Of Offsets On Right set to **1**, change Incremental Offset On Right to **30** (metric users, **10**).

6. Verify that Alignment Label Set is set to _No Labels and click OK to accept the rest of the defaults shown in Figure 6.6.

7. Select the left offset alignment just created along the easterly and northerly right-of-way of ROAD D to activate the Offset Alignment contextual tab.

8. From the Offset Alignment contextual tab ➢ Modify panel, click the Alignment Properties icon to open the Alignment Properties dialog.

9. Change to the Masking tab and click the Add Masking Region button.

10. Enter **264.90** for the first station and **326.47** for the second station when prompted (metric users, enter **81.46** and **98.78**) and click OK. Alternatively, you could have used the station picker that becomes available once the station cell is active and in editing mode.

Notice that the alignment is now masked at the intersection of the alignment with the right-of-way at the north end.

11. Repeat the process for the rest of the intersections for both of the offset alignments by using the station picker and snapping to the intersection of the offset alignments and the right-of-way lines so that the areas in between the right-of-way lines are masked.

Once complete, the Masking tab of the Alignment Properties dialog should look like Figure 6.7 for the case of the left offset.

FIGURE 6.7
Creating an alignment mask for the left offset with both U.S. (top) and metric (bottom) values.

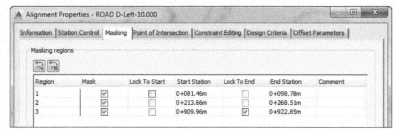

12. Click OK to close the dialog.

Offset alignments are simple to create, and they are dynamically linked to a centerline alignment.

13. To test this, grip the centerline alignment, select the endpoint grip, and stretch the alignment to the west.

Notice the change and then undo this change to return to the original state.

OFFSET GRIPS AND MORE

Offset alignments have two main grips: the arrow and the plus sign. The arrow is used to change the offset value, and the plus sign is used to create a transition, called a *widening*, such as a turning lane. When a widening is present, there will be a third grip present in the form of a filled gray circle that enables the transition grips. To access the Create Widening command, from the Home tab ➤ Create Design panel, select the Alignment drop-down. Widening criteria can also be found in the Create Offset Alignments dialog and the Offset Alignment contextual tab. The widening in the Offset Alignments contextual tab can be added as a new alignment or as an element within the existing offset alignment.

Also, offset alignments with widening remain dynamic to their host alignment. Offset alignment objects can be found in Prospector in the Alignments branch.

When this exercise is complete, you can close the drawing. A finished copy of this drawing is available from the book's web page with the filename `0601_AlignmentFromObjects_FINISHED` `.dwg` (`0601_AlignmentFromObjects_METRIC_FINISHED.dwg`).

Creating by Layout

Now that you've made an alignment from polylines, let's look at another creation option: Create By Layout. You'll use the same street layout (Figure 6.4) that was provided by a planner, but instead of converting from polylines, you'll trace the alignments. Although this seems like duplicate work, it will pay dividends in the relationships created between segments.

1. Open the `0602_AlignmentByLayout.dwg` (`0602_AlignmentByLayout_METRIC.dwg`) file.

2. From the Home tab ➤ Create Design panel, choose the Alignment ➤ Alignment Creation Tools option.

The Create Alignment – Layout dialog appears.

3. Change the Name field to **ROAD D** if it is not already set.

4. Verify that Alignment Style is set to Proposed and Alignment Label Set is set to Major And Minor Only.

5. Click OK to accept the other settings shown in Figure 6.8.

FIGURE 6.8
Create Alignment –
Layout dialog

The Alignment Layout Tools toolbar for ROAD D appears (Figure 6.9).

FIGURE 6.9
The Alignment
Layout Tools tool-
bar for the ROAD
D alignment

6. Click the down arrow next to the Tangent-Tangent (No Curves) tool at the far left and select the Tangent-Tangent (With Curves) option (see Figure 6.10).

FIGURE 6.10

The Tangent-Tangent (With Curves) tool

This tool places a curve automatically based on a default setting that is defined under the Curve And Spiral Settings option from the same menu. Later, you'll adjust the curve based on your design's preferred layout.

7. Turn on the Endpoint Osnap and snap to the north endpoint of the ROAD D centerline.

8. Continue to pick the vertices endpoints of the red polyline along the ROAD D centerline, from north to south and then east to finish creating this alignment.

9. After selecting the last endpoint along the red polyline, press ↵ to end the command.

10. Click the X button at the upper right on the Alignment Layout Tools toolbar for ROAD D to close it.

Keep this drawing open for the next portion of the exercise.

Zoom in around the areas with arcs. Notice that some of them follow very closely the desired layout, while others are off by a huge margin from what the planner envisioned as design parameters for those arcs. That's okay—you will fix them in a later exercise.

The alignment you just made is one of the most basic. Let's create additional alignments and use a few of the other tools to complete your initial layout. In this exercise, you will build the alignment at the center of the site that will access the cul-de-sac area, but this time you will use a floating curve to ensure the two segments you will be creating maintain their relationship.

DESIGN AND THEN REFINE

It bears repeating that when creating Civil 3D objects, it is good practice to get something in place and *then* refine it. With Land Desktop or other packages, you didn't want to define the object until it was fully designed. In Civil 3D, you define the object in a preliminary state and then refine your design.

---

11. From the Home tab ➢ Create Design panel, choose Alignment ➢ Alignment Creation Tools.

The Create Alignment – Layout dialog appears.

12. In the Create Alignment – Layout dialog, do the following:

    a. Change the Name field to **ROAD G**.

    b. Set the Alignment Style field to Proposed.

    c. Set the Alignment Label Set field to Major And Minor Only.

13. Click OK to display the Alignment Layout Tools toolbar for ROAD G.

14. Select the Fixed Line (Two Points) tool, as shown in Figure 6.11.

FIGURE 6.11
The Fixed Line (Two Points) tool

15. At the Specify start point: prompt, using Endpoint Osnap, select the north endpoint of the polyline, and working north to south, draw the first fixed-line segment to the south end of the segment.

When you've finished, the command line will read Specify start point: in case you want to draw another line. You can either press ↵ to end the command or draw the next entity without ending the command.

16. Click the down arrow next to the Add Fixed Curve (Three Point) tool on the toolbar and select More Floating Curves ➢ Floating Curve (From Entity End, Through Point), as shown in Figure 6.12.

FIGURE 6.12
Selecting the Floating Curve tool

17. At the Select entity to attach to: prompt, select the fixed-line segment you drew in steps 14 and 15.

Make sure you select the line segment somewhere south of the segment's midpoint to connect to the southern endpoint instead of the northern endpoint. If you cannot select the alignment segment, enable Selection Cycling (Ctrl+W).

18. At the Specify Pass Through Point: prompt, pick the endpoint between the two arcs (the point of compound curvature).

Notice that you are generating the segments from low station to high station. If you perform these steps backward, you can reverse a segment using the Reverse Sub-Entity Direction button on the Alignment Layout Tools toolbar.

19. Use the same command to draw the last arc segment, using the previous alignment arc segment as your entity to attach and the end of the polyline as the through point.

20. Press ↵ to end the command.

21. Close the Alignment Layout Tools toolbar.

22. Pick the ROAD G alignment and then pick the grip on the lower end of the line and pull it away from its location.

Notice that the line and the arcs are in sync and tangency is maintained (see Figure 6.13).

FIGURE 6.13
Floating curves maintain their tangency.

23. Press Esc to cancel the grip edit.

When this exercise is complete, you can close the drawing. A finished copy of this drawing is available from the book's web page with the filename 0602_AlignmentByLayout_FINISHED.dwg (0602_AlignmentByLayout_METRIC_FINISHED.dwg).

ALL ABOARD! RAIL ALIGNMENTS

Rail alignments were introduced in Civil 3D 2013 to allow for the differences between rail design and other types of design. For example, railways are characterized by long sweeping curves, and the curve geometry is expressed differently on railway construction plans. Rail design also has its own type of superelevation called *cant*, which is handled differently than road superelevation. These differences are accounted for when you use rail alignments in Civil 3D. Let's look at a quick, simple example:

1. Start a new blank drawing from the `_AutoCAD Civil 3D (Imperial)` NCS template that ships with Civil 3D. Metric users should use the `_AutoCAD Civil 3D (Metric)` NCS template.

2. From the Home tab ➢ Create Design panel, choose the Alignment section ➢ Alignment Creation Tools option.

   The Create Alignment – Layout dialog appears.

3. Change the name to **Mastering Railway** and set Type to Rail.

4. On the General tab, make these changes:
   - ◆ Set Alignment Style to Proposed.
   - ◆ Set Alignment Label Set to All Labels.

5. Switch to the Design Criteria tab.

6. Change the starting design speed to **30** mi/hr (or **50** km/hr for metric users).

7. Select the Use Criteria-Based Design check box.

   If the design criteria file doesn't default to the one that references railway design standards, you may need to click the ellipsis next to the design criteria file, which by default shows `_Autodesk Civil 3D Imperial Rail Cant Design Standards.xml` or `_Autodesk Civil 3D Metric Rail Cant Design Standards.xml` available to select and use.

8. Verify that Use Design Criteria File and Use Design Check Set are also checked.

9. Click OK.

   The Alignment Layout Tools toolbar appears.

10. Select the Fixed Line (Two Points) tool.

11. Click anywhere on the screen to define the start point, and define the second point by entering **@330,0** on the command line (or **@100,0** for metric users).

12. Press ↵ to end the command.

13. From the More Floating Curves branch, select Floating Curve (From Entity End, Radius, Length).

14. At the `Select entity to attach to:` prompt, select the right side of the line segment that you just drew.

15. At the `Specify curve direction [Clockwise cOunterclockwise] <Clockwise>:` prompt, press ↵ to accept the default, Clockwise.

16. At the `Specify radius or [Degree of curvature]:` prompt, enter **D** ↵ to switch to entering the radius by degree of curvature.

17. At the `Specify degree of curvature or [Radius]:` prompt, enter **3** ↵.

18. At the `Specify curve length or [deltaAngle Tanlen Chordlen midOrd External]:` prompt, enter **C** ↵ to define by chord length.

19. At the `Specify chord length or [curveLen deltaAngle Tanlen midOrd External]:` prompt, enter **100** ↵.

20. Press ↵ to end the command. Click the X on the corner to close the Alignment Layout Tools toolbar.

    Note that this will result in a different curve for Imperial and metric users.

When this exercise is complete, you can close the drawing. A saved finished copy of this drawing is available from the book's web page with the filename `0603_RailAlignment_FINISHED.dwg` (`0603_RailAlignment_METRIC_FINISHED.dwg`).

Best-Fit Alignments

Often designers have to re-create an alignment for an existing road that does not have defined horizontal geometry. Civil 3D has multiple tools to re-create the alignment using a best-fit algorithm. You can either re-create a full best-fit alignment or use best-fit lines or best-fit curves in an alignment. You will look at both methods to achieve this within the following section.

The Create Best Fit Alignment command can use AutoCAD blocks, AutoCAD entities, AutoCAD points, Civil 3D COGO points, or Civil 3D feature lines. You can also pick points by simply clicking the screen. The Line and Curve drop-down menus on the Alignment Layout toolbar include options for Floating and Fixed Lines By Best Fit as well as Best Fit curves in all three flavors: Fixed, Float, and Free. It is similar to what was covered in Chapter 1, "The Basics," in the section "Best-Fit Entities." Let's see how it works with alignments:

1. Open the 0604_AlignmentBestFit.dwg (0604_AlignmentBestFit_METRIC.dwg) file, which you can download from this book's web page.

2. From the Home tab ➤ Create Design panel, choose the Alignment section ➤ Alignment Creation Tools option.

   The Create Alignment – Layout dialog appears.

3. Enter **Best Fit Lines** in the Name field.

4. Leave the rest at their defaults and click OK.

   The Alignment Layout Tools toolbar opens.

5. Click the down arrow next to the Fixed Line (Two Points) tool on the toolbar and select the Fixed Line – Best Fit option.

   The Tangent By Best Fit dialog opens (Figure 6.14).

FIGURE 6.14
The Tangent By Best Fit dialog

Here, you can choose various methods to create a best-fit line alignment:

◆ From COGO Points

◆ From Entities

◆ From AutoCAD Points

◆ By Clicking On The Screen

6. Pick the From COGO Points radio button and click OK.

   At the Select Point objects or [Numbers Groups]: prompt, select points 1–11 using a combination of selection on the screen and transparent commands.

7. On point selection, select manually points 1 to 6.

8. When it comes to select the point 7, at the command line enter the transparent command for point number: **'pn** ↵. In the point number selection, enter **7-11** ↵. Press the Esc key once to exit transparent mode.

As you continue defining the tangent, you will see a red dashed line being formed. In your selections, this line looks at all the endpoints selected in order to create the best-fit line alignment segment (Figure 6.15).

FIGURE 6.15
The best-fit line
being formed

9. Press ↵ to open the Regression Data tab of the Panorama window shown in Figure 6.16.

FIGURE 6.16
Regression
Data tab of the
Panorama
window

On the Regression Data tab of the Panorama window, you can choose to exclude end-points or force them to be pass-through endpoints by checking the appropriate boxes.

As you check and uncheck boxes in the Regression Data chart, notice the changes that occur on your best-fit line alignment.

10. For this exercise you will try to make sure that the line will pass through point 1 and exclude point 6. Therefore, put a check mark in the Pass Through check box for point 1 and one in the Exclude check box for point 6, as shown in Figure 6.16.

11. Click the green check mark on the upper-right side of Panorama to accept the selection and dismiss the Panorama window.

You will notice that the line is drawn temporarily until you click the green check mark and exit the Panorama window or if you are still in the Panorama window, when you click the Save button.

12. Without exiting the Alignment Layout Tools toolbar, you will build a best-fit floating curve using the remainder of COGO points. Expand the curve creation tools and select the Floating Curve – Best Fit option, as shown in Figure 6.17.

FIGURE 6.17
The Floating Curve – Best Fit option

13. At the Select entity to attach to: prompt, select the previously defined segment close to the right end.

The Curve By Best Fit dialog appears.

14. Select the From COGO Points option and click OK.

15. At the Select point objects or [Number Groups]: prompt, enter **G** and press ↵ to select a point group.

The Point Groups Selection dialog will appear.

16. Select the Curve Point Group and click OK. You will notice the curve being created and the Regression Data tab appearing again, this time for the curve (see Figure 6.18).

FIGURE 6.18
The floating curve temporary layout and Regression Data tab of the Panorama window

17. Click the green check mark to finish the creation of the curve and click the X on the toolbar to exit the creation of the alignment workflow.

The best-fit line alignment is complete.

Keep this drawing open for the next portion of the exercise.

One of the benefits of doing individual best-fit segments (lines or curves) is that it is easy to exclude points. However, sometimes you will want a single "rough and dirty" alignment full of curves and lines without having to define them individually. Next, you will create a full best-fit alignment.

For the creation of the full best-fit alignment, you will use the same COGO points that you used for the first part of the exercise. You will do this in order to compare the results of both methods. If you create segments using best-fit line or best-fit curve, for example, you can use the Edit Best Fit Data For All Entries tool to edit these segments after they are created.

18. From the Home tab ➤ Create Design panel, choose the Alignment section ➤ Create Best Fit Alignment.

The Create Best Fit Alignment dialog appears.

19. Set the input type to COGO Points; on the drop-down list of Path 1 Point Group, select the _All Points point group.

20. Deselect the Create Spirals check box.

21. Change Alignment Name to **Best Fit Alignment**.

22. Verify that Alignment Style is set to Layout, Alignment Label Set is set to _No Labels, and the Show Report box is checked, as shown in Figure 6.19. Then click OK to accept all the other defaults.

FIGURE 6.19
The Create Best Fit Alignment dialog

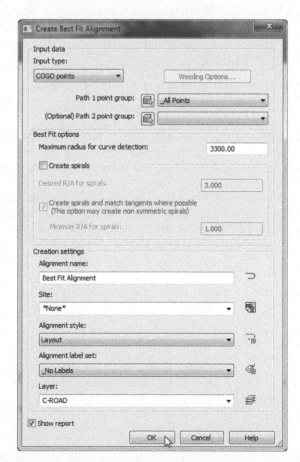

The Best Fit Report dialog opens, as shown in Figure 6.20.

FIGURE 6.20
The Best Fit Report
dialog

Pt No.	Point Northing	Point Easting	Offset to Entity	Northing on Entity	Easting on Entity
0	0.0000	0.0000	0.17	0.1708	-0.0016
1	35.0000	100.0000	-33.90	1.0967	100.3129
2	-35.0000	200.0000	37.02	2.0137	199.6584
3	35.0000	300.0000	-32.06	2.9426	300.2959
4	-55.0000	400.0000	58.86	3.8578	399.4567
5	55.0000	500.0000	-50.21	4.7901	500.4634
6	-65.0000	600.0000	70.71	5.7028	599.3474
7	65.0000	700.0000	-58.37	6.6368	700.5387
8	-35.0000	800.0000	42.55	7.5512	799.6073
9	35.0000	900.0000	-26.52	8.4801	900.2448
10	0.0000	1000.0000	9.40	9.4001	999.9132

Regression Graph:

Min. offset:	0.17	Max. offset:	70.71
Min. R:	634.95	Max. R:	634.95
Length:	1899.67	Overall average error:	35.82

Review the results in the Best Fit Report. Notice that if you select a row, it will highlight the location on the regression graph.

23. Click the close (X) button to dismiss the dialog.

Unlike the Regression Data tab in the Panorama window, the Best Fit Report is purely informational and does not allow you to select to exclude or pass through a specific point. While the Create Best Fit Alignment procedure is fast, it may not be precise. Therefore, this command may be useful for providing a draft alignment, and then you can manually create your final alignment using results similar to those shown in the Best Fit Report that meet your specific design criteria.

The completed best-fit alignment is shown together with the alignment made with the best-fit lines and curves in Figure 6.21. Although a best-fit alignment may not give you exactly what you are looking for (especially if you like nice, whole-number radii), it generates a good starting point that you can then edit to fit your design needs.

FIGURE 6.21
The best-fit
alignment

When this exercise is complete, you can close the drawing. A finished copy of this drawing is available from the book's web page with the filename 0604_AlignmentBestFit_FINISHED.dwg (0604_AlignmentBestFit_METRIC_FINISHED.dwg).

Reverse and Compound Curve Creation

Next, let's look at a more complicated alignment—building reverse and compound curves by connecting two curves:

1. Open the 0605_ReverseCompoundAlignment.dwg (0605_ReverseCompoundAlignment_METRIC.dwg) file.

2. For this exercise, confirm that your Endpoint Osnap is active using the Osnap settings since you will need to snap to endpoints for this exercise.

   Also, disable polar tracking.

3. From the Home tab ➤ Create Design panel, choose Alignment ➤ Alignment Creation Tools.

   The Create Alignment – Layout dialog appears.

4. In the Create Alignment – Layout dialog, do the following:

   a. Change the Name field to **Reverse-Compound**.

   b. Set the Alignment Style field to Layout.

   c. Set the Alignment Label Set field to Major Minor And Geometry Points.

5. Click OK to display the Alignment Layout Tools toolbar for the alignment.

6. Start by drawing a fixed line from the west endpoint heading east along the tangent to the place where this tangent meets the magenta arc, using the same Fixed Line (Two Points) tool as used in an earlier exercise. Do the same thing for the end tangent of the alignment, starting from the end of the cyan arc and finishing at the east endpoint of that tangent.

7. Press Enter to finish drawing the line segments.

   You will notice that the second segment will not have any labels applied to it, since it is not connected to the first segment created.

8. Use the Floating Curve (From Entity, Radius, Through Point) tool to connect a curve from the endpoint of the first drawn tangent.

9. At the Select entity to attach to: prompt, pick the right end of the west tangent. At the Specify radius or [Degree of curvature]: prompt, enter **200** ↵ (for metric, **60.96** ↵).

10. At the Is curve solution angle [Greaterthan180 Lessthan180] <Lessthan180>: prompt, press ↵ to accept the default.

11. At the Specify end point: prompt, click the other end of the arc, where the magenta arc meets the green arc.

12. The command repeats; at the Select entity to attach to: prompt, select the right side of the curve you just created.

13. At the Specify radius or [Degree of curvature]: prompt, enter **300** ↵ (for metric, **91.44** ↵).

14. At the Is curve solution angle [Greaterthan180 Lessthan180] <Lessthan180>: prompt, press ↵ to accept the default.

    The program detects that you are attaching a curve to a curve.

15. At the Is curve compound or reverse to curve before? [Compound Reverse] <Compound>: prompt, enter **R** ↵ to specify that it is a reverse curve.

16. At the Specify end point: prompt, click the endpoint of the second arc or the connecting point between the green and blue arcs.

17. The command repeats. Repeat steps 12–15, but enter **250** (for metric, **76.20**) for a radius and choose Compound as the type of curve.

18. At the Specify end point: prompt, click the endpoint of the third arc or the connecting point between the blue and cyan arcs.

19. Press ↵ to end the command. You should be able to see the stationing through all the arcs you created so far.

20. For the final arc you will a conversion tool. Use the Convert AutoCAD Line And Arc tool to define the last arc segment that connects the previously defined curve to the second tangent segment. Click the tool, select the arc, and press ↵.

    You will notice that upon the connection of the last arc to the segment, the missing labels will be added to the tangent since now it is connected to the main chain. You can see the final result of the layout in Figure 6.22.

FIGURE 6.22
Segment layout for the reverse and compound curve alignment

The alignment now contains a perfect series of reverse-compound-reverse curves. Move any of the pieces, and you'll see the other segments react to maintain the relationships shown in Figure 6.23. The flexibility of the Civil 3D tools allows you to explore an alternative solution (the reverse curve) as opposed to the basic solution. Flexibility is one of the strengths of Civil 3D.

FIGURE 6.23
Curve relationships during a grip edit

You've completed your initial reverse and compound curve layout. Unfortunately, the curve design may not be acceptable to the designer, but you'll look at those changes later in the section "Component-Level Editing."

When this exercise is complete, you can close the drawing. A finished copy of this drawing is available from the book's web page with the filename 0605_ReverseCompoundAlignment_FINISHED.dwg (0605_ReverseCompoundAlignment_METRIC_FINISHED.dwg).

Creating with Design Constraints and Check Sets

Civil 3D allows you to use design constraints and design check sets during the process of creating alignments and design profiles. Typically, these constraints check for things such as curve radius, length of tangents, and so on. Design constraints use information from AASHTO or other design manuals to set curve requirements. Check sets allow users to create their own criteria to match local requirements, such as subdivision or county road design. In this exercise, you'll make one quick set of design checks:

1. Open the 0606_AlignmentCheck.dwg (0606_AlignmentCheck_METRIC.dwg) file.

2. On the Settings tab in Toolspace, expand the Alignment ➤ Design Checks branch.

3. Right-click the Line category and select New to display the New Design Check dialog.

4. Change the name to **Subdivision Tangent**.

5. Click the Insert Property drop-down menu and select Length.

6. Click the greater-than/equals symbol (>=) button and then enter **100** (for metric, **30.48**) in the Expression field, as shown in Figure 6.24.

FIGURE 6.24
The completed
Subdivision Tangent
design check

When complete, your dialog should look like Figure 6.24.

7. Click OK to accept the settings in the dialog.

8. Right-click the Curve category and select New to display the New Design Check dialog.

9. Change the name to **Subdivision Radius**.

10. Click the Insert Property drop-down menu and select Radius.

11. Click the greater-than/equals symbol (>=) button and then enter **200** (for metric, **60.96**) in the Expression field, as shown in Figure 6.25.

FIGURE 6.25
The completed
Subdivision Radius
design check

12. Click OK to accept the settings in the dialog.

13. Right-click the `Design Check Sets` folder and select New to display the Alignment Design Check Set dialog.

14. On the Information tab, change the name to **Mastering Subdivision** and then switch to the Design Checks tab.

15. Choose Line from the Type drop-down list and select the Subdivision Tangent line check that you just created.

16. Click the Add button to add the Subdivision Tangent check to the set.

17. Choose Curve from the Type drop-down list and select the Subdivision Radius curve check that you just created.

18. Click the Add button again to complete the set, as shown in Figure 6.26.

FIGURE 6.26
The completed Mastering Subdivision design check set

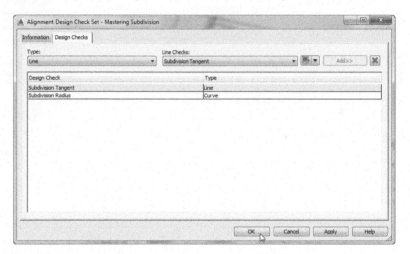

19. Click OK to accept the settings in the dialog.

You can keep this drawing open to continue to the next exercise or use the finished copy of this drawing available from the book's web page `0606_AlignmentCheck_FINISHED.dwg` (`0606_AlignmentCheck_METRIC_FINISHED.dwg`).

Once you've created a number of design checks and design check sets, you can apply them as needed during the design and layout stage of your projects.

DESIGN CHECKS VS. DESIGN CRITERIA

What's the difference between design checks and design criteria? A design check uses basic properties such as radius, length, grade, and so on, to check a particular portion of an alignment or profile. These constraints are generally dictated by a governing agency based on the type of road involved. Design criteria use speed and related values from design manuals such as AASHTO to establish these geometry constraints. Think of design criteria as a suite of check sets with different sets for each city, type of street, design speed, and so on.

In the next exercise, you'll see the results of your Mastering Subdivision check set in action:

1. If it's not still open from the previous exercise, open the `0606_AlignmentCheck_ FINISHED.dwg` (`0606_AlignmentCheck_METRIC_FINISHED.dwg`) file.

2. Change to the Prospector tab in Toolspace and expand the Alignments ➢ Centerline Alignments branches.

3. Right-click ROAD D and select Properties.

4. Change to the Design Criteria tab and set the start station design speed to **30 mi/h** (or metric, **48 km/h**), as shown in Figure 6.27.

FIGURE 6.27
Setting up
design checks
from Alignment
Properties

5. Verify that all of the check boxes are selected and that Use Design Check Set is set to Mastering Subdivision, as shown in Figure 6.27.

Note that the Use Criteria-Based Design check box must be selected to activate the other two.

6. Click OK to accept the settings in the dialog.

You could have alternatively set the design criteria when you were originally creating the alignment.

Notice that all the curves along the alignment fail to meet the design criteria.

If you hover your cursor over one of the exclamation-point symbols, as shown in Figure 6.28, it will indicate which design criteria and design checks have been violated. Make sure you have Show Rollover Tooltips enabled.

FIGURE 6.28
Completed alignment layout with design criteria and design checks failure indicator

When this exercise is complete, you can close the drawing. A finished copy of this drawing is available from the book's web page with the filename 0606_AlignmentChecked_FINISHED.dwg (0606_AlignmentChecked_METRIC_FINISHED.dwg).

Now that you've created an alignment that didn't pass the design checks, let's look at different ways of modifying alignment geometry. As you correct and fix alignments that violate the assigned design checks, the warning symbols indicating those violations will disappear.

Editing Alignment Geometry

The general power of Civil 3D lies in its flexibility in design. The documentation process is tied directly to the objects involved, so making edits to those objects doesn't create hours of work in updating the documentation. With alignments, there are three major ways to edit the object's horizontal geometry without modifying the underlying construction:

Graphical Grip Editing   Select the object and use the various grips to move critical points. This method works well for realignment, but precise editing for things such as a radius or direction can be difficult without the ability to enter values.

Tabular Design   Use Panorama to view all the alignment segments and their properties; type in values to make changes. This approach works well for modifying lengths or radius values, but setting a tangent perpendicular to a line in the drawing or placing a control point in a specific location is better done graphically.

Component-Level Editing   Use the Alignment Layout Parameters dialog to view the properties of an individual piece of the alignment. This method makes it easy to modify one piece of an alignment that is complicated and that consists of numerous segments, whereas picking the correct field in a Panorama view can be difficult.

In addition to these methods, you can use the Alignment Layout Tools toolbar to make edits that involve removing components or adding to the underlying component count. The following exercises look at the three simple edits and then explain how to add and remove components of an alignment without redefining it.

Grip Editing

You already used graphical editing techniques when you created alignments from polylines, but those techniques can also be used with considerably more precision than shown previously. The Alignment object has a number of grips that reveal important information about the elements' creation (see Figure 6.29).

FIGURE 6.29
Alignment grips

You can use the grips in Figure 6.29 to do the following actions:

Grip 1 The square pass-through grip at the beginning of the alignment indicates a segment point that can be moved at will to change the length and angle of the line. This grip doesn't attach to any other components.

Grip 2 The square pass-through grip in the middle of the tangents allows the element to be moved while maintaining the length and angle. Other components attempt to hold their respective relationships, but moving the grip to a location that would break the alignment will not be allowed by the software. The change will be limited to the point where the break would occur.

Grip 3 The triangular grip at the intersection of tangents indicates a Point of Intersection (PI) relationship. The curve shown is a function of these two tangents and is free to move on the basis of incoming and outgoing tangents while still holding a radius.

Grip 4 The triangular and circular radius grips near the middle of the curve allow the user to modify the radius directly. The tangents must be maintained, so any selection that would break the alignment geometry isn't allowed.

Grip 5 The circular pass-through grip on the end of the curve allows the radius of the curve to be indirectly changed by changing the Point of Curvature (PC) of the alignment. You make this change by changing the curve length, which in effect changes the radius.

In the following exercise, you'll use grip edits to make one of your alignments match the planner's intent more closely:

1. Open the `0607_AlignmentEditing.dwg` (`0607_AlignmentEditing_METRIC.dwg`) file.

2. In Prospector, expand the Alignments ➤ Centerline Alignments branch.

3. Right-click ROAD D and select Zoom To if the alignment is not within view.

4. Zoom in to the first curve of the ROAD D alignment, near station 10+00 (0+300 for metric users).

   This curve was inserted in a previous exercise using the default settings and doesn't match the guiding polyline well. If the warning symbol is in the way after zooming in, please use the regen command to update the size of the warning symbol.

5. Select the ROAD D alignment to activate the grips.

6. Select the triangular grip shown in Figure 6.30 and use a Midpoint Osnap to place it on the original polyline arc outline.

   When the triangular grip is used, the radius is changed without changing the PI.

FIGURE 6.30
Grip-editing the
ROAD D curve

Keep this drawing open for the next exercise.

Your alignment of ROAD D now follows the planned layout. With no knowledge of the curve properties or other driving information, you've quickly reproduced the design's intent.

Tabular Design

When you're designing to meet jurisdictional standards, one of the most important elements is meeting curve radius requirements. It's easy to work along an alignment in a tabular view, verifying that the design meets the criteria. In this exercise, you'll verify that your curves are suitable for the design:

1. Continuing in the drawing from the previous exercise, zoom to the ROAD D alignment and select it to activate the Alignment contextual tab.

2. From the Alignment contextual tab ➤ Modify panel, choose Geometry Editor.

   You can also access the same location by selecting the alignment, right-clicking, and from the context menu selecting the Edit Alignment Geometry option.

   The Alignment Layout Tools toolbar opens.

3. Select the Alignment Grid View tool.

   Panorama appears as shown in Figure 6.31, with all the elements of the alignment listed along the left. You can click into many of the fields to modify their values. You can use the scroll bar along the bottom to review the properties of the alignment if necessary. Note that the columns can be resized, as well as toggled off, by right-clicking the column headers. The segment selected in the alignment grid view is also highlighted in the model, which can also make identifying the segment easier. Note that the design check failure indicators that are shown on the plan also appear in the table.

FIGURE 6.31
Alignment Entities
vista for ROAD D
alignment

CREATING AND SAVING CUSTOM PANORAMA VIEWS

If you right-click a column heading in Panorama and select the Customize Columns option at the bottom of the menu, you're presented with a Customize Columns dialog. This dialog allows you to set up any number of column views, such as Road Design or Stakeout, to show a set of different columns. These views can be saved, allowing you to switch between views easily.

---

4. Change the radius value of segment 4 to **400** (or **121.92** for metric users).

5. Click the close X button (notice that in the Panorama window, there is no green check mark to accept the changes) to dismiss Panorama and then close the Alignment Layout Tools toolbar.

   Keep this drawing open for the next exercise.

Panorama allows for quick and easy review of designs and for precise data entry, if required. Grip editing is commonly used to place the line and curve of an alignment in an approximate working location, but then you use the tabular view in Panorama to make the values more reasonable—for example, to change a radius of 292.56 to 300.00. Also note that for this part of the exercise, when you changed the radius, the violation for the design checks were cleared for the curve, providing feedback that you meet design requirements.

Component-Level Editing

Once an alignment gets more complicated, the tabular view in Panorama can be hard to navigate, and deciphering which element is which can be difficult. In this case, reviewing individual elements by picking them onscreen can be easier:

1. Continuing in the drawing from the previous exercise, zoom to the ROAD D alignment and select it to activate the contextual Alignment tab if not still active from the previous exercise.

2. If the Alignment Layout Tools toolbar for ROAD D is not still open from the previous exercise, from the Alignment contextual tab ➤ Modify panel, choose Geometry Editor.

3. Select the Sub-Entity Editor tool to open the Alignment Layout Parameters dialog for ROAD D.

   The Alignment Layout Parameters dialog opens. The dialog contents will be blank.

   Each line, arc, or spiral member of the alignment is referred to as a *subentity*. The Sub-Entity Editor allows you to select any segment member and edit its properties in the Alignment Layout Parameters dialog.

4. Select the Pick Sub-Entity tool on the Alignment Layout Tools toolbar.

5. Pick the curve that begins near station 16+00 on this alignment to display its properties in the Alignment Layout Parameters dialog (see Figure 6.32).

FIGURE 6.32
The Alignment Layout Parameters dialog for the last curve on the ROAD D alignment

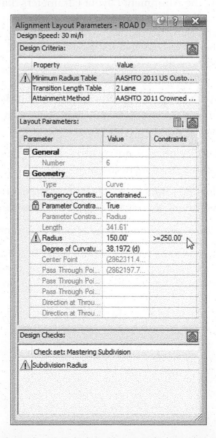

Notice that the Tangency Constraint value currently reports Constrained On Both Sides (Free).

6. Change Parameter Constraint Lock to **False**.

Notice that this will enable the ability to set many of the values that previously were grayed out and could not be set.

7. Change Parameter Constraint Lock to the original status. Change the value in the Radius field to **175** (for metric, **53.34**) and watch the screen see the geometry update.

This value is too far from the original design intent to be a valid alternative. You will reinvestigate the tangency constraints in the next exercise.

8. Change the value in the Radius field to **200** (for metric, **60.96**) and again watch the update.

This value is closer to the design and is acceptable despite being less than the minimum radius for the 30 mi/hr design speed.

9. Close the Alignment Layout Parameters dialog and the Alignment Layout Tools toolbar.

Notice that the stationing updates.

You may keep this drawing open to continue to the next exercise or use the finished copy of this drawing available from the book's web page, `0607_AlignmentEditing_FINISHED.dwg` (`0607_AlignmentEditing_METRIC_FINISHED.dwg`).

By using the Alignment Layout Parameters dialog, you can concisely review all the individual parameters of a component. In each of the editing methods discussed so far, you've modified the elements that were already in place. You will look at how to change the makeup of the alignment itself, not just the values driving it. But first, let's look at some of the constraints to understand how they work.

Understanding Alignment Constraints

In the previous exercise, you were exposed to constraints. The various constraints will help keep geometry together to maintain tangency or to maintain a radius.

◆ A fixed segment is not constrained to its adjoining segments, so it does not maintain tangency to segments on either side.

◆ A floating segment maintains tangency at one of its endpoints, but the other end is not constrained; therefore, tangency will not be maintained at the unconstrained end.

◆ A free entity is constrained at both endpoints, thus maintaining tangency at both ends.

You may have noticed in Panorama the Tangency Constraint field that you looked at briefly in the previous exercise. You can click any segment and change the constraints (Figure 6.33). You can also change the constraints in the Sub-Entity Editor.

FIGURE 6.33
The tangency
constraints in
Panorama

In this exercise, you will experiment with constraints and their effect on the behavior of an alignment:

1. If your file is not still open from the previous exercise, open the 0607_AlignmentEditing_FINISHED.dwg (0607_AlignmentEditing_METRIC_FINISHED.dwg) file.

2. Select the ROAD D alignment to activate the Alignment contextual tab.

3. From the Alignment contextual tab ➤ Modify panel, choose Geometry Editor.

4. In the Alignment Layout Tools toolbar, select Alignment Grid View.

5. Click in the Tangency Constraint field for the third curve and change it to Not Constrained (Fixed).

    Notice that when you change the third curve from Constrained On Both Sides (Free) to Not Constrained (Fixed), the segment before the curve changes from Not Constrained (Fixed) to Constrained By Next (Floating).

6. Click the alignment to grip-edit the curve using the circular grip on the midpoint of the curve.

    Notice how the curve radius increases to account for the change (Figure 6.34). Also notice that the tangents are also changing to account for the change.

FIGURE 6.34
Gripping an alignment with the tangent before the curve set to Constrained By Next (Floating) and the curve set to Not Constrained (Fixed)

You may need to move Panorama out of the way to do this, but don't close it yet.

7. Press Esc on your keyboard to cancel the grip edit. If you inadvertently moved the curve, you can use the Undo command.

8. In Panorama, click in the Tangency Constraint field for the same curve and change it to Constrained By Previous (Floating).

   The line before the curve segment will change back to Not Constrained (Fixed).

9. Click the alignment to grip-edit the curve again using the same midpoint grip.

   Notice how the curve changes its radius but the first line maintains its bearing, while the following segment since it is floating adjusts to the new radius (Figure 6.35).

FIGURE 6.35
Gripping an alignment with the tangent before the curve set to Not Constrained (Fixed) and the curve using Constrained By Previous (Floating)

10. Press Esc on your keyboard to cancel the grip edit. If you inadvertently moved the curve, you can use the Undo command.

11. Click in the Tangency Constraint field for the same curve and change it to Constrained By Next (Floating).

    The lines before it and after it will change to Not Constrained (Fixed).

12. Click the alignment to grip-edit the curve using the midpoint grip.

    Notice that the curve now maintains its tangency with the following line but not the previous line (Figure 6.36).

FIGURE 6.36
Gripping an alignment with the curve set to Constrained By Next (Floating) and the following line set to Not Constrained (Fixed)

13. Press Esc on your keyboard to cancel the grip-edit action. If you inadvertently moved the curve, you can use the Undo command.

14. Click in the Tangency Constraint field for the third curve of the alignment and change it to Constrained On Both Sides (Free).

15. Grip-edit the curve using the same midpoint grip. See that the curve maintains its tangency with both the previous and following lines (see Figure 6.37).

FIGURE 6.37
Gripping an alignment with the third curve on the alignment set to Constrained On Both Sides (Free) with both adjoining lines set to Not Constrained (Fixed)

16. Press Esc on your keyboard to cancel the grip edit. If you inadvertently moved the curve, you can use the Undo command.

17. Close the Alignment Layout Tools toolbar.

When you access the Alignment Properties dialog representing an alignment containing curves, some additional options become available that were not available when the alignment was originally created. In the Point Of Intersection tab, you can select whether you want to visually show points of intersection by a change in alignment direction or by individual curves and curve groups. You can also choose to not display any implied points of intersection (see Figure 6.38).

FIGURE 6.38
The Point Of Intersection tab

In the Constraint Editing tab, you can select if you want to always perform any implied tangency constraint swapping and whether to lock all parameter constraints (Figure 6.39).

FIGURE 6.39
The Constraint
Editing tab

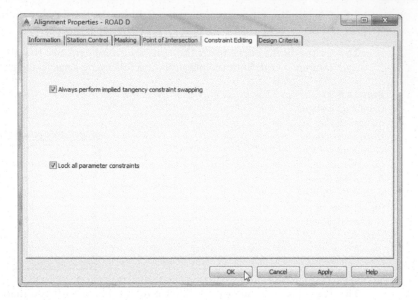

Changing Alignment Components

One of the most common changes is adding a curve where there was none before or changing the makeup of the curves and tangents already in place on an alignment. Other design changes can include swapping out curves for tangents or adding a second curve to smooth a transition area.

As it turns out, your perfect reverse curve isn't allowed by the current ordinances for subdivision design! In this example, you'll go back to the design and place a minimum-length tangent between the curves:

1. Open the 0608_AlignmentComponents.dwg (0608_AlignmentComponents_METRIC .dwg) file.

2. Select the alignment named Reverse-Compound to activate the Alignment contextual tab.

3. From the Alignment contextual tab ➢ Modify panel, choose Geometry Editor.

   The Alignment Layout Tools toolbar appears.

4. Select the Delete Sub-Entity tool.

5. When prompted to select a subentity, pick the curve (C2) along alignment to remove it and press ↵ to end the command.

   Note that even if the last two curves and tangents are still part of the alignment, they lost the connection to the first part of the alignment.

6. Select the Floating Line (From Curve End, Length) option.

7. At the `Select Entity to Attach to:` prompt, click the south end of curve 3 and then specify a length of **100** ↵ (for metric, **30.48** ↵).

8. Select the Free Curve Fillet (Between Two Entities, Through Point) option.

9. Select the first curve (C1) segment to the west and then the line just drawn.

10. For the through point, use an Endpoint Osnap to select the free end of the tangent line just drawn and press ↵ to end the command. Notice how the stationing is now shown the full length of the completed alignment.

11. Close the Alignment Layout Tools toolbar.

Your reverse curve with tangent section is complete, as shown in Figure 6.40.

FIGURE 6.40
Reverse curve with tangent segment

When this exercise is complete, you can close the drawing. A finished copy of this drawing is available from the book's web page with the filename `0608_AlignmentComponents_FINISHED .dwg` (`0608_AlignmentComponents_METRIC_FINISHED.dwg`).

So far in this chapter, you've created and modified the horizontal alignments, adjusted them onscreen according to the planners initial layout, and tweaked the design using a number of different methods. Now let's look beyond the lines and arcs and get into the design properties of the alignment.

Alignments as Objects

Alignments can represent things such as highways. Such items have design properties that help define them, and many of these design properties can be built into your Alignment properties. In addition to obvious properties such as names and descriptions, you can include functionality such as superelevation, station equations, reference points, and station control. The following sections will look at other properties that can be associated with an alignment and how to edit them.

Alignment Properties

While the properties of the alignment were originally assigned during creation, later in design there are often changes that are required. In this exercise, you'll learn an easy way to change the object style and how to add a description.

Most of an alignment's basic properties can be modified in Prospector. In this exercise, you'll change the name in a couple of ways:

1. Open the `0609_AlignmentProperties.dwg` (`0609_AlignmentProperties_METRIC.dwg`) file and make sure Toolspace is open.

2. In Prospector, expand the Alignments ➢ Centerline Alignments branch.

   Notice that a series of alignments are listed as members.

3. Select the Centerline Alignments branch, and the individual alignments appear in the Item View (see Figure 6.41).

FIGURE 6.41
The Alignments branch listed in the Item View of Prospector

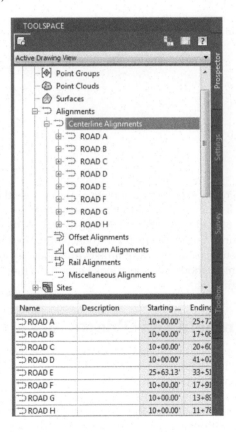

Name	Description	Starting ...	Ending
ROAD A		10+00.00'	25+7:
ROAD B		10+00.00'	17+08
ROAD C		10+00.00'	20+6(
ROAD D		10+00.00'	41+0:
ROAD E		25+63.13'	33+5|
ROAD F		10+00.00'	17+9|
ROAD G		10+00.00'	13+8!
ROAD H		10+00.00'	11+7!

4. Down in the Item View, click in the Name field for ROAD A and pause briefly before clicking again.

   The text highlights for editing.

5. Click in the Description field for ROAD A and enter a description (such as **West-East**). Press ↵.

6. Click in the Style field for ROAD A (you may have to scroll left/right to find the Style field), pause briefly, and click again; the Select Label Style dialog appears.

7. Select Basic from the drop-down menu and click OK.

   The screen updates. Keep this drawing open for the next portion of the exercise.

   That's one method to change Alignment properties. The next is to use the Properties palette.

8. Open the Properties palette by using the Ctrl+1 keyboard shortcut or some other method.

9. Select the ROAD B alignment in the drawing using the Prospector's Select option that is available when you right-click the object's name.

   The Properties palette looks like Figure 6.42.

FIGURE 6.42
ROAD B in the
Properties palette

10. Click in the Description field, and the Description dialog will open. Enter a description (such as **North-South Leg**) and click OK, as shown in Figure 6.42.

11. Press Esc on your keyboard to deselect all objects and close the Properties palette if you'd like.

    Keep this drawing open for the next portion of the exercise.

The final method involves getting into the Alignment Properties dialog, which is your access point to information beyond the basics.

12. In Prospector, right-click ROAD H and select Properties. This is the alignment for the south cul-de-sac.

The Alignment Properties dialog for ROAD H opens.

13. Change to the Information tab if it isn't selected.

14. Enter a description in the Description field (such as **South Cul-De-Sac**).

15. Set Object Style to Existing.

16. Click the Apply button.

Notice that the display style in the drawing updates immediately.

17. Click OK to accept the settings in the dialog.

Keep this drawing open for the next portion of the exercise.

Now that you've updated your alignments, you can make them all the same style for ease of viewing. The best way to do this is in the Prospector Item view.

18. In Prospector, expand the Alignments ➢ Centerline Alignments branch.

19. Select one of the alignments in the Item View.

20. Press Ctrl+A to select them all, or pick the top and then Shift+click the bottom item.

The idea is to pick *all* of the alignments.

21. Right-click the Style column header and select Edit (see Figure 6.43).

FIGURE 6.43
Editing alignment
styles en masse via
Prospector

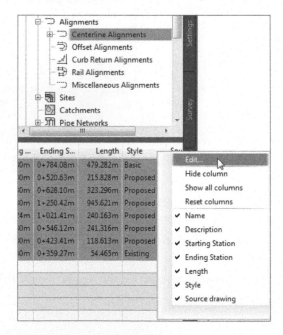

22. Select Layout from the drop-down list in the Select Label Style dialog that appears and click OK.

23. Press Esc to deselect all of the alignments.

Notice that all alignments pick up this style. Although the dialog is named Edit Label Style, you are actually assigning styles to the objects.

DON'T FORGET THIS TECHNIQUE

This technique of selecting all, right-clicking the column heading, selecting Edit, and modifying the value works on every object that displays in the Toolspace Item View, including parcels, pipes, corridors, assemblies, and so on. It can be painfully tedious to change a large number of objects from one style to another using any other method. If you left-click the column header instead of right-click, the alignments will sort alphabetically based on the values in that column.

You can save the drawing and if needed compare your results against the finished file that can be downloaded from the book's web page under the filename `0609_AlignmentProperties_FINISHED.dwg` (`0609_AlignmentProperties_METRIC_FINISHED.dwg`).

Let's look at some other properties you can modify and update.

The Right Station

Every alignment has stationing applied to help locate design geometry points. This stationing may start at zero or may start at a predefined value based on previous construction. Stationing can also be fixed in both directions, requiring station equations that help translate between two disparate points that are the basis for the stationing in the drawing.

Sometimes alignments can be drawn initially in the wrong direction. Thankfully, Civil 3D has a command to fix that:

1. Open the `0610_AlignmentStations.dwg` (`0610_AlignmentStations_METRIC.dwg`) file and make sure Toolspace is open.

2. Since the ROAD D alignment does not have the alignment labels running from north to south, you will want to reverse its direction, so pick it to activate the Alignment contextual tab.

3. From the Alignment contextual tab ➤ Modify drop-down panel, choose Reverse Direction.

A warning dialog appears, reminding you of the consequences of such a change.

4. Click OK to dismiss the warning dialog.

The stationing reverses, with 10+00 (or 0+304.80 for metric users) now at the north end-point of the alignment.

The warning message lets you know that when the direction is reversed, things happen to the settings defined for the alignment. Take note of what can change when an alignment is reversed. For example, if you had masking applied to the alignment, you would need to redefine it.

5. Press Esc to deselect the alignment.

Keep this drawing open for the next portion of the exercise.

This technique allows you to reverse an alignment almost instantly. The warning that appears is critical, though! When an alignment is reversed, the information that was derived from its original direction may not translate correctly, if at all. One prime example of this would be design profiles: they don't reverse themselves when the alignment is reversed, and this can lead to serious design issues if you aren't paying attention.

Beyond reversing, it's common for alignments to not start with zero. For example, the ROAD E alignment may be a continuation of an existing street, and it makes sense to make the starting station for this alignment the station where this alignment intersects ROAD A, the alignment from the existing street. In this next portion of the exercise, you'll set the beginning station.

6. Select the ROAD E alignment to activate the Alignment contextual tab.

7. From the Alignment contextual tab ➤ Modify panel, choose Alignment Properties icon.

8. Switch to the Station Control tab of the Alignment Properties dialog.

This tab controls the base stationing and lets you create station equations.

9. In the Reference Point section of the dialog, enter **2563.13** (for metric, **781.24**) in the Station field (see Figure 6.44).

FIGURE 6.44
Setting a new
starting station
on the ROAD E
alignment

10. Click OK to dismiss the warning message that appears and click OK to dismiss the dialog.

11. Press Esc to deselect the alignment.

The Station Information section in the top right will update. These options can't be edited but provide a convenient way for you to review the alignment's Length and Station values.

Keep this drawing open for the next portion of the exercise.

In addition to changing the value for the start of the alignment, you could use the Pick Reference Point button, as shown in Figure 6.44, to select another point as the stationing reference point.

Station equations can occur multiple times along an alignment. They typically come into play when plans must match existing conditions or when the stationing has to match other plans, but the lengths in the new alignment would make that impossible without some translation. In this last portion of the exercise, you'll add a station equation on ROAD C at the intersection with ROAD B.

12. Select the ROAD C alignment to activate the Alignment contextual tab.

13. From the Alignment contextual tab ➤ Modify panel, choose the Alignment Properties icon.

14. On the Station Control tab of the Alignment Properties dialog, click the Add Station Equation button. You will get a warning notification. Click OK to go to the next step.

15. Use an Endpoint Osnap to select the intersection of the two alignments.

16. Change the Station Ahead value to **1000** (for metric, **304.8**). You will get a warning notification. Click OK to go to the next step.

17. Click the Apply button and notice the change in the Station Information section, as shown in Figure 6.45.

FIGURE 6.45
ROAD C station
equation in place

18. Click OK to accept the settings in the dialog and review the stationing that has been applied to the alignment.

You can save the drawing and if needed compare your results against the finished file that can be downloaded from the book's web page under the filename 0610_AlignmentStations_ FINISHED.dwg (0610_AlignmentStations_METRIC_FINISHED.dwg).

Stationing constantly changes as alignments are modified during the initial stages of a development or as late design changes are applied to the plans. With the flexibility shown here, you can reduce the time you spend dealing with minor changes that seem to ripple across an entire project.

Assigning Design Speeds

One driving part of transportation design is the design speed. Civil 3D considers the design speed a property of the alignment, and it can be used in labels or calculations as needed. In this exercise, you'll add a series of design speeds to ROAD D. Later in the chapter, you'll label these sections of the road using a label set:

1. Open the 0611_AlignmentDesignSpeed.dwg (0611_AlignmentDesignSpeed_METRIC .dwg) file.

2. Bring up the Alignment Properties dialog for ROAD D.

3. Switch to the Design Criteria tab.

4. Verify that the Design Speed field for Number 1 is 30 mi/hr (or 48 km/hr for metric users).

This speed is typical for a subdivision street.

5. Click the Add Design Speed button.

6. Click to select row 2 and then click in the Start Station.

A small Pick On Screen button appears to the right of the Start Station value, as shown in Figure 6.46.

FIGURE 6.46
Setting the design speed for a Start Station field

7. Click the Pick On Screen button and then use an Osnap to pick the PC on the west portion of the site, near station 9+65.78 (or station 0+294.37 for metric users).

8. Enter a value of **20** (for metric, **32**) in the Design Speed field for the line you just added.

9. Click the Add Design Speed button again.

Notice that the additional row is added to the top of the list.

10. Select the new row. Then click in the Start Station field for the new row and enter **2050** ↵ (for metric, **620.10** ↵).

Notice that the rows reorder according to the station values in the Start Station column.

11. Enter a value of **30** (for metric, **48**) for this design speed.

When complete, the tab should look like Figure 6.47.

FIGURE 6.47
The design speeds assigned to ROAD D alignment with both U.S. (top) and metric (bottom) values

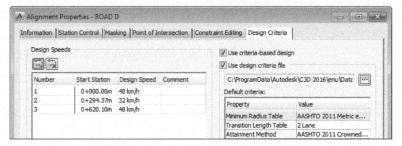

12. Click OK to accept the settings in the Alignment Properties dialog.

You can save the drawing and if needed compare your results against the finished file that can be downloaded from the book's web page under the filename 0611_AlignmentDesignSpeed_FINISHED.dwg (0611_AlignmentDesignSpeed_METRIC_FINISHED.dwg).

In a subdivision, these values can be inserted for labeling purposes. In a highway design, they can be used to drive the superelevation calculations that are critical to a working design. Chapter 11, "Superelevation," looks at this subject.

Labeling Alignments

Labeling in Civil 3D is one of the program's strengths, but it's also an easy place to get lost. There are many options for different labeling situations, and keeping them straight can be difficult.

THE POWER OF LABEL SETS

When you think about it, any number of items can be labeled on an alignment. These include major and minor stations, geometry points, design speeds, and profile information. Each of these objects will have its own style. Applying all of these individual labeling styles one after the other would be tedious, so Civil 3D has provided you with *label sets*.

A label set can contain many different types of alignment labels. These sets are available during the creation and labeling process, making the application of many different types of labels less burdensome. Out of the box, a number of sets are available, primarily designed for combinations of major and minor station styles along with geometry information.

You'll learn how to create individual label styles in Chapter 18. You will use the out-of-the-box styles and label sets over the next couple of exercises.

Major Station   Major station labels typically include a tick mark and a station callout, while the minor station labels include a tick mark only.

Geometry Points   Geometry points refers to the PC, PT, and other points along the alignment that define the geometric properties.

In this exercise, you'll apply a label set to all of your alignments and then see how an individual label can be changed from the set:

1. Open the `0612_AlignmentLabelSets.dwg` (`0612_AlignmentLabelSets_METRIC .dwg`) file.

2. Select the ROAD D alignment on the screen.

3. Right-click to open the context menu for the object and select Edit Alignment Labels to display the Alignment Labels dialog shown in Figure 6.48.

FIGURE 6.48
The Alignment Labels dialog for ROAD D

4. Click the Import Label Set button near the bottom of this dialog to display the Select Label Set dialog.

5. In the Select Label Set drop-down list, select All Labels and click OK.

The Alignment Labels dialog now populates with the additional labels imported from the label set, as shown in Figure 6.49.

FIGURE 6.49
The All Labels label set

6. Click OK to accept the settings in the Alignment Labels dialog.

7. Deselect the alignment by pressing the Esc key and repeat this process to import the All Labels set for the other alignment in the drawing.

8. When you've finished, zoom in on any of the major station labels (for example, on ROAD G, the 1+00 label, or the 0+020 label for metric users). Open the AutoCAD Properties palette using the Ctrl+1 shortcut key.

9. Select the label and notice how all of the label set group labels are selected. Notice also the properties for this group, as displayed in the AutoCAD Properties palette.

10. Press Esc to deselect.

11. Hold down the Ctrl key and select the label.

Notice that a single label is selected, not the label set group, and the Labels contextual tab is activated.

CTRL+CLICK? WHAT'S THAT ABOUT?

Prior to AutoCAD Civil 3D 2008, clicking an individual label picked the label and the alignment. Because labels are part of a label set object now, Ctrl+click is the *only* way to edit an individual label in a label set.

12. With the individual major station selected, in the Properties palette you will see the properties for that individual label.

13. Use the Major Station Label Style drop-down list to change from <default> to Perpendicular With Line.

14. Change the Flipped Label value to True to move the label from the left side of the alignment to the right side.

This command can be helpful if your plans become busy and you need to move a label to the other side for better visibility.

15. Close the Properties palette and press Esc to deselect the label item.

Keep this drawing open for the next exercise.

By using alignment label sets, you'll find it easy to standardize the appearance of labeling and stationing across alignments. Building label sets can take some time if you take into account building the label styles also, but it's one of the easiest, most effective ways to enforce standards. Building label sets will be discussed further in Chapter 18.

STATION OFFSET LABELING

Beyond labeling an alignment's basic stationing and geometry points, you may want to label points of interest in reference to the alignment. Station offset labeling is designed to do just that. In addition to labeling the alignment's properties, you can include references to other object types in your station offset labels. The objects available for referencing are as follows:

◆ Alignments

◆ COGO points

◆ Parcels

◆ Profiles

◆ Surfaces

◆ Survey figures

In this last portion of this exercise, you'll use an alignment reference to create a label suitable for labeling the station information for the center point of the cul-de-sac along ROAD D.

1. Using the drawing from the previous exercise, from the Annotate tab ➤ Labels & Tables panel ➤ Add Labels drop-down, choose Alignment ➤ Add Alignment Labels. The Add Labels dialog appears with Feature set to Alignment.

2. In the Label Type drop-down list, select Station Offset – Fixed Point.

The Station Offset label type creates a label that floats with the alignment. If the alignment is edited graphically, the label will move with it, and the station and offset information that it displays will remain constant. An example of this would be a label style that acts as a matchline. The counterpart label type is Station Offset – Fixed Point. This type of label will hold its position if the alignment is modified and the station and offset information change. An example of this kind of label would be labeling of a property corner on a subdivision plat.

3. In the Station Offset Label Style drop-down, select Station And Offset.

4. Leave the Marker Style field at the default setting, but remember that you could use any of these styles, including the option to use none to mark the selected point.

5. Click the Add button.

6. At the Select Alignment: prompt, select the ROAD D alignment.

7. At the Specify station along alignment: prompt, use the Center Osnap to snap to the center of the right-of-way arc at the cul-de-sac (see Figure 6.50).

FIGURE 6.50
The alignment station offset label in use

8. At the Specify station offset: prompt, use the Center Osnap to snap to the center of the right-of-way arc at the cul-de-sac (see Figure 6.50) again and press ↵ to end the command.

9. Close the Add Labels dialog.

10. Select the label if needed and use the square grip to drag the label to a convenient location (see Figure 6.50). Label grips will be discussed further in Chapter 18.

You can save the drawing and compare your results against the finished file that can be downloaded from the book's web page (0612_AlignmentLabelSets_FINISHED.dwg or 0612_AlignmentLabelSets_METRIC_FINISHED.dwg).

Using station offset labels and their reference object ability, you can label most site plans quickly with information that dynamically updates. Because of the flexibility of labels in terms of style, you can create design labels that are used to aid in modeling yet never plot and aren't seen in the final deliverables. More advanced alignment labels are discussed in Chapter 18.

Alignment Tables

There isn't always room to label alignment geometry along the alignment. Sometimes doing so doesn't make sense, or a reviewing agency wants to see a table showing the radius of every curve in the design. Beyond labels that can be applied directly to alignment objects, you can also create tables to meet your requirements.

You can create four types of tables:

◆ Line

◆ Curve

◆ Spiral

◆ Segment

Each of these is self-explanatory except perhaps the segment table. That table generates a mix of all the lines, curves, and spirals that make up an alignment, essentially re-creating the alignment in a tabular format. In this section, you'll generate a new line table and segment table.

All the tables work in a similar fashion. In any drawing, to add a table, follow these steps:

1. From the Annotate tab ➤ Labels & Tables panel, choose the drop-down from the Add Tables button.

2. From the Add Tables drop-down, choose the object type (such as Alignment).

3. Pick a table type (such as Add Segment) that is relevant to your work.

The Alignment Table Creation dialog appears (see Figure 6.51).

FIGURE 6.51
The Alignment Table Creation dialog for the Add Segment table type

4. Select a table style from the drop-down list or create a new one.

The Select By Label Or Style area determines how the table is populated. All the label style names for the selected type of component are listed, with a check box to the right of each one. Placing a check mark in the Apply column next to one of these label styles enables the Selection Rule setting, which has the following two options:

Add Existing   Any label using this style that currently exists in the drawing is converted to a tag format, substituting a key number such as L1 or C27, and added to the table. Any labels using this style created in the future will *not* be added to the table. The order in which each of the labels are converted might not be the order you desire, so you might need to renumber the label tags.

Add Existing And New   Any label using this style that currently exists in the drawing is converted to a tag format and added to the table. In addition, any labels using this style created in the future will be added to the table.

Another way of selecting labels for an alignment table is to pick each one individually by clicking the green button under the Select By Label Or Style area.

To the right of the Select section is the Split Table section, which determines how the table is stacked up in modelspace once it's populated. You can modify these values after a table is generated, so it's often easier to leave them alone during the creation process.

Finally, the Behavior section provides two options for Reactivity Mode: Static and Dynamic. This section determines how the table reacts to changes in the labeled objects. In some cases in surveying, this disconnect is used as a safeguard to the platted data, but in general, the point of a 3D model is to have live labels that dynamically react to changes in the object. Be sure to cancel out of the Alignment Table Creation dialog before proceeding to the next exercise.

Before you draw any tables, you need to apply labels so the tables will have data to populate. In this exercise, you'll place some labels on your alignments, and then you'll move on to drawing tables:

1. Open the `0613_AlignmentTable.dwg` (`0613_AlignmentTable_METRIC.dwg`) file.

2. From the Annotate tab ➢ Labels & Tables panel, click the Add Labels icon to open the Add Labels dialog.

3. In the Feature field, select Alignment.

4. In the Label Type field, select Multiple Segment from the drop-down list.

   With these options, you'll click each alignment one time, and every subcomponent will be labeled with the style selected here.

5. Verify that the Line Label Style field is set to Line Label Style: Bearing Over Distance (not General Line Label Style: Bearing Over Distance).

   You won't be left with these labels—you just want them for selecting elements later.

6. Verify that the Curve Label Style field is set to Delta Over Length & Radius.

   Since you have no spirals, no Spiral label style needs to be specified, so leave it at the default.

7. Click the Add button, and select each of the two alignments; then press ↵ to end the command.

   Make sure to not select the alignment multiple times during the labeling process since this will result in duplicate labels for the same segments.

8. Click the Close button to dismiss the Add Labels dialog.

   Keep this drawing open for the next exercise.

Now that you have labels to play with, let's build some tables.

CREATING A LINE TABLE

Most line tables are simple: a line tag, a bearing, and a distance. You'll also see how Civil 3D can translate units without having to change units in Drawing Settings:

1. Using the drawing from the previous exercise, from the Annotate tab ➤ Labels & Tables panel, click the Add Tables drop-down arrow and choose Alignment ➤ Add Line to open the Table Creation dialog.

2. Verify that a check mark appears in the Apply column for the Alignment Line: Bearing Over Distance label, as shown in Figure 6.52, and that the Add Existing And New rule is selected.

FIGURE 6.52
Creating an alignment line table

3. Click OK to accept the settings in the Table Creation dialog.

4. At the `Select upper left corner:` prompt, select an insertion point onscreen, and the table will generate.

   Keep this drawing open for the next exercise.

You will notice that all the labels that have been selected to be displayed in the tables will have their styles modified to display the label in Tag mode. After you've made one table, creating other tables is similar. Be patient as you create tables—you must tweak a lot of values to make them look just right. By drawing one onscreen and then editing the style, you can quickly achieve the results you want.

CREATING AN ALIGNMENT SEGMENT TABLE

An individual segment table allows a reviewer to see all the components of an alignment. In this exercise, you'll draw the segment table for ROAD D:

1. Using the drawing from the previous exercise, select the ROAD D alignment, and from the Alignment contextual tab in the Labels And Tables panel, click the Add Tables icon. From the drop-down list, choose Add Segments to open the Alignment Table Creation dialog.

Notice that when a segment table is selected, you have the option to add the table based on the label entities assigned to an alignment, which wasn't an option when creating line and curve tables.

2. In the Select Alignment field, choose the ROAD D alignment from the drop-down list (Figure 6.53) and click OK.

FIGURE 6.53
Creating an align-
ment segment
table

3. At the Select upper left corner: prompt, select an insertion point on the screen, and the table will generate.

When this exercise is complete, you can close the drawing. A finished copy of this drawing is available from the book's web page with the filename 0613_AlignmentTable_FINISHED.dwg (0613_AlignmentTable_METRIC_FINISHED.dwg).

The Bottom Line

Create an alignment from an object. Creating alignments based on polylines is a tradi-tional method of building engineering models. With built-in tools for conversion, correction, and alignment reversal, it's easy to use the linework prepared by others to start your design model. These alignments lack the intelligence of crafted alignments, however, and you should use them sparingly.

Master It Open the Masterit_0601.dwg (Masterit_0601_METRIC.dwg) file and create alignments from the linework found there, having as alignment style the Layout style, using the All Labels label set, and making sure that the source objects are erased.

Create a reverse curve that never loses tangency. Using the alignment layout tools, you can build intelligence into the objects you design. One of the most common errors introduced into engineering designs is curves and lines that aren't tangent, requiring expensive revi-sions and resubmittals. The free, floating, and fixed components can make smart alignments in a large number of combinations available to solve almost any design problem.

Master It Open the `Masterit_0602.dwg` (`Masterit_0602_METRIC.dwg`) file and create an alignment using the linework on the right as a guide. Create a reverse curve with both radii equal to 200 (or 60 for metric users) and with a pass-through point at the intersection of the two arcs.

Replace a component of an alignment with another component type. One of the goals in using a dynamic modeling solution is to find better solutions, not just the first solution. In the layout of alignments, this can mean changing components along the design path or changing the way they're defined. The ability of Civil 3D to modify alignments' geometric construction without destroying the object or forcing a new definition lets you experiment without destroying the data already based on an alignment.

Master It Convert the first curve along the alignment in the `Masterit_0603.dwg` (`Masterit_0603_METRIC.dwg`) file to a floating arc that is constrained by the next segment. Then change the radius of the curves to 150 (or 45 for metric users). Make sure that the tangency is maintained all across the alignment.

Create alignment tables. Sometimes there is just too much information displayed on a drawing, and to make it clearer, tables are used to show bearings and distances for lines, curves, and segments. With their dynamic nature, these tables are kept up-to-date with any changes.

Master It Open the `Masterit_0604.dwg` (`Masterit_0604_METRIC.dwg`) file and generate a line table, a curve table, and a segment table. Use whichever style you want to accomplish this.

Chapter 7

Profiles and Profile Views

Profile information is the backbone of vertical design. The Autodesk® AutoCAD® Civil 3D® software takes advantage of sampled data, design data, and external input files to create profiles for a number of uses. Profiles will be an integral part of corridors, as we'll discuss in Chapter 9, "Basic Corridors." In this chapter, we'll look at using profile-creation tools, editing profiles, and generating and editing profile views. You will also apply labels like you did in Chapter 6, "Alignments."

 In this chapter, you will learn to:

◆ Sample a surface profile with offset samples.

◆ Lay out a design profile on the basis of a table of data.

◆ Add and modify individual entities in a design profile.

◆ Apply a standard band set.

The Elevation Element

The whole point of building a three-dimensional model is to include the elevation element that's been missing for years on two-dimensional plans. But to get there, designers and engineers still depend on a flat 2D representation of the vertical dimension as shown in a profile view (see Figure 7.1).

FIGURE 7.1
A typical profile view of the surface elevation along an alignment

A profile is nothing more than a series of data pairs in a station, elevation format. There are basic curve and tangent components, but these are purely the mathematical basis for the paired data sets. In AutoCAD Civil 3D, you can generate profile information in one of the following five ways:

Sampling from a Surface   Sampling from a surface involves taking vertical information from a surface object every time the sampled alignment crosses a TIN line of the surface. This is perfect for generating a profile for the existing ground.

Using a Layout to Create a Profile   Using a layout to create a profile allows you to input design information, setting critical station and elevation points, calculating curves to connect linear segments, and typically working within design requirements laid out by a reviewing agency.

Creating a Best-Fit Profile   Similar to the ability to generate a best-fit alignment that we discussed in Chapter 6, you can also create a best-fit profile. You may find yourself using this method when you are trying to generate defined geometry for an existing road.

Creating a Profile from a File   Creating from a file lets you reference a specially formatted text file to pull in the station and elevation pairs. Doing so can be helpful in dealing with other analysis packages or spreadsheet tabular data.

Creating a Superimposed Profile   You can project a profile based on another alignment into a profile view. This can be done for comparison. Label sets can be applied to superimposed profiles.

Creating a Profile from a Corridor   You can define a profile by using a corridor's feature line as the source for its definition. This can be helpful for times when you want to display the profiles of the flow line of the curb in the same profile view with the centerline, for example.

The following sections look at the first four methods of creating profiles.

Surface Sampling

Working with surface information is the most elemental method of creating a profile. This information can represent any of the surfaces already in your drawing, such as an existing surface or any number of other surface-derived data sets. Surfaces can also be sampled at offsets, as you'll see in the next series of exercises. Follow these steps:

1. Open the `0701_ProfileSampling.dwg` file (or the `0701_ProfileSampling_METRIC.dwg` file for metric users) shown in Figure 7.2. Remember, all data files can be downloaded from this book's web page at www.sybex.com/go/masteringcivil3d2016.

FIGURE 7.2
The drawing
you'll use for this
exercise

2. From the Home tab ➤ Create Design panel, choose Profile ➤ Create Surface Profile to
display the Create Profile From Surface dialog (Figure 7.3).

FIGURE 7.3
The Create Profile
From Surface
dialog

A QUICK TOUR OF THE CREATE PROFILE FROM SURFACE DIALOG

This dialog has a number of important features, so take a moment to see how it breaks down:

◆ The upper-left quadrant is where you will specify the alignment. You can select the alignment from a drop-down list, or you can use the pick button to select it in the drawing. The Station Range area shows the starting and ending stations of the alignment and sets the To Sample range automatically to run from the beginning to the end of the alignment. You can control it manually by entering the station ranges in the To Sample text boxes or graphically in the drawing by using the pick buttons provided.

◆ The upper-right quadrant is where you specify the surface that will be sampled and allows you to add sample offsets. You can select a surface from the list, or you can click the Pick On Screen button. Beneath the Select Surfaces box is a Sample Offsets check box. The offsets aren't applied in the left and right direction uniformly. You must enter a negative value to sample to the left of the alignment or a positive value to sample to the right. You can add multiple offsets in a comma-delimited list here, such as -50, -25, -10, -5, 0, 5, 10, 25, 50. In all cases, whether or not you are sampling offsets, the profile isn't generated until you click the Add button.

◆ In the bottom half, the Profile List box displays all profiles associated with the alignment currently selected in the Alignment drop-down menu. This area is generally static (it won't change), but you can modify the Update Mode, Layer, and Style columns by clicking the appropriate cells in this table. You can stretch and rearrange the columns to customize the view. The columns can be modified in this location only as they are created. Upon returning to the Create Profile From Surface dialog, the profiles previously created will have static values and can be changed in the Profile Properties dialog instead.

3. Select ROAD A from the Alignment drop-down list if it isn't already selected.

4. In the Select Surfaces box, select MC3D2016-EG.

5. Click Add to add the centerline profile to the Profile List section.

6. Check the box next to Sample Offsets.

7. Enter **-25, 25** (or **-7.62, 7.62** for metric users) to sample at the left and right right-of-way lines and click Add again.

8. In the profile list, select the cell in the Style column that corresponds to the negative (left offset) value (see Figure 7.4) to activate the Pick Profile Style dialog.

FIGURE 7.4

The Create Profile From Surface dialog with styles assigned on the basis of the Offset value

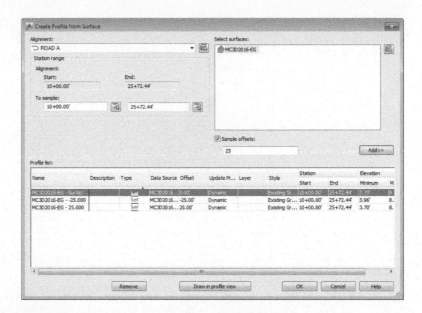

If you need to widen the columns, you can do so by double-clicking the line between the column headings.

9. Select the Left Sample Profile option from the drop-down list and click OK to dismiss the Pick Profile Style dialog.

   The style changes from Existing Ground Profile to Left Sample Profile in the table.

10. Select the cell in the Style column that corresponds to the positive (right offset) value to activate the Pick Profile Style dialog.

11. Select the Right Sample Profile option from the drop-down list and click OK to dismiss the Pick Profile Style dialog.

12. Click Draw In Profile View to dismiss this dialog and open the Create Profile View Wizard, as shown in Figure 7.5.

FIGURE 7.5
The Create Profile
View – General
wizard page

13. Verify that the Select Alignment drop-down list shows ROAD A and that Land Desktop Profile View is selected in the Profile View Style drop-down list. Click Next.

14. On the Create Profile View – Station Range wizard page, verify that the Automatic option has been selected (Figure 7.6). Click Next.

FIGURE 7.6
The Create Profile
View – Station
Range wizard page

15. On the Create Profile View – Profile View Height wizard page, verify that the Automatic option has been selected (Figure 7.7). Click Next.

FIGURE 7.7
The Create Profile
View – Profile
View Height wiz-
ard page

We will cover split profile views in a later exercise.

16. On the Create Profile View – Profile Display Options wizard page, look at the settings but do not make any changes (Figure 7.8). Click Next.

FIGURE 7.8
The Create Profile
View – Profile
Display Options
wizard page

17. On the Create Profile View – Data Bands wizard page, verify that the band set is set to EG-FG Elevations And Stations (Figure 7.9).

Notice in the Set Band Properties area that the Profile1 and Profile2 columns are both set to MC3D2016-EG-Surface (1). We will look at data bands in greater detail a bit later.

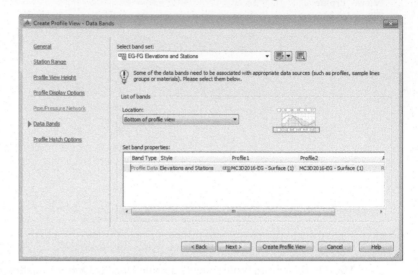

Notice that you could continue to click Next to step through the remainder of the wizard; however, you have no need to adjust further options at this time.

18. Click the Create Profile View button to dismiss the wizard.

19. Pick a point on the screen somewhere to the right of the site to draw the profile view, as shown in Figure 7.10.

FIGURE 7.10
The complete
profile view for
ROAD A

If the Events tab in Panorama appears, telling you that you've sampled data or an error in the sampling needs to be fixed, then click the green check mark or the X to dismiss Panorama.

Keep the drawing open for the next portion of the exercise.

Profiles are dependent on the alignment they're derived from, so they're stored as profile branches under their parent alignment on the Prospector tab, as shown in Figure 7.11.

FIGURE 7.11
Alignment profiles on the Prospector tab

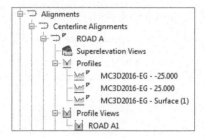

By maintaining the profiles under the alignments, it is much simpler to review what has been sampled and modified for each alignment. Note that the profiles from surface that you just created are dynamic and continuously update, as you'll see in the next portion of this exercise.

20. From the View tab ➤ Model Viewports panel, choose the drop-down list on the Viewport Configuration button and select Two: Horizontal.

21. Click in the top viewport to activate it.

22. On the Prospector tab, expand the Alignments ➤ Centerline Alignments branch.

23. Right-click ROAD A, and select the Zoom To option.

24. Click in the bottom viewport to activate it.

25. Expand the Alignments ➤ Centerline Alignments ➤ ROAD A ➤ Profile Views branch.

26. Right-click the profile view named ROAD A1, and select Zoom To.

Your screen should now look similar to Figure 7.12.

FIGURE 7.12
Splitting the screen for plan and profile editing

27. Click in the top viewport.

28. Zoom out so you can see more of the plan view.

29. Pick the ROAD A alignment to activate the grips, and stretch the western end grip to lengthen and/or move the alignment, as shown in Figure 7.13.

FIGURE 7.13
Grip-editing the
alignment

30. Click to complete the edit.

The profile view automatically adjusts to reflect the change in the starting point of the alignment. Note that the offset profiles move dynamically as well.

31. Press Ctrl+Z enough times to undo the movement of your alignment and return it to its original location.

32. Select the top viewport and then switch back to a single viewport by clicking the view-port controls in the upper-left corner of one of the modelspace viewports and selecting Viewport Configuration List ➢ Single.

Save and close the drawing. A finished copy of this drawing is available from the book's website with the filename 0701_ProfileSampling_FINISHED.dwg (0701_ProfileSampling_METRIC_FINISHED.dwg).

By maintaining the relationships between the alignment, the surface, the sampled informa-tion, and the offsets, the software creates a much more dynamic feedback system for designers. This system can be useful when you're analyzing a situation with a number of possible solu-tions, where the surface information will be a deciding factor in the final location of the align-ment. Once you've selected a location, you can use this profile view to create a vertical design, as you'll see in the next section.

LEFT TO RIGHT AND RIGHT TO LEFT?

What would happen if the alignment direction for ROAD A were reversed and drawn right to left? In that case, you would notice that the profile view would show drawn left to right if its style was con-figured with that property. It is often desirable to have the plan and profile go in the same direction.

One option is to rotate the plan view 180 degrees. If you have your labeling all set to be plan-readable, it will follow along nicely.

Another option is to generate a profile view object style that is set to read right to left instead of left to right.

In the following short exercise, you will generate a profile view that displays right to left:

1. Open the `0702_ProfileViewMatch.dwg` file (or the `0702_ProfileViewMatch_METRIC` `.dwg` file for metric users), where you will notice that the ROAD A alignment is drawn from right to left while its profile view is shown displayed from left to right.

2. Select the profile view (grid), and from the Profile View contextual tab ➢ Modify View panel, choose Profile View Properties.

3. On the Information tab, click the drop-down edit button to the right of the current object style (Land Desktop Profile View) and select Copy Current Selection.

   You will learn more about managing and editing these styles in Chapter 19, "Object Styles."

4. On the Information tab, change the name to Land Desktop Profile View: Right to Left.

   You may revise the description if desired.

5. In the Profile View Style dialog, on the Graph tab, change the profile view direction to Right To Left.

6. Click OK to dismiss the Profile View Style dialog.

7. Click OK to dismiss the Profile View Properties dialog.

You may need to move the profile view since the insert point of the profile view will now be in the lower-right corner instead of the lower-left corner as it was previously.

When this exercise is complete, you may close the drawing. A finished copy of this drawing is available from the book's website with the filename `0702_ProfileViewMatch_FINISHED.dwg` (`0702_ProfileViewMatch_METRIC_FINISHED.dwg`).

Changing a profile view style is straightforward, but because of the large number of settings contained in a profile view style, the changes can be graphically dramatic. A profile view style includes information such as labeling on the axis, vertical scale factors, grid clipping and configuration, and component coloring.

Using various styles lets you make changes to the view to meet requirements without changing any of the design information associated with the profile. To learn more about editing and creating profile styles, refer to Chapter 19.

Layout Profiles

Certification Objective

The sampled surface information contained in a surface profile is normally dynamic with the surface definitions. Moving into the design stage, you'll see how these improvements are a benefit as you look at the nature of creating design profiles. By working with layout profiles as a collection of segments that understand their relationships with each, you will realize the power of the AutoCAD Civil 3D software as a design tool in addition to being a drafting tool.

You can create layout profiles in two basic ways:

PVI-Based Layout PVI-based layouts are the most common, using tangents between points of vertical intersection (PVIs) and then applying curve parameters to connect them. PVI-based editing allows editing in a more conventional tabular format.

Entity-Based Layout   Entity-based layouts operate like horizontal alignments in the use of free, floating, and fixed entities. The PVI points are derived from pass-through points and other parameters that are used to create the entities. Entity-based editing allows for the selection of individual entities and editing in an individual component dialog.

You'll work with both methods in the next series of exercises to illustrate a variety of creation and editing techniques. First you'll focus on the initial layout, and then you'll edit the various layouts.

LAYOUT BY PVI

PVI layout is the most common methodology in transportation design. Using long tangents that connect PVIs by derived parabolic curves is a method most engineers are familiar with, and it's the method you'll use in the first exercise:

1. Open the 0703_ProfileLayoutPVI.dwg (0703_ProfileLayoutPVI_METRIC.dwg) file.

2. From the Home tab ➤ Create Design panel, choose Profile ➤ Profile Creation Tools.

3. At the Select profile view to create profile: prompt, pick the ROAD A profile view by clicking one of the grid lines to display the Create Profile – Draw New dialog.

4. Set Name to ROAD A FG.

5. On the General tab, set Profile Style to Design Profile and Profile Label Set to Complete Label Set, as shown in Figure 7.14.

FIGURE 7.14
The General tab of
the Create Profile
– Draw New dialog

6. Switch to the Design Criteria tab to examine the options provided.

Criteria-based design for profiles is similar to what you learned in Chapter 6 for alignments in that the software compares the design speed to a selected design table (typically AASHTO 2011 in North America) and sets minimum values for curve K values. This can be helpful when you're laying out long highway design projects, but most site and subdivision designers have other criteria to design against. We won't be using design criteria in this exercise, so you can leave everything unchecked.

7. Click OK to display the Profile Layout Tools toolbar shown in Figure 7.15.

FIGURE 7.15
Profile Layout
Tools toolbar

Notice that the toolbar is *modeless*, meaning it stays open even if you do other AutoCAD operations such as Pan or Zoom.

8. On the Profile Layout Tools toolbar, click the drop-down arrow next to the Draw Tangents button on the far left.

9. Select the Curve Settings option.

The Vertical Curve Settings dialog opens (Figure 7.16).

FIGURE 7.16
The Vertical Curve
Settings dialog

The Select Curve Type drop-down menu should be set to Parabolic, and the Length values in both the Crest Curves and Sag Curves areas should be 150.000′ (or 45.720 m for metric users), as shown in Figure 7.16. Selecting a Circular or Asymmetric curve type activates the other options in this dialog.

> ### To K or Not to K
>
> You don't have to choose. Realizing that users need to be able to design using both, the software lets you modify your design based on what's important. You can enter a K value to see the required length and then enter a length with a nice round value that satisfies the K. The choice is up to you.

10. Click OK to dismiss the Vertical Curve Settings dialog.

11. On the Profile Layout Tools toolbar, click the drop-down arrow next to the Draw Tangents button on the far left again. This time, select the Draw Tangents With Curves option.

12. Use a Center Osnap to pick the center of the circle at the far left in the profile view.

13. Continue working your way across the profile view, picking the center of each circle left to right with a Center Osnap.

14. Right-click or press ↵ after you select the center of the last circle.

15. The profile labels will default to a location; however, you can click any of the profile labels and use the grips to move them to a more legible location.

Your drawing should look similar to Figure 7.17.

FIGURE 7.17
A completed layout profile with labels

16. Close the Profile Layout Tools toolbar. Save the drawing.

When this exercise is complete, you may close the drawing. A finished copy of this drawing is available from the book's website with the filename 0703_ProfileLayoutPVI_FINISHED.dwg (0703_ProfileLayoutPVI_METRIC_FINISHED.dwg).

The layout profile is labeled with the complete label set you selected in the Create Profile dialog. As you'd expect, this labeling and the layout profile are dynamic. If you select the profile and then zoom in on this profile line, not the labels or the profile view, you'll see something like Figure 7.18.

FIGURE 7.18
The types of grips
on a layout profile

The PVI-based layout profiles include the following unique grips:

Vertical Triangular Grip   The vertical triangular grip at the PVI point is the PVI grip. Moving this alters the inbound and outbound tangents, but the curve remains in place with the same design parameters of length and type.

Angled Triangular Grips   The angled triangular grips on either side of the PVI are sliding PVI grips. Selecting and moving moves the PVI, but movement occurs only along the tangent of the selected grip. The curve length isn't affected by moving these grips, but the PVI station and elevation will be, as well as the grade of the other tangent.

Circular Pass-Through Grips   The circular pass-through grips near the PVI and at each end of the curve are curve grips. Moving any of these grips makes the curve longer or shorter without adjusting the inbound or outbound tangents or the PVI point.

Although this simple pick-and-go methodology works for preliminary layout, it lacks a certain amount of control typically required for final design. For that, you'll use another method of creating PVIs:

1. Open the `0704_ProfileLayoutPVITransparent.dwg` (`0704_ProfileLayoutPVITransparent_METRIC.dwg`) file.

2. Verify that the Transparent Commands toolbar (Figure 7.19) is displayed somewhere on your screen. If it is not shown, from the View tab ➤ Interface panel, choose Toolbars ➤ CIVIL ➤ Transparent Commands.

FIGURE 7.19
The Transparent
Commands
toolbar

3. From the Home tab ➤ Create Design panel, choose Profile ➤ Profile Creation Tools.

4. Pick the ROAD C profile view by clicking one of the grid lines to display the Create Profile – Draw New dialog.

5. Set the name to **ROAD C FG**.

6. On the General tab, set Profile Style to Design Profile and Profile Label Set to Complete Label Set. Click OK to display the Profile Layout Tools toolbar.

7. On the Profile Layout Tools toolbar, make sure the curve settings are set to 150 (45.72 for metric users) by accessing the dialog for these settings; then click the drop-down arrow next to the Draw Tangents button on the far left and select the Draw Tangents With Curves option, as in the previous exercise.

8. Use an Endpoint Osnap to snap to the endpoint of the existing surface profile where this intersects the left edge of the profile view.

9. On the Transparent Commands toolbar, select the Profile Station Elevation transparent command.

   For those who prefer using the command line, the key-in command for this transparent command is 'PSE.

10. When prompted to select a profile view, click a grid line on the ROAD C profile view to select it.

    If you move your cursor within the profile grid area, a vertical red line appears. Notice that the tooltip currently shows the station value of the cursor.

11. When prompted for a station, enter **1250** ↵ (or **381** ↵ for metric users) at the command line.

    If you move your cursor within the profile grid area, a horizontal line appears (see Figure 7.20), but it can move only vertically along the station just specified.

FIGURE 7.20
Using the Profile Station Elevation transparent command

12. When prompted to specify an elevation, enter **8** ↵ (or **2.438** ↵ for metric users) at the command line to set the elevation for the second PVI.

13. Press Esc only once.

The Profile Station Elevation transparent command is no longer active, but the Draw Tangents With Curves button that you previously selected on the Profile Layout Tools toolbar continues to be active.

14. When prompted to specify a point, select the Profile Grade Station transparent command on the Transparent Commands toolbar.

For those who prefer using the command line, the key-in command for this transparent command is 'PGS.

Notice that you did not need to select a profile view this time; that's because you are still in the same command (Draw Tangents With Curves in this case). The transparent command will default to the same profile view that was previously selected.

15. When prompted to specify the grade, enter **-.13** ↵ at the command line for the profile grade.

16. When prompted for the station, enter **1520** ↵ (or **463.30** ↵ for metric users) at the command line.

17. Press Esc only once to deactivate the Profile Grade Station transparent command.

18. When prompted to specify the grade, select the Profile Grade Elevation transparent command on the Transparent Commands toolbar.

For those who prefer using the command line, the key-in command for this transparent command is 'PGE.

19. When prompted to specify the grade, enter **0.31**↵ at the command line for the profile grade.

20. Enter **8.39** ↵ (or **2.557** ↵ for metric users) for the profile grade elevation.

21. Press Esc only once to deactivate the Profile Grade Elevation transparent command.

22. When prompted to specify the grade, select the Profile Grade Length transparent command on the Transparent Commands toolbar.

For those who prefer using the command line, the key-in command for this transparent command is 'PGL.

23. When prompted to specify the grade, enter **-.19**↵ at the command line for the profile grade.

24. Enter **200**↵ (or **60.96**↵ for metric users) for the profile grade length.

25. Press Esc only once to deactivate the Profile Grade Elevation transparent command.

26. Use an Endpoint Osnap to select the end of the existing surface profile on the far-right side of the profile view.

27. Press ↵ to complete the profile.

Your profile should look like Figure 7.21.

FIGURE 7.21
A layout profile
created using
the Transparent
Commands
toolbar

28. Close the Profile Layout Tools toolbar.

When this exercise is complete, you may close the drawing. A finished copy of this drawing is available from the book's website with the filename `0704_ProfileLayoutPVITransparent_FINISHED.dwg` (`0704_ProfileLayoutPVITransparent_METRIC_FINISHED.dwg`).

Using PVIs to define tangents and fitting curves between them is the most common approach to create a layout profile, but you'll look at an entity-based design in the next section.

LAYOUT BY ENTITY

In this exercise you will lay out a design profile using the concepts of fixed, floating, and free entities in much the same way that you used them for laying out alignments in Chapter 6:

1. Open the `0705_ProfileEntityLayout.dwg` (`0705_ProfileEntityLayout_METRIC.dwg`) file.

2. From the Home tab ➤ Create Design panel, choose Profile ➤ Profile Creation Tools.

3. Pick the ROAD B profile view by clicking one of the grid lines to display the Create Profile – Draw New dialog.

4. For Name, enter **ROAD B FG**.

5. On the General tab, set Profile Style to Design Profile and Profile Label Set to Complete Label Set; then click OK to display the Profile Layout Tools toolbar.

OOPS, YOU CLOSED THE PROFILE LAYOUT TOOLS TOOLBAR!

If at any point you inadvertently close the Profile Layout Tools toolbar, have no fear. You can reopen it by selecting the profile that you were editing and selecting Geometry Editor from the Profile contextual tab. If you created the profile but there aren't any entities to select, you can select it in Prospector by expanding the Alignments ➤ Centerline Alignments ➤ *Alignment Name* ➤ Profiles branch. Right-click the profile and choose Delete to start again from scratch. Unfortunately, there isn't a Select option like you have with alignments, so deleting the profile is the only option.

---

6. On the Profile Layout Tools toolbar, click the drop-down arrow next to the Tangent Creation button and select the Fixed Tangent (Two Points) option.

7. Using a Center Osnap, pick the circle at the left edge of the profile view labeled A.

   A rubber-band line appears.

8. Using a Center Osnap, pick the circle labeled B.

   A tangent is drawn between these two circles.

9. Using a Center Osnap, pick the circle labeled B again as the start point and the circle labeled C as the endpoint.

   A tangent is drawn between these two circles. Notice that the tangent does not automatically continue from the previous two-point fixed tangent; therefore, you have to select the B circle again.

10. Using a Center Osnap, pick the circle labeled D as the start point and the circle labeled E as the endpoint.

    A tangent is drawn between these two circles.

11. On the Profile Layout Tools toolbar, click the drop-down arrow next to the Vertical Curve Creation button and select the More Free Vertical Curves ➤ Free Vertical Parabola (PVI Based) option.

    Notice that the image shown to the left of the drop-down arrow for the Tangent Creation button and Vertical Curve Creation button will match the last type of entity you selected from the drop-down menu.

12. At the `Pick point near PVI or curve to add curve:` prompt, pick the circle labeled B as the PVI.

13. At the `Specify curve length or [Passthrough K]:` prompt, enter **150** ↵ (or **45.72** ↵ for metric users) as the curve length.

14. Press ↵ to end the command.

    Your drawing should now look similar to Figure 7.22. Notice that although you have added the tangent between D and E, it is not yet labeled since it is not connected with the main portion of the profile created up until this point.

FIGURE 7.22
Some tangent and vertical curve entities placed on ROAD B

15. On the Profile Layout Tools toolbar, click the drop-down arrow next to the Vertical Curve Creation button and select the Free Vertical Curve (Parabola) option.

16. When prompted to select the first entity, click the tangent between B and C. Then click the tangent between D and E as the next entity.

Remember to pick the tangent line and not an end circle.

17. At the `Specify curve length or [Radius K]:` prompt, enter **100** ↵ (or **30.48** ↵ for metric users) as the curve length and press ↵ again to end the command.

Notice that with this command the tangents do not have to meet at a PVI, unlike the previous Free Vertical Curve (PVI Based) curve.

18. On the Profile Layout Tools toolbar, click the drop-down arrow next to the Vertical Curve Creation button and select the Floating Vertical Curve (Parameter, Through Point) option.

19. At the `Select entity to attach to:` prompt, select the tangent between D and E to attach the floating vertical curve.

Remember to pick the tangent line and not the end circle. Also, you have to select the tangent between the midpoint and the endpoint of the tangent at the circle labeled E. Selecting too close to the endpoint at the circle labeled D will give a result of `End of selected entity already has an attachment.`

20. At the `Enter K value or [Radius]:` prompt, enter **73.10** (**22.30** for metric users) for the K value and ↵; then at the `Specify End Point:` prompt using the Center Osnap, select the circle labeled F as the endpoint for the curve.

You will notice when using this tool that once you select the first entity and define the parameter, a rubber-band curve appears. If you move the cursor on the wrong side of the tangent endpoint, it will become a large red circle with an X across it indicating that you cannot select that point.

21. On the Profile Layout Tools toolbar, click the drop-down arrow next to the Tangent Creation button and select the Float Tangent (Through Point) option.

22. At the `Select entity to attach to:` prompt, select the curve from E and F making sure to select it between the midpoint of the curve and the circle labeled F to attach the floating tangent.

A rubber-band line appears.

23. At the `Select through point:` prompt, using a Center Osnap, select the circle labeled G.

24. Press ↵ or right-click to end the Fixed Tangent (Through Point) command; then close the Profile Layout Tools toolbar.

Your drawing should look like Figure 7.23.

When this exercise is complete, you may close the drawing. A finished copy of this drawing is available from the book's website with the filename `0705_ProfileEntityLayout_FINISHED`
`.dwg` (`0705_ProfileEntityLayout_METRIC_FINISHED.dwg`).

With the entity-creation method, grip editing works in a similar way to other layout methods based on the fixed, floating, and free constraints.

FIGURE 7.23
Completed
profile built
using entities.

PROFILE LAYOUT TOOLS

Although we have touched on many of the available tools in the Profile Layout Tools toolbar, shown in Figure 7.24, there are still many that we have not discussed.

FIGURE 7.24
Profile Layout
Tools toolbar

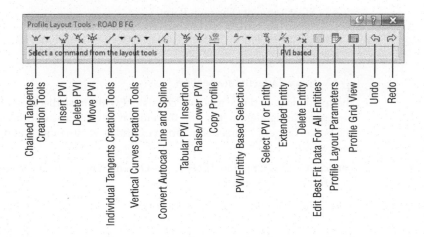

Chained Tangents Creation Tools The Chained Tangents Creation Tools drop-down button contains four options:

- Draw Tangents lays out a profile point to point with no curves.

- Draw Tangent With Curves lays out a profile from point to point with the curve type and length determined from the Curve Settings options.

- Curve Settings sets the type of curve (parabolic, circular, asymmetric) along with specific geometric properties that define each type of curve.

- Convert Free Curve (Through Point) is a new feature introduced with this release that allows free curves that are constrained by using pass-through points to be converted to free curves based on a parameter.

Insert PVI   The Insert PVI button adds a new PVI at the specified location, consequently breaking an existing tangent and generating two new tangents connected to the new PVI.

Delete PVI   The Delete PVI button removes an existing PVI at the specified location, consequently taking two tangents and replacing them with a single tangent.

Move PVI   The Move PVI button allows you to select an existing PVI and relocate it to a specified location while keeping the two existing tangents. You can get the same result by grip-editing the PVI with the vertical triangular grip, as described earlier. In fact, one might argue that the grip-editing approach is better because it shows you a preview of your edit as you make it. The Move PVI command does not.

Individual Tangents Creation Tools   The Individual Tangents Creation Tools Drop-down button contains six tools:

◆   Fixed Tangent (Two Points)

◆   Fixed Tangent – Best Fit

◆   Float Tangent (Through Point)

◆   Float Tangent – Best Fit

◆   Free Tangent

◆   Solve Tangent Intersection

The fixed, float, and free tools are consistent with those discussed in Chapter 6 when we were generating alignments, and therefore many of these options should be self-explanatory. The Solve Tangent Intersection option extends two tangents that do not currently connect to form a PVI.

Vertical Curves Creation Tools Drop-Down   The Vertical Curves Creation drop-down button contains 15 options:

◆   Fixed Vertical Curve (Three Points)

◆   Fixed Vertical Curve (Two Points, Parameter)

◆   Fixed Vertical Curve (Entity End, Through Point)

◆   Fixed Vertical Curve (Two Points, Grade At Start Point)

◆   Fixed Vertical Curve (Two Points, Grade At End Point)

◆   Fixed Vertical Curve – Best Fit

◆   Floating Vertical Curve (Parameter, Through Point)

◆   Floating Vertical Curve (Through Point, Grade)

◆   Floating Vertical Curve – Best Fit

◆   Free Vertical Curve (Parabola)

◆   Free Vertical Curve (Circular)—a feature introduced with this release

◆   Free Vertical Parabola (PVI Based)

◆   Free Asymmetrical Parabola (PVI Based)

◆ Free Circular Curve (PVI Based)

◆ Free Vertical Curve – Best Fit

Once again the fixed, floating, and free terminology should be familiar from Chapter 6. By trying these various options, you will become comfortable with their capabilities, and you will find the ones that best fit your design needs.

Convert AutoCAD Line And Spline   The Convert AutoCAD Line And Spline button takes a singular line/spline and converts it into a profile object, either a tangent or a three-point vertical curve, as applicable.

Insert PVIs - Tabular   The Insert PVIs - Tabular Insertion button allows you to enter PVI station and elevation information in a table-like dialog, which is helpful if you want to create multiple PVIs at once using station and elevation information. This table allows you to insert PVIs and curves anywhere geometrically possible in the profile. You are not required to enter the PVIs in any specific order when using this method of entry.

Raise/Lower PVIs   The Raise/Lower PVIs button allows you to raise or lower the entire profile or a subset of PVIs within a specified station range. This button will be discussed in a later exercise in the section "Other Profile Edits."

Copy Profile   The Copy Profile button allows you to copy either the entire profile or a portion of the profile within a specified station range. This button will be discussed later in the section "Other Profile Edits."

PVI/Entity Based Selection   The PVI Based/Entity Based selection button allows you to choose to select and display profile layout parameters based on either PVI or entity. By switching the selection to Entity and selecting a curve entity in the Profile Layout Parameters discussed shortly, you will be able to change the parameter constraint. This represents a new enhancement introduced in 2015.

Select PVI or Entity   The Select PVI or Entity button opens the Profile Layout Parameters dialog for the selected PVI or entity.

Extend Entities   The Extend Entities button extends a fixed or floating profile tangent or curve located at the end of the profile.

Delete Entity   The Delete Entity button removes a selected curve or tangent.

Profile Layout Parameters   The Profile Layout Parameters button opens the Profile Layout Parameters dialog, which shows numeric data for editing the selected entity or PVI.

Profile Grid View   The Profile Grid View button opens the Profile Entities tab in Panorama, showing information about all the entities and PVIs in the profile. This is where you have access to make edits on all the entities of the profile.

Undo/Redo   The Undo button reverses that last command and the Redo button reverses the last undo operation. This includes commands and operations that are not part of creating or editing a profile.

The Best-Fit Profile

You've surveyed along a centerline, and you need to closely approximate the tangents and vertical curves as they were originally designed and constructed.

The Create Best Fit Profile option is in the Home tab ➤ Create Design panel, in the Profile drop-down. Once you select a profile view, the Create Best Fit Profile dialog appears (Figure 7.25).

FIGURE 7.25
Create Best Fit
Profile dialog

Similar to the best-fit alignment we discussed in Chapter 6, a best-fit profile can be based on an Input Type setting of AutoCAD Blocks, AutoCAD 3D Polylines, AutoCAD Points, COGO Points, Surface Profile, or Feature Lines. The most common option is Surface Profile.

The command attempts to run a complex algorithm to determine the best-fit profile, including both tangents and vertical curves. However, the only best-fit option available for determining vertical curves is the maximum curve radius. The maximum curve radius does not apply in a design that uses parabolic curves, the most common curves found in roadway design. Once the analysis is run, a Best Fit Report is provided; however, unlike the Best Fit command for lines and curves as discussed in Chapter 1, "The Basics," this command has no options for selecting or deselecting points.

Creating a Profile from a File

Working with profile information in the AutoCAD Civil 3D environment is nice, but it isn't the only place where you can create or manipulate this sort of information. Many programs and analysis packages generate profile information. One common case is the plotting of a hydraulic grade line against a stormwater network profile of the pipes. When information comes from outside the program, it is often output in a variety of formats. If you convert this data to a text file in the format required by AutoCAD Civil 3D, the profile information can be imported directly.

There is a specific format that is required for creating a profile from a text file. Each line is a PVI definition (station and elevation) listed in ascending order. The station should not include the plus character (use 100, not 1+00 or 0+100). Curve information is an optional third bit of data on any line except for the first and last lines in the file. The vertical curve that is created will be a parabolic curve, which is the most popular type of vertical curve. Note that each line is space delimited. Here's one example of a profile text file:

```
0 550.76
127.5 552.24
200.8 554 100
256.8 557.78 50
310.75 561
```

In this example, the third and fourth lines include the curve length as the optional third piece of information. The only inconvenience of using this input method is that the information in Civil 3D doesn't directly reference the text file. Once the profile data is imported, no dynamic relationship exists with the text file, but other methods can be used to edit the profile once imported.

In this exercise, you'll import a small text file to see how the function works:

1. Open the 0706_ProfilefromFile.dwg (0706_ProfileFromFile_METRIC.dwg) file.

2. From the Home tab ➤ Create Design panel, choose Profile ➤ Create Profile From File.

   The Import Profile From File – Select File dialog appears.

3. Browse to and select the 0706_ProfileFromFile.txt file (or the 0706_ ProfileFromFile_METRIC.txt file for metric users), and click Open to display the Create Profile – Draw New dialog.

4. For Alignment, choose ROAD G, and set Name to **ROAD G FG**.

5. On the General tab, set Profile Style to Design Profile and Profile Label Set to Complete Label Set; then click OK.

   Your drawing should look like Figure 7.26. The ROAD G profile view should be updated to reflect the newly imported design profile for the specified alignment.

FIGURE 7.26
Completed profile created from a file

When this exercise is complete, you may close the drawing. A finished copy of this drawing is available from the book's website with the filename 0706_ProfileFromFile_FINISHED.dwg (0706_ProfileFromFile_METRIC_FINISHED.dwg).

Now that you've tried the three main ways of creating profiles, you'll edit a profile.

Editing Profiles

The methods just reviewed let you quickly create profiles. You saw how sampled profiles reflect changes in the surface along the parent alignment and how to lay out a design profile using a few different techniques. You also imported a text file with profile information. In all these cases, you just left the profile as originally designed with no analysis or editing.

In the following sections, you will begin to look at some of the profile-editing methods available. The most basic is a more precise grip-editing methodology, which you'll learn about first. Then you'll see how to modify the PVI-based layout profile, how to change out the components that make up a layout profile, and how to use some other miscellaneous editing functions.

Grip-Editing Profiles

Once a profile layout is in place, sometimes a simple grip edit will suffice. But for precision editing, you can use the grips along with transparent commands or dynamic input, as in this short exercise:

1. Open the 0707_ProfileEditing.dwg (0707_ProfileEditing_METRIC.dwg) file.

2. Zoom to the ROAD D profile view and pick the ROAD D FG profile (the blue line) to activate its grips.

3. Locate the PVI around Sta. 19+50 (or 0+594.36 for metric users) and pick the vertical triangular grip on the vertical crest curve to begin a grip stretch of the PVI, as shown in Figure 7.27.

FIGURE 7.27

Grip-editing a PVI

The command line states Specify stretch point or [Base point Copy Undo eXit]:.

4. On the Transparent Commands toolbar, select the Profile Station Elevation command. That's 'PSE for the command-line users.

5. At the Select a profile view: prompt, pick a grid line on the ROAD D profile view to select.

6. At the Specify station: prompt, enter **1975** ↵ (or **601.98** ↵ for metric users).

7. At the Specify elevation: prompt, enter **7.50**↵ (or **2.286**↵ for metric users).

8. Click the vertical triangular grip for the PVI near station 14+00 (or 0+426.72 for metric users).

9. If dynamic input is not turned on already, click the Dynamic Input icon at the bottom of your screen if available, or press the F12 key to enable it.

   You should see two editable tooltips on your screen, one for station and one for elevation. You may need to zoom out to see them.

10. Enter **1425** ↵ (or **434.34** ↵ for metric users).

    The value you type in will populate the dynamic tooltip.

When this exercise is complete, you may save the drawing, but keep it open for the following exercise. A copy of this drawing at this stage is available from the book's web page with the filename 0707_ProfileEditingGrips_FINISHED.dwg (0707_ProfileEditingGrips_METRIC_FINISHED.dwg).

The grips can go from quick-and-dirty editing tools to precise editing tools when you use them in conjunction with the transparent commands or dynamic input. They lack the ability to precisely control a curve length, though, so you'll look at editing a curve next.

Editing Profiles Using Profile Layout Parameters

Beyond the simple grip edits, but before changing out the components of a typical profile, you can modify the values that generate an individual component. In this exercise, you'll use the Profile Layout Parameters dialog to modify the curve properties on your design profile:

1. Continue working on the previous file, or open the 0707_ProfileEditingGrips_FINISHED.dwg (0707_ProfileEditingGrips_METRIC_FINISHED.dwg) file.

2. Zoom to the ROAD D profile view and pick the ROAD D FG profile (the blue line) to activate the Profile contextual tab.

3. From the Profile contextual tab ➤ Modify Profile panel, choose Geometry Editor.

4. On the Profile Layout Tools toolbar, click the Profile Layout Parameters button to open the Profile Layout Parameters dialog, and place the dialog somewhere on your screen so that you can still see the profile view.

5. On the Profile Layout Tools toolbar, click the Select PVI button.

   If the Select Entity button is showing on the toolbar instead, from the PVI/Entity Based selection button select the PVI Based option.

6. Zoom in to click near the PVI at station 34+70 (or 1+057.66 for metric users) to populate the Profile Layout Parameters dialog (Figure 7.28).

FIGURE 7.28
The Profile Layout
Parameters dialog

Parameter	Value
⊟ **General**	
Curve Type	Crest
Passing Sight Distance	4983.84'
Stopping Sight Distance	2184.66'
Headlight Distance	
⊟ **Geometry**	
Lock type	Manual
Lock	False
Grade In	0.11%
Grade Out	-0.21%
A (Grade Change)	0.32%
PVI Station	34+70.00'
PVI Elevation	7.55'
Profile Curve Length	150.00'
High Point Station	34+45.50'
High Point Elevation	7.50'
Low Point Station	
Low Point Elevation	
Curve Radius	47616.65'
K Value	476.167

Values that can be edited are in black; the rest, shown grayed out, are mathematically derived and can be of some design value but can't be directly modified. The two buttons at the top of the dialog adjust how much information is displayed. The one on the left is the Show More/Show Less button, and the one on the right is the Collapse All Categories/Expand All Categories button.

7. In the Profile Layout Parameters dialog, change the K value to **500** ↲ (or **152.4** ↲ for metric users).

Notice that the curve changes, but the label does not update. This is because you are still in the command. Once you end the command, all appropriate labels will update.

8. Change the selection to Entity Based from the PVI/Entity Based Selection drop-down of the toolbar.

9. Click the PVI/Entity Selection button and select the curve at station 38+05 (or 1+159.76 for metric users) to repopulate the Profile Layout Parameters dialog with that curve's data.

10. In the Profile Layout Parameters dialog, change Parameter Constraint Lock to False, thus enabling the choice of constraints.

11. In the Constraint Type Desc field, change the value to Through Point.

    On making this change you will notice that all the other settings are grayed out, leaving you with the option of defining only the Through Point Station and Elevation parameters.

12. Change the station to **38+10** and the elevation to **7.00** (**1+161.28** for station and **2.134** for elevation for metric users).

    The ability to change the parameter constraint is a new enhancement introduced with this release.

13. Close the Profile Layout Parameters dialog by clicking the X in the upper-right corner and press Enter to exit selection mode. Close the Profile Layout Tools toolbar as well.

When this exercise is complete, you may save the drawing, but keep it open for the following exercise. A copy of this drawing at this stage is available from the book's web page with the filename 0707_ProfileEditingParameter_FINISHED.dwg (0707_ProfileEditingParameter_METRIC_FINISHED.dwg).

Editing Profiles Using Profile Grid View

In this exercise, you'll use the Profile Grid View command to view and modify the profile within Panorama:

1. Continue using the file from the previous exercise, or if you did not complete the previous exercise, open the 0707_ProfileEditingParameter_FINISHED.dwg (0707_ProfileEditingParameter_METRIC_FINISHED.dwg) file.

    If you have closed the Profile Layout Tools toolbar, click the ROAD D FG profile, and then from the Profile: ROAD D FG contextual tab ➢ Modify Profile panel, click Geometry Editor.

2. On the Profile Layout Tools toolbar, change the selection to PVI Based from the PVI/Entity Based Selection drop-down if it is not already set to that mode.

3. Click the Profile Grid View tool to activate the Profile Entities tab in Panorama.

    Panorama allows you to view all the profile components at once, in a compact form.

4. Scroll right in Panorama until you see the Profile Curve Length column.

    You can show and hide columns by right-clicking the column headings. You can also resize the columns by dragging the breaks between the columns or by double-clicking the break between two columns to autosize to the column contents.

5. Double-click the Profile Curve Length value for Entity No. 5 (see Figure 7.29) and change the value from 300 to **250** (or from 91.44 to **76.2** for metric users).

FIGURE 7.29
Direct editing of
the curve length in
Panorama

6. Close Panorama and the Profile Layout Tools toolbar, and zoom out to review your edits.

Your complete profile should now look like Figure 7.30.

FIGURE 7.30
The completed
editing of the
curve length in the
layout profile

When this exercise is complete, you may save the drawing, but keep it open for the following exercise. A copy of this drawing at this stage is available from the book's web page with the filename 0707_ProfileEditingGrid_FINISHED.dwg (0707_ProfileEditingGrid_METRIC_FINISHED.dwg).

You can use these tools to modify the PVI points or tangent parameters, but they won't let you add or remove an entire component. You'll do that in the next section.

PVIS IN LOCKDOWN

You may have noticed while editing the profile in Panorama that the last column is named Lock. You can also lock a PVI at a specific station and elevation in the Profile Layout Parameters dialog. PVIs that are locked cannot be moved with edits to adjacent entities. However, it's important to note that a PVI can be unlocked by simply clicking the lock icon in the profile view.

Component-Level Editing

In addition to editing basic parameters and locations, sometimes you have to add or remove entire components. In this exercise, you'll delete a curve, remove a PVI, insert a new PVI, and add a new curve into the layout profile:

1. Continue using the file from the previous exercise, or if you did not complete the previous exercise, open the 0707_ProfileEditingGrid_FINISHED.dwg (0707_ProfileEditingGrid_METRIC_FINISHED.dwg) file.

   If you have closed the Profile Layout Tools toolbar, click the ROAD D FG profile, and then from the Profile: ROAD D FG contextual tab ➤ Modify Profile panel, click Geometry Editor.

2. On the Profile Layout Tools toolbar, click the Delete Entity button.

3. Pick the curve near the 31+40 station (or the 0+957.07 station for metric users) and right-click or press ↵ to end the command.

The profile is adjusted accordingly. Since the deleted curve was defined as a free curve, on deletion, the tangents will still be connected to each other by means of the PVI.

4. On the Profile Layout Tools toolbar, click the Delete PVI button.

5. Pick a point near the PVI that resulted from the deletion of the previous curve.

6. Right-click or press ↵ to end the command.

The PVI is deleted, and the layout is updated.

7. On the Profile Layout Tools toolbar, click the Insert PVI button.

8. At the prompt, using the transparent command for Profile Station and Elevation ('**PSE**) select the ROAD D profile view and define the new PVI at station **24+00** (**0+731.52** for metric users) and the elevation of **5.25** (**1.60** for metric users).

9. Press Esc twice, once to exit the transparent command and again to exit the Insert PVI command.

10. On the Profile Layout Tools toolbar, expand the Vertical Curves Creation Tools.

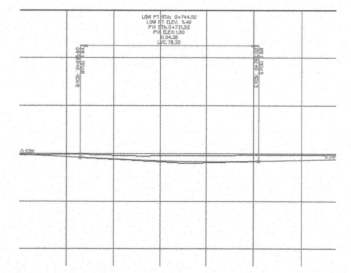

11. From the More Free Vertical Curves section, select Free Asymmetrical Parabola (PVI Based).

12. At the prompt for the PVI click the screen in the vicinity of the previously created PVI at station 24+00 (0+731.52 for metric users).

13. At the Specify Length1: prompt, enter **150** (**45.72** for metric users) and click Enter.

14. At the Specify Length2: prompt, enter **100** (**30.48** for metric users) and press Enter.

15. Right-click or press the Enter key again to end the command. Close the toolbar.

Your layout should update to reflect the new changes, and the drawing should look similar to Figure 7.31.

FIGURE 7.31
The completed editing of the curve using component-level editing

When this exercise is complete, you may save the drawing, but keep it open for the following exercise. A copy of the drawing at this stage is available from the book's web page with the filename 0707_ProfileEditingComponent_FINISHED.dwg (0707_ProfileEditingComponent_METRIC_FINISHED.dwg). Editing profiles using any of these methods gives you precise control over the creation and layout of your vertical design. In addition to these fine-tuning tools, there are other tools worth investigating, and you'll look at them next.

Other Profile Edits

Some handy tools exist on the Profile Layout Tools toolbar for performing specific actions. These tools aren't normally used during the preliminary design stage, but they come into play as you're working to create a final design for grading or corridor design. They include raising or lowering a whole layout in one shot, as well as copying profiles. The 2015 release introduced a new tab within the Profile Properties dialog that allows users to control the locking of the vertical alignment to the horizontal alignment geometry points. You will experiment with all these options in the following exercise:

1. Continue using the file from the previous exercise, or if you did not complete the previous exercise, open the 0707_ProfileEditingComponent_FINISHED.dwg (0707_ProfileEditingComponent_METRIC_FINISHED.dwg) file.

   If you have closed the Profile Layout Tools toolbar, click the ROAD D FG profile, and then from the Profile: ROAD D FG contextual tab ➤ Modify Profile panel, click Geometry Editor.

2. On the Profile Layout Tools toolbar, click the Copy Profile button to display the Copy Profile Data dialog, shown in Figure 7.32.

FIGURE 7.32
The Copy Profile
Data dialog

3. Click OK to create a new layout profile directly on top of ROAD D FG.

4. In Prospector, expand the Alignments ➤ Centerline Alignments ➤ ROAD D ➤ Profiles branches to see that a profile named ROAD D FG [Copy] has been added.

5. Press Esc to clear the selection of the original profile and then click the profile again to select it.

   This time the ROAD D FG [Copy] profile is selected because it is on top since it was the last object created. The Profile Layout Tools toolbar now references the new profile.

6. On the Profile Layout Tools toolbar, click the Raise/Lower PVIs button to display the Raise/Lower PVI Elevation dialog, shown in Figure 7.33.

FIGURE 7.33
The Raise/Lower PVI Elevation dialog

7. Set Elevation Change to **-1** (or **-0.3** for metric users).

8. Click the Station Range radio button, and set the Start value to **14+25** (or **0+434.34** for metric users) and the End value to **19+75** (**0+601.98** for metric users) to modify the profile in between the starting and ending PVIs.

9. Click OK to close the Raise/Lower PVI Elevation dialog.

   Generating a copy is useful if you want to remember a conceptual profile layout but would like to experiment with a different layout. The copies do not stay dynamically related to one another.

   Let's continue to explore, turning now to the new enhancement to Profile Properties.

10. Switch the modelspace to a two-viewport layout from the View tab ➤ Model Viewports panel ➤ Viewport Configuration drop-down by selecting Two: Horizontal Setup.

    Make sure that on the top viewport you zoom to the ROAD D alignment, while on the bottom viewport you have the ROAD D profile view.

11. Select the ROAD D FG profile either from the profile view or through Prospector and access the Profile Properties dialog.

Figure 7.34 shows the new Profile Locking tab.

FIGURE 7.34
The Profile Locking tab of the Profile Properties dialog allows you to lock your vertical alignment to the horizontal geometry points or the alignment start.

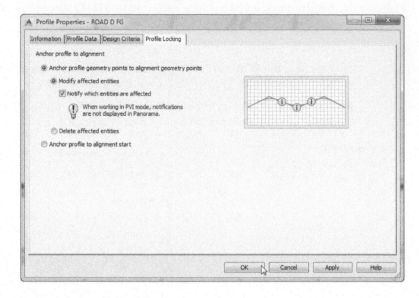

Here you have the option of locking the vertical alignment (profile) to the horizontal alignment's geometry points. When locked, after making changes to the horizontal alignment, the affected profile's subentities will be modified either through deletion or a change in their parameters to keep the profile vertical geometry in sync with the horizontal alignment.

Anchoring the profile to the alignment start will lock the start point of the alignment to the start point of the profile. Subentity geometry will remain unchanged.

12. Close the Profile Properties dialog; then in plan view, zoom to the curve around station 28+00 (0+853 for metric users).

13. Grip-edit the alignment's curve by selecting the triangular grip, sliding it toward the inside of the curve as shown in Figure 7.35, and clicking a new location not too far from the original location.

FIGURE 7.35
Grip-editing the alignment curve by sliding the triangular grip toward the inside of the curve

Upon editing the alignment, you will notice that in the profile view, the subentities affected by this change display notification symbols, as shown in Figure 7.36. These notification symbols show you where changes have been applied to the profile in order to synchronize the start and end stations with the alignment.

FIGURE 7.36
On alignment change, notification symbols are displayed for the items affected by the change.

A horizontal geometry change affected this element. Make sure this element is still valid.

14. Select the profile with the notification symbols.

15. On the contextual tab ➤ Notifications panel, expand Horizontal Changes and select Dismiss All Notifications to clear the notification warnings.

If you did not dismiss the notifications and then saved and closed the drawing, if the drawing is opened later, the notifications would no longer be there.

If you are used to the profile not being locked with the horizontal alignment, you'll notice changes. Namely, with Profile Locking on, you will notice that even if the alignment changed its length as reflected in the plan and profile views, the design profile ends are tied to the new beginning and end stations on the alignment, and the properties for the subentities in between are modified to accommodate this change.

When this exercise is complete, you can save and close the drawing. A finished copy of this drawing at this stage is available from the book's web page with the filename `0707_ProfileEditingOther_FINISHED.dwg` (`0707_ProfileEditingOther_METRIC_FINISHED.dwg`).

Using the layout and editing tools discussed in these sections, you should be able to create profiles for many different types of designs.

Up to now, you have learned how to use some of the available tools for modifying profiles, but you might be wondering about intersecting roads and how their profiles will interact with one another. Have no fear; we will discuss those in Chapter 10, "Advanced Corridors, Intersections, and Roundabouts," when we discuss corridor intersections.

Profile Views

Certification
Objective

Working with vertical data is an integral part of building the model. Once profile information has been created in any number of ways, displaying it to make sense is another task. It can't be stated enough that profiles and profile views are not the same thing. The profile view displays the profile data. A single profile can be shown in an infinite number of views, with different grids, exaggeration factors, labels, or linetypes. In the following sections, you'll look at the various methods available for creating profile views.

Creating Profile Views During Sampling

The easiest way to create a profile view is to draw it as an extended part of the surface-sampling procedure, as shown in the first exercise in this chapter. By combining the profile-sampling step with the creation of the profile view, you avoid one more trip to the menus. This is the most common method of creating a profile view, but we'll cover manual creation in the next section.

Creating Profile Views Manually

Once an alignment has profile information associated with it, any number of profile views might be needed to display the proper information in the right format. To create a second, third, or even tenth profile view once the sampling is done, you must use a manual creation method. In this exercise, you'll create a profile view manually for an alignment that already has a surface profile associated with it:

1. Open the 0708_ManualProfileView.dwg (0708_ManualProfileView_METRIC.dwg) file.

2. From the Home tab ➤ Profile & Section Views panel, choose Profile View ➤ Create Profile View to display the Create Profile View Wizard.

   This is the same wizard that was discussed in the surface-sampling example.

3. In the Select Alignment drop-down list, select ROAD G from the drop-down list.

4. Set the Profile View name as **ROAD G Full Grid**.

5. In the Profile View Style drop-down list, select the Full Grid style.

6. Click the Create Profile View button and pick a point onscreen to draw the profile view, as shown in Figure 7.37.

When this exercise is complete, you may save the drawing. A copy of this drawing at this stage is available from the book's web page with the filename 0708_ManualProfileView_FINISHED.dwg (0708_ManualProfileView_METRIC_FINISHED.dwg).

Using this creation method, you've made a short, simple profile view, but in the next exercise you will look at a longer alignment as well as some more of the options available in the Create Profile View Wizard.

FIGURE 7.37
The completed profile view of ROAD G using the Full Grid profile view style

Real World Scenario

SO YOU WANT TO DELETE A PROFILE VIEW?

Getting rid of a profile view is easy, but be careful not to inadvertently delete your profiles at the same time. If you use a crossing window when selecting the objects to delete, then you will also be deleting your profiles that hold the data shown in your profile view.

The easiest way to get rid of a profile view is to click one of the grid lines to activate the profile view object and press the Delete key on your keyboard.

Alternatively, you can delete the profile view by expanding the branches in Prospector until you see the profile view you want to get rid of and then right-clicking it and selecting the Delete option.

Splitting Views

Dividing up the data shown in a profile view can be time-consuming. The Profile View Wizard is used for simple profile view creation, but the wizard can also be used to create manually limited profile views, staggered (or stepped) profile views, multiple profile views with gaps between the views, and stacked profiles (aka three-line profiles). You'll now look at these variations on profile view creation.

CREATING MANUALLY LIMITED PROFILE VIEWS

Continuous profile views like the ones you made in the exercises prior to this point work well for design purposes, but they are often unusable for plotting or documentation purposes. In this exercise, you'll use the Profile View Wizard to create a manually limited profile view. This variation will allow you to control how long and how high each profile view will be, thereby making the views easier to plot:

1. Open the 0709_ManualLimitedProfileView.dwg file (or the 0709_ ManualLimitedProfileView_METRIC.dwg file).

2. From the Home tab ➢ Profile & Section Views panel, choose Profile View ➢ Create Profile View to display the Create Profile View Wizard.

3. Verify that the Select Alignment drop-down list shows Frontenac Drive, Profile Name is set to Frontenac Drive Limited Full Grid, and Full Grid is selected in the Profile View Style drop-down list; then click Next.

4. On the Station Range wizard page, select the User Specified Range radio button.

5. Enter **0** for the start station and **800** for the end station (or **0** and **245** for metric users), as shown in Figure 7.38.

   It isn't necessary to include the + when entering station data.

FIGURE 7.38
The start and end stations for the user-specified profile view

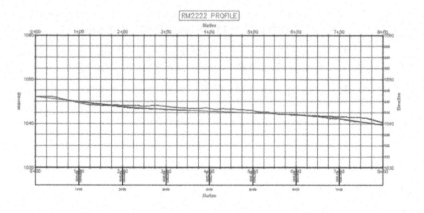

Notice that the preview picture now shows a clipped portion of the total profile.

6. Click Next.

7. On the Profile View Height wizard page, select the User Specified radio button.

8. Set the minimum height to **1030** and the maximum height to **1060** (or **314** and **322** for metric users).

   It isn't necessary to include the foot mark (') or m for meters when entering elevations.

9. Click the Create Profile View button and pick a point onscreen to draw the profile view.

   Your screen should look similar to Figure 7.39.

FIGURE 7.39
Applying user-specified station and height values to a profile view

When this exercise is complete, you may save the drawing, but keep it open for the following exercise. A copy of the drawing at this stage is available from the book's

web page with the filename 0709_ManualLimitedProfileView_FINISHED.dwg (0709_
ManualLimitedProfileView_METRIC_FINISHED.dwg).

CREATING SPLIT PROFILE VIEWS

When large variations occur in profile height, the profile view must often be split just to keep
from wasting much of the page with empty grid lines. In this exercise, you use the Create Profile
View Wizard to create a staggered, or stepped, view:

1. Continue using the file from the previous exercise, or if you did not complete the
   previous exercise, open the 0709_ManualLimitedProfileView_FINISHED.dwg (0709_
   ManualLimitedProfileView_METRIC_FINISHED.dwg) file.

2. From the Home tab ➤ Profile & Section Views panel, choose Profile View ➤ Create Profile
   View to display the Create Profile View Wizard.

3. Verify that the Select Alignment drop-down list shows RM2222, Profile View Name is set
   to RM2222 Staggered Full Grid, and Full Grid is selected in the Profile View Style drop-
   down list; then click Next.

4. Verify that Station Range is set to Automatic to allow the view to show the full length,
   and click Next.

5. In the Profile View Height field, select the User Specified option and set the values to **880**
   and **970** (or **268** and **294** for metric users), as shown in Figure 7.40.

FIGURE 7.40
Split Profile View
settings

6. Check the Split Profile View option and set the view styles to First View, Intermediate
   View, and Last View, as shown in Figure 7.40.

7. Click the Create Profile View button and pick a point onscreen to draw the staggered display, as shown in Figure 7.41.

FIGURE 7.41
A staggered (stepped) split profile view created via the wizard

The profile view is split into views according to the settings that were selected in the Create Profile View Wizard in step 6. The first portion of the profile view shows the profile from 0 to the station where the elevation change of the profile exceeds the limit for height. If more splits were required, the command would have created them accordingly. Each of these portions is part of the same profile view and can be adjusted via the Profile View Properties dialog.

The profile view splits can be controlled manually on the Elevations tab of the Profile View Properties dialog box. Here you can add and remove splits, control the station at which a given split occurs, and control the datum elevation at each split station by changing the Split Profile View option to Manual (see Figure 7.42).

FIGURE 7.42
The Elevations tab of the Profile View Properties dialog showing manual control of a split profile view

When this exercise is complete, you may save the drawing, but keep it open for the following exercise. A copy of the drawing at this stage is available from the book's web page with the filename 0709_StaggeredProfileView_FINISHED.dwg (0709_StaggeredProfileView_METRIC_FINISHED.dwg).

CREATING GAPPED PROFILE VIEWS

Profile views must often be limited in length and height to fit a given sheet size. Gapped views are a way to show the entire length and height of the profile by breaking the profile into different sections with gaps, or spaces, between each view.

When you are using the Plan Production tools (covered in Chapter 15, "Plan Production"), the gapped profile views are automatically created.

In this exercise, you will use a variation of the Create Profile View Wizard called the Create Multiple Profile Views Wizard to create gapped views automatically:

1. Continue using the file from the previous exercise, or if you did not complete the previous exercise, open the 0709_StaggeredProfileView_FINISHED.dwg (0709_StaggeredProfileView_METRIC_FINISHED.dwg) file.

2. From the Home tab ➤ Profile & Section Views panel, choose Profile View ➤ Create Multiple Profile Views to display the Create Multiple Profile Views Wizard.

3. Verify that the Select Alignment drop-down list shows RM2222, Profile View Name is set to RM2222 Gapped Full Grid, and Full Grid is selected in the Profile View Style drop-down list, as shown in Figure 7.43; then click Next.

FIGURE 7.43
The Create Multiple Profile Views – General wizard page

4. On the Station Range wizard page, verify that the Automatic option is selected.

5. Set the length of each view to **900** (or **275** for metric users), and click Next.

6. On the Profile View Height wizard page, verify that the Automatic option is selected.

    Note that you could use the Split Profile View options from the previous exercise here as well, if you use the User Specified profile view height.

7. Click Next.

8. On the Profile Display Options wizard page, scroll across until you get to the Labels column and verify that Style is set to _No Labels on both profiles; then click Next.

9. On the Data Bands wizard page, verify that the band set is EG-FG Elevations And Stations, and click the Multiple Plot Options link in the left sidebar of the wizard to jump ahead to that wizard page.

    We will cover the data bands in further depth a little later in this chapter.

The Multiple Plot Options wizard page shown in Figure 7.44 is unique to the Create Multiple Profile Views Wizard. This wizard page controls whether the gapped profile views will be arranged in a column, a row, or a grid. The RM2222 alignment is fairly short, so the gapped views will be aligned in a row. However, it could be prudent with longer alignments to stack the profile views in a column or a compact grid, thereby saving screen space.

FIGURE 7.44
The Create Multiple Profile Views – Multiple Plot Options wizard page

10. Click the Create Profile Views button and pick a point onscreen to create a view similar to Figure 7.45.

FIGURE 7.45
The staggered and gapped profile views of the RM2222 alignment

The gapped profile views are the four profile views on the bottom of the screen, and just like the staggered profile view, they show the entire alignment from start to finish. Unlike the staggered view, however, the gapped view is separated by a gap, creating four individual profile views. In addition, the gapped profile views are independent of each other, so they can be modified to have their own styles, properties, and labeling. This is also the primary way to create divided profile views for sheet production.

When this exercise is complete, you can save and close the drawing. A copy of the drawing at this stage is available from the book's web page with the filename `0709_GappedProfileView_FINISHED.dwg` (`0709_GappedProfileView_METRIC_FINISHED.dwg`).

CREATING STACKED PROFILE VIEWS

In some parts of the United States, a three-line profile view is a common requirement. In this situation, the centerline is displayed in a central profile view, with left and right offsets shown in profile views above and below the centerline profile view. These are then typically used to show top-of-curb design profiles in addition to the centerline design. In this exercise, you look at how the Create Profile View Wizard makes generating these stacked views a simple process:

1. Open the `0709_StackedProfileView.dwg` (`0709_StackedProfileView_METRIC.dwg`) file.

   This drawing has sampled profiles for the RM2222 alignment at center as well as left and right offsets.

2. From the Home tab ➤ Profile & Section Views panel, choose Profile View ➤ Create Profile View to display the Create Profile View Wizard.

3. Verify that the Select Alignment drop-down list shows RM2222, Profile View Name is set to RM2222 Stacked Full Grid, and Full Grid is selected in the Profile View Style drop-down list.

4. Check the Show Offset Profiles By Vertically Stacking Profile Views option on the General wizard page.

   Notice that when you check this box, an additional link named Stacked Profile is added to the left sidebar of the wizard.

5. Click Next.

6. On the Create Profile View – Station Range wizard page, verify that Station Range is set to Automatic, and click Next.

7. On the Create Profile View – Profile View Height wizard page, verify that Profile View Height is set to Automatic, and click Next.

8. On the Create Profile View – Stacked Profile wizard page, set the gap between views to **15** (or **4** for metric users).

9. Set the view styles to Top Stacked View, Middle Stacked View, and Bottom Stacked View, as shown in Figure 7.46. Click Next.

FIGURE 7.46
The Create Profile
View – Stacked
Profile wizard
page

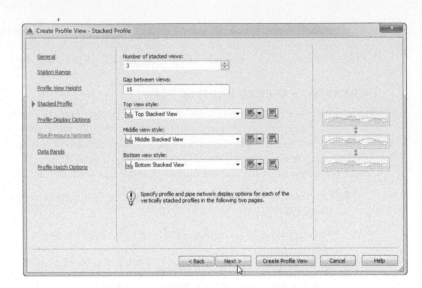

10. On the Create Profile View – Profile Display Options wizard page, select Top View in the Select Stacked View To Specify Options For list box.

11. Toggle the Draw option for the left offset profile (RM2222-EG - -30.000, or RM2222-EG - -10.000 for metric users), as shown in Figure 7.47.

FIGURE 7.47
Setting the
stacked view
options for each
view, in this case
for the top view

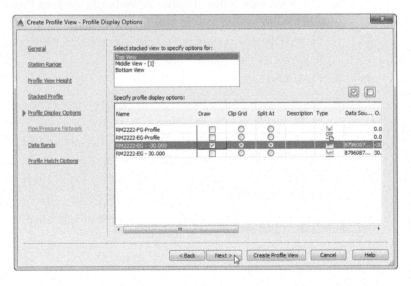

If you need to widen the columns, you can do so by double-clicking the line between the column headings.

Remember that the negative offset denotes a left profile, whereas a positive offset denotes a right profile. You can also check the Offset column to verify the offset.

12. Select Middle View - [1] in the Select Stacked View To Specify Options For list box.

13. Toggle the Draw option for the sampled centerline profile (RM2222-EG-Profile) as well as the layout centerline profile (RM2222-FG-Profile).

14. Select Bottom View in the Select Stacked View To Specify Options For list box.

15. Toggle the Draw option for the right offset profile (RM2222-EG - 30.000, or RM2222-EG - 10.000 for metric users), and click Next.

16. On the Data Bands wizard page, verify that the band set is set to EG-FG Elevations And Stations.

17. Click the Create Profile View button and pick a point on the screen to draw the stacked profiles, as shown in Figure 7.48.

FIGURE 7.48
Completed stacked profiles

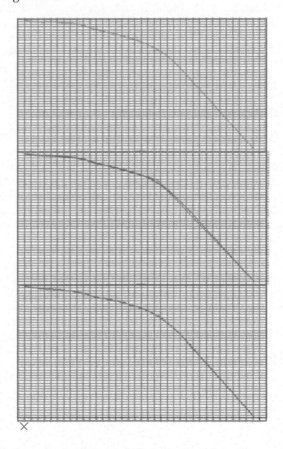

When this exercise is complete, you can save and close the drawing. A copy of the drawing at this stage is available from the book's web page with the filename 0709_StackedProfileView_FINISHED.dwg (0709_StackedProfileView_METRIC_FINISHED.dwg).

Like the gapped profile views that you generated in a previous exercise, the profile views are independent of one another, so they can be modified to have their own styles, properties, and labeling associated with them. The stacking here simply automates a process that many users previously found tedious. At this point you do not have finished grade information at the offsets, but you can add it to these views later by editing the Profile View Properties for those profile views.

When you create a profile, that profile will appear in any profile views that reference the same alignment. In the Profile View Properties dialog, you can always turn the Draw option off for any profile that should not appear in a given profile view.

STYLES: WHERE TO LOOK

The exercises in this chapter have many different styles created to show variety. You'll learn more about styles in Chapter 18, "Label Styles," and Chapter 19. It's okay to take a peek ahead once in a while.

Editing Profile Views

The profile view is one of the most sophisticated and flexible objects in the AutoCAD Civil 3D package. After a profile view is created, many modifications can be made to it without modifying the style or assigning a different style. In this series of exercises, you'll look at a number of changes that can be applied to any profile view in a given drawing.

SUPERELEVATION VIEWS

Although not the focus of this chapter, superelevation views behave much like profile views. Once design speeds have been assigned to an alignment and superelevation has been calculated, you'll find the Create Superelevation View command on the Alignment contextual tab ➤ Modify panel. You can access the view's properties via a contextual tab after selecting a view.

Profile View Properties

Picking a profile view and then selecting Profile View Properties from the Profile View contextual tab ➤ Modify View panel yields the dialog shown in Figure 7.49. The properties of a profile include the style applied, station and elevation limits, the number of profiles displayed, the bands associated with the profile view, and any hatching that has been included. If a pipe network is displayed, the Pipe Networks tab will appear. Also, if objects are projected in the profile view, then a Projections tab will be enabled and displayed as well. These tabs should look similar to the links in the sidebar of the Create Profile View Wizard.

FIGURE 7.49
Typical Profile
View Properties
dialog

ADJUSTING THE PROFILE VIEW STATION LIMITS

There are oftentimes when a profile view needs to be manually adjusted. For example, the most common change is to limit the length of the profile view that is being shown so it fits on a specific size of paper or viewport. You can make some of these changes during the initial creation of a profile view (as shown in a previous exercise), but you can also make changes after the profile view has been created.

One way to do this is to use the Profile View Properties dialog to make changes to the profile view. The profile view is an AutoCAD Civil 3D object, so it has properties and styles that can be adjusted in this dialog to make the profile view look like you need it to look.

1. Open the `0710_ProfileViewProperties.dwg` (`0710_ProfileViewProperties_METRIC .dwg`) file.

2. Zoom to the ROAD D Full Grid profile view.

3. Pick a grid line, and from the Profile View contextual tab ➢ Modify View panel, choose the Profile View Properties icon button to display the Profile View Properties dialog.

4. On the Stations tab, click the User Specified Range radio button, and set the value of the end station to **2200** (or **670** for metric users), as shown in Figure 7.50.

   Note that you do not need to type the + symbol.

FIGURE 7.50
Adjusting the end
station values for
ROAD D

5. Click OK to dismiss the dialog and press Esc to clear the selection.

   The profile view will now reflect the updated end station value.

   One of the nice things about Civil 3D is that copies of a profile view retain the properties of that view, making a gapped view easy to create manually if it was not created with the wizard.

6. Press F8 on your keyboard to enable Ortho mode.

7. Enter **Copy** ↵ on the command line.

8. Pick the ROAD D Full Grid profile view you just modified.

   Make sure you are selecting the grid representing the profile view and not the linework that represents the profile.

9. Press Enter to complete the selection.

10. Pick a base point and move the crosshairs to the right.

11. When the crosshairs reach a point where the two profile views do not overlap, pick that as your second point, and press ↵ to end the Copy command.

12. Pick a grid line on the copy just created, and from the Profile View contextual tab ➢ Modify View panel, choose Profile View Properties to display the Profile View Properties dialog.

13. On the Stations tab, set the Start field to **2200** (or **670** for metric users) and the End field to **4102.42** (or **1250.42** for metric users).

14. Click OK to dismiss the dialog.

   The total length of the alignment will now be displayed on the two profile views, with a gap between the two views at station 22+00 (or 0+760 for metric users).

You may want to move the copied profile view since it holds the station location, thus shifting it to the right. You could also copy the profile view in place and then change the settings, with no need to move the profile view.

Once this exercise is complete, your drawing will look like Figure 7.51.

FIGURE 7.51
A manually cre-
ated gap between
profile views

You can save and close the drawing. A copy of the drawing at this stage is available from the book's web page with the filename `0710_ProfileViewProperties_FINISHED.dwg` (`0710_ProfileViewProperties_METRIC_FINISHED.dwg`).

In addition to creating gapped profile views by changing the profile view properties, you could show phase limits by applying a different style to the profile in the second view.

ADJUSTING THE PROFILE VIEW ELEVATIONS

Another common issue is the need to control the height of the profile view. Civil 3D automatically sets the datum and the top elevation of profile views on the basis of the data to be displayed. In most cases this is adequate, but in others this simply creates a view too large for the space allocated on the sheet or does not provide the adequate room for layout PVIs to be placed.

1. Open the `0710_ProfileViewElevations.dwg` (`0710_ProfileViewElevations_METRIC .dwg`) file.

2. Zoom to the RM2222 Full Grid profile view, which is the first on the left.

3. Pick a grid line, and from the Profile View contextual tab ➤ Modify View panel, choose Profile View Properties to display the Profile View Properties dialog.

4. On the Elevations tab, in the Elevation Range section, select the User Specified Height radio button and set the maximum height to **1090** (or **332** for metric users), as shown in Figure 7.52.

FIGURE 7.52
Modifying the
height of the pro-
file view

Profile View Properties - RM2222 Full Grid			

Information | Stations | Elevations | Profiles | Bands | Hatch

Elevation range

	Minimum:	Maximum:	Height:
○ Automatic height	259.065m	318.842m	
● User specified height	256.000m	332.000m	76.000m

☐ Split profile view

○ Manual

● Automatic

Station rounding:
Exact station

Datum rounding:
Exact elevation

Split profile view data:

No.	Split Station	Adjusted Datum	Profile View Style

OK | Cancel | Apply | Help

5. Click OK to dismiss the dialog, and press Esc to clear the selection.

The profile view of RM2222 should reflect the updated elevation range, as shown in Figure 7.53.

FIGURE 7.53
The updated profile view with the heights manually adjusted

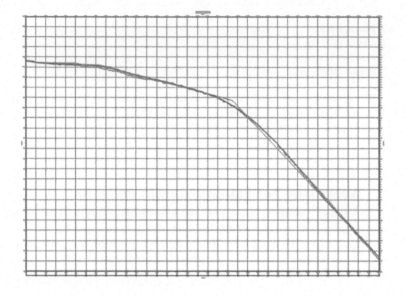

USING PROFILE DISPLAY OPTIONS

AutoCAD Civil 3D allows the creation of hundreds of profiles for any given alignment, which makes it easy to evaluate multiple design solutions, but it can also mean that profile views get crowded. In this exercise, you'll look at some profile display options that allow the toggling of various profiles within a profile view:

1. Continue using the file from the previous exercise, or open the 0710_ ProfileViewElevations_FINISHED.dwg (0710_ProfileViewElevations_METRIC_ FINISHED.dwg) file.

2. Click the grid for the last profile view on the right RM2222 Full Grid (1) (1).

3. From the Profile View contextual tab ➤ Modify View panel, choose Profile View Properties to display the Profile View Properties dialog.

4. Switch to the Profiles tab.

5. Uncheck the Draw option for RM2222-FG-Profile and click OK.

You might need to make the columns wider to be able to distinguish between the options. In any case, your profile view dialog settings should look similar to Figure 7.54.

FIGURE 7.54
The RM2222 profile view settings with the Draw option toggled off for RM2222-FG-Profile

Toggling off the Draw option for the FG layout has created a profile view in which a profile of the desired design will not be drawn.

The FG profile still exists under the RM2222 alignment; it simply isn't shown in the current profile view.

When this exercise is complete, you can save and close the drawing. A copy of the drawing at this stage is available from the book's web page with the filename 0710_ProfileViewToggle_FINISHED.dwg (0710_ProfileViewToggle_METRIC_FINISHED.dwg).

Now that you've modified profile views using a number of methods, let's look at another option that is available on the Profile View Properties dialog: Profile View Bands.

ADDING PROFILE VIEW BANDS

Data bands are horizontal elements that display additional graphical and numerical information about the profile or alignment that is referenced in a profile view. Bands can be applied to both the top and bottom of a profile view, and there are six different band types:

Profile Data Bands Display information about the selected profile. This information can include simple elements such as elevation or more complicated information such as the cut-fill between two profiles at a given station.

Vertical Geometry Bands Create a schematic view of the elements making up a profile. Typically used in reference to a design profile, vertical data bands make it easy for a designer to see the locations of tangents and vertical curves along an alignment as well as information about the tangents and vertical curves.

Horizontal Geometry Bands Create a schematic view of the horizontal alignment elements, giving the designer or reviewer information about line, curve, and spiral segments and their relative location to the profile data being displayed.

Superelevation Data Bands Display the various options for superelevation values at the critical points along the alignment.

Sectional Data Bands Can display information about the sample line locations and the distance between them as well as other section-related information.

Pipe Network Bands Can display specific information such as part, offset, elevation, or direction about each pipe or structure being shown in the profile view.

In this exercise, you'll add bands to give feedback on the EG and layout profiles as well as horizontal and vertical geometry:

1. Open the 0711_ProfileViewBands.dwg (0711_ProfileViewBands_METRIC.dwg) file.

2. Zoom to the ROAD D Full Grid profile view.

3. Pick a grid line, and from the Profile View contextual tab ≻ Modify View panel, choose Profile View Properties to display the Profile View Properties dialog.

4. On the Bands tab (Figure 7.55), in the List Of Bands area, verify that the Location drop-down is set to Bottom Of Profile View, and notice that an Elevations And Stations band has already been set during the creation of this profile view.

FIGURE 7.55
The Bands tab of the Profile View Properties dialog

Selecting the type of band from the Band Type drop-down menu changes the Select Band Style drop-down menu so that it includes only styles that are available for the band type you select. Next to the Select Band Style drop-down menu are the usual Style Edit/Copy button and a preview button.

Once you've selected a style from the Select Band Style drop-down, clicking the Add button places it on the profile. The Location drop-down list in the List Of Bands section of this dialog allows you to switch between the bands shown at the bottom of the profile view or the top of the profile view; you'll look at that in a moment.

5. Change the Band Type drop-down to the Profile Data option and choose the Cut Data option from the Select Band Style drop-down.

6. Click the Add button. The Geometry Points To Label In Band dialog will open (Figure 7.56).

FIGURE 7.56

The Geometry Points To Label In Band dialog showing the Alignment Points tab (left) and the Profile Points tab (right)

7. Click OK to accept the defaults in the Geometry Points To Label In Band dialog.

8. Leave Band Type set to Profile Data, and choose the Fill Data option from the Select Band Style drop-down.

9. Click the Add button, which will open the Geometry Points To Label In Band dialog once again. Click OK to accept the defaults and dismiss that dialog.

10. Change the Location drop-down to Top Of Profile View.

11. Change the Band Type drop-down to the Horizontal Geometry option and choose the Geometry option from the Select Band Style drop-down.

12. Click the Add button to add the Horizontal Geometry band to the table in the List Of Bands area.

13. Change the Band Type drop-down to the Vertical Geometry option.

Do not change the Select Band Style field from its current selection (Geometry).

14. Click the Add button to also add the Vertical Geometry band to the table in the List Of Bands area.

15. Click OK to exit the dialog and press Esc to deselect.

Your profile view should look like Figure 7.57.

FIGURE 7.57
Applying bands to
a profile view

There are obviously problems with the bands. The Vertical Geometry band is a mess and is located above the title of the profile view, whereas the Horizontal Geometry band over-writes the title. In addition, the elevation information has only the existing ground profile being referenced. Next, you'll fix those issues.

16. Pick a grid line on ROAD D Full Grid profile view.

17. From the Profile View contextual tab ➤ Modify View panel, choose Profile View Properties to display the Profile View Properties dialog.

18. On the Bands tab, verify that the Location drop-down in the List Of Bands area is set to Bottom Of Profile View.

19. Verify that the Match Major/Minor Increments To Vertical Grid Intervals option at the bottom of the page is selected.

Checking this option ensures that the major/minor intervals of the profile data band match the major/minor profile view style's major/minor grid spacing.

Three Profile Data bands are listed in the table in the List Of Bands area (Elevations And Stations, Cut Data, and Fill Data). If you need to widen the columns, you can do so by double-clicking the line between the column headings.

20. Scroll right and notice the two columns labeled Profile1 and Profile2.

21. For all three rows, change the value of Profile2 to **ROAD D FG**, as shown in Figure 7.58.

FIGURE 7.58
Setting the profile
view bands to ref-
erence the ROAD
D FG profile

22. Change the Location drop-down to Top Of Profile View.

    The Horizontal Geometry and Vertical Geometry bands are now listed in the table.

23. Scroll to the right again, and set the value of Profile1 in the Vertical Geometry band to **ROAD D FG**.

    Notice that some of the Profile1 and Profile2 boxes are not available for editing, such as those in the horizontal geometry band in the Top Of Profile View; this is because profile information isn't needed for this band.

24. Scroll back to the left and set the Gap value for the Horizontal Geometry band and the one for the Vertical Geometry band to **2″** (or **35 mm** for metric users).

    This value controls the distance from one band to the next for all bands for both top and bottom locations, except the first in the list of bands, for which this value defines the offset of the band from the bottom or top of the profile view, respectively.

25. Click OK to dismiss the dialog.

    Your profile view should now look like Figure 7.59.

FIGURE 7.59
Completed profile view with the bands appropriately spaced

You can save and close the drawing. A finished copy of this is available from the book's web page with the filename 0711_ProfileViewBands_FINISHED.dwg (0711_ProfileViewBands_METRIC_FINISHED.dwg).

Bands use the Profile1 and Profile2 designation as part of their style construction. By changing the profile referenced as Profile1 or Profile2, you change the values that are calculated and displayed (e.g., existing versus proposed elevations). These bands are just additional items that are driven by object styles, which you will learn more about in Chapter 19.

In the next section, you'll look at using band sets to make working with bands more efficient.

BAND SETS

Band sets are simply collections of bands, much like the profile label sets or alignment label sets. In this exercise, you'll save a band set and then apply it to a second profile view:

1. Open the 0711_ProfileViewBandsSet.dwg (0711_ProfileViewBandsSet_METRIC .dwg) file.

2. Pick a grid line in the ROAD D Full Grid profile view (the top profile view), and from the Profile View contextual tab ➤ Modify View panel, choose Profile View Properties to display the Profile View Properties dialog.

3. On the Bands tab, click the Save As Band Set button to display the Band Set – New Profile View Band Set dialog.

4. On the Information tab, in the Name field, enter **Cut Fill Elev Station and Horiz Vert Geometry**, as shown in Figure 7.60.

FIGURE 7.60
The Information tab for the Band Set – New Profile View Band Set dialog

5. Click OK to dismiss the Band Set – New Profile View Band Set dialog.

6. Click OK to dismiss the Profile View Properties dialog.

7. Press Esc to clear your selection; then pick a grid line in the ROAD A Full Grid profile view (profile view on the bottom), and from the Profile View contextual tab ➢ Modify View panel, choose Profile View Properties to display the Profile View Properties dialog.

8. On the Bands tab, click the Import Band Set button, and the Band Set dialog opens.

9. Select the Cut Fill Elev Station And Horiz Vert Geometry option from the drop-down list and click OK.

10. Select Top Of Profile View from the Location drop-down list.

11. Scroll over on the Vertical Geometry row and set Profile1 to **ROAD A FG**.

12. Select Bottom Of Profile View from the Location drop-down list.

13. Scroll over and change Profile2 to **ROAD A FG** for all three rows. Also make sure that Profile1 is set to MC3D2016-EG for all three.

14. Click OK to exit the Profile View Properties dialog.

Your ROAD A Full Grid profile view (Figure 7.61) now looks like the ROAD D Full Grid profile view with the exception of the finished grade labels.

FIGURE 7.61
Completed profile view after importing the band set and assigning profiles

Band sets allow you to create uniform labeling and callout information across a variety of profile views. By using a band set, you can take a collection of settings and styles that you've assigned to a single profile view and apply them to a number of profile views. The simplicity of enforcing standard profile view labels and styles makes using profiles and profile views simpler than ever.

You can save and close the drawing. A finished copy of this drawing is available from the book's web page with the filename 0711_ProfileViewBandsSet_FINISHED.dwg (0711_ ProfileViewBandsSet_METRIC_FINISHED.dwg).

UNDERSTANDING PROFILE VIEW HATCH

Sometimes it is necessary to hatch cut/fill areas in a profile view. The settings on the Hatch tab of the Profile View Properties dialog are used to specify upper and lower cut/fill boundary limits for associated profiles (see Figure 7.62).

FIGURE 7.62
Shape style selection on the Hatch tab of the Profile View Properties dialog

Shape styles from the General Multipurpose Styles branch found on the Settings tab of Toolspace can also be selected here. These settings include the following:

Cut Area   Click this button to add hatching to a profile view in areas of cut (the layout profile is at a lower elevation than the sampled surface profile).

Fill Area   Click this button to add hatching to a profile view in areas of fill (the layout profile is at a higher elevation than the sampled surface profile).

Multiple Boundaries   Click this button to add hatching to a profile view in areas of a cut/fill where the area must be averaged between two existing profiles (for example, finished ground at the centerline vs. the left and right top of a curb).

From Criteria   Click this button to add hatch in areas where quantity takeoff criteria are used to define a hatch region.

Figure 7.63 shows a cut and fill hatched profile based on the criteria shown previously in Figure 7.62.

FIGURE 7.63
A portion of the RM2222 profile shown with cut and fill shading

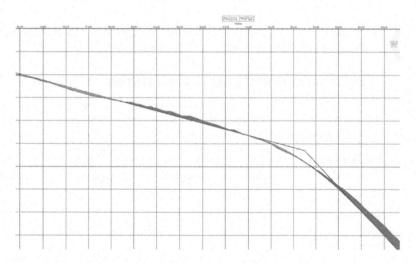

MASTERING PROFILES AND PROFILE VIEWS

One of the most difficult concepts to master in AutoCAD Civil 3D is the notion of which settings control which display property. Although the following two rules may sound overly simplistic, they are important to remember and will help you work through your understanding of the software:

◆   Every object has a label and an object style.

◆   Every label has a label style.

Furthermore, if you can remember that there is a distinct difference between a profile object and the profile view object you place it in, you'll be well on your way to mastering profiles and profile views. When in doubt, select an object and observe the options that become available on the contextual ribbon tab. Label styles and object styles will be discussed further in Chapters 18 and 19, respectively.

Profile View Labeling Styles

Now that the profile view is created, the profile view grid spacing is set, and the titles all look good, it's time to add some specific callouts and detail information. Civil 3D uses profile view labels and bands for annotating. The specific label styles will be discussed further in Chapter 18, but for now we will just discuss how to apply the labels.

VIEW ANNOTATION

Profile view annotations label individual points in a profile view, but they are not always tied to a specific profile object like a pipe. Profile view labels can be station elevation labels, depth labels, or projection labels; projection labels are tied to entities or projected from plan view. Station elevation labels can be used to label a single point or the depth between two points in a profile while recognizing the vertical exaggeration of the profile view and applying the scaling factor to label the correct depth. In this exercise, you'll use both the station elevation label and the depth label:

1. Open the 0712_ProfileViewLabels.dwg (0712_ProfileViewLabels_METRIC.dwg) file.

2. Zoom to the ROAD D Full Grid profile view.

3. From the Annotate tab ➤ Labels & Tables panel, choose Add Labels (not the drop-down list) to open the Add Labels dialog.

4. In the Feature drop-down, select Profile View.

5. In the Label Type drop-down, verify that Station Elevation is selected.

6. In the Station Elevation Label Style drop-down, verify that Station And Elevation is selected.

7. Verify that the marker style is set to Basic Circle With Cross.

8. Click the Add button.

9. When prompted to select a profile view, click a grid line in the ROAD D Full Grid profile view, and a vertical red line will appear.

10. Zoom in around station 11+40 (or 0+347 for metric users) so that you can see the point where the EG and layout profiles cross.

11. Turn off your running Osnaps and pick this profile crossover point visually; then pick the same point to set the elevation and press ↵.

    Your label should look like Figure 7.64, although the actual values will vary slightly.

FIGURE 7.64
A profile view station and elevation label

> **SNAPPING TO PROFILES AND PROFILE VIEWS**
>
> For a number of releases now, users have been asking for the ability to simply snap to the intersection of two profiles. We mention this because you'll try to snap and wonder if you've lost your mind. You haven't—it just doesn't work. If you are after a solution (it isn't elegant), you can draw lines on top of the profiles.

12. In the Add Labels dialog, change both Label Type and Depth Label Style to the Depth option.

13. Click the Add button.

14. Pick the ROAD D Full Grid profile view by clicking one of the grid lines.

15. Pick a point along the layout profile; then pick a point along the EG profile at approximately the same station and press ↵.

The depth between the two profiles will be measured, as shown in Figure 7.65. Your value may vary from what is shown.

FIGURE 7.65
A depth label
applied to the
ROAD D Full Grid
profile view

16. Close the Add Labels dialog.

You can save and close the drawing. A finished copy of this drawing is available from the book's web page with the filename 0712_ProfileViewLabels_FINISHED.dwg (0712_ ProfileViewLabels_METRIC_FINISHED.dwg).

Depth labels can be handy in earthworks situations where cut and fill become critical, and individual spot labels are important to understanding points of interest, but most design documentation is accomplished with labels placed along the profile view axes in the form of data bands and band sets discussed earlier in this chapter.

Profile Labels

It's important to remember that the profile and the profile view aren't the same thing. The labels discussed in the following sections are those that relate directly to the profile but are visible for a specific profile view. This usually means station-based labels, individual tangent and curve labels, or grade breaks.

Applying Labels

As with alignments, you can apply labels as a group of objects separate from the profile. In this portion of the exercise, you'll learn how to add labels along a profile object:

1. Open the `0712_ProfileLabels.dwg` (`0712_ProfileLabels_METRIC.dwg`) file.

2. Zoom to the ROAD D Full Grid profile view and pick the ROAD D FG profile (the blue line) to activate the Profile contextual tab.

Edit Profile
Labels

3. From the Profile contextual tab ➢ Labels panel, choose Edit Profile Labels to display the Profile Labels dialog (see Figure 7.66).

FIGURE 7.66
An empty Profile
Labels dialog

Selecting the type of label from the Type drop-down menu changes the Style drop-down menu to include styles that are available for that label type. Next to the Style drop-down menu are the usual Style Edit/Copy button and Preview button.

Once you've selected a style from the Style drop-down menu, clicking the Add button places it on the profile. The middle portion of this dialog displays information about the labels that are being applied to the profile selected; you'll look at that in a moment.

4. Choose the Major Stations option from the Type drop-down menu.

The name of the second drop-down menu changes to Profile Major Station Label Style to reflect this option.

5. Verify that Perpendicular With Tick is selected in this menu.

6. Click the Add button to apply this label to the profile.

7. Choose Horizontal Geometry Points from the Type drop-down menu.

The name of the Style drop-down menu changes to Profile Horizontal Geometry Point.

8. Select the Horizontal Geometry Station option, and click the Add button again to display the Geometry Points dialog.

This dialog lets you apply different label styles to different geometry points if necessary.

9. Deselect the Alignment Beginning and Alignment End rows, as shown in Figure 7.67, and click OK to dismiss the dialog.

FIGURE 7.67
The Geometry
Points dialog
appears when you
apply labels to
horizontal geom-
etry points.

10. On the Profile Labels dialog, click the Apply button.

11. Drag the dialog out of the way to view the changes to the profile, as shown in Figure 7.68.

FIGURE 7.68
Labels applied to
major stations and
alignment geom-
etry points

12. In the middle of the Profile Labels dialog, change the Increment value in the Major Stations row to **50** (or **10** for metric users), as shown in Figure 7.69.

FIGURE 7.69
Modifying the
major station
labeling increment

This modifies the labeling increment only, not the grid or other values.

13. Click OK to dismiss the Profile Labels dialog.

You can save and close the drawing. A finished copy of this drawing is available from the book's web page with the filename `0712_ProfileLabels_FINISHED.dwg` (`0712_ProfileLabels_METRIC_FINISHED.dwg`).

Using Profile Label Sets

Applying labels one at a time to both crest and sag curves and to tangents, grade breaks, and geometry can be tedious. Thankfully, Civil 3D gives you the ability to use label sets, as in alignments, to make the process quick and easy. Just as you saved and imported band sets in a previous example, you can save and import label sets as well.

In all of the previous examples, you used either the complete label set or the _No Labels label set, which you specified on the Profile Display Options wizard page.

SOMETIMES YOU DON'T WANT TO SET EVERYTHING

Resist the urge to modify the beginning or ending station values in a label set. If you save a specific value, that value will be applied when the label set is imported. For example, if you set a station label to end at 15+00 because the alignment is 15+15 long, that label will always stop at 15+00, even if the target profile is 5,000' long!

Label sets are the best way to apply profile labeling uniformly. When you're working with a well-developed set of styles and label sets, it's quick and easy to go from sketched profile layout to plan-ready output. We will discuss profile label sets in further detail and go over an example in Chapter 18.

Profile Utilities

One common requirement is to compare profile data for objects that are aligned similarly but not parallel. Another is the ability to project objects from a plan view into a profile view. The abilities to superimpose profiles and project objects are both discussed in this section.

Superimposing Profiles

In a profile view, a profile is sometimes superimposed to show one profile adjacent to another (for example, a ditch adjacent to a road centerline). In this brief exercise, you'll superimpose one of your street designs onto the other to see how they compare over a certain portion of their length:

1. Open the `0713_SuperImposeProfile.dwg` (`0713_SuperImposeProfile_METRIC.dwg`) file.

2. From the Home tab ➤ Create Design panel, choose Profile ➤ Create Superimposed Profile.

3. At the `Select source profile:` prompt, zoom to the ROAD C TRAIL Full Grid profile view on the right and pick the ROAD C TRAIL FG profile (the blue line).

4. At the `Select destination profile view:` prompt, click one of the grid lines in the ROAD C Full Grid profile view to display the Superimpose Profile Options dialog shown in Figure 7.70.

FIGURE 7.70
The Superimpose Profile Options dialog

On the Limits tab you can control the start and end stations of the superimposed profile, in the event that you do not want the entire profile to be superimposed. On the Accuracy tab, you can control the handling of curves through the mid-ordinate settings. Superimposed curves aren't curves at all; they are lots of small segments that approximate a curve. The smaller the mid-ordinate distance values, the smaller and more numerous the segments will be.

5. Click OK to dismiss the dialog, accepting the default settings.

6. Zoom in on the ROAD C Full Grid profile view to see the superimposed data, as shown in Figure 7.71.

FIGURE 7.71
The ROAD C TRAIL FG layout profile superimposed on the ROAD C Full Grid profile view

Note that the vertical curves in the ROAD C TRAIL FG layout profile have been approximated on the ROAD C Full Grid profile view, using a series of PVIs. Superimposing works by projecting a line from the target alignment (ROAD C) to a perpendicular intersection with the other source alignment (ROAD C TRAIL).

The target alignment is queried for an elevation at the intersecting station, and a PVI is added to the superimposed profile. Note that this superimposed profile is still dynamic! A change in the ROAD C TRAIL FG layout profile will be reflected on the ROAD C Full Grid profile view.

When this exercise is complete, you can save and close the drawing. A finished copy of this drawing is available from the book's web page with the filename `0713_SuperImposeProfile_FINISHED.dwg` (`0713_SuperImposeProfile_METRIC_FINISHED.dwg`).

Projecting Objects in Profile View

Some AutoCAD and some AutoCAD Civil 3D objects can be projected from a plan view into a profile view. The list of available AutoCAD objects includes points, blocks, 3D solids, and 3D polylines. The list of available AutoCAD Civil 3D objects includes COGO points, feature lines, and survey figures. These objects can be projected to the object's elevation, a manually selected elevation, a surface, or a profile. In the following exercise, you'll project a 3D object into a profile view:

1. Open the `0714_ProjectToProfile.dwg` (`0714_ProjectToProfile_METRIC.dwg`) file.

2. From the Home tab ➢ Profile & Section Views panel, choose Profile View ➢ Project Objects To Profile View.

3. At the `Select objects to add to profile view:` prompt, select the three power poles and the fire hydrant object located along the left and right of the ROAD C alignment and press ↵.

4. At the `Select a profile view:` prompt, select the ROAD C Full Grid profile view by clicking one of the grid lines to display the Project Objects To Profile View dialog.

5. Verify that Style is set to Power Pole for the power poles object and to Hydrant (existing) for the hydrant object, Elevation Options is set to Surface ➤ MC3D2016-EG, and Label Style is set to Projection Dimension Below, as shown in Figure 7.72.

FIGURE 7.72
A completed
Project Objects To
Profile View dialog

6. Click OK to dismiss the dialog, and review your results, as shown in Figure 7.73.

FIGURE 7.73
The COGO point
objects projected
into a profile view

We actually wanted the second power pole along the alignment to show on the proposed surface. No problem. Follow the next steps.

7. Click the power pole in profile view to activate the Cogo Point contextual tab. Together with this tab another tab is activated, the Projected Object tab. Switch to this contextual tab.

8. From the Projected Object contextual tab ➤ Modify Projected Object panel, choose Projection Properties to display the Profile View Properties dialog.

9. In the Profile View Properties dialog, click the cell in the Elevation Options column for the Cogo Point 2 object, and from the drop-down select Profile ➤ ROAD C FG, as shown in Figure 7.74. Click OK.

FIGURE 7.74
Selecting the
ROAD C FG profile
elevation

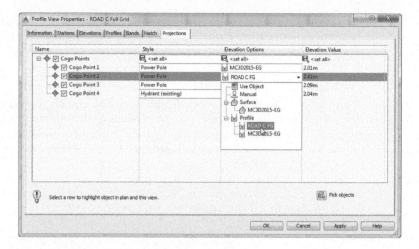

The projected power pole is now adjusted to match the elevation of the ROAD C FG profile, as shown in Figure 7.75.

FIGURE 7.75
The COGO point
object projected
onto the ROAD C
FG profile

You can save and close the drawing. A finished copy of this drawing is available from the book's web page with the filename 0714_ProjectToProfile_FINISHED.dwg (0714_ProjectToProfile_METRIC_FINISHED.dwg).

Once an object has been projected into a profile view, the Profile View Properties dialog will display a new Projections tab. Projected objects will remain dynamically linked with respect to their plan placement. If you move them manually in profile view after placing them dynamically, a warning will appear to confirm that you want to break the dynamic setting.

Because profile views and section views are similar in nature, objects can be projected into section views in the same fashion. However, projecting a feature line drawn parallel to an alignment into a profile view will give you a different result than projecting it onto a section view. On a profile view, it will look more like a superimposed profile. On a section view, it will look more like a pipe crossing since it will appear only where it intersects the section line.

Creating a Quick Profile

There are going to be times when all you want is to quickly look at a profile and not keep it for later use. When this is the case, instead of creating an alignment, a profile, and a profile view, you can create a quick profile. A quick profile is a temporary object that will not be saved with the drawing. You can create a quick profile for 2D or 3D lines or polylines, lot lines, feature lines, survey figures, and even a series of points.

From the Home tab ➤ Create Design panel, choose Profile ➤ Quick Profile. The command line will state `Select object or [by Points]:`. Once you select your object (or points), the Create Quick Profiles dialog is displayed (Figure 7.76).

FIGURE 7.76
The Create Quick
Profiles dialog

You can select which surface you want to sample as well as what profile view style and 3D entity profile style to use. Upon clicking OK, you will be prompted for a location to place the profile. A quick profile is a temporary profile that will be erased once a save operation is performed on the drawing. You cannot access Profile View Properties for a quick profile, but you can select a different style to use for this profile view by using the Properties palette. You cannot sample other sources or create new layout profiles once the profile view is created, but you can project objects and superimpose other profiles and pipe networks into this view.

The Bottom Line

Sample a surface profile with offset samples.   Using surface data to create dynamic sampled profiles is an important advantage of working with a three-dimensional model. Quick viewing of various surface centerlines and grip-editing alignments makes for an effective preliminary planning tool. Combined with offset data to meet review agency requirements, profiles are robust design tools in Civil 3D.

Master It   Open the MasterIt_0701.dwg (MasterIt_0701_METRIC.dwg) file and sample the ground surface along Alignment A, along with offset values at 15′ left and 15′ right (or 4.5 m left and 4.5 m right) of the alignment. Generate a profile view showing this information using the Major Grids profile view style with no data band sets.

Lay out a design profile on the basis of a table of data.   Many programs and designers work by creating pairs of station and elevation data. The tools built into Civil 3D let you input this data precisely and quickly.

Master It   Continue in the previous file or open MasterIt_0701_FINISHED.dwg (MasterIt_0701_METRIC_FINISHED.dwg). Create a layout profile on Alignment A using the Layout profile style and the Complete Label Set with the following information for Imperial users:

Station	PVI Elevation	Curve Length
0+00	822.00	
1+80	825.60	300′
6+50	800.80	

Or use the following information for metric users:

Station	PVI Elevation	Curve Length
0+000	250.400	
0+062	251.640	100 m
0+250	244.840	

Add and modify individual entities in a design profile. The ability to delete, modify, and edit the individual components of a design profile while maintaining the relationships is an important concept in the 3D modeling world. Tweaking the design allows you to pursue a better solution, not just a working solution.

Master It Continue in the previous file or open MasterIt_0702_FINISHED.dwg (MasterIt_0702_METRIC_FINISHED.dwg). For the layout profile created in the previous exercise, modify the curve so that it is 200¢ (or 60 m for metric users). Then insert a PVI at Station 4+90, Elevation 794.60 (or at Station 0+150, Elevation 242.840, for metric users), and add a 300′ (or 96 m for metric users) parabolic vertical curve at the newly created PVI.

Apply a standard band set. Standardization of appearance is one of the major benefits of using styles in labeling. By applying band sets, you can quickly create plot-ready profile views that have the required information for review.

Master It Continue in the previous file or open MasterIt_0703_FINISHED.dwg (MasterIt_0703_METRIC_FINISHED.dwg). Apply the Cut And Fill band set to the layout profile created in the previous exercise with the appropriate profiles referenced in each of the bands.

Chapter 8

Assemblies and Subassemblies

Roads, ditches, trenches, and berms usually follow a predictable pattern known as a *typical section*. Assemblies are how you tell the Autodesk® AutoCAD® Civil 3D® software what these typical sections look like. Assemblies consist of smaller components called *subassemblies*. For example, a typical road section assembly contains subassemblies such as lanes, sidewalks, and curbs.

In this chapter, the focus will be on understanding where these assemblies come from and how to build and manage them.

In this chapter, you will learn to:

◆ Create a typical road assembly with lanes, curbs, gutters, and sidewalks.

◆ Edit an assembly.

◆ Add daylighting to a typical road assembly.

Subassemblies

A *subassembly* is a building block of a typical section, known as an *assembly*. Examples of subassemblies include lanes, curbs, sidewalks, channels, trenches, daylighting, and any other component required to complete a typical corridor section.

An extensive selection of subassemblies has been created for use in Civil 3D. More than 100 subassemblies are available in the tool palettes, and each subassembly has a list of adjustable *parameters*. There are also more than a dozen generic links you can use to further refine your most complex assembly needs. From ponds and berms to swales and roads, the design possibilities are almost infinite.

To expand the possibilities even more, you can use the Subassembly Composer to create custom subassemblies from scratch. Subassembly Composer is a separate program whose sole purpose is to build custom subassemblies. You can learn more about Subassembly Composer in the bonus chapter named "Custom Subassemblies" that is available on the book's website, www .sybex.com/go/masteringcivil3d2016.

The Tool Palettes

You will add subassemblies to a design by clicking them from the subassembly tool palette, as you'll see later in this chapter. By default, Civil 3D has several tool palettes created for corridor modeling.

 You can access these tool palettes from the Home tab by clicking the Tool Palettes button on the Palettes panel or by pressing Ctrl+3.

When Civil 3D is installed, you have an initial set of the most commonly used assemblies and subassemblies ready to go. The Tool Palettes window consists of multiple customizable tabs that categorize the assemblies and subassemblies so that they are easy to find.

The top, default tab in the Tool Palettes window is the Assemblies tab. On this tab you will find a selection of predefined, completed assemblies (Figure 8.1). These are a great starting point for beginners who are looking for examples of how subassemblies are put together into an assembly. There are examples of simple roadway sections as well as more advanced items, such as intersections and roundabouts. To use one, click the desired assembly tool on the Tool Palettes window and then click within the drawing area and press ↵ to end the command.

FIGURE 8.1
Tool Palettes predefined assemblies

GETTING TO THE TOOL PALETTES

The exercises in this chapter depend heavily on the use of the Tool Palettes window of AutoCAD. To avoid redundancy, we will assume that you have the Tool Palettes window open for each exercise and not include instructions to open it. In case you need a reminder, the easiest way to open the Tool Palettes window is either by going to the Home tab ➤ Palettes panel or by pressing Ctrl+3 on your keyboard.

The Corridor Modeling Catalogs

All of the assemblies and subassemblies that ship with Civil 3D are included in the Tool Palettes window. However, if any mysteriously disappear, they can be reloaded from the Content Browser.

The Corridor Modeling Catalogs are installed by default on your local hard drive in `C:\ ProgramData\Autodesk\C3D 2016\enu\Tool Catalogs\Road Catalog\ AutoCAD Civil 3D Imperial Corridor Catalog.atc` or `AutoCAD Civil 3D Metric Corridor Catalog.atc` for metric users. You access it on the Home tab by expanding the Palettes panel and clicking the Content Browser button to open the Content Browser interface.

Choose either the metric or Imperial corridor catalogs to explore the entire collection of subassemblies available in each category (see Figure 8.2).

FIGURE 8.2
The front page of the Corridor Modeling Catalog

Adding Subassemblies to a Tool Palette

To add subassemblies to your Tool Palettes window, you can use the i-drop to grab subassemblies from the catalog and drop them onto the Tool Palettes window. To use the i-drop, follow these steps:

1. Click the small blue *i* next to any subassembly and continue to hold down your left mouse button until you're over the desired tool palette.

2. Release the button, and your subassembly should appear on the tool palette (see Figure 8.3).

Note that if you i-drop drag the items from the home screen such as Assemblies, you get the full palette named Assemblies. If you use i-drop to drag just a subassembly onto a palette, then only that subassembly is added to the palette.

FIGURE 8.3
Using the i-drop to add the RailSingle subassembly to a tool palette

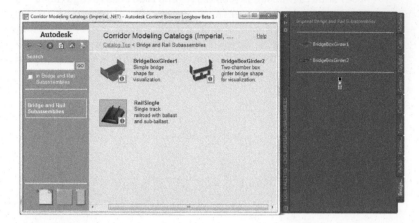

Building Assemblies

You build an assembly from the Home tab ➤ Create Design panel by choosing Assembly ➤ Create Assembly and selecting an insertion point in the graphic. The result is the main assembly baseline marker. This is the point on the assembly that gets attached to your design alignment and profile. Figure 8.4 shows a typical assembly baseline.

FIGURE 8.4
Creating an assembly (left); an assembly baseline marker (right)

When an assembly is created, you have the option of telling Civil 3D what type of assembly this will be:

- Undivided Crowned Road

- Undivided Planar Road

- Divided Crowned Road

- Divided Planar Road

- Railway

- Other

These categories will help the software determine the axis of rotation options in superelevation, if needed.

Once an assembly is created and assigned a type, you start piecing it together using various subassemblies to meet your design intent. In the next section, we explain how you can create a simple and common assembly type, an undivided crowned road.

Creating a Typical Road Assembly

The process for building an assembly requires the use of the Tool Palettes window (accessible using Ctrl+3) and the AutoCAD Properties palette (accessible using Ctrl+1), both of which can be docked. You'll quickly learn how to best orient these palettes with your limited screen real estate. If you run dual monitors, you may find it useful to place both of these palettes on your second monitor.

The exercise that follows builds a typical assembly, as shown in Figure 8.5, using Lane SuperelevationAOR, UrbanCurbGutterGeneral, UrbanSidewalk, and DaylightMaxOffset subassemblies.

FIGURE 8.5
A typical road
assembly

Let's have a more detailed look at each component you'll use in the following exercise. A quick peek into the subassembly help file will give you a breakdown of attachment options; input parameters; target parameters; output parameters; behavior; layout mode operation; and the point, link, and shape codes.

The LaneSuperelevationAOR Subassembly   The LaneSuperelevationAOR subassembly is an all-purpose subassembly for lanes. It can superelevate for an inside or outside lane if needed and allows for up to four layers of materials. The input parameters available are Side, Width, Default Slope, Pave1 Depth, Pave2 Depth, Base Depth, Subbase Depth, Use Superelevation, Slope Direction, Potential Pivot, Inside Point Code, and Outside Point Code. The default width of 12′ (3.6 m) can be adjusted in the Parameters section of the Properties palette or can be overridden with an offset alignment, feature line, or polyline to control its width. Figure 8.6 shows the image provided in the subassembly help file for this subassembly.

FIGURE 8.6
LaneSuperelevationAOR
subassembly help diagram

The UrbanCurbGutterGeneral Subassembly The UrbanCurbGutterGeneral subassembly is another standard component that creates an attached curb and gutter. Looking into the subassembly help file, you'll see a diagram of UrbanCurbGutterGeneral with input parameters for Side, Insertion Point, Gutter Slope Method, Gutter Slope, Gutter Slope Direction, Subbase Depth, Subbase Extension, Subbase Slope Method, Subbase Slope, and the subassembly's seven dimensions. You can adjust these parameters to match many standard curb-and-gutter configurations. Figure 8.7 shows the image provided in the subassembly help file for this subassembly.

FIGURE 8.7
UrbanCurbGutterGeneral
subassembly help diagram

The UrbanSidewalk Subassembly The UrbanSidewalk subassembly creates a sidewalk and terrace buffer strips. The help file lists the following six input parameters for the UrbanSidewalk subassembly: Side, Inside Boulevard Width, Sidewalk Width, Outside Boulevard Width, Slope, and Depth. These input parameters let you adjust the sidewalk width, material depth, and buffer widths to match your design specification. Figure 8.8 shows the image provided in the subassembly help file for this subassembly.

FIGURE 8.8
UrbanSidewalk
subassembly help
diagram

The UrbanSidewalk subassembly can return quantities of concrete (or other sidewalk construction material) but not gravel bedding or other advanced material layers. If you needed to track these materials, you could use generic subassemblies (covered later in this chapter) or build a custom subassembly using Subassembly Composer (covered in the online bonus chapter, "Custom Subassemblies").

The DaylightMaxOffset Subassembly   The DaylightMaxOffset subassembly is a nice "starter" for creating simple, single-slope daylight instructions for your corridor. In Civil 3D, an offset dimension is measured from the baseline, and a width is measured from the attachment point. Therefore, the maximum offset in our example is measured from the centerline of the road, which is the baseline. The slope will attempt a default of 4:1, but it will adjust if it needs to in order to keep inside your specified maximum offset (such as a right-of-way line). Options are also available for rounding. Figure 8.9 shows the image provided in the subassembly help file for this subassembly.

FIGURE 8.9
DaylightMaxOffset
subassembly help
diagram for the
cut scenario

WHAT'S WITH THE FUNNY NAMES?

You'll notice that all subassemblies have names with no spaces. This is because of the underlying .NET coding that makes up a subassembly. When you place one of these in your project, it will retain the name from the tool palette.

Prior to Civil 3D 2013, each subassembly was required to have a unique name; therefore, it was suffixed with a number. This is no longer the case. Nonetheless, later in this chapter you'll see how to rename them to something more user friendly if you so desire.

In the following exercise, you'll build a typical road assembly using the subassemblies discussed previously. Follow these steps:

1. Start a new blank drawing from the `_AutoCAD Civil 3D (Imperial) NCS` template that ships with Civil 3D. Metric users can use the `_AutoCAD Civil 3D (Metric) NCS` template.

2. Confirm that your Tool Palettes window is showing the subassembly set appropriate for your drawing units (imperial or metric).

   If you need to change your active Tool Palettes window from Metric to Imperial or vice versa, right-click the Tool Palettes control bar located at the top of the window if docked (Figure 8.10, left) or on the opposite edge of the palette from the tabs if undocked (Figure 8.10, right).

FIGURE 8.10
Right-click the
Tool Palettes con-
trol bar to change
assembly sets if
needed.

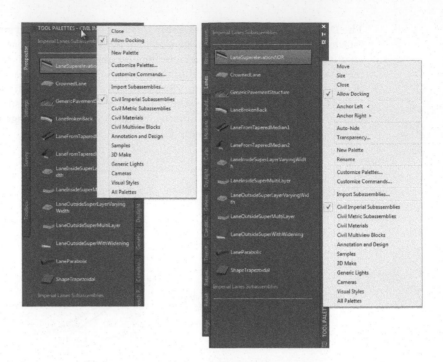

3. Verify that your drawing scale is set to 1=10′ (1:50 for metric users).

4. From the Home tab ➤ Create Design panel, choose Assembly ➤ Create Assembly.

   The Create Assembly dialog opens.

5. In the Create Assembly dialog, follow these steps:

   a. Enter **Urban 14′ Single-Lane** (or **Urban 4.5m Single-Lane**) in the Name text box.

   b. Set Assembly Type to Undivided Crowned Road.

   c. Confirm that Assembly Style is set to Basic and Code Set Style is set to All Codes, and click OK.

6. Pick a location in your drawing to place your red assembly baseline marker.

   The program will automatically zoom you into the assembly.

7. Locate and select the Lanes tab on the Tool Palettes window.

   Position the palette on your screen so that you can clearly see the assembly baseline.

8. Click the LaneSuperelevationAOR button on the Tool Palettes window.

   The AutoCAD Properties palette appears (if it is not already open).

9. Locate the Advanced Parameters section on the Design tab of the AutoCAD Properties palette (Figure 8.11).

FIGURE 8.11
Advanced
Parameters on the
Properties palette

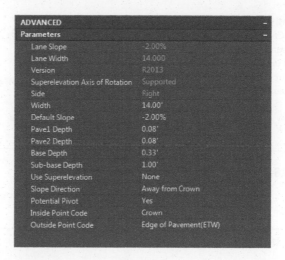

This section lists the LaneSuperelevationAOR parameters.

10. Change the Width parameter to **14'** (**4.5m**).

Your Properties palette should resemble Figure 8.11.

11. At the Select marker point within assembly or [Insert Replace Detached]: prompt, select anywhere on the red assembly baseline marker to place the first lane.

Note that it is placed on the right side as specified in the Advanced Parameters section.

12. Before ending the command, click the red assembly baseline marker again to place the left lane.

For most subassemblies, Civil 3D has the intelligence to automatically detect the side and place a subassembly on the appropriate side regardless of what is specified in the Advanced Parameters section.

13. Press ⏎ to end the command.

14. Switch to the Curbs tab in the Tool Palettes window.

15. Click the UrbanCurbGutterGeneral button on the Tool Palettes window.

16. Accept the parameter defaults, so no changes are needed.

Remember that the Side parameter will automatically be detected, so there is no need to change it.

17. At the Select marker point within assembly or [Insert Replace Detached]: prompt, select the circular marker located at the top right of the LaneSuperelevationAOR subassembly located on the right side of the assembly.

This marker represents the top-right edge of pavement (see Figure 8.12).

FIGURE 8.12
UrbanCurbGutterGeneral
subassembly
placed on the
LaneSuperelevationAOR
subassembly

18. Press ↵ to end the command.

You will add the left curb later. Keep this drawing open for the next portion of the exercise.

IF YOU GOOF...

Often, the first instinct when a subassembly is misplaced is to undo or erase the wayward piece. However, if you have spent a lot of time diligently tweaking parameters, there is a way to fix things without redoing the subassembly.

MOVING A SUBASSEMBLY

Select the errant subassembly component and use the Move option from the Subassembly contextual tab ➤ Modify Subassembly panel. Use this instead of the base AutoCAD Move tool to get the best results. Using regular AutoCAD Move may cause unexpected results in the corridor. The subassembly move command does not require a base point. It will prompt you to select the marker point where the assembly should have been placed.

INSERTING A SUBASSEMBLY

Sometimes you forget to place a subassembly component, or your design changes and you want to include a subassembly that wasn't there before. Prior to Civil 3D 2013, you had to delete the subassembly components from the outside in until you got to where you wanted to insert your missing subassembly and then had to re-create the deleted subassembly pieces.

In this version of Civil 3D, you may have noticed that every time you place an assembly the command line states `Select marker point within assembly or [Insert Replace Detached]:`. If you enter **I**, the command line will state `Select the subassembly to insert after or [Before]:`. The ability to insert a subassembly will come in handy when the planner decides to add a sidewalk at the shoulder of your road.

REPLACING A SUBASSEMBLY

Similar to the insert operation, you can also replace a subassembly component with another component. Again, you will find this helpful when the planner decides to make changes to your design.

DELETING A SUBASSEMBLY

To delete a subassembly component, you can simply select the subassembly component and press the Delete key. The assembly will connect the subassemblies on either side at the connection points previously used with the deleted component.

> **CHANGING SUBASSEMBLY PARAMETERS**
>
> If you placed everything correctly but forgot to change a parameter or two, there's an easy fix for that, too. Cancel out of any active subassembly placement and select the subassembly you want to change. Most subassembly parameters can be changed from the AutoCAD Properties palette. For more heavy-duty modifications (such as specifying the side), you will want to get into the Subassembly Properties discussed later in this chapter.

19. In the Curbs tab, click the UrbanSidewalk button on the Tool Palettes window.

20. In the Advanced Parameters area of the AutoCAD Properties palette, change the following parameters, leaving all other parameters at their default values:

    Sidewalk Width: **5′ (1.5 m)**

    Inside Boulevard Width: **2′ (0.7 m)**

    Outside Boulevard Width: **2′ (0.7 m)**

    It may be hard to ignore the Side parameter, but setting it is not required with Civil 3D side autodetection.

21. At the Select marker point within assembly or [Insert Replace Detached]: prompt, select the circular marker on the UrbanCurbGutterGeneral subassembly that represents the top rear of the curb to attach the UrbanSidewalk subassembly (see Figure 8.13).

FIGURE 8.13
BasicSidewalk subassembly placed on the UrbanCurbGutterGeneral subassembly

22. Switch to the Daylight tab on the subassemblies Tool Palettes window, and select the DaylightMaxOffset subassembly.

23. In the Advanced Parameters area of the AutoCAD Properties palette, change Max Offset From Baseline to **50′ (17 m)**, leaving all other parameters at their default values.

24. At the Select marker point within assembly or [Insert Replace Detached]: prompt, select the circular marker on the outermost point of the sidewalk subassembly.

25. Press Enter or Esc to complete the command.

    Your drawing should now resemble Figure 8.14.

FIGURE 8.14
The completed right side of the assembly with DaylightMaxOffset

To complete the left side, you will use the Mirror Subassemblies command.

26. Select the curb, sidewalk, and daylight subassemblies on the right side of the baseline.

The Subassembly contextual tab will show a variety of tools, including Mirror (Figure 8.15).

FIGURE 8.15
The Subassembly contextual tab with subassembly modification tools

27. From the Subassembly contextual tab ➢ Modify Subassembly panel, choose Mirror and then click the circular point marker located at the top left of the left LaneSuperelevationAOR subassembly.

Your assembly should now resemble Figure 8.5 from earlier in the chapter.

You have now completed a typical road assembly.

A finished copy of this drawing is available from the book's web page (0801_Typical RoadAssembly_FINISHED.dwg or 0801_TypicalRoadAssembly_METRIC_FINISHED.dwg).

ASSEMBLY LABELS

You may notice the 4.00:1 label shown in Figure 8.14. These labels are governed by the code set style, which in this exercise is set to All Codes. If you would like to add this label or other labels, follow these simple steps:

1. Switch to the Settings tab in Toolspace.

2. Expand the General ➢ Multipurpose Styles ➢ Code Set Styles branch.

3. Right-click All Codes and select Edit to display the Code Set Style – All Codes dialog.

4. On the Codes tab, locate the Link branch.

5. In the Label Style column of the Daylight link row, click the Style button to display the Pick Style dialog.

You may need to widen the column headings in order to view the full names.

6. Use the drop-down list to select Steep Grades.

7. Click OK to dismiss the Pick Style dialog.

8. Click OK to dismiss the Code Set Style – All Codes dialog.

Now all Daylight links in any assembly that uses the All Codes code-set style will display a grade label. You may find it helpful to provide other labels on your subassemblies to be able to easily differentiate visually between the assemblies that are similar. For example, now you can tell the difference between the assembly that uses the 4:1 daylight and the one that uses the 5:1 daylight.

Subassembly Components

A subassembly consists of three basic parts: *links*, *marker points*, and *shapes*, as shown in Figure 8.16. Each piece plays a role in your design and is used for different purposes at each stage of the design process.

FIGURE 8.16
Schematic showing parts of a subassembly

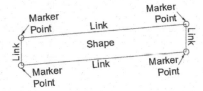

LINKS

Links are the linear components to your assembly. A link usually represents the outer edges of a subassembly but can also be used as a spacer between subassemblies.

Links can have codes assigned to them that help Civil 3D identify stratum, materials, and shapes. One link may have several codes assigned to it. For example, the sidewalk subassembly contains a four-sided trapezoid. Each side of the trapezoid is a link. All four links have a sidewalk code assigned so that the cross-sectional area of the concrete can be calculated.

The bottom, left, and right links of the trapezoid each have an additional datum code assigned, while the top link has an additional top code assigned. Top and datum codes are used to build surfaces. Coded links will be your primary source of data when creating proposed surfaces from your corridors.

As shown in Figure 8.17, the inner and outer boulevard width links are coded top, sod, and datum.

FIGURE 8.17
Link codes on the UrbanSidewalk subassembly

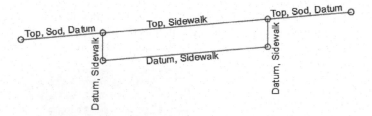

MARKER POINTS

Marker points are located at the endpoints of every link and usually are depicted by the circles you see on the subassemblies. As you experienced in the previous exercise, the markers are used in assembly creation to "click" subassemblies together and will also "hook" to attach to alignments and/or profiles, known as *targets*.

Marker points are also coded and responsible for generating linework in your corridor. In Figure 8.18, notice the two coded markers representing each side of the sidewalk. When assemblies are inserted into a corridor, Civil 3D will play connect the dots with each code in between each occurrence of the assembly. In the case of the UrbanSidewalk, linework will be created by connecting the Sidewalk_In point codes and the Sidewalk_Out point codes. We will revisit how a corridor is built in Chapter 9, "Basic Corridors."

FIGURE 8.18
Point codes on the
UrbanSidewalk

SHAPES

Shapes are the areas inside a closed formation of links. For example, Figure 8.19 shows the UrbanSidewalk, which contains one shape. Shapes are used in end-area material quantity calculations. At the time an assembly is created, you do not need to consider what materials these shapes represent. After your corridor is complete, you can specify what materials the codes represent upon computing materials.

FIGURE 8.19
Shape codes on the
UrbanSidewalk
subassembly

Jumping into Help

Each subassembly is capable of accomplishing different tasks in your design. For a detailed rundown of each parameter and what can be done with a subassembly, you will need to open the help files.

There are several ways to access the help files. Help for each subassembly can be accessed from the Corridor Modeling Catalogs or the tool palettes by right-clicking any subassembly and selecting Help, as shown from the tool palettes in Figure 8.20.

FIGURE 8.20
Getting to the subas-
sembly help file for
UrbanCurbGutterGeneral

ATTACHMENT AND INPUT PARAMETERS

When you access subassembly help using one of the previous methods, it will take you to the help file specific to the subassembly you selected the Help option for. At the top, you will see a diagram showing the location of the numeric parameters that can be edited in the Properties palette, as shown in Figure 8.21.

FIGURE 8.21
The top portion of subassembly help shown with subassembly parameters

For most subassemblies, the default attachment point will be the topmost-inside marker point. The help file will tell you whether this differs for the subassembly you are looking at. Scroll farther down to see detailed explanations of each input parameter.

TARGET PARAMETERS

The Target Parameters section is a list of what attachments can be set for a subassembly. There are three types of targets: a target surface, a target elevation, and a target offset. The help file will also tell you whether the target is optional or required. We will cover target parameters and setting targets in Chapter 9.

OUTPUT PARAMETERS

Output parameters are values calculated when the corridor is built, such as the cross-slope of a lane. In several subassemblies, there is an advanced option called Parameter Reference that can use an output parameter from a previous subassembly in the assembly instead of using the value entered in the subassembly properties. We discuss this concept further in the bonus chapter, "Custom Subassemblies," available on this book's web page.

READING A CODING DIAGRAM

The coding diagram lists all the codes used on the subassembly you are working with. All coded points, links, and shapes are listed here. Not all subassembly components have explicit names, such as L9 shown in Figure 8.22. If the point, shape, or link is not included in the table, it is considered uncoded. Code Set Styles have a category for uncoded points, shapes, and links called <no codes>.

FIGURE 8.22
Coding diagram and name table for UrbanCurbGutter General

Point / Link	Code	Description
P1	Flange	Flange point of the gutter
P2	Flowline_Gutter	Gutter flowline point
P3	TopCurb	Top-of-curb
P4	BackCurb	Back-of-curb
L1 – L3	Top, Curb	Finish grade on the curb and gutter
L7	Subbase Datum	
S1	Curb	Curb-and-gutter concrete area
S2	Subbase	

Coding Diagram

Commonly Used Subassemblies

Once you gain some skills in building assemblies, you can explore the subassembly tool palettes to find subassemblies that have more advanced parameters so that you can get more out of your corridor model. For example, if you must produce detailed schedules of road materials such as asphalt, coarse gravel, fine gravel, subgrade material, and so on, the catalog includes lane subassemblies that allow you to specify those thicknesses for automatic volume reports.

The following sections include some examples of different components you can use in a typical road assembly. Many more alternatives are available within the subassembly tool palettes provided in the software. The help file provides a complete breakdown of each subassembly provided; you'll find this useful as you search for your perfect subassembly.

Each of these subassemblies can be added to an assembly using the same process specified in the first exercise in this chapter. Choose your alternative subassembly instead of the basic parts specified in the exercise, and adjust the parameters accordingly.

COMMON LANE SUBASSEMBLIES

The LaneSuperelevationAOR subassembly is suitable for many roads, including undivided roads (as shown in the previous example) and divided roads (as shown in Figure 8.23). However, you may need different road lane configurations for your locality or design situation.

FIGURE 8.23
LaneSuperelevation
AOR in a divided
highway

LaneParabolic   The LaneParabolic subassembly (Figure 8.24) is used for road sections that require a parabolic lane in contrast to the linear grade of LaneSuperelevationAOR. The LaneParabolic subassembly also adds options for four material depths. This is useful in jurisdictions that require two lifts of asphalt, base material, and sub-base material; taking advantage of these additional parameters gives you an opportunity to build corridor models that can return more detailed quantity takeoffs and volume calculations.

FIGURE 8.24
The LaneParabolic
subassembly help
diagram

Note that the LaneParabolic subassembly doesn't have a Side parameter. The parabolic nature of the component results in a single attachment point that would typically be the assembly centerline marker.

LaneBrokenBack   For designs that call for two lanes that must each have a unique slope, the LaneBrokenBack subassembly (Figure 8.25) can be used. This subassembly provides parameters to change the road-crown location and specify the width and slope for each lane. Like LaneParabolic, the LaneBrokenBack subassembly provides parameters for additional material thicknesses.

FIGURE 8.25
The LaneBrokenBack
subassembly and
parameters

The LaneBrokenBack subassembly, like LaneSuperelevationAOR, allows for the use of target alignments and profiles to guide the subassembly horizontally and/or vertically for both of the lanes.

COMMON SHOULDER AND CURB SUBASSEMBLIES

There are many types of curbs, and the UrbanCurbGutterGeneral subassembly can't model them all. Sometimes you may need a mountable curb, or perhaps you need a shoulder instead. In those cases, the Curbs tool palette provides many alternatives:

UrbanCurbGutterValley (1, 2, or 3)   The UrbanCurbGutterValley subassemblies are great if you need mountable curbs. UrbanCurbGutterValley 1, 2, and 3, shown in Figure 8.26,

Figure 8.27, and Figure 8.28, respectively, vary slightly in how they handle the sub-base slope. UrbanCurbGutterValley 1 also differs because it comes to a point instead of offering a width at the top of curb.

FIGURE 8.26
UrbanCurbGutterValley1
subassembly help
diagram

FIGURE 8.27
UrbanCurbGutterValley2
subassembly help
diagram

FIGURE 8.28
UrbanCurbGutterValley3
subassembly help
diagram

BasicShoulder   BasicShoulder (see Figure 8.29) is another simple yet effective subassembly for use with road sections that require a shoulder. The predefined shape for this subassembly is called Pave1, which is useful if you are planning to treat this as a paved shoulder and include it in your material quantity calculations.

FIGURE 8.29
BasicShoulder
subassembly help
diagram

ShoulderExtendSubbase and ShoulderExtendAll   Shoulders that can work with your lanes in a superelevation situation, as these two do, are extremely helpful. These two subassemblies, shown in Figure 8.30, will "play nice" with your breakover-removal settings, as you will see in Chapter 11, "Superelevation."

FIGURE 8.30
ShoulderExtendSubbase
subassembly help
diagram (top) and
ShoulderExtendAll
subassembly help
diagram (bottom)

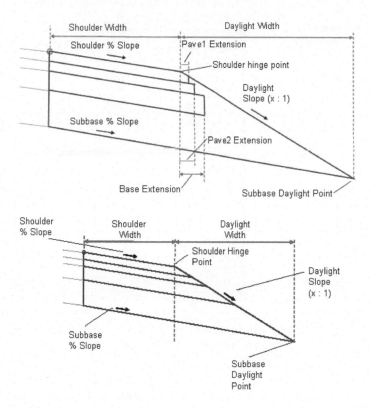

Editing an Assembly

As you saw earlier in this chapter, the AutoCAD Properties palette is an option for changing subassembly parameters for one or more subassemblies of the same type. However, there are a handful of settings that can be controlled only in the Civil 3D Subassembly Properties dialog. For example, the side (left or right) is a parameter that must be changed in the Subassembly Properties dialog or on the Construction tab of the Assembly Properties dialog.

EDITING A SINGLE SUBASSEMBLY'S PARAMETERS

Once your assembly is created, you can edit individual subassembly components as follows:

1. Pick the subassembly component you'd like to edit.

This will bring up the Subassembly contextual tab.

2. From the Subassembly contextual tab ➢ Modify Subassembly panel, choose the Subassembly Properties option.

The Subassembly Properties dialog appears.

3. Switch to the Parameters tab, shown in Figure 8.31, to access the same parameters you saw in the AutoCAD Properties palette when you first placed the subassembly.

FIGURE 8.31
Subassembly
Properties –
Parameters tab

4. Click the Subassembly Help ellipsis button at the bottom right of the dialog if you want to access the help page that gives detailed information about the use of this particular subassembly.

Do not confuse the Subassembly Help ellipsis button with the plain Help button, which will just give you help on the Subassembly Properties dialog.

5. Close the help file when you've finished viewing it.

6. On the Parameters tab of the Subassembly Properties dialog, click inside any field in the Default Input Value column to make changes.

EDITING THE ENTIRE ASSEMBLY

Sometimes it's more efficient to edit all the subassemblies in an assembly at once. To do so, pick the assembly baseline marker or any subassembly that is connected to the assembly you'd like to edit. This time, select the Assembly Properties option from the Modify Assembly panel of either the Subassembly or Assembly contextual tab to display the Assembly Properties dialog, shown in Figure 8.32.

Renaming the Assembly

The Information tab in the Assembly Properties dialog shown in Figure 8.32 gives you an opportunity to rename your assembly and provide an optional description. It is good practice to be consistent and detailed in your assembly names (for example, **Divided 4-Lane 12′ w Paved Shoulder**). With informative assembly names, you will eliminate much of the guesswork when it comes to building corridors later.

FIGURE 8.32
Assembly
Properties –
Information tab

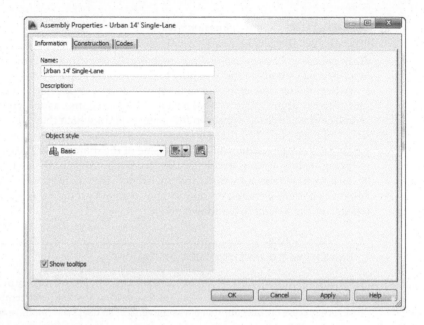

Changing Parameters

The Construction tab in the Assembly Properties dialog, as shown in Figure 8.33, houses each subassembly and its parameters. At the top of the dialog you can change the Assembly Type setting using the drop-down list. In addition, you can change the parameters for individual subassemblies by selecting the subassembly in the Item pane on the left side of the Construction tab and changing the desired parameter in the Input Values pane on the right side.

FIGURE 8.33
Assembly
Properties –
Construction tab

Renaming Groups and Subassemblies

Note that the left side of the Construction tab displays a list of groups. Under each group is a list of the subassemblies in use in your assembly. A new group is formed every time a subassembly is connected directly to the assembly baseline marker or an offset assembly is added.

With side autodetection, you will notice that the groups have already been named Right and Left with the appropriate symbol next to the group name, as shown in Figure 8.33. The subassemblies in each group appear in the same order in which they were originally placed, usually from the inside out. The first subassembly under the Right group is LaneSuperelevationAOR. If you dig into its parameters on the right side of the dialog, you'll learn that this lane is attached to the right side of the assembly marker, the UrbanCurbGutterGeneral is attached to right side of the LaneSuperelevationAOR, and the UrbanSidewalk is attached to the right side of the UrbanCurbGutterGeneral. In this example, the next group, Left, is identical but attached to the left side of the assembly baseline marker.

RENAMING TO INCLUDE LEFT OR RIGHT?

The automatic naming conventions are somewhat simple but usually provide enough information. In previous editions of Civil 3D, many users would change the subassembly names to reference what side they were on; this approach was convenient so users did not have to dig into the subassembly parameters to determine which side of the assembly a certain group was on when it came time to attach targets to a corridor. However, since AutoCAD Civil 3D 2013, both the subassembly and the assembly group are listed in the Target Mapping dialog, as you will see in Chapter 9, so there is no longer any need to add the left or right information to the subassembly name.

If you want, you can rename any of the groups or subassemblies on the Construction tab of the Assembly Properties dialog by right-clicking the group or subassembly you want to rename and choosing Rename. From this same context menu you can also delete the group or subassembly.

There is no official best practice for renaming your groups and subassemblies, but you may find it useful to keep the designation of what type of subassembly it is or other distinguishing features. For example, if a lane is to be designated as a transition lane or a generic link used as a ditch foreslope, it would be useful to name them descriptively.

Creating Assemblies for Non-Road Uses

There are many uses for assemblies and their resulting corridor models aside from road sections. The Corridor Modeling Catalog also includes components for retaining walls, rail sections, bridges, channels, pipe trenches, and much more. In Chapter 9, you'll use a channel assembly and a pipe trench assembly to build corridor models. Let's investigate how those assemblies are put together by building a channel assembly for a stream section:

1. Start a new blank drawing from the _AutoCAD Civil 3D (Imperial) NCS template that ships with Civil 3D. Metric users can use the _AutoCAD Civil 3D (Metric) NCS template. You can also continue working in your drawing from the first exercise in this chapter.

2. Confirm that your Tool Palettes window is showing the subassembly set (Imperial or metric) appropriate for your drawing units.

3. From the Home tab ➢ Create Design panel, choose Assembly ➢ Create Assembly.

   The Create Assembly dialog opens.

4. In the Create Assembly dialog, configure these options:

   Enter **Channel** in the Name text box.

   Set Assembly Type to Other.

   Confirm that Assembly Style is set to Basic and that Code Set Style is set to All Codes, and click OK.

5. Pick a location in your drawing to place your red assembly baseline marker.

6. Locate the Trench Pipes tab on the Tool Palettes window.

7. Click the Channel subassembly on the Tool Palettes window.

   The AutoCAD Properties palette appears.

8. Locate the Advanced Parameters area on the AutoCAD Properties palette.

   You'll place the channel with its default parameters and make adjustments through the Assembly Properties dialog, so don't change anything for now. Note that there is no Side parameter. This subassembly will be centered on the assembly baseline marker.

9. At the Select marker point within assembly or [**I**nsert **R**eplace **D**etached]: prompt, select the red assembly baseline marker, and a channel is placed on the assembly (see Figure 8.34).

FIGURE 8.34
The Channel subassembly with default parameters

10. Press Esc to leave the assembly insertion command and dismiss the Properties palette.

11. Click the assembly baseline marker, and then on the Assemblies contextual tab ➢ Modify Assembly palette, click Assembly Properties.

    The Assembly Properties dialog appears.

12. Switch to the Construction tab.

    Notice that while the typical road assembly in the previous exercise generated a Left group and a Right group, the Channel subassembly generated a Centered group.

13. Select the Channel entry on the left side of the dialog (under the Centered group).

14. Click the Subassembly Help ellipsis button located at the bottom right on the dialog's Construction tab.

The Subassembly Reference page of the AutoCAD Civil 3D 2016 help file appears.

15. Familiarize yourself with the diagram, shown in Figure 8.35, and the input parameters for the Channel subassembly.

FIGURE 8.35
The Channel subassembly help diagram

Especially note the Attachment Point, Bottom Width, Depth, and Side slope parameters. The attachment point indicates where your baseline alignment and profile will be applied.

16. Minimize or close the help file.

To match the engineer's specified design, you need a stream section 6′ (2 m) deep with a bottom that's 3′ (1 m) wide, 1:1 sideslopes, and no backslopes.

17. Change the following parameters in the Assembly Properties dialog, leaving all other parameters at their default values:

Depth: **6′ (2 m)**

Bottom Width: **3′ (1 m)**

Sideslope: **1** (value will automatically change to be displayed as 1.00:1)

Left and Right Backslope Width: **0′ (0 m)**

ZERO SUBASSEMBLY VALUES

Some subassemblies do not like zero values, so you may be taught to enter 0.001 or some other value that is so small that it is as if you enter 0. However, there are also some subassemblies that like zero values. If you look in the help file for the Channel subassembly, you will notice that in the Behavior section it explains that if a zero value is specified for left or right extensions and backslope widths, those links are omitted or are not drawn. So if a zero is what you want, be sure to check the help files before using a zero in your subassemblies!

---

18. Click OK, and confirm that your completed assembly looks like Figure 8.36.

FIGURE 8.36
The channel
assembly with
customized
parameters

A finished copy of this drawing is available from the book's web page (0802_ ChannelAssembly_FINISHED.dwg or 0802_ChannelAssembly_METRIC_FINISHED.dwg).

 Real World Scenario

PIPE TRENCH ASSEMBLY

Projects that include piping, such as sanitary sewers, storm drainage, gas pipelines, or similar structures, almost always include trenching. The trench must be carefully prepared to ensure the safety of the workers placing the pipe as well as to provide structural stability for the pipe in the form of bedding and compacted fill.

The corridor is an ideal tool for modeling pipe trenching. With the appropriate assembly combined with a pipe-run alignment and profile, you not only can design a pipe trench but also can use cross-section tools to generate section views, materials tables, and quantity takeoffs. The resulting corridor model can also be used to create a surface for additional analysis.

The following exercise will lead you through building a pipe trench corridor based on an alignment and profile that follow a pipe run and a typical trench assembly:

1. Start a new blank drawing from the _AutoCAD Civil 3D (Imperial) NCS template that ships with Civil 3D. Metric users can use the _AutoCAD Civil 3D (Metric) NCS template.

You can also continue working in your drawing from the previous exercise.

2. Confirm that your Tool Palettes window is showing the subassembly set (Imperial or metric) appropriate for your drawing units.

3. From the Home tab ➤ Create Design panel, choose Assembly ➤ Create Assembly.

4. In the Create Assembly dialog, set these properties:

Enter **Pipe Trench** in the Name text box to change the assembly's name.

Set Assembly Type to Other.

Confirm that Assembly Style is set to Basic and Code Set Style is set to All Codes, and click OK.

5. Pick a location in your drawing for the assembly; somewhere in the center of your screen where you have room to work is fine.

6. Locate the Trench Pipes tab on the Tool Palettes window.

7. Click the TrenchPipe1 button on the Tool Palettes window.

Continues

Continued

The AutoCAD Properties palette appears.

8. Locate the Advanced Parameters area of the AutoCAD Properties palette.

This section lists the TrenchPipe1 parameters. You'll place TrenchPipe1 with its default parameters and make adjustments through the Assembly Properties dialog, so don't change anything for now. Note that similar to the Channel subassembly, there is no Side parameter. This subassembly will be placed centered on the assembly baseline marker.

9. At the `Select marker point within assembly or [Insert Replace Detached]:` prompt, select the assembly baseline marker.

A TrenchPipe1 subassembly is placed on the assembly, as shown here.

10. Press Esc to leave the assembly-creation command and dismiss the AutoCAD Properties palette.

11. Select the assembly baseline marker to activate the Assembly contextual tab.

12. From the Assembly contextual tab ➤ Modify Assembly panel, choose Assembly Properties.

The Assembly Properties dialog appears.

13. On the Construction tab, select the TrenchPipe1 assembly entry on the left side of the dialog.

14. Click the Subassembly Help ellipsis button located at the bottom right.

The Subassembly Reference page of the AutoCAD Civil 3D 2016 help file appears.

15. Familiarize yourself with the diagram, shown in the following image, and with the input parameters for the TrenchPipe1 subassembly.

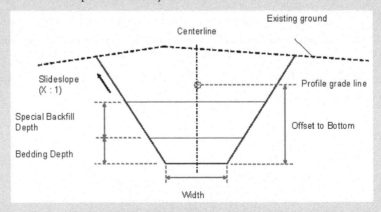

In this case, the profile grade line will attach to a profile drawn to represent the pipe invert. Because the trench will be excavated deeper than the pipe invert to accommodate gravel bedding, you'll want to provide information for the bedding depth parameter. Also note under the Target Parameters section in Help that this subassembly requires a surface target to determine where the sideslopes terminate.

16. Minimize or close the help file.

To match the engineer's specified design, the pipe trench should be 3′ (1 m) deep and 4′ (1.3 m) wide with 2:1 sideslopes and 1′ (0.3 m) of gravel bedding.

17. In the Assembly Properties dialog – Construction tab, change the following parameters, leaving all other parameters at their default values:

Width: **4′ (1.3** m)

Sideslope: **2** (This value will automatically change to be displayed as 2:1.)

Bedding Depth: **1′ (0.3** m)

Offset To Bottom: **3′ (1** m)

18. Click OK.

19. Confirm that your completed assembly looks like the image shown here.

A finished copy of this drawing is available from the book's web page (0803_PipeTrenchAssembly_FINISHED.dwg or 0803_PipeTrenchAssembly_METRIC_FINISHED.dwg).

This assembly will be used to build a pipe trench corridor in Chapter 9.

Specialized Subassemblies

Despite the more than 100 subassemblies available in the Corridor Modeling Catalog, sometimes you may not find the perfect component. Perhaps none of the channel assemblies exactly meets your design specifications and you'd like to make a more customized assembly, or neither of the sidewalk subassemblies allows for the proper boulevard slopes. Maybe you'd like to try to do some preliminary lot grading using your corridor or mark a certain point on your subassembly so that you can extract important features easily.

You can handle most of these situations by using subassemblies from the Generic Subassembly Catalog (see Figure 8.37). These simple yet flexible components can be used to build almost anything, although they lack the coded intelligence of some of the more intricate subassemblies (such as knowing if they're paved or grass and understanding things like sub-base depth and so on).

TOOL PALETTES - CIVIL IMPERIAL SUBASSEMBLIES

FIGURE 8.37
The Generic Subassembly tool palette

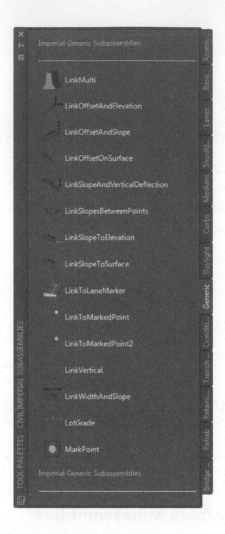

Using Generic Links

Let's look at two examples where you might take advantage of generic links.

The first example involves the typical road section you built in the first exercise in this chapter. You saw that UrbanSidewalk applies one continuous cross-slope across the inside boulevard (terrace), sidewalk, and outside boulevard (buffer strip). If you need a terrace that's 3′ (1 m) wide with a 3 percent slope, and then a 5′ (1.5 m) sidewalk with a 2 percent slope, followed by another buffer strip that is 6′ (2 m) wide with a slope of 5 percent, you can use generic links to assist in the construction of the proper assembly.

In this exercise, you will be creating a new assembly based on the typical road assembly made in the first exercise.

1. Open `0801_TypicalRoadAssembly_FINISHED.dwg` or `0801_TypicalRoadAssembly_METRIC_FINISHED.dwg`, available on the book's website.

2. In Prospector, locate and expand the Assemblies group.

3. Right-click Urban 14' Single-Lane or Urban 4.5m Single-Lane and select Zoom To.

4. Select the lane and curb subassemblies as well as the assembly baseline marker and Mtext below; then on the Home tab ➤ Clipboard panel, click Copy Clip.

5. On the Home tab ➤ Clipboard panel, click Paste. Pick a location directly under the Urban Single-Lane assembly to paste the copied assembly and regen the drawing.

   Notice that the Mtext updated to the name of the copy of the assembly. This is because it's a field.

   You could have used the Copy command. However, when the assembly baseline marker is part of the Copy command selection set, the entire assembly is copied even if some of the subassemblies are not included in the selection set. If this were your method in this exercise, all you would need to do next would be to delete the unwanted subassemblies.

   While you could place the subassembly anywhere, you will find that as you gather more and more assemblies in a drawing, having them organized in a logical manner with similar assemblies in a common area makes them easier to manage.

LABELING ASSEMBLIES

When you start getting multiple similar assemblies in your drawing, you may find it helpful to add Mtext next to the assembly with the assembly's name so that you know which assembly is which. By using a field within Mtext, these labels will remain dynamic to their associated object (that is, if you change the name of the assembly, the Mtext will change as well). You can do this using the following simple steps:

1. Enter **MTEXT** on the command line.

2. Specify the location of your Mtext box.

3. From the Text Editor contextual tab ➤ Insert panel, click Field to display the Field dialog.

4. Verify that Field Category is set to Objects and Field Names is set to Object.

5. Click the Select Object button next to Object Type.

6. At the Select object: prompt, select an assembly baseline marker.

7. Set Property to Name, select your format preference, and click OK to dismiss the Field dialog.

8. On the Text Editor tab ➤ Close panel, click Close Text Editor.

You now have a dynamic field that will maintain the name of the associated assembly; however, you may need to run a REGEN in order for the field to update. It's also helpful to know that if you copy an assembly and its label at the same time, the new label will reference the new assembly.

---

6. Select the new assembly baseline marker; then on the Assembly contextual tab ➤ Modify Assembly panel, click Assembly Properties.

The Assembly Properties dialog appears.

7. On the Information tab, change Name to **Urban 14′ Single-Lane with Terraced Sidewalk** (or **Urban 4.5m Single-Lane With Terraced Sidewalk**) and click OK.

   If you copied the Mtext label containing a field, you may want to run a REGEN to update the label or play with the grips to stack the text legibly.

8. Locate the Generic tab on the Tool Palettes window.

9. Click the LinkWidthAndSlope subassembly (you may need to scroll down to find it), and the AutoCAD Properties palette appears.

10. Scroll down to the Advanced Parameters section of the Properties palette and change the parameters as follows to create the first buffer strip, leaving all other parameters at their default values:

    Width: **3′ (1 m)**

    Slope: **3%**

11. At the Select marker point within assembly or [Insert Replace Detached]: prompt, select the circular marker at the rear top of the curb on the right UrbanCurbGutterGeneral subassembly as well as the circular marker on the left UrbanCurbGutterGeneral subassembly, both of which represent the top back of the curb.

12. Switch to the Curbs tab of the Tool Palettes window, and click the UrbanSidewalk button.

13. In the Advanced Parameters area of the Properties palette, change the parameters as follows to create the sidewalk, leaving all other parameters at their default values:

    Inside Boulevard Width: **0′ (0 m)**

    Sidewalk Width: **5′ (1.5 m)**

    Outside Boulevard Width: **0′ (0 m)**

    Slope: **2%**

14. At the Select marker point within assembly or [Insert Replace Detached]: prompt, select the upper-right circular marker on the right LinkWidthAndSlope subassembly and the upper-left circular marker on the left LinkWidthAndSlope subassembly.

15. Switch to the Generic tab of the Tool Palettes window, and click the LinkWidthAndSlope button.

    The AutoCAD Properties palette appears.

16. In the Advanced Parameters area, change the parameters as follows to create the second buffer strip, leaving all other parameters at their default values:

    Width: **6′ (2 m)**

    Slope: **5%**

17. At the Select marker point within assembly or [Insert Replace Detached]: prompt, select the upper-right circular marker on the right UrbanSidewalk subassembly,

as well as the upper-left circular marker on the left UrbanSidewalk subassembly, both of which represent the outside edge of the sidewalk. When complete, press Esc to end the command.

18. Select the right daylight subassembly from the Urban Single-Lane assembly. On the Subassembly contextual tab ➤ Modify Subassembly panel, click Copy.

19. Select the outermost marker on the right side of the new assembly that you are working on and then press the Esc key to finish to end the command. Do the same for the left daylight.

The completed assembly should look like Figure 8.38 (shown with the typical road assembly from the first exercise for comparison).

FIGURE 8.38
The completed Urban Single-Lane assembly from the first exercise (top) and the Urban Single-Lane with Terraced Sidewalks assembly (bottom)

The finished copy of this drawing is available from the book's web page (0804_Generic LinksAssembly_FINISHED.dwg or 0804_GenericLinksAssembly_METRIC_FINISHED.dwg). You've now created a custom sidewalk terrace for a typical road.

Daylighting with Generic Links

The next example involves the channel section you built earlier in this chapter. This exercise will lead you through using the LinkSlopeToSurface generic subassembly, which will provide a surface target to the channel assembly that will seek the target assembly at a 25 percent slope. For more information about surface targets, see Chapter 9.

In this exercise, you will be creating another new assembly based on the channel assembly exercise.

1. Open 0802_ChannelAssembly_FINISHED.dwg or 0802_ChannelAssembly_METRIC_ FINISHED.dwg, available on the book's website.

2. In Prospector, locate and expand the Assemblies group.

3. Right-click Channel and select Zoom To.

4. Locate the Generic tab on the Tool Palettes window.

5. Click the LinkSlopeToSurface button.

6. In the Advanced Parameters area of the Properties palette, change the Slope parameter to **25%**, leaving all other parameters at their default values.

7. At the Select marker point within assembly or [**I**nsert **R**eplace **D**etached]: prompt, select the circular marker at the upper right on the channel subassembly as well as the circular marker on the upper left on the channel subassembly. Press Esc to end the command.

The left surface target link appears, but it is sloping to the right instead of the left. This is one subassembly that doesn't automatically "flip" to the appropriate side.

8. Select the LinkSlopeToSurface subassembly to activate the Subassembly contextual tab.

9. From the Subassembly contextual tab ➤ Modify Subassembly panel, choose Subassembly Properties.

10. On the Parameters tab, locate the Side input value, and click the default input value field.

11. In the Pick Default Value dialog, select Left as the new input value, and click OK.

12. Click OK to dismiss the Subassembly Properties dialog.

The completed assembly should look like Figure 8.39.

FIGURE 8.39
The completed
channel assembly

The finished copy of this drawing is available from the book's web page (0805_ChannelLink Daylight_FINISHED.dwg or 0805_ChannelLinkDaylight_METRIC_FINISHED.dwg).

Adding a surface link to the channel assembly provides a surface target for the assembly. Now that you've added the LinkSlopeToSurface, you will be able to specify your existing ground as the surface target for a corridor, and the subassembly will grade between the top of the bank and the surface for you. You can achieve additional flexibility for connecting to existing ground with the more complex daylight subassemblies, as discussed in the next section.

Working with Daylight Subassemblies

In previous examples, you worked with a generic daylight subassembly, but now let's take a closer look at what they can do for you.

A daylight subassembly tells Civil 3D how to extend a link to a target surface. The instructions might specify that a ditch or berm be inserted before looking for existing ground. Others provide a straight shot but with contingencies for certain design conditions. Figure 8.40 shows the many options you have for adding a daylight subassembly to an assembly.

FIGURE 8.40
Daylight subassemblies in the Tool Palettes window

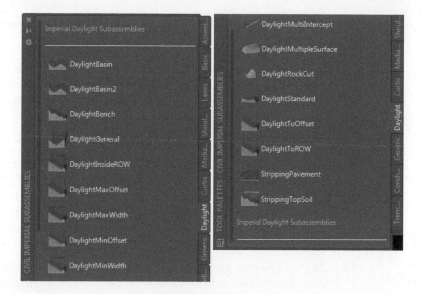

In the following exercise, you'll use the DaylightInsideROW subassembly. This subassembly contains parameters for specifying the maximum distance from the centerline or offset alignments. If the 4:1 slope hits the surface inside the right-of-way (ROW), no adjustment is made to the slope. If 4:1 causes the daylight to hit outside of the ROW, the slope adjusts to stay inside the specified location.

In this exercise, you will be creating a new assembly based on the typical road assembly you made in the first exercise.

1. Open `0804_GenericLinksAssembly_FINISHED.dwg` or `0804_GenericLinksAssembly_METRIC_FINISHED.dwg`, available from the book's website.

2. Locate the Urban 14' Single-Lane or Urban 4.5m Single-Lane assembly.

3. Select the lane, curb, and sidewalk subassemblies as well as the assembly baseline marker and the Mtext displaying the assembly name. On the Home tab ➢ Clipboard panel, click Copy Clip.

5. On the Home tab ➢ Clipboard panel, click Paste and pick a location directly above the Urban Single-Lane assemblies to paste the copied assembly.

6. Click the copied assembly baseline marker, and then on the Assemblies contextual tab ➢ Modify Assembly palette, click Assembly Properties and close the Event Viewer in the Panorama palette if it appears.

   The Assembly Properties dialog appears.

7. On the Information tab, change the name to **Urban 14' Single-Lane Daylight ROW** (or **Urban 4.5m Single-Lane Daylight ROW**), and click OK. Run a REGEN to update Mtext.

8. Locate the Daylight tab on the Tool Palettes window.

9. Right-click the DaylightInsideROW button on the Tool Palettes window and select Help.

   The Subassembly Reference page opens in a new window.

10. Familiarize yourself with the options for the DaylightInsideROW subassembly, especially noting the optional parameters for a lined material, a mandatory daylight surface target, and an optional ROW offset target that can be used to override the ROW offset specified in the parameters.

11. Close the Help dialog. Click the DaylightInsideROW button on the Tool Palettes window.

12. In the Advanced Parameters area of the Properties palette, change the parameter ROW Offset From Baseline to **33′** (**10** m), leaving all other parameters at their default values.

13. At the Select marker point within assembly or [**I**nsert **R**eplace **D**etached]: prompt, select the circular marker on the farthest-right link on the new assembly. The Select marker point within assembly or [**I**nsert **R**eplace **D**etached]: prompt is still active.

14. On the Properties palette, in the Advanced Parameters area, change the parameter ROW Offset From Baseline to **-33′** (**-10** m) and then place the subassembly on the left side of the new assembly. Press Esc to end the command.

   Notice that there is no Left or Right parameter. The negative value in the ROW Offset From Baseline parameter is what tells Civil 3D the daylight is to the left. Some subassemblies will contain an offset parameter instead of a side parameter to direct to which side it should flip. In the case of an offset parameter, left will be indicated by a negative value, and right will be indicated by a positive value.

15. You can now dismiss the Properties palette and close the Event Viewer in the Panorama palette if it appears.

   The completed assembly should look like Figure 8.41.

FIGURE 8.41
An assembly with the DaylightInsideROW subassembly attached to each side

Urban 14′ Single—Lane Daylight ROW

You may keep this drawing open to continue to the next exercise or use the finished copy of this drawing available from the book's web page (DaylightROWAssembly_FINISHED.dwg or DaylightROWAssembly_METRIC_FINISHED.dwg).

WHEN TO IGNORE DAYLIGHT INPUT PARAMETERS

The first time you attempt to use daylight subassemblies, you may become overwhelmed by the large number of parameters.

The good news is that many of these parameters are unnecessary for most uses. For example, many daylight subassemblies, such as DaylightGeneral (shown here), include multiple cut-and-fill widths for complicated cases where the design may call for test scenarios. If your design doesn't require this level of detail, leave those parameters set to zero.

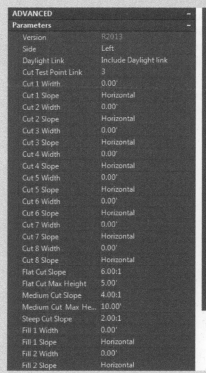

Some daylight subassemblies include guardrail options. If your situation doesn't require a guardrail, leave the default parameter set to Omit Guardrail and ignore it from then on. Another common, confusing parameter is Place Lined Material, which can be used for riprap or erosion-control matting. If your design doesn't require this much detail, ensure that this parameter is set to None and ignore the thickness, name, and slope parameters that follow.

If you're ever in doubt about which parameters can be omitted, investigate the help file for that subassembly.

ALTERNATIVE DAYLIGHT SUBASSEMBLIES

More than a dozen daylight subassemblies are available, varying from a simple cut-fill parameter to a more complicated benching or basin design. Your engineering requirements may dictate something more challenging than the exercise in the previous section. Here are some alternative daylight subassemblies and the situations where you might use them. For more information on any of these subassemblies and the many other daylighting choices, see the AutoCAD Civil 3D 2016 Subassembly Reference page in the help file.

DaylightToROW and DaylightInsideROW   The DaylightToROW subassembly differs slightly from the DaylightInsideROW, as shown in Figure 8.42. DaylightToROW constantly adjusts the slope to stay a certain distance away from your ROW, as specified by the Offset Adjustment input parameter. For example, you can have a ROW alignment specified but use this subassembly to tell Civil 3D to always stay 3′ inside the ROW line. The DaylightInsideROW uses the typical slope but adjusts up to a maximum slope in order to stay inside of the ROW. In both subassemblies, you must specify an offset value or an offset target to use as the ROW.

FIGURE 8.42
DaylightToROW
subassembly help
diagram (top) and
DaylightInsideROW
subassembly help
diagram (bottom)

BasicSideSlopeCutDitch   In addition to including cut-and-fill parameters, the BasicSideSlopeCutDitch subassembly (see Figure 8.43) creates a ditch in a cut condition. This is most useful for road designs that require a roadside ditch through cut sections but omit it when passing through areas of fill. If your corridor model is revised in a way that changes the location of cut-and-fill boundaries, the ditch will automatically adjust. Note that this subassembly is located on the Basic tab, whereas the other subassemblies in this section are located on the Daylight tab.

FIGURE 8.43
BasicSideSlopeCutDitch
subassembly help
diagram

When you insert this subassembly, you will notice that it does not look anything like the help diagram and instead will display the *Layout Mode* text on the design assembly, as shown in Figure 8.44. This will not display on the completed corridor. There are several subassemblies where this will occur—which is another good reason to always check the help file for an accurate representation of what the final product will look like.

FIGURE 8.44
BasicSideSlopeCutDitch
in layout mode

DaylightBasin   Many engineers must design berms to contain roadside swales when the road design is in the fill condition. The process for determining where these berms are required is often tedious. The DaylightBasin subassembly (see Figure 8.45) provides a tool for automatically creating these "false berms." The subassembly contains parameters for the specification of a basin (which can be easily adapted to most roadside ditch cross sections as well) and parameters for containment berms that appear only when the subassembly runs into areas of roadside cut.

FIGURE 8.45
The DaylightBasin
subassembly help
diagram

Advanced Assemblies

As you get to know Civil 3D better, you will want it to do more for you. With the tools you are given and your own creativity and problem-solving skills, you can use Civil 3D to create some complex designs. Offset assemblies and marked point assemblies are powerful tools you have at your fingertips.

Offset Assemblies

Offset assemblies are an advanced option when you want to model a coordinating component of the design whose cross section is related to the main assembly. An example of where an offset assembly would be helpful is a main road adjacent to a meandering bike path. The bike path generally follows the main road, but its alignment is not always parallel, and the profile might be altogether different. Figure 8.46 shows what the assembly for a bike path to the left of a road would look like.

FIGURE 8.46
An example of an assembly with an offset to the left representing a bike path

To use an offset assembly, from the Home tab ➤ Create Design panel, choose Assembly ➤ Add Assembly Offset. You will be prompted to select the main assembly and place the offset in the graphic. The location of the offset assembly in relation to the main assembly will have no effect on the final design.

Once the offset assembly is placed, the construction of the offset assembly is identical to any other assembly. We will use an example of an assembly with an offset in Chapter 10, "Advanced Corridors, Intersections, and Roundabouts."

Marked Points Used with Partner Subassemblies

The marked point assembly is a small but powerful subassembly found in the Generic palette. It consists of a single marker, and you can place it on an assembly to flag a location. You can use the marked point by itself to generate a feature line where no coded marker currently exists, say in the midpoint of a lane link. Marked points really perform when used with one of the subassemblies designed to tie into a marked point.

When using a marked point, name it right away, and make note of that name for using it with a partner subassembly (Figure 8.47).

FIGURE 8.47
Name the marked point in the Advanced Parameters area of the Properties palette

LINKING TO A MARKED POINT

In the example shown in Figure 8.48, a LinkToMarkedPoint2 subassembly is placed on the right side of the bike path pavement. The LinkToMarkedPoint2 subassembly has been created to look for the marked point on the left side of the sidewalk buffer.

FIGURE 8.48
Add the name of the marked point before you place it on the assembly.

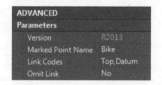

When placing a marked point, enter a descriptive and unique Point Name value under Advanced Parameters. Remember to enter that same descriptive and unique name into the partner subassembly's corresponding field called Marked Point Name. Upon doing this, you will not see the geometry tie together on the assembly, but it will in the resulting corridor, as you will see in Chapter 10.

All subassemblies that use the marked point will appear with the "Layout Mode" placeholder. The following subassemblies are designed to look for a marked point:

- Channel
- ChannelParabolicBottom
- LinkToMarkedPoint
- LinkToMarkedPoint2
- LinkSlopesBetweenPoints
- MedianDepressed
- MedianRaisedConstantSlope
- MedianRaisedWithCrown
- OverlayBrokenBackBetweenEdges
- OverlayBrokenBackOverGutters
- OverlayCrown
- OverlayParabolic
- UrbanReplaceCurbGutter1
- UrbanReplaceCurbGutter2
- UrbanReplaceSidewalk

MAKING SURE YOUR MARKED POINT PROCESSES

Always place the marked point before placing the links that use it to avoid having to reorder subassemblies in the Construction tab of Assembly Properties. If the marked point is listed below its partner subassembly in the Construction tab, the connection between the two subassemblies will not occur.

To reorder subassemblies in this dialog, right-click the subassembly and select Move Up or Move Down as needed.

Organizing Your Assemblies

The more geometry changes that occur throughout your corridor, the more assemblies you will have. Civil 3D offers several tools to keep your assemblies organized and available for future use.

Storing a Customized Subassembly on a Tool Palette

Customizing subassemblies and creating assemblies are both simple tasks. However, you'll save time in future projects if you store these items for later use.

A typical jurisdiction usually has a finite number of allowable lane widths, curb types, and other components. It would be extremely beneficial to have the right subassemblies with the parameters already available on your Tool Palettes window.

The following exercise will lead you through storing a customized subassembly on a tool palette.

In this exercise you will be storing some of the subassemblies you made in earlier exercises; therefore, any of the previously saved files (which you can download from this book's web page) can be used, if you do not have one open from a previous exercise.

You can add a tool only from a saved drawing, so make sure you save the drawing you are working in before following these steps:

1. Be sure your Tool Palettes window is displayed.

2. Right-click the Tool Palettes control bar located at the top of the window or side opposite of tabs if undocked and select New Palette to create a new tool palette.

3. Enter **My Road Parts** in the Name text box.

4. Select one of the sidewalk subassemblies from the Urban 14′ Single-Lane assembly.

   You'll know it's selected when you see it highlighted and the grip appears.

5. Click any link in the assembly (not the grip), and while holding down the left mouse button, drag the assembly into the Tool Palettes window. Release the mouse button.

   It may take you several tries to get the click-and-drag timing correct, but it will work. You'll know it is working when the cursor appears with a plus sign in the tool palette.

   When you release the mouse button, an entry appears on your tool palette with the name of the subassembly component that you are adding as well as a graphic of the subassembly.

6. Select and right-click this entry, and select the Properties option.

   The Tool Properties dialog appears (see Figure 8.49).

FIGURE 8.49
The Tool
Properties dialog

7. If desired, change the image, description, and other parameters in the Tool Properties dialog, and click OK.

8. Try this process for other subassemblies in the drawing.

The resulting tool palette could look similar to Figure 8.50.

FIGURE 8.50
A tool palette with five customized subassemblies

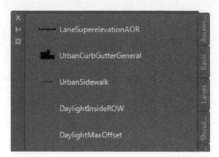

Note that the tool palette entries for each subassembly pull from the C3DStockSubassemblies .dll file installed locally. The subassembly will not pull from this drawing as do blocks. If you share this tool palette, there is no need to share the drawing.

Storing a Completed Assembly on a Tool Palette

In addition to storing individual subassemblies on a tool palette, it's often useful to store entire completed assemblies. Many jurisdictions have several standard roadway sections; once each standard assembly has been built, you can save time on future projects by pulling in a stored version of this assembly.

The process for storing an assembly on a tool palette is nearly identical to the process of storing a subassembly. Simply select the assembly baseline, hover your cursor over the assembly baseline, left-click, hold, and drag to a palette of your choosing.

It's usually a good idea to create a library drawing in a shared network location for common completed assemblies and to create all assemblies in that drawing before dragging them onto the tool palette. By using this approach, you'll be able to test your assemblies for validity before they are rolled into production. Alternatively, you can right-click the new palette name and choose Import Subassemblies to display the Import Subassemblies dialog. Here you can choose a source file and then specify whether you want the subassemblies from that source file to import into the palette (optional) and/or the Catalog Library/My Imported Tools.

ORGANIZING ASSEMBLIES WITHIN PROSPECTOR

There are multiple features that help you keep a drawing with many assemblies organized. In Prospector, you will see your listing of assemblies and an Unassigned Subassemblies entry.

Unassigned subassemblies are orphaned parts that are not attached to any main assembly. They may be left over from some assembly customization, or they may just be a mistake. In either case, you will want to clean them out. On Prospector, under Assemblies ➤ Unassigned Subassemblies, you can right-click each unassigned subassembly and select Remove From Modelspace.

To remove any unused assemblies from the drawing, right-click the Assemblies collection and select Erase All Unreferenced Assemblies.

In this same context menu, you can also choose to remove the display of the assemblies from modelspace. This hides the display of the assembly but retains its definition in the drawing.

You can still use a hidden assembly in a corridor. If you need it visible again for editing purposes, right-click the assembly and select Insert To Modelspace.

The niftiest part of this method of organizing assemblies is that they can now be part of your Civil 3D template without being visible.

The Bottom Line

Create a typical road assembly with lanes, curbs, gutters, and sidewalks.   Most corridors are built to model roads. The most common assembly used in these road corridors is some variation of a typical road section consisting of lanes, curbs, gutters, and sidewalks.

> **Master It**   Create a new drawing from either the Civil 3D metric or Imperial template. Build a symmetric assembly using LaneSuperelevationAOR, UrbanCurbGutterValley2, and LinkWidthAndSlope for terrace and buffer strips adjacent to the UrbanSidewalk. Use widths and slopes of your choosing.

Edit an assembly.   Once an assembly has been created, it can be easily edited to reflect a design change. Often, at the beginning of a project you won't know the final lane width. You can build your assembly and corridor model with one lane width and then change the width and rebuild the model immediately.

> **Master It**   Working in the drawing from the preceding exercise, edit the width of each LaneSuperelevationAOR to **14′ (4.3** m), and change the cross slope of each LaneSuperelevationAOR to **-3.00**%.

Add daylighting to a typical road assembly.   Often, the most difficult part of a designer's job is figuring out how to grade the area between the last engineered structure point in the cross section (such as the back of a sidewalk) and the existing ground. An extensive catalog of daylighting subassemblies can assist you with this task.

> **Master It**   Working in the drawing from the preceding exercise, add the DaylightMinWidth subassembly to both sides of your typical road assembly. Establish a minimum width between the outermost subassembly and the daylight offset of 10′ (3 m).

Chapter 9

Basic Corridors

The corridor object is a three-dimensional model that combines the horizontal geometry of an alignment, the vertical geometry of a profile, and the cross-sectional geometry of an assembly.

Corridors range from extremely simple roads to complicated highways and interchanges, but they aren't limited to just road travel ways. Corridors can be used to model many linear designs. This chapter focuses on building several simple corridors that can be used to model and design roads, channels, and trenches.

In this chapter, you will learn to:

- ◆ Build a single baseline corridor from an alignment, profile, and assembly.

- ◆ Use targets to add lane widening.

- ◆ Create a corridor surface.

- ◆ Add an automatic boundary to a corridor surface.

Understanding Corridors

In its simplest form, a corridor combines an alignment, a profile, and an assembly (see Figure 9.1).

FIGURE 9.1
A corridor shown in 3D view

You can also build corridors with complex combinations of alignments, profiles, and assemblies to make complicated intersections, interchanges, or branching streams (see Figure 9.2).

FIGURE 9.2
An intersection
modeled with a
corridor

The horizontal properties of the alignment, the vertical properties of the profile, and the cross-sectional properties of the assembly are merged to form a dynamic model that can be used to build surfaces, sample cross sections, generate quantities, and much more.

Most commonly, corridors are used to model roads, but they can also be adapted to model berms, streams (see Figure 9.3), trails, and even parking lots.

FIGURE 9.3
A stream
modeled with
a corridor

Recognizing Corridor Components

Certification
Objective

First, let's look at some important corridor components you will want to become familiar with before proceeding. *Baseline*, *region*, *assembly*, *frequency*, and *target* are all parts of a corridor that you will encounter even on your first design.

BASELINE

The first component for any corridor is a *baseline*. The baseline is composed of two Autodesk® AutoCAD® Civil 3D® objects, an alignment providing the horizontal layout, and a profile providing the vertical layout. The baseline generates the backbone on which the assembly is placed. Corridors can contain more than one baseline. Therefore, a network of roads can be modeled using one corridor.

In most of the examples in this chapter, the baseline will correspond to the centerline alignment with a profile representing the elevation at the crown of a proposed road. However, this is not always the case, as we will explore in more depth in Chapter 10, "Advanced Corridors, Intersections, and Roundabouts." As your designs become more detailed, you may have corridors with multiple baselines.

REGION

When the geometry along a baseline changes enough to warrant a new assembly, a new *region* is needed. Regions specify the station range where a specific assembly is applied to the design. There may be many regions along a baseline to accommodate design geometry, but the regions may not overlap. Therefore, each region has a start station and an end station, with the end station of one region often matching the start station of the next region.

ASSEMBLY

Marker points, *links*, and *shapes* are coded into the subassemblies that the assembly contains, as you saw in Chapter 8, "Assemblies and Subassemblies." Assemblies are the third Civil 3D object that is required to generate the corridor by providing cross-sectional information to be applied along some or all of the length of the baseline. Figure 9.4 shows a symmetric roadway assembly that consists of lanes, curbs, sidewalks, and daylight links.

FIGURE 9.4
Typical roadway assembly

FREQUENCY

Frequency refers to how often the assembly is applied to the corridor design. You can set the frequency for the corridor as a whole or for each region.

The frequency value will vary depending on the situation. The default frequencies of the stock Civil 3D templates are 25′ in Imperial units and 20 m for metric units. But like many of the settings in Civil 3D, these defaults can be changed in your drawing or template settings by using the following simple steps:

1. On the Settings tab of Toolspace, expand the Corridor ➤ Commands branch.

2. Right-click the Create Corridor command and choose Edit Command Settings to display the Edit Command Settings – Create Corridor dialog.

3. Expand Assembly Insertion Defaults.

4. Change Frequency Along Tangents, Frequency Along Curves, Frequency Along Spirals, Frequency Along Profile Curves, or any other of the multitude of default settings associated with creating a corridor.

A new feature in Civil 3D 2016 is an alternative to configuring frequency along curvatures. Instead of using a constant distance value for frequency, frequency can be triggered by the mid-ordinate distant value. This frequency setting can be applied to curves in the alignment or curves in offset targets (targets will be discussed in the next section), resulting in more frequent insertions of assemblies along smaller curves and less frequent insertions of assemblies along larger curves. This produces a more precise and accurate 3D model without a lot of manual overrides on the region level.

In addition to the frequencies based on the alignment or profile entity, Civil 3D can place frequency lines at special stations such as horizontal geometry stations, superelevation critical stations, profile geometry stations, profile high/low stations, and offset target geometry stations. You can also manually create additional frequency stations for things such as driveways or culvert crossings.

TARGET

As you learned in Chapter 8, three types of targets can be configured in a corridor: a target surface, a target elevation, and a target offset. Targets can be used in lieu of additional assemblies to change corridor geometric characteristics such as cross slope (elevation targets) and lane width (offset target). Surface targets can be used in daylighting or roadway rehabilitation scenarios. Some targets are optional, whereas others are required. For a detailed explanation on targeting for each stock assembly, refer to the help files.

CORRIDOR FEATURE LINES

When a corridor is created, corridor feature lines are generated. These feature lines can represent back of curb, top of curb, flow lines, edges of pavement, crowns, and any other breakline that would be produced based on your proposed typical roadway section. Corridor feature lines are drawn along the corridor, connecting marker points of identical codes in between assembly frequencies, as shown in Figure 9.5. This takes traditional roadway design to another level: A collection of cross sections occurring at specified frequencies becomes a dynamic three-dimensional object model.

FIGURE 9.5
The anatomy of a corridor

Later in this chapter, you will take a closer look at corridor feature lines.

This exercise gives you hands-on experience in building a corridor model from an alignment, a profile, and an assembly:

1. Open the 0901_RoadCorridor.dwg file or 0901_RoadCorridor_METRIC.dwg file. You can download these files from www.sybex.com/go/masteringcivil3d2016.

   Note that the drawing has several alignments, profile views containing the existing and design profiles for each, an assembly, and an existing ground surface.

2. From the Home tab ➤ Create Design panel, choose Corridor to display the Create Corridor dialog.

3. In the Name text box, name the corridor **North River Crossing**.

   Keep the default values for Corridor Style and Corridor Layer.

4. Set Alignment to ROAD C and set Profile to FG-ROAD C (take extra care not to select EG-ROAD C by mistake).

   Notice that you can use the small green selection button to select the object on the screen instead of using the drop-down list if you prefer.

5. Verify that Assembly is set to Urban 14' Single-Lane (or Urban 4.5m Single-Lane for metric users).

6. Verify that Target Surface is set to Existing Surface.

7. Verify that the Set Baseline And Region Parameters check box is selected.

   The Create Corridor dialog should now look similar to Figure 9.6.

FIGURE 9.6
The Create
Corridor
dialog

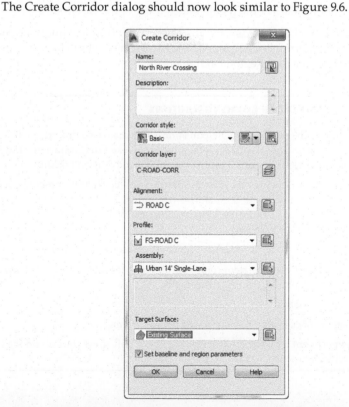

8. Click OK to accept the settings and to display the Baseline And Region Parameters dialog, as shown in Figure 9.7.

FIGURE 9.7
The Baseline And Region Parameters dialog

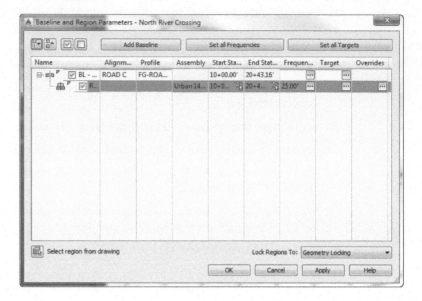

Notice that there is currently one baseline containing one region. The Start Station and End Station values of the region match those of the baseline.

Most of the other settings have already been set from the information you provided in the Create Corridor dialog, but let's take a few minutes to look at some of the settings in the Baseline And Region Parameters dialog.

UNDERSTANDING THE LOCKING REGIONS

At the bottom of the Baseline And Region Parameters dialog is a drop-down list for locking regions. In versions prior to Civil 3D 2013, all regions were locked to the station. However, now there are two options for locking regions: Geometry Locking and Station Locking.

By default, on new drawing files, this drop-down will be set to Geometry Locking. If you open a drawing created in a previous version, the drop-down will be set to Station Locking, but you can change it to Geometry Locking if you desire. You can update this default in your existing templates as needed by using the following steps:

1. On the Settings tab of Toolspace, expand the Corridor ➤ Commands branch.
2. Right-click the Create Corridor command and choose Edit Command Settings to display the Edit Command Settings – Create Corridor dialog.
3. Expand Assembly Insertion Defaults.
4. Change the Lock Region To value to the desired setting.

You can experiment with either option to see how it will affect your corridor as you make changes to the corridor's baseline.

9. Click the ellipsis button in the Frequency column in the first row associated with the baseline (BL) to display the Frequency To Apply Assemblies dialog.

By clicking the ellipsis in the first row that is associated with the baseline, you will be setting the frequency for all of the regions within that baseline. In this instance you have only one region, but setting them all at once is a good habit to get into when applicable. You could also click the Set All Frequencies button, which would set the frequency for all the baselines and all the baseline regions.

10. Examine the settings in the Frequency To Apply Assemblies dialog, as shown in Figure 9.8.

FIGURE 9.8
The Frequency To Apply Assemblies dialog

You can vary the default frequency distance for the portions of the region along tangents, curves, spirals, and profile curves. You can also base frequency along alignment and offset curves by curvature (mid-ordinate distance) instead of by increment. In addition, you can add frequency lines at various geometry points. At the bottom of the dialog you can add a user-defined station.

11. Click OK to accept the settings in the Frequency To Apply Assemblies dialog.

12. Click the ellipsis button in the Targets column in the baseline row to display the Target Mapping dialog.

The ellipsis buttons in this column behave the same way as the ellipsis buttons in the Frequency column. Notice that there is also a Set All Targets button, which can be used to set the targets for all of the baselines and all of the baseline regions.

13. Examine the settings in the Target Mapping dialog, as shown in Figure 9.9.

FIGURE 9.9
The Target Mapping dialog

Target	Object Name	Subassembly	Assembly Group
⊟ Surfaces	\<Click here to set all\>		
Target Surface	Existing Surface	DaylightMaxOffset	Right
Target Surface	Existing Surface	DaylightMaxOffset	Left
⊟ Width or Offset Targets			
Width Alignment	\<None\>	LaneSuperelevationAOR	Right
Target Alignment of Inside ...	\<None\>	UrbanSidewalk	Right
Target Alignment of Sidew...	\<None\>	UrbanSidewalk	Right
Target Alignment of Outsid...	\<None\>	UrbanSidewalk	Right
Target Alignment	\<None\>	DaylightMaxOffset	Right
Width Alignment	\<None\>	LaneSuperelevationAOR	Left
Target Alignment of Inside ...	\<None\>	UrbanSidewalk	Left
Target Alignment of Sidew...	\<None\>	UrbanSidewalk	Left
Target Alignment of Outsid...	\<None\>	UrbanSidewalk	Left
Target Alignment	\<None\>	DaylightMaxOffset	Left
⊟ Slope or Elevation Targets			
Outside Elevation Profile	\<None\>	LaneSuperelevationAOR	Right
Target Profile of Slope	\<None\>	UrbanSidewalk	Right
Outside Elevation Profile	\<None\>	LaneSuperelevationAOR	Left
Target Profile of Slope	\<None\>	UrbanSidewalk	Left

The information in this dialog will vary depending on the subassemblies assigned to the assembly used for this corridor baseline but will always be broken into three categories: Surfaces, Width Or Offset Targets, and Slope Or Elevation Targets. Notice that because you selected Existing Surface as the target surface when creating the corridor, Existing Surface is already set as the target surface for the left and right subassemblies targeting a surface.

14. Click OK to accept the settings in the Target Mapping dialog.

15. Click OK to accept the settings in the Baseline And Region Parameters dialog.

If at any point you want to return to the information shown in this dialog, you can do so on the Parameters tab of the Corridor Properties dialog, which you will look at a little later in this chapter.

You will see a dialog warning you that the corridor definition has been modified and giving you two options: Rebuild The Corridor or Mark The Corridor As Out-Of-Date. Select the Rebuild The Corridor option.

If you click the check box at the bottom of this warning dialog that says "Always perform my current choice," you will not see this warning dialog again.

UNDERSTANDING THE LOCKING REGIONS

If you select the check box (or any others) to hide a message and later want to receive the warning dialog again, you can reactivate it in the future by entering **Options** on the command line. On the System tab, click the Hidden Message Settings button.

You will receive an error message in Panorama, as shown in Figure 9.10, that reads "Intersection with target could not be computed," "Intersection Point doesn't exist," or something similar. You will rectify this issue in the following steps.

FIGURE 9.10
Corridor error in Panorama

If Panorama did not automatically display, from the Home tab ➤ Palettes expanded panel, choose Event Viewer.

16. Dismiss Panorama.

Your corridor should look similar to Figure 9.11.

FIGURE 9.11
A portion of the nearly completed corridor

Now, let's try to figure out why those messages appeared in Panorama. In plan view, at the last station on the east end of the alignment, notice that on the left side some of the feature lines are not connecting (shown in Figure 9.11). Daylighting could not occur at the final station because the alignment is extending outside the outer edge of the surface. Furthermore, a look at the corridor in the Object Viewer shows a "waterfall" (see Figure 9.12).

FIGURE 9.12
A "waterfall"
at the end of
the alignment
viewed in the
Object Viewer

VIEWING THE CORRIDOR IN THE OBJECT VIEWER

If you'd like to view the corridor in the Object Viewer, do the following:

1. Select one of the corridor lines to activate the Corridor contextual tab.

2. From the Corridor contextual tab ➢ General Tools panel, choose Object Viewer.

3. Use the View Control drop-down from the top of the Object Viewer to view the corridor from various isometric views, or press and hold the left button on your mouse and move the object around to view it from various custom angles.

4. After you have examined the corridor, click the X in the upper-right corner to dismiss the Object Viewer.

The fact that the alignment is extending outside the outer edge of the surface isn't the only cause of the error in Panorama. If you take a look at the profile view for ROAD C, the FG-ROAD C profile does not extend to the end of the alignment, which explains the waterfall. A waterfall occurs when the profile used in the corridor is not providing elevation data along a station range of the alignment. Therefore, the corridor dives down to elevation zero in that station range. In this case, you need to shorten the corridor so that it builds along the station range matching FG-ROAD C.

17. Select the corridor to activate the Corridor contextual tab.

18. From the Corridor contextual tab ➤ Modify Corridor panel, choose the Corridor Properties icon to display the Corridor Properties dialog.

19. In the Corridor Properties dialog, switch to the Parameters tab.

Notice in Figure 9.13 that the end station for the region is 20+43.16′ (or 0+622.76m for metric users), which is based on the full length of the alignment. However, the design profile ends at 19+95′ (or 0+608m for metric users). Even though there is no elevation assigned at 20+43.16′ (or 0+622.76m for metric users), the corridor assumes an elevation of zero at this station, which creates this waterfall effect. To fix this, you need to tell the corridor to end the region at the final station of the design profile.

FIGURE 9.13
Corridor
Properties
dialog,
Parameters
tab

Note that even though the display value shows only two (or three) decimal places, the corridor examines up to eight decimal places of precision, which means that the value being displayed as the final station of the design profile may be a rounded-up value. If this is the case, this too will create a waterfall effect.

20. Click into the End Station field for the region and enter **1995** (or **608** for metric users).

Entering the value with station notation (the plus sign) is not needed.

Notice that you could alternatively click the station picker button in this cell to select the station on the plan.

21. Click OK to accept the settings in the Corridor Properties dialog.

22. If you didn't click the check box at the last warning dialog, you will receive the same warning again. If so, select the Rebuild The Corridor option to allow the corridor to rebuild.

No new errors will appear in Panorama.

A quick look in the Object Viewer should reveal that the waterfall is gone. When this exercise is complete, you can close the drawing. A finished copy of this drawing is available from the book's website with the filename 0901_RoadCorridor_FINISHED.dwg or 0901_RoadCorridor_METRIC_FINISHED.dwg.

REBUILDING YOUR CORRIDOR

A corridor is a *dynamic* model—which means that if you modify any of the objects used to create the corridor, the corridor must be rebuilt to reflect those changes. For example, if you make a change to the design profile, you must rebuild the corridor to bring it up to date. The same principle applies to changes to alignments, assemblies, target surfaces, and any other corridor building blocks or parameters.

You can access the Rebuild command by right-clicking the corridor name in Prospector, as shown in Figure 9.14.

FIGURE 9.14
In Prospector, expand the Corridors branch and right-click the corridor name to rebuild it.

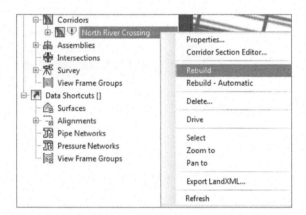

You can also rebuild the corridor or rebuild all corridors by selecting the corridor object and choosing Rebuild Corridor or Rebuild All Corridors from the Corridor contextual tab ➤ Modify Corridor panel, as shown in Figure 9.15.

FIGURE 9.15
Rebuilding the corridor from the Corridor contextual tab

> **AVOIDING LENGTHY REBUILDS**
>
> For large, complex corridors, you may want to consider leaving the Rebuild Automatic option unchecked. Every time a change is made that affects a region in your corridor, those regions that have been modified will go through the rebuilding process. This is an improvement from previous versions of Civil 3D, which rebuilt the full corridor even if a modification affected only one region. Nonetheless, the larger or more complex the corridor is and the more regions you are modifying, the longer the rebuild process will take.

TWEAKING CORRIDORS

Your corridor may not be perfect on your first iteration of the design. Become comfortable getting into and working with the Parameters tab of the Corridor Properties dialog. You will spend the majority of your time modifying your corridor on this tab.

Whether you are building your first corridor or your five hundredth, odds are good that you will run into one of the following common issues:

Problem   The waterfall effect—your corridor seems to fall off a cliff, meaning the beginning or ending station of your corridor drops down to elevation zero.

   Typical Cause   The range of your corridor is longer than the design profile.

   Fix   This is exactly what you ran into in the first exercise. The corridor takes the initial station range from your alignment. However, sometimes you don't tie into existing ground at the exact alignment start and end stations, so you need to adjust the corridor stations accordingly.

   If you need to check the exact start and end stations of the design profile, the best place to do so is the Profile Data tab in the Profile Properties dialog (as shown in Figure 9.16). Edit your corridor region to begin and end at the design profile station.

FIGURE 9.16
Check your Profile Properties dialog to verify the station range of the design profile.

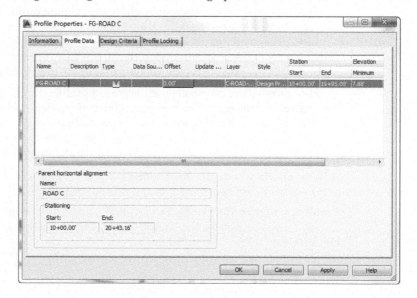

Alternatively, you can use the station picker button to select the first and last corridor region stations by snapping to the first and last frequency lines that correspond to your profile geometry.

Problem   Your corridor seems to take longer to build and has irregular frequency stations. Also, your daylighting may not extend out to where you expect it (see Figure 9.17).

FIGURE 9.17
An example
of unexpected
corridor
frequency

Typical Cause   You accidentally chose the existing profile instead of the design profile for your baseline profile. Most corridors are set up to place a frequency line at every vertical geometry point, and a profile, such as the existing profile, has many more vertical geometry points than a layout profile (in this case, the design profile). These additional points on the existing profile are the cause of the unexpected frequency lines.

Fix   Always use care to choose the correct profile. Either physically select the profile onscreen or make sure your naming conventions clearly define your finished grade as finished grade. If your corridor is already built, select the corridor, right-click, and choose Corridor Properties, as shown in Figure 9.18. On the Parameters tab of the Corridor Properties dialog, change the profile from the existing profile to the design profile.

Adding a surface target throws another variable into the mix. Here is a list of some of the most typical problems new users face and how to solve them:

Problem   Your corridor doesn't show daylighting even though you have a daylight subassembly on your assembly. You may also get an error message in Event Viewer, as shown in Figure 9.19.

FIGURE 9.18
The context menu available on the Corridor object

FIGURE 9.19
Error messages associated with absence of daylighting

Typical Cause You forgot to set the surface target when you created your corridor.

Fix Select the corridor, right-click, and choose Corridor Properties. On the Parameters tab of the Corridor Properties dialog, click the Set All Targets button. The Target Mapping dialog opens, and its first category is Surfaces. Click the <Click Here To Set All> text in the Object Name column field to display the Pick A Surface dialog. In this dialog, you can choose a surface for the daylight subassembly to target.

Problem Your corridor seems to be missing areas of daylighting. You may also get an error message in Event Viewer, as shown in Figure 9.20.

FIGURE 9.20
Error messages associated with missing areas of daylighting

Typical Cause The Daylight link cannot find the target surface within the parameters you've set in the subassembly properties. This could also mean that the target surface doesn't fully extend the full length of your corridor or your target surface is too narrow at certain locations.

Fix Add more data to your target surface. The daylighting subassemblies in your corridor need a surface to tie into at the slope, grade, or distance specified in subassembly properties.

You can also revisit your daylight subassembly settings to give the program a narrower offset or steeper slope or grade. Alternatively, you can adjust your alignment and/or profile to require less cut or fill, which would cause daylighting to occur over a shorter distance. Lastly, you can adjust your station range on the Parameters tab in Corridor Properties, as you did in the previous exercise.

If this is not possible, omit daylighting through those specific stations, and once your corridor is built, do hand-grading using feature lines or grading objects. You can also investigate other subassemblies such as LinkOffsetAndElevation that will meet your design intention without requiring a surface target.

Working with Corridor Feature Lines

Corridor feature lines are first drawn connecting marker points of the same code in between assembly frequencies. For example, a feature line will work its way down the corridor and connect all the Daylight points occurring from assembly to assembly. If there are Daylight points on the entire length of your corridor, then the feature line is drawn for the entire length of your corridor. If a region is defined along that same corridor without Daylight points, then the daylight feature line will end at that region.

The Feature Lines tab of the Corridor Properties dialog has a drop-down menu called Branching (see Figure 9.21) with two options: Inward and Outward.

FIGURE 9.21
The Feature Lines tab of the Corridor Properties dialog

In the case of a two-lane road transitioning to a four-lane road, you would have two lane edges transitioning to four lane edges in the corridor. When branching inward, the feature lines representing those two lane edges will be drawn to the innermost lane edges of the four-lane road on their respective sides. When branching outward, the feature lines representing the two lane edges will be drawn to the outermost lane edges on their respective sides. This setting is particularly important for surface building purposes. Also on this tab is a check box labeled Connect Extra Points. If checked, this will cause the feature lines representing those two lane edges to branch out and connect to both the inner and outer lane edges on their respective sides (see Figure 9.22).

FIGURE 9.22
Feature line branching and connectivity options

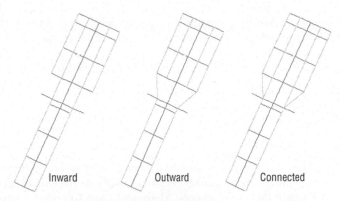

As mentioned earlier, a feature line will connect the same point codes in between assembly frequencies by default. However, the Feature Lines tab of the Corridor Properties dialog allows you to eliminate certain feature lines on the basis of the point code. For example, if for some reason you did not want your Daylight points connected with a feature line, you could toggle that feature line off using the check box in the Connect column.

Corridor feature lines represent the linear features of your corridor like crown, pavement edge, flow line, back and top of curb, and sidewalk edges. Feature lines can also be generated for the edges of all pavement layers, base layers, and sub-base layers. You will be using feature lines in Chapter 14, "Grading," for grading purposes. The difference between the two types of feature line is that corridor feature lines live in the Corridor object.

There are several types of objects you can extract from the Corridor object. If you select the corridor to activate the Corridor contextual tab, you will notice that the Launch Pad panel, shown in Figure 9.23, offers tools for extracting points, alignments, profiles, polylines, and feature lines. The latter four objects are created from the corridor feature lines.

FIGURE 9.23
Launch Pad panel of the Corridor con-textual tab

A step-by-step explanation of how to extract a corridor feature line is given in the next exercise.

In the case of extracting a feature line, you have the choice of keeping the line dynamically linked to the corridor geometry or making it an entirely separate entity. When the feature line is linked, it automatically updates when the corridor updates. It cannot be modified. It can be used for grading, but it cannot be used for targeting in that corridor. If the feature line is not linked, it will not update with the corridor. It will be a duplicate of the corridor feature line, but it can be modified. It can also be used for targeting in that corridor. Both types of feature lines can be used as breaklines in surface models.

Once an alignment, profile, or 3D polyline has been extracted, its geometry can be adjusted independently. In this case, the profile, alignment, or polyline no longer retains a link to the corridor from which it originated. Once a profile, alignment, or 3D polyline has been extracted, you can use it as a target back in the corridor that formed it. In the following exercise, a corridor feature line is extracted to produce an alignment and profile:

1. Open the `0902_CorridorFeatureLine.dwg` or `0902_CorridorFeatureLine_METRIC` `.dwg` file.

2. From the Home tab ➤ Create Design panel, choose Alignment ➤ Create Alignment From Corridor.

   Alternatively, you can select the corridor by selecting the corridor feature line that you want to create an alignment from to activate the Corridor contextual tab. From the Launch Pad panel, choose Alignment From Corridor. *If you do this, then skip the next step.*

3. At the `Select a corridor feature line:` prompt, select the feature line labeled in the drawing as TOP OF CURB FEATURE LINE.

4. In the Name text box of the Create Alignment From Objects dialog, name the alignment **Road D East Top Curb**.

5. Verify that Type is set to Offset.

6. On the General tab of the Create Alignment From Objects dialog, verify the following settings:

   ◆ Alignment Style is set to Basic.

   ◆ Alignment Label Set is set to _No Labels.

   ◆ The Create Profile check box is selected.

   The dialog should match Figure 9.24.

7. Click OK to accept the settings in the Create Alignment From Objects dialog and display the Create Profile – Draw New dialog.

8. In the Name text box of the Create Profile – Draw New dialog, name the profile **FG-Road D East Top Curb**.

9. On the General tab of the Create Profile – Draw New dialog, verify that the profile style is set to Design Profile and that the profile label set is set to _No Labels.

   The dialog should match Figure 9.25.

FIGURE 9.24
The completed
Create Alignment
From Objects
dialog

FIGURE 9.25
The Create
Profile – Draw
New dialog

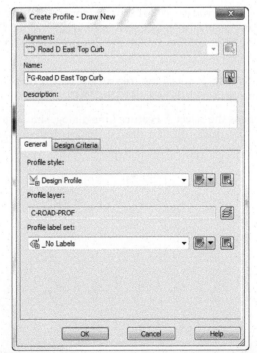

10. Click OK to accept the settings in the dialog and then press ↵ to exit the command. If corridor is still selected, press Esc to deselect.

11. In Prospector, expand Alignments ➤ Offset Alignments ➤ Road D East Top Curb ➤ Profiles to review the completed alignment and profile (see Figure 9.26).

FIGURE 9.26
The completed alignment and profile shown on the Prospector tab of Toolspace

There are additional offset alignments listed on Prospector that were created to construct the intersection of Road C and Road D. You will be learning about intersections in the next chapter.

Next, you will extract a corridor feature line and keep it dynamically linked to the corridor.

12. From the Home tab ➤ Create Design panel, choose Feature Line ➤ Create Feature Line From Corridor.

Alternatively, you can select the corridor by selecting the corridor feature line that you want to create a feature line from to activate the Corridor contextual tab and then selecting Feature Lines From Corridor from the Launch Pad panel. *If you do this, then skip the next step.*

13. At the `Select a corridor feature line:` prompt, select the feature line labeled in the drawing as DAYLIGHT FEATURE LINE.

This opens the Select A Feature Line dialog, similar to the one shown in Figure 9.27.

FIGURE 9.27
Selecting the Daylight feature line with the Select A Feature Line dialog

The Select A Feature Line dialog will open when there are overlapping feature lines available at the location selected.

14. Select the Daylight feature line from the Select A Feature Line dialog.

15. Click OK to close the Select A Feature Line dialog and display the Create Feature Line From Corridor dialog.

16. Select the Name check box and name the feature line **Road D Daylight East**.

17. Verify that Style is set to Corridor Grading.

18. Verify that the Create Dynamic Link To The Corridor check box is selected.

All other settings can be left at their defaults. The dialog should match Figure 9.28.

19. Click OK to accept the settings in the dialog and then press ↵ to exit the command. If the corridor is still selected, press Esc to deselect.

FIGURE 9.28
The Create Feature Line From Corridor dialog with the option to create a dynamic link turned on

20. Select the newly created auto corridor feature line.

Note that it can be selected but does not have grips.

21. From the Feature Line contextual tab ➢ Modify panel, click the Edit Geometry and Edit Elevations buttons to reveal these hidden panels if they are not displaying.

Note which options on the contextual tab are grayed out and which are not, as shown in Figure 9.29.

FIGURE 9.29
Auto Corridor
Feature Line
contextual tab

These alignments and feature lines can now be used for further design. Remember that feature lines created from the corridor but not dynamically linked to the corridor are no longer connected to the corridor and will not update as you make modifications to the corridor.

When this exercise is complete, you can close the drawing. A finished copy of this drawing is available from the book's web page with the filename 0902_CorridorFeatureLine_FINISHED .dwg or 0902_CorridorFeatureLine_METRIC_FINISHED.dwg.

Understanding Targets

Every subassembly is programmed with parameters. Some of these parameters are fixed values like pavement thickness. A lot of subassemblies are programmed with targeting parameters. Examples of targeting parameters would be lane width and cross slope. Lane width and cross slope can be variable. Therefore, if this is the case, you could use alignment and profile targets to define the variable lane width and cross slope.

Alignments, profiles, feature lines, survey figures, and polylines can be configured as targets for subassemblies with width or cross slope. Surface targets are used with daylighting and road-way rehabilitation subassemblies. Ever since the release of Civil 3D 2014, you can select these targets through external references. Not all subassemblies contain targeting parameters. You can refer to the help file for target information regarding any subassembly you plan to use.

When you built the corridor in the first exercise, the opening dialog prompted you for a surface target. Next we will cover linear targets.

Using Target Alignments and Profiles

So far, the corridor examples you looked at have a constant cross section. In this section, we'll take a look at what happens when a portion of your corridor needs to transition to a wider section and then transition back to normal.

Many subassemblies have been programmed to allow for not only a baseline attachment point but also additional outer attachment points that can target alignments, feature lines, and profiles. Be sure to check the subassembly help file to make sure the subassembly you are using will accept targets if you need them. In Chapter 8, you learned that you can right-click any subassembly in the Tool Palettes window to enter the help file. For instance, the BasicLane subassembly will show None in the Target Parameters area of the help file, but LaneSuperElevationAOR lists Lane Width and Outside Elevation.

Think of a subassembly as a rubber band that is attached both to the baseline of the corridor (such as the road centerline) and to the target alignment. As the target alignment, such as a lane widening, gets further from the baseline, the rubber band is stretched wider. As that target alignment transitions back toward the baseline, the rubber band changes to reflect a narrower cross section.

Figure 9.30 shows what happens to a cross section when various targets are set for the left edge of a traveled way for a lane subassembly. Figure 9.30a shows the assembly as it was originally placed in the drawing. The width from the original assembly is 14′ with a cross slope of

2 percent to the edge of pavement. Figure 9.30b shows how the geometry changes if an alignment target is set for the edge of pavement. Notice that because there is no profile specified to change the elevation, the 2 percent cross slope is held and the lane width is the only geometry that changes. Figure 9.30c shows that if both an alignment and profile are specified for an edge of pavement alignment, the design cross slope and width both change. Last, you see the assembly with just a profile target assigned to the edge of pavement in Figure 9.30d. In this case, the width stays at 14', but the elevation of the edge of pavement is dictated by the profile.

FIGURE 9.30
How geometry changes with a target on the left: original assembly geometry (a), assembly with width alignment target only (b), assembly with both alignment and profile target (c), and assembly with only profile target set (d)

The following exercise shows you how to set targets using an offset alignment with a widening configured to build a right turn lane in the corridor:

1. Open the 0903_TargetPractice.dwg or 0903_TargetPractice_METRIC.dwg file. Note that this drawing has an incomplete corridor.

   You will be creating an offset alignment and modifying the alignment with a widening. Then you will use the Target Mapping dialog to configure the outer lane edge to follow the alignment.

2. From the Home tab ➤ Create Design panel, choose Alignment ➤ Create Offset Alignment.

3. At the Select an alignment: prompt, select the ROAD D alignment.

   You might need to pan toward where it intersects ROAD A to avoid a selection conflict with the corridor.

4. In the Create Offset Alignments dialog, configure the following:

   ◆ No. Of Offsets On Left: **0**

   ◆ No. Of Offsets On Right: **1**

   ◆ Incremental Offset On Right: **14′ (4.5 m)**

◆ Alignment Style: Offsets

◆ Alignment Label Set: _No Labels

5. Click OK to dismiss.

The offset alignment has been created. Notice how it lines up with the right edge of pavement in Figure 9.31.

FIGURE 9.31
Offset Alignment representing the edge of pavement before adding a widening

In the previous exercise, you created an alignment from a feature line in the corridor. The difference between an alignment from a corridor and an offset alignment is that the offset alignment remains dynamic to the centerline alignment. If the centerline alignment geometry changes, the offset alignment geometry will change with it, maintaining its offset value.

6. From the Home tab ➢ Create Design panel, choose Alignment ➢ Create Widening.

7. At the Select an alignment: prompt, select the new offset alignment.

8. At the Create widening portion as a new alignment: prompt, enter **No**.

9. At the Select start station: prompt, type **1638** ↵ (or **502** ↵ for metric users).

10. At the Select end station: prompt, type **1738** ↵ (or **527** ↵ for metric users).

11. At the Enter widening offset: prompt, type **28** ↵ (or **9** ↵ for metric users), the offset distance from the centerline alignment to the widening alignment.

The Offset Alignment Parameters palette appears as shown in Figure 9.32. Though you won't be making any changes to the defaults at this time, observe that you can change or extend the transition parameters at the entry and exit if desired.

FIGURE 9.32
Offset
Alignment
Parameters
palette

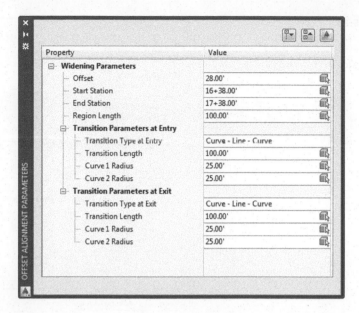

12. Dismiss the Offset Alignment Parameters palette by clicking the X in the upper corner.

13. Select the corridor to activate the Corridor contextual tab.

14. From the Corridor contextual tab ➤ Modify Corridor panel, choose the Corridor Properties icon.

15. On the Parameters tab, locate the baseline named BL - ROAD D - (13) for Imperial and metric units.

    There are multiple baselines in this corridor. As mentioned earlier in the chapter, a corridor can contain multiple baselines and baselines can contain multiple regions.

16. In the Target column for region RG - Urban 14' Single-Lane - (6) (for Imperial units) or RG - Urban 4.5m Single-Lane - (2) (for metric units), click the ellipsis button to display the Target Mapping dialog. You may need to make the Name column wider to see the row name.

17. In the Width Or Offset Targets ➤ Width Alignment branch for Lane SuperelevationAOR for the Right Assembly Group, click <None> to display the Set Width Or Offset Target dialog.

    New to Civil 3D 2016 is the Alignments Bylayer feature, shown in this dialog.

18. With the Select Object Type To Target drop-down set to Alignments, use the Select From The Drawing button to select the offset alignment that you just created.

19. Press Enter when finished selecting to return to the Set Width Or Offset Target dialog.

20. Click the Add button.

    The alignment should appear in the listing of selected entities to target at the bottom of the dialog, as shown in Figure 9.33.

FIGURE 9.33
The Set Width
Or Offset
Target dialog

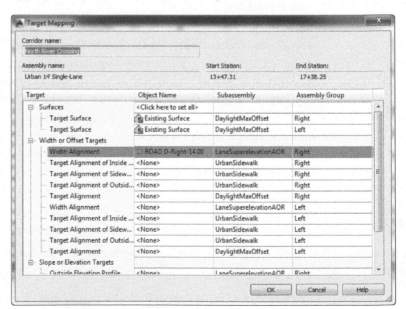

21. Click OK to accept the settings in the Set Width Or Offset Target dialog.

The Target Mapping dialog should now look like Figure 9.34.

FIGURE 9.34
Targets set for
surface and
lane width for
the right side

22. Click OK to accept the settings in the dialog

23. Click OK to accept the settings in the Corridor Properties dialog and allow the corridor to rebuild.

The corridor should now be following the ETW alignment and resemble Figure 9.35.

FIGURE 9.35
The completed exercise in plan view

A finished copy of this drawing is available from the book's web page (`0903_TargetPractice_FINISHED.dwg` or `0903_TargetPractice_METRIC_FINISHED.dwg`).

CORRIDOR PROPERTIES MODIFICATIONS MADE EASY

It can be tedious to modify alignments, profiles, starting stations, ending stations, frequencies, and targets along a corridor. Each of these items can be modified in the item view at the bottom of Prospector, as shown here.

Continues

Continued

In the following quick exercise, you will use Toolspace to access and modify Frequency values for the North River Crossing corridor region:

1. Open the `0904_CorridorFrequency.dwg` or `0904_CorridorFrequency_METRIC.dwg` file.

2. In Prospector, expand and highlight the North River Crossing corridor.

3. Click the Frequency ellipsis button for the BL - ROAD E - (14) baseline to display the Frequency To Apply Assemblies dialog.

4. Set the Along Curves value to By Curvature and then set the Mid-ordinate Distance To Define Curvature value to **0.1′** (or **0.03** m for metric users).

5. Click OK.

The corridor will rebuild, and the additional frequency lines should be visible in the plan, as shown here.

When this exercise is complete, you can close the drawing. A finished copy of this drawing is available from the book's web page with the filename `0904_CorridorFrequency_FINISHED.dwg` or `0904_CorridorFrequency_METRIC_FINISHED.dwg`.

Editing Sections

Once your corridor is built, chances are you will want to examine it section by section, make some adjustments, and check for problems. For a station-by-station look at a corridor, select the corridor and from the Corridor contextual tab ➤ Modify Corridor Sections panel, choose Section Editor (see Figure 9.36).

FIGURE 9.36
Some of the many tools, including the Section Editor, available on the Corridor contextual tab

Once you are in the Section Editor, you are in a purely data-driven view. That means that this is a live, editable section of the corridor and is not for plotting purposes. We will discuss plotting cross sections in Chapter 12, "Cross Sections and Mass Haul."

The Section Editor allows for multiple viewport configurations so that you can see the plan, profile, and section all at the same time, as demonstrated in the following exercise:

1. Open the `0904_CorridorFrequency_FINISHED.dwg` or `0904_CorridorFrequency_METRIC_FINISHED.dwg` file.

2. Select the corridor, and from the Corridor contextual tab ➤ Modify Corridor Sections panel choose Section Editor.

3. From the Section Editor contextual tab ➤ View Tools panel, choose Viewport Configuration to display the Corridor Section Editor: Viewport Configuration dialog, as shown in Figure 9.37.

FIGURE 9.37
The Corridor Section Editor: Viewport Configuration dialog

4. Set Layout to Three: Above and Viewport 1 to Plan, Viewport 2 to Profile, and Viewport 3 to Section with a 50 percent horizontal split and a 50 percent vertical split.

5. Click OK to accept the settings in the Viewport Configuration dialog. Your screen should now look similar to Figure 9.38.

FIGURE 9.38
The Corridor
Section Editor
with Viewport
Configuration
set to Three:
Above

6. You may receive a warning dialog asking if you would like to turn on Viewport Configuration; if so, select Yes.

7. To exit the Section Editor, click the Close button on the Close panel.

8. Close the drawing. You don't need to save changes.

The Section Editor contextual tab offers many commands other than just Viewport Configuration, as shown in Figure 9.39.

FIGURE 9.39
The Corridor
Section Editor
contextual tab

The Station Selection panel on the Section Editor contextual tab allows you to move forward and backward through your corridor to see what each section looks like. For complex corridors, you can switch between baselines.

If you want to edit a section, you may do so geometrically in the viewport showing the section in the Section Editor or through the Parameter Editor palette but not both. To graphically edit a link, hold down the Ctrl key on the keyboard while selecting the item. This will activate grips that you can use to relocate or stretch the link (Figure 9.40).

FIGURE 9.40
A Daylight
link ready for
grip-editing
in the Section
Editor

If you would rather use the Parameter Editor to make more precise changes to your section, do the following:

1. From the Section Editor contextual tab ➤ Corridor Edit Tools panel, choose Parameter Editor.

2. Advance the Select A Station list until you reach the station of interest.

    The Parameter Editor button will not be active for stations without an assembly applied.

3. Look through the listing of subassemblies and their current parameter values.

4. When you find a value you want to edit, click in the Value field to override the design value, as shown in Figure 9.41.

FIGURE 9.41
The Corridor
Parameter
Editor

When you change the value, a check mark will appear in the Override column. You will find that some of the values are uneditable.

The changes you make can be applied to just the section you are viewing or to a range of stations in the region you are working in (use the Apply To A Station Range button in the Corridor Edit Tools panel to apply the changes to a region).

ACK! STUCK IN BIZARRO COORDINATE SYSTEM

If you accidentally exit your drawing without exiting the Section Editor, you will return to a drawing in a rotated coordinate system, as shown here. It may be difficult to see your design, but don't panic.

At the command line, type **Plan** ↵ **W** ↵. You will see your project, but there is still another step.

From the View tab ➤ Coordinates panel, set the current UCS to World, as shown in the following graphic. The UCS icon will return to normal, and you can continue working.

If your viewport configuration was set to three views, you can return to a single view on the View tab ➤ Model Viewports panel. Click the drop-down from the Viewport Configuration button and select Single. Whichever viewport is current when you select Single will be the only one visible after you complete the command.

Creating a Corridor Surface

Certification
Objective

A corridor provides the raw components for surface creation. Just as you would use points, breaklines, and boundaries to make a surface, a corridor surface uses corridor points as point data, feature lines and links as breaklines, and various commands for using corridor geometry as an outer boundary.

The Corridor Surface

Civil 3D does not automatically build a corridor surface when you build a corridor. From examining subassemblies, assemblies, and the corridors you built in the previous exercises, you have probably noticed that there are many "layers" of points, links, and feature lines. Some represent the top of the finished ground of your road design, some represent subsurface gravel or concrete thicknesses, and some represent subgrade, among other possibilities. You can choose to build a surface from any one of these layers or from all of them. Figure 9.42 shows an example of a TIN surface built from the links that are coded Top, which would represent final finished ground.

FIGURE 9.42
A surface built
from Top code
links

When you create a surface from a corridor, the surface is dependent on the Corridor object. This means that if you change something about your corridor and then rebuild the corridor, the surface will also update.

A corridor surface shows up as a surface under the Surfaces branch in Prospector with a slightly modified icon that denotes it is related to the corridor.

After you create the initial corridor surface, you can create a static export of the surface by changing to the Home tab ➤ Create Ground Data panel and choosing Surfaces ➤ Create Surface From Corridor. The Create Corridor Surfaces dialog will appear. If you have created multiple surfaces inside multiple corridors, all of the surfaces will be listed. Fill the check box next to each surface to be exported and then click OK. A detached surface will not react to corridor changes and can be used to archive a version of your surface. To remind you that this surface is not related to a corridor, the icon in the Surfaces branch in Prospector will not show the corridor icon.

Corridor Surface Creation Fundamentals

You create corridor surfaces on the Surfaces tab in the Corridor Properties palette using the following three steps (which are examined in detail later):

1. Click the Create A Corridor Surface button to add a surface item.

2. Choose the data type, either links or feature lines.

3. Choose the data to add and click the Add Surface Item button.

You can choose to create your corridor surface on the basis of links, feature lines, or a combination of both.

CREATING A SURFACE FROM LINK DATA

Most of the time, you will build your corridor surface from links. As discussed earlier, each link in a subassembly is coded with a name such as Top, Pave, Datum, and so on. Choosing to build a surface from Top links will create a surface that triangulates between the points at the link vertices that represent the final finished grade.

The most commonly built link-based surfaces are Top for contours and Datum for earthworks; however, you can build a surface from any link code in your corridor. Figure 9.43 shows a schematic of how links are used to form the most common surfaces—in this case a top surface, as shown in the top image of Figure 9.43, and a datum surface, as shown in the bottom image of Figure 9.43.

FIGURE 9.43
Schematic of Top links connecting to form a surface (top) and schematic of Datum links connecting to form a surface (bottom)

OVERHANG CORRECTION FOR CONFUSED DATUM SURFACES

A common situation with assemblies is a material that juts out past another material, such as curb sub-base. Triangulated surfaces cannot contain caves or perfectly vertical faces because both of those scenarios result in two elevation points for a given (x,y) coordinate pair, so Civil 3D needs to go around the material in a logical manner. What the software sees as logical and what you actually want from the surface may not always be the same thing, as shown next.

If you have a datum surface doing an unexpected zigzag, change the Overhang Correction setting to Bottom Links. There is also an option to set Overhang Correction to Top Links. This Overhang Correction setting is in the Corridor Properties dialog on the Surfaces tab. After your corridor rebuilds, the result will resemble the bottom image of Figure 9.43. You can set a different overhang correction for each surface listed on the Corridor Properties Surfaces tab.

When building a surface from links, you have the option of checking a box in the Add As Breakline column. Checking this box will add the actual link lines themselves as additional breaklines to the surface. In most cases, especially in intersection design, checking this box forces better triangulation.

CREATING A SURFACE FROM FEATURE LINES

There might be cases where you would like to build a simple surface from your corridor—for example, by using just the crown and edge-of-travel way. If you build a surface from feature lines only or a combination of links and feature lines, you have more control over what Civil 3D uses as breaklines for the surface.

If you added all the topmost corridor feature lines to your surface item and built a surface, you would get a result that's similar to the result you would get if you had added the Top link codes.

CREATING A SURFACE FROM BOTH LINK DATA AND FEATURE LINES

A link-based surface can be improved by the addition of feature lines. A link-based surface does not automatically include the corridor feature lines but instead uses the link vertex points to create triangulation. Therefore, the addition of feature lines ensures that triangulation occurs where desired along ridges and valleys. This is especially important for intersection design, curves, and other corridor surfaces where triangulation around tight corners is critical. Figure 9.44 shows the Surfaces tab of the Corridor Properties dialog where a Top link surface will be improved by the addition of Back_Curb, ETW, and Top_Curb feature lines.

If you are having trouble with triangulation or contours not behaving as expected, experiment with adding a few feature lines to your corridor surface definition.

FIGURE 9.44
The Surfaces tab indicates that the surface will be built from Top links as well as from several feature lines.

CREATING A CORRIDOR SURFACE FOR EACH LINK

To the right of the Create Corridor Surface button is the Create A Corridor Surface For Each Link button. Clicking this button populates the Surface List area with a multitude of corridor surfaces; as the button name would suggest, you will now have a corridor surface for each of the link codes.

This may not be desirable for many people because you rarely need a surface for every link, but once they are created, you can always remove the unwanted corridor surfaces using the Delete Surface Item button.

USING THE CORRIDOR SURFACE NAME TEMPLATE

The third button at the upper left of the Surfaces tab of the Corridor Properties dialog is the Surface Name Template button. When you click this button, the Name Template dialog shown in Figure 9.45 appears.

FIGURE 9.45
The Name Template dialog for corridor surfaces

Here you can set the formatting for the corridor name as well as the number style, starting number, and increment value. The Property fields are Corridor Name and Next Corridor Surface Counter. Based on the name shown in Figure 9.45, the next surface created for the corridor named North River Crossing will be named North River Crossing Surface – (1). The Number style can be set to 1, 2, 3 … or 01, 02, 03 … or a multitude of other styles based on the number of leading zeros.

COMPLETING OTHER SURFACE TASKS

You can do several other tasks on the Surfaces tab. For each corridor surface, you can set a surface style, revise the default name assigned by the Name Template, and provide a description for your corridor surface. Alternatively, you can do all those things once the corridor surface appears under the Surface branch in Prospector.

Adding a Surface Boundary

Surface boundaries are critical to any surface but especially so for corridor surfaces. Tools that automatically and interactively add surface boundaries, using the corridor intelligence, are available. Figure 9.46 shows a corridor surface before and after the addition of a boundary. Notice how the extraneous contours have been eliminated along the line of intersection between the existing ground and the proposed ground (the daylight line), thereby creating a much more accurate surface.

FIGURE 9.46
A corridor surface before the addition of a boundary (top) and after the addition of a boundary (bottom)

You can create corridor surface boundaries using the Boundaries tab of the Corridor Properties dialog. Each corridor surface will be listed. To add the boundary, right-click the corridor surface and select the desired boundary type.

BOUNDARY TYPES

There are several tools to assist you in corridor surface boundary creation. They can be automatic, semiautomatic, or manual in nature, depending on the complexity of the corridor.

You access these options on the Boundaries tab of the Corridor Properties dialog by right-clicking the name of your surface item, as shown in Figure 9.47.

FIGURE 9.47
Corridor surface boundary options for a corridor containing a single baseline

The following corridor boundary methods are listed in order of desirability. Corridor Extents As Outer Boundary is the most user-friendly, whereas Add From Polygon is fast but needs constant updating because it is not dynamically linked to the corridor.

Corridor Extents As Outer Boundary   With this selection, Civil 3D will shrink-wrap the corridor, taking into account intersections and various daylight options on different alignments. Corridor Extents As Outer Boundary will probably be your most-used boundary option unless you are modeling other parts of your roadway network in separate corridors. This topic will be covered in more detail in Chapter 10.

Add Automatically   The Add Automatically boundary tool allows you to pick a point code and use the associated feature lines as your corridor boundary. This tool is available only for single-baseline corridors. This tool is automatic, is easy to apply, and will remain dynamically linked to the corridor.

Add Interactively   The Add Interactively boundary tool allows you to work your way around a corridor and choose which corridor feature lines you would like to use as part of the boundary definition.

Choosing this option is better than using Add From Polygon if Add Automatically and Corridor Extents are not available. This method is also good for defining hide boundaries in your corridor surface (hide boundaries were discussed in Chapter 4, "Surfaces"). It takes a bit of patience to trace the corridor, but the result is a dynamically linked boundary that changes when the corridor changes. Using this method, once you select a feature line, a thick line will trace around the corridor following your mouse; to switch to a different feature line, simply click the new feature line at the transition location. When it's complete, you can close the boundary just as you would a polyline.

Add From Polygon   The Add From Polygon tool allows you to choose a closed 2D or 3D polyline or polygon in your drawing that you would like to add as a boundary for your corridor surface. This method is quick, but unlike the other methods, the resulting boundary is not dynamic to your design.

The next exercise leads you through creating a corridor surface with a shrink-wrap and an interactive boundary:

1. Open the 0905_CorridorBoundary.dwg or 0905_CorridorBoundary_METRIC.dwg file.

2. Select the corridor to activate the Corridor contextual tab.

3. From the Corridor contextual tab ➤ Modify Corridor panel, choose the Corridor Properties icon.

4. On the Surfaces tab of the Corridor Properties dialog, click the Create A Corridor Surface button in the upper-left corner of the dialog.

   You should now have a surface item in the bottom half of the dialog.

5. Click the surface item under the Name column and change the default name of your surface to **North River Crossing - Top**.

6. Verify that Links has been selected from the drop-down list in the Data Type selection box.

7. Verify that Top has been selected from the drop-down list in the Specify Code selection box.

8. Click the Add Surface Item button to add Top Links to the Surface Definition, set the Overhang Correction to Top Links, and fill in the Add As Breakline check box.

9. Click OK to accept the settings in this dialog. Choose Rebuild The Corridor when prompted and examine your surface.

   The road surface should look fine; however, because you have not yet added a boundary to this surface, undesirable triangulation is occurring outside your corridor area and the area bounded by ROAD A, B, C, and D.

10. Expand the Surfaces branch in Prospector.

    Note that you now have a corridor surface listed in addition to the existing surface that was already in the drawing.

11. Select the corridor again to activate the Corridor contextual tab if not already selected.

12. From the Corridor contextual tab ➤ Modify Corridor panel, choose Corridor Properties icon.

    If you do not see the Corridor Properties button on the Modify Corridor panel, you may have inadvertently chosen the corridor surface and may be viewing the Surface contextual ribbon.

13. On the Boundaries tab of the Corridor Properties dialog, right-click North River Crossing – Top in the listing.

14. Select Corridor Extents As Outer Boundary, which will define the outer boundary of the surface.

15. Click OK to accept the settings in the Corridor Properties dialog, and choose Rebuild The Corridor when prompted.

16. Examine your surface, and note that the triangulation terminates at the outer limits of the corridor.

17. Select the corridor again to activate the Corridor contextual tab if not still selected.

18. From the Corridor contextual tab ➤ Modify Corridor panel, choose the Corridor Properties icon.

19. On the Boundaries tab of the Corridor Properties dialog, right-click North River Crossing – Top in the listing.

20. Select Add Interactively.

    The Corridor Properties dialog will temporarily disappear while you define this boundary. You will now digitize around the area enclosed by ROAD A, B, C, and D, tracing over the edge of the corridor defining the enclosed area. You may find it helpful to turn on your endpoint Osnap setting, but it isn't necessary.

21. Using your scroll button, zoom into the northwest corner of the intersection of ROAD A and ROAD B.

    Be careful to avoid exiting the command while doing so.

22. Pick the edge of the corridor. If you see the Select A Feature Line dialog open, select Edge and click OK.

23. Drag the cursor to the left along the edge of the corridor until you see a red, dashed line representing your interactive boundary beginning to trace over the Edge feature line, as shown in Figure 9.48.

24. Pan to the left along the edge of the corridor until the red, dashed line makes a stop.

    It will make a stop when it reaches another baseline.

25. Click the stopping point and then click the link ahead of the stopping point to continue the generation of the interactive boundary.

26. Repeat step 25 whenever the interactive boundary makes a stop until you reach the point of closing your boundary.

FIGURE 9.48
Defining an
interactive
boundary

If you accidentally click the wrong location, just type **U** for undo to redefine the last segment. If the interactive boundary doesn't want to follow the edge of your corridor in certain areas, click the link the edge at the location just before the bad behavior begins. If the Select A Feature Line dialog opens displaying two Edge feature lines, just pick the top one and click OK.

27. To close your boundary, click the link just before the start point and type **C** for close.

The Corridor Properties dialog will reappear.

28. On the Boundary tab of the Corridor Properties dialog, there are two boundaries listed.

29. Select Corridor Boundary(2) and click in the Use Type column to change the setting to Hide Boundary, as shown in Figure 9.49.

FIGURE 9.49
Configuring
the interac-
tive bound-
ary as a Hide
boundary

30. Click OK to dismiss the Corridor Properties dialog. Rebuild the corridor if prompted.

31. (Optional) Experiment with making changes to your finished grade profile, assembly, or alignment geometry and rebuilding both your corridor and finished ground surface to see the boundary in action.

When this exercise is complete, you can close the drawing. A finished copy of this drawing is available from the book's web page with the filename 0905_CorridorBoundary_FINISHED.dwg or 0905_CorridorBoundary_METRIC_FINISHED.dwg.

REBUILD: LEAVE IT ON OR OFF?

Once you rebuild your corridor, your corridor surface will need to be updated. Typically, the best practice is to leave Rebuild – Automatic off for corridors and keep it on for corridor surfaces. The corridor surface will want to rebuild only when the corridor is rebuilt. For large corridors, this may cause a bit of a memory lag, so try it both ways to see what you like best.

COMMON SURFACE-CREATION PROBLEMS

Here are some common problems you may encounter when creating surfaces:

Problem Your corridor surface does not appear or seems to be empty.

Typical Cause You might have created the surface item but not added any data. Another cause could be the surface style is set to No Display or to display contours at a wide interval, or the surface was created on a frozen layer.

Fix Open the Corridor Properties dialog and switch to the Surfaces tab. Select a data type from the drop-down menus in the Data Type and Specify Code selection boxes, and click the Add Surface Item button. Make sure your dialog shows both a surface item and a data type, as shown in Figure 9.50.

FIGURE 9.50
A surface cannot be created without both a surface item and a data type.

Problem Your corridor surface does not seem to respect its boundary after a change to the assembly or surface-building data type (in other words, you switched from link data to feature lines).

Typical Cause Automatic and interactive boundary definitions are dependent on the codes used in your corridor. If you remove or change the codes used in your corridor, the boundary needs to be redefined.

Fix Open the Corridor Properties dialog and switch to the Boundaries tab. Remove any boundary definitions that are no longer valid (if any) by right-clicking the boundary and selecting Remove Boundary. Once the outdated boundary has been removed, you can redefine the corridor surface boundaries using any of the applicable boundary types.

Problem Your corridor surface seems to have gaps at points of curvature (PCs) and points of tangency (PTs) near curb returns.

Typical Cause You may have encountered an error in rounding station values at these locations and as a result created gaps in your corridor. This is commonly caused by osnapping to start and end region stations using two-dimensional linework as a guide when some segments of that linework do not touch.

Fix Be sure your corridor region definitions produce no gaps. You might consider using the PEDIT command to join lines and curves representing corridor elements that will need to be modeled later. You might also consider setting a COGO point at these locations (PCs, PTs, and so on) and using the Node object snap instead of the Endpoint object snap to select the same location each time you are required to do so.

Performing a Volume Calculation

One of the most powerful aspects of Civil 3D is having instant feedback on your design iterations. Once you create a preliminary road corridor, you can immediately compare a corridor surface to existing ground and get a good understanding of the earthwork magnitude. When you make an adjustment to the finished grade profile and then rebuild your corridor, you can see the effect that this change has on your earthwork within minutes, if not sooner.

Even though volumes were covered in detail in Chapter 4, it is worth revisiting the subject here in the context of corridors.

This exercise uses a TIN-to-TIN composite volume calculation to compare the existing ground surface and the datum corridor surface; average end area and other section-based volume calculations are covered in Chapter 12.

1. Open the 0906_CorridorVolume.dwg or 0906_CorridorVolume_METRIC.dwg file.

    Note that this drawing has a completed North River Crossing corridor, as well as a top corridor surface and a datum corridor surface.

2. From the Analyze tab ➢ Volumes And Material panel, choose Volumes Dashboard to display the Volumes Dashboard tab in the Panorama.

3. Click the Create New Volume Surface button to display the Create Surface dialog.

4. Change the name to **Vol - Road Datum** and set Style to Elevation Banding (2D).

5. Click the <Base Surface> field to display the ellipsis button; once it's visible, click the ellipsis button to select Existing Surface. Then click OK.

6. Click the <Comparison Surface> field to display the ellipsis button.

7. Once it's visible, click the ellipsis button to select North River Crossing – Datum and then click OK.

8. Click OK to accept the settings in the Create Surface dialog.

A Cut/Fill breakdown should appear in the Volumes Dashboard tab of Panorama, as shown in Figure 9.51. Your numbers may vary.

FIGURE 9.51
Panorama showing an example of a volume surface and the cut/fill results

9. Make a note of these numbers.

10. Leave Panorama open on your screen (make it smaller, if desired), and pan over to the proposed profile for Road D.

11. Select the Finished Ground profile and move the vertical triangular grip on the second PVI to the center of the circle shown in the profile view.

Notice that the volume calculations have changed to Out Of Date because the corridor isn't set to rebuild automatically.

12. In Prospector, expand Corridors, select the North River Crossing corridor, right-click, and choose Rebuild.

Notice that the corridor changes, and therefore the corridor surfaces (which are both set to Rebuild Automatic) change as well. However, the volume surface did not automatically rebuild.

13. On the Volumes Dashboard tab of Panorama, right-click the volume surface and select Rebuild.

Notice the new values for cut and fill.

14. Close Panorama using the X in the upper corner.

When this exercise is complete, you can close the drawing. A finished copy of this drawing is available from the book's web page with the filename 0906_CorridorVolume_FINISHED.dwg or 0906_CorridorVolume_METRIC_FINISHED.dwg.

Building Nonroad Corridors

As discussed in the beginning of this chapter, corridors are not just for roads. Once you have the basics about corridors down, your ingenuity can take hold.

Corridors can be used for far more than just road designs. You will explore some more advanced corridor models in Chapter 10, but there are plenty of simple, single-baseline applications for alternative corridors such as channels, berms, retaining walls, duct banks and more.

You can take advantage of several specialized subassemblies or build your own custom assembly using the Subassembly Composer. Figure 9.52 shows an example of a channel corridor.

FIGURE 9.52
A simple channel corridor, viewed in 3D, built from the channel subassembly and a generic link subassembly

One of the subassemblies discussed in Chapter 8 is the channel subassembly. The following exercise shows you how to apply this subassembly to design a simple drainage channel:

1. Open the `0907_CorridorChannel.dwg` or `0907_CorridorChannel_METRIC.dwg` file.

   Note that there is an alignment that represents a drainage channel centerline, a profile that represents the drainage channel normal water line, and an assembly created using the Channel and LinkSlopetoSurface subassemblies.

2. From the Home tab ➤ Create Design panel, choose Corridor to display the Create Corridor dialog.

3. In the Name text box, name your corridor **Drainage Channel**.

   Keep the default values for Corridor Style and Corridor Layer.

4. Verify that Alignment is set to Channel CL and Profile is set to Channel NWL.

   NWL stands for *normal water level*.

5. Verify that Assembly is set to Project Channel.

6. Verify that Target Surface is set to Existing Ground.

7. Verify that the Set Baseline And Region Parameters check box is checked.

8. Click OK to accept the settings in the Create Corridor dialog and to display the Baseline And Region Parameters dialog.

9. Click the Set All Frequencies button.

10. Change the values for Along Tangents and Curve Increment to **10'** (3 m for metric users).

11. Click OK to accept the settings in the Frequency To Apply Assemblies dialog.

12. Click OK to accept the settings in the Baseline And Region Parameters dialog.

13. You may receive a dialog warning that the corridor definition has been modified. If you do, select the Rebuild The Corridor option.

14. Select the corridor to activate the contextual tab.

15. From the Corridor contextual tab ➢ Modify Corridor Sections panel, choose Section Editor.

16. From the Section Editor contextual tab ➢ Station Selection panel, you can navigate through the drainage channel cross sections by clicking the forward and backward arrows.

The cross section should look similar to Figure 9.53.

FIGURE 9.53
The completed Drainage Channel corridor viewed in the Section Editor

This corridor can be used to build a surface for a TIN-to-TIN volume calculation or to create sections and generate material quantities, cross-sectional views, and anything else that can be done with a more traditional road corridor.

When you are finished viewing the sections, dismiss the dialog by clicking the X on the Section Editor contextual tab ➢ Close panel. When this exercise is complete, you can close the drawing. A finished copy of this drawing is available from the book's web page with the filename 0907_CorridorChannel_FINISHED.dwg or 0907_CorridorChannel_METRIC_FINISHED.dwg.

 Real World Scenario

CREATING A PIPE TRENCH CORRIDOR

Another use for a corridor is a pipe trench. A pipe trench corridor is useful for determining quantities of excavated material, limits of disturbance, trench-safety specifications, and more. This graphic shows a completed pipe trench corridor.

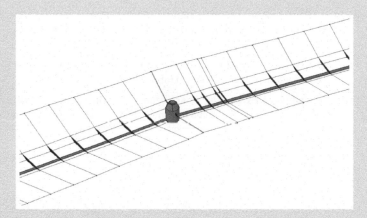

One of the subassemblies discussed in Chapter 8 is the TrenchPipe1 subassembly. The following exercise leads you through applying this subassembly to a pipe trench corridor:

1. Open the `0908_CorridorPipeTrench.dwg` or `0908_CorridorPipeTrench_METRIC.dwg` file.

   Note that there is a pipe network with a corresponding alignment, profile view, and pipe trench assembly. Also note that there is a profile drawn that corresponds with the inverts of the pipe network.

2. From the Home tab ➤ Create Design panel, choose Corridor.

3. In the Name text box, name the corridor **Pipe Trench**.

   Keep the default values for Corridor Style and Corridor Layer.

4. Verify that Alignment is set to Pipe Centerline and Profile is set to Bottom Of Pipe Profile.

5. Verify that Assembly is set to Pipe Trench.

6. Verify that Target Surface is set to Existing Ground.

7. Verify that the Set Baseline And Region Parameters check box is selected.

8. Click OK to accept the settings in the Create Corridor dialog and display the Baseline And Region Parameters dialog.

9. Click the Set All Frequencies button.

10. Change the values for Along Tangents and Curve Increment to **10'** (**3** m for metric users).

11. Click OK to accept the settings in the Frequency To Apply Assemblies dialog and click OK again to accept the settings in the Baseline And Region Parameters dialog.

12. You may receive a dialog warning that the corridor definition has been modified. If you do, select the Rebuild The Corridor option.

    The corridor will build.

13. Select the corridor to activate the Corridor contextual tab.

Continues

Continued

14. From the Corridor contextual tab ➤ Modify Corridor Sections panel, choose Section Editor. Browse the cross sections through the trench.

15. When you are finished viewing the sections, dismiss the Section Editor by clicking the X on the Section Editor contextual tab ➤ Close panel.

You may notice that at the sharp bends in the pipe alignment the corridor frequency lines cross one another. This is called a *bow-tie* and will be discussed further in the next chapter.

When this exercise is complete, you can close the drawing. A finished copy of this drawing is available from the book's web page with the filename 0908_CorridorPipeTrench_FINISHED.dwg or 0908_CorridorPipeTrench_METRIC_FINISHED.dwg.

The Bottom Line

Build a single baseline corridor from an alignment, profile, and assembly. Corridors are created from the combination of alignments, profiles, and assemblies. Although corridors can be used to model many things, most corridors are used for road design.

Master It Open the MasterIt_0909.dwg or MasteringIt_0909_METRIC.dwg file. Build a corridor named Corridor A on the basis of the Alignment A alignment, the FG profile, and the Basic Assembly. Set EG as the target surface. Set all frequencies to **10′** (or **3** m for metric users).

Use targets to add lane widening. Targets are an essential design tool used to manipulate the geometry of the road.

Master It Open the MasterIt_0910.dwg or MasterIt_0910_METRIC.dwg file. Set Right Lane to target Alignment A-Right.

Create a corridor surface.   The corridor model can be used to build a surface. This corridor surface can then be analyzed and annotated to produce finished road plans.

> **Master It**   Open the `MasterIt_0911.dwg` or `MasterIt_0911_METRIC.dwg` file. Create a corridor surface for the Alignment A corridor from Top links. Name the surface Corridor A-Top.

Add an automatic boundary to a corridor surface.   A surface can be improved with the addition of a boundary. Single-baseline corridors can take advantage of automatic boundary creation.

> **Master It**   Open the `MasterIt_0912.dwg` or `MasterIt_0912_METRIC.dwg` file. Use the Automatic Boundary Creation tool to add a boundary using the Daylight code.

Chapter 10

Advanced Corridors, Intersections, and Roundabouts

This chapter focuses on taking your corridor-modeling skills to a new level by introducing more tools to your corridor-building toolbox, such as intersecting roads, cul-de-sacs, advanced techniques, and troubleshooting. You will use advanced corridor targets and work with conditional subassemblies.

This chapter assumes that you've worked through the examples in the chapters on alignments, profiles, profile views, assemblies, and basic corridors. Without a strong knowledge of the foundational skills, many of the tasks in this chapter will be difficult.

In this chapter, you will learn to:

◆ Create corridors with multiregion baselines.

◆ Add alignment and profile targets to a region for a cul-de-sac.

◆ Create a surface from a corridor and add a boundary.

Using Multiregion Baselines

In the previous chapter, you modeled corridors with one baseline and one region. A question many people ask when working with corridors is, "At what point do I need another region?" The answer is simple: If you need a different assembly, you need a different region.

In the following example, you will step through adding an additional region to an existing baseline:

1. Open the drawing 1001_MultiRegionCorr.dwg (1001_MultiRegionCorr_METRIC .dwg), which you can download from this book's web page, www.sybex.com/go/ masteringcivil3d2016.

    This drawing has been split into two modelspace viewports so that you can observe the results of your efforts in 3D.

2. Select the corridor and, from the Corridor contextual tab ➢ Modify Corridor panel, select Corridor Properties.

    On the Parameters tab of the Corridor Properties dialog, notice that there is a baseline containing a single region.

3. Click the icon in the End Station column for the region to pick a new end station in the drawing, as shown in Figure 10.1.

FIGURE 10.1
Changing the
region end station

The Corridor Properties dialog temporarily disappears. The drawing contains linework representing the edge of pavement for this network of roadways in this subdivision. You will be using your Endpoint Osnap along with this linework to define multiple regions in this corridor.

4. In the drawing, with your cursor anchored to ROAD C, stretch the station picker south and Osnap to the end point of the left arc where it intersects ROAD C's edge of pavement, as shown in Figure 10.2.

FIGURE 10.2
Using Osnaps to
help define regions

The Corridor Properties dialog reappears. Notice the new End Station value.

5. Click Apply, and rebuild the corridor if prompted.

6. Move the Corridor Properties dialog aside to review the corridor in the drawing area.

Notice that the corridor region now stops exactly at the beginning of the curb return leading into ROAD B; you would not want the curb and gutter, sidewalk, and daylighting to shoot through the intersection on the right side of the road. In this situation, you need another assembly, one without curb and gutter on the right. Since it is needed only in the intersection area, you'll add a region that picks up where the first region left off and ends at the end point of the opposite curb return.

7. Back in the Corridor Properties dialog, Parameters tab, right-click the region and select Insert Region – After.

8. In the Create Corridor Region dialog, using the drop-down menu under Assembly, select Left Daylight-Right Pavement, as shown in Figure 10.3.

FIGURE 10.3
Assigning an assembly after inserting a new region

9. Click OK to close the Create Corridor Region dialog.

10. Click the ellipsis button in the Target column of the new region to open the Target Mapping dialog.

    This assembly contains a daylighting subassembly, so you'll need to set the surface target.

11. In the Object Name column next to Target Surface, click <None> to open the Pick A Surface dialog.

12. Select Existing Surface and click OK to close.

13. Click OK to close the Target Mapping dialog.

14. Click OK to close Corridor Properties and rebuild the corridor if prompted. Also, close the Event Viewer if open.

    The new region was added, but it is extending to the end of ROAD C, which wasn't the intent. Next, you will split that region in two and assign another assembly to finish this part of the corridor.

15. Select the corridor and open Corridor Properties using the contextual ribbon.

16. On the Parameters tab, right-click the second region and select Split Region.

17. Use your Endpoint Osnap to select the point where the curb return on the opposite side of ROAD B meets the edge of pavement of ROAD C. Press ↵.

    If you see a warning dialog referring to 0+00 being outside of the station limits, click OK and continue.

    Back on the Parameters tab, you now have three regions listed under your baseline. The last region requires an assembly change since this is the section on the corridor that requires curb and gutter, sidewalk, and daylighting on both sides.

18. On the third region in the Assembly column, click to open the Edit Corridor Region dialog. Using the drop-down menu under Assembly, select Full Section and then click OK to close.

19. Set the surface targets for both sides of the road as described in steps 10–13.

20. Change the end station for the third region to **1995** (**608** for metric).

21. Click OK to close Corridor Properties and rebuild the corridor if prompted.

The corridor along ROAD C is nearly complete with the exception of the curb returns, as shown in Figure 10.4.

FIGURE 10.4
Corridor with
multiple-baselines

The files 1001_MultiRegionCorr_FINISHED.dwg and 1001_MultiRegionCorr_METRIC_FINISHED.dwg are available on this book's web page for you to check your work.

Instead of moving into building out the regions required for the curb returns, you're going to switch gears for a bit and look at building a cul-de-sac region. Then after you build the cul-de-sac, you'll learn how to use the intersection tool, which automates the process of creating regions, assigning assemblies, and designating targets.

Modeling a Cul-de-Sac

Even if you never plan to design one in real life, understanding what is going on in a cul-de-sac corridor model will set you on the right path for building more complex models. If you truly understand the principles explained in the section that follows, then expanding your repertoire to include intersections and roundabouts will become much easier.

Using Multiple Baselines

Up to this point, every corridor you've built has had a single baseline. When you worked with corridor surfaces, you were working with a complex corridor with multiple baselines. A cul-de-sac by itself can be modeled in two baselines, as shown in Figure 10.5. The procedures that follow will work for most cul-de-sacs, including symmetrical, asymmetrical, and hammerhead styles. You will need a centerline alignment and design profile for the road leading into the cul-de-sac as well as an edge of pavement (EOP) alignment and design profile defining the cul-de-sac bulb.

FIGURE 10.5
Example cul-de-sac
alignment setup

In the example shown in Figure 10.5, the centerline of the road, Baseline 1, will require a typical crowned assembly, which will terminate when it reaches the point in the cul-de-sac geometry where the bulb defining curvature begins. From that point, the baseline is swapped out for an alignment and profile that define the edge of the cul-de-sac.

As you've seen, when assemblies are applied to a baseline, the geometry of the subassemblies project perpendicularly from the baseline. In the example of Figure 10.5, the curb and gutter subassembly as well as the rest of the subassemblies it carries (sidewalk, daylighting) need to be projected from the edge of the cul-de-sac bulb because that's the way their real-life counterparts are built. The assembly used on this baseline will have the curb and gutter subassembly on one side and the lane subassembly on the opposite side (Figure 10.6). The lane subassembly will stretch to meet the centerline alignment and profile as its targets.

FIGURE 10.6
Assembly used for
designing off the
edge of pavement

It helps to think of the assembly as radiating away from the baseline, from the assembly base outward, toward a target (Figure 10.7). Because the assemblies are applied to the baseline in a perpendicular manner, using the edge of pavement for a baseline in curved areas (such as cul-de-sac bulbs or curb returns) will result in a smooth, properly graded pavement surface.

FIGURE 10.7
It helps to think of the assemblies radiating away from the base-line toward the targets.

Establishing EOP Design Profiles

One of the most challenging parts of complex corridor (in other words, cul-de-sac, intersection, or roundabout) is establishing design profiles for non-centerline alignments. You must have design profiles for both the centerline and edge of pavement alignments, but it does not have to be a painful process to obtain them.

Using a simple, preliminary corridor and the profile-creation tools you learned about in Chapter 7, "Profiles and Profile Views," you'll find that establishing an edge of pavement profile can go quickly.

In the exercise that follows, you will work through the steps of creating an EOP profile:

1. Open the `1002_EOPProfile.dwg` (`1002_EOPProfile_METRIC.dwg`) file, which you can download from this book's web page, www.sybex.com/go/masteringcivil3d2016.

   This drawing contains the corridor you worked on in the previous exercise, plus an additional baseline and region built for ROAD E. You may also notice that there is an alignment tracing around what would be the edge of pavement in the cul-de-sac for ROAD E.

2. Click the corridor, and open Corridor Properties from the contextual ribbon.

3. On the Surfaces tab of Corridor Properties, do the following:

   a. Click the Create A Corridor Surface button.

    b. Rename the surface to **North River Crossing – Top**.

    c. Change the surface style to Border Only.

    d. Under Add Data, verify that the Data Type setting is set to Links and the Specify Code setting is set to Top.

    e. Click the Add Surface Item button. Set Overhang Correction to Top Links.

You will not be adding a boundary at this time.

4. Click OK to close the Corridor Properties dialog and rebuild the corridor when prompted.

You should now see a green surface boundary in your drawing.

5. Press Esc to clear the selection. Select the red edge of pavement alignment for the cul-de-sac, and in the Alignment contextual tab ➢ Launch Pad panel, click Surface Profile.

6. In the Create Profile From Surface dialog, highlight North River Crossing – Top and click Add.

7. Click the Draw In Profile View button.

8. Leave all the defaults in the Create Profile View dialog and click Create Profile View.

9. Click in the graphic to the right of the surface to place the profile view.

The profile you are seeing has a large gap in the middle. The two short segments at the beginning and end of this profile show what the proposed grade would be according to the corridor surface, which terminates at the PC and PT of the cul-de-sac bulb. The cul-de-sac alignment actually overlaps the corridor surface so you were able to show the proposed grades in profile view leading into and exiting the cul-de-sac.

Next, you will fill in the large gap with your own profile by snapping to the red profile segments to ensure that you are matching grade at the edge of pavement of your cul-de-sac.

10. Select the profile view. (Hint: Click a grid line rather than the profile itself.) From the Profile View contextual tab ➢ Launch Pad panel, click Profile Creation Tools.

    a. For Name, prefix the alignment name with **FG** instead of EG.

    b. For Profile Style, select Design Profile.

11. Click OK to accept the defaults in the Create Profile dialog.

12. Click Draw Tangents Without Curves from the left end of the Profile Layout Tools toolbar and Osnap to the end of the first red segment where the preliminary surface ends (station 0+00, elevation 9.149 or 0+000, elevation 2.784 for metric).

13. Next, snap to the beginning of the last red segment where the preliminary surface begins (station 3+69.17, elevation 9.149 or 0+113.26, elevation 2.784 for metric). Press Enter to end the command.

You'll now add a high point along the corridor edge of pavement.

14. Click the Insert PVIs – Tabular button on the Profile Layout Tools toolbar.

15. Enter station **1+62.04** and elevation **11.58** (or station **0+049.54**, elevation **3.528** for metric) and click OK.

16. Close the Profile Layout Tools toolbar.

Your profile should look like Figure 10.8.

FIGURE 10.8
A completed cul-de-sac profile

You now have a proposed profile that is acceptable to use in the cul-de-sac baseline. Check your work against 1002_EOPProfile_FINISHED.dwg or 1002_EOPProfile_METRIC_FINISHED .dwg to see how your stations and elevations compare. You do not need to save the drawing file and may close it.

Putting the Pieces Together

You have all the pieces in place to perform the first iterations of this cul-de-sac design.

The following exercise will walk you through the steps to put the cul-de-sac together. You will complete several steps and let the corridor build to observe what is happening at each stage. This exercise will also encourage you to get comfortable using the Corridor Properties dialog to make design modifications.

1. Open the 1003_Cul-de-SacDesign.dwg (1003_Cul-de-SacDesign_METRIC.dwg) file, which you can download from this book's web page.

This drawing contains the cul-de-sac centerline alignment and profile, the EOP alignment and profile, and the assemblies needed to complete the process.

2. Click the corridor.

3. From the contextual tab ➤ Modify Corridor panel, click Add Baseline.

4. In the Create Corridor Baseline dialog, select ROAD E CUL-DE-SAC from the drop-down list. Click OK to continue.

5. In the Select a Profile dialog, select FG-ROAD E CUL-DE-SAC from the drop-down list. Click OK to continue.

6. From the contextual tab ➤ Modify Region panel, select Add Regions.

7. At the Select a baseline: prompt, click over the cul-de-sac alignment in the drawing.

8. At the Specify the region start station: prompt, type **0** ↵.

9. At the Specify the region end station: prompt, type **369.17** (**113.26** for metric) ↵.

10. In the Create Corridor Region dialog, under Assembly, select Curb Returns from the drop-down list. Click OK to continue.

11. In the Target Mapping dialog, in the Object Name column, click <None> next to Target Surface and select Existing Surface from the Pick A Surface dialog.

12. Click OK to dismiss the Pick A Surface dialog, and click OK again to dismiss the Target Mapping dialog.

13. Press the Esc button on your keyboard to end the command.

The curb return assembly has been wrapped around the cul-de-sac, as shown in Figure 10.9. However, the curve frequency needs to be increased to mimic the curvature of the cul-de-sac bulb. Also, an offset and elevation target will have to be set so that the pavement of the assembly stretches to connect horizontally and vertically to the centerline design of ROAD E.

FIGURE 10.9
Cul-de-sac region before configuring frequency and targets

14. On the contextual tab ➢ Modify Region panel, select Edit Frequency.

15. At the Select a region to edit: prompt, click anywhere inside the cul-de-sac portion of the corridor. Be careful not to select inside the "donut hole" in the center of the cul-de-sac.

16. In the Frequency To Apply Assemblies dialog, change the Along Curves setting to By Curvature and the Mid-ordinate Distance To Define Curvature value to **0.1** (**0.03** for metric). Click OK to dismiss the dialog.

17. Press the Esc key to end the command.

18. To stretch the pavement to meet the horizontal and vertical centerline of ROAD E, on the contextual tab ➢ Modify Region panel, select Edit Targets.

19. At the `Select a region to edit:` prompt, click anywhere inside the cul-de-sac portion of the corridor. Be careful not to select inside the "donut hole" in the center of the cul-de-sac.

20. In the Target Mapping dialog in the Width or Offset Targets section, click <none> in the Object Name column next to Width Alignment. Note the name of the subassembly in the Subassembly column.

21. In the Set Width Or Offset Target dialog, set the Select Object Type To Target drop-down list to Alignments; then under Select Alignments, click ROAD E.

SELECT TARGET BYLAYER

A new feature in the Set Width Or Offset Target dialog box is the Select Bylayer button, which will present you with a list of layers containing alignments enabling you to select the alignment bylayer.

---

22. Click the Add button to place it on the list below.

23. Click OK to continue.

24. Back in the Target Mapping dialog in the Slope or Elevation Targets section, click <none> in the Object Name column next to Outside Elevation Profile.

Note the name of the subassembly in the Subassembly column.

25. In the Set Slope Or Elevation Target dialog, set the Select Object Type To Target drop-down list to Profiles then select ROAD E as the alignment.

26. Under Select Profiles, choose FG-ROAD E and click the Add button to place it on the list below.

You may need to change the width of the Name column to see the full profile name.

27. Click OK to dismiss the dialog.

28. Click OK again to close the Target Mapping dialog and press Esc to end the command.

The corridor is completely modeled (see Figure 10.10).

FIGURE 10.10
The completed
cul-de-sac corridor

29. With the corridor still selected, open Corridor Properties from the contextual tab.

30. On the Parameters tab, inspect the baselines and regions that are accumulating in your corridor, as shown in Figure 10.11.

31. When finished inspecting, you can close the Corridor Properties dialog.

FIGURE 10.11
Multiple base-
lines and regions
in Corridor
Properties

The files `1003_Cul-de-SacDesign_FINISHED.dwg` and `1003_Cul-de-SacDesign_METRIC_FINISHED.dwg` are available for you to check your work.

Troubleshooting Your Cul-de-Sac

People make several common mistakes when modeling their first few cul-de-sacs:

Your cul-de-sac appears with a large gap in the center. If your curb line seems to be modeling correctly but your lanes are leaving a large empty area in the middle (see Figure 10.12), chances are pretty good that you forgot to assign targets or perhaps assigned the incorrect targets.

FIGURE 10.12
A cul-de-sac without targets

You can fix this problem by opening the Target Mapping dialog for your region and checking to make sure you assigned the road centerline alignment and FG profile for your targets. Also, check to see whether you assigned these targets to the wrong subassembly.

To pinpoint the location of errors, use the Edit Targets tool from the Modify Region panel of the Corridor contextual ribbon. Edit targets one region at a time to avoid confusion.

Your cul-de-sac appears to be backward. Occasionally, you may find that your lanes wind up on the wrong side of the EOP alignment, as shown in Figure 10.13. The direction of your alignment will dictate whether the lane should be on the left or right side. In the example from the previous exercise, the alignment was running counterclockwise around the cul-de-sac bulb; therefore, the lane was on the left side of the assembly.

FIGURE 10.13
A cul-de-sac with
the lanes modeled
on the wrong side
without targets

You can fix this problem by changing the assembly applied to the region to one that was created for the correct side or by reversing the alignment.

Your cul-de-sac drops down to 0.   A common problem when you first begin modeling cul-de-sacs, intersections, and other corridor components is that one end of your baseline drops down to 0. You probably won't notice the problem in plan view, but once you build your surface or rotate your corridor in 3D (see Figure 10.14), you'll see it. This problem will always occur if your region station range extends beyond the proposed profile.

FIGURE 10.14
A corridor viewed
in 3D showing a
drop down to 0
(bottom)

To fix this problem, make sure your region station range corresponds with the design profile length. You may need to extend the design profile in some cases, but usually restricting the station range of the region will do the trick.

Your cul-de-sac seems flat.   When you're first learning the concept of targets, it's easy to mix up baseline alignments and target alignments. In the beginning, you may accidentally choose your EOP alignment as a target instead of the road centerline. If this happens, your cul-de-sac will look similar to Figure 10.15.

FIGURE 10.15
A flat cul-de-sac
with the wrong
lane target set

You can fix this problem by opening the Target Mapping dialog for this region and making sure the target alignment is set to the road centerline and the target profile is set to the road centerline FG profile.

Moving Up to Intersections

Now that you have a thorough understanding of cul-de-sacs, you're ready to take on intersections.

The steps that follow apply to all intersections, regardless of whether it is a T-shaped intersection, a four-way intersection, perfectly perpendicular, or skewed at an angle.

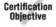
**Certification
Objective**
When you build your corridor model, chances are that it will not be graded perfectly, and you may need to tweak it to perfect it. This is why you build the model in the first place, so you

can easily see whether and where the model fails. Design flaws are difficult to catch right away when you're dealing with a two-dimensional model.

Plan what alignments, profiles, and assemblies you'll need to create the right combination of baselines, regions, and targets to model an intersection that will interact the way you want. It helps to create a simple sketch, as shown in Figure 10.16.

Figure 10.17 shows a sketch of required baselines. As you saw in the previous example, *baselines* are the horizontal and vertical foundations of a corridor. Each baseline consists of an alignment and its corresponding finished ground (FG) profile. You may never have thought of edge of pavement in terms of profiles, but after you build a few intersections, thinking that way will become second nature. The Intersection tool on the Create Design panel of the Home tab will create EOP baselines as curb return alignments for you, but it will rely on your input for curb return radii.

FIGURE 10.16
Plan your inter-
section model in
sketch form.

FIGURE 10.17
Required baselines
for modeling a typ-
ical intersection

Figure 10.18 breaks each baseline into regions where a different assembly or different target will be applied. Once the intersection has been created, target mapping as well as other particulars can be modified as needed. Note that the two regions that begin at the curving alignment of the intersection can be combined into one region with two targets by using the Target to Nearest Offset option in the Set Width Or Offset Target dialog.

FIGURE 10.18
Required regions for modeling an intersection created by the Intersection tool

Region with typical assembly

Region with intersection assembly targeting Second Road Centerline

Region with intersection assembly targeting Main Road Centerline

Region with typical assembly

Region with typical assembly that leaves off left lane and curb

Using the Intersection Wizard

Certification Objective

All the work of setting baselines, creating regions, setting targets, and applying the correct frequencies can be done manually for an intersection. However, Autodesk® AutoCAD® Civil 3D® software contains an automated Intersection tool that can handle many types of intersections.

On the basis of the schematic you drew of your intersection, your main road will need several assemblies to reflect the different road cross sections. Figure 10.19 shows the full range of potential assemblies you may need in an intersection and the design situations in which they may arise.

FIGURE 10.19
Various assembly
schematics and
applications

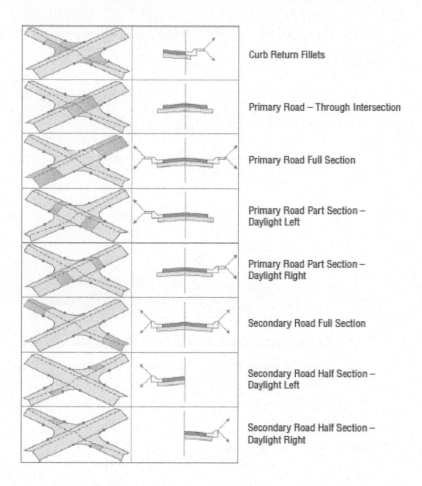

Curb Return Fillets

Primary Road – Through Intersection

Primary Road Full Section

Primary Road Part Section –
Daylight Left

Primary Road Part Section –
Daylight Right

Secondary Road Full Section

Secondary Road Half Section –
Daylight Left

Secondary Road Half Section –
Daylight Right

This exercise will take you through building a typical intersection with a couple of right-turn lanes using the Create Intersection Wizard:

1. Open the `1004_Intersection.dwg` (`1004_Intersection_METRIC.dwg`) file, which you can download from this book's web page.

   You'll start by building a four-way intersection for ROAD A and ROAD D.

2. From the Home tab ➤ Create Design panel, choose the Intersections ➤ Create Intersection tool.

3. At the `Select intersection point:` prompt, choose the intersection of the two existing alignments.

   Hint: The Intersection Osnap will automatically turn on and be active.

4. At the `Select main road alignment <or press enter key to select from list>:` prompt, click the ROAD A alignment that runs from west to east.

The Create Intersection – General dialog will appear (Figure 10.20).

FIGURE 10.20
The General page
of the Create
Intersection Wizard

5. Set Intersection Corridor Type to All Crowns Maintained and click Next.

6. In the Geometry Details page (Figure 10.21), verify that ROAD A is the primary road by looking at the Priority list.

   If ROAD A is not at the top of the list, use the arrow buttons on the right side to reorder the roads.

FIGURE 10.21
The Geometry
Details page of the
Create Intersection
Wizard

7. Click the Offset Parameters button, and do the following in the Intersection Offset Parameters dialog:

    a. Set the offset values for both the left and right sides to **14'** (**4.5 m**) for both ROAD A and ROAD D.

    b. Fill in the check box for Create New Offsets From Start To End Of Centerlines.

    This will ensure that the turn lanes you're about to create will have targets to meet.

    At this step, the screen should resemble Figure 10.22.

FIGURE 10.22
Intersection Offset
Parameters dialog

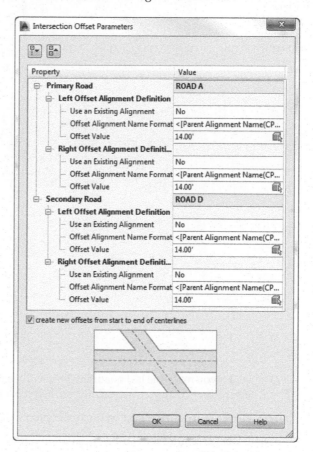

    c. Click OK to close the Intersection Offset Parameters dialog.

8. On the Geometry Details page, click the Curb Return Parameters button to enter the Intersection Curb Return Parameters dialog.

    a. For the NE and SW quadrants, place a check mark next to Widen Turn Lane For Incoming Road.

You will be creating right-turn lanes for ROAD A. Notice how the dialog changes when the check box is filled to show widening parameters.

b. Click the Next button at the top of the dialog to move from quadrant to quadrant.

You will see a schematic name of the quadrant listed at the top of the dialog that corresponds to the glyph. As shown in Figure 10.23, the temporary glyph will help you determine which quadrant you are currently modifying.

FIGURE 10.23
Adding lane widening to the NE – Quadrant of the intersection

When you reach the last quadrant, you will see that the Next button is grayed out. This means that you have successfully worked through all four curb returns.

c. Click OK to return to the wizard's Geometry Details page.

Some locales require that lane slopes flatten out to a 1 percent cross-slope in an intersection. If this is the case for you, you can change the lane slope parameters in the Intersection Lane Slope Parameters dialog (Figure 10.24). In this exercise, you will leave this setting at –2 percent.

FIGURE 10.24
Lane slope parameters control the cross-slope in the intersection.

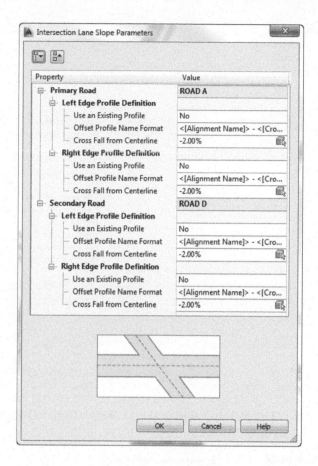

Civil 3D performs the task of generating the curb return profile. The profile will be at least as long as the rounded curb plus the turn lanes that are added in this exercise. If you want to have Civil 3D generate even more than the length needed, you can specify that in the Intersection Curb Return Profile Parameters dialog (Figure 10.25). This dialog is actually a series of dialogs based on quadrant, as was the Curb Return Parameters dialog. According to Figure 10.25, the alignment and profile for the SE – Quadrant curb return will be extended 25" beyond its PCs and PTs. And how is this useful? You'll find out in the upcoming section called "Creating Intersections Manually."

You will be keeping all default settings in both the Lane Slope Parameters area (Figure 10.24) and the Curb Return Profile Parameters area (Figure 10.25).

FIGURE 10.25
Intersection Curb
Return Profile
Parameters
options extend
the Civil
3D–generated
profile beyond
the curb returns
by the value
specified.

9. Click Next to continue to the Corridor Regions page of the Create Intersection Wizard (Figure 10.26).

FIGURE 10.26
The Corridor
Regions page
of the Create
Intersection
Wizard drives the
assemblies used in
the intersection.

The Corridor Regions page is where you control which assemblies are used for the different design locations around the intersection. Clicking each entry in the Corridor Region Section Type list will give you a preview of what each assembly type should look like and where in the intersection it's applied (as shown at the bottom of Figure 10.26). If your assemblies have the same names as the default assemblies, they will be pulled from the current drawing. Alternatively, you can click the ellipsis to select any assembly from the drawing, which is what you will be doing in this example.

If you didn't have all the necessary assemblies created in your drawing at this point, you could still create your intersection with the default assemblies. You could always modify the default assemblies with your own criteria and subassemblies after they are brought in.

10. On the Corridor Regions page, do the following:

a. Click Add To An Existing Corridor to place the intersection in the North River Crossing corridor.

b. Verify that Select Surface To Daylight is set to Existing Surface.

c. In the Corridor Region Section Type list, set the following:

CORRIDOR REGION SECTION TYPE	ASSEMBLY TO APPLY
Curb Return Fillets	Curb Returns
Primary Road Full Section	Full Section
Primary Road Half Section – Daylight Left	Left Half
Primary Road Half Section – Daylight Right	Right Half
Secondary Road Full Section	Full Section
Secondary Road Half Section – Daylight Left	Left Half
Secondary Road Half Section – Daylight Right	Right Half

Giving each assembly a friendly, meaningful name will keep things less confusing.

11. Click Create Intersection.

After a few moments of processing, you will see a corridor appear at the intersection of the roads. Use the REGEN command if you do not see the frequency lines. Your corridor should now resemble Figure 10.27. Executing a Regen command after creating an intersection is sometimes necessary.

FIGURE 10.27
The completed
intersection

12. Select the corridor, and from the Corridor contextual tab ➤ Modify Corridor panel, select Corridor Properties.

    a. Switch to the Parameters tab of the Corridor Properties dialog and highlight one of the regions toward the bottom in the list, as shown in Figure 10.28.

FIGURE 10.28
One way to modify
regions is to use
the Parameters
tab in Corridor
Properties. The
selected region
will highlight
graphically.

Notice how the region highlighted in the Parameters tab is outlined in the graphic. This will help you determine which region to edit.

To move from region to region without searching through the overwhelming list of baselines and regions, use the Select Region From Drawing button.

    b. Click Cancel to close Corridor Properties and press Esc to deselect.

ASSEMBLY SETS

When you are ready to create an intersection, you do not need to have all the special assemblies created ahead of time. On the Corridor Regions page of the Create Intersection Wizard, you will see a list of the assemblies Civil 3D plans to use. If the assemblies are not already part of the drawing, they will get pulled in automatically when you click Create Intersection.

The default intersection assemblies are general and may not work for your design situation. You will want to create and save an assembly set of your own.

1. In a file that contains all of your desired assemblies, work through the Create Intersection Wizard to get to the Corridor Regions page.

2. Click the ellipsis to select the appropriate assembly to use for each corridor region section type.

3. Once the list is complete, click the Save As A Set button.

Civil 3D creates an XML file that stores the list of the assemblies. It also creates a copy of each assembly as a separate DWG file. Save the set in a network shared location so your office colleagues can use the set as well.

The next time an intersection is created, you can use the assembly set by clicking Browse and selecting the XML file. Civil 3D will pull in your assemblies, saving lots of time!

Next you will create a three-way intersection.

13. In your drawing, pan northward to the intersection of ROAD C and ROAD D.

14. From the Home tab ➢ Create Design panel, choose the Intersections ➢ Create Intersection tool.

15. At the Select intersection point: prompt, choose the intersection of the two existing alignments.

You will not be prompted to pick a main/primary road alignment for three-way intersections. The Intersection tool automatically configures the through road as the primary road.

16. On the General page of the Intersection wizard, set the Intersection Corridor Type to All Crowns Maintained and click Next.

17. On the Geometry Details page, accept the defaults and click Next.

18. On the Corridor Regions page, do the following:

    a. Click Add To An Existing Corridor to place the intersection in the North River Crossing corridor.

    b. Verify that Select Surface To Daylight is set to Existing Surface.

    c. In the Corridor Region Section Type list, set the following:

CORRIDOR REGION SECTION TYPE	ASSEMBLY TO APPLY
Curb Return Fillets	Curb Returns
Primary Road Full Section	Full Section
Primary Road Half Section – Daylight Left	Left Half
Primary Road Half Section – Daylight Right	Right Half
Secondary Road Full Section	Full Section
Secondary Road Half Section – Daylight Left	Left Half
Secondary Road Half Section – Daylight Right	Right Half

    d. Before creating this intersection, click the Save As A Set button so this configuration of assemblies can be reused on the other two three-way intersections.

    e. Name your file **NorthRiver** and click Save to continue.

19. Click the Create Intersection button to add this intersection to the North River Crossing corridor.

20. Repeat steps 14–19 for the intersection of ROAD C and ROAD B with the following exceptions:

    a. On the Corridor Regions page, click Browse to choose the assembly set you just created.

    b. In the Select Assembly Set File dialog, select the NorthRiver.xml file and click Open to import.

This may take a few seconds, so wait for it.

c. Do not forget to add the intersection to the North River Crossing corridor.

d. Create the intersection.

21. Repeat steps 15–19 for the intersection of ROAD A and ROAD E with the following exceptions:

a. You will not need to browse for the assembly set. The wizard will remember the last assembly set used.

b. Do not forget to add the intersection to the North River Crossing corridor.

c. Create the intersection.

22. Select the corridor to expose its grips.

Note the two diamond grips located on the centerline of ROAD E.

23. Click in the diamond grip closest to the intersection.

24. Drag it back just south of to the diamond grip furthest from the intersection.

Notice that the intersection creates a short baseline region beyond the curb returns along ROAD E that could potentially interfere with other regions previously created.

25. Osnap to the outer edge of the intersection's baseline region along ROAD E to resolve the overlap.

You should have four intersections in addition to your cul-de-sac modeled in your drawing, as shown in Figure 10.29.

FIGURE 10.29
Four intersections
and a cul-de-sac,
all modeled in
the North River
Crossing corridor

26. Save and close the drawing when you have completed the exercise.

The files 1004_Intersection_FINISHED.dwg and 1004_Intersection_METRIC_FINISHED .dwg are available for your review.

Creating Intersections Manually

You will begin this section by visiting an intersection with unusual circumstances that must be built manually. Then we will discuss other issues you can experience with intersections.

1. Open the 1004_Intersection_FINISHED.dwg (1004_Intersection_METRIC_FINISHED .dwg) file, which you can download from this book's web page.

2. Zoom into the intersections of the ROAD A and ROAD B alignments.

3. From the Home tab, on the Create Design panel ➤ Intersections tool, select Create Intersection and pick the intersection of ROAD A and ROAD B.

4. At the Select main road alignment <or press enter key to select from list>: prompt, click the ROAD A alignment that runs from west to east.

5. On the General page of the Create Intersection Wizard, for Intersection Corridor Type select All Crowns Maintained. Then click Next.

6. On the Geometry Details page, you'll be using the defaults for all parameters, so click Next.

7. On the Corridor Regions page, do the following:

   a. Turn on Add To Existing Corridor.

   b. Set the assemblies to the following:

CORRIDOR REGION SECTION TYPE	ASSEMBLY TO APPLY
Curb Return Fillets	Curb Returns
Primary Road Full Section	Full Section
Primary Road Half Section – Daylight Left	Left Half
Primary Road Half Section – Daylight Right	Right Half
Secondary Road Full Section	Full Section
Secondary Road Half Section – Daylight Left	Left Half
Secondary Road Half Section – Daylight Right	Right Half

   c. Click Create Intersection.

The intersection will be created. Event Viewer will open displaying a number of errors, as shown in Figure 10.30.

FIGURE 10.30
Errors resulting from creating final intersection

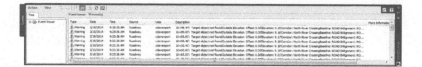

Upon looking through the errors in Event Viewer, you'll discover that they are all the same error occurring at different stations. Each mentions a target object not being found. The subassembly involved is LaneSuperelevationAOR, and the Target name is Outside Elevation. Since the Intersection tool uses profiles for elevation targets, there must be a problem with one of the profiles that the tool created. A quick way to figure out which one is to examine the intersection in 3D.

8. On the ribbon, make the View tab current and do the following:

   a. On the Model Viewports panel ➢ Viewport Configuration tool, select Two: Vertical to split your drawing window into two viewports.

   b. Click in the right viewport to make it current.

   c. On the Views panel ➢ Named View list, make the SE Isometric named view current and zoom back into the intersection of ROAD A – ROAD B.

Your viewport configuration should be similar to Figure 10.31.

FIGURE 10.31
A combination of viewport configurations can help you keep an eye on your corridor design.

For some reason, you have two quadrants in this intersection that decided to set down at elevation zero. You could spend a lot of time trying to seek out the reasons for this, but if you're like most of us, you're in a time crunch and would like to finish up this roadway model. Before we delve into creating manual intersections, it's important that you look at a couple of things before moving on.

If you look at the profile properties for both the NE and SE quadrants on the Prospector under Alignments ➤ Curb Returns, you'll see that the profile is empty of station and elevation data (Figure 10.32), so this is one area where the Intersection tool failed. However, according to the errors, the targeting problems are occurring along the ROAD B baseline, so what is happening there?

FIGURE 10.32
Curb return profile is empty of station and elevation data

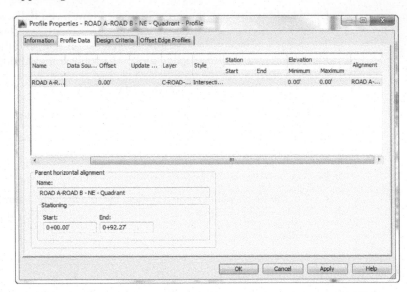

If you open up Corridor Properties, scroll all the way down to the bottom of the list on the Parameters tab, select one of the regions, click the Target ellipsis, and open the Set Slope Or Elevation Target dialog for the left lane, you'll see that the "bad" profiles show up for targeting there as well.

Even if you made manual overrides to cause your corridor to use relevant data, you will still receive errors in Event Viewer because the Intersection tool does not want to let go of the profiles and settings it created. The upside to this behavior is that autogenerated intersections will always update.

The downside to this behavior is when you are in situations like this where the tool failed in an area and you need to make manual adjustments. The best thing to do here is to "turn the intersection off." The Intersection tool did do a lot of the heavy lifting for you, so all is not lost.

9. Press the Esc key a few times to make sure nothing is currently selected. This is always a good thing to do when you are about to press the Delete key.

10. In the left viewport, click the intersection marker (X with a circle imposed at the center). When you do so, the Intersection contextual ribbon will appear.

Examine the contextual ribbon. Notice the tools for editing offset, curb return, lane slopes, and curb return parameters. If any of the parameters set in the Intersection wizard need to change, these tools can be used to reconfigure the intersection.

11. Press the Delete key.

The contextual ribbon closes, the intersection marker and label disappear, and the entry for this intersection on Prospector will no longer be found.

The next step is to re-create the two curb return profiles with relevant station and elevation data.

12. In Prospector, in Alignments ➢ Curb Return Alignments, right-click ROAD A-ROAD B – NE Quadrant and choose Select.

13. Select Surface Profile from the Launch Pad panel on the contextual ribbon.

14. In the Create Profile From Surface dialog, do the following:

a. Under Select Surfaces, select North River Crossing Surface – Top.

b. Click the Add button to add it to the profile list.

c. Click Draw In Profile View.

15. In the Create Profile View dialog, click Create Profile View and place the profile in an open area in your drawing.

If you take a look at the profile, the surface that is being displayed in profile is doing exactly what your corridor is doing: taking a dive down to elevation 0 where the quadrant begins and ends. Here is where you get to fill in the gap like you did in the previous cul-de-sac exercise.

16. On the Home tab ➢ Create Design Panel, select Profile and open the Profile Creation Tools.

17. At the Select profile view to create profile: prompt, select the profile view for the curb return.

18. In the Create Profile dialog, change the text in the Name field to **FG-<[Alignment Name]>**. Click OK to continue.

19. On the Profile Layout Tools toolbar, select Draw Tangents, and using your Endpoint Osnap, bridge the gap as shown in Figure 10.33.

FIGURE 10.33
Filling in the elevation gap in profile view

20. Press ↵ to end the command. Close the Profile Layout Tools toolbar.

    You have created an actual profile that can be used in the NE quadrant of this intersection. Next, you'll address the SE quadrant.

21. Repeat steps 12–20 for the curb return alignment called ROAD A-ROAD B – SE Quadrant.

22. Using the left viewport, pan back over to the troubled intersection.

23. Select the corridor to reveal the contextual ribbon.

24. On the contextual ribbon, select Corridor Properties and do the following:

    a. On the Parameters tab, locate BL – ROAD A-ROAD B – NE – Quadrant (the name of the baseline may have a counter behind it depending on how many times the Intersection command was executed).

    It may be helpful to simplify the list using the Collapse All Categories button in the top left of the dialog. You may use the Select Region From Drawing button as an alternative to searching the list.

    b. In the Profile column, click the profile name for that baseline to change the selection.

    c. In the Select A Profile dialog, change the selection to FG-ROAD A-ROAD B – NE – Quadrant. Click OK to continue.

    d. Next, locate BL – ROAD A-ROAD B – SE – Quadrant.

    e. In the Profile column, click the profile name for that baseline to change the selection.

    f. In the Select A Profile dialog, change the selection to FG-ROAD A-ROAD B – SE – Quadrant. Click OK to continue.

    g. Click OK in the Corridor Properties and rebuild the corridor if prompted.

    Event Viewer will pop up.

25. In Event Viewer, clear all the events being reported using the Action button.

Although the right viewport is now showing a good-looking intersection, you'll want to take the following steps to ensure that Event Viewer isn't picking up any more problems with the corridor.

26. On the contextual ribbon, on the Modify Regions tab, select Edit Targets.

27. At the Select a region to edit: prompt, select the RG – Full Section region along ROAD B north of the intersection, as indicated by Figure 10.34.

FIGURE 10.34
Selecting the RG – Full Section region along ROAD B north of the intersection

RG - Full Section - (53)

28. In the Target Mapping dialog, under Slope Or Elevation Targets ➤ Outside Elevation Profile for the Left assembly group, click in the Object Name column.

29. In the Set Slope Or Elevation Target dialog, do the following:

    a. In the Selected Entities To Target section, select both profiles on the list.

    b. Click the Delete Selected Item button to remove both profile targets from the list.

    Neither of these targets are needed since you are not widening the road in this area.

    c. Click OK to close.

30. Click OK to close the Target Mapping dialog.

The Select a region to edit: prompt should still be active.

31. Select the RG – Left Half region in the north part of the intersection along ROAD B, as indicated by Figure 10.35.

FIGURE 10.35
Selecting the
RG – Left Half
region along ROAD
B north of the
intersection

32. Repeat steps 28–30. Just be aware that sometimes the Intersection tool will throw in the alignment as an elevation target instead of the bad profile. If you find that to be the case, remove the alignment from the list.

The Select a region to edit: prompt should still be active.

33. Select the RG – Full Section region in the south part of the intersection along ROAD B, as indicated by Figure 10.36.

FIGURE 10.36
Selecting the
RG – Full Section
region along ROAD
B south of the
intersection

34. Repeat steps 28–30.

35. Press ↵ to end the command.

Now if you were to clear the events out of Event Viewer and rebuild the corridor, you would receive no errors. It's better to reserve the error list for those items that you need to address.

The files 1005_ManualIntersection_FINISHED.dwg and 1005_ManualIntersection_METRIC_FINISHED.dwg are available for your review.

Troubleshooting Your Intersection

The best way to learn how to build advanced corridor components is to go ahead and build them, make mistakes, and try again. This section provides some guidelines on how to "read" your intersection to identify what steps you may have missed.

Your lanes appear to be backward.   Occasionally, you may find that your lanes wind up on the wrong side of the EOP alignment, as in Figure 10.37. The most common cause is that your assembly is backward from what is needed based on your alignment direction.

FIGURE 10.37
An intersection
with the lanes
modeled on the
wrong side

Fix this problem by editing your subassembly to swap the lane to the other side of the assembly. If the assembly is used in another region that is correct, just make a new assembly that is the mirror image of the other assembly and apply the new one to the alignment.

Since so many design elements rely on the alignment as their base, it is better to add a new assembly rather than reversing the direction of the alignment.

Your intersection drops down to zero.   A common problem when modeling corridors is the cliff effect, where a portion of your corridor drops down to zero. You probably won't notice in plan view, but if you rotate your corridor in 3D using Object Viewer (see Figure 10.38), you'll see the problem. The most common cause for this phenomenon is incorrect region stationing.

FIGURE 10.38
A corridor viewed
in 3D, showing a
drop down to zero

Fix this problem by making sure your baseline profile exists where you need it, and make note of the station range. Set your station range in the corridor to be within the correct range.

Your lanes extend too far in some directions.   There are several variations on this problem, but they all appear similar to Figure 10.39. All or some of your lanes extend too far down a target alignment, or they may cross one another, and so on.

FIGURE 10.39
The intersection lanes extend too far down the main road alignment.

This occurs when a target alignment and profile have been omitted for one or more regions. In the case of Figure 10.39, the EOP Left baseline region was set to only one alignment. In an intersection, you need two targets in a corner region to model the road correctly. You would see a similar issue appear if the Selection Choice If Multiple Targets Are Found option were set to Target Farthest From Offset.

Your lanes don't extend far enough.   If your intersection or portions of your intersection look like Figure 10.40, you neglected to set the correct target alignment and profile.

FIGURE 10.40
Intersection lanes don't extend out far enough.

You can fix this problem by opening the Target Mapping dialog for the appropriate regions and double-checking that you assigned targets to the right subassembly. It's also common to accidentally set the target for the wrong subassembly if you use Map All Targets or if you have poor naming conventions for your subassemblies.

Finishing Off Your Corridor

Now it's time for you to fill in another kind of gap in the corridor. You will be filling in the corridor between the intersections you created.

1. Open the 1005_ManualIntersection_FINISHED.dwg (1005_ManualIntersection_ METRIC_FINISHED.dwg) file, which you can download from this book's web page.

2. On Prospector, expand the Intersections branch and select the ROAD A-ROAD E intersection.

3. Right-click and select Zoom To to zoom into the ROAD A-ROAD E intersection and select the corridor to reveal its grips.

4. Grab the rightmost diamond-shaped region grip, which coincides with ROAD A-ROAD C intersection, and drag it over to the adjacent diamond-shaped region grip in the ROAD A-ROAD E intersection, as shown in Figure 10.41.

FIGURE 10.41
Stretching the region to match up with the adjacent region

Notice how your intersections become out of date according to the yellow alert shield that appears next to each.

5. Right-click ROAD A-ROAD E and select Update Regions And Rebuild Corridor.

6. When the Intersections – Update Corridor Regions dialog opens, select Continue With Update.

7. Notice how the stretched region returns to its original position.

This could be a problem if you are relying on the dynamic dependencies of your intersections to keep your corridor updated. Next, you'll try an alternative method of filling in the gaps.

8. Select the corridor, and on the contextual ribbon select Add Region from the Modify Corridor panel; then do the following:

a. In the Select A Baseline dialog, choose the second BL – ROAD A baseline from the list.

The three instances of the Intersection command each created a ROAD A baseline to use. We're choosing the one associated with the ROAD A-ROAD E intersection.

b. Click OK to continue.

c. At the Specify region start station prompt, snap to the diamond grip, as shown in Figure 10.42.

FIGURE 10.42
Defining the region start station

When selecting the region start station, it must be an earlier station than the region end station that you will select next.

d. At the Specify region end station prompt, snap to the diamond grip, as shown in Figure 10.43.

FIGURE 10.43
Defining the region end station

e. In the Create Corridor Region dialog, select the Full Section assembly and click OK to apply.

f. In the Target Mapping dialog, in the Object Name column next to Surfaces, click <Click Here To Set All> and then select Existing Surface.

g. Click OK to continue.

h. Click OK to close the Target Mapping dialog.

Your new baseline region should resemble Figure 10.44.

FIGURE 10.44
Filling in the gap with a new baseline region

The Add Region command is still active.

i. Repeat step 8 for the rest of the empty regions along ROAD A.

j. When the regions along ROAD A are complete, press ↵ to end the Add Regions command.

Optionally, you may repeat step 8 to fill in the gaps in this corridor along the remaining areas of ROADs B, C, and D.

The files `1006_FillingCorridorGaps_FINISHED.dwg` and `1006_FillingCorrodorGaps_METRIC_FINISHED.dwg` are available for your review.

Using an Assembly Offset

In Chapter 9, "Basic Corridors," you completed a road-widening example with a simple lane transition. Earlier in this chapter, you worked with intersections and cul-de-sacs. These are just a few of the techniques for adjusting your corridor to accommodate a widening, narrowing, interchange, or similar circumstances. There is no single method for building a corridor model; every method discussed so far can be combined in a variety of ways to build a model that reflects your design intent.

Another tool in your corridor-building arsenal is the assembly offset. In Chapter 8, "Assemblies and Subassemblies," you had your first glimpse of an offset assembly, but in the example that follows you will have a chance to use one for a bike path design.

Notice in Figure 10.45 how the frequency lines in the corridor are running perpendicular to the main alignment. The bike path is an alignment that is not a constant offset through the length of the corridor. In this scenario, the cross section of the bike path itself is skewed. This could prove problematic when computing end area volumes for the bike path pavement. This is the result of using an assembly where all of the design is based on one main baseline assembly.

FIGURE 10.45
A bike path modeled with a traditional assembly

There are several advantages to using an offset assembly instead of creating an additional, separate assembly. The offset assembly requires its own alignment and profile for design. In the corridor that results, a secondary set of frequency lines is generated perpendicular to the offset alignment, as shown in Figure 10.46. Additionally, you can use a marked point assembly to model the ditch between the bike path and the main road.

FIGURE 10.46
Modeling a bike path with an assembly offset

There are many uses of offset assemblies besides bike paths. Typical examples of when you'll use an assembly offset include transitioning ditches, divided highways, and interchanges. The assembly in Figure 10.47, for example, includes two assembly offsets.

FIGURE 10.47
An assembly with two offsets representing roadside swale centerlines

When you use an assembly with an offset in your corridor, you must assign an alignment and profile to it. The only restriction to the offset assembly is that it can't use the same alignment or profile as the main part of the assembly. In the case where you want your offsets to follow the same elevation, you will need to use the Superimposed Profile tool to effectively make a copy of the desired profile.

In this exercise, you will model a bike path with an assembly offset:

1. Open the 1007_BikePath.dwg (1007_BikePath_METRIC.dwg) file, which you can download from this book's web page.

2. Locate the assembly in the Prospector tab, right-click, and click Zoom To.

   You'll see an incomplete assembly called Road With GR And Bikepath.

3. Click the main assembly marker, and then from the Assembly contextual tab ➢ Modify Assembly panel, click Add Offset.

4. At the Specify offset location: prompt, click to the left of the Road With GR And Bikepath assembly, leaving enough room for the bike lane and ditch.

   Your result should look like Figure 10.48. The warning symbols indicate that you can no longer use the assembly for roads where superelevation occurs at points other than the centerline. Superelevation at the crown will still work, which is the situation used here.

FIGURE 10.48
Road With GR And
Bikepath assembly,
so far

5. Press Ctrl+3 to open the subassembly tool palette.

6. Switch to the Basic tab, and select the BasicLane subassembly.

7. In the Advanced parameters in the Properties palette, set Side to Right and Width to 5' (1 m).

8. Click to place the subassembly on the offset assembly, and click the offset assembly again to form the left side.

   Your assembly should now look like Figure 10.49.

FIGURE 10.49
Road With GR And
Bikepath assembly
with the BasicLane
subassembly as a
bike path

Next, you will use a MarkPoint assembly to set the stage for building a ditch between the bike path and the main road.

9. Switch to the Generic tab in the subassembly tool palette, and click the MarkPoint subassembly.

10. Change Point Name on the Properties palette to **BIKE** (use all capital letters).

11. Click the outermost point of the left shoulder subassembly.

Your marker will look like Figure 10.50. Note that the point code defaults to MarkedPoint in the subassembly parameters but can be renamed as needed.

FIGURE 10.50

A close-up of the MarkPoint subassembly

12. From the Generic tab of the subassembly tool palette, click the LinkSlopesBetweenPoints subassembly, and do the following:

    a. Set Marked Point Name to **BIKE** (again, use all capital letters).

    b. Set Ditch Width to **0.5' (0.15** m).

    c. Click the right side of the bike path.

    The offset assembly will now look like Figure 10.51.

FIGURE 10.51

The LinkSlopes: BetweenPoints subassembly in layout mode

13. Add a LinkSlopeToSurface generic link subassembly, and do the following:

    a. Set Side to Left and Slope to 25 percent .

    b. Place the subassembly on the left side of the bike path. Press Esc to finish adding subassemblies and save the drawing.

    The completed assembly will look like Figure 10.52.

FIGURE 10.52

The completed assembly with offset

Next, you will create a corridor using this new assembly:

14. From the Home tab ➤ Create Design panel, click Corridor and do the following:

    a. Name the corridor **Bike Path**.

    b. Set Alignment to USH 10.

    c. Set Profile to USH 10 Roadway CL Prof.

    d. Set Assembly to Road with GR And Bikepath.

    e. Set Target Surface to Existing Intersection.

    f. Verify that there is a check mark next to Set Baseline And Region Parameters.

    g. Click OK.

In the Baseline And Region Parameters dialog, notice that the Offset – (1) is not associated with an alignment (your numbers may vary).

15. Click the Alignment field for Offset – (1), select Bike Path from the drop-down list, and click OK.

16. Click the Profile field for Offset – (1) and do the following:

    a. From the Select An Alignment drop-down list, select Bike Path.

    b. From the Select A Profile drop-down list, select Bike Path FG, and click OK.

The Bike Path alignment is slightly shorter than the main USH 10 alignment, which would cause the "waterfall" effect explained in Chapter 9.

17. To prevent corridor errors, do the following:

    a. Set the start station for the Offset – (1) region to **0+25.00** (**0+010.0** for metric users).

    b. Set the end station to **40+00** (**1+220** for metric users).

    c. Click OK and rebuild the corridor.

Your completed corridor will resemble the example shown earlier in Figure 10.46.

18. Select the corridor by clicking on one of the frequency lines anywhere near the middle of the alignment, and click Section Editor.

You may want to change your annotation scale to 1′ = 1″ (1: 1 for metric users) to get an unobstructed view of your masterpiece.

19. Explore the finished design by clicking through the Corridor Editor.

At each station, the offset assembly ties back to the main assembly because of the use of the LinkSlopeBetweenPoints subassembly. Your design in the Section Editor should resemble Figure 10.53.

FIGURE 10.53
Inside the Corridor
Section Editor

20. On the Section Editor contextual tab ➤ Close panel, click Close.

Completed versions of these drawings (1007_BikePath_FINISHED.dwg and 1007_ BikePath_METRIC_FINISHED.dwg) are located with the rest of the dataset for your review.

21. Save and close the drawing.

THE TROUBLE WITH BOWTIES

In your adventures with corridors, chances are pretty good that you'll create an overlapping link or two. These overlapping links are known not so affectionately as *bowties*. Here's an example.

Bowties are problematic for several reasons. In essence, the corridor model has created two or more points at the same *x* and *y* locations with a different *z*, making it difficult to build surfaces, extract feature lines, create a boundary, and apply codeset styles that render or hatch.

When your corridor surface is created, the TIN has to make some assumptions about crossing breaklines that can lead to strange triangulation and incoherent contours, such as in the following image:

When you create a corridor that produces bowties, the corridor won't behave as expected. Using the Corridor contextual tab ➤ Launch Pad panel to extract polylines or feature lines from overlapping corridor areas yields an entity that is difficult to use for additional grading or manipulation because of extraneous, overlapping, and invalid vertices. If the corridor contains many overlaps, you may have trouble even executing the extraction tools. The same concept applies to extracted alignments, profiles, and COGO points.

If you try to add an automatic or interactive boundary to your corridor surface, either you'll get an error or the boundary jig will stop following the feature line altogether, making it impossible to create an interactive boundary.

To prevent these problems, the best plan is to try to avoid link overlap. Be sure your baseline, offset, and target alignments don't have redundant or PI locations that are spaced excessively close.

If you initially build a corridor with simple transitions that produce a lot of overlap, try using an assembly offset and an alignment besides your centerline as a baseline. Another technique is to split your assembly into several smaller assemblies and to use your target assemblies as baselines, similar to using an assembly offset. This method was used to improve the river corridor shown in the previous images. The following image shows the two assemblies that were created to attach at the top of bank alignments instead of the river centerline.

The resulting corridor is shown here.

The TIN connected the points across the flat bottom and modeled the corridor perfectly, as you can see in the following image.

Continues

Continued

Another method for eliminating bowties is to notice the area where they seem to occur and then adjust the regions. If your daylight links are overlapping, perhaps you can create an assembly that doesn't include daylighting and create a region to apply that new assembly.

If overlap can't be avoided in your corridor, don't panic. If your overlaps are minimal, you should still be able to extract a polyline or feature line—just be sure to weed out vertices and clean up the extracted entity before using it for projection grading. You can create a boundary for your corridor surface by drawing a regular polyline around your corridor and adding it as a boundary to the corridor surface under the Surfaces branch in Prospector. The surface-editing tools, such as Swap Edge, Delete Line, and Delete Point, can also prove useful for the final cleanup and contour improvement of your final corridor surface.

As you gain more experience building corridors, you'll be able to prevent or fix most overlap situations, and you'll also gain an understanding of when they aren't having a detrimental effect on the quality of your corridor model and resulting surface.

Understanding Corridor Utilities

You'll now take advantage of some of the corridor utilities found in the Launch Pad panel (Figure 10.54) of the contextual tab.

FIGURE 10.54
A bounty of corridor utilities on the Launch Pad panel

The utilities on this panel are as follows:

Superelevation   This button will jump you to the alignment superelevation parameters. See Chapter 11, "Superelevation," for a detailed look at how Civil 3D creates banked curves for your design speed.

Create Sample Lines   Corridors and sample lines are both linked to alignments. Civil 3D gives you a shortcut to the sample line creation tool. Chapter 12, "Cross Sections and Mass Haul," explores the creation and uses of sample lines.

Feature Lines From Corridor   This utility extracts a grading feature line from a corridor feature line. This grading feature line can remain dynamic to the corridor, or it can be a static extraction. Typically, this extracted feature line will be used as a foundation for some feature-line grading or projection grading. If you choose to extract a dynamic feature line, it can't be used as a corridor target because of possible circular references.

Alignment From Corridor   This utility creates an alignment that follows the horizontal path of a corridor feature line. By default, the alignment is categorized as an offset alignment, but it is not tied to the baseline. You can use this alignment to create target alignments, profile views, special labeling, or anything else for which a traditional alignment could be used. Extracted alignments are not dynamic to the corridor. If you place a check box next to the Create Profile option, the resulting profile will be related to the new alignment rather than the baseline.

Profile From Corridor   This utility creates a profile that follows the vertical path of a corridor feature line. This profile appears in Prospector under the baseline alignment and is drawn on any profile view that is associated with that baseline alignment. This profile is typically used to extract edge of pavement (EOP) or swale profiles for a finished profile view sheet or as a target profile for additional corridor design. Extracted profiles are not dynamic to the corridor.

Points From Corridor   This utility creates Civil 3D points that are based on corridor point codes. You select which point codes to use as well as a range of corridor stations. A Civil 3D point is placed at every point-code location in that range. These points are a static extraction and don't update if the corridor is edited. For example, if you extract COGO points from your corridor and then revise your baseline profile and rebuild your corridor, your COGO points won't update to match the new corridor elevations.

Polyline From Corridor   This utility extracts a 3D polyline from a corridor feature line. The extracted 3D polyline isn't dynamic to the corridor. You can use this polyline as is or flatten it to create road linework.

Using Corridor Utilities in Practice

There are many uses for the utilities outlined in this section. Once you get the hang of using some of the corridor utilities, you should find that they are straightforward. In the exercise that follows, you will dabble in the corridor utilities:

1. Open the file 1008_CorrUtils.dwg (1008_CorrUtils_METRIC.dwg).

2. Select the corridor by clicking one of the frequency lines (these are the magenta lines that are perpendicular to the alignment).

3. From the Corridor contextual tab ➢ Launch Pad panel, click Feature Lines From Corridor.

4. At the Select a Corridor Feature Line: prompt, click the south daylight line (this will be the line that is not a constant offset from the centerline alignment).

    The Select A Feature Line dialog will appear if you click the daylight line in a cut or fill region. This is because Civil 3D makes two distinct feature lines in these areas. Recall from Chapter 9 that feature lines are formed as a result of marker points with the same name in the assembly connecting together at frequency stations. In other words, why do you have two feature lines here? Because the daylight subassembly creates two marker points at the catch point.

You want the Daylight feature line because it is continuous through the length of the corridor. Daylight_Cut appears only in the cut areas (red), and Daylight_Fill appears only in the fill areas (green). Where the corridor transitions from cut to fill (or fill to cut), you will see a yellow line. Only the Daylight feature line will appear in the transition regions.

5. If needed, highlight Daylight and click OK.

6. In the Create Feature Line From Corridor dialog (Figure 10.55), clear the check box labeled Create Dynamic Link To The Corridor.

FIGURE 10.55
Creating a feature line from a corridor without the dynamic link to the corridor

7. Leave all other options at their defaults and click OK.

8. You should still be in the Create Feature Line From Corridor command, and the command line should return to the `Select a Corridor Feature Line:` prompt. If you accidentally exited the Feature Lines From Corridor command, start it again from the Launch Pad panel. Click the daylight line on the north side of the road.

9. Repeat steps 5–7 to create a second feature line out of the north daylight feature line.

10. Press Esc to end the command.

11. Select the corridor again if it is not already selected.

12. From the Corridor contextual tab ➤ Launch Pad panel flyout, click Points From Corridor.

13. In the Create COGO Points dialog, do the following:

    a. Toggle on the option For Entire Corridor Range.

    b. Name the new point group **Corridor Stakeout**.

    c. In the Select column, clear all the check boxes except Daylight and ETW, as shown in Figure 10.56. (Hint: Press the Ctrl key as you click to unselect multiple items at once.)

    d. Click OK.

FIGURE 10.56
Creating points for stakeout along corridor feature lines

14. Save and close the drawing.

Completed versions of this exercise are available with the rest of the dataset.

Using a Feature Line as a Width and Elevation Target

You've gained some hands-on experience using alignments and profiles as targets in an intersection and in a cul-de-sac design. Civil 3D adds options for corridor targets beyond alignments and profiles. You can use grading feature lines, survey figures, or polylines to drive horizontal and vertical aspects of your corridor model.

Imagine using an existing polyline that represents a curb for your lane-widening projects without duplicating it as an alignment or grabbing a survey figure to assist with modeling an existing road for a rehabilitation project. Better yet, what if the object you are targeting is visible to the corridor drawing only as an XRef? The next exercise will lead you through an example where a lot-grading feature line is integrated with a corridor model through an external reference:

1. Open the 1009_FeatureLineTarget.dwg (1009_FeatureLineTarget_METRIC.dwg) file, which you can download from this book's web page. Note that the file 1009_XREF.dwg (or 1009_XREF_METRIC.dwg) must be extracted to the same folder as the main file in order to see it for use in this exercise.

   This drawing includes a completed assembly and a partially completed corridor. Your task will be to use the feature lines that run through the project as targets in the corridor. These lines are in an external reference file.

2. Zoom to the corridor and select it. From the Corridor contextual tab ➤ Modify Corridor panel, choose Corridor Properties.

3. Switch to the Parameters tab in the Corridor Properties dialog.

4. Click the ellipsis button in the Targets field in the RG – Subdivision region.

   The Target Mapping dialog appears.

   Note that the number following the region will vary. The higher the number, the more previous attempts at building the corridor the authors have made before handing the drawing over to you.

5. In the Target Mapping dialog, locate Width Or Offset Targets in the Object Name column. Click the <None> field next to Target Alignment for the Slope-Left subassembly.

   The Set Width Or Offset Target dialog appears.

6. Choose Feature Lines, Survey Figures And Polylines from the Select Object Type To Target drop-down list (see Figure 10.57).

FIGURE 10.57
The Select Object Type To Target drop-down list at the top of the Set Width Or Offset Target dialog

7. In the Set Width Or Offset Target dialog, click the Select From Drawing button. At the `Select feature lines, survey figures or polylines to target:` prompt, select the north feature line to the left of the alignment and then press ↵.

   The Set Width Or Offset Target dialog reappears, with an entry in the Selected Entries To Target area.

8. Click OK to return to the Target Mapping dialog.

   If you stopped at this point, the horizontal location of the feature line would guide the Slope-Left subassembly, and the vertical information would be driven by the slope set in the subassembly properties. Although this has its applications, most of the time you'll want the feature line elevations to direct the vertical information. The next few steps will teach you how to dynamically apply the vertical information from the feature line to the corridor model.

9. In the Object Name column in the Slope Or Elevation Targets section, click the <None> field next to Target Profile for the Slope-Left subassembly.

10. Make sure Feature Lines, Survey Figures And 3D Polylines is selected in the Select Object Type To Target drop-down.

11. Click the Select From Drawing button. At the Select feature lines, survey figures or 3D polylines to target: prompt, select the north feature line to the left of the alignment again and then press ↵.

    The Set Slope Or Elevation Target dialog reappears, with an entry in the Selected Entries To Target area.

12. Click OK to return to the Target Mapping dialog.

13. Repeat steps 4–12 for Slope-Right on the right side of the corridor using the south feature line to the right of the alignment.

14. Click OK to return to the Corridor Properties dialog.

15. Click OK to close the Corridor Properties dialog and choose Rebuild The Corridor. Press Esc to deselect.

    The corridor will rebuild to reflect the new target information and should look similar to Figure 10.58.

FIGURE 10.58
The corridor now uses the grading feature lines as width and elevation targets.

South feature line (right of alignment)   North feature line (left of alignment)

Once you've linked the corridor to these feature lines, any edits to the feature lines will be incorporated into the corridor model. You can establish this feature line at the beginning of the project and then make horizontal edits and elevation changes to perfect your design. The next few steps will lead you through making some changes to this feature line and then rebuilding the corridor to see the adjustments.

16. Select the text that resides in the XRef. From the External Reference context tab ➢ Edit panel, click Open Reference.

    This opens the external reference so you can modify the feature lines.

17. Select one of the feature lines so that you can see its grips. Experiment with the feature lines by moving several grips.

18. When you have edited several areas in the external reference file (1009_XREF.dwg or 1009_XREF_METRIC.dwg), save and close the drawing.

After the external reference closes, you should be back in the corridor drawing. A message will appear in the lower-right corner of your screen indicating External Reference File Has Changed.

19. In the bubble message, click the link to reload 1009_XREF.dwg (for metric users, 1009_XREF_METRIC.dwg).

20. Press Esc to deselect and then select the corridor. From the Corridor contextual tab ➢ Modify Corridor panel, click Rebuild Corridor.

The corridor will rebuild to reflect the changes to the target feature lines.

See 1009_FeatureLineTarget_FINISHED.dwg (1009_FeatureLineTarget_METRIC_FINISHED.dwg) to view a completed version of this exercise.

Edits to targets—whether they're feature lines, alignments, profiles, or other Civil 3D objects—drive changes to the corridor model, which in turn drives changes to any corridor surfaces, sections, section views, associated labels, and other objects that are dependent on the corridor model.

CONDITIONAL LOVE

Driveways are a common source of grief for designers. They pop up along corridors at irregular intervals, making them difficult to model with a traditional assembly. Luckily, you have the powerful *conditional subassemblies* available to you. Conditional subassemblies allow designers to test scenarios and have the assembly react to different conditions. In programmer-speak, the conditional subassemblies allow "if-then" statements within an assembly.

There are two conditional subassemblies available to Civil 3D users: ConditionalCutOrFill and ConditionalHorizontalTarget.

The ConditionalCutOrFill subassembly will check for a range of depth of cut or fill and apply the desired subassembly accordingly. For example, you may have a shoulder subassembly with daylight for cut scenarios, but after a cut of more than 10¢, you want a retaining wall subassembly to be placed instead.

The ConditionalHorizontalTarget subassembly checks for the presence of a specific offset object or objects. For example, you will use the existence of a driveway to trigger the assembly to apply geometry in the following example:

Continues

Continued

1. Open the drawing 1010_Conditional.dwg (or 1010_Conditional_METRIC.dwg).

   There are five total assemblies in this drawing. The one that is modified in this exercise is the DRIVEWAY CONDITIONAL. The other four assemblies in the drawing are there to illustrate the assemblies that would be needed to accomplish the corridor modeling task without the use of conditional subassemblies. In other words, one assembly has the power of four!

2. In the right viewport, zoom in to the assembly labeled DRIVEWAY CONDITIONAL.

3. Open the Tool Palettes if they are not already open. Switch to the Conditional tab.

4. Click the ConditionalHorizontalTarget subassembly. In the Properties palette, set the side to **Right**. Change the type to **Target Found**. Leave all other parameters as default.

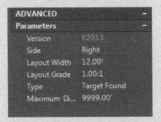

5. Click the marker point at the top-right edge of the lane to place the subassembly in the drawing.

6. Again, click the ConditionalHorizontalTarget subassembly. In the Properties palette, set the side to Right. Change Layout Grade to **-1.00:1** and change the type to **Target Not Found**.

The Layout Width and Layout Grade values do not have any effect on the resulting corridor. Changing Layout Grade only helps to visually separate the different conditions so they do not overlap graphically.

7. Click the same marker point at the top-right edge of the lane to place the subassembly in the drawing.

8. Press Esc to clear any previous selections. Select one of the new subassemblies. From the Subassembly contextual tab, click Assembly Properties.

9. In the Assembly Properties dialog, switch to the Construction tab.

10. Right-click the first ConditionalHorizontalTarget in the listing and select Rename. Change the name to **DRIVEWAY**.

11. Right-click the second ConditionalHorizontalTarget in the listing and select Rename. Change the name to **NO DRIVEWAY**.

12. Click OK to close the Assembly Properties dialog. Press Esc to clear the selection.

13. Select the shoulder and the daylight subassemblies from the right side of the Driveway Right assembly.

14. From the Subassemblies contextual tab ➤ Modify Subassembly panel, click Copy.

15. At the Select marker point within assembly for the copied subassemblies: prompt, click the marker point at the end of the DRIVEWAY subassembly. This will be the geometry that is created when the driveway target is found.

16. Press Esc to clear the selection.

17. Select the shoulder and the magenta link subassemblies from the right side of the Driveway Left assembly.

18. From the Subassemblies contextual tab ➤ Modify Subassembly panel, click Copy.

19. At the Select marker point within assembly for the copied subassemblies: prompt, click the marker point at the end of the NO DRIVEWAY subassembly, completing the right side of the assembly.

20. Press Esc to clear the selection; then select all the subassemblies that you have added in this exercise.

21. From the Subassemblies contextual tab ➤ Modify Subassembly panel, click Mirror.

22. Click the top-left edge of pavement marker point of the left lane of the Driveway Conditional assembly.

23. In Toolspace ➤ Prospector, expand Corridors. Right-click USH 10 – w Driveways and select Properties.

24. In the Corridor Properties dialog, switch to the Parameters tab. Click the ellipsis in the Target column of the DRIVEWAY CONDITIONAL region row.

25. In the Target Mapping dialog, click the <Click Here To Set All> option in the Object Name column in the Surfaces row. Highlight the surface Existing Intersection and click OK.

26. Under Width or Offset Targets, click the <None> field next to Target Offset for the DRIVEWAY subassembly (in the assembly group Right).

27. Under Select Object Type To Target, use the drop-down list to switch to Feature Lines, Survey Figures And Polylines, and then click Select By Layer.

Continues

Continued

28. Place a check mark next to the C-TOPO-FEAT layer and click OK. Click OK again to close the Set Width Or Offset Target dialog.

29. Repeat steps 26–28 for NO DRIVEWAY on the right and again for both DRIVEWAY and NO DRIVEWAY on the left assembly group.

30. Click OK to close the Target Mapping dialog and then click OK (click Rebuild The Corridor if prompted to do so) to close the Corridor Properties dialog.

See 1010_Conditional_FINISHED.dwg (1010_Conditional_METRIC_FINISHED.dwg) to view a completed version of this exercise.

Tackling Roundabouts: The Mount Everest of Corridors

If you really understand what went on earlier in this chapter, you are almost ready for roundabout design. You may want to wait to tackle your first roundabout until after reading Chapter 14, "Grading."

The same concepts apply to a roundabout as for a standard road junction, but you will have several more regions, baselines, and corresponding profiles.

The following sections will help you prepare files for roundabout design. We will not take you through every detail of corridor creation, but once you master the topics of intersection design, a roundabout is an extension of the same concepts.

A roundabout is best done in several corridors:

Preliminary Corridor for Circulatory Road   This is a corridor used to determine the elevations of the approach road profiles. The circular portion of the roadway will set the elevations for all of the alignments leading into it. Using similar techniques to those used earlier in the chapter, you create a corridor surface from this corridor and use it as a tie-in for approach road profiles.

Main Corridor with Approaches and Circulatory Road   This corridor is the main part of your design. You will spend lots of time in the corridor properties tweaking stations, adding baselines and regions, and targeting the appropriate locations.

Curb Island Corridors (Optional)   There are many different philosophies about the best way to show curb islands. If showing them in a section is not important, you can omit this altogether. Some people prefer to use grading feature lines (as discussed in Chapter 14). In the following sections, you will go "all out" and use the dynamic capabilities of the corridor model to make curb islands.

Drainage First

Based on your existing ground surface, determine the general direction that you want water to flow away from the center of the roundabout. Use grading tools and a feature line to create the general drainage direction of the roundabout.

Chapter 14 will go into much more depth on creating grading. You will certainly want to have an understanding of grading basics before you tackle a roundabout.

Create a feature line that represents the highest elevations. In the example shown in Figure 10.59, the feature line slopes downward and acts as a ridge to separate water flow. The grading tools are then used to create grading objects and a corresponding surface model called Roundabout Grading.

FIGURE 10.59
Feature lines and
grading create
a preliminary
surface to ensure
proper drain-
age through the
roundabout.

The Roundabout Grading surface will be the basis for your profile elevations through the rest of the design process.

Roundabout Alignments

Roundabouts need alignments to guide the design for the same reasons that an intersection needs them. Alignments will be baselines and targets for the approaches and rotary. Create alignments manually with the tools you learned to use earlier in this chapter, or start with the handy roundabout layout tool.

The roundabout layout tool creates horizontal data based on the location of the center of the roundabout and the approach alignments.

In the exercise that follows, you will create the Civil 3D alignments needed to create a roundabout:

1. Open the 1011_RoundaboutLayout.dwg (1011_RoundaboutLayout_METRIC.dwg) file, which you can download from this book's web page.

2. From the Home tab ➤ Create Design panel, select Intersections ➤ Create Roundabout, as shown in Figure 10.60.

FIGURE 10.60
Access the Create
Roundabout tool
from the Home
tab.

3. At the `Specify roundabout center point:` prompt, use your Intersection Osnap to select the point where the alignments intersect.

The alignments leading into the roundabout are often referred to as *approaches*.

4. At the `Select approach road:` prompt, select all four alignments leading into the roundabout, and press ↵ when you have finished.

You now see the Create Roundabout – Circulatory Road page of the wizard, shown in Figure 10.61.

FIGURE 10.61

The first roundabout layout screen for designing the main circulatory road

5. Verify that you are using the correct standards for your units. Click the ellipsis next to the Roundabout Design Standard File field, and verify that you are using the correct XML standards file. Imperial users should be using `Autodesk Civil 3D Imperial Roundabouts Presets.xml`. Metric users should be using `Autodesk Civil 3D Metric Roundabouts Presets.xml`.

a. If Roundabout Design Standard File is set correctly, click Cancel and continue to step 6.

b. If it is not set correctly, browse to the `C:\ProgramData\Autodesk\C3D 2016\enu\Data\Corridor Design Standards\` folder.

   c. Browse to either the Imperial or Metric units folder and select the correct roundabout presets XML file.

   d. Click Open to return to the Create Roundabout dialog.

6. From the Predefined Parameters To Import drop-down, choose R = 75 (Rg = 25m).

This will be the radius from the center of the roundabout to the outermost circular edge of pavement. This will also adjust other settings in the dialog.

7. Set Alignment Layer to C-ROAD and Alignment Label Set to Major And Minor Only. Click Next.

Now, you'll design the approach road exit and entry geometry. The options in the Create Roundabout – Approach Roads page of the wizard (see Figure 10.62) can be set independently for each approach, or you can click Apply To All, which will set the geometry for all four approaches.

FIGURE 10.62
Approach road widths at entry and exit

8. On the Create Roundabout – Approach Roads page, do the following:

   a. Set Predefined Parameters To Import to R = 75 (Rg = 25m).

    b. Change the alignment layer to C-ROAD. Hint: You can type in the layer name or pick it from the drop-down.

    c. For Alignment Label Set, choose Major And Minor Only.

    d. Leave all other settings at their defaults.

    e. Click the Apply To All button, and click Next.

9. In the Create Roundabout – Islands screen (see Figure 10.63), again set Predefined Parameters To Import to R = 75 (Rg = 25m).

FIGURE 10.63
Roundabout
Islands parameters

10. Click Apply To All and then click Next.

The final screen of the Create Roundabout Wizard deals with pavement markings and signage. Notice that you can specify your own blocks for the signs that will be placed in this process.

Everything created in this last step is an AutoCAD polyline or block. The polylines have a global width set to indicate pavement marking thicknesses. These thicknesses are set in the Markings And Signs page (Figure 10.64).

FIGURE 10.64
Pavement mark-
ings galore!

11. Leave all defaults in the Create Roundabout – Markings And Signs page (Figure 10.64), and click Finish.

    Your roundabout should resemble Figure 10.65. Since standards vary by region, the metric drawing will have slightly different default pavement markings.

    Finally, you will add a turn lane in the NW quadrant of the roundabout. When you're creating slip turn lanes, remember that the turn radius must be large enough to fillet the exit and entry roads without overlapping the other alignments.

    When selecting the approach entry and exit alignments, you need to click the shorter approach alignments created by Civil 3D rather than the original approach road. For this reason, the exercise has you select inside the islands, just to be sure.

FIGURE 10.65
Completed round-
about alignment
layout

12. From the Home tab ➢ Create Design panel, select Intersections ➢ Add Turn Slip Lane.

13. When prompted to select the entry approach, select the north approach alignment inside the curb island.

14. When prompted for the exit approach, select the west approach alignment inside the curb island, as shown in Figure 10.66.

FIGURE 10.66
Entry and exit
approach align-
ments for the slip
lane

15. In the Draw Slip Lane dialog shown in Figure 10.67, set the lane width to **14'** (4 m) and the radius to **150'** (45 m).

FIGURE 10.67
Adding a slip lane

Draw Slip Lane

Slip Lane parameters

Segmentation line length:	1	Lane width:	14
Length of deceleration lane:	80	Radius:	150
Length of acceleration lane:	70	Taper length:	70

Draw pavement markings

	Draw	Linetype:	Width:	Offset:
Outer edge	☑	Continuous	0.3	0.15
Decelerating transition line	☑	Continuous	0.3	0.15
Accelerating transition line	☑	Continuous	0.3	0.15

Alignment style:
Proposed

Alignment name prefix:
SlipLane

Alignment layer:
C-ROAD

Alignment label set:
Major and Minor only

OK   Cancel   Help

16. For Alignment Layer, choose C-ROAD, and for Alignment Label Set, choose Major And Minor Only. Click OK.

Your roundabout will now look like Figure 10.68.

FIGURE 10.68
The completed slip lane alignments

17. Save and close the drawing.

The completed files, 1011_RoundaboutLayout_FINISHED.dwg and 1011_RoundaboutLayout_METRIC_FINISHED.dwg, are available for your review if desired.

You now have all the alignments you need to start your roundabout design. At this point, you can add geometry to the alignments and modify what Civil 3D has created for you.

The horizontal layout is complete, but the roundabout design is far from done. No vertical data has been created; that is up to you.

This is as far as we will take you in this book in regard to building a roundabout step by tedious step. Rest assured, however, that if you have truly mastered corridors, the technique for completing a roundabout is similar to that used for any intersection.

The remainder of this chapter gives you an overview of how to accomplish the rest on your own.

Center Design

All profiles need to meet at the elevations inside the traveled way in the circular pavement area of the roundabout. Therefore, the main circle design comes first.

To see an example of a completed roundabout corridor, open the drawing 1011_RoundaboutExample_FINISHED.dwg or 1011_RoundaboutExample_METRIC_FINISHED.dwg. Use these examples as a guide to "reverse engineer" your own roundabouts when you've mastered other forms of intersections.

You can use any of the circular alignments created by Civil 3D as the basis for this step, as long as your assembly works with the design. Remember to make note of which direction the alignment goes, to ensure that the assembly you create is not backward.

Extract profiles for the main circle design from the Existing Intersection and Roundabout Grading surfaces, as shown in Figure 10.69.

FIGURE 10.69
Extract surface profiles around the main circular alignment.

The assembly you create for this preliminary design will also be used in the main design. Decide which alignment will be used as the circular design basis and create an assembly based on your alignment location and desired geometry, as shown in Figure 10.70.

FIGURE 10.70
Center assembly
for roundabout

This assembly can be used in several steps of the process. First, it is used in a preliminary corridor called RAB MAIN. It can also be recycled to be the centerpiece of your main corridor. In the example, the main circle alignment created by Civil 3D, Roundabout_OUTER_EDGE, was used as the baseline for this initial corridor. There are no targets or frequencies set in this corridor. Like the cul-de-sac example earlier in this chapter, this is a preliminary corridor, used to ensure that profiles from the approach roads tie in at the correct elevations.

In the example drawings, a Top link surface was created from the RAB MAIN corridor. At this point, the roundabout will resemble Figure 10.71.

FIGURE 10.71
Preliminary cen-
ter corridor and
surface

Profiles for All

You have all the preliminary surfaces in place, and you have all the alignments you need, so it is time to extract profiles from your various surfaces.

In the `1011_RoundaboutExample_FINISHED.dwg` and `1011_RoundaboutExample_METRIC_FINISHED.dwg` files, the surface profiles for all the approach alignments were created by sampling the existing ground, drainage surface, and preliminary RAB MAIN corridor surface. These profiles will look something like Figure 10.72.

FIGURE 10.72
Surface profiles needed for design

When you create your design, you will see all your design considerations in the profile views. No matter how you decide to tie into existing ground and slope upward toward the surface, your design must tie into the preliminary center surface, as shown in Figure 10.73.

FIGURE 10.73
Design profiles must tie into the center.

Use techniques you learned earlier in this chapter to assist you. Labels are an especially valuable tool for roundabouts. Keep your profile views organized because you will have at least three for each approach. If you have a slip turn lane, you will have a profile for that as well.

Tie It All Together

Stretch your legs and go for more coffee. It is time to put this thing together into a completed corridor. When you model the corridor initially, ignore curb islands—you will add them as individual corridors in a later step.

A simple roundabout can be completed using as few as three assemblies. In our example, however, the slip turn lane necessitates a total of four assemblies. In addition to the RAB Main assembly you saw in Figure 10.70, you will need three more assemblies, as shown in Figure 10.74.

FIGURE 10.74
Assemblies
needed for the
main roundabout
corridor

These assemblies will be tied to the EOP alignments and profiles as baselines, similar to a traditional intersection. Each quadrant of the roundabout will target at least two alignments and profiles, as shown in Figure 10.75.

FIGURE 10.75
Roundabout cor-
ridor regions and
targets

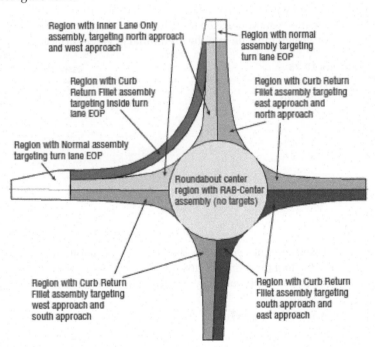

Keep in mind the direction of your alignments. If you build the corridor in stages, check the corridor periodically to make sure it is building correctly.

Create a corridor surface from your completed roundabout lanes. You will likely have to use the Add Interactively tool to add the boundary correctly.

Finishing Touches

The median islands are the last parts to go on the corridor. You can create them using simple grading objects, but since this is a book about mastering skills and this is a chapter about corridors, you should examine the dynamic way.

Create a simple assembly containing the curb and gutter for the curb islands. This will be the assembly that you use with the median corridors (Figure 10.76).

FIGURE 10.76
Simple assembly
containing just
the curb and
gutter on the
median islands

Each median island will need its own alignment. Take note of the direction of the alignments to make sure they are compatible with the curb island assembly. If necessary, change the direction of the alignments using the Reverse Direction tool in the Modify panel of the contextual ribbon tab. Figure 10.77 shows the bypass island and north island with directions.

FIGURE 10.77
Several median
island alignments
with direction
shown

The good news is that the elevation data for the medians is already complete. Your main corridor's surface will act as the profile for each individual median. This also means that once the curb return corridors are created, they will be dynamic to the main corridor. After these little corridors are created and surface model information has been obtained, you can set them to Rebuild – Automatic and forget all about them.

Extract a profile for all the curb return alignments from the Top link surface model from the main roundabout corridor, as shown in Figure 10.78. You do not need to see this profile in a view, so you can click OK to extract.

FIGURE 10.78
Extract the profile for medians from your main roundabout surface.

When the design roundabout corridors are complete and surfaces are made, the next step is to merge the surfaces. Create a final surface model and paste the main roundabout design in first. After the main corridor is pasted in, paste the smaller median corridor surfaces, as shown in Figure 10.79. The center median is already taken care of by the first baseline.

FIGURE 10.79
The completed roundabout

Your next step is to use the corridor fine-tuning techniques you learned earlier in this chapter to ensure that your grades are correct and the design is correct. To see an example of a completed corridor using these steps, take a look at `1011_RoundaboutExample_FINISHED.dwg` (`1011_RoundaboutExample_FINISHED_METRIC.dwg`), which you can download from this book's web page.

The Bottom Line

Create corridors with non-centerline baselines.   Although for simple corridors you may think of a baseline as a road centerline, other elements of a road design can be used as a baseline. In the case of a cul-de-sac, the EOP, the top of curb, or any other appropriate feature can be converted to an alignment and profile and used as a baseline.

Master It   Open the `MasterIt1001.dwg` (`MasterIt1001_METRIC.dwg`) file, which you can download from www.sybex.com/go/masteringcivil3d2016. Add the cul-de-sac alignment and profile to the corridor as a baseline. Create a region under this baseline that applies the Intersection Typical assembly.

Add alignment and profile targets to a region for a cul-de-sac.   Adding a baseline isn't always enough. Some corridor models require the use of targets. In the case of a cul-de-sac, the lane elevations are often driven by the cul-de-sac centerline alignment and profile.

Master It   Continue working in the `MasterIt1001.dwg` (`MasterIt1001_METRIC.dwg`) file. You need to have completed the previous exercise before continuing. Add the Second Road alignment and Second Road FG profile as targets to the cul-de-sac region. Adjust Assembly Application Frequency to **5′ (1 m)** for tangents and curves.

Create a surface from a corridor and add a boundary.   Every good surface needs a boundary to prevent bad triangulation. Bad triangulation creates inaccurate contours and can throw off volume calculations later in the process. Civil 3D provides several tools for creating corridor surface boundaries, including an Interactive Boundary tool.

Master It   You need to have completed the previous exercise before continuing. Keep working in the `MasterIt1001.dwg` (`MasterIt1001_METRIC.dwg`) file. Create an interactive corridor surface boundary for the entire corridor model.

Chapter 11

Superelevation

Superelevation and cant are methods for changing the cross section of a design to keep cars and trains safely and comfortably on their paths when driving along a curve or series of curves. Superelevation tools also provide a convenient way to force the slope of a road for drainage purposes, without the need for additional assemblies.

Once you have a good grasp of alignments, assemblies, and corridors, you can further advance your design with the superelevation and cant tools within the Autodesk® AutoCAD® Civil 3D® software. Whether you are trying to tie into an existing road's superelevation or creating new data, you will find the tools you need.

In this chapter, you will learn to:

◆ Add superelevation to an alignment.

◆ Create a superelevation assembly.

◆ Create a rail corridor with cant.

◆ Create a superelevation view.

Preparing for Superelevation

Before superelevation can be applied to the design, you will need a *design criteria file* appropriate for your locale, design speeds applied to an alignment, an assembly with subassemblies that recognize superelevation, and an understanding of superelevation critical stations.

Critical Stations

Critical stations mark "milestones" in the gradual transition of crown to full super to crown in a superelevated region of an alignment. These points are located by means of calculations driven by the design criteria file.

End Normal Shoulder (ENS)   This is the first station in the Transition In region. Normal shoulder slope is maintained, as shown in Figure 11.1, but at subsequent stations, shoulder slope gradually becomes planar.

FIGURE 11.1
End Normal
Shoulder, the
first station in
the Transition In
region

End Normal Crown (ENC)   Normal lane slope is maintained, as shown in Figure 11.2, but at subsequent stations lane slope gradually becomes planar. ENC also marks the beginning of runout distance in the region.

FIGURE 11.2
End Normal
Crown, where the
outside lane slope
starts to flatten

Level Crown (LC)   One side of the assembly will flatten to 0.00 percent, as shown in Figure 11.3. This occurs in the Transition In region as well as the Transition Out region. It marks the beginning of runoff distance in the Transition In region and the beginning of runout distance in the Transition Out region.

FIGURE 11.3
Level Crown,
where the outside
lane flattens

Reverse Crown (RC)   The outside lane becomes planar with the inside lane matching slope (normal), as shown in Figure 11.4. This occurs in the Transition In region as well as the Transition Out region in the runoff distance.

FIGURE 11.4
Reverse Crown,
where the outside
lane becomes
planar with the
inside lane

Low Shoulder Match (LMS)   The inside shoulder becomes planar with the lanes and outside shoulder. This occurs in the runoff distance in the Transition In and Transition Out regions.

Begin Full Super (BFS) Both lanes are planar and are at their maximum rate of superelevation (e_{max}), as shown in Figure 11.5. This occurs at the end of the Transition In region.

FIGURE 11.5
Begin Full Super,
with both lanes at
maximum slope

End Full Super (EFS) EFS has the same cross-slope conditions as Begin Full Super (Figure 11.5). This station marks the beginning of the Transition Out region and marks the beginning of the runoff distance for that region.

Begin Normal Crown (BNC) BNC has the same cross-slope conditions as End Normal Crown (Figure 11.2). This station in the Transition Out region marks the end of the runout distance.

Begin Normal Shoulder (BNS) BNS has the same cross-slope conditions as End Normal Shoulder (Figure 11.1). This station marks the end of the Transition Out region.

Now that you are familiar with the terminology used to describe transition stations, you are ready to examine design criteria.

Design Criteria Files

Having the correct design criteria file in place is the first step to applying superelevation to your corridor. These XML-based files contain instructions to the software about when to flag your design for geometry problems both horizontally and vertically. Design criteria determine how your road behaves when superelevation is applied to the design.

Several design criteria files are supplied with Civil 3D upon installation. The out-of-the-box standards for roads include AASHTO 2001, AASHTO 2004, and AASHTO 2011 for both metric and Imperial units. Several of the country kits include design criteria files for your locality if you are outside the United States. If country or state kits do not exist for your situation, you can create your own user-defined files.

To create your own design criteria, follow these steps:

1. Select any alignment.

2. From the Alignment context tab ➤ Modify panel, click the Design Criteria Editor.

   It is easier to modify an existing table in your desired units than to start from an empty file.

3. Be sure to click the Save As icon before making any changes.

USER-DEFINED CRITERIA FILES

If you create design criteria files for your region or design scenario, you will need to be able to share the file with anyone who will be working with your design.

Inside your organization, the best way to handle the design criteria file is to move it to a shared network location. If the design criteria file is stored in a shared location, be sure to have your IT personnel set the file to read-only to prevent inexperienced users from modifying it.

The default location for road design standards is `C:\ProgramData\Autodesk\C3D 2016\enu\ Data\Corridor Design Standards\`.

The default location for rail design standards is `C:\ProgramData\Autodesk\C3D 2016\enu\ Data\Railway Design Standards\`.

Once you browse to a design criteria file for an alignment, the location will be saved with the alignment.

If you are collaborating with someone without direct access to your design criteria files, you will need to send that person the XML file with your DWG. The XML file will not automatically go along for the ride if you use the eTransmit command.

Inside the Design Criteria Editor (Figure 11.6), you will see three headings: Units, Alignments, and Profiles. The Units page tells Civil 3D what type of values it will be using in the file. The Alignments page is used for checking design, creating superelevation, and widening outside curves. The Profiles page provides tabular data for minimum K-value used to check vertical design.

FIGURE 11.6
Inside the Design
Criteria Editor

Civil 3D will graphically flag alignments when the design speed specified in Alignment Properties has a radius less than the value specified in the Minimum Radius Table. The Minimum Radius Table values from AASHTO use superelevation rates in the table names, but this does not lock you into that rate for applying superelevation to the corridor. In other words, just because you use a more conservative value in your radius check, that doesn't mean you can't superelevate at a steeper rate. The tables are independent of one another.

Also in the Alignments branch you will find the superelevation attainment equations. These equations determine the distance between superelevation critical stations. Familiarize yourself with the terminology and locations represented by these stations, as shown in Figure 11.7.

FIGURE 11.7
Diagram of super-elevation critical stations and regions calculated by Civil 3D

In the following exercise, you will modify an example design criteria file and save it:

Design Criteria Editor

1. Open the 1101_Criteria.dwg (1101_Criteria_METRIC.dwg) file, which you can download from this book's web page at www.sybex.com/go/masteringcivil3d2016. This exercise will also require 1101_CriteriaExample.xml (1101_CriteriaExample_METRIC.xml).

2. Select the USH 10 alignment that already exists in the drawing.

3. On the Alignment contextual tab ➢ Modify panel, select Design Criteria Editor.

4. Click the Open button at the top of the dialog, and browse to the 1101_CriteriaExample.xml (1101_CriteriaExample_METRIC.xml) file. Click Open.

5. Expand the Alignments branch, and expand the Superelevation Tables branch.

   There is only one superelevation table in this example for 4% maximum slope.

6. Right-click Superelevation Tables and select New Superelevation Table.

7. Double-click the new table and rename it **Example 6% Super**.

8. Right-click Example 6% Super and select New SuperelevationTypeByTable.

9. Expand the new branch, right-click SuperelevationTypeByTable, and select New Superelevation Design Speed, as shown in Figure 11.8.

FIGURE 11.8
Adding a design speed to the design criteria file

When you expand the SuperelevationTypeByTable branch, you will see that Civil 3D has created a new table with a default design speed of 10 regardless of the units you are working in.

10. Double-click Design Speed 10 and change the design speed to **30** mi/hr (**50** km/hr).

Notice that you need only the numeric value; Civil 3D fills in the rest of the table name for you.

11. Highlight your new design speed table.

The right side of the dialog will display an empty table containing columns labeled Radius and Superelevation Rate.

12. Select the first row of the table. Click the first field in the Radius column to start entering data. Add several radius and superelevation values, as follows:

CURVE RADIUS (FEET)	CURVE RADIUS (METERS)	SUPERELEVATION %
300	90	6
1000	300	4.5
1500	450	3.2
2000	600	2.6
4000	1250	NC

When you have completed your data entry from the table, the U.S. units Design Criteria Editor will resemble Figure 11.9.

FIGURE 11.9
Adding example data using the Design Criteria Editor

13. Add a note in the Comments field that reads **Example Data Only!**

14. Click the Save And Close button at the bottom of the editor.

15. Click Save Changes and exit when prompted.

16. Save and close the current drawing.

Compare your work with `1101_CriteriaExample_FINISHED` if desired.

Ready Your Alignment

Superelevation stations are connected to alignment curves (unless you create a user-defined curve in a tangent section). The design speed from Alignment Properties is needed at each curve to specify which superelevation rate tables to use from the design criteria. The design speed has an effect on the distance between superelevation critical stations and the cross slope used when the road is at full-super.

It is a good idea to get your alignment geometry and design speed locations finalized before attaching superelevation. If a change is made to your alignment, the superelevation stationing will be marked as out of date.

Super Assemblies

As a general rule, if the lane subassembly has the word *super* somewhere in its name, it will respond to superelevation. If you want to verify that the lane you are choosing will behave the way you want it to in a superelevation situation, you can right-click it from the tool palette and access the subassembly help.

As long as you stay away from the Basic tab, all of the shoulder and curb subassemblies have parameters you can set to dictate how the assembly is to behave when an adjacent lane superelevates.

Most subassemblies that are capable of superelevating are intended for use where the pivot point for the cross section is at the center crown of the road. When the pivot point is at the center of the road, the baseline profile dictates the final elevation of the crown of the road. Figure 11.10 shows an example of a two-lane highway (top image) and a four-lane divided highway (bottom image) that are designed to be used with the superelevation tools.

FIGURE 11.10
Two-lane and four-lane road assemblies designed to be used in super

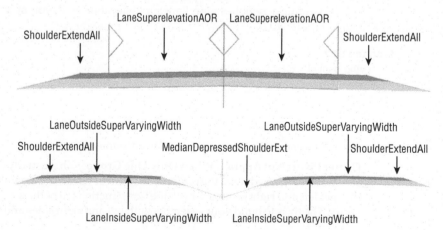

AXIS OF ROTATION

The following is a list of the limitations and other factors to be aware of if you decide to take these new assemblies for a spin:

◆ Don't use an offset assembly with an axis of rotation superelevation assembly. The result in the corridor may not come out as expected.

◆ When working with curbs, medians, and shoulders, keep an eye out for the parameter Superelevation Axis Of Rotation. If this parameter reads Unsupported, it means that the subassembly will not adjust for superelevation other than at the center. None of the curb and gutter subassemblies adjust for breakover or rollover, but most of the shoulder assemblies do. This is a hard-coded parameter that cannot be changed by the end user. However, a custom subassembly could be composed that would accomplish this. Custom subassemblies will be covered in Bonus Chapter 1, "Custom Subassemblies."

AXIS OF ROTATION SUPPORT

The axis of rotation (AOR) subassembly can be used when the centerline of the road is not the pivot point for superelevation. The flag symbols (as shown in Figure 11.11) indicate potential pivot points on the assembly.

FIGURE 11.11
AOR subassemblies used on an undivided, crowned roadway

The flag symbols on LaneSuperelevationAOR indicate where the lane can be pinned down and used as a pivot point. When the axis of rotation is not the centerline of the road, the lane geometry is used to determine the change in elevation that will occur as a result.

When building assemblies with LaneSuperelevationAOR, you may see warnings appear, as shown in Figure 11.12.

FIGURE 11.12
A warning symbol on an assembly using Lane Superelevation AOR

Here are some of the warnings you may encounter:

Center Pivots Not Applied When Only One Group   This usually occurs when you start your assembly with a median at the center. The construction of the assembly then does not have distinct left and right groups. Check the Construction tab of the assembly Properties dialog to verify. The fix is to build your assembly with left and right sides and add the median last.

Unsupported Subassemblies   This warning will appear when you're attempting to use an assembly that has the Superelevation Axis Of Rotation parameter absent from its parameters.

Unsupported In Assemblies Containing Offsets   Using an offset assembly will interfere with the software's ability to calculate the correct slope and curve widening on a superelevated road. Therefore, offset assemblies are not recommended for use with the AOR subassembly. You can still use offsets in traditional center-pivot-based superelevation.

No Center Pivots Found   Make sure your assembly properties list the assembly as the correct type. For example, if you accidentally set Assembly Type to Divided Crowned Road when it is actually an undivided crowned road, you will receive this message. Check the Construction tab of the assembly Properties dialog to verify.

You can still add assemblies with warnings to a corridor; however, the superelevation may not behave as expected.

 Real World Scenario

THE TIPPING POINT

In some design situations that use superelevation, the crown of the road is not the ideal pivot point. In the following example, you will create a four-lane divided highway that pivots inside the curve rather than at the crowns during superelevation.

1. Open the file 1102_AORAssembly.dwg (1102_AORAssembly_METRIC.dwg).

   This drawing contains an assembly that was started for you. Note that a generic link has been placed on the right side of the main assembly marker as a spacer for the subassemblies that you will be adding in the next steps.

2. Open your subassembly tool palette (Ctrl+3 will work) and select the Lanes tab.

3. Select the LaneSuperelevationAOR subassembly.

4. In the Parameters section of the AutoCAD Properties palette, change Side to Right and set Use Superelevation to Right Lane Outside (as shown here).

Continues

Continued

5. Click the outer circular marker point on the generic link located on the right side to place the subassembly. Press Esc to complete the placement of the lane subassembly.

6. Select the newly placed LaneSuperelevationAOR subassembly.

7. From the Subassembly: LaneSuperelevationAOR contextual tab ➤ Modify Subassembly panel, click Mirror.

8. Click the outer same marker point as you selected in step 5 on the generic link.

   A dialog will appear asking you to confirm that you want to place the mirrored subassembly on the same side. Click OK.

9. Press Esc to deselect the first lane subassembly; then select the newly placed SuperelevationAOR subassembly and view its AutoCAD properties.

10. Change the Use Superelevation parameter to Right Lane Inside, as shown here.

11. Select both of the new LaneSuperelevationAOR subassemblies and the generic link. From the Subassemblies contextual tab ➤ Modify Subassembly panel, click Mirror.

12. Click the baseline assembly marker to mirror all three subassemblies to the left side of the assemblies. Press the Esc key.

    Be sure to set the subassembly parameters to the correct superelevation lane and side property. Note that the inside lane must have Use Superelevation set to Left Lane Inside, and the outside lane must be set to Left Lane Outside.

13. On the tool palette, switch to the Generic tab. Select the MarkPoint subassembly, change Point Name to **MEDIAN**, and place it by clicking the red circle on the inside-right edge of the pavement (as shown next).

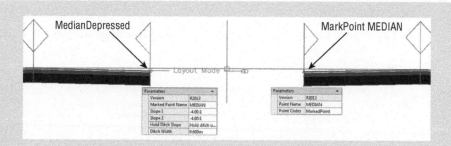

14. On the Medians tab, select Median Depressed and change Marked Point Name to **MEDIAN**.

    Note that the Marked Point name is case sensitive and must match the point name exactly or the median will not form correctly.

15. Leave all other parameters at their defaults and place the median on the inside left of the subassembly, as shown in the previous image. Press Esc when complete.

16. As the final step in building this assembly, select both of the original generic link spacers, and in the Properties palette, Advanced Parameters section, set the Omit Link property to Yes.

    If time permits, add the ShoulderExtendAll subassembly from the Shoulder tab to the outermost edges using only the default settings. Press Esc when complete.

17. Select the Route 66 alignment that runs through the plan view of the project. (Hint: Zoom out to see it.)

18. On the Alignment contextual tab ➢ Modify panel, click Superelevation ➢ Calculate/Edit Superelevation, and click the Calculate Superelevation Now option when notified that no data exists.

Continues

Continued

19. On the Calculate Superelevation – Roadway Type page, set Roadway Type to Divided Crown With Median.

20. Set the pivot method to Inside Of Curve.

21. Set the median treatment to Distorted Median, and click Next.

22. On the Calculate Superelevation – Lanes page, set the normal lane width to **12´** (**4** m) and the normal lane slope to **-2.00**%.

23. Place a check mark next to Symmetric Roadway and click Next.

24. On the Calculate Superelevation – Shoulder Control page, leave the settings at their defaults and click Next.

25. On the Calculate Superelevation – Attainment page, set the design criteria file to `Autodesk Civil 3D Imperial (2011) Roadway Design Standards.xml` (metric users use `Autodesk Civil 3D Metric (2011) Roadway Design Standards.xml`).

26. Set the superelevation rate table to AASHTO 2011 US Customary eMax 6% (AASHTO 2004 Metric eMax 6%) using the 4 Lane transition length table.

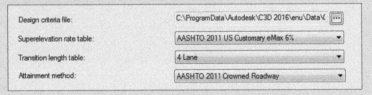

27. Select Automatically Resolve Overlap and click Finish.

The Panorama palette will pop up displaying the Superelevation Tabular Editor containing the results of your superelevation calculation. Because the Automatically Resolve Overlap option was turned on, no warnings should appear in Panorama.

28. Click the green check mark to dismiss Panorama.

29. In the Prospector tab of Toolspace, expand the Corridors branch, select the corridor Route 66, right-click, and select Rebuild.

30. Select the corridor in plan and enter the Section Editor to examine your corridor. (Hint: Review "Editing Sections" in Chapter 9, "Basic Corridors.")

You should observe that superelevation is occurring based on your specified pivot point inside the curves. Close the Section Editor.

Check out `1102_AORAssembly_FINISHED.dwg` and `1102_AORAssembly_METRIC_FINISHED.dwg` to see a complete version of this example.

Applying Superelevation to the Design

Civil 3D takes into account other factors such as curve station locations and assembly geometry. Superelevation information is associated with the alignment but is handled in a separate calculation area. In this section, you will apply and configure superelevation to an alignment.

Start with the Alignment

To begin applying superelevation to the design, configure your Alignment Properties.

1. Open the `1103_Super.dwg` (`1103_Super_METRIC.dwg`) file, which you can download from this book's web page.

2. Select the USH 10 alignment that already exists in the drawing.

3. From the Alignment contextual tab, select Superelevation ➤ Calculate/Edit Superelevation.

4. When prompted by the dialog, click Calculate Superelevation Now.

5. On the Calculate Superelevation – Roadway Type page, select the Undivided Crowned radio button.

6. From the Pivot Method drop-down, choose Center Baseline, as shown in Figure 11.13, and click Next.

FIGURE 11.13
Roadway type
specification for
superelevation

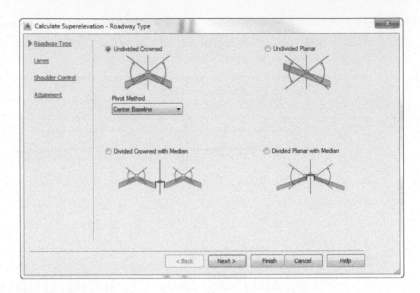

7. On the Calculate Superelevation – Lanes page, verify that the Symmetric Roadway check box is selected.

8. Set Normal Lane Width to **12´** (4 m), and set Normal Lane Slope to **-2.00%**, as shown in Figure 11.14; click Next.

FIGURE 11.14
Lane information

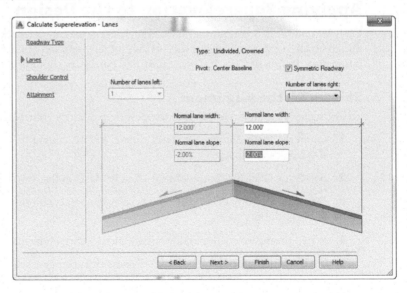

9. On the Calculate Superelevation – Shoulder Control page, make sure the Calculate check box is selected on the right side of the page.

Only the Outside Edge Shoulders options should be active. Since this is an undivided road, the options for the inside median shoulders are grayed out.

10. Set Normal Shoulder Width to **6′** (**2 m**), and set Normal Shoulder Slope to **-5.00%**.

11. For Shoulder Slope Treatment, set the following:

    ◆ Set the Low Side option to Breakover Removal.

    ◆ Set the High Side option to Default Slopes.

    ◆ Place a check mark next to Maximum Shoulder Rollover and set the value to **8.00%**.

    Your Shoulder Control screen should look like Figure 11.15.

FIGURE 11.15
Shoulder Control and Breakover Removal parameters

12. Click Next.

13. On the Calculate Superelevation – Attainment page, click the ellipsis button to set the design criteria file to `Autodesk Civil 3D Imperial (2004) Roadway Design Standards.xml` (`Autodesk Civil 3D Metric (2004) Roadway Design Standards.xml`).

14. Set the superelevation rate table to AASHTO 2004 US Customary eMax 4% (AASHTO 2004 Metric eMax 4%).

15. Set the transition length table to 2 Lane.

16. Set the Attainment method to AASHTO 2004 Crowned Roadway.

17. Place a check mark next to Apply Curve Smoothing and set Curve Length to **50′** (**20 m**).

    Leave all other settings at their defaults, as shown in Figure 11.16.

FIGURE 11.16
Finalizing the
superelevation
on the Attainment
screen

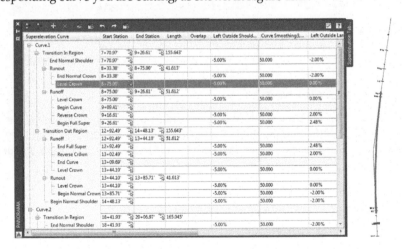

18. Click Finish.

You should now see the Superelevation Tabular Editor appear inside Panorama with the data resulting from the wizard. Examine your alignment; you should now have labels showing the superelevation critical stations created by the wizard.

As you click in the table, you will see helpful glyphs showing you which superelevation station and corresponding curve you are editing, as shown in Figure 11.17.

FIGURE 11.17
Superelevation
table with glyphs
in the graphic

Compare your work with 1103_Super_FINISHED.dwg or 1103_Super_METRIC_FINISHED.dwg.

Transition Station Overlap

It is not uncommon to have overlap warnings in your superelevation table. You should resolve the transition station overlap before you continue your design.

Overlap occurs when there is not enough room between curves to fully transition out of one curve and back into the next. Transition station overlap will always occur when a reverse curve or compound curve exists in your alignment. As you can see in Figure 11.18, Curve 1 does not complete its transition out until station 9+16.64, but according to the attainment calculations, Curve 2 will begin affecting the shoulder starting at station 5+98.21.

FIGURE 11.18
Superelevation table showing overlap between two curves

Superelevation Curve	Start Station	End Station	Length	Overlap	Left Outside Should...	Left Outside Lane	Right Outside Lane	Right Outside Shou...
Curve.1								
Transition In Region	1+79.81'	4+20.56'	240.750'					
End Normal Shoulder	1+79.81'				-5.00%	-2.00%	-2.00%	-5.00%
Runout	2+60.06'	3+13.56'	53.500'					
End Normal Crown	2+60.06'				-2.00%	-2.00%	-2.00%	-5.00%
Level Crown	3+13.56'				0.00%	0.00%	-2.00%	-5.00%
Runoff	3+13.56'	4+20.56'	107.000'					
Level Crown	3+13.56'				0.00%	0.00%	-2.00%	-5.00%
Reverse Crown	3+67.06'				2.00%	2.00%	-2.00%	-5.00%
Begin Curve	3+84.89'							
Begin Full Super	4+20.56'				4.00%	4.00%	-4.00%	-5.00%
Transition Out Region	6+75.89'	9+16.64'	240.750'					
Runoff	6+75.89'	7+82.89'	107.000'					
End Full Super	6+75.89'			⚠	4.00%	4.00%	-4.00%	-5.00%
End Curve	7+11.56'			⚠				
Reverse Crown	7+29.39'			⚠	2.00%	2.00%	-2.00%	-5.00%
Level Crown	7+82.89'			⚠	0.00%	0.00%	-2.00%	-5.00%
Runout	7+82.89'	8+36.39'	53.500'					
Level Crown	7+82.89'			⚠	0.00%	0.00%	-2.00%	-5.00%
Begin Normal Crown	8+36.39'			⚠	-2.00%	-2.00%	-2.00%	-5.00%
Begin Normal Shoulder	9+16.64'			⚠	-5.00%	-2.00%	-2.00%	-5.00%
Curve.2								
Transition In Region	5+98.21'	8+38.96'	240.750'					
End Normal Shoulder	5+98.21'			⚠	-5.00%	-2.00%	-2.00%	-5.00%
Runout	6+78.46'	7+31.96'	53.500'					
End Normal Crown	6+78.46'			⚠	-5.00%	-2.00%	-2.00%	-2.00%
Level Crown	7+31.96'			⚠	-5.00%	-2.00%	0.00%	0.00%
Runoff	7+31.96'	8+38.96'	107.000'					
Level Crown	7+31.96'			⚠	-5.00%	-2.00%	0.00%	0.00%
Reverse Crown	7+85.46'			⚠	-5.00%	-2.00%	2.00%	2.00%
Begin Curve	8+03.30'			⚠				
Begin Full Super	8+38.96'			⚠	-5.00%	-4.00%	4.00%	4.00%

You have several options for fixing superelevation overlap:

◆ You can choose to have Civil 3D rectify the overlap for you.

◆ You can manually modify the stations in the table.

◆ You can change the stationing for superelevation by modifying the superelevation view, which we will discuss later in this chapter.

IMPORT OR EXPORT SUPERELEVATION DATA TO CSV

You may spend hours getting your superelevation stations to work out correctly. However, it just takes one wrong button click to blow away all your time-consuming edits to the tabular input. To be safe, back up your superelevation tables by exporting them to a file. You'll find the Export Superelevation Data button at the top of the tabular input.

Continues

Continued

Import from file   Export to file   Clear all superelevation data

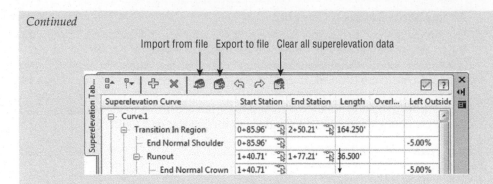

The nice thing about a CSV file is that it can easily be edited in an external spreadsheet program, such as Microsoft Excel. If you choose to modify your superelevation stations outside of Civil 3D, there are a few things to keep in mind:

◆ You must keep the same number of columns and column names.

◆ It is OK to add or delete rows.

◆ Blank shoulder or lane slope fields will be treated as 0.00 percent. However, if all of your lane and shoulder slope fields are blank, the row will be omitted from the import.

◆ It is OK to rename the superelevation critical stations.

◆ If your CSV file contains more superelevation regions in it than the alignment has curves, you must create additional user-defined curves in the Superelevation Curve Manager before importing the data. See "User-Defined Curves: Forcing Superelevation" for more information on user-defined curves.

◆ Importing data from a CSV file will override any data for existing stations in the file.

When you need to reimport the superelevation data, it is a best practice to clear any data before clicking Import From File.

To have Civil 3D clear the overlap for you, click the warning symbol that appears in the Superelevation Tabular Editor. Civil 3D resolves overlap by omitting noncritical stations or by compressing the transition length between certain stations. In the case of a reverse curve, Civil 3D will pivot the road from full-super to full-super, without transitioning back to normal crown. Be sure to verify that the software has made the update that meets the requirements of your locale.

Real World Scenario

USER-DEFINED CURVES: FORCING SUPERELEVATION

By default, superelevation stations are calculated per curve. In most situations, the curves on the alignment will correspond to the needed superelevation regions. However, there are several situations where you want to force superelevation to occur on a tangent. In those situations, you can create a user-defined curve.

To create a user-defined curb, select the alignment along which you want to create superelevation. From the Alignment contextual tab ➤ Modify panel, click Superelevation ➤ Calculate/Edit Superelevation.

If your alignment already has curves with superelevation data attached to them, Civil 3D will open the Superelevation Curve Manager palette right away. If no superelevation data exists for the alignment, you will be prompted to either calculate superelevation now or open the Superelevation Curve Manager. If your alignment has no curves, click the Open The Superelevation Curve Manager option.

Once you are in the Superelevation Curve Manager, you will have access to any curves—if they exist. If you are working with an alignment that contains no curves, this palette will be blank.

To create a user-defined curve, click the Create User-Defined Curve button. You will be prompted to select an entity to associate to the user-defined curve.

The entity (or entities) you select must be a tangent segment that does not already have a user-defined curve associated with it. The segment geometry will be used as the Begin Curve and End Curve stations. If you pick more than one entity, they must be adjacent to each other.

After you pick your elements, you will have the ability to add "fake" curve information. If you plan to use Civil 3D to calculate superelevation, you must have a design speed assigned to the alignment.

Continues

Continued

You can specify a radius and curve direction in the Superelevation Curve Manager palette (as shown here) so that the Superelevation Wizard knows which way you intend to tip the road.

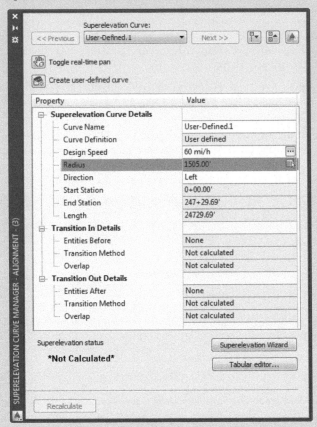

After a user-defined curve has been assigned a design speed and radius, the Superelevation Wizard can be used to calculate superelevation similar to a traditional, "real" curve.

If you are planning to import all your stations from a CSV file or manually create stations and cross-slopes in the tabular editor, then you may omit design speed and radius.

As shown in this image, you can manually add superelevation stations by clicking the plus sign in the Superelevation Tabular Editor. Initially, the lane and shoulder slopes will be blank in a manually added station. Use the Superelevation Tabular Editor to rename the special regions and set the slopes as needed.

Calculating Cants for Rail

In the civil engineering industry, the terms *superelevation* and *cant* are used interchangeably. Inside Civil 3D, the terms have distinct meanings. Superelevation tools in Civil 3D are used for roads; the cross-slope changes within a curve are expressed by a percentage. Cant applies to railways in Civil 3D and is expressed as a difference in height between the outer and inner rails (Figure 11.19).

FIGURE 11.19

Example cant curve data table

Cant Curve	Start Station	End Station	Length	Applied Cant	Equ
⊟ Curve.1					
⊟ Transition In Region	4+75.44'	8+42.44'	367.000'		
End Level Rail	4+75.44'			0.000"	0.000
Begin Curve	6+58.94'				2.047
Begin Full Cant	8+42.44'			0.400"	2.047
⊟ Transition Out Region	13+86.97'	15+22.24'	135.264'		
End Full Cant	13+86.97'			0.400"	2.047
Begin Level Rail	15+22.24'			0.000"	2.047
⊟ Curve.2					
⊟ Transition In Region	15+22.24'	17+91.31'	269.074'		
End Level Rail	15+22.24'			0.000"	0.000

Preparing for Cants

To work with cant, the following must be in place:

Alignment Type Set to Rail   Normally, you would set the alignment type when you first define the alignment. If you forget to set this initially, you can change it at any time in the Alignment properties on the Information tab.

Alignment Design Speed   Like motorways and superelevation, rail requires a design speed in order to apply cant. Cant design standards are provided with the software and can be edited in the same manner as other design criteria files.

Cant Calculation   Like superelevation, cant is attached to an alignment and its curves. As shown in Figure 11.20, the icon's location in the Alignment contextual tab should be reminiscent of the superelevation button.

FIGURE 11.20

Accessing the Cant Calculation tools from the Rail Alignment contextual tab

Rail Assembly   When working with an assembly for rail, the type must be set to Railway. You can set this on assembly creation or in the Assembly properties after the fact.

There is one subassembly that is purpose-built for cant, the RailSingle subassembly, shown in Figure 11.21. If you are working with a drawing created in a release prior to 2013, make sure you replace the old assemblies with this new rail subassembly to ensure cant takes place. You can verify the version by checking Advanced Parameters ➢ Version in the AutoCAD Properties palette.

FIGURE 11.21
The RailSingle
subassembly

Creating a Rail Assembly

You will find the RailSingle subassembly in the Bridge And Rail tab of the tool palettes. The following exercise will walk you through creating a typical rail bed design:

1. Open the drawing 1104_Rail.dwg (1104_Rail_METRIC.dwg), which you can download from this book's website.

   This drawing contains an alignment and design profile.

2. On the Home tab ➢ Create Design panel, choose Assembly ➢ Create Assembly.

3. Name the assembly **Rail w Service Road**.

4. Set Assembly Type to Railway, and click OK.

5. Click to place the assembly in a blank area anywhere in the graphic.

6. Open the subassembly tool palettes if they are not already open. In the subassembly tool palettes, locate the Bridge And Rail palette, and click RailSingle. In the Properties palette, make the following changes:

   a. Set the subballast width to **20′ (6 m)**.

   b. Set the subballast side slope to **0.001:1**.

   Leave all other parameters at their defaults.

7. Click the assembly to place the RailSingle subassembly.

8. Switch to the Basic tab of the subassembly tool palettes, and click GenericPavementStructure.

   This will be your service road, constructed out of the same material as the subballast.

9. Enter the following data into the Properties palette, remembering that the codes are case sensitive:

   a. Set Side to **Left**.

   b. Set Width to **8′ (2.5 m)**.

   c. Set Depth to **1′ (0.3 m)**.

   d. Set DeflectOuterVerticalFace to **Yes**.

   e. Set Outer Edge Slope to **2.00:1**.

   f. Set TopLink Codes to **Top**, and set BottomLink Codes to **Datum**.

   g. Set Shape Codes to Subballast.

10. When your parameters resemble Figure 11.22, click to place the GenericPavementStructure to the left of the subballast rail subassembly.

FIGURE 11.22
Advanced
Parameters for
service road

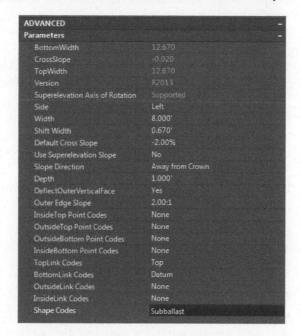

ADVANCED	
Parameters	
BottomWidth	12.670
CrossSlope	-0.020
TopWidth	12.670
Version	R2013
Superelevation Axis of Rotation	Supported
Side	Left
Width	8.000'
Shift Width	0.670'
Default Cross Slope	-2.00%
Use Superelevation Slope	No
Slope Direction	Away from Crown
Depth	1.000'
DeflectOuterVerticalFace	Yes
Outer Edge Slope	2.00:1
InsideTop Point Codes	None
OutsideTop Point Codes	None
OutsideBottom Point Codes	None
InsideBottom Point Codes	None
TopLink Codes	Top
BottomLink Codes	Datum
OutsideLink Codes	None
InsideLink Codes	None
Shape Codes	Subballast

11. Remain in the GenericPavementStructure tool, but change the width to **0.1'** (0.03 m) and the side to Right.

12. Click to place the structure on the right side of the rail subassembly.

13. Switch to the Generic palette, and click LinkSlopeToSurface.

14. Set Slope to **-50**, and click the "tip" of the generic pavement structure on both sides of the assembly.

Your completed assembly will look like Figure 11.23.

FIGURE 11.23
Your completed rail
assembly

15. Save and close the drawing.

Compare your work with 1104_Rail_FINISHED.dwg or 1104_Rail_METRIC_FINISHED .dwg to see how you fared.

Applying Cant to the Alignment

Like superelevation in a roadway alignment, cant is related to a rail alignment. The following exercise will walk you through applying cant to the alignment. You should experience a distinct feeling of déjà vu if you completed earlier exercises involving applying superelevation to the alignment.

1. Open the drawing 1105_RailAlignment.dwg (1105_RailAlignment_METRIC.dwg), which you can download from this book's website.

   This drawing contains a corridor with rail; your task is to update the alignment to apply cant. Observe the section views in the drawing (shown in the lower modelspace viewport in the file). Zoom into one of these section views so that the cant can be seen immediately after it is calculated. Each is created at a location on the curve that should have cant applied. However, these views currently show flat rails.

2. Select the alignment from the upper viewport. From the Rail Alignment contextual tab ➤ Modify panel, click Cant ➤ Calculate/Edit Cant.

3. Click Calculate Cant Now.

4. Keep the pivot method as Low Side Rail, and click Next.

5. Place a check mark next to Automatically Resolve Overlap.

6. Set the Applied Cant Table setting to Freight Train Applied Cant Table (metric users, use Mixed Passenger And Freight Cant).

7. Leave all other settings at their defaults, and click Finish.

   Panorama opens showing the Cant Tabular Editor, as shown in Figure 11.24.

FIGURE 11.24
The Cant Tabular Editor

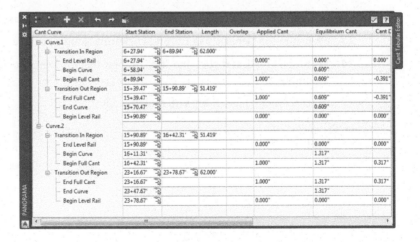

Cant Curve	Start Station	End Station	Length	Overlap	Applied Cant	Equilibrium Cant	Cant D
Curve.1							
Transition In Region	6+27.94'	6+89.94'	62.000'				
End Level Rail	6+27.94'				0.000"	0.000"	0.000"
Begin Curve	6+58.94'					0.609"	
Begin Full Cant	6+89.94'				1.000"	0.609"	-0.391"
Transition Out Region	15+39.47'	15+90.89'	51.419'				
End Full Cant	15+39.47'				1.000"	0.609"	-0.391"
End Curve	15+70.47'					0.609"	
Begin Level Rail	15+90.89'				0.000"	0.000"	0.000"
Curve.2							
Transition In Region	15+90.89'	16+42.31'	51.419'				
End Level Rail	15+90.89'				0.000"	0.000"	0.000"
Begin Curve	16+11.31'					1.317"	
Begin Full Cant	16+42.31'				1.000"	1.317"	0.317"
Transition Out Region	23+16.67'	23+78.67'	62.000'				
End Full Cant	23+16.67'				1.000"	1.317"	0.317"
End Curve	23+47.67'					1.317"	
Begin Level Rail	23+78.67'				0.000"	0.000"	0.000"

8. In Prospector, right-click and rebuild the Hiawatha corridor.

   You should observe in the lower viewport that your section views show the cant applied to the design. Check your design against 1105_RailAlignment_FINISHED.dwg or 1105_RailAlignment_METRIC_FINISHED.dwg if desired.

Superelevation and Cant Views

Superelevation and cant views are a graphic representation of the roadway or rail superelevation. Grip edits to the graphical view will also edit the superelevation stations. The view itself is not intended for plotting. The superelevation view plots station against lane slope to form a graph of the left and right edges of the pavement.

In the following exercise, you will create a superelevation view:

1. Open the drawing 1106_SuperView.dwg (1106_SuperView_METRIC.dwg), which you can download from this book's website.

   The alignment in this file already has superelevation calculated for it. Your task is to create the superelevation view.

2. Select the Route 66 alignment by clicking it in the graphic.

3. From the Alignment contextual tab ➤ Modify panel, click Superelevation ➤ Create Superelevation View, as shown in Figure 11.25.

FIGURE 11.25
Creating a superelevation view

4. In the Create Superelevation View dialog, set the colors for the lane and shoulder slopes, as shown in Figure 11.26, by double-clicking the ByBlock field and picking the colors indicated.

FIGURE 11.26
Set colors for different assembly components to easily differentiate them in the superelevation view.

5. Click OK and then click in the graphic to place the superelevation view. Your result should look like Figure 11.27.

FIGURE 11.27
The superelevation
view for the Route
66 alignment

6. Save the file for use in the next exercise.

At first glance, the superelevation view may seem difficult to read, but with a little explanation it can shed a lot of light on what is going on with your lane and shoulder slopes. The superelevation graphic plots the station value against the percent cross-slope of each edge of pavement and edge of shoulder. The upper line shows the lane edges, and the lower line shows the shoulder edges.

Where no superelevation is applied, the graph data for the lanes remains at -2 percent, while the shoulders are shown at their default cross-slope of -5 percent. As the assembly twists into position during superelevation, the distances between the lines become greater as the outside lane edge slopes up to a maximum superelevation of 4 percent.

There are a few more observations you can make about your superelevation view. No overlap exists between the two curves' superelevation data. You can tell this by observing the center portion of the graph; the superelevation lines go back to the default cross-slope. The astute observer can ascertain by looking at this graph that a maximum breakover slope of 8 percent was used on the shoulder. How can you tell? By seeing that when the lanes are in max super (i.e., the lane is at +4 percent slope), the shoulder slope jumps up to -4 percent.

Using a Superelevation View to Edit Data

Next, you will use the superelevation view to edit superelevation data. Editing superelevation data by the superelevation view is an alternative to editing the data in tabular form, as you learned about earlier.

The diamond-shaped grips can be slid in one axis to modify stationing (the horizontally oriented grips) or slope (the vertically oriented grips). The rectangular grip can be moved to reduce the maximum lane slope when it is in a full-super state, as shown in Table 11.1.

In the following exercise, you will use the superelevation view to remove the normal crown area in the middle of the alignment. In other words, you will force the curves to transition directly from one to the other. You will also adjust the rate of maximum superelevation.

TABLE 11.1: Superelevation view grips

SUPERELEVATION VIEW SYMBOL	MEANING
	Blue, vertical, diamond-shaped grips are at superelevation critical stations where a grade break occurs at that station. Vertically oriented grips can be moved up or down to change the slopes associated with them.
	Blue, horizontal, diamond-shaped grips are at superelevation stations. Horizontally oriented grips change the value of superelevation stations.
	Blue, rectangular grips will appear at locations of constant slope. These can be moved up or down to change the superelevation cross-slope.
	Gray, vertical, diamond-shaped grips are at superelevation critical stations, but no grade breaks occur at the location. Vertically oriented grips can be moved up or down to change the slopes associated with them.
	The plus sign next to any grip indicates that more than one item is the same slope at that station.

1. Continue working in the drawing 1106_SuperView.dwg (1106_SuperView_METRIC.dwg). You need to have completed the previous exercise before continuing.

2. Isolate the right-outside lane line in the superelevation view by holding down Ctrl as you click the red line.

   Hint: If you are not sure which line represents the various superelevation slopes, pause your cursor over the line to get a tooltip showing the line's information.

3. Pause your cursor (without clicking) over the blue grip at station 5+73.47 (0+175.06 in the metric drawing).

4. Select Remove Grade Break from the grip menu, as shown in Figure 11.28. Press Esc after the grip is removed.

FIGURE 11.28
The grip menu at the superelevation critical station

5. Repeat steps 3 and 4 to remove the grade break at 8+35.56 (0+258.53 in the metric drawing).

6. Press Esc to clear your selection.

7. Hold down Ctrl and select the green line representing the left-outside lane.

8. Using the same technique as before, remove the grade break at stations 6+93.47 (0+207.56 in the metric drawing) and 9+39.31 (0+286.03 in the metric drawing). Press Esc to clear the selection when complete.

9. Turn on dynamic input (F12 on your keyboard) if it is not already on.

10. Click your superelevation view to select it. All of the grips should be available.

11. Click the flat blue grip in the first left-outside shoulder region just after station 1+09.41 (0+039.60 in the metric drawing). The grip will be associated with the cyan line.

12. In the dynamic input box, enter **-4.5**, as shown in Figure 11.29, and then press Enter.

FIGURE 11.29
Changing the slope using grips and dynamic input

The shoulder slope has been changed slightly to match existing conditions.

13. Save the file.

Compare your work to 1106_SuperView_FINISHED.dwg or 1106_SuperView_METRIC_FINISHED.dwg if desired.

The Bottom Line

Add superelevation to an alignment.   Civil 3D has convenient and flexible tools that will apply superelevation to an alignment curve using AASHTO standards.

> **Master It**   Open the MasterIt1101.dwg (MasterIt1101_METRIC.dwg) file, which you can download from www.sybex.com/go/masteringcivil3d2016. Verify that the design speed of the road is 20 miles per hour (35 km per hour) and apply superelevation to the entire length of the alignment. Use AASHTO 2011 design criteria with an eMax of 6 percent for a two-lane, crowned roadway. Use the option to automatically resolve overlap.

Create a superelevation assembly.   For superelevation to happen, you need to have an assembly that is capable of superelevation.

> **Master It**   Continue working in MasterIt1101.dwg (MasterIt1101_METRIC.dwg). You must have completed the previous exercise before starting this one. Create an undivided crowned road assembly named AOR similar to the one in the top image shown earlier in the chapter in Figure 11.10. Set each lane to be **14′ (4.5 m)** wide and each shoulder to be **6′ (2 m)** wide. Set the Use Superelevation parameter to Right Lane Outside and Left Lane Outside. Leave all other options at their defaults. If time permits, build a corridor based on the alignment and assembly.

Create a rail corridor with cant.   Cant tools allow users to create corridors that meet design criteria specific to rail needs.

> **Master It**   In the drawing MasterIt1102.dwg (MasterIt1102_METRIC.dwg), create a Railway assembly named Rail with the RailSingle subassembly using the default parameters for width and depth. Add a LinkSlopeToSurface generic link with 50 percent slope to each side. Add cant to the alignment in the drawing using the default settings for attainment. Create a corridor named Rail from these pieces using the design profile and daylighting to the existing intersection.

Create a superelevation view.   Superelevation views are a great place to get a handle on what is going on in your roadway design. You can visually check the geometry as well as make changes to the design.

> **Master It**   Open the drawing MasterIt1103.dwg (MasterIt1103_METRIC.dwg). Create a superelevation view for the alignment. Show only the left and right outside lanes as blue and red, respectively.

Cross Sections and Mass Haul

Cross sections are used in the Autodesk® AutoCAD® Civil 3D® program to allow the user to have a graphic confirmation of design intent as well as to calculate the quantities of materials used in a design. All that is needed for section creation is an alignment and a surface. Other objects, such as pipes, structures, and corridor components, can be sampled in a sample line group, which is used to create the graphical section displayed in a section view. These section views and sections remain dynamic throughout the design process, reflecting any changes made to the sampled information. The result is a plot-worthy set of section views and accurate end area volume information.

In this chapter, you will learn to:

- ◆ Create sample lines.
- ◆ Create section views.
- ◆ Define and compute materials.
- ◆ Generate volume reports.

Section Workflow

When the time comes that you want to see how the information along your alignment will appear plotted, you can create sample lines. If your goal is to show your completed design, at this point you should have a completed corridor, corridor top surface, and corridor datum surface.

Comparing Sample Lines and Frequency Lines

Sample lines are created at any stations where you want to create a *section view*. Sample lines are also used to compute end area volumes.

A common point of confusion with new users is the difference between *frequency lines* and *sample lines*. Table 12.1 explains the differences.

TABLE 12.1: Sample lines vs. frequency lines

SAMPLE LINES AND SECTION VIEWS	FREQUENCY LINES AND SECTION EDITOR
Sample lines can be created without a corridor present (e.g., when you want to see existing surface sections along the alignment).	Frequency lines are only part of a corridor.
Sample lines occur at any station where a section view or end area is needed.	Frequency lines occur anywhere the design needs to be calculated or modified (e.g., at certain station intervals, a driveway).
Sample lines are used for end area volume computation.	Frequency lines are used to apply assembly calculations to the design (e.g., locating slope-intercept).
Sample lines can be skewed at an angle other than 90° from the baseline.	Frequency lines are always perpendicular to the baseline.
Sample line swath width is usually uniform and dependent on user plotting needs.	Frequency lines' length from baseline depends on assembly and will vary from station to station.
Section views are read-only reflections of the design.	Design can be modified in the Section Editor at each frequency line.
Section views are readily adapted to plotting.	Plotting should never occur from the Section Editor.

When you create your sample line group, you will have the option to sample any surface in your drawing, including corridor surfaces, the corridor assembly itself, and pipes. The sections are then sampled along the alignment with the left and right *swath widths* specified and at the intervals specified. After you create sample lines, you can create section views or define materials for end area volume calculations.

Creating Sample Lines

A sample line is a powerful tool needed for both section view creation and end area material computations. Sample lines are created in batches and stored in *sample line groups*. A sample line group is always associated with an alignment and can be found under the associated alignment in Prospector, as shown in Figure 12.1.

FIGURE 12.1
A view of Prospector; sample lines are stored in sample line groups and are dependent on an alignment

You can also see in Figure 12.1 that quite a few additional items are dependent on sample lines, such as *sections, section view groups, mass haul lines, mass haul views,* and *material lists.* If you click a sample line, you will be presented with three types of grips, as shown in Figure 12.2.

FIGURE 12.2
The three grips on a typical sample line

The grips are intended for changes to a sample line that cannot be accomplished through the sample line group properties. The diamond-shaped grip at the alignment location will allow you to slide the sample line to a different station. The triangular grips at the ends of a sample line allow you to extend the sample line swath width while maintaining its angle in relation to the alignment. The square grips on the sample line will allow you to change the length and angle of the sample line. If you have used the square grip to skew a sample line but want to return it to its original perpendicular state, select the sample line, right-click, and then select Make Orthogonal from the menu, as shown in Figure 12.3. Note that this command is available only from the context menu, not in the ribbon tab.

FIGURE 12.3
Removing the skew with the Make Orthgonal command

To create a sample line group, follow these steps:

1. Change to the Home tab ➤ Profile & Section Views panel and choose Sample Lines.

2. Select the appropriate alignment.

   The Create Sample Line Group dialog, shown in Figure 12.4, will appear.

3. Name the sample line group and verify the sample line and label styles.

FIGURE 12.4
Click the Sample Lines icon to open the Create Sample Line Group dialog.

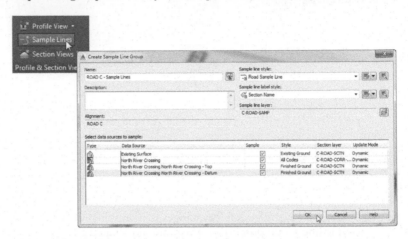

Every source object that is available will be displayed at the bottom of this box. If you want to omit specific data from the section view, you can clear the check box. Set the applicable style for each item by clicking in the column to the right of the object. The section layer should be preset as specified in your template Object Layers settings.

Once you've selected the sample data and clicked OK, the Sample Line Tools toolbar will become active (Figure 12.5).

FIGURE 12.5
From the Sample Line Tools toolbar, choose By Range Of Stations.

The By Range Of Stations option is used most often. You can use At A Station to create one sample line at a specific station. From Corridor Stations will insert a sample line at the same locations as corridor frequency stations. Pick Points On Screen allows you to pick any two (or more) points to define a sample line. This option can be useful in special situations, such as sampling a pipe on a skew or cross sections for drainage area calculations. The last option, Select Existing Polylines, lets you define sample lines from existing polylines. Like Pick Points On Screen, this tool is useful in the case of cross sections for drainage area calculations.

To define sample lines, you need to specify a few settings. Figure 12.6 shows these settings in the Create Sample Lines – By Station Range dialog.

FIGURE 12.6
Create Sample
Lines – By Station
Range dialog

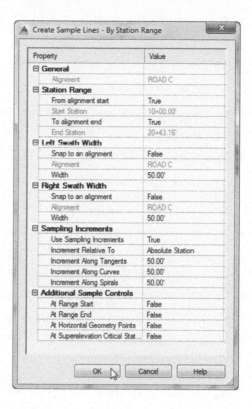

Station Range   Station Range controls where on your alignment sample lines are created. By default, the dialog picks up the start and end stations of the alignment. Change the station range by changing From Alignment Start or To Alignment End to False and setting the desired stations.

Left/Right Swath Width   Swath width is the offset from the alignment along which you create sample lines. When using sample lines for end area volume calculations, be sure that the swath width is large enough to encompass the design but not so large that they overlap in curve areas. You can change the Snap To An Alignment option to True if you want to force your sample lines to stop at an alignment that is not a constant offset from the centerline.

Sampling Increments   Sampling Increments allows you to choose the interval at which sample lines are created. Notice that you can control the sample line interval separately along tangents, curves, and spirals.

Additional Sample Controls   Additional Sample Controls adds a sample line at the beginning, end, and other special stations, such as horizontal geometry (PC, PT, and so on) and superelevation critical stations.

In the following exercise, you'll create sample lines for ROAD C alignment:

1. Open the 1201_SampleLines.dwg (1201_SampleLines_METRIC.dwg) file, which you can download from this book's web page at www.sybex.com/go/masteringcivil3d2016.

2. From the Home tab ➤ Profile & Section Views panel, choose Sample Lines.

3. At the `Select an alignment, <or press enter key to select from list>:` prompt, press ↵ to display the Select Alignment dialog.

4. Select the ROAD C alignment and click OK.

   The Create Sample Line Group dialog opens.

5. In the Create Sample Line Group dialog, follow these steps:

   a. Name the group **ROAD C - Sample Lines**.

   b. Set Existing Surface to the Existing Ground style, if not already set, by selecting that style from the Style column. (Hint: The first click will activate the cell, and the second click will give you the list of styles.)

   c. Set the style for both the Top and Datum corridor surfaces to Finished Ground.

      The column is too narrow to view the full names of the items, so to see the name of the item, pause your cursor over the name or expand the column.

   d. Set the corridor North River Crossing style to All Codes.

6. Leave the default settings for Sample Line Style and Sample Line Label Style.

7. When your dialog looks similar to Figure 12.4 (your sampled items may be listed in a different order), click OK.

8. On the Sample Line Tools toolbar, click the Sample Line Creation Methods drop-down arrow and then choose By Range Of Stations.

9. In the Create Sample Lines – By Station Range dialog, leave the swath widths and sampling increments at their defaults (this will be 50.00" for Imperial units and 20.00 m for metric units).

10. Make sure that both the At Range Start and At Range End options are set to False, as shown earlier in Figure 12.6.

11. Click OK, and press ↵ to end the command.

12. If you receive a Panorama view telling you that your corridor is out of date and may require rebuilding, dismiss it by clicking the green check box.

    You should now have dashed lines at even station intervals; these are your new sample lines.

13. Save the drawing for use in the next exercise.

Check your completed drawings at this stage against 1201_SampleLines_A.dwg or 1201_SampleLines_A_METRIC.dwg if desired.

Editing the Swath Width of a Sample Line Group

There may come a time when you need to show information outside the limits of your section views or not show as much information. To edit the width of a section view, you will have to change the swath width of a sample line group. These sample lines can be edited manually on an individual basis, or you can edit the entire group at once.

SAMPLE LINE AND SECTION VIEW WORDS OF WISDOM

It is extremely rare to encounter situations where you need to touch each sample line or section view individually. From the contextual tab, select a sample line or section view to access many tools that will save time (and your sanity).

YOU WANT TO CHANGE ALL THE SAMPLE LINE LENGTHS

To change many swath widths at once, use this process:

1. Click the sample line contextual tab ➤ Modify panel ➤ Group Properties icon to open the Sample Line Group Properties dialog; then switch to the Sample Lines tab.

2. Select the first station of the range you want to change and hold down Shift as you click the last row. All the stations in between will be selected as well.

3. Click the offset distance to change the swath widths as desired. Upon entering the desired value, all the selected offsets will reflect that value.

Continues

Continued

You will need to change both the left and right offsets because they are independent from each other.

YOU WANT TO ADD OR REMOVE SECTION DATA IN MANY VIEWS

A common situation with sections is that surface or corridor data you've created after you created sample lines does not appear in your cross sections. This is easily rectified; follow these steps:

1. Click the Sample More Sources button. (Hint: You can get to this directly from the contextual tab or from the Sample Line Group Properties dialog's Sections tab.)

   Data that exists but that is not recognized by the sample lines will appear to the left. The sampled data that is recognized and used by the sample lines will appear on the right.

2. Highlight the data you want to add and click Add.

In this exercise, you'll edit the widths of an entire sample line group:

1. Continue working on the 1201_SampleLines.dwg (1201_SampleLines_METRIC.dwg) file or open 1201_SampleLines_A.dwg (1201_SampleLines_A_METRIC.dwg).

2. Select a sample line.

3. From the Sample Line contextual tab ➤ Modify panel, click Group Properties.

4. Switch to the Sample Lines tab.

5. Click to select the first sample line in the listing at station 10+50.00 (0+320.00).

   a. Scroll down to the bottom of the list.

   b. While holding the Shift key, select the last station in the listing. This will highlight all rows.

    c. Click your mouse in the Left Offset column and change it to **100"** (**30 m**). Press ↵ to complete the edit.

    The left offsets will change in the listing. If you have a long list of sample lines in a project, it may take a moment to update.

    d. With all of the rows still highlighted, make the same change to the Right Offset column.

6. Click OK.

After a moment, the sample lines will resize to reflect your change. The Event Viewer panorama might appear.

7. Save the drawing.

Check your completed drawings against 1201_SampleLines_FINISHED.dwg or 1201_SampleLines_METRIC_FINISHED.dwg if desired.

Creating Section Views

Once the sample line group is created, it is time to create views. You can create a single view or many views arranged together (Figure 12.7).

FIGURE 12.7
Section views arranged to plot by page

A section view is a reflection of the road design for the specific location defined by its corresponding sample line and can be used for plotting purposes. No edits to the corridor, surface, or other design elements can be made from a section view. The view contains horizontal and vertical grids, tick marks for axis annotation, the axis annotation itself, and a title. Views can also be configured to show horizontal geometry, such as the centerline of the section, edges of pavement, and rights of way. Tables displaying end areas or volumes can also be shown with the sections.

Also new to the current release is the possibility to change the direction of the section view (similar to the profile view) using the style dialog box. This is helpful for the hydrology users, for whom the analyzed rivers are built downstream, but the section views need to be created upstream. You can find more detailed information about the editing of the styles that define the views in Chapter 19, "Object Styles."

Creating a Single-Section View

There are occasions when all section views are not needed. In these situations, you can create a single-section view. In this exercise, you'll create a single-section view of station 15 + 00.00 (0+460.00 for metric users) from a sample line:

1. Open the 1202_SectionViews.dwg (1202_SectionViews_METRIC.dwg) file, which you can download from this book's web page.

   You will want to switch to this drawing because there are a few steps completed for you that you will learn about later in the chapter.

2. Select the sample line at 15+00.00 (0+460.00 for metric users).

3. From the Sample Line contextual tab ➤ Launch Pad panel, choose Create Section View ➤ Create Section View.

4. Verify that your alignment and sample line group name are correct on the General page of the wizard, shown in Figure 12.8.

FIGURE 12.8
The General page of the Create Section View Wizard

You can navigate from one page to another by either clicking Next at the bottom of the screen or clicking the links on the left side of the screen.

5. Click Next to view the Offset Range page.

   The top of Figure 12.9 shows the Offset Range page, which should match your sample line swath width. In this case, you will leave this set to Automatic. No action is needed on the Offset Range page.

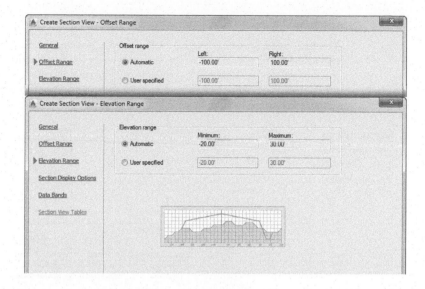

FIGURE 12.9
The Offset Range page (top) and Elevation Range page (bottom) of the Create Section View Wizard

6. Click Next to view the Elevation Range page.

The bottom of Figure 12.9 shows the Elevation Range page. The values shown here are taken from your design maximum and minimum elevations. In this case, and in most cases, you will leave this set to Automatic. No action is needed on the Elevation Range page.

7. Click Next to view the Section Display Options page. Change all three surface label sets to _No Labels by clicking in the Label Set column for each surface item.

The fourth page contains the section display options, as shown in Figure 12.10. This page reflects the styles and data you selected when creating your sample lines. If you forgot to set a style or want to omit additional data, you can change your options here.

FIGURE 12.10
The Section Display Options page of the Create Section View Wizard

8. Click Next to view the Data Bands page.

The fifth page, shown in Figure 12.11, lets you specify the data band options. Here, you can select band sets to add to the section view, pick the location of the band, and choose the surfaces to be referenced in the bands. The data bands used in this example show only offset distance (rather than offset and elevation), and therefore no action is needed on the Data Bands page.

FIGURE 12.11
The Data Bands page of the Create Section View Wizard

9. Click Next to view the Section View Tables page.

The sixth and last page, shown in Figure 12.12, is where you set up the section view tables. Note that this screen will be available only if you have already computed materials for the sample line group. On this page, you can select the type of table and the table style and select the position of the table relative to the section view. The graphic on the lower-right side of the window will help to illustrate the table placement and changes as you update these settings.

FIGURE 12.12
The Section View Tables page of the Create Section View Wizard

10. With the table type set to Total Volume and Select Table Style set to Basic, click Add.

As shown in Figure 12.12, you will have a row of data indicating that a material table will come in to the right of your view. Make sure that X Offset is set to 0.5 (10 for metric users).

11. Click the Create Section View button.

12. Pick any point in the drawing area to place your section view.

13. Examine your section view.

The display should resemble Figure 12.13.

14. Save the drawing for use in the next exercise.

FIGURE 12.13
The finished
section view

Check your completed drawings at this stage against 1201_SectionViews_A.dwg or 1201_SectionViews_A_METRIC.dwg if desired.

Creating Multiple Section Views

Certification
Objective

Even though many times you can create individual section views, most of the times you will get them packed in the groups so that they are easy to set in page and plot. In the exercise that follows, you will create section views intended to plot together on a sheet:

1. Continue working in 1202_SectionViews.dwg (1202_SectionViews_METRIC.dwg) or open 1202_SectionViews_A.dwg (1201_SectionViews_A_METRIC.dwg). You do not need to have completed the previous exercise to continue.

2. Change your drawing scale to **1" = 20'** (**1:500** for metric users) from the lower-right corner of the application window and select any sample line.

3. From the Sample Line contextual tab ➤ Launch Pad panel, choose Create Section View ➤ Create Multiple Section Views.

Alternatively, you can access this tool from the Home tab ➤ Profile & Section Views panel ➤ Section Views ➤ Create Multiple Views.

4. On the General page, set the Section View Style option to Road Section, if not already set, and leave all the other settings at the default. Click Next.

5. On the Section Placement page, click the ellipsis button next to the path for Template For Cross Section Sheet.

6. From the default cross section sheet template, select ARCH D Section 20 Scale (ISO A1 Section 1 to 500 for metric users), as shown in Figure 12.14, and click OK.

FIGURE 12.14

When you're creating multiple views, the scale and spacing of the final product depend on layouts from sheet templates.

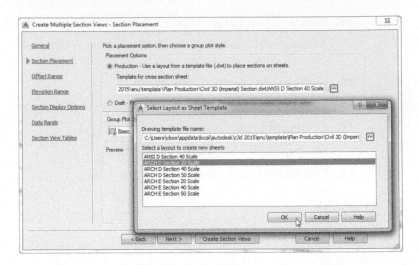

The Civil 3D default cross section template should be `Civil 3D (Imperial) Section .dwt` or `Civil 3D (Metric) Section.dwt`. Each scale listed in the dialog box (Figure 12.14) relates to a layout tab in the section template file. You can also set up your own templates based on these layouts, but it is important to note that the viewports set for the sections must be assigned the section type in the Viewport object AutoCAD properties.

7. Leave Group Plot Style set to Basic and click Next.

When placing a single section view instead of multiple section views, you will not see the Section Placement Page shown in Figure 12.14. Use the Production option when your final purpose is to use the plan production tools for section sheets found on the Output tab. The Draft option forces Civil 3D to behave like version 2010 and prior. Do not use the Draft option if you intend to run the Create Section Sheets command with the section views.

Group Plot Style controls how the views are arranged on a page. In this example, the grid will come from the group plot style rather than the section view style.

You can skip the rest of the wizard because you will keep the default input for the remainder of the settings.

8. Click the Create Section Views button.

9. Click anywhere off to the right of the graphic to place the views.

You should see views arranged on the screen (Figure 12.15). Metric users will see two pages of section views, and Imperial unit users will see three pages of section views. Notice that the scale chosen in the Select Layout As Sheet dialog box matches the annotative scale of the drawing, creating a neat, coherent set of section views.

FIGURE 12.15
One of the pages
of cross-section
views

10. Save the drawing for use in the next exercise.

Check your completed drawings at this stage against 1202_SectionViews_B.dwg or 1202_SectionViews_B_METRIC.dwg if desired.

Section Views and Annotation Scale

In the previous section, you created section views using a cross-section sheet template. You chose a scale for the section sheet layout at the same time that you picked a page size. Coincidentally, the scale you used in the exercise was already set as the annotation scale. Since both scales agreed with each other, everything came out nicely.

Depending on what portion of the design you are working on, the scale of the sections and the scale you are comfortable working with may not agree. Additionally, you may just forget to set the scale ahead of placing section views.

Ideally, your section views and their sheets should be in a drawing separate from the corridor and the rest of the design. In Chapter 16, "Advanced Workflows," you will learn how to do this using data shortcuts.

DELETE SECTION VIEWS THE PAIN-FREE WAY

The best way to remove an unwanted batch of section views from your graphic is to delete them through Prospector. In the following image, you can see that the intrepid user tried (and apparently failed) multiple times before creating the desired view group.

Continues

Continued

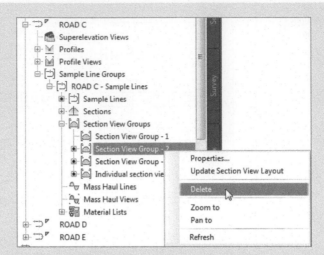

If you delete views graphically, you'll create more work for yourself. First, the section view group stays behind in Prospector, as you could see in the previous image.

As indicated by the dot in front of the group in the first image, three section views groups contain information.

The second problem with graphically deleting your section views is that Civil 3D interprets this maneuver as removing data from the sample lines. The next time you create sections, not all of the data you expect will be there. In this case, you would need to use the Sample More Sources tool to bring back the missing data.

The best way to delete section view groups is by right-clicking the group in Prospector and selecting Delete, as shown in the first image in this sidebar.

It is helpful to learn how to work with annotation scale and section views. In the following exercise, you will go through a brief lesson in reorganizing sections:

1. If you completed the previous exercise, continue working in your open file; otherwise, open 1202_SectionViews_B.dwg (1202_SectionViews_B_METRIC.dwg).

2. Select the Annotation scale in the lower-right portion of the screen.

3. Change the scale to **1"=10'** (**1:250** mm).

   The views probably look pretty funky—and not in a good way. The page has gotten smaller, but the views have not updated.

4. Select any section view by clicking the station value.

5. From the Section View contextual tab ➤ Modify View panel, click Update Group Layout.

6. Save and close the drawing.

   The views should now be reorganized to a better-looking state.

Check your completed drawings against 1202_SectionViews_FINISHED.dwg or 1202_SectionViews_METRIC_FINISHED.dwg if desired.

SECTION VIEW OBJECT PROJECTION

Civil 3D has the ability to project AutoCAD points, blocks, 3D solids, 3D polylines, Civil 3D COGO points, feature lines, and survey figures to section views. Each of the objects listed can be projected to a section view and labeled appropriately.

In the following exercise, you will project several COGO points and an AutoCAD cylinder solid to a section view:

1. Open the drawing 1203_SectionProjection.dwg (1203_SectionProjection_METRIC.dwg).

2. On the Home tab ➤ Profile & Section Views panel, choose Section Views ➤ Project Objects To Multiple Section Views.

3. When prompted at the command line Select a sample line or a section view:, select any sample line in the drawing.

4. In the Project Objects To Multiple Section Views dialog, switch the projection rule to the By Distance option.

5. Change Distance Before and Distance After to **25** (**10** for metric users).

   The distance before and distance after tell Civil 3D how far away from the sample line to look for objects for projection.

Continues

Continued

This tool will pick up all of the object types listed in the Name column that it encounters. If you do not want a certain type of object to be projected to a section view, clear the check box. For Cogo Points, Feature Lines, and Survey Figures, the default behavior for the tool is to use the object style section settings. You can override this by clicking in the Style field and choosing a projection style. For all other objects listed in this dialog box, a projection style must be specified. The elevation for the projected object can be taken from the object or a surface or set to Manual, in which case you will be able to edit the Elevation Value field.

Many other Civil 3D objects, such as pipes, structures, and surfaces, do not appear in this list because they can be picked up by sample lines for display in section views.

6. Leave the default settings for all other options and click OK.

7. Examine your section views. For example, take a look at the section at station 10+50.00 (0+320.00 for metric users). You should now see additional information in that section view representing objects that would have not been visible in section view without this command.

8. Save and close the drawing.

Check your completed drawings against 1203_SectionProjection_FINISHED.dwg or 1203_SectionProjection_METRIC_FINISHED.dwg if desired.

Real World Scenario

SHOWING ROW LINES IN CROSS-SECTION VIEWS

The trick you are about to learn will come in handy for more than just showing right-of-way locations in cross section. Any item that is alignment-based can work the same way.

1. Open the drawing 1204_SectionROW.dwg (1204_SectionROW_METRIC.dwg).

2. Select any sample line and then, from the Sample Line contextual tab ➤ Modify panel, click Group Properties.

3. Switch to the Section Views tab.

4. Locate the Profile Grade column for the section view group. You may need to expand the columns to read their names.

5. Select Section View Group – 1 and then click the ellipsis button in the Profile Grade column, as shown here.

The offset alignments representing the ROW location have been added to the drawing. An existing ground profile has been created for you as well. You will use this information to place the ROW symbol in the cross-section graphic.

6. Set ROAD C-Left-ROW as the active alignment in the list and click Add.

7. Repeat step 6 for ROAD C-Right-ROW.

8. Set the Marker Style option for both left and right alignments to ROW.

Continues

Continued

9. Click OK several times until you are out of all dialog boxes.

You should now have a ROW symbol whose insertion offset was determined by the alignment and whose elevation was from the surface profile.

Check your completed drawings against 1204_SectionROW_FINISHED.dwg or 1204_SectionROW_METRIC_FINISHED.dwg if desired.

Calculating and Reporting Volumes

Once alignments are sampled, volumes can be calculated from the sampled surface or from the corridor section shape. These volumes are calculated in a materials list and can be displayed as a label on each section view or in an overall volume table, as shown in Figure 12.16.

The volumes can also be displayed in an Extensible Markup Language (XML) report, as shown in Figure 12.17.

Once you create a materials list, you can edit it to include more materials or modify the existing materials. For example, you can enter soil expansion (fluff or swell) and shrinkage factors to make the volumes more accurately match the true field conditions. This can make cost estimates more accurate, which can result in fewer surprises during the construction phase of any given project.

Total Volume Table						
Station	Fill Area	Cut Area	Fill Volume	Cut Volume	Cumulative Fill Vol	Cumulative Cut Vol
10+50.00	33.99	9.21	0.00	0.00	0.00	0.00
11+00.00	30.21	13.10	59.45	20.66	59.45	20.66
11+50.00	28.66	14.98	54.51	26.00	113.95	46.65
12+00.00	29.88	13.49	54.20	26.36	168.15	73.02
12+50.00	106.20	0.00	126.00	12.49	294.15	85.51
13+00.00	42.35	1.82	137.55	1.69	431.71	87.19
13+50.00	44.74	0.95	80.64	2.57	512.34	89.77
14+00.00	41.83	2.25	80.15	2.96	592.50	92.73
14+50.00	40.09	3.65	75.85	5.46	668.34	98.19
15+00.00	85.70	1.06	116.47	4.37	784.82	102.55
15+50.00	67.58	0.00	141.93	0.99	926.75	103.54
16+00.00	83.54	0.00	139.92	0.00	1066.67	103.54
16+50.00	87.14	0.00	158.04	0.00	1224.71	103.54
17+00.00	79.03	0.00	153.86	0.00	1378.57	103.54
17+50.00	49.90	0.00	119.38	0.00	1497.94	103.54
18+00.00	51.88	1.16	94.23	1.08	1592.18	104.62
18+50.00	49.50	0.18	93.87	1.25	1686.05	105.87
19+00.00	46.51	0.73	88.90	0.85	1774.95	106.71
19+50.00	41.77	2.41	81.74	2.91	1856.70	109.62
20+00.00	0.00	0.00	38.68	2.23	1895.37	111.85

Volume Report

Project: C:\Mastering\Ch12\1205_Materials_C_METRIC.dwg

Alignment: ROAD C
Sample Line Group: ROAD C - Sample Lines
Start Sta: 0+320.000
End Sta: 0+620.000

Station	Cut Area (Sq.m.)	Cut Volume (Cu.m.)	Reusable Volume (Cu.m.)	Fill Area (Sq.m.)	Fill Volume (Cu.m.)	Cum. Cut Vol. (Cu.m.)	Cum. Reusable Vol. (Cu.m.)	Cum. Fill Vol. (Cu.m.)	Cum. Net Vol. (Cu.m.)
0+320.000	1.24	0.00	0.00	3.08	0.00	0.00	0.00	0.00	0.00
0+340.000	1.63	28.66	28.66	2.54	56.21	28.66	28.66	56.21	-27.55
0+360.000	1.63	32.64	32.64	2.50	50.45	61.30	61.30	106.67	-45.37
0+380.000	0.00	16.34	16.34	9.04	115.43	77.64	77.64	222.10	-144.45
0+400.000	0.28	2.76	2.76	3.75	127.91	80.41	80.41	350.01	-269.60
0+420.000	0.35	6.23	6.23	3.77	75.27	86.64	86.64	425.27	-338.64
0+440.000	0.56	9.07	9.07	3.53	73.03	95.71	95.71	498.30	-402.59
0+460.000	0.00	5.60	5.60	10.37	138.94	101.31	101.31	637.25	-535.93
0+480.000	0.00	0.00	0.00	6.69	170.56	101.31	101.31	807.80	-706.49
0+500.000	0.00	0.00	0.00	7.75	144.44	101.31	101.31	952.24	-850.93
0+520.000	0.00	0.00	0.00	6.79	145.42	101.31	101.31	1097.66	-996.35
0+540.000	0.00	0.00	0.00	9.11	158.98	101.31	101.31	1256.64	-1155.33
0+560.000	0.17	1.70	1.70	4.09	132.03	103.01	103.01	1388.67	-1285.67
0+580.000	0.21	3.79	3.79	4.00	80.92	106.79	106.79	1469.59	-1362.80
0+600.000	0.53	7.38	7.38	3.54	75.39	114.18	114.18	1544.98	-1430.80
0+620.000	0.00	5.29	5.29	0.00	35.41	119.47	119.47	1580.39	-1460.92

Computing Materials

Certification
Objective

Materials can be created from surfaces or from corridor shapes. Surfaces are great for earthwork because you can add cut or fill factors to the materials, whereas corridor shapes are great for determining quantities of asphalt or concrete. In this exercise, you will practice calculating earthwork quantities for the ROAD C corridor:

1. Open the 1205_Materials.dwg (1205_Materials_METRIC.dwg) file, which you can download from this book's web page.

2. From the Analyze tab ➤ Volumes And Materials panel, choose Compute Materials.

   The Select A Sample Line Group dialog appears.

3. Select the ROAD C alignment and the ROAD C – Sample Lines group and click OK.

   The Compute Materials dialog appears.

4. In the Quantity Takeoff Criteria drop-down box, select Earthworks from the drop-down menu.

5. Click the Object Name cell for the Existing Ground surface and select Existing Surface from the drop-down menu.

6. Click the Object Name cell for the Datum surface and select North River Crossing North River Crossing – Datum (this is the name of the corridor followed by the name of the surface) from the drop-down menu.

7. Verify that your settings match those shown in Figure 12.18 and then click OK.

FIGURE 12.18
The settings for the Compute Materials dialog

Graphically, nothing will happen. However, in the background Civil 3D has computed material data.

8. Save the drawing for use in the next exercise.

Check your completed drawings at this stage against 1205_Materials_A.dwg or 1205_Materials_A_METRIC.dwg if desired.

Creating a Volume Table in the Drawing

Certification
Objective

In the preceding exercise, materials were computed that represent the total dirt to be moved or used in the sample line group. In the next exercise, you insert a table into the drawing so you can inspect the volumes.

1. If you completed the previous exercises, continue working in 1205_Materials.dwg (1205_Materials_METRIC.dwg); otherwise, open 1205_Materials_A.dwg (1205_Materials_A_METRIC.dwg).

2. From the Analyze tab ➤ Volumes And Materials panel, choose Total Volume Table.

The Create Total Volume Table dialog appears.

3. Verify that your settings match those shown in Figure 12.19.

FIGURE 12.19
The Create Total Volume Table dialog settings

4. Verify that Reactivity Mode at the bottom of the dialog is set to Dynamic.

5. Clear the check box next to Split Table and click OK.

6. Pick a point in the drawing to place the volume table.

   The table indicates a cumulative fill volume of 1896.91 cubic yards (1580.39 cubic meters) and a cumulative cut volume of 111.85 cubic yards (119.47 cubic meters).

7. Save the drawing for use in the next exercise.

   Check your completed drawings at this stage against 1205_Materials_B.dwg or 1205_Materials_B_METRIC.dwg if desired.

Adding Soil Factors to a Materials List

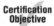
Certification
Objective

Civil 3D allows for more accurate earthwork computations by providing entry of cut factors, fill factors, and refill factors.

Cut Factor   Sometimes known as expansion factor, or "fluff" factor, the *cut factor* is always expressed as a number greater than or equal to 1.0. Cut volume is multiplied by this value to determine the volume of soil after excavation has taken place. For example, soil that expands 5 percent after excavation would use a cut factor of 1.05.

Fill Factor   Commonly known as compaction factor, the *fill factor* is used to determine the volume of material after it has been mechanically compacted. Counter to most people's intuition, this value is also expressed as a value greater than or equal to 1.0. A material that compacts to 90 percent of its original volume would use a fill factor of 1.1. The fill volume is divided by the fill factor to determine the final amount of fill needed on a site.

Refill Factor   The *refill factor* dictates what amount of the cut material can be reused as fill. This value is expressed as a percentage of the cut volume (with cut factor applied). This factor is used only when the material quantity type is set to Cut And Refill.

In the following exercise, the materials need to be modified to bring them closer in line with true field numbers. For this exercise, the shrinkage factor will be assumed to be 80 percent, which is entered into Civil 3D as 1.2. The expansion on cut will be 115 percent, or, as entered into Civil 3D, 1.15. In addition to these numbers (which Civil 3D represents as cut factor for swell and fill factor for shrinkage), for this exercise, you will assume a Refill Factor value of 1.00.

1. If you completed the previous exercise, continue working in 1205_Materials.dwg (1205_Materials_METRIC.dwg); otherwise, open 1205_Materials_B.dwg (1205_Materials_B_METRIC.dwg).

2. From the Analyze tab ➢ Volumes And Materials panel, choose Compute Materials.

   The Select A Sample Line Group dialog appears.

3. Select the ROAD C alignment and the ROAD C – Sample Lines group and click OK.

   The Edit Material List dialog appears. You will use different criteria that allow the input of the previously mentioned values.

4. Click the Import Another Criteria button, and from the Select A Quantity Takeoff Criteria dialog, select the Cut And Fill criteria; then click OK.

5. In the Compute Materials – ROAD C – Sample Lines dialog, click the <Click Here To Set All> cell and set the EG surface to Existing Surface. Click the cell for the DATUM surface and set it to North River Crossing North River Crossing – Datum surface. Click OK.

6. In the Edit Material List dialog for the alignment, you will now have two material lists, as shown in Figure 12.20. Expand Material List – (2), as shown in the figure.

FIGURE 12.20
The Edit Material List dialog

7. Enter a cut factor of **1.15** in the Cut Factor cell for the Ground Removed row and a fill factor of **1.2** in the Fill Factor cell of the Ground Fill row.

8. Verify that all other settings are the same as in Figure 12.20 and click OK.

9. From the Analyze tab ➢ Volumes And Materials panel, choose Total Volume Table.

   The Create Total Volume Table dialog appears.

10. Set the Select Material List drop-down to Material List – (2), uncheck the Split Table check box if it's selected, leave all the other settings at their defaults, and click OK.

11. Place the new table next to the one already present and examine the total volume table again for the changed values when the factors are considered and applied.

    Notice that the new Cumulative Fill Volume value is 2276.30 cubic yards (1896.47 cubic meters) and the new Cumulative Cut Volume value is 128.63 cubic yards (137.39 cubic meters).

12. Save the drawing for use in the next exercise.

    Check your completed drawings at this stage against 1205_Materials_FINISHED or 1205_Materials_METRIC_FINISHED.dwg if desired.

Generating a Volume Report

Civil 3D provides you with a way to create a report that is suitable for printing or for transferring to a word processing or spreadsheet program. In this exercise, you'll create a volume report for the North River Crossing corridor.

1. If you completed the previous exercise, continue working in 1205_Materials .dwg (1205_Materials_METRIC.dwg); otherwise, open 1205_Materials_FINISHED.dwg (1205_Materials_METRIC_FINISHED.dwg).

2. From the Analyze tab ➢ Volumes And Materials panel, choose Volume Report.

   The Report Quantities dialog appears.

3. Verify that Material List – (2) is selected in the dialog and click OK. Calculating the volume report may take a few moments depending on your computer specifications.

4. You may get a warning message that says, "Scripts are usually safe. Do you want to allow scripts to run?" Click Yes.

   Civil 3D temporarily takes over your web browser to display the volume report. This is the same information that you placed in your drawing, but since it's in this form, you can more readily copy and paste it into Microsoft Excel, Microsoft Word, or another program.

5. Note the cut-and-fill volumes and compare them to your volume table in the drawing. You will notice the same values for the report as they are displayed in the table.

6. Close the report when you have finished viewing it.

7. Close the drawing without saving it.

Adding Section View Final Touches

Before you move away from section views, a few last touches are needed in your sections. First, you will add last-minute data to the sections. You will also add labels to the sections.

Adding Data with Sample More Sources

It is a common occurrence that data is created from the design after sample lines have been generated. For example, you may need to add surface data or pipe network data to existing section views. To accomplish this, you need to add that data to the sample line group using the Sample More Sources command. In other words, any data that was created after the sample lines were generated will need to be added using the sampling from more sources.

In this exercise, you'll add a pipe network to a sample line group and inspect the existing section views to ensure that the pipe network was added correctly:

1. Open the 1206_FinalTouches.dwg (1206_FinalTouches_METRIC.dwg) file, which you can download from this book's web page.

2. Select one of the section views by clicking the station label.

3. From the Section View contextual tab ➢ Modify Section panel, click the Sample More Sources button.

4. In the Section Sources dialog, click ROAD C Sanitary on the left side of the dialog to highlight it, as shown in Figure 12.21, and then click Add.

FIGURE 12.21
Adding sanitary pipe network to the cross-section view via Sample More Sources

The sanitary network will now appear on the right side of the dialog.

5. Click OK to dismiss the Section Sources dialog.

Take a look at the sections. You should now see pipes and structures in the various section views.

Sometimes the sections views placed on the sheets might come close to overlapping the sheet border. To fix or avoid this, make sure you have well-defined settings for the generation of section views sheets in your template to take into account any future data added using Sample More Sources.

6. Save the drawing for use in the next exercise.

Check your completed drawings at this stage against 1206_FinalTouches_A.dwg or 1206_FinalTouches_A_METRIC.dwg if desired.

Adding Cross-Section Labels

The best way to label cross sections that contain corridor data is to use the code set style. Using the code set style, you can control which parts of the corridor are labeled. You can learn more about creating code set styles in Chapter 18, "Label Styles." In the meantime, you will look at how to change the active code set style on a cross-section view group.

In the following exercise, you will use the view group properties to add labels:

1. Continue working in 1206_FinalTouches.dwg (1206_FinalTouches_METRIC.dwg) or open 1206_FinalTouches_A.dwg (1206_FinalTouches_A_METRIC.dwg).

2. Select one of the section views by clicking its station label.

3. From the Section View contextual tab ➤ Modify View panel, choose View Group Properties.

4. On the Sections tab, locate the Style column for the corridor and click the All Codes field.

   This is the code set style that is current in the views.

5. Click the field again to switch the style to Codes With Labels from the drop-down list, as shown in Figure 12.22, and click OK to dismiss the Code Set Style dialog. Click OK once more to dismiss the Section View Group Properties dialog. Press Esc to deselect the selected section view.

FIGURE 12.22
Changing the active code set style for all views in the group

You will notice that the only labels that you see are the pavement grade labels. To show the elevation and offset labels, you will use a feature introduced in the 2014 release of the software. This feature uses labels from within the section label styles part of the Settings tab in Toolspace. The advantage of using these new labels is that you can automatically stagger labels, making it easier to manage their placement in the section view.

The point labels within the code sets are considered legacy elements and are still available to display if needed. If you ever need to create the section views using the legacy code set labels for points, you can change the default section view Corridor Point Code Labeling Method setting from Section Label Set to Section Code Set Style, as shown in Figure 12.23. Note that you need to do this before creating the cross-section views.

FIGURE 12.23
Change the command settings before creating section views to maintain legacy point labels.

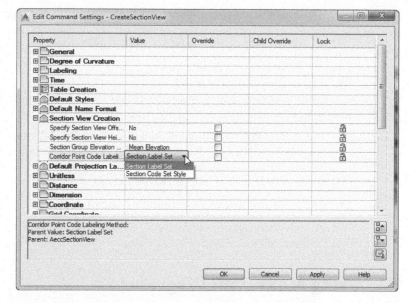

6. Select one of the section views by clicking its station label and, from the Section View contextual tab ➤ Modify View panel, choose View Group Properties.

7. Click within the cell for Label Set assigned to the corridor, which is located to the left of the Code With Labels cell that you assigned previously.

8. In the Select Label Set dialog, in the drop-down menu select Corridor Points. Click OK twice to apply the label set and dismiss the dialog. Press Esc to deselect the section view.

   You should now have lovely little labels on all of the views, as shown in Figure 12.24. Next, you will convert one of the section views to display the legacy labels for corridor points.

FIGURE 12.24
Slope, elevation, and offset labels from the code set style and corridor section labels

9. At the command line, enter **CORRIDORSECTIONLABELSCONV**. Hit the Enter key, and at the `Select section views you want to convert:` prompt, pick the section view at station 11+50.00 (0+340.00 for metric users); then press the Enter key to accept the selection.

10. At the `Convert all corridor point labels to [Code set style labels corridor Points style labels] <Code set style labels>:` prompt, press Enter once more to accept the default.

   The section view will be converted to legacy mode and the code set style–defined labels for points will be now displayed for the converted section view. Note that the same workflow can work in reverse, with the only difference being that you will need to re-assign the desired label set to the converted section view.

11. Check the result of you work and then save and close the drawing.

   Check your work against the file 1206_FinalTouches_FINISHED.dwg or 1206_FinalTouches_METRIC_FINISHED.dwg if desired.

Using Mass Haul Diagrams

Mass haul diagrams help designers and contractors gauge how far and how much soil needs to be moved around a site. Figure 12.25 shows the mass haul diagram for a road named Syrah Way. The free haul area is material the contractor has agreed to move at no extra charge. The fact that the mass haul line is always above zero indicates that the project is in a net cut situation through the length of the Syrah Way alignment.

FIGURE 12.25
Syrah Way Mass Haul diagram (the legend was added for illustration purposes only)

Taking a Closer Look at the Mass Haul Diagram

In an ideal design situation, there is no leftover cut material, and no extra material needs to be brought in. This would mean that net volume equals zero. When the line appears above the zero volume point, it is showing net cut values.

As the mass haul diagram continues, it shows the cumulative effect of net cut and fill for the alignment. When the net cut and net fill converge at the zero volume, the earthwork along the alignment is balanced. When the line appears below the zero volume point, it is showing net fill values, as you can see in Figure 12.26.

FIGURE 12.26

The volume, net cut, and net fill on an idealized mass haul diagram shown with profile

Here is some of the terminology you will encounter:

Balanced The state where the cumulative cut and fill volumes are equal.

Origin Point The beginning of the mass haul diagram, typically at station 0+00, but it can vary depending on your stationing.

Borrow A negative value, typically at the end of the mass haul diagram, that indicates fill material that will need to be brought into the site.

Waste A positive value, typically at the end of the mass haul diagram, that indicates cut material that will need to be hauled out of the site.

Free Haul Earthwork that a contractor has contractually agreed to move. This typically specifies a contracted distance.

Over Haul Earthwork that the contractor has not contractually agreed to move. This excess can be used for borrow pits or waste piles.

Creating a Mass Haul Diagram

Now, let's put it all together and build a mass haul diagram in Civil 3D for Syrah Way, and you'll see how easy it is:

1. Open the 1207_MassHaul.dwg (1207_MassHaul_METRIC.dwg) file.

   Remember, you can download all the data files from this book's web page.

2. From the Analyze tab ➤ Volumes And Materials panel, choose Mass Haul.

   The Create Mass Haul Diagram Wizard opens.

3. On the General page, complete these steps:

   a. Verify that you are creating a mass haul diagram for the Syrah Way alignment.

b. Verify that you are using the Syrah Way – Sample Lines group.

c. Leave all other options at their defaults, as shown in Figure 12.27, and click Next. On the Mass Haul Display Options page, no changes are needed.

FIGURE 12.27
The General options page of the Create Mass Haul Diagram Wizard

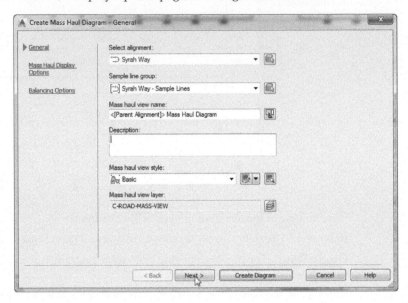

4. Click Next.

5. In the Balancing Options page, place a check mark next to Free Haul Distance.

6. Set the distance to **200** (**60** for metric users), as shown in Figure 12.28, and click Create Diagram.

FIGURE 12.28
The Balancing Options page of the Create Mass Haul Diagram Wizard

7. Find a clear spot on your drawing to place the mass haul diagram.

The diagram should look similar to Figure 12.25 (shown previously). Note that the legend was added for explanation purposes and is not generated by Civil 3D. We created this using AutoCAD text and hatching tools.

8. Save the drawing and keep it open for the next exercise.

Check your completed drawing at this stage against 1207_MassHaul_A.dwg or 1207_MassHaul_A_METRIC.dwg if desired.

Editing a Mass Haul Diagram

When you create a mass haul diagram, you can easily modify parameters and get instant feedback on it. Follow these steps to see how:

1. If you completed the previous exercise, continue working in 1207_MassHaul.dwg (1207_MassHaul_METRIC.dwg); otherwise, open 1207_MassHaul_A.dwg (1207_MassHaul_A_METRIC.dwg).

2. Select anywhere on the mass haul object or grid.

If you look at your mass haul diagram, you can see that nearly all the earthwork for Syrah Way involves net cut, which means hauling away dirt.

The Balancing options give you a chance to change or add waste and borrow pits. You will now make a few changes and observe what happens to the mass haul diagram.

3. From the Mass Haul View contextual panel ➤ Modify panel, select Balancing Options.

The Mass Haul Line Properties dialog opens with the settings you used when initially generating the mass haul diagram.

4. Free Haul Distance is presently set for 200 (60 for metric users). Change it to **500′ (150** m).

5. Drag the dialog away from the screen to see the changes and then click Apply.

You can further tweak this amount to cut down on the net cut values by adding a dump site.

6. Click the Add Dump Site button.

    a. Set the station to **1+31.00 (0+040.00)**.

    b. Set the capacity to **850** cubic yards (**650** cubic meters).

7. When your dialog resembles Figure 12.29, click OK.

FIGURE 12.29
The Mass Haul
Line Properties
dialog: adding a
dump site

The mass haul diagram will immediately update to reflect the changes. If the mass haul view does not reflect the desired layout, don't worry. Upon saving the drawing, closing it, and opening it again, the desired layout should be displayed.

8. Save and close the drawing.

If you'd like to compare how you did, open the file 1207_MassHaul_FINISHED.dwg or 1207_MassHaul_METRIC_FINISHED.dwg.

The Bottom Line

Create sample lines. Before any section views can be displayed, sections must be created from sample lines.

> **Master It** Open MasterIt_1201.dwg (MasterIt_1201_METRIC.dwg) and create sample lines along the USH 10 alignment every 50 feet (20 meters for metric users). Sample all data, and set the left and right swath widths to 50 (20 for metric users).

Create section views. Just as profiles can be shown only in profile views, sections require section views to be displayed. Section views can be plotted individually or all at once. You can break them up into groups for plotting into sheets.

> **Master It** In the previous exercise, you created sample lines. In that same drawing, create section views for all the sample lines. For U.S. units, use a cross-section scale of

1" = 20′ on an Arch D size layout sheet. For metric units, use a cross-section scale of 1:500 on an ISO A0 size sheet. For all other options, use the default settings and styles.

Define and compute materials.　Materials are required to be defined before any quantities can be displayed. You learned that materials can be defined from surfaces or from corridor shapes. Corridors must exist for shape selection, and surfaces must already be created for comparison in materials lists.

Master It　Continuing using `MasterIt_1201.dwg` (`Master It_1201_METRIC.dwg`), create a materials list that compares Existing Intersection with HWY 10 DATUM Surface. Use the Earthworks Quantity takeoff criteria. Be sure you have completed all the previous "Master It" exercises before continuing.

Generate volume reports.　Volume reports give you numbers that can be used for cost estimating on any given project. Typically, construction companies calculate their own quantities, but developers often want to know approximate volumes for budgeting purposes.

Master It　Continue using `MasterIt_1201.dwg` (`MasterIt_1201_METRIC.dwg`). Be sure you have completed all the previous "Master It" exercises before continuing. Use the materials list created earlier to generate a volume report. Create a web browser–based report and a total volume table that can be displayed on the drawing.

Chapter 13

Pipe Networks

In this chapter, you'll look at two different types of pipe systems used in Autodesk® AutoCAD® Civil 3D® installations. *Pipe networks* refer to the gravity-based object type in Civil 3D that works best for sewer systems. *Pressure networks* are a separate object type that works best for systems such as water and gas.

First, you will take an in-depth look at pipe networks. In the latter part of this chapter, you'll learn about pressure networks.

In this chapter, you will learn to:

◆ Create a pipe network by layout.

◆ Create an alignment from network parts and draw parts in profile view.

◆ Label a pipe network in plan and profile.

◆ Create a dynamic pipe table.

Setting Up a Pipe Network

Before you can draw pipes in your project, some setup is needed. The setup discussed in this first section should be done in your Civil 3D template so it can be applied to multiple projects. In this section, you'll examine what is needed for an example waste water network.

Pipe networks contain the following object types:

Pipes *Pipes* are components of a pipe network that primarily represent underground pipes or culverts. The standard catalog has pipe shapes that are circular, elliptical, egg-shaped, and rectangular and are made of materials that include PVC, RCP, DI, and HDPE. You can use Part Builder (discussed later in this chapter) to create your own shapes and materials if the default shapes and dimensions can't be adapted for your design.

Structures *Structures* are the components of a pipe network that represent manholes, catch basins, inlets, joints, and any other type of junction between two pipes. The standard catalog includes inlets, outlets, junction structures with frames (such as manholes with lids or catch basins with grates), junction structures without frames (the same as the previous ones, less the frame), and simple shape structures.

When working with bringing data from Autodesk® Infraworks® 360, a generic catalog was provided for structures in both metric and Imperial units for a close match of structures in between the two platforms, and this includes access and inlet type structures.

Null Structures *Null structures* are needed when two pipes are joined without a structure; they act as a placeholder for a pipe endpoint. They have special properties, such as allowing pipe cleanup at pipe intersections. Most of the time, you'll create a style for them that doesn't plot or is invisible for plotting purposes. (See Chapter 19, "Object Styles," for more information on creating structure styles.)

Understanding Parts List—Waste Water Systems

A *parts list* contains the pieces needed to complete a pipe design. Both pipe networks and pressure networks use parts lists to help you organize design elements and determine how they will appear in a drawing. For example, you'll want to have different parts available when working with waste water than you'll want when working with storm sewers.

Pipe network parts lists (for gravity systems) contain pipes, structures, pipe and structure rules, pipe and structure styles, render material, and the ability to associate a quantity takeoff pay item number with each item. You'll learn more about pressure network parts lists later in this chapter.

The following are examples of pipe network parts lists:

◆ Storm sewer:

  ◆ Catch basin/inlet structures

  ◆ Manhole structures

  ◆ Concrete pipe

  ◆ HDPE pipe

◆ Waste water (gravity), as shown in Figure 13.1:

  ◆ Manhole structures

  ◆ HDPE pipe

  ◆ PVC pipe

FIGURE 13.1
A waste water parts list

In the upcoming section, you will explore planning and creating a parts list. You'll start by examining your local requirements, and then you will compare those needs with what is available in the software.

Planning a Typical Pipe Network

Let's look at a typical waste water design. You'll start by going through the waste water specifications for the jurisdiction in which you're working. The following is an example of a completed checklist for the example's jurisdiction, Sample County:

Waste Water Network in Sample County

♦ *Recommended structures*: The recommended structures are standard concentric manhole, small-diameter cleanout.

♦ *Structure behavior*: All structures have 1.5′ (0.50 m) sump, rims, and a 0.10′ (0.03 m) invert drop across all structures. All structures' rim elevations are designed at finished road grade.

♦ *Structure representation*: Manholes are shown in plan view as a circle with an *S* inside. Cleanouts are shown as a hatched circle (see Figure 13.2).

FIGURE 13.2
Waste water manhole in plan view (left) and a cleanout in plan view (right)

Manholes are shown in profile view with a coned top and rectangular bottom. Cleanouts are shown as a rectangle (see Figure 13.3).

FIGURE 13.3
Profile view of a waste water manhole (left) and a cleanout (right)

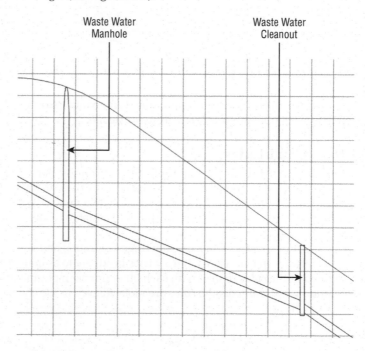

Waste Water Manhole

Waste Water Cleanout

Recommended pipes 8″ (200 mm), 10″ (250 mm), and 12″ (300 mm) PVC pipe, per manufacturer specifications.

Pipe behavior Pipes must have a minimum cover of 4′ (1.22 m) to the top of the pipe; the maximum slope for all pipes is 10 percent, although minimum slopes can be adjusted to optimize velocity as follows:

PIPE SIZE	MINIMUM SLOPE
8″ (200 mm)	0.40%
10″ (250 mm)	0.28%
12″ (300 mm)	0.22%

Pipe representation In plan view, pipes are shown with a CENTER2 linetype line that has a thickness corresponding to the inner diameter of the pipe. In profile view, pipes show both inner and outer walls, with a hatch between the walls to highlight the wall thickness (see Figure 13.4).

FIGURE 13.4
Waste water pipe in plan view (a) and in profile view (b)

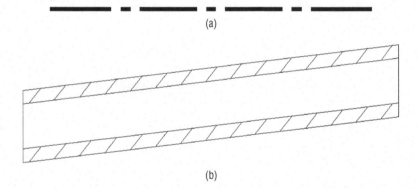

(a)

(b)

Now that you know your requirements for Sample County, the next step is to begin entering this information into your Civil 3D template file.

Using Part Rules

Rules define the constraints on things like minimum slope, sump depths, and pipe-invert drops across structure. Rules are assigned to parts in the parts list. Depending on the type of network and the complexity of your design, you may have many rules. Civil 3D allows you to establish structure and pipe rules that will assist in respecting these constraints during initial layout and edits.

Rules don't restrict you from drawing the location and lengths you want. As you draw your pipe network in plan view, Civil 3D tries to adhere to as many rules as it can. If the constraints defined in the rules conflict with each other (for example, maximum slope may be violated to maintain minimum depth), rules are violated even in the layout stage.

Furthermore, rules will never change your design without your direct guidance. For example, if the surface tied to a structure changes, the rim elevation *will* change, but the pipe invert elevations *will not* change.

To see where the design needs to be altered, you will need to view the violations in the Status column of Panorama. Panorama is the only place where rule violations are flagged; there is no graphic representation of rule violations in plan view.

Structures and pipes have separate rule sets. When creating rules, don't be thrown off by the fact that the category always reads Storm Sewer, as you'll see in Figure 13.6. You can use these rules regardless of the type of parts list you are creating. You can then add these rule sets to specific parts in your parts list, which you'll build later in this chapter.

UNDERSTANDING STRUCTURE RULES

Structure rule sets are located on the Settings tab of Toolspace, under the Structure branch, as shown in Figure 13.5.

FIGURE 13.5
On the Settings tab of Toolspace, right-click a structure rule set to edit it.

Right-click the rule set and choose Edit. In the Rules tab, click the Add Rule button on the Rules tab in the Structure Rule Set dialog. The Add Rule dialog will appear, which will allow you to access all the various structure rules (see Figure 13.6). Although it looks like you can, you won't be able to change the values until you finalize adding the rule. The rules that are available for the structures are different from the ones that are available for and apply to pipes.

You will have a chance to work with this firsthand in the upcoming exercise.

FIGURE 13.6
In the Add Rule dialog, the category always shows Storm Sewer, but you can use rules for whatever type you want.

Maximum Pipe Size Check Rule

The Maximum Pipe Size Check rule (see Figure 13.7) examines all pipes connected to a structure and flags a violation in Prospector if any pipe is larger than your rule. This is a violation-only rule—it won't change your pipe size automatically.

FIGURE 13.7
The Maximum
Pipe Size Check
rule option

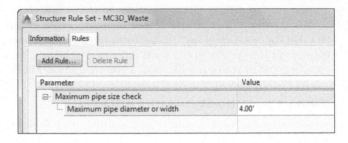

Pipe Drop Across Structure Rule

The Pipe Drop Across Structure rule (see Figure 13.8) tells any connected pipes how their inverts (or alternatively, their crowns or centerlines) must relate to one another.

FIGURE 13.8
The Pipe Drop
Across Structure
rule options

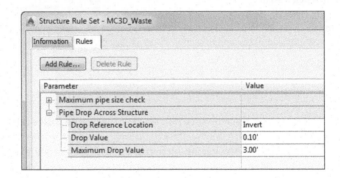

When a new pipe is connected to a structure that has the Pipe Drop Across Structure rule applied, the following checks take place:

◆ A pipe drawn to be exiting a structure has an invert equal to or lower than the lowest pipe entering the structure based on the minimum drop across structure setting.

◆ A pipe drawn to be entering a structure has an invert equal to or higher than the highest pipe exiting the structure based on the minimum drop across structure setting.

◆ The minimum specified drop distance is calculated by measuring between the lowest entering pipe and the highest exiting pipe. If at any time this value is lower or higher than the rule setting, it will be flagged in the Status column of the Panorama view, as noted previously.

In the hypothetical waste water example, you're required to maintain a 0.10′ (3 cm) invert drop across all structures. You'll use this rule in your structure rule set in the next exercise.

Set Sump Depth Rule

Sump depth is additional structure depth below the lowest pipe invert. The Set Sump Depth rule (Figure 13.9) establishes sump depth for structures.

FIGURE 13.9
The Set Sump Depth rule option

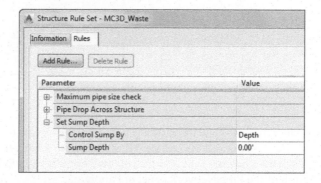

It's important to add a sump depth rule to all of your structure rule sets. If no sump rule is used, Civil 3D will assume a 2' sump for English units and 2 meters in metric units! If you forget to set this before placing structures, you will need to edit the individual structure properties or make the rule and retroactively apply it to the network.

In the hypothetical waste water example, all the structures have a 1.5' (0.5 m) sump depth. You'll use this rule in your structure rule set in the next exercise.

UNDERSTANDING PIPE RULES

Pipe rule sets are located on the Settings tab of Toolspace, under the Pipe branch. After you right-click a pipe rule set and choose Edit (as shown in Figure 13.10), you can access all the pipe rules by clicking the Add Rule button on the Rules tab of the Pipe Rule Set dialog.

FIGURE 13.10
Accessing the pipe rules dialog from the Settings tab

Cover And Slope Rule

The Cover And Slope rule (Figure 13.11) allows you to specify your desired slope range and cover range. As you place your pipe network, Civil 3D tries to use the minimum and maximum depths and minimum and maximum slopes to set the initial pipe depth and slope.

FIGURE 13.11
The Cover And
Slope rule options

Depending on your site conditions, applying this rule to every pipe may not be feasible. In this situation, the rule becomes what is referred to as *violation only*. You will still be able to place pipes that violate the rule, and the rule will cause a violation message to show in the Status column of the Pipe Network panel of Panorama.

If part of your design changes and you'd like Civil 3D to make another attempt to enforce the Cover And Slope rule, you can use the Apply Rules feature, which is discussed later in this chapter.

Cover Only Rule

The Cover Only rule (Figure 13.12) is designed for use with pipe systems where slope can vary or isn't a critical factor. Like Cover And Slope, this rule is used on first placement. Manual edits can cause rules to be violated. The rule will show as a violation in the Status column of the Pipe Network panel, but no changes to your design take place until you use the Apply Rules command.

FIGURE 13.12
The Cover Only
rule options

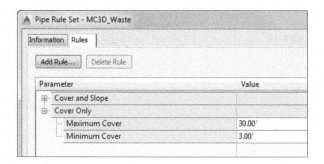

Length Check Rule

Length Check is a violation-only rule; it won't change your pipe length size automatically. The Length Check options (see Figure 13.13) allow you to specify minimum and maximum pipe lengths.

FIGURE 13.13
The Length Check
rule options

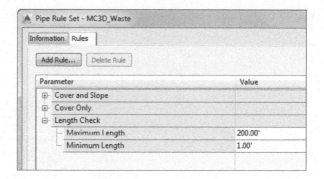

Pipe To Pipe Match Rule

The Pipe To Pipe Match rule (Figure 13.14) is also designed for use where there are no true structures (only null structures), including situations where pipe is placed to break into an existing pipe. This rule determines how pipe inverts are assigned when two pipes come together, similar to the Pipe Drop Across Structure rule.

FIGURE 13.14
The Pipe To
Pipe Match rule
options

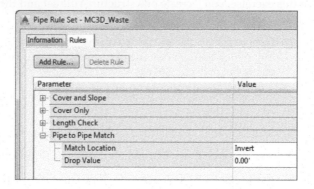

Set Pipe End Location Rule

Without the Set Pipe End Location rule (Figure 13.15), Civil 3D assumes you are measuring pipes from center of structure to center of structure. With the rule in place, you have the capability to determine where the pipe end is located on the structure. The options are Structure Center (the default without the rule), Structure Inner Wall, or Structure Outer Wall.

End Offset and Start Offset are used if you would like to have your pipes protrude past the inner or outer wall on the respective ends. The offset is ignored if the location for the end is set to the center of the structure. The value must be positive and will be ignored if the additional length causes the pipe end to be located past the center of the structure.

Graphically, you probably won't be able to tell that this setting is active until you add labels. The Set Pipe End Location will make a difference in the length and slope labels on pipes.

FIGURE 13.15
The Set Pipe End
Location rule
options

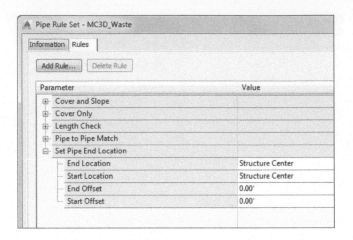

CREATING STRUCTURE AND PIPE RULE SETS

In this exercise, you'll create one structure rule set and three pipe rule sets for a hypothetical waste water project:

1. Open the 1301_RulesTemplate.dwg (1301_RulesTemplate_METRIC.dwg) drawing, which you can download from this book's web page at www.sybex.com/go/masteringcivil3d2016.

2. On the Settings tab of Toolspace, expand the Structure branch, right-click Structure Rule Set, and click New.

3. Switch to the Information tab and enter **Waste Water** in the Name text box.

4. Switch to the Rules tab, and click the Add Rule button.

5. In the Add Rule dialog, choose Pipe Drop Across Structure in the Rule Name drop-down. Click OK.

6. Expand the new rule and confirm that the parameters in the Structure Rule Set dialog are the following:

   ◆ Drop Reference Location: Invert

   ◆ Drop Value: 0.1′ (0.03 m)

   ◆ Maximum Drop Value: 3′ (1 m)

   These parameters establish a rule that will match your hypothetical municipality's standard for the drop across waste water structures.

7. Click the Add Rule button again.

8. In the Add Rule dialog, choose Set Sump Depth in the Rule Name drop-down. Click OK.

9. Expand the new rule. Change the Sump Depth parameter to **1.5′ (0.5 m)** in the Structure Rule Set dialog to meet the hypothetical municipality's standard for sump in waste water structures and click OK.

10. On the Settings tab of Toolspace, expand the Pipe branch, right-click Pipe Rule Set and choose New.

11. Switch to the Information tab and enter **8 Inch Waste Water Pipe** (for metric, **200 mm Waste Water Pipe**) for the name.

12. Switch to the Rules tab. Click Add Rule.

13. In the Add Rule dialog, choose Cover And Slope in the Rule Name drop-down. Click OK.

14. Expand the Cover And Slope rule and then modify the parameters to match the constraints established by your hypothetical municipality for 8" (200 mm) pipe, as follows:

- Maximum Cover: 10′ (3 m)

- Maximum Slope: 10%

- Minimum Cover: 4′ (1.5 m)

- Minimum Slope: 0.40%

15. Click OK.

16. In the Settings tab of Toolspace, expand Pipe Rule Set and select the rule set you just created. Right-click and choose Copy.

17. Switch to the Information tab and enter **10 Inch Waste Water Pipe** (for metric, **250 mm Waste Water Pipe**) in the Name text box.

18. Switch to the Rules tab, expand the Cover And Slope rule, and then modify the parameters to match the constraints established by your hypothetical municipality for a 10" (250 mm) pipe, as follows.

- Maximum Cover: 10′ (3 m)

- Maximum Slope: 10%

- Minimum Cover: 4′ (1.5 m)

- Minimum Slope: 0.28%

19. Click OK when you have finished modifying the rule set. Repeat the process to create a rule set for the 12" (300 mm) pipe using the following parameters:

- Maximum Cover: 10′ (3 m)

- Maximum Slope: 10%

- Minimum Cover: 4′ (1.5 m)

- Minimum Slope: 0.22%

20. You should now have one structure rule set and three pipe rule sets.

21. Save and close your drawing.

For your reference, completed versions of the drawing (1301_RulesTemplate_FINISHED .dwg and 1301_RulesTemplate_METRIC_FINISHED.dwg) are available with the rest of this book's download.

Putting Your Parts List Together

Everything you've done in this chapter up to this point is leading up to the creation of the parts list. Your parts lists should reside in your Civil 3D template file. Having this information in your template will prevent you from needing to re-create the parts list for every project. You will have multiple parts lists for each type of system you are creating and possibly for each jurisdiction you work in. You might even consider setting up a template for each jurisdiction.

1. Open the 1302_PartsListTemplate.dwg (1302_PartsListTemplate_METRIC.dwg) drawing.

2. From the Settings tab, expand the Pipe Network branch, and expand Parts Lists.

   In the drawing, there are currently two parts lists: Standard and Storm Sewer.

3. Right-click Parts Lists and select Create Parts List.

4. In the Network Parts List dialog, switch to the Information tab and name the parts list **Sample County Waste Water**.

5. Switch to the Pipes tab.

6. Right-click New Parts List and select Add Part Family, as shown in Figure 13.16.

FIGURE 13.16
Add a part family for your new parts list.

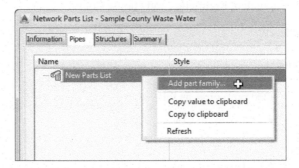

The Part Catalog dialog will appear.

7. As shown in Figure 13.17, place a check mark next to PVC Pipe (PVC Pipe SI in the metric catalog) and click OK.

FIGURE 13.17
Choosing a part
family to add

At this step, the parts list name should appear at the top of the pipe list.

8. Expand the pipe list name to see the new PVC Pipe family you just added.

9. Right-click PVC Pipe (PVC Pipe SI for metric users) and select Add Part Size, as shown in Figure 13.18.

FIGURE 13.18
Add a new part
size to the PVC
Pipe part family.

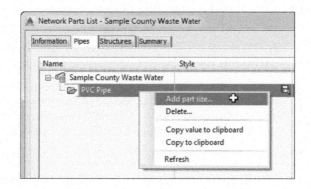

10. In the Part Size Creator dialog, click the drop-down in the Inner Pipe Diameter field, as highlighted in Figure 13.19.

11. Select 8 Inch (metric: 200 mm). Click OK.

FIGURE 13.19
Set the diameter and material for all the needed pipes.

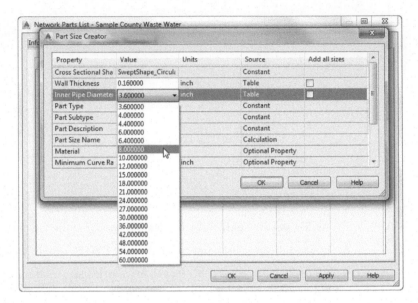

12. Expand the new PVC Pipe category to examine the result. Repeat steps 9 through 11 for 10" (250 mm) and 12" (300 mm) pipes.

In this example, the pipes will share the same style. Using the disk icon in the PVC Pipe part family row of the table, you will apply your style choice to the entire PVC family.

For the columns Render Material and Pay Item, leave the defaults. Render materials and pay items do not affect the design portion of the pipe network. Render materials are used if you want to give a realistic material to the object for visualization purposes. You will take an in-depth look at assigning pay items to a parts list in Chapter 17, "Quantity Takeoff."

13. In the PVC Pipe part family row, click the disk icon in the Style column.

14. Set Pipe Style to Single Line (Waste Water) and click OK.

15. For each pipe size, click the Pipe Rule Set icon in the Rules column, choose the respective rule in the Pipe Rule Set dialog, and then click OK.

At the end of the process, your Pipes tab will look like Figure 13.20.

FIGURE 13.20
The completed Pipes tab

16. Switch to the Structures tab and expand New Parts List.

Notice there is already a null structure in the listing.

17. Expand the Null Structure part family and click the Structure Style icon for the null structure.

18. Change the Null Structure style to Null and click OK.

19. Right-click the main heading New Parts List and select Add Part Family.

20. In the Part Catalog dialog, locate the Junction Structures With Frames grouping and place a check mark next to Concentric Cylindrical Structure and Cylindrical Structure Slab Top Circular Frame (in the metric drawings, the structure descriptions end with SI), as shown in Figure 13.21. Click OK.

FIGURE 13.21
Adding structure part families.

21. Right-click Concentric Cylindrical Structure and select Add Part Size.

22. In the Part Size Creator dialog, select an Inner Structure Diameter of 48″ (1,200 mm).

23. Leave all other size options at their defaults and click OK.

24. Repeat steps 22 through 24 to add the 60′ (1,500 mm) structure.

If the Add Part Size option is not available in the list, make sure you don't have multiple parts selected. In this case, just select another part family and switch back to the desired part family you need to add new part sizes.

25. Use the disk icon to set the style for both concentric cylindrical structures to Waste Water Manhole.

26. Right-click Cylindrical Structure Slab Top Circular Frame and select Add Part Size.

27. Set Inner Structure Diameter to 15^2 (450 mm) and click OK.

28. Using the same process you used in step 25, set Structure Style to Cleanout.

29. Use a similar procedure to set the rules for the three new structures to Waste Water.

If you expand all the structure part families, your network parts list will look like Figure 13.22.

FIGURE 13.22
The completed
Structures tab in
your new parts list

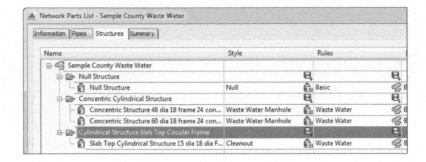

30. Click OK to close the network parts list.

31. Save and close the drawing.

For your reference, completed versions of the drawing (1302_PartsListTemplate_FINISHED.dwg and 1302_PartsListTemplate_METRIC_FINISHED.dwg) are available with the rest of this book's download.

Creating a Waste Water Network

Earlier, you prepared a parts list for a typical waste water network. This chapter will lead you through several methods for using that parts list to design, edit, and annotate a pipe network.

A pipe network, such as the one in Figure 13.23, can have many branches. In most cases, the pipes and structures in your network will be connected to each other; however, they don't necessarily have to be physically touching to be included in the same pipe network.

FIGURE 13.23
A typical Civil 3D
pipe network.

There are several ways to create pipe networks. You can do so using the Civil 3D pipe layout tools. You can also create pipe networks from certain AutoCAD and Civil 3D objects, such as lines, polylines, alignments, and feature lines.

Establishing Pipe Network Parameters

This section will give you an overview of establishing pipe network parameters. Use this section as a reference for the exercises in this chapter. When you're ready to create a pipe network by layout, select the Home tab ➤ Create Design panel and choose Pipe Network ➤ Pipe Network Creation Tools. The Create Pipe Network dialog appears (see Figure 13.24), and you can establish your settings.

FIGURE 13.24
The Create Pipe
Network dialog

Before you can create a pipe network, you must give your network a name, but more important, you need to assign a parts list for your network. As you saw earlier, the parts list provides a toolkit of pipes, structures, rules, and styles to automate the pipe network design process. It's also important to select a reference surface in this interface. This surface will be used for rim elevations and rule application.

When creating a pipe network, you'll be prompted for the following options:

Network Name   Choose a name for your network that is meaningful and will help you identify it in Prospector and other locations.

Network Description   The description of your pipe network is optional. You might make a note of the date, the type of network, and any special characteristics.

Network Parts List   Choose the parts list that contains the parts, rules, and styles you want to use for this design.

Surface Name Choose the surface that will provide a basis for applying cover rules as well as provide an insertion elevation for your structures (in other words, rim elevations). You can change this surface later or for individual structures. For proposed pipe networks, this surface is usually a finished ground surface or a composite surface of the existing and proposed surfaces, which can be set to No Display in the drawing.

Alignment Name Choose an alignment that will provide station and offset information for your structures in Prospector as well as any labels that call for alignment stations and/or offset information. Because most pipe networks have several branches, it may not be meaningful for every structure in your network to reference the same alignment. Therefore, you may find it better to leave your Alignment option set to None in this dialog and set it for individual structures later using the layout tools or Structure list in Prospector. The same suggestion applies for the pipe list.

Structure Label Style and Pipe Label Style As you create the network, you'll have the option to add labels as you go. If you choose to use a label style that displays text (that is, not the <None> option), these labels will apply only to the plan view. Section and profile pipe network labels are added in a separate area. You will learn about adding labels later in this chapter. For more information about creating label styles, see Chapter 18, "Label Styles."

Using the Network Layout Creation Tools

Creating a pipe network with layout tools is much like creating other Civil 3D objects. After naming and establishing the parameters for your pipe network, you'll be presented with a special toolbar that you can use to lay out pipes and structures in plan, which will also drive a vertical design.

Certification Objective

After establishing your pipe network parameters in the Create Pipe Network dialog (shown earlier in Figure 13.24), click OK; the Network Layout Tools toolbar will appear (see Figure 13.25).

FIGURE 13.25
The Network Layout Tools toolbar

Clicking the Pipe Network Properties tool displays the Pipe Network Properties dialog, which contains the settings for the entire network. If you mistyped any of the parameters in the original Create Pipe Network dialog, you can change them here. In addition, you can set the default label styles for the pipes and structures in this pipe network.

The Pipe Network Properties dialog contains the following tabs:

Information   On this tab, you can rename your network, provide a description, assign a predefined type of utility type to the network, and choose whether you'd like to see network-specific tooltips. Utility Type will be set to Undefined for data brought from Autodesk® Infraworks® 360.

Layout Settings   Here you can change the default label styles, network parts list, reference surface and alignment, and master object layers for plan pipes and structures, as well as name templates for your pipes and structures (see Figure 13.26).

FIGURE 13.26
The Layout Settings tab of the Pipe Network Properties dialog

Profile   On this tab, you can change the default profile label styles and master object layers for profile pipes and structures (see Figure 13.27). Note the introduction of a new type of label style, the crossing pipe label style that allows you to label the elevation and station of the pipe at the crossing point in the profile view only. Make sure that an appropriate label style is assigned or set to <none>.

FIGURE 13.27
The Profile tab of
the Pipe Network
Properties dialog

FIGURE 13.27
The Profile tab of
the Pipe Network
Properties dialog

Section Here you can change the master object layers for network parts in a section view
(see Figure 13.28).

FIGURE 13.28
The Section tab of
the Pipe Network
Properties dialog

Statistics This tab gives you a snapshot of your pipe network information, such as minimum and maximum elevation information, pipe and structure quantities, and the assigned
reference objects to the network such as alignments and surfaces (see Figure 13.29).

FIGURE 13.29
The Statistics
tab of the
Pipe Network
Properties dialog

The Select Surface tool on the Network Layout Tools toolbar allows you to switch between reference surfaces while you're placing network parts if needed. However, you should create a merged surface containing your existing surface plus your final design. Whenever possible, you should use a surface that incorporates the entire site (for example, existing and proposed pasted together) to avoid needing to switch between surfaces.

The Select Alignment tool on the Network Layout Tools toolbar lets you switch between reference alignments while you're placing network parts, which is similar to the Select Surface tool.

The Parts List tool allows you to switch parts lists for the pipe network.

The Structure drop-down (the image on the left in Figure 13.30) lets you choose which structure you'd like to place next, and the Pipes drop-down (the image on the right in Figure 13.30) allows you to choose which pipe you'd like to place next. Your choices come from the active network parts list.

FIGURE 13.30
The Structure
drop-down (left)
and the Pipes
drop-down (right)

The options for the Draw Pipes And Structures category let you choose what type of parts you'd like to lay out next. You can choose Pipes And Structures, Pipes Only, or Structures Only.

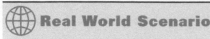 **Real World Scenario**

PRECOOKED PIPE NETWORKS IN YOUR TEMPLATE

The following tip is a revelation from a client—as many of the coolest tricks are. Even book authors have more to discover every day!

If you know that you will most likely have pipe networks in your project, you can create a few preset pipe networks in your template.

These "dummy" networks should be empty, but you can set the layout settings ahead of time. This will save you the steps of setting the correct parts catalog, object layers, object styles, and label styles.

PLACING PARTS IN A NETWORK

Network parts can be placed in a manner similar to those of other Civil 3D objects or AutoCAD objects such as polylines. You can use your mouse, transparent commands, dynamic input, object snaps, and other drawing methods when laying out your pipe network.

If you choose Pipes And Structures, a structure is placed wherever you click, and the structures are joined by pipes. If you choose Pipes Only, you can connect previously placed structures. If you have Pipes Only selected and there is no structure where you click, a null structure is placed to connect your pipes.

 Use the Structures Only option when you want to add a structure along an existing pipe run. Watch for the "boxing glove" glyph to appear, indicating that the pipe network recognizes the connection. Clicking to connect to the pipe breaks the pipe into two pieces and places a structure (or null structure) at the break point.

 While you're actively placing pipes and structures, you may want to connect to a previously placed part. For example, there may be a service or branch that connects into a structure along the main trunk. Begin placing the new branch. When you're ready to tie into a structure, you'll get a circular connection marker as your cursor comes within connecting distance of that structure. If you click to place your pipe when this marker is visible, a structure-to-pipe connection will form, and the end of the pipe will automatically be set as the center or attachment point for the structure. If you add a structure to the end of a pipe, the connection marker will be a box marker instead of a circular marker.

 As you create pipes, the default behavior is to draw them upstream to downstream. The Toggle Upslope/Downslope tool changes the flow direction of your pipes as they're placed. In Figure 13.31, structure 9 was placed before structure 10. It is recommended to leave the setting on its default value (downslope) because changing it would cause issues with the way in which the rules are applied.

FIGURE 13.31
Using the
Downslope
toggle (a) and the
Upslope toggle (b)
to create a pipe
network leg

Click Delete Pipe Network Object to delete pipes or structures of your choice. AutoCAD Erase can also delete network objects, but be careful that you don't accidentally remove more objects than you intend. Also, the AutoCAD Erase command might cause corruption when used to erase pipe networks parts; therefore, it isn't a recommended method. Always try to use the Delete tool available under the Network Layout Tools toolbar, or delete objects either using Pipe Network Vistas or using the Prospector tab ➤ Pipe Networks branch of Toolspace.

Clicking Pipe Network Vistas brings up the Pipes and Structures tabs in Panorama (see Figure 13.32), where you can make tabular edits to your pipe network while the Network Layout Tools toolbar is active.

FIGURE 13.32
Pipe Network
Vistas via
Panorama for
pipes (top)
and structures
(bottom)

The Pipe Network Vistas interface is similar to what you encounter in the Prospector tab ➤ Pipe Networks branch of Toolspace. The advantage of using Pipe Network Vistas is that you can make tabular edits without leaving the Network Layout Tools toolbar. You can edit pipe properties, such as Invert and Slope, on the Pipes tab, and you can edit structure properties, such as Rim and Sump, on the Structures tab.

CREATING A WASTE WATER NETWORK

This exercise will apply the concepts taught in this section and give you hands-on experience using the Network Layout Tools toolbar:

1. Open 1303_Pipes.dwg (1303_Pipes_METRIC.dwg), which you can download from this book's web page.

2. Expand the Surfaces branch in Prospector.

   This drawing has several surfaces that have a _No Display style applied to simplify the drawing. The surface you will be working from is a composite of the existing conditions, corridor surfaces, and grading surfaces.

OPTIMIZING THE COVER BY STARTING UPHILL

If you're using the Cover And Slope rule for your pipe network, you'll achieve better cover optimization if you begin your design at an upstream location and work your way down to the connection point.

The Cover And Slope rule prefers to hold minimum slope over optimal cover. In practice, this means that as long as minimum cover is satisfied, the pipe will remain at minimum slope. If you start your design from the upstream location, the pipe is forced to use a higher slope to achieve minimum cover. The following graphic shows a pipe run that was created starting from the upstream location (right to left):

When you start from the downhill side of your project, the Minimum Slope rule is applied as long as minimum cover is achieved. The following graphic shows a pipe run that was created starting from the downstream location (left to right):

Notice how the slope remains constant even as the pipe cover increases. Maximum cover is a violation-only rule, which means it never forces a pipe to increase slope to remain within tolerance; it provides only a warning that maximum cover has been violated.

3. Expand the Alignments and Centerline Alignments branches, and notice that there are several road alignments (no action is required).

4. On the Home tab ➢ Create Design panel ➢ Pipe Network drop-down, select Pipe Network Creation Tools.

5. In the Create Pipe Network dialog (shown previously in Figure 13.24), give your network the following information:

    ◆ Network Name: **Waste Water Network**

    ◆ Network Parts List: Waste Water

    ◆ Surface Name: Composite

    ◆ Alignment Name: **Syrah Way**

    ◆ Structure Label Style: Data With Connected Pipes (Waste Water)

    ◆ Pipe Label Style: Length Description And Slope

6. Click OK.

    The Network Layout Tools toolbar will appear.

7. From the structure list, expand the Concentric Cylindrical Structure (SI for metric) branch, and choose Concentric Structure 48 Dia 18 Frame 24 Cone (metric: Concentric Structure 1,200 Dia 450 Frame 600 Cone).

8. From the pipe list, expand the PVC pipe (SI for metric) branch and choose 8 Inch PVC (200 mm PVC).

9. Click the Draw Pipes And Structures tool. Working right to left, snap using an Intersection Osnap to the X labeled 1 in the drawing to place the first structure. Snap the X labeled 2 to place the second structure.

10. Without exiting the command, go back to the Network Layout Tools toolbar and change the Pipe drop-down from 8 Inch PVC to 10 Inch PVC (200 mm PVC to 250 mm PVC) and then place structures at the Xs labeled 3, 4, and 5.

The labels show that the diameter of the pipe between these structures is 10″ (250 mm).

11. Press ↵ to exit the command.

Next, you'll add a branch of the network from ROAD B. You may want to use the label grip to drag the label off to the side. This will form the leaders as shown in Figure 13.33, making the next step easier. Be sure to deselect the labels before proceeding using the Esc key.

FIGURE 13.33
Labels shown in a dragged state

12. Go back to the Network Layout Tools toolbar, and select 8 Inch PVC (200 mm PVC) from the pipe list.

13. Click the Draw Pipes And Structures tool button again.

14. Working north to south, click to place the next structure at the X labeled 6.

15. Tie into the ROAD A branch by moving your cursor near structure 2. You will be ready to click when you see the "sunshine" glyph, indicating that the pipe will tie into the structure.

16. Press ↵ to exit the command.

Observe your pipe network, including the labeling that automatically appeared as you drew the network.

17. Expand the Pipe Networks ➤ Networks branch in Prospector in Toolspace, and locate your Waste Water Network.

18. Expand Waste Water Network, and click the Pipes branch.

    The list of pipes appears in the preview pane.

19. Click the Structures branch; the list of structures appears in the preview pane.

20. Close the Network Layout Tools toolbar, and save the drawing.

For your reference, completed versions of the drawing (1303_Pipes_FINISHED.dwg and 1303_Pipes_METRIC_FINISHED.dwg) are available with the rest of this book's download.

Creating a Storm Drainage Pipe Network from a Feature Line

If you already have an object in your drawing that represents a pipe network (such as a polyline, an alignment, or a feature line), you can take advantage of the Create Pipe Network From Object command in the Pipe Network drop-down.

This option can be used for applications such as converting surveyed pipe runs into pipe networks and bringing forward legacy drawings that used AutoCAD linework to represent pipes. The Create Pipe Network From Object option creates a pipe for every linear segment of your object and places a structure at every vertex of your object. Each object you convert will initially go to a separate network. However, once you have several networks, you can easily merge them if needed.

This exercise will give you hands-on experience building a pipe network from a feature line with elevations and merging it with an existing network:

1. Open the 1304_PipesFromObject.dwg (1304_PipesFromObject_METRIC.dwg) file.

    This drawing contains the feature line you will use to generate a storm network.

2. Expand the Surfaces branch in Prospector.

    This drawing has several surfaces that have a _No Display style applied to simplify the drawing (no action is required).

3. Expand the Alignments and Centerline Alignments branches, and notice that there are several road alignments.

    In the drawing, a cyan feature line runs through Syrah Way (the horizontal road) and then goes onto Frontenac Drive. This feature line represents utility information for a storm-drainage line. The elevations of this feature line correspond with invert elevations that you'll apply to your pipe network.

4. On the Home tab ➤ Create Design panel ➤ Pipe Network drop-down, select Create Pipe Network From Object.

5. At the Select Object or [Xref]: prompt, select the cyan feature line near the eastern end of the feature line.

    You'll see a preview (see Figure 13.34) of the pipe-flow direction that is based on where you selected the line. In this case, the east end of the feature line is considered the upstream end.

FIGURE 13.34
The flow-direction
preview

   6. At the `Flow Direction [OK Reverse] <Ok>:` prompt, press ↵ to choose OK.

   The Create Pipe Network From Object dialog appears, as shown in Figure 13.35.

FIGURE 13.35
Converting a
feature line to a
pipe network

7. In the dialog, give your pipe network the following information:

- Network Name: **Storm Network**
- Network Parts List: Storm Sewer
- Pipe To Create: 12 Inch Concrete Pipe (300 mm Concrete Pipe)
- Structure To Create: From the Rectangular Junction Structure NF (SI for metric) collection 2 × 2 (750 × 750 mm Rectangular Structure)
- Surface Name: Composite
- Alignment Name: <none>
- Erase Existing Entity check box: Selected
- Use Vertex Elevations check box: Selected
- Vertex Elevation Reference: Invert

If you select Use Vertex Elevations, the pipe rules for your chosen parts list will be ignored. If it becomes necessary later, you can use the Apply Rules tool as discussed in the next section of this chapter.

8. Click OK. A pipe network will be created.

Next, you will merge this network with another network that exists in the drawing.

9. Select a pipe or structure from the newly created network. From the Pipe Networks contextual tab ➤ Modify panel, select Merge Networks.

10. In the Select Pipe Network To Be Merged Into Another Network dialog, highlight Storm Network and click OK.

11. In the Select Destination Pipe Network dialog, highlight Existing Storm Network and click OK.

12. Save and close the drawing.

This exercise combined all your object-created networks into a more manageable single network.

For your reference, completed versions of the drawing (1304_PipesFromObject_FINISHED .dwg and 1304_PipesFromObject_METRIC_FINISHED.dwg) are available with the rest of this book's download.

Editing a Pipe Network

You can edit pipe networks in several ways:

- Using drawing layout edits such as grip, move, and rotate
- Grip-editing the pipe size
- Using vertical movement edits using grips in profile (see the "Editing Pipe Networks in Profile View Using Grips" section later in this chapter)

- Using tabular edits in the Pipe Networks branch in Prospector or from Pipe Network Vistas (via Panorama) from the Network Layout Tools toolbar

- Right-clicking a network part to access tools such as Swap Part or Pipe/Structure Properties

- Returning to the Network Layout Tools toolbar by right-clicking the object and choosing Edit Network

- Selecting the pipe network in Toolspace ➤ Prospector, right-clicking, and choosing Edit Network

- Selecting a network part to access the Pipe Networks contextual tab

You will have the chance to explore most of these methods in the following sections.

Changing Flow Direction

By default, Civil 3D pipes are drawn upstream to downstream. It is easy to forget the Toggle Upslope/Downslope tool located on the Network Layout Tools. If you forget to use it, don't fret; you can change the flow direction after the pipes are placed.

To change flow direction, select any part from a pipe network to open the Pipe Networks contextual tab. Select Change Flow Direction from the drop-down portion of the Modify panel. Change Flow Direction allows you to reverse the pipe's understanding of which direction it flows, which comes into play when you're using the Apply Rules command and when you're annotating flow direction with a pipe label–slope arrow.

Changing the flow direction of a pipe doesn't modify the pipe's inverts in any way. By default, a pipe's flow direction depends on how the pipe was drawn and how the Toggle Upslope/Downslope tool was set when the pipe was drawn:

Downslope   If the toggle was set to Downslope (the default setting), the pipe flow direction is set to Start To End, which means the first endpoint you placed is considered the start of flow and the second endpoint is established as the end of flow.

Upslope   If the toggle was set to Upslope when the pipe was drawn, the pipe flow direction is set to End To Start, which means the first endpoint placed is considered the end for flow purposes and the second endpoint the start.

After pipes are drawn, by default they will have a Start To End flow direction. This is among the four options of flow that can be assigned by going to Pipe Properties or by going to Prospector ➤ Pipe Networks ➤ Networks ➤ Network Name ➤ Pipes Branch:

Start To End   A pipe label–flow arrow shows the pipe direction from the first pipe endpoint drawn to the second endpoint drawn, regardless of invert or slope.

End To Start   A pipe label–flow arrow shows the pipe direction from the second pipe endpoint drawn to the first pipe endpoint drawn, regardless of invert or slope.

Bi-Directional   Typically, this is a pipe with zero slope that is used to connect two bodies that can drain into each other, such as two stormwater basins, septic tanks, or overflow vessels. The direction arrow is irrelevant in this case. This might be the case as well when gravity networks are used to represent pressure networks, such as in the case of force main waste water lines.

By Slope   A pipe label–flow arrow shows the pipe direction as a function of pipe slope. For example, if End A has a higher invert than End B, the pipe flows from A to B. If B is edited to have a higher invert than A, the flow direction flips from B to A.

Editing Your Network in Plan View

When selected, a structure has two types of grips, shown in Figure 13.36. The first is a square grip located at the structure insertion point. You can use this grip to grab the structure and stretch/move it to a new location using the insertion point as a base point. Stretching a structure results in the movement of the structure as well as any connected pipes. Moving a structure allows the reposition of the structure to a new place while the connected pipes remain at the original location. You can also scroll through Stretch, Move, and Rotate by using your spacebar once you've grabbed the structure by this grip.

FIGURE 13.36
Two types of structure grips

The second structure grip is a rotational grip that you can use to spin the structure around its insertion point. This is useful for aligning eccentric structures, such as rectangular junction structures. Note that even though they will be rotated in plan view, the specified rotation may not be properly represented in the profile view.

In plan view, many common AutoCAD Modify commands work with structures. You can execute the following commands normally: Move, Copy, Rotate, Align, and Mirror. (Scale doesn't have an effect on structures.) You can use the AutoCAD Erase command to erase network parts. Note that erasing a network part in plan completely removes that part from the network. Once erased, the part disappears from plan, profile view, Prospector, and so on. Always remember that even though the AutoCAD Erase command is supported, its use is not recommended in the management of network parts.

When selected, a pipe end has two types of grips (see Figure 13.37). The first is a square endpoint-location grip. Using this grip, you can change the location of the pipe end without constraint. You can move it in any direction, make it longer or shorter, and take advantage of Stretch, Move, Rotate, and Scale by using your spacebar.

FIGURE 13.37
Two types of pipe-
end grips

The second grip (triangular) is a pipe-length grip. This grip lets you extend a pipe along its current bearing and slope.

A pipe midpoint also has two types of grips (see Figure 13.38). The first is a square location grip that lets you move the pipe using its midpoint as a base point.

FIGURE 13.38
Two types of pipe
midpoint grips

The second grip is a triangular-shaped pipe-diameter grip. Stretching this grip gives you a tooltip showing allowable diameters for that pipe, which are based on your parts list. Use this grip to make quick visual changes to the pipe diameter.

A WORD ABOUT PAY ITEMS

Be careful about using the grip to change the pipe diameter. Note that if a pay item is associated with a pipe in your parts list, changing the pipe diameter graphically does not change the associated pay item. For more information on associating pipe parts to pay items, see Chapter 17.

Using the Pipe Network Vista Effectively

To access the full tabular version of your pipe network, the best place to go is to the Pipe Networks contextual tab ➢ Modify panel ➢ Edit Pipe Network button.

Clicking Edit Pipe Network will display the Network Layout Tools toolbar, from which you can click the Pipe Network Vistas (aka Panorama) tool. This will display the grid view shown in Figure 13.39.

FIGURE 13.39
Selecting multiple rows and right-clicking the column name allows you to edit multiple items at once.

Note that pipes and structures are listed on separate tabs. Many items can be edited from this view. Subtle shading of the columns indicates which rows can be modified. If a column has a light gray background, this means the value is calculated or for information only.

The Status column indicates any rule violations that exist in the network. When a rule violation exists, a red symbol will appear with the number of violations. When you pause your cursor over one of these symbols, a tooltip will inform you which rule has been violated.

You can adjust many things in this interface, but you'll find it cumbersome for some tasks. The interface is best used for the following:

Batch Changes to Styles, Render Materials, Reference Surfaces, Reference Alignments, Rule Sets, and So On   Use your Shift or Ctrl key to select the desired rows and then right-click the column header of the property you'd like to change. Choose Edit and then select the new value from the drop-down. If you find yourself doing this on every project for most network parts, confirm that the correct values are set in your parts list and in the Pipe Network Properties dialog.

Batch Changes to Pipe Description   Use your Shift key to select the desired rows and then right-click the Description column header. Choose Edit and then enter your new description. If you find yourself doing this on every project for most network parts, check your parts list. If a certain part will always have the same description, you can add it to your parts list and prevent the extra step of changing it here.

Changing Pipe or Structure Names   You can change the name of a network part by typing in the Name field. If you find yourself doing this on every project for every part, check that you're taking advantage of the Name templates in your Pipe Network Properties dialog (which can be further enforced in your Pipe Network command settings).

This interface can be useful for changing pipe inverts, crowns, and centerline information. Keep in mind that Civil 3D will allow you to make changes that violate your pipe rules. Edits to a single pipe or structure are dynamic to parts that are directly connected, but Civil 3D will not reapply the rules for you automatically.

Editing Using the Pipe Networks Contextual Tab

You can perform many edits at the individual part level by selecting it. The Pipe Networks contextual tab will appear for the object you have selected.

If you realize you placed the wrong part at a certain location—for example, if you placed a catch basin where you need a drainage manhole—use the Swap Part option on the Pipe Networks contextual tab (see Figure 13.40). You'll be given a list of all the relevant parts from the parts list associated with the Pipe Network.

FIGURE 13.40

Selecting a network part brings up the Pipe Networks contextual tab with many options, including Swap Part.

The same properties listed in Prospector (or Pipe Network Vistas) can be accessed on an individual part level by selecting a pipe or structure and choosing Pipe Properties or Structure Properties from the Pipe Networks contextual tab. A dialog like the Structure Properties dialog in Figure 13.41 will open, with several tabs that you can use to edit that particular part.

FIGURE 13.41

The Part Properties tab in the Structure Properties dialog gives you the opportunity to perform many edits and adjustments.

THE LABELS & TABLES PANEL

Many objects have a Labels & Tables panel in their contextual tabs. This panel (Figure 13.42) is where you do the most annotation labeling for pipes.

FIGURE 13.42
The Labels &
Tables panel

Add Labels For the best control over what styles are used in your label, use the Add Pipe Network Labels option. From there, you can add labels for the selected pipe network using the suboptions such as Entire Network Plan, Entire Network Profile, Entire Network Section, Single Part Plan, Single Part Profile, Single Part Section, Spanning Pipes Plan, and Spanning Pipes Profile.

Add Tables You can add a structure or pipe table.

Reset Labels This Reset Labels is different from the Reset Label option you see when right-clicking directly on a pipe or structure label. By using this specific contextual ribbon command, pipe networks that are in the drawing via data reference will be labeled using styles from the source drawing. For more information on source drawings and data references, see Chapter 16, "Advanced Workflows."

THE GENERAL TOOLS PANEL

The General Tools panel (Figure 13.43) is common to all Civil 3D objects' contextual tabs.

FIGURE 13.43
The General Tools panel in the Pipe Networks contextual tab

Properties This toggles the Properties palette on and off.

Object Viewer This allows you to view the selected object or objects in 3D via a separate window.

Isolate Objects Selected objects will be the only objects visible on the screen. This is useful if you are working in a tight area and do not want to see extraneous objects, and it is much quicker than clicking to turn off or freeze layers.

These tools are available via the General Tools panel drop-down.

Select Similar This is the best tool ever invented! Select an example object or objects and then click Select Similar. All objects of the same type and layer will be selected. This works great on base AutoCAD objects, not just Civil 3D objects.

Quick Select or QSelect This opens the Quick Select dialog, which allows custom filtering.

Draw Order Icons These icons allow you to move objects either to the front or back of other visible objects or above or behind a specific object.

The Modify Panel

The Modify panel (shown previously in Figure 13.40) is where you edit an existing pipe network. The Modify panel contains the following tools:

Network Properties   This opens the Pipe Network Properties dialog.

Pipe Properties   This opens the Pipe Properties dialog.

Edit Pipe Style   This tool resides in the Pipe Properties drop-down and opens the Pipe Style dialog. If you are seeing the Modify panel because you have selected a structure, you will be prompted to select a pipe. For more on pipe styles, see Chapter 19.

Structure Properties   This opens the Structure Properties dialog.

Edit Structure Style   This tool resides in the Structure Properties drop-down and opens the Structure Style dialog. For more on structure styles, see Chapter 19.

Edit Pipe Network   This opens the Network Layout Tools toolbar.

Connect/Disconnect Part   These allow you to connect pipes to structures that may have been disconnected and to disconnect pipes from structures.

Swap Part   This allows you to replace a structure or pipe type with another one from a Swap Part Size dialog that is part of the current network parts list.

Split/Merge Network   These allow you to take an existing network and split it into two networks or take an existing pipe network and merge it into another pipe network.

The Modify panel has a flyout that contains the following tools:

Rename Parts   This opens the Rename Pipe Network Parts dialog. Here, you can rename pipes and structures, modify pipe numbering, and decide how you want to handle conflicting names or numbers.

Apply Rules   Apply Rules is an important yet easy-to-miss tool that will help you recalculate pipe slopes if changes need to be made. The easiest way to use this tool is to key in **APPLYRULES** with no objects selected. The reason for this is that it will give you a chance to pick an upstream part and a downstream part and automatically select items between. If you have items selected at the time you click Apply Rules, the rules will be rechecked only for the selected items, often leading to unexpected results. This command can be also accessed from the Modify panel of the Pipe Networks contextual tab.

Change Flow Direction   This changes the path of the selected objects. It is important to have this option set correctly if you are going to use any of the analysis programs.

The Network Tools Panel

The Parts List drop-down on the Network Tools panel (Figure 13.44) contains the following tools:

FIGURE 13.44
The Network Tools
panel shown with
the Parts List
menu expanded

Create Parts List   Allows you to create a new parts list via the Network Parts List – New Parts List dialog.

Create Full Parts List   Takes all the parts available in the parts catalog and creates a list called Full Catalog.

Edit Parts List   Opens the Parts List dialog, where you can select the network with which you want to work. A common mistake people make when getting to the parts lists this way is clicking OK. To edit, copy, or make a new list, use the drop-down to the right of the Parts List name.

Set Network Catalog   Opens the Pipe Network Catalog Settings dialog, where you can indicate whether you want to use Imperial or metric parts, and also sets the location of the catalog folder.

Part Builder   Opens the Getting Started screen of the Part Builder tool. For more information about Part Builder, see the section "Understanding Part Builder" later in this chapter.

You'll also find Draw Parts In Profile on the Network Tools panel. This tool adds the selected pipe network objects into an existing profile view.

THE ANALYZE PANEL

The Analyze panel (Figure 13.45) contains three tools for performing various checks on a pipe network. Using the drop-down menu for Interference Check, you have these options:

Create Interference Check   This allows you to create an interference check between parts, whether or not they are on the same network.

Interference Check Properties   When you select the Interference Check Properties tool, you will be prompted to select an Interference, and then the Interference Check Properties dialog will open:

FIGURE 13.45
The Analyze panel with Interference Check expanded

- ◆ The Information tab displays basic information such as the name of the interference check, style, render material, and layer.

- ◆ The Criteria tab contains specific editable items, such as whether to apply 3D proximity check, which uses either distance or scale factor.

- ◆ The Statistics tab is a combined listing of the other tabs but also allows you to see the networks used for the interference check.

Interference Properties   The Interference Properties tool gives you information about a single interference location in your drawing. This differs from the Interference Check Properties in that you can't change the criteria from here. You see only the following information about a specific instance of interference:

- ◆ Information tab (where you can name the individual interference objects and change the style and render material)

- ◆ Statistics tab (which contains read-only information about the networks causing the selected interference and its location)

Edit Interference Style   This tool prompts you to select an interference object (by default a brown, circular block in the default stock template). After selecting the interference object, this opens the Interference Style dialog, where you can change the visual parameters for the interference object. For more on object styles, see Chapter 19.

Getting back to the ribbon, next you will see the Storms Sewers commands that interact with the Hydraflow Storm Sewers Extension. Hydraflow is a separate program that is included with Civil 3D. An in-depth discussion of Hydraflow is beyond the scope of this book; see the Hydraflow Storm Sewers Extension help files for more information.

Choosing Edit In Storm And Sanitary Analysis opens the Storm and Sanitary Analysis (SSA) program. For more on SSA, see this book's website for a bonus chapter, "Storm and Sewer Analysis."

THE LAUNCH PAD PANEL

The Launch Pad panel (Figure 13.46) contains the following tools:

FIGURE 13.46
The Launch Pad panel

Alignment From Network   Allows you to create an alignment from pipe network parts

Storm Sewers   Launches the Hydraflow Storm Sewers program

Hydrographs   Launches the Hydraflow Hydrographs program

Express   Opens the Hydraflow Express program

Hydraflow Storm Sewers, Hydraflow Hydrographs, and Hydraflow Express are separate programs that are included with Civil 3D. An in-depth discussion of these programs is beyond the scope of this book; see the relevant Hydraflow help files for more information.

Editing with the Network Layout Tools Toolbar

You can also edit your pipe network by retrieving the Network Layout Tools toolbar. This is accomplished by selecting a pipe network object and choosing Edit Network from the contextual tab. You can also access the contextual tab via the Modify tab of the ribbon and click Pipe Network on the Design panel.

Once the toolbar is up, you can continue working exactly the way you did when you originally laid out your pipe network.

This exercise will give you hands-on experience in making a variety of edits to a waste water and storm drainage pipe network:

1. Open the 1305_PipeEditing.dwg (1305_PipeEditing_Metric.dwg) file.

   This drawing includes a waste water network and a storm drainage network, as well as some surfaces and alignments. For metric users, the structure family names end with SI.

2. Select the structure STM STR 3 in the drawing. It is labeled with the structure name showing.

3. From the Pipe Networks contextual tab ➤ Modify panel, click Swap Part.

4. Select the 2 × 4 (1,500 × 750) structure from the Rectangular Junction Structure NF (Rectangular Structure Slab Top Rectangular Frame SI for metric users) and click OK.

5. Select the newly replaced catch basin so that you see the two structure grips.

6. Use the rotational grip and your nearest Osnap to align the catch basin to the centerline of the pipe, as shown in Figure 13.47.

FIGURE 13.47
Rotate the catch
basin into place
along the curb.

7. Press Esc to clear the selection.

8. In the Prospector tab of Toolspace ➢ Pipe Networks ➢ Networks ➢ Waste Water Network,
    select the Structures branch.

    At the bottom of Toolspace, you should see a list of structures present in the network.

9. Scroll through the Structures list and locate SAN STR 7. (You will probably need to
    expand the width of the Name column to view the structure names.)

10. Right-click SAN STR 7 and click Pan To.

11. Again, right-click SAN STR 7 in the list. This time, click Delete. Select Yes at the prompt.

    Next, you will use the AutoCAD dynamic input tool to force pipe lengths to the
    desired value.

12. At the command line, type **DYNMODE** and press ↵.

13. Type **3** and press ↵.

    Your DYNMODE setting may already be set to a value of 3, meaning dimensional input
    will appear. This step ensures that dynamic input will allow you to enter a total length
    for the pipe.

14. If dynamic input is not already on, press F12 to enable it. Make sure that nothing is
    selected by pressing the Esc key until everything is cleared. Select the waste water pipe
    that is labeled in the north of the drawing along the Frontenac Drive alignment.

15. Click the triangular Endpoint grip on the right end of the pipe.

    Notice the tooltips at your cursor with information about the length of the pipe.

16. Press the Tab key to switch the input to the overall length of the pipe. Enter **200** (**60.96** m),
    as shown in Figure 13.48, and then press Enter.

FIGURE 13.48
Lengthen the pipe
to 200′ (60.96 m).

Note that this is the 3D Center To Center Pipe length. Next, you will add a structure to the end of the pipe you just modified.

17. With the pipe still selected from the Pipe Networks contextual tab ➤ Modify panel, click Edit Pipe Network.

18. From the Structures list, set the structure to SMH from the Concentric Cylindrical Structures NF family.

19. From the Draw Pipes And Structures drop-down, set the option to Structures Only. Place the structure in the drawing at the end of the pipe you lengthened previously. Make sure you can see the connection glyph before you click to add the structure.

20. Press Esc to clear the selection.

21. Select STM STR 3 in the drawing (this is the structure you modified at the beginning of this exercise), and from the Pipe Networks contextual tab ➤ Modify panel, click Structure Properties.

22. Switch to the Part Properties tab, scroll down to the Sump Depth field, and change the value to **0** (0 m).

23. Click OK to exit the Structure Properties dialog. Press Esc to clear the selection.

24. Select any pipe or structure from the Waste Water Network.

25. From the Pipe Networks contextual tab ➤ Modify panel, click Edit Pipe Network.

26. From the Network Layout Tools, click Pipe Network Vistas.

This will bring up the Panorama interface, which will allow you to rename the structures.

27. Make sure that the active Panorama tab is set to Structures.

28. In the Name column heading, widen the column so you can see the full name of the structures in the list. (You can widen a column in all spreadsheet-like views in Civil 3D, much as you would in Microsoft Excel.)

29. Double-click the cell in the Name column for SAN STR 1.

30. Clear the text that is there and type **MH 1**.

31. Repeat steps 29 and 30 for SAN STR 2 through SAN STR 4, renaming each but keeping the number. Close the vista and then close the toolbar.

32. Save and close the drawing.

For your reference, completed versions of the drawing (1305_PipeEditing_FINISHED .dwg and 1305_PipeEditing_METRIC_FINISHED.dwg) are available with the rest of this book's download.

Creating an Alignment from Network Parts

On some occasions, certain legs of a pipe network require their own stationing. Perhaps most of your pipes are shown on a road profile, but the legs that run offsite or through open space require their own profiles. Whatever the reason, it's often necessary to create an alignment from network parts. To do so, follow these steps:

1. Open the 1306_Alignment.dwg (1306_Alignment_METRIC.dwg) file.

2. Select the CB1 structure, which will be the first structure in the network on the east side of the Syrah Way alignment.

By launching the command with the CB1 selected, it is assumed this structure will be the start point of your new alignment.

3. On the Pipe Networks contextual tab ➢ Launch Pad panel, select Alignment From Network.

The command line will read Select next Network Part or [Undo].

4. Select the STM STR 7 structure, which will be the last structure on the alignment.

Notice that all the pipes and structures between the two selected structures have been highlighted. If any of the pipes or structures are not connected, the selecting set won't work as expected.

5. Press ↵, and a Create Alignment – From Pipe Network dialog will appear that is almost identical to the one you see when you create an alignment from the Alignments menu.

♦   Leave the default site to <None>.

♦   Name your alignment **Storm CL**.

♦   Leave the default Alignment type.

♦   Set Alignment Style to Layout and set Alignment Label Set to Major And Minor Only.

◆ Notice the Create Profile And Profile View check box on the last line of the dialog. Leave the box selected and click OK.

The Create Profile From Surface dialog will appear (see Figure 13.49).

FIGURE 13.49
The Create Profile From Surface dialog

6. Select the Composite surface, and click Add.

7. Click Draw In Profile View.

The Create Profile View Wizard will appear (see Figure 13.50). Make sure your settings match those in the figure.

FIGURE 13.50
The Create Profile View Wizard

8. Click Pipe/Pressure Network to jump to that page.

   You should see a list of pipes and structures in your drawing.

9. Verify that Yes is selected for each pipe and structure in the Storm Network only. By default, only the previously selected pipes and structures will be set to Yes on this tab.

10. Click Create Profile View and place the profile view to the right of the site plan. Notice that the profile shows the pipe network from upstream to downstream.

    Seven structures and six pipes will be drawn in a profile view, which is based on the newly created alignment (see Figure 13.51).

FIGURE 13.51
The completed profile view

11. Press Esc to deselect any features and then select the created alignment; from the contextual tab ➢ Modify panel drop-down, choose Reverse Direction. At the warning prompt, click OK.

    Notice how the profile view updates and the pipe network is displayed from downstream to upstream.

12. Save and close the drawing.

   For your reference, completed versions of the drawing (1306_Alignment_FINISHED.dwg and 1306_Alignment_METRIC_FINISHED.dwg) are available with the rest of this book's download.

Drawing Parts in Profile View

Certification
Objective

To add pipe network parts to an existing profile view, select a network part and choose Draw Parts In Profile from the Network Tools panel of the Pipe Networks contextual tab. When you're using this command, it's important to note that only selected parts are drawn in your chosen profile view.

   Profiles and profile views are always cut with respect to an alignment. Therefore, pipes are shown in the profile view on the basis of how they appear along that alignment or how they cross that alignment. Unless your alignment *exactly follows the centerline of your network parts*, your pipes will likely show some drafting distortion.

Let's look at Figure 13.52 as an example. This particular jurisdiction requires that all utilities be profiled along the road centerline. There are a road centerline and a storm network that jogs across the road to connect with another catch basin.

FIGURE 13.52
These pipe lengths will be distorted in profile view.

At least two potentially confusing elements show up in your profile view. First, the distance between structures (2D Length – Center To Center) isn't the same between the plan and the profile (see Figure 13.53) because the storm pipe doesn't run parallel to the alignment. Because the labeling reflects the network model, all labeling is true to the 2D Length – Center To Center or any other length you specify in your label style.

FIGURE 13.53
Pipe labels in plan view (top) and profile view (bottom)

The second potential issue is that the invert of your crossing storm pipe is shown at the point where the storm pipe *crosses the alignment* and not at the point where it connects to the storm sewer structure (see Figure 13.54).

FIGURE 13.54
The invert of a
crossing pipe
is drawn at the
location where
it crosses the
alignment.

Editing Pipe Networks in Profile View Using Grips

Although you can't make changes to certain part properties (such as pipe length) in profile view, pipes and structures both have special grips for changing their vertical properties in profile view.

When selected, a structure has two grips in profile view (see Figure 13.55). The first is a triangular-shaped grip representing a rim insertion point. This grip can be dragged up or down, and it affects the rim elevation of the structure at the insertion point.

FIGURE 13.55
A structure has
two grips in profile
view.

Moving this grip can affect your structure insertion point in two ways, depending on how your structure properties were established:

Automatic Surface Adjustment set to True   If your structure has Automatic Surface Adjustment set to True, grip-editing this Rim Insertion Point grip changes the surface adjustment value. If your reference surface changes, your rim will change along with it, plus or minus the surface adjustment value.

Automatic Surface Adjustment set to False   If your structure has the Automatic Surface Adjustment set to False, grip-editing this Rim grip modifies the insertion point of the rim. No matter what happens to your reference surface, the rim will stay locked in place.

Typically, you'll use the Rim Insertion Point grip only in cases where you don't have a surface for your rims to target or if you know there is a desired surface adjustment value. It's tempting to make a quick change instead of making the improvements to your surface that are fundamentally necessary to get the desired rim elevation. One quick change often grows in scope. Making the necessary design changes to your target surface will keep your model dynamic and, in the long run, will make editing your rim elevations easier.

The second grip is a triangular grip located at the sump depth. This grip doesn't represent structure invert. In Civil 3D, only pipes truly have invert elevation. The structure uses the connected pipe information to determine how deep it should be. When the sump has been set at a depth of 0, the sump elevation equals the invert of the deepest connected pipe.

This grip can be dragged up or down. It affects the modeled sump depth in one of two ways, depending on how your structure properties are established:

Control Sump By Depth   If your structure is set to control sump by depth, editing with the Sump grip changes the sump depth.

The depth is measured from the structure insertion point. For example, if the original sump depth was 0, grip-editing the sump 0.5′ (15.24 cm) lower would be the equivalent of creating a new sump rule for a 0.5′ (15.24 cm) depth and applying the rule to this structure. This sump will react to hold the established depth for any changes that would affect the invert of the lowest connected pipe. This triangular grip is most useful in cases where most of your pipe network will follow the sump rule applied in your parts lists, but selected structures need special treatment.

Control Sump By Elevation   If your structure is set to control sump by elevation, adjusting the Sump grip changes that elevation.

When sump is controlled by elevation, sump is treated as an absolute value that will hold regardless of the structure insertion point or invert elevation. For example, if you grip-edit your structure so its depth is 8.219′ (2.51 m), the structure will remain at that depth regardless of what happens to the inverts of your connected pipes. The Control Sump By Elevation parameter is best used for existing structures that have surveyed information of absolute sump elevations that won't change with the addition of new connected pipes.

When selected, a pipe end has three grips in profile view (see Figure 13.56). You can grip-edit the invert, crown, and centerline elevations at the structure connection using these grips, resulting in the pipe slope changing to accommodate the new endpoint elevation.

FIGURE 13.56
Three grips for a pipe end in profile view

When selected, a pipe in profile view has one grip at its midpoint (see Figure 13.57). You can use this grip to move the pipe vertically while holding the slope of the pipe constant.

FIGURE 13.57
Use the midpoint
grip to move a pipe
vertically.

You can access pipe or structure properties by choosing a part, right-clicking, and choosing Pipe or Structure Properties, or from the contextual ribbon tab.

Removing a Part from Profile View

If you have a part in profile view that you'd like to remove from the view without deleting it from the pipe network entirely, you have a few options.

AutoCAD Erase can remove a part from profile view; however, that part is then removed from every profile view in which it appears. If you have only one profile view or if you're trying to delete the pipe from every profile view, this is a good method to use.

Be careful when using the Del key or the Erase command on objects in plan view. Keep in mind that deleting any object from plan view removes the object outright, which includes pipe network parts. Use your Esc key liberally before selecting items to remove; this will help you avoid unintended deletion of items. Of course, if you accidentally blow away something, Undo will bring it back, but it isn't recommended since pipe network corruption might occur.

A better way to remove parts from a particular profile view is through the Profile View Properties. You can access these properties by selecting the profile view and from the contextual tab select Profile View Properties from the Modify View panel.

The Pipe Networks tab of the Profile View Properties dialog (see Figure 13.58) provides a list of all pipes and structures that are shown in that profile view. You can deselect the check boxes next to parts you'd like to omit from this view.

FIGURE 13.58
Deselect parts to
omit them from a
view.

At the bottom of the Profile View Properties dialog is a check box for Show Only Parts Drawn In Profile View. This check box is off by default so that you can see every possible pipe and structure. When it is checked on, the Pipe Network tab will hide any pipes that are not visible in the profile view you are examining.

Don't forget about the Show Only Crossing Pipes option. When this option is on, the list will narrow to only pipes that cross the alignment related to the profile view. This is a great help when you need to override the style of crossing pipes to show them as ellipses rather than linear pipes. Style overrides are discussed in more detail in the "Adding Pipe Network Labels" section.

Showing Pipes That Cross the Profile View

If you have pipes that cross the alignment related to your profile view, you can show them with a crossing style. A pipe must cross the parent alignment to be shown as a crossing in the profile view. The location of a crossing pipe is always shown *at the elevation where it crosses the alignment* (see Figure 13.59).

FIGURE 13.59
A pipe crossing a profile

When pipes enter directly into profiled structures, they can be shown as ellipses through the Display tab of the Structure Style dialog (see Figure 13.60). See Chapter 19 for more information about creating structure styles.

FIGURE 13.60
Pipes that cross directly into a structure can be shown as part of the structure style.

The first step to display a pipe crossing in profile is to add the pipe that crosses your alignment to your profile view, either by selecting the pipe and from the contextual tab selecting Draw Parts In Profile from the Network Tools panel and then selecting the profile view, or by checking the appropriate boxes on the Pipe Network tab of the Profile View Properties dialog. When the pipe is added, it's distorted when it's projected onto your profile view—in other words, it's shown as if you wanted to see the entire length of pipe in profile (see Figure 13.61).

FIGURE 13.61
The pipe crossing
is distorted.

The next step is to override the pipe style *in this profile view only*. Changing the pipe style through pipe properties won't give you the desired result because that will affect the visibility of every single instance of the pipe. You must override the style on the Pipe Networks tab of the Profile View Properties dialog (see Figure 13.62).

FIGURE 13.62
Use Style Override
to display cor-
rectly a crossing
in the Profile View
Properties dialog.

Locate the pipe you just added to your profile view and scroll to the last column on the right (Style Override). Select the Style Override check box and choose your pipe crossing style. Click OK. Your pipe should appear as an ellipsis.

If your pipe appears as an ellipsis but suddenly seems to have disappeared in the plan and other profiles, chances are good that you didn't use Style Override but accidentally changed the pipe style. Go back to the Profile View Properties dialog and make the necessary adjustments; your pipes will appear as you expect.

Adding Pipe Network Labels

Once you've designed your network, it's important to annotate the design. This section focuses on pipe network–specific label components in plan and profile views (see Figure 13.63).

Like with all Civil 3D objects, you can find the Pipe and Structure label styles in the Pipe and Structure branches of the Settings tab in Toolspace; they are covered in Chapter 18.

FIGURE 13.63
Sample of pipe network labels in plan view (top) and in profile view (bottom)

Creating a Labeled Pipe Network Profile with Crossings

This exercise will apply several of the concepts in this chapter to give you hands-on experience producing a pipe network profile that includes pipes that cross the alignment. You will have another chance to practice creating an alignment from a pipe network and associating the new alignment to the parts. You will also practice overriding pipe display in the Profile View Properties. There are storm pipes that cross the centerline nearly perpendicular to the alignment. You will show these as ellipses in the profile view.

1. Open the `1307_PipeLabels.dwg` (`1307_PipeLabels_METRIC.dwg`) file.

   It's important to start with this drawing rather than use the drawing from an earlier exercise.

   Note that surface numbering may differ between drawings, so these numbers have been omitted from the exercise.

2. Locate in plan view the waste water Structure 16 (near station 5+15 or 0+160 of Cabernet Court), select it to open the Pipe Networks contextual tab, and then select Alignment From Network on the Launch Pad panel.

3. When prompted to `Select Next Network Part`, select structure 18 and press ⏎ to create an alignment from the waste water network.

4. Choose the following options in the Create Alignment – From Pipe Network dialog:

   ◆ Site: <None>

   ◆ Name: **SMH16 to SMH18 Alignment**

   ◆ Alignment Type: Miscellaneous

   ◆ Alignment Style: _None

   ◆ Alignment Label Set: _No Labels

   ◆ Create Profile And Profile View check box: Selected

5. Click OK.

6. In the Create Profile From Surface dialog, highlight the EG and Corridor FG surfaces and click Add.

7. Change the Style for Corridor FG – Surface to Design Profile by clicking the Style column cell for the profile and selecting the specified style.

8. Click Draw In Profile View to open the Create Profile View dialog.

9. Set Profile View Style to Land Desktop Profile View and click the Next button in the Create Profile View Wizard until you reach the Pipe/Pressure Network Display page.

   You should see a list of pipes and structures in your drawing. Make sure Yes is selected for each pipe and structure under Waste Water Network.

10. Click Create Profile View. At the `Select profile view origin:` prompt, click to place the profile view to the right of the site plan.

11. Press the Esc key to complete the command. Select either a pipe or a structure in the profile view to open the Pipe Networks contextual tab. On the Labels & Tables panel, select Add Labels ➤ Entire Network Profile. Press Esc to deselect pipe networks parts.

The alignment information is missing from your structure labels because the alignment was created after the pipe network.

12. Select one of the pipes in the drawing from either plan or profile view.

13. From the Pipe Networks contextual tab ➤ Modify panel, click Edit Pipe Network.

14. From the Network Layout Tools, click Pipe Network Vistas.

15. Verify that you are on the Structures tab of Panorama.

16. Select structures 16 through 18 in Panorama using Shift+click. You may need to left-click the Name column header to sort by name.

17. Scroll to the right until you see the Reference Alignment column.

18. Right-click the column header and select Edit. Choose SMH16 To SMH18 Alignment from the Select Alignment dialog and click OK.

19. Close Panorama by clicking the green check mark on the Pipes and Structures tabs. You may need to enter **REGENALL** at the command line to see your updated structure labels. Close the Network Layout Tools toolbar.

20. Pan your drawing until you see the Storm layout located on Syrah Way in the plan view.

The waste water pipe network has already been laid out on the Syrah Way profile view. You want to show the storm where it crosses the waste water, so you can adjust the pipe elevations if necessary.

21. Press Esc a few times to make sure no other parts are selected. Then select the four pipes that cross perpendicular to the Syrah Way alignment.

22. In the Pipe Networks contextual tab ➤ Network Tools panel, select Draw Parts In Profile.

23. Select the Syrah Way profile view.

24. Press Esc to ensure no extra objects are selected; then select the profile view and pick Profile View Properties from the Modify View panel of the Profile View contextual tab.

25. On the Pipe Networks tab of the Profile View Properties dialog, place a check mark next to Show Only Crossing Pipes.

26. Select all four Storm Network pipes shown in Figure 13.62, and override the pipe style in this profile view by placing a check mark next to <Not Overridden> in the Style Override column.

You will be prompted to pick the pipe style and select the Pipe Crossing Pipe (Storm) style.

27. Click OK when you have selected the style.

28. When overrides have been set for all four pipes, click OK and Esc to deselect any items.

Your crossing pipes will resemble Figure 13.64.

FIGURE 13.64
The completed
exercise with
crossing pipes

29. Adjust the elevations of the crossing pipes as needed. Once you are done with editing, close the Network Layout Tools toolbar.

30. Select the four crossing pipes in the profile view. From the contextual tab, expand the Add Labels button within the Labels & Tables panel and select the Single Part Profile. Your crossing pipes will be labeled.

    Note that there are two labels applied to each of the pipes. One is a profile label, and the other is a crossing pipe label, with the latter being a new label feature with this release of the software.

31. Hit the Esc key a few times, select the profile view label (the vertical displayed one) for each of the pipes, and delete it using the Delete Key or the Erase command.

32. Drag the remainder label to a dragged state to better suit the label position outside of the pipe. Save and close the drawing.

    The crossing profile view label displays labels, which are in this case the type of pipe, the station of the crossing along the assigned pipe alignment, and the invert elevation of the pipe at the alignment crossing.

    You can control the accuracy of the pipe crossing representation by changing the value of the facetdev variable.

For your reference, completed versions of the drawing (1307_PipeLabels_FINISHED.dwg and 1307_PipeLabels_METRIC_FINISHED.dwg) are available with the rest of this book's download.

Using Pipe and Structure Labels

In earlier exercises, you had a sneak peek at adding labels for structures. Civil 3D makes no distinction between a plan label and a profile label. The same label style can be used in both places. In this chapter, you will use label styles that are already part of the drawing.

To create your own pipe labels from scratch, see Chapter 18.

SPANNING PIPE LABELS

In addition to single-part labels, pipes shown in either plan or profile view can be labeled using the Spanning Pipes option. This feature allows you to choose more than one pipe; the length that is reported in the label is the cumulative length of all pipes you choose.

Unlike parcel-spanning labels, no special label-style setting is required to use this tool. The Spanning Pipes option is on the Annotate tab. Select Add Labels ➤ Pipe Network ➤ Spanning Pipes Profile or Spanning Pipes Plan to access the command. Within these labels you can add and display specific parameters for spanned labels such as Drop Across Span, Slope Across Span, and Number Of Pipes In Span.

Creating an Interference Check

Certification
Objective

When designing, you must make sure pipes and structures are appropriately separated. You can perform some visual checks by rotating your model in 3D and plotting pipes in profile and section views (see Figure 13.65). Civil 3D also provides a tool called Interference Check that makes a 3D sweep of your pipe networks and lets you know whether anything is too close for comfort.

FIGURE 13.65
Two pipe networks may interfere vertically where crossings occur (left). Viewing your pipes in profile view can also help identify conflicts (right).

The following exercise will lead you through creating a pipe network and using Interference Check to scan your design for potential pipe network conflicts:

1. Open the 1308_Interference.dwg (1308_Interference_METRIC.dwg) file.

   The drawing includes a waste water pipe network and a storm drainage pipe network.

2. Select a part from either network in plan view, and on the Pipe Networks contextual tab ➤ Analyze panel, choose Interference Check ➤ Create Interference Check, as shown in Figure 13.66.

FIGURE 13.66
Creating an interference check

You'll see the Select another part from the same network or different network: prompt.

3. Select a part from the network that hasn't already been chosen.

The Create Interference Check dialog will appear (Figure 13.67).

FIGURE 13.67
The Create Interference Check dialog

4. Name the interference check **Collision**, and confirm that Waste Water and Storm Network appear in the Network 1 and Network 2 boxes.

5. Click the 3D Proximity Check Criteria button, and the Criteria dialog will appear (see Figure 13.68).

FIGURE 13.68
Criteria for the 3D proximity check

6. You're interested in finding all network parts that are within a certain tolerance of one another, so place a check mark next to Apply 3D Proximity Check. Then enter **1.5** (**0.5** for metric users) in the Use Distance box.

This setting creates a buffer to help find parts in all directions that might interfere. If you forget to check Apply 3D Proximity Check, only direct, physical collisions will be listed as collisions.

7. Click OK to exit the Criteria dialog, and click OK to run the Interference Check.

   You should see a dialog that alerts you to three interferences.

8. Click OK to dismiss this dialog.

9. On the Prospector tab of Toolspace, expand the Pipe Networks ➤ Interference Checks branch. Right-click Collision and select Zoom To.

   A small marker will appear at each location where interference occurs, as shown in Figure 13.69.

FIGURE 13.69
The interference marker in plan view

10. Make sure there is no item selected by pressing the Esc key a few times. Then select any one of the interference markers, the pipes that intersect, and the nearby inlets.

11. From the Multiple contextual tab ➤ General Tools panel, click Object Viewer.

12. In the upper-left corner of Object Viewer, click the Visual Style drop-down. Change Visual Style to Conceptual. Choose SW Isometric in the upper-right corner of Object Viewer.

    The interference marker will appear in 3D, as shown in Figure 13.70.

FIGURE 13.70
The interference marker in 3D

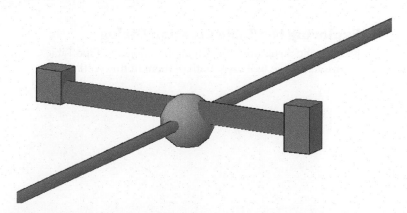

13. Use the ViewCube in Object Viewer to navigate in 3D.

14. Once you have examined the 3D objects, close Object Viewer. Save and close the drawing.

Note that each instance of interference is listed in the preview pane for further study.

For your reference, completed versions of the drawing (`1308_Interference_FINISHED` `.dwg` and `1308_Interference_METRIC_FINISHED.dwg`) are available with the rest of this book's download.

Editing your pipe network will flag the interference check as "out of date." You can rerun Interference Check by right-clicking Interference Check in Prospector. You can also access the Interference Check Properties to edit your criteria in this context menu.

Creating Pipe Tables

Just as with parcels and labels, the process of labeling pipes can turn into a mess when all the labels are set on the plan (see Figure 13.71). In this section, you will explore the process of creating tables for pipes and structures.

FIGURE 13.71
Crowded pipes and
structure labels on
a plan

Exploring the Table Creation Dialog

Because the Structure Table Creation dialog and Pipe Table Creation dialog are similar (see Figure 13.72), we will cover both of them in this section.

FIGURE 13.72
The Structure
Table Creation
dialog box

- The Table Style option allows you to select a table look or style. You can select the available styles from the arrow to the right of the Table Style name. You can also create new, copy, edit, or pick a table style from an existing table in the drawing. For more on table styles, see Chapter 18.

- The Table Layer option shows the layer where the table is placed.

- With the By Network radio button selected, you can select the network to create a table from the drop-down, or you can use the Pick icon to select the network from the drawing.

- With the Multiple Selection radio button selected and by using the Pick icon, you can select structures or pipes (depending on which table type is selected) from the drawing. You can pick pipes or structures regardless of the network.

- The Split Table check box allows you to split the table if it becomes too large. You can specify the maximum number of rows per table and the maximum number of tables per stack. Additionally, you can set the offset distance between the stacked tables.

- ◆ You can choose whether you want the split tables tiled across or down.

- ◆ In the Behavior section, choose Static or Dynamic. A static table will not update if any changes are made to the pipe network, such as swapping a part. Dynamic will update the table to those changes.

In the following exercise, you will create a pipe network table for the waste water structures:

1. Open the 1309_PipeTable.dwg (1309_PipeTable_METRIC.dwg) file.

2. Click the structure named MH1. This is a structure from the waste water network.

3. From the Pipe Networks contextual tab ➢ Labels & Tables panel, select Add Tables ➢ Add Structure.

   The Structure Table Creation dialog opens.

4. Verify that the By Network option is set to Waste Water. Click OK to accept the default settings (shown in Figure 13.72).

5. At the Select Upper Left Corner: prompt, place the table to the right of your plan.

   The table should look similar to Figure 13.73.

FIGURE 13.73
The finished structure table

STRUCTURE TABLE			
STRUCTURE NAME:	DETAILS:	PIPES IN:	PIPES OUT
MH2	48" RIM = 824.50 SUMP = 818.8 INV IN = 818.72 INV OUT = 820.81	Pipe 10, 12" PVC INV IN =816.72	Pipe 1, 8" PVC INV OUT =820.81
MH1	48" RIM = 823.35 SUMP = 814.9 INV IN = 814.92 INV OUT = 814.92	Pipe 1, 8" PVC INV IN =814.92	Pipe 2, 8" PVC INV OUT =814.92
SAN STR 11	48" RIM = 822.99 SUMP = 816.9 INV OUT = 816.90		Pipe 10, 12" PVC INV OUT =816.90
SAN STR 10	48" RIM = 815.82 SUMP = 775.0 INV IN = 775.06	Pipe 9, 8" PVC INV IN =775.06	
MH3	48" RIM = 811.05 SUMP = 806.1 INV IN = 806.21 INV OUT = 306.21	Pipe 2, 8" PVC INV IN =806.21	Pipe 3, 8" PVC INV OUT =806.21
SAN STR 4	48" RIM = 797.37 SUMP = 776.8 INV IN = 776.90 INV OUT = 776.90	Pipe 8, 8" PVC INV IN =776.90	Pipe 9, 8" PVC INV OUT =776.90
SAN STR 5	48" RIM = 793.30 SUMP = 788.7 INV IN = 788.83 INV OUT = 789.81	Pipe 3, 8" PVC INV IN =788.83	Pipe 4, 8" PVC INV OUT =789.81
SAN STR 6	48" RIM = 791.47 SUMP = 777.4 INV IN = 777.47 INV OUT = 777.47	Pipe 7, 8" PVC INV IN =777.47	Pipe 8, 8" PVC INV OUT =777.47
SAN STR 3	48" RIM = 785.43 SUMP = 778.2 INV IN = 778.28 INV OUT = 778.28	Pipe 6, 8" PVC INV IN =778.28	Pipe 7, 8" PVC INV OUT =778.28
SAN STR 9	48" RIM = 783.64 SUMP = 779.0 INV IN = 779.09 INV OUT = 779.09	Pipe 5, 8" PVC INV IN =779.09	Pipe 6, 8" PVC INV OUT =779.09

The process of creating tables for pipes is similar to the process for creating tables for structures.

6. Press Esc to clear the current selection and click any waste water pipe.

Note that as long as you have the Pipe Networks contextual tab open, you can create a table for either pipes or structures.

7. From the Pipe Networks contextual tab ➢ Labels & Tables panel, select Add Tables ➢ Add Pipe.

The Pipe Table Creation dialog opens (Figure 13.74).

FIGURE 13.74
The Pipe Table
Creation dialog

8. Verify that the By Network option is set to Waste Water. Click OK to accept the default settings.

9. At the `Select Upper Left Corner:` prompt, place the table to the right of the structure table.

The pipe table should look similar to Figure 13.75. (Metric users will see Reinforced Concrete in the Material column.)

For your reference, completed versions of the drawing (`1309_PipeTable_FINISHED.dwg` and `1308_PipeTable_METRIC_FINISHED.dwg`) are available with the rest of this book's download.

FIGURE 13.75
The finished pipe
table

NAME	SIZE	LENGTH	SLOPE	MATERIAL
Pipe 1	8"	139.54'	4.22%	PVC
Pipe 2	8"	177.33'	4.91%	PVC
Pipe 3	8"	248.11'	7.00%	PVC
Pipe 4	8"	122.89'	6.00%	PVC
Pipe 5	8"	105.12'	3.00%	PVC
Pipe 6	8"	80.50'	1.00%	PVC
Pipe 7	8"	81.15'	1.00%	PVC
Pipe 8	8"	56.44'	1.00%	PVC
Pipe 9	8"	199.99'	0.92%	PVC
Pipe 10	12"	45.00'	0.40%	PVC

Pipe Table

The Table Panel Tools

When you click a table, the Table contextual tab opens and has several tools available (Figure 13.76). You'll look at each in this section.

FIGURE 13.76
The Table contex-
tual tab

THE GENERAL TOOLS PANEL

The tools here are the same as mentioned earlier when the pipe network tools were discussed.

THE MODIFY PANEL

The Modify panel contains the following tools:

Table Properties   This tool opens the Table Properties dialog. With it, you can set the table style and choose whether to split the table with all the options mentioned earlier. In addition, you can force realignment of stacks, and if the reactivity mode is set to Static, you can force content updating.

Edit Table Style   This tool is located in the Table Properties drop-down and opens the Table Style dialog. For more on editing table styles, see Chapter 18.

Static Mode   This tool turns a dynamic table into a static table.

Update Content This tool forces an update on a table.

Realign Stacks This tool readjusts the table columns back to the default setting. This is especially useful after changing the annotation scale of the view or viewport.

Add Items This tool adds pipe data to the table that was added after the table was created.

Remove Items This tool removes pipe or structure objects from a table.

Replace Items This tool allows you to replace the current select set with a new one.

Setting and Using a Pressure Pipes Network

Pressure pipes work differently than gravity-flow pipe systems within Civil 3D. Much of the need for custom parts such as valves or hydrants is eliminated with these systems. In this section, you'll learn how easy it is to model water, gas, or other pressurized systems in 3D.

Pressure Network Parts List

Like gravity-based networks, a pressure network starts with a parts list. All of the parts available in Civil 3D are based on standards established by the American Water Works Association (AWWA) and are listed in both inches and millimeters.

Pressure parts lists contain pipes, fittings, and appurtenances. You'll find the style for each object in the parts list, but instead of rules, pressure pipe design checks are tucked into the command settings.

The following are examples of Pressure Pipe Network parts lists:

◆ Water main and service connections:

◆ Ductile iron pipe

◆ Tees, elbows, and crosses

◆ Valves

◆ Gas main:

◆ PVC pipe

◆ Valves

Under the Hood of the Pressure Network

Before you can create a Pressure parts list, you must determine the catalog from which you will be working. Set the pressure network catalog by going to the Home tab ➤ Create Design panel (expand the panel to view the additional tools) and selecting Set Pressure Network Catalog, as shown in Figure 13.77.

FIGURE 13.77
Setting the pressure network catalog

Create Figure from Object   Create Network Parts List
Create Subassembly from Polyline   Create Full Parts List
Create Polyline From Corridor   Set Pipe Network Catalog
Create Boundary From Corridor   Part Builder
Set Pressure Network Catalog
Create Design

Set the path to the Pressure Pipes Catalog folder to C:\ProgramData\Autodesk\ C3D 2016\enu\Pressure Pipes Catalog. Click the folder icon to choose either the metric or Imperial database, depending on your needs.

The catalog database file determines the join type between pressure network parts. In modern water main construction, the most commonly used join type is the push-on type, which is the default pressure database. As shown in Figure 13.78, with Imperial units you have three options:

FIGURE 13.78
Setting your catalog database file

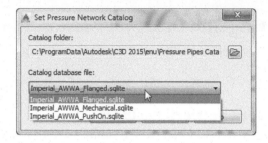

◆ Imperial_AWWA_Flanged

◆ Imperial_AWWA_Mechanical

◆ Imperial_AWWA_PushOn

Metric_AWWA_PushOn is currently the only available option for metric users.

These differ slightly in their options for pipes, fittings, and appurtenances. Only one type of pressure network catalog can be active at a time. A parts list can have parts from only one catalog in it; for example, you cannot mix and match push-on with mechanical parts. You can, however, have multiple Pressure parts lists in your template; each can pull parts from the various catalog database files. You can place parts from different parts lists into the same pressure network, as long as the parts are meant for the same diameter and pressure.

CREATING A PRESSURE PARTS LIST

In the Settings tab of Toolspace, you will find the listing for pressure networks. The Pressure Networks ➤ Parts List branch is where you will create a parts list. In the case of pressure networks, a parts list contains three components:

Pressure Pipes   Ductile iron of various sizes can be added. Like the gravity networks, each part can have a style. Furthermore, different sizes within the part families can have styles, which can help you identify them in the graphic.

Fittings   Fittings such as tees, crosses, and elbows are specified in this tab.

Appurtenances   Valves are specified in the Appurtenances tab.

BURSTING WITH PARTS

To create a complete list of all pressure network parts available in your active part catalog, type **CreatePressurePartListFull** at the command line and press ↵.

Keep in mind that the three different catalogs available to U.S. Imperial units vary with regard to which parts are available. For example, the following graphic shows the variation of the fittings available to Push-on, Flanged, and Mechanical catalogs:

Push-On fittings

Flanged fittings

Mechanical fittings

Your next question is probably, "Okay, so can I make my own parts?" The answer is, "It depends on your modeling skills and available time."

Pressure pipe network parts are 3D solids with a few extra bells and whistles that tell the program how they connect to other parts. If you are comfortable drafting 3D solids using the tools from the 3D modeling workspace, the procedure is fairly painless.

The Part Publishing Wizard tools built into AutoCAD will allow you to create a `*.CONTENT` package—for example, `Hydrant.CONTENT`. Once the content package is created, you can import it into the pressure pipe catalog of your choice by launching the Content Catalog Editor.

The Content Catalog Editor is automatically installed with Civil 3D 2016 and can be found from your Windows Start menu along with the other Autodesk AutoCAD Civil 3D 2016 utilities.

For more information on creating parts through the Part Publishing Wizard, see `PartPublishingWizardUsersGuide.docx` located in `C:\Program Files\Autodesk\AutoCAD 2016\C3D\Sample\Civil 3D API\Part Publishing Wizard`.

In the following exercise, you will create a Pressure Network parts list:

1. Open the `1310_Pressure.dwg` (`1310_Pressure_METRIC.dwg`) drawing, which you can download from this book's web page.

    This file is set up with a layer state that makes other objects gray. This will help you focus on the placement of pressure pipe network objects.

2. On the Home tab ➤ Create Design panel, click the arrow to view additional tools and select Set Pressure Network Catalog.

3. In the Set Pressure Network Catalog dialog, verify that Catalog Database File is set to `Imperial_AWWA_PushOn.sqlite` (`Metric_AWWA_PushOn.sqlite`).

   You might need to change the Catalog Folder path to access the correct catalog database file for the metric drawing.

4. Click OK.

5. On the Settings tab of Toolspace ➤ Pressure Network, expand the Pressure Network branch, right-click Parts Lists, and select New.

6. In the Pressure Network Parts List dialog, switch to the Information tab. Rename the Pressure Network parts list to **Watermain**.

7. Switch to the Pressure Pipes tab. Right-click New Parts List and select Add Material.

8. In the Pressure Network Catalog dialog, place a check mark next to Ductile Iron and click OK.

9. The name of the Pipe Parts list will update to Watermain. Expand the Watermain branch.

10. Right-click Ductile Iron and select Add Size.

11. Set the Nominal Diameter value to **10"** (**250** mm).

12. Set the Cut Length value to **20'** (**6** m).

13. Leave all other default values, as shown in Figure 13.79, and click OK.

FIGURE 13.79
Adding ductile iron pipe to the Pressure Network parts list

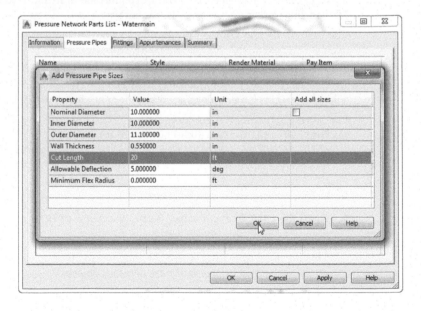

14. Switch to the Fittings tab, right-click New Parts List, and select Add Type.

15. In the Pressure Network Catalog dialog, place a check mark next to all three fitting types (Cross, Elbow, and Tee) as shown in Figure 13.80, and then click OK.

FIGURE 13.80
Adding fittings
to the Pressure
Network parts list

Metric users will have only the options for Elbow and Tee.

16. Expand the Watermain branch under the Fittings tab if it is not already expanded.

Metric users can skip to step 20.

17. Right-click Ductile Iron Cross and select Add Size.

18. Change Nominal Diameter to **10 × 10 × 14 × 14** (note that zeroes have been dropped from the name).

19. Leave the Allowable Deflection value as 5 degrees and click OK.

20. Right-click Ductile Iron Elbow and click Add Size.

21. Set Bend Angle to **11.25** and set Nominal Diameter to **10 × 10 (250 × 250** mm) (note that zeroes have been dropped from the name).

22. Leave the Allowable Deflection value at 5 degrees, which is the default for the size you picked. Click OK.

23. Repeat steps 20 and 21 for 22.5-degree and 45-degree elbows, with a nominal diameter of **10 × 10 (250 × 250** mm) (note that zeroes have been dropped from the name).

24. Right-click Ductile Iron Tee and select Add Size.

25. Set Nominal Diameter to **10" (250** mm) (note that zeroes have been dropped from the name).

26. Leave Allowable Deflection as 5 degrees. Click OK.

27. Switch to the Appurtenances tab.

28. Right-click New Parts List and select Add Type.

29. Place a check mark next to Gate Valve – Push-On – Ductile Iron – 200 psi (Gate Valve – Push-On – Ductile Iron – 16 Bar) and click OK.

30. Expand the Watermain branch under the Appurtenances tab.

31. Right-click the new gate valve and select Add Size.

32. Change the Nominal Diameter value to **10 × 10** (**250 × 250** mm) (note that zeroes have been dropped from the name) and click OK.

33. Click OK again to finish creating the Watermain Pressure Network parts list and then save the drawing for use in the next exercise.

You can check your results against 1310_Pressure_A.dwg (1310_Pressure_A_METRIC.dwg), which can be downloaded from the book's website.

Creating a Pressure Network

After you have set your pressure network catalog, created your Pressure Network parts list, and set your design parameters, it is time to draw your first network.

PRESSURE NETWORKS IN PLAN VIEW

As you work with pressure pipes, you will see some useful glyphs appear as you draw.

As shown in Figure 13.81, selecting a pressure pipe will give you tools to modify and continue your design.

FIGURE 13.81
Glyphs on a pressure pipe end

Location   Deflection   Continue Layout   Lengthen

Location The Location glyph moves the pipe both horizontally and vertically and will disconnect it from the adjoining fittings or appurtenances.

Deflection The Deflection glyph will change the angle at which the pipe sits in the adjoining fitting. When this glyph is active, you will see a fan-shaped guide indicating the allowable deflection from the fitting properties in the Pressure Network parts list. You are able to move the pipe beyond the guide but will receive design check errors when analyzing the network. You will take a closer look at design checks later in this chapter.

Continue Layout Continue Layout will help you pick up where you left off when working with pressure pipes. When you use this glyph from the end of a pipe, it will create a bend using the elbows from your Pressure Network parts list.

Lengthen   Lengthen will allow you to stretch or shorten a pipe. When used with dynamic input, you can set pipes to a specified 3D length. See the section on working with pipes and dynamic input earlier in the "Editing with the Network Layout Tools Toolbar" section.

As shown in Figure 13.82, you will encounter more glyphs when working with fittings and appurtenances.

FIGURE 13.82
Glyphs on a cross fitting

Slide   The Slide glyph is similar to Lengthen, but it can modify a pipe's length when a fitting or appurtenance is already attached.

Flip   The Flip glyph will mirror the part at its center. Flip glyphs are especially handy when working with tees, because it is often necessary to change the outlet direction of a tee after it is inserted. Be cautious when using the Flip glyph with elbows because it may disconnect the adjoining pipe.

Location   Changing the location of a fitting or appurtenance will move the pipe and maintain the connection.

Continue Layout   When you use this grip from a fitting or appurtenance, you are restricted to creating your pipe within the object's deflection tolerance.

Rotation   This grip allows you to rotate your fitting around its z-axis by a defined angle. Note that this grip is available only when the fitting is not connected to any pipe. Upon connection, the grip becomes unavailable.

In this exercise, you will create a pressure network. Use the Xs as guides for placement, but don't worry if your pipe network is slightly off from the guides. Because of the 3D nature of the pipes, the restrictions on placement angles within the pressure network parts, and object snap behavior, duplicating an example network exactly would be quite tedious. Get a feel for the pressure network creation tools and have fun! You need to have completed the previous exercise before continuing.

1. Continue working in the drawing 1310_Pressure.dwg (1310_Pressure_METRIC.dwg), or if you have not completed the previous exercise, open 1310_Pressure_A.dwg (1310_ Pressure_A_METRIC.dwg).

   Make sure that your catalog is set to the Push-On part catalog, as shown in the previous exercise.

As you work through this exercise, you will get the best results if you turn off object snaps, object snap tracking, polar tracking, and/or ortho. Because the pressure pipe tools already have restrictions on how they can be drafted, sometimes these tools conflict with where you want to place the pipe.

2. From the Home tab ➤ Create Design panel, click Pipe Network ➤ Pressure Network Creation Tools, as shown in Figure 13.83.

FIGURE 13.83
Selecting Pressure Network Creation Tools

3. In the Create Pressure Pipe Network dialog, name the network **Watermain North**, and then do the following:

   a. Set Parts List to Watermain.

   b. Set Surface Name to Composite.

   c. Set Alignment Name to Syrah Way.

   d. Set the pipe, fitting, and appurtenance labels styles as shown in Figure 13.84.

FIGURE 13.84
Creating your new Watermain North system using pressure pipe network tools

4. Click OK.

   The ribbon will change to show you the Pressure Network Plan Layout contextual tab, as shown in Figure 13.85.

FIGURE 13.85
The Pressure
Network Plan
Layout toolbar

5. On the Pressure Network Plan Layout contextual tab ➢ Network Settings panel, set the default cover to **4.5′ (1.5 m)**.

6. On the Layout panel, set your Size And Material drop-down to Pipe–10 In–Push On–Ductile Iron–350 psi–AWWA C151 (Pipe–250 mm–Push On–Ductile Iron–25 Bar–AWWA C151).

7. Start to place a waterline by clicking the X labeled 1 toward the east end of Syrah Way.

8. Place the first bend by clicking near the X labeled 2, to the left.

   At the bend, you are restricted to the bend angles listed in your part network. The Compass glyph (Figure 13.86) that appears represents the elbow angles to the left and right of your pipe. If you had not included multiple elbow angles in your Pressure Pipe Network parts list, only the default elbow angle of 11.25 degrees would be available.

FIGURE 13.86
The Pressure Pipe
Fitting glyph
reflects your elbow
angles.

9. Click the X labeled 3 to place the next pipe end.

10. Continue working east to west until you click near the X labeled 8. Press the Esc key.

    To keep the pressure pipe on track, you will use the allowable deflection of the elbow to move the pipe closer to the edge of the road.

    Make sure your object snaps are off for the next steps because they will interfere with the pipe modification glyphs.

11. Select the pipe section between the X labeled 7 and the X labeled 8 and then use the Deflection glyph to move the end of the pipe up north toward (see Figure 13.87) the approximate center of the green circle in the drawing.

FIGURE 13.87
Use the Deflection glyph to move the pipe.

12. Click the Continue Layout glyph to continue the layout.

13. Place the next pipe end at the X labeled 9.

14. Continue working west until you reach near the X labeled 10.

    Don't worry if you are off the desired location; you can always use the glyphs to edit the pipe location after the fact.

15. Press Esc after placing this pipe.

16. On the Pressure Network Plan Layout contextual tab ➤ Insert panel, change the fitting to Tee–10 in × 10 in- push on-ductile iron-350 psi-AWWA C111/C153 (Tee–250 mm × 250 mm-push on-ductile iron-25 bar-AWWA C110/C111/C153).

17. Click Add Fitting.

    As you hover your cursor near the end of the pipe, you will see the Add Connection glyph, as shown in Figure 13.88.

FIGURE 13.88
Add the fitting to the end of the pipe.

18. When the connection glyph is visible, click to add the tee.

19. Press Esc to complete the task.

    At this point, the tee is in the graphic, but it is not positioned in such a way that would make it useful in continuing the design north and south along the intersecting road (Frontenac Drive). To fix this situation, you will disconnect it from the pipe, rotate it, and then reconnect it to the pipe.

20. Click the tee in the graphic to select it and then right-click the part and select Disconnect From Pressure Part, as shown in Figure 13.89. (Note that this command is not available in the contextual tab.)

FIGURE 13.89
Disconnecting the part in preparation for rotating it

21. At the `Select connected pressure part:` prompt, select the pipe connected to the tee.

    Now that the part is disconnected, you are free to rotate it into place. Select the part to reveal its glyphs. A Rotation glyph is visible on the object, which you will use to rotate the part 90 degrees counterclockwise.

22. Press F12 to turn on dynamic input if it is not already on.

23. Select the tee and then, as shown in Figure 13.90, click the Rotation glyph and enter **90**.

FIGURE 13.90
Rotate the tee to correct its position before reconnecting.

The tee is now in the correct position, but it must be reconnected to the pipe.

24. Select the Location grip and move the tee to the east until you see the Connection glyph similar to the one you saw in Figure 13.88.

25. When you see the Connection glyph, click to set the tee.

You will know the tee is connected properly when the Rotation glyph no longer appears on the selected fitting. Another graphic indication that the tee is connected will be the reappearance of the Slide glyph on the connected end.

26. Working north from the tee, click the Continue Layout grip to continue the layout.

27. Click to place an elbow at the X labeled 11 and finally the X labeled 12. Press Esc.

28. Select the tee again, and working south from the tee, click the Continue Layout grip to continue the layout.

29. Click to place a pipe ending at the X labeled 13 and press Esc.

30. From the Home tab ➢ Layers panel, click Layer Freeze.

31. Click one of the Xs to freeze the _PLACEMENT SYMBOLS layer and press ↵ to complete.

If you no longer see the Pressure Network Plan Layout contextual tab, you can get back to it by selecting any pressure network part and, from the Pressure Networks contextual tab ➢ Modify panel, clicking Edit Network ➢ Plan Layout Tools.

32. Press Esc several times to deselect any items selected on the screen. On the Pressure Network Plan Layout contextual tab ➢ Insert panel, verify that Appurtenance is set to the gate valve-10 inch-push on-ductile iron-200 psi-AWWA C111/C500 (gate valve-250 mm-push on-ductile iron-16 bar for metric users).

33. Click Add Appurtenance.

34. Place the appurtenance in the drawing by clicking near the end of the north pipe.

Be sure to look for the single square Connection glyph that indicates you are connecting to the end of the pipe. If you see the double "boxing gloves" glyph, it means you are about to break the pipe.

Be sure to look for the Attachment glyph before clicking, as shown previously in Figure 13.88. Don't be shy about zooming in close to get a good look at the object with which you are working.

35. Repeat the process to place another valve at the south end. Press the Esc key when you've finished.

36. Close the contextual tab to exit the editing mode.

37. Save and close the drawing.

You can find completed versions of this drawing with the dataset for comparison: 1310_Pressure_FINISHED.dwg (1310_Pressure_METRIC_FINISHED.dwg).

IMPORTING AN INDUSTRY MODEL

One of the options you have with Civil 3D 2016 is to create a pressure network from an industry model.

An *industry model* is a type of AutoCAD drawing file that contains data from one of the handful of Autodesk-created templates, most commonly from Autodesk® Map 3D software. The Map 3D stand-alone product comes with premade infrastructure data classes such as waste water, water, gas, and electric, just to name a few. Not just any Map 3D file will do. A drawing containing pipe and valve information will be recognized as an industry model only if it was created based on one of the industry-specific templates. The ability to create an industry model is not available on the Map 3D workspace that is part of Civil 3D.

PRESSURE PIPE NETWORKS IN PROFILE VIEW

Pressure pipe networks can do things in profile view that gravity pipes cannot. With pressure pipes, the profile view can be used to change straight pipes to curves and delete parts from the project altogether. It is not a good idea to attempt to add parts to your pressure network in profile view because the resulting location in plan cannot be controlled.

To access these tools, select any pressure part, and from the Pressure Networks contextual tab ➤ Modify panel, choose Edit Network ➤ Profile Layout Tools, as shown in Figure 13.91.

FIGURE 13.91
Locating the Profile Layout tools

In the following exercise, you will draw the pressure pipe network in profile view and modify the layout using the Follow Surface command:

1. Open the 1311_PressureProfile.dwg (1311_PressureProfile_METRIC.dwg) drawing, which you can download from this book's web page.

2. Select any pressure network part in the drawing.

3. From the Pressure Networks contextual tab ➤ Launch Pad panel, select Alignment From Network.

4. At the `Select first Pressure Network Part (Pipe or Fitting or Appurtenance):` prompt, click the Gate Valve at the far right of the drawing.

5. At the `Select next Pressure Network Part or [Undo]:` prompt, select the Gate Valve at the northwest part of the project.

6. Press ↵ to continue.

    The next few steps are the same as when you created an alignment and profile from a gravity pipe network. You will be prompted to create an alignment, sample the surface, and create a profile view.

7. In the Create Alignment – From Pressure Network dialog, change the name to **Syrah Water**.

8. Verify that Create Profile And Profile View is checked. Leave all other styles and settings at their defaults and click OK.

9. In the Create Profile From Surface dialog, highlight the Composite surface and click Add.

10. Click Draw In Profile View.

11. In the Create Profile View Wizard, set Profile View Style to Land Desktop Profile View, and leaving all other settings at their defaults, click Create Profile View.

12. Place the view by clicking a location in the drawing off to the side of the project.

    You should see the profile view with your pressure pipe network present in all its glory. As you can see in Figure 13.92, the pipe looks good, except it appears that the pipe cover is inadequate toward the end of the alignment. You can fix this in the steps that follow.

FIGURE 13.92
Pressure network
in profile

13. Select a part from the network if the Pressure Networks contextual tab is not already visible.

14. From the Pressure Networks contextual tab ➤ Modify panel, select Edit Network ➤ Profile Layout Tools.

The Pressure Network Profile Layout contextual tab will appear, as shown in Figure 13.93.

FIGURE 13.93
The Pressure Network Profile Layout contextual tab

15. From the Pressure Network Profile Layout contextual tab ➤ Modify panel, select Follow Surface.

16. At the `Select first pressure part in profile:` prompt, select the leftmost valve in the profile view.

17. At the `Select next pressure part in profile [Enter to finish]:` prompt, click the rightmost valve in the profile view and then press ↵ to finish selecting parts. All connected parts in between will become selected.

18. At the `Enter depth below surface <0.0000>:` prompt, enter **4.5** (**1.5** for metric users).

Your profile view will change to resemble Figure 13.94.

FIGURE 13.94
The pressure pipe follows the surface.

19. Save and close the drawing.

Even though you have not used any labels in this exercise, be aware that the plan and profile view labels are used in the same way as the labels used for gravity pipe networks. With this release of the software, crossing pipe labels in profile views can be used for pressure pipes as well.

Completed versions of the drawing (1311_PressureProfile_FINISHED.dwg and 1311_PressureProfile_METRIC_FINISHED.dwg) are available with the rest of this book's download.

Using Design Checks

Pressure networks differ from the networks you created earlier in this chapter. Because the fluid in a pressure network can go uphill, the rules you saw in gravity systems no longer apply. The main concerns for a pressure network are pressure loss and depth of cover.

You can locate the Depth Check values on the Settings tab of Toolspace. Locate and expand the Pressure Network branch and expand the Commands branch. Double-click RunDepthCheck to edit the command settings. A dialog like the one in Figure 13.95 will open.

FIGURE 13.95
Edit the RunDepthCheck command settings to validate your design.

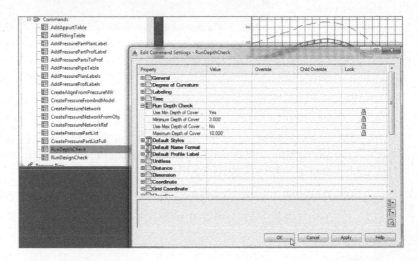

Also in the command settings you will find a separate listing for RunDesignCheck. Double-click (or right-click and click Edit Command Settings) to enter these settings. You can set an acceptable range of values for pipe bends and radius of curvature for curved pipes. The Deflection Validation settings are found under RunDesignCheck, as shown in Figure 13.96.

FIGURE 13.96
Turning on the Deflection Validation settings

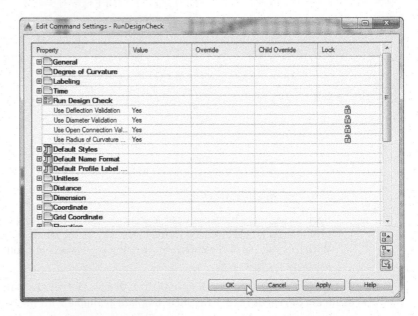

Once you have created your pressure network, you should check your initial design for flaws. From the Pressure Networks contextual tab, you can check your design to see whether it meets the requirements you set up in the command settings.

Depth Check verifies that all pipes and fittings are within the acceptable range of values for depth.

Design Check will check for improperly terminating pipes, mismatched pipe and fitting diameters, any curved pipe whose radius has exceeded acceptable values, and pipes that have exceeded the maximum deflection you set up in the parts list.

In the following exercise, you will modify the command settings and run a depth check on the pipe network:

1. Open the `1312_DesignCheck.dwg` (`1312_DesignCheck_METRIC.dwg`) drawing, which you can download from this book's web page.

2. In the Settings tab of Toolspace, expand Pressure Network ➤ Commands, right-click RunDepthCheck, and select Edit Command Settings (you could also double-click the command to access it).

3. Expand the Run Depth Check category and verify that Minimum Depth Of Cover is set to 6′ (2 m).

4. Click in the Value column and change Use Max Depth Of Cover Validation to Yes.

5. Click OK.

6. Select a pressure network part if you do not already see the Pressure Networks contextual tab.

7. From the Pressure Networks contextual tab ➤ Analyze panel, select Depth Check.

   The Depth Check command will allow you to perform the analysis in either plan or profile view. Either way you choose to select your pressure pipe network, the result will be the same.

8. At the `Select a path along a Pressure Network in plan or profile view:` prompt, click the first pressure network object to the left in the profile view.

9. At the `Select next point on path [Enter to finish]:` prompt, select the Gate Valve to the far right in the profile view and press ↵.

   The Run Depth Check dialog will appear. The settings should be the same values as those in steps 3 and 4.

10. Click OK.

   In both plan view (Figure 13.97, top) and profile view (Figure 13.97, bottom), warnings will appear if any Depth Check violations are found.

FIGURE 13.97
Depth Check
result in plan
(top) and profile:
(bottom) views

11. Save and close the drawing.

For your reference, completed versions of the drawing (1312_DesignCheck_FINISHED .dwg and 1312_DesignCheck_METRIC_FINISHED.dwg) are available with the rest of this book's download.

Understanding Part Builder

Part Builder is an interface that allows you to build and modify pipe network parts for gravity systems. You access Part Builder by selecting the Create Design drop-down from the Home tab. At first, you may use Part Builder to add a few missing pipes or structure sizes. As you become more familiar with the environment, you can build your own custom parts from scratch.

Parts created by Part Builder will not be available for use in pressure networks, so this section applies only to parts needed for gravity systems.

🌐 Real World Scenario

A WORD OF CAUTION ABOUT PART BUILDER

Every time one of our clients asks about Part Builder, we cringe. Our advice is, "If all you need to do is add a size to an existing part, no problem. If you want to create new geometry from scratch? Run. Run, screaming."

This is not a tool you can master by dabbling in it for a few hours. Even after you understand Part Builder, it can take days to build a complex part that functions correctly. Think of Part Builder as a half-step away from programming, and you will have more realistic expectations.

Before you buckle down to learn about Part Builder, ask yourself a few questions:

◆ Do I really understand pipes and structures well enough to tackle this?

◆ Is it worth taking extra time from a billable project to learn this feature?

◆ Is the part I need unique and not available from another source (such as colleagues or purchased from an Autodesk reseller)?

If you can answer yes to all these questions, you have our blessing. In many cases, the new pressure network tools eliminate the need for custom parts.

This section is intended to be an introduction to Part Builder and a primer in some basic skills required to navigate the interface. It isn't intended to be a robust "how-to" for creating custom parts. Civil 3D includes three detailed tutorials for creating three types of custom structures. The tutorials lead you through creating a cylindrical manhole structure, a drop inlet manhole structure, and a vault structure. You can find these tutorials by going to Help ➢ Tutorials and then navigating to Part Builder Tutorials.

BACK UP THE PART CATALOGS

Here's another warning: Before you explore Part Builder in any way, it's critical that you make a backup copy of the part catalogs. Doing so will protect you from accidentally removing or corrupting default parts as you're learning and will provide a means of restoring the original catalog.

The catalog (as discussed in the previous section) can be found by default at:

```
C:\ProgramData\Autodesk\C3D 2016\enu\Pipes Catalog\
```

To make a backup, copy this entire directory and then save that copy to a safe location, such as another folder on your hard drive or network, or to a CD.

We recommend that you do this and use the backup file for the exercises here. To do this, you will have to point to the new location by clicking the drop-down in the Home tab ➢ Create Design panel and selecting Set Pipe Network Catalog Location. Select the icon next to the `Catalog` folder and point it to your saved location. When you locate the backup folder, pick either Imperial or Metric and then click OK.

The parts in the Civil 3D pipe network catalogs are *parametric*. Parametric parts are dynamically sized according to a set of variables, or parameters. In practice, this means you can create one part and use it in multiple situations.

You can create one parametric model that understands how the different dimensions of the pipe are related to each other and what sizes are allowable. When a pipe is placed in a drawing, you can change its size. The pipe will understand how that change in size affects all the other pipe dimensions such as wall thickness, outer diameter, and more; you don't have to sort through a long list of individual pipe definitions.

Part Builder Orientation

Each drawing "remembers" which part catalog it is associated with. If you're in a metric drawing, you need to make sure the catalog is mapped to metric pipes and structures, whereas if you're in an Imperial drawing, you'll want the Imperial catalog. By default, the Civil 3D templates should be appropriately mapped out of the box, but it's worth the time to check. Set the catalog by changing to the Home tab and selecting Set Pipe Network Catalog from the drop-down on the Create Design panel. Verify the appropriate folder and catalog for your drawing units in the Pipe Network Catalog Settings dialog (see Figure 13.98), and you're ready to go.

FIGURE 13.98
Choose the appropriate folder and catalog for your drawing units.

Understanding the Organization of Part Builder

The vocabulary used in the Part Builder interface is different from the rest of Civil 3D, so we will first examine the basics.

Open Part Builder by going to the Home tab ➢ Create Design panel and selecting the Part Builder icon from the drop-down.

The first screen that appears when you start Part Builder is Getting Started – Catalog Screen (see Figure 13.99).

FIGURE 13.99
The Getting
Started – Catalog
Screen dialog

At the top of this window is a drop-down for selecting the part catalog type. Depending on what you need to modify, you can set this to either Pipe or Structure. Once you pick the catalog type, you will see the main catalog name. In Figure 13.99, you see US Imperial Pipe Catalog.

Below the catalog name is a list of part categories. In Part Builder vocabulary, a part or structure *category* is a grouping based on the shape for pipes and function for structures. Inside the category, you will see the part families listed. The US Imperial Pipe Catalog has four default categories:

◆ Circular Pipes

◆ Egg-Shaped Pipes

◆ Elliptical Pipes

◆ Rectangular Pipes

You can create new categories for different-shaped pipes, such as Arch Pipes.

The US Imperial Structure Catalog also has four default categories: Inlets-Outlets, Junction Structures With Frames, Junction Structures Without Frames, and Simple Shapes. You can create new categories for custom structures. You can expand each category folder to reveal one or more part families. For example, the US Imperial Circular Pipes category has six default families:

◆ Concrete Pipe

◆ Corrugated HDPE Pipe

◆ Corrugated Metal Pipe

◆ Ductile Iron Pipe

◆ HDPE Pipe

◆ PVC Pipe

Pipes that reside in the same family typically have the same parametric behavior, with differences only in size.

As Table 13.1 shows, a series of buttons on the Getting Started – Catalog Screen dialog lets you perform various edits to categories, families, and the catalog as a whole.

TABLE 13.1:   The Part Builder catalog tools

ICON	FUNCTION
	The New Parametric Part button creates a new part family.
	The Modify Part Sizes button allows you to edit the parameters for the selected part family.
	The Catalog Regen button refreshes all the supporting files in the catalog when you've finished making edits to the catalog.
	The Catalog Test button validates the parts in the catalog when you've finished making edits to the catalog.
	The New Category button creates a new category.
	The Delete button deletes a part family. Use this button with caution, and remember that if you accidentally delete a part family, you can restore your backup catalog as mentioned in the beginning of this section.

Exploring Part Families

The best way to become oriented to the Part Builder interface is to explore one of the standard part families:

1. Open Part Builder, and then in the Getting Started – Catalog Screen dialog, click the Part Catalog drop-down and select Pipe.

2. Expanding the US Imperial Pipe Catalog ➤ Circular Pipe family, select Concrete Pipe (Concrete Pipe SI for metric users) and click the Modify Part Sizes button.

3. It is not unusual to receive a message stating that the file contains previous-version AEC objects. If you get such a message, click Close to continue.

   A Part Builder pane will appear with AeccCircularConcretePipe_Imperial.dwg (AeccCircularConcretePipe_Metric.dwg for metric users) on the screen, along with the Content Builder Toolspace, as shown in Figure 13.100.

FIGURE 13.100
DWG file as shown in Content Builder

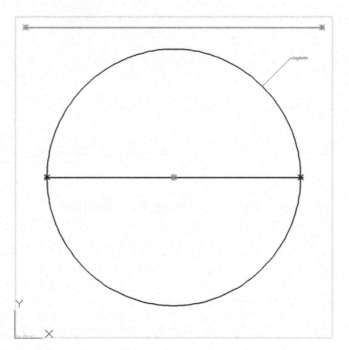

4. Close Part Builder by clicking the X on the Part Builder pane.

5. Click No when asked to save the changes to the concrete pipe.

6. Click No when asked to save the drawing.

The Part Builder pane, or Content Builder (Figure 13.101), is well documented through the Autodesk Knowledge Network available for the Autodesk AutoCAD Civil 3D.

FIGURE 13.101
Content Builder

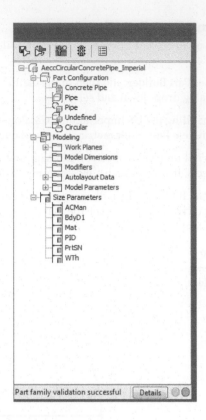

Adding a Part Size Using Part Builder

The hypothetical municipality requires a 12″ (300 mm) waste water cleanout. After studying the catalog, you decide that Concentric Cylindrical Structure NF (SI for metric users) is the appropriate shape for your model, but the smallest inner diameter size in the catalog is 48″ (1,200 mm). The following exercise gives you some practice in adding a structure size to the catalog—in this case, adding a 12″ (300 mm) structure to the US Imperial Structures catalog (Metric Structures Catalog for metric users).

You can make changes to the US Imperial Structures catalog from any drawing that is mapped to that catalog, which is probably any Imperial drawing you have open, as follows:

1. For this exercise, start a new drawing from _AutoCAD Civil 3D (Imperial) NCS.dwt (_AutoCAD Civil 3D (Metric) NCS.dwt).

2. On the Home tab, select the drop-down on the Create Design panel and select Part Builder.

3. In the Getting Started – Catalog Screen dialog, choose Structure from the drop-down in the Part Catalog selection box.

4. Expand the Junction Structures Without Frames category.

5. Highlight the Concentric Cylindrical Structure NF (SI for metric users) part family.

6. Click the Modify Part Sizes button.

   The Part Builder interface opens `AeccStructConcentricCylinderNF_Imperial.dwg` (`AeccStructConcentricCylinderNF_Metric.dwg` for metric users) along with the Content Builder pane.

7. Zoom extents if necessary.

8. In the Content Builder pane, expand the Size Parameters branch.

9. Right-click the SID (Structure Inner Diameter) parameter and choose Edit.

   The Edit Part Sizes dialog appears.

10. Locate the SID column (see Figure 13.102) and double-click inside the box.

FIGURE 13.102
Examining the available part sizes

   Note that a drop-down shows the available inner diameter sizes 48", 60", 72", and 96" (1,200 mm, 1,400 mm, 1,600 mm, and 1,800 mm).

11. Locate the Edit button. Make sure you're still active in the SID column cell and then click Edit.

    The Edit Values dialog appears.

12. In the Edit Values dialog, click Add and type **12** (metric users type **300**), as shown in Figure 13.103.

FIGURE 13.103
Add the 12" (300 mm) value to the Edit Values dialog.

13. Click OK to close the Edit Values dialog, and click OK again to close the Edit Part Sizes dialog.

14. Click the small X in the upper-right corner of the Content Builder pane to exit Part Builder. If you don't see it, hover over the window top bar, and it should be available.

15. The message "Save Changes To Concentric Cylindrical Structure NF?" will appear. Click Yes.

    You could also click Save in Content Builder to save the part and remain active in the Part Builder interface.

You're back in your original drawing. If you created a new parts list in any drawing that references the US Imperial Structures catalog (Metric Structures Catalog for metric users), the 12" (300 mm) structure will be available for selection.

 Real World Scenario

I THOUGHT I TOOK CARE OF THAT SUMP?

In the "Editing with the Network Layout Tools Toolbar" section, you were instructed to make the Sump Depth 0. So why isn't the bottom of the structure even with the pipe in the profile graphic? Structures are created using the outermost edges, and in the case of most structures, this includes a 6" (150 mm) sump defined as a part parameter.

Since you learned some about editing parts within Part Builder, you can now add a 0 value to the Floor Thickness list, as follows:

1. From the Home tab ➤ Create Design panel drop-down, click Part Builder.

2. Change the active part catalog to Structure.

3. Expand the Junction Structures With Frames family.

4. Select the Concentric Cylindrical Structure (SI for metric users) part and click the Modify Part Sizes button.

5. In the Content Builder area on the left side of the screen, right-click Size Parameters and select Edit Values.

6. In the Edit Part Sizes dialog, click your cursor in the FTh field. This will enable the Edit button on the top-left corner.

7. Click the Edit button. In the Edit Values dialog, click Add.

8. Type **0** for the new value and click OK.

9. Click OK again to close the Edit Part Sizes dialog.

10. Move your cursor to the top of the Content Builder palette until you see the X appear. Click the X to close Part Builder.

11. When you are prompted with Save Changes To Concentric Cylindrical Structure (SI for metric), click Yes.

12. Run the **PartCatalogRegen** command and select structure from the selection. Hit Enter and then press Esc to exit the command.

13. Back in Toolspace, switch to the Settings tab and expand Pipe Network ➤ Parts Lists ➤ Storm Sewer.

14. Right-click Storm Sewer and click Edit.

15. On the Structures tab of the Network Parts List dialog, expand Storm Sewer and the Concentric Cylindrical Structure (SI for metric users) part family.

16. Right-click any of the structures within that part family and choose Edit.

17. Notice the row called Floor Thickness. Verify that the Floor Thickness value of 0 is available for selection, and upon selecting it, finish by clicking OK. Click OK once more to close the Network Parts List dialog.

Note that this thickness will be applied only to parts going forward. You are stuck with the floor thickness at the time you placed the structure unless you use the Swap Part tool to force the parts to "refresh" from the parts list.

Sharing a Custom Part

You may need to go beyond adding pipe and structure sizes to your catalog and build custom part families or even whole custom chapters. Perhaps instead of building them yourself, you'll be able to acquire them from an outside source.

The following section can be used as a reference for adding a custom part to your catalog from an outside source, as well as sharing custom parts that you've created. The key to sharing a part is to locate three files that Civil 3D needs in order to use that part.

Adding a custom part size to your catalog requires these steps:

1. Locate the partname.dwg, partname.xml, and (optionally) partname.bmp files of the part you'd like to obtain.

2. Make a copy of the partname.dwg, partname.xml, and (optionally) partname.bmp files.

3. Insert the partname.dwg, partname.xml, and (optionally) partname.bmp files in the correct folder of your catalog.

4. Run the **PARTCATALOGREGEN** command in Civil 3D and select the specific catalog you need to regen.

If you added both structures and pipes, within the same command you can regen both pipes and structures. You may get errors on adding new parts from outside sources. Your best resources on this matter will be the Autodesk Knowledge Network for Civil 3D or the Autodesk Community forums.

Adding an Arch Pipe to Your Part Catalog

This exercise will teach you how to add a premade custom part to your catalog. You can make changes to the US Imperial Pipes (Metric Pipes for metric users) catalog from any drawing that is mapped to that catalog, which is probably any Imperial (metric) drawing you have open.

1. For this exercise, start a new drawing from the _AutoCAD Civil 3D (Imperial) NCS .dwt file (_AutoCAD Civil 3D (Metric) NCS.dwt).

2. In Windows Explorer, create a new folder called **Arch Pipes** in your Pipes Catalog directory.

For the purposes of the exercise, you should add the new pipe files into this directory. Remember, the real path is located here:

```
C:\ProgramData\Autodesk\C3D 2016\enu\Pipes Catalog\US Imperial Pipes\
```

```
(C:\ProgramData\Autodesk\C3D 2016\enu\Pipes Catalog\Metric Pipes\)
```

This directory should now include five folders: `Arch Pipes`, `Circular Pipes`, `Egg-Shaped Pipes`, `Elliptical Pipes`, and `Rectangular Pipes`.

3. Copy the `Concrete Arch Pipe.dwg` (`Concrete Arch Pipe_METRIC.dwg`), `Concrete Arch Pipe.bmp` (`Concrete Arch Pipe_METRIC.bmp`), and `Concrete Arch Pipe.xml` (`Concrete Arch Pipe_METRIC.xml`) files into the `Arch Pipes` folder.

4. Return to your drawing and enter **PARTCATALOGREGEN** at the command line.

5. Type **P** and press ↵ to regenerate the Pipe catalog; then press ↵ again to exit the command.

   If you created a new parts list or edited an existing one, the arch pipe would be available for selection at this point in any drawing that references the US Imperial Pipes catalog.

6. To confirm the addition of the new pipe shape to the catalog, locate, open, and browse the catalog HTM file found at this location:

```
C:\ProgramData\Autodesk\C3D 2016\enu\Pipes Catalog\
US Imperial Pipes\Imperial Pipes.htm
```

```
(C:\ProgramData\Autodesk\C3D 2016\enu\Pipes Catalog\Metric Pipes\Metric Pipes
.htm)
```

The Bottom Line

Create a pipe network by layout.   After you've created a parts list for your pipe network, the first step toward finalizing the design is to use Pipe Network By Layout.

Master It   Open the `MasterIt_1301.dwg` or `MasterIt_1301_METRIC.dwg` file. Use Network Creation Tools to create a waste water pipe network named Mastering. Use the Composite surface, and name only structure and pipe label styles. Don't choose an alignment at this time. Create 8" (200 mm) PVC pipes and a manhole called SMH. There are blocks in the drawing to assist you in placing manholes. Begin at the START HERE marker, and place a manhole at each marker location. You can erase the markers when you've finished.

Create an alignment from network parts and draw parts in profile view.   Once your pipe network has been created in plan view, you'll typically add the parts to a profile view based on either the road centerline or the pipe centerline.

Master It   Continue working in the `MasterIt_1301.dwg` or `MasterIt_1301_METRIC` `.dwg` file. You need to have completed the previous exercise before beginning this one. Create an alignment named Mastering from your pipes so that station zero is located at the START HERE structure. Create a profile view from this alignment and show the pipes and profiles for the EG and Corridor FG surfaces on the profile view. Use defaults for everything, except change the Corridor FG profile style to FG Profile on the profile view.

Label a pipe network in plan and profile.   Designing your pipe network is only half the process. Engineering plans must be properly annotated.

Master It   Continue working in the `MasterIt_1301.dwg` or `MasterIt_1301_METRIC`.`dwg` file. You need to have completed the previous exercise before beginning this one. Add the Length Description And Slope pipe label style to profile pipes and the Data With Connected Pipes (Sanitary) structure label style to profile structures. Assign the alignment created in the previous "Master It" exercise to all pipes and structures.

Create a dynamic pipe table.   It's common for municipalities and contractors to request a pipe or structure table for cost estimates or to make it easier to understand a busy plan.

Master It   Continue working in the `MasterIt_1301.dwg` or `MasterIt_1301_METRIC.dwg` file. You need to have completed the previous exercise before beginning this one. Create a pipe table for all pipes in your network. Use the default table style.

Chapter 14

Grading

Beyond creating streets, sewers, cul-de-sacs, and inlets, much of what happens to the ground as a site still needs to be determined. Planning for the earthwork of a site is a crucial part of bringing a project together. This chapter examines feature lines and grading groups, which are the two primary tools of site design. Feature lines and grading groups work in tandem, providing the site designer with tools to completely model the land.

In this chapter, you will learn to:

- ◆ Convert existing linework into feature lines.

- ◆ Model a simple breakline with a feature line.

- ◆ Model planar site features with grading groups.

Working with Grading Feature Lines

There are two types of feature lines: corridor feature lines and grading feature lines. Corridor feature lines are discussed in Chapter 9, "Basic Corridors," and grading feature lines are the focus of this chapter. It's important to note that grading feature lines can be extracted from corridor feature lines, and you can choose whether to dynamically link them to the corridor.

Terrain modeling can be defined as the manipulation of triangles created by connecting points and vertices to achieve Delaunay triangulation, as discussed in Chapter 4, "Surfaces." In the Autodesk® AutoCAD® Civil 3D® platform, the creation of the Feature Line object adds a level of control and complexity not available to 3D polylines. In this section, you'll look at the feature line, various methods of creating feature lines, some simple elevation edits, planar grading and editing functionality, and labeling of the newly created feature lines.

Accessing Grading Feature-Line Tools

You can access the Feature Line creation tools from the Home tab's Create Design panel, as shown in Figure 14.1.

FIGURE 14.1
The Feature Line
drop-down on
the Create Design
panel

You can access the Feature Line editing tools via the Feature Line contextual tab (see Figure 14.2). To activate the Feature Line contextual tab, just select a feature line, or from the Modify tab ➤ Design panel, choose Feature Line.

FIGURE 14.2
The Feature Line
contextual tab
can be accessed by
selecting an exist-
ing feature line

When you're working with feature lines, one thing to remember is that they belong in a site, as shown in Figure 14.3. Alignments, parcels, and feature lines within the same site snap to each other vertically, which can cause some confusion when you're trying to build surfaces.

FIGURE 14.3
Feature lines are
located in the
Sites branch in
Prospector.

UNDERSTANDING PARENT SITES

If you notice some weird elevation data along your feature line, be sure to check out the parent site. If the concept of a site or sites in general doesn't make much sense to you, be sure to review Chapter 5, "Parcels," before going too much further. Sites are a major part of the way feature lines interact with each other, and many users who have problems with grading are the same users who ignore sites.

The next few sections break down the various tools in detail. You'll use almost all of them in this chapter, so in each section you'll spend some time getting familiar with these tools and the basic concepts behind them.

Creating Grading Feature Lines

Certification
Objective
There are five primary methods for creating feature lines, as shown previously in Figure 14.1. They generate similar results but have some key differences:

Create Feature Line   The Create Feature Line tool allows you to create a feature line from scratch, assigning elevations as you go. These elevations can be based on direct data input at the command line, slope information, elevation difference, or surface elevations.

Create Feature Lines From Objects   The Create Feature Lines From Objects tool converts lines, arcs, polylines, and 3D polylines into feature lines. This process also allows you to assign elevations. You can assign a single elevation to all vertices on the feature line. You can also acquire elevations from grading groups and surfaces if the feature line has been drawn over either. You also have the option to delete the original object and weed the vertices of the new feature line.

Create Feature Lines From Alignment   The Create Feature Lines From Alignment tool allows you to build a new feature line from an alignment, using a profile to assign elevations. This feature line can be dynamically tied to the alignment and the profile, which limits your ability to edit it directly but makes it easy to generate feature lines based on horizontal and vertical controls of alignments and profiles. If the feature line created from an alignment is not dynamically linked, any of the feature-line editing commands can be used. This could be useful if you wanted to place a vertical curve in your feature line.

Create Feature Line From Corridor   The Create Feature Line From Corridor tool is used to export a grading feature line from a corridor feature line. The feature line created from a corridor feature line can be dynamically linked to the corridor. If the feature line is dynamically linked, then it can't be edited with the feature-line editing tools.

Create Feature Line From Stepped Offset   The Create Feature Line From Stepped Offset tool is used to create an offset feature line, allowing you to specify a vertical offset value in terms of elevation difference, grade, slope, and actual elevation for the entire feature line or each vertex. You can also define variable stepped offsets at each feature line vertex. This tool can also be used on feature lines, survey figures, polylines, or 3D polylines. The feature line created from a stepped offset does not keep a dynamic link to the original feature line.

You'll explore some of these methods over the next few exercises. In this first exercise, you will create the edge of a tennis court with a feature line:

1. Open the 1401_CreatingFeatureLines.dwg or 1401_CreatingFeatureLines_METRIC.dwg file. (Remember, all data can be downloaded from www.sybex.com/go/masteringcivil3d2016.)

    This drawing contains some AutoCAD entities and Civil 3D points representing basic geometry for a recreational center at the entrance of the subdivision.

2. From the Home ➤ Create Design panel, choose Feature Line ➤ Create Feature Line to display the Create Feature Lines dialog.

    You need to associate feature lines with a site. Just like parcels, grading objects will react with like objects in a site if they touch, horizontally in particular. So by isolating this feature line, you can ensure that everything will be drawn properly before committing it to a site.

3. Verify that Rec Center is the Site name.

4. Fill in the check box next to Style and select Grading Edge Of Pavement as the style name using the drop-down.

The Create Feature Lines dialog should now look like Figure 14.4.

FIGURE 14.4
The Create Feature
Lines dialog

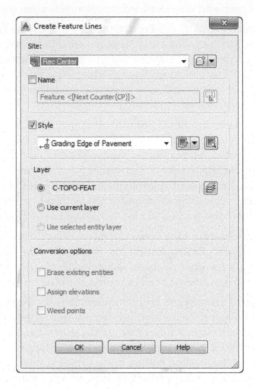

5. Click OK to dismiss the Create Feature Lines dialog.

6. At the `Specify start point:` prompt, use a Node Osnap to specify your start point as point #1.

7. At the `Specify elevation or [Surface]:` prompt, enter **S** ↵ to use a surface to set the elevation.

Since there are multiple surfaces in the drawing, the Select Surface dialog appears. If there were only one surface in this drawing, the surface would automatically be selected and you would not be prompted with this dialog.

8. In the Select Surface dialog, use the drop-down to choose Existing Surface and click OK.

9. At the `Surface elevation:` prompt, press the Enter key to accept the default surface elevation offered on the command line.

10. At the `Specify the next point or [Arc]`: prompt, use a Node Osnap to pick point #2.

11. At the `Specify grade or [SLope Elevation Difference SUrface Transition]`: prompt, enter **−0.83** ⏎ to set this grade between these two points.

12. At the `Specify the next point or [Arc Length Undo]`: prompt, use a Node Osnap to pick point #3.

13. At the `Specify grade or [Slope Elevation Difference SUrface Transition]`: prompt, enter **0** ⏎ to set this grade between these two points.

14. At the `Specify the next point or [Arc Length Close Undo]`: prompt, use a Node Osnap to pick point #4.

15. At the `Specify grade or [SLope Elevation Difference SUrface Transition]`: prompt, enter **0.83** ⏎ to set this grade between these two points.

16. At the `Specify the next point or [Arc Length Close Undo]`: prompt, type **C** ⏎ to close the feature line.

The feature-line command will end. Your screen should look like Figure 14.5 with a red rectangular feature line drawn through the points.

FIGURE 14.5
Setting the grade between points

This method of creating a feature line by picking each vertex and specifying its elevation or grade before picking the next may seem tedious to some users. In the next portion of the exercise, you will convert an existing polyline to a feature line and acquire elevations for the vertices from a surface.

ASSIGNING NAMES

Looking back at Figure 14.4, note that there is an unused option for assigning a Name value to each feature line. Using feature-line names is not mandatory, but will make it easier to discern which feature line is which when inspecting the Feature Line collection in the Site branch in Prospector.

17. From the Home tab ➤ Create Design panel, choose Feature Line ➤ Create Feature Lines From Objects.

18. At the Select lines, arcs, polylines or 3d polylines to convert to feature lines or [Xref]: prompt, notice the options for selection and note that by typing **X** and then pressing the Enter key, you may pick these types of entities from an external reference. This will save you the trouble of opening the external reference, copy clipping, closing the reference, and pasting to original coordinates. Select the green closed polyline, which represents the edge of the recreation center building.

19. Press the Enter key.

The Create Feature Lines dialog will appear.

20. Verify that Rec Center is the name of the site.

21. Verify that the Style check box is filled, and select Grading Building as the style for the feature line using the drop-down.

This Create Feature Lines dialog has some differences from that shown in Figure 14.4. Notably, the Conversion Options near the bottom of the dialog are now active, so take a look at the options presented:

Erase Existing Entities   This option deletes the object and replaces it with a Feature Line object. This avoids the creation of duplicate linework but could be harmful if you wanted to keep your linework for planimetric purposes.

Assign Elevations   This option lets you set the feature-line elevations from a surface or grading group, essentially draping the feature line on the selected object.

Weed Points   Weed Points decreases the number of nodes along the object. This option is handy when you're converting digitized information into feature lines.

22. Check the Assign Elevations box.

The Erase Existing Entities option is checked by default, and you will not select the Weed Points option.

23. Click OK to dismiss the Create Feature Lines dialog.

The Assign Elevations dialog appears. Here you can assign a single elevation for the feature line, assign the elevations from a grading if one is present in the drawing, or select a surface to pull elevation data from.

24. Verify that Existing Surface is selected.

25. Verify that the Insert Intermediate Grade Break Points option is checked.

    This setting inserts a vertical point of intersection (elevation point) at every point along the feature line where it crosses an underlying TIN line.

26. Click OK to dismiss the Assign Elevations dialog.

27. Select the feature line that was just created, and the grips will look like Figure 14.6.

FIGURE 14.6
Conversion to
a Feature Line
object

SQUARE GRIPS VS. CIRCULAR GRIPS

Note that Figure 14.6 shows two types of grips: square and circular. Feature lines offer feedback via the grip shape:

Square Grips   Square grips are PI points. They can be moved in the x, y, and z directions, manipulating both the horizontal and vertical design.

Circular Grips   Circular grips are elevation points. Elevation points can be slid along a given feature line, adjusting the vertical design, but cannot be moved in the x or y direction deviating from the original bearing of the feature line. In this part of the exercise, the elevation points are located where the original polyline intersected the TIN lines of the EG surface representing the intermediate grade break points you created.

This combination of PIs and elevation points makes it easy to modify a feature line with a number of changes in design grade, enabling it to maintain its linear design intent if the endpoints are moved.

When this exercise is complete, you can close the drawing. A saved copy of this drawing (1401_CreatingFeatureLines_FINISHED.dwg or 1401_CreatingFeatureLines_METRIC_FINISHED.dwg) is available from the book's web page.

 Real World Scenario

USING STYLES WITH FEATURE LINE OBJECTS

Although using styles with feature lines is optional, doing so makes it easy to recognize the type of breaklines being represented (flowline, crown, and so on). Using styles with feature lines provides another advantage: Split Point Resolution.

When two feature lines in the same site cross, the point of intersection on both becomes a single split point because there cannot be more than one elevation at the same point when grading. The last feature line modified will have the winning elevation. The other feature line will spike up or down to match or join to the other's elevation at that point. One way to control this is by managing the Split Point Resolution hierarchy, which is simply a list of your feature-line styles in the order of priority. The style at the top of the list will always have the winning elevation. The style at the bottom of the list will always lose.

Split Point Resolution can be managed on the Prospector by expanding Sites, expanding the Feature Line site, right-clicking the Feature Line branch, and clicking Properties. Split Point Resolution is managed on the Options tab.

Editing Feature Line Information

From the Feature Line contextual tab, you can examine several more commands on the Modify panel, as shown in Figure 14.7, before you get into editing objects.

FIGURE 14.7

The Modify panel on the Feature Line contextual tab

The Modify panel of the Feature Line contextual tab provides commands for editing various properties of the feature line, editing the feature line style, editing the feature line geometry, and moving or copying to sites as follows:

Feature Line Properties   The top half of the Feature Line Properties tool is a button that will access the Feature Line Properties dialog. The Feature Line Properties dialog has two tabs: Information and Statistics. The Information tab of the Feature Line Properties dialog allows you to edit the name or feature line style and, if present, remove the dynamic link. The Statistics tab of the Feature Line Properties dialog allows you to view various physical properties such as minimum and maximum grade.

The bottom half of the Feature Line Properties tool is a drop-down containing two commands:

Feature Line Properties   This command accesses the same Feature Line Properties dialog as discussed earlier when you click the button.

Edit Feature Line Style   This command is used to access various display characteristics of the feature line such as color and linetype. Feature line styles will be discussed further in Chapter 19, "Object Styles."

Edit Geometry   The Edit Geometry toggle opens and closes the Edit Geometry panel on the Feature Line contextual tab (see Figure 14.8). This panel will remain open until the Edit Geometry button is toggled off (it's highlighted when toggled on). The Edit Geometry panel will be discussed later in this chapter in the "Editing Feature Line Geometry" section.

FIGURE 14.8

The Edit Geometry panel on the Feature Line contextual tab

Edit Elevations   The Edit Elevations toggle opens the Edit Elevations panel on the Feature Line contextual tab (see Figure 14.9). This panel will remain open until the Edit Elevations button is toggled off (it's highlighted when toggled on). The Edit Elevations panel will be discussed later in this chapter in the "Editing Feature Line Elevations" section.

FIGURE 14.9
The Edit
Elevations panel
on the Feature
Line contextual
tab

Add To Surface As Breakline The Add To Surface As Breakline tool allows you to select a feature line or feature lines to add to a surface as breaklines. Once feature lines are added to the surface, they will be listed as a Breakline Set in Prospector ➤ Surface ➤ Surface Name ➤ Definition ➤ Breaklines.

Apply Feature Line Names The Apply Feature Line Names tool allows you to apply names to a selection of feature lines based on a new naming template. This tool can be helpful when you want to rename a group or just assign names to Feature Line objects. This tool cannot be used on a feature line that is dynamically linked to an alignment and profile or corridor.

Apply Feature Line Styles The Apply Feature Line Styles tool changes the styles of selected feature lines.

Move To Site If you expand the Modify panel, you will notice two additional commands. The first command is Move To Site. This command allows you to associate the selected feature line with a new site.

Copy To Site The other command in the expanded Modify panel is Copy To Site. This command allows you to duplicate the selected feature with a new site while leaving the original feature line in its current site. The two feature lines are not dynamically linked.

Once the Feature Line contextual tab has been activated, the Quick Profile tool is available on the Launch Pad panel. The Quick Profile tool generates a temporary profile of the feature line based on user parameters in the Create Quick Profiles dialog (Figure 14.10).

FIGURE 14.10
The Create Quick
Profiles dialog

Note the following about this operation:

- Civil 3D creates a temporary phantom alignment that will not display in Prospector as the basis for a quick profile. A unique alignment number is assigned to this alignment.

- Panorama will display a message to tell you that a quick profile has been generated and to remind you that "this is a temporary object and will be deleted on save command or on exit from drawing." You can close Panorama or move the Panorama palette out of the way if necessary.

Feature lines aren't the only things from which you can create a quick profile. You can also create a quick profile for 2D or 3D lines or polylines, lot lines, survey figures, or even a series of points. When a quick profile is created from 3D objects, there is an additional option to draw the 3D entity profile.

The Edit Geometry and Edit Elevations toggles provide even more commands, which make feature lines considerably more grading-friendly than standard 3D polylines. The Edit Geometry functions and the Edit Elevations functions are described in the next sections. While these sections reference the Edit Geometry and Edit Elevations panels of the Feature Line contextual tab, these panels are also available on the Modify tab. When used from the Modify tab, many of these commands can also be used to edit parcel lines, survey figures, 3D polylines, and 2D polylines, in addition to feature lines, as discussed in the sections that follow.

Editing Feature-Line Geometry

Feature-line revisions often require adding PIs, breaking apart feature lines, trimming, and performing other horizontal operations without destroying the vertical information. To access the commands for editing feature-line horizontal information, select the feature line to access the Feature Line contextual tab and toggle on the Edit Geometry panel, as shown in Figure 14.11.

Figure 14.11
The Edit Geometry panel on the Feature Line contextual tab

The first two tools are designed to manipulate the PI points that make up a feature line:

Insert PI   The Insert PI tool allows you to insert a new PI, controlling both the horizontal and vertical design.

Delete PI   The Delete PI tool removes a PI. If the PI is located at the beginning or end of a feature line, the beginning or end segment is removed. If the PI is removed at a PC, the arc is removed and the segment leading into the arc gets stretched to the next PI. If the PI is removed at a PT, the arc segment gets stretched to the next PI.

The next few tools act like their AutoCAD counterparts, but they are used specifically with feature lines because elevations are involved, and they will add PIs accordingly:

Break   The Break tool allows two feature lines to be created from one. Additionally, if a feature line is part of a surface definition, both new feature lines are added to the surface definition to maintain integrity. Elevations at the new PIs are assigned on the basis of an interpolated elevation.

Trim The Trim tool operates much like the AutoCAD Trim command, trimming a feature line and adding a new end PI on the basis of an interpolated elevation.

Join The Join tool creates one feature line from two or more, making editing and control easier. You can set the tolerance distance from the settings associated with the Join tool on the Settings tab of Toolspace by doing the following:

1. Expand the Grading ➢ Commands branch.

2. Right-click JoinFeatures and select Edit Command Settings.

3. In the Edit Command Settings – JoinFeatures dialog, expand the Feature Line Join property to change the tolerance.

Reverse The Reverse tool changes the direction of a feature line and flips any labels applied to the feature line on the opposite side.

Edit Curve The Edit Curve tool allows you to modify or delete the radius that has been applied to a Feature Line object. Once the feature line is selected, the Edit Feature Line Curve dialog will display. For each curve, you can modify the radius while viewing information on the curve length, chord length, and tangent length. There is also an option to maintain tangency if the curve is not already tangent to attached linework. After entering a value for the radius, a preview of the resulting curve will appear. Values that won't compute will not be accepted. In that case, a warning message will appear. There is also an option to pick two points to define a radius length. You can click the Apply button to continue making edits to other curves of the feature line or click the OK button to complete the command and dismiss the dialog.

Fillet The Fillet tool inserts a curve at PIs along a feature line and will join feature lines sharing a common PI that are not actually connected. You can apply a radius to a single PI or to all PIs on a feature line.

The last few tools refine feature lines, making them easier to manipulate and use in a surface:

Fit Curve The Fit Curve tool analyzes a number of elevation points and attempts to define a working arc through them all. This tool is often used when the corridor utilities are used to generate feature lines. These derived feature lines can have a large number of unnecessary PIs in curved areas. You can modify the tolerance and the minimum number of segments by entering O to select Options on the command line during the prompt to display the Fit Curve Options dialog.

Alternatively, you can set the default values for these options from the settings associated with the Fit Curve tool on the Settings tab of Toolspace by doing the following:

1. Expand the Grading ➢ Commands branch.

2. Right-click FitCurveFeature and select Edit Command Settings.

3. In the Edit Command Settings – FitCurveFeature dialog, expand the Feature Line Fit Curve property to change the tolerance and specify the minimum number of segments.

Smooth   The Smooth tool takes a series of disjointed feature-line segments and creates a best-fit curve. This tool is great for creating streamlines or other natural terrain features that are known to curve, but there's often not enough data to fully draw them that way. You can also straighten previously smoothed feature lines on the Modify tab ➤ Edit Geometry panel by choosing the Smooth command and typing **S** for Straighten. Notice that the Smooth command accessed through the Feature Line contextual tab does not give you the Straighten option.

Weed   The Weed tool allows the user to remove elevation points and PIs on the basis of various criteria. Once you select the feature line or multiple feature lines or a partial feature line, the Weed Vertices dialog will display. This dialog will allow you to weed based on any combination of angle, grade, or length; in addition, you can remove points based on their 3D distance between one another.

♦   Weeding by angle considers the horizontal angles at each bend of the feature line and will delete a vertex smaller than the value entered.

♦   Weeding by grade looks at three points, considering the middle point as a PVI. If the difference in grade is less than the entered amount, the PVI will be deleted.

♦   Weeding by length looks at three points and will delete the middle point if the distance between the outside points is less than the value entered.

♦   Weeding by 3D distance looks at the slope distance between two adjacent points and will delete the following vertex if the slope distance is less than the value entered.

At the bottom of the Weed Vertices dialog, it states how many of the total number of vertices will be weeded. This is great for cleaning up corridor-generated feature lines as well.

Similar to the Join and Fit Curve tools, you can set the default settings associated with the Weed command on the Settings tab of Toolspace by doing the following:

1.   Expand the Grading ➤ Commands branch.

2.   Right-click WeedFeatures and select Edit Command Settings.

3.   In the Edit Command Settings – WeedFeatures dialog, expand the Feature Line Weed property to change the various default values.

Stepped Offset   The Stepped Offset tool allows offsetting in a horizontal and vertical direction, making it easy to create stepped features such as stairs or curbs.

In this exercise, you'll manipulate some feature lines that were roughed in to define the pool area at the recreational center:

1.   Open the 1402_FeatureLineGeometry.dwg or 1402_FeatureLineGeometry_METRIC .dwg file.

2.   Zoom into the area where the sidewalk intersects the edge of the concrete at the southwest edge of the building, and select the edge of the concrete, as shown in Figure 14.12.

FIGURE 14.12
Picking the edge
of concrete feature
line at the south-
west edge of the
building

3. If the Edit Geometry panel isn't visible, from the Feature Line contextual tab ➤ Modify panel, choose Edit Geometry to toggle on the Edit Geometry panel.

4. From the Feature Line contextual tab ➤ Edit Geometry panel, choose the Break tool.

5. At the `Select an object to break:` prompt, select the edge of concrete feature line again.

6. At the `Specify second break point or [First point]:` prompt, enter **F** ↵ to pick the first point of the break.

7. At the `Specify first break point:` prompt, using a Node Osnap, select the node of point #5, as shown in Figure 14.13.

FIGURE 14.13
Using the node
object snap to
select a point

8. At the Specify second break point: prompt, using a Node Osnap, select the node of point #6, leaving a gap, as shown in Figure 14.14.

FIGURE 14.14
The feature line after executing the Break command

The feature lines representing the sidewalk and the edge of concrete at the pool area were roughed in and are not joined. Feature lines that represent continuous line work are much easier to manage when they are joined.

9. With the small segment drawn from point #6 to the edge of the building still selected, from the contextual tab ➤ Edit Geometry panel, click Join.

10. At the Select the connecting feature line, polyline or 3D polyline or [Multiple]: prompt, select all the magenta feature lines representing the sidewalk and the edge of concrete, as shown in Figure 14.15.

FIGURE 14.15
Selecting the feature lines representing the sidewalk and edge of concrete

11. Press ↵ to end the command.

12. Press Esc to deselect.

If you zoom out slightly, you may notice the green feature line representing the edge of pavement that is wrapping around the back of the building. It needs to connect up with the magenta feature line you just joined. Although there is a special Trim command that you must use with feature lines, the AutoCAD Extend command is the tool to use when you need to lengthen feature lines to meet others.

13. Execute the AutoCAD Extend command (you can type **Ex** ↵ at the command line).

14. At the `Select boundary edges ... Select objects or <select all>:` prompt, select the magenta feature line as the boundary edge.

15. Press ↵ to advance to the next prompt.

16. At the `Select object to extend or shift-select to trim or [Fence Crossing Project Edge Undo]:` prompt, select the green feature line to the rear of the building close to the end of the segment that must be extended.

17. Press Esc to end the command.

The edge of pavement feature line should be extended to the joined feature line, as shown in Figure 14.16.

FIGURE 14.16
The extended edge of pavement feature line

18. Select the magenta feature line.

19. From the contextual tab ➤ Edit Geometry panel, click the Trim tool.

20. At the `Select cutting edges:` prompt, select the green feature line that was just extended.

21. Press ↵ to advance to the next prompt.

22. At the `Select objects to trim:` prompt, select the end of the joined feature line that extends south of the green one.

23. Press Enter to end the command.

Next you'll join the magenta feature line to the green one. Similar to the AutoCAD Join command, the entity selected first will pass its properties onto those selected after.

24. Select the magenta feature line if not already selected.

25. From the contextual tab ➤ Edit Geometry panel, click the Join tool.

26. At the `Select the connecting feature line, polyline or 3D polyline or [Multiple]:` prompt, select the green feature line.

27. Press ↵ to end the command.

28. Press Esc to deselect.

At this point in the exercise, your drawing should look like Figure 14.17 containing one feature line representing the edges of the sidewalk joining the edge of concrete around the pool area.

FIGURE 14.17
One feature line representing the edges of the sidewalk joining the edge of concrete around the pool area

Next, you will round one of the corners of the pool area to accommodate landscape.

29. Select the magenta feature line.

30. From the contextual tab ➤ Edit Geometry panel, click the Fillet tool.

31. Hover the cursor over the southwest corner of the magenta feature line, as shown in Figure 14.18.

FIGURE 14.18
Filleting the
southwest corner
of the magenta
feature line

As you hover near the corner, you will see a preview of the fillet with the current radius value following the cursor. Just as with the AutoCAD Fillet command, you could use the options at the command prompt to change the radius value.

32. Click near the corner to place the fillet using the default radius value.

33. Press Esc twice to end the command and deselect.

To adjust the radius value of the curve, do the following:

34. Select the magenta feature line.

35. From the contextual tab ➤ Edit Geometry panel, click the Edit Curve tool.

36. At the Select feature line curve to edit or [Delete]: prompt, select the magenta feature line on the curve.

37. In the Edit Feature Line Curve dialog, type **24′ (8 m)** for a new radius value. If you press Tab after entering the radius value, then you can see a preview of the curve before clicking OK.

38. Click OK to close the dialog.

39. Press Esc to end the command.

40. With the feature line still selected, notice the PI labeled extra PI next to the parking lot.

Sometimes when you piece together your linework, you can end up with extra vertices. Before proceeding to applying elevations to your PIs, you should delete any extras you don't need.

41. From the contextual tab ➤ Edit Geometry panel, click the Delete PI tool.

You will see triangular glyphs appear at each vertex of the feature line. When your cursor nears a vertex, the glyph turns green indicating that it will be deleted if you click now.

42. At the Specify Point: prompt, hover your cursor over the extra PI and left-click.

43. Press Esc three times to end the command and deselect.

Your site should now look like Figure 14.19.

FIGURE 14.19
Site with completed geometry adjustments

When this exercise is complete, you can close the drawing. A saved copy of this drawing (1402_FeatureLineGeometry_FINISHED.dwg or 1402_FeatureLineGeometry_METRIC_FINISHED.dwg) is available from the book's web page.

MODIFYING FEATURE LINES

When you're modifying the radius of a feature line curve, it's important to remember that you must have enough tangent length on either side of the curve segment to make a curve fit; if you don't, the program will not make the change or it will create a nontangent curve. If this is the case, adjust the feature line's geometry on either side of the arc until there is a mathematical solution.

Sometimes you may need to use the Weed Vertices or Delete PI tool to remove vertices and create enough room to fillet feature lines. When you're creating feature lines, you may need to plan ahead to ensure that vertices will not be placed too closely together.

EDITING FEATURE LINE ELEVATIONS

To access the commands to edit feature line elevation, from the Feature Line contextual tab ➤ Modify panel, choose the Edit Elevations toggle to open the Edit Elevations panel.

The first tool in this panel is the Elevation Editor, which will activate a palette in Panorama where you can inspect station, elevation, length, and grade information about the feature line selected in a tabular grid format. You can edit elevation and grade in this interface. When you are working in a row in the Elevation Editor, the corresponding point will be shown with a temporary triangular glyph on the plan.

A number of tools are available for modifying and manipulating feature-line elevations. You will be using a few of them in the upcoming exercises. In this first exercise, you'll take a brief look at the Grading Elevation Editor tools:

1. Open the 1403_EditingFeatureLineElevations.dwg or 1403_EditingFeatureLineElevations_METRIC.dwg file.

2. Select the red feature line representing the tennis court area to activate the Feature Line contextual tab.

3. On the Feature Line contextual tab ➤ Edit Elevations panel, choose the Elevation Editor tool. Then press Esc to deselect the feature so you can observe feature line glyphs while working in the Grading Elevation Editor.

   The Grading Elevation Editor in Panorama will open, as shown in Figure 14.20.

FIGURE 14.20
The Grading Elevation Editor

A series of symbols appears in the far-left column of the Grading Elevation Editor; these are the same glyph symbols used on the feature line grips. A triangular symbol denotes a PI, and a circular symbol denotes an elevation point. In this example, you don't have any elevation points.

4. Click in the Station column for the first PI at Station 0+00.00 (or 0+000.00).

   As a row is selected in the Grading Elevation Editor, the PI or the elevation point that was selected will be highlighted on the graphic with a small glyph.

   You can use the Grading Elevation Editor to make changes to the Station, Elevation, Length, Grade Ahead, and Grade Back settings. The exception is that you cannot edit stationing or length for PI points, as indicated by triangle glyphs in the Grading Elevation Editor.

   Across the top of the Grading Elevation Editor are multiple tools that will be used as you edit the data in the table:

Select   Clicking the Select tool allows you to select the feature line on the screen for editing in the Grading Elevation Editor. You can also select a parcel or survey figure.

Zoom To   The Zoom To tool will do exactly as it says. If a station is highlighted in the Panorama and you select the Zoom To tool, your plan view will be zoomed to that station on the feature line on the screen. When multiple stations are selected, the Zoom To tool will fit those multiple stations into your drawing window.

Quick Profile   The Quick Profile tool will generate a temporary profile based on the feature line selected. This is the same tool discussed earlier that was available on the Feature Line contextual tab ➤ Launch Pad panel. The Create Quick Profiles dialog will open, allowing you to select which surfaces you want to display, as well as what profile view style and 3D entity profile you want.

Raise/Lower   Clicking the Raise/Lower tool will activate the Set Increment text box. This will allow you to raise or lower selected station points by the value entered in the text box. If no station points are selected, it will raise or lower the entire feature line to the elevation displayed in the text box. This is an actual elevation, not an elevation difference, and you must press the Enter key to apply the elevation.

Raise Incrementally and Lower Incrementally   The Raise Incrementally/Lower Incrementally tools will raise or lower the station point or points by the amount listed in the Set Increment text box. This is an elevation difference.

Set Increment   The Set Increment tool activates the text box used with the Raise Incrementally and Lower Incrementally tools. This text box must be activated and supplied a value before proceeding with these tools. Negative values are not accepted in the Set Increment text box.

Flatten Grade Or Elevations   The Flatten Grade Or Elevations tool enables you to assign either one elevation to selected station points or a constant slope between selected station points. If you want to flatten the elevations, the elevation of the first selected station point will be applied to the other selected points. If nothing is selected, the elevation of the first point on the list will be used. If you want to apply a constant grade across a selected group of station points, the elevation of the first and last points in the selection will be held, and all points in between will be flattened to the grade calculated between the first and last points. When this tool is selected, the Flatten dialog will open asking if you want to flatten by constant elevation or by constant grade.

Insert Elevation Point   The Insert Elevation Point tool will let you select a spot on the feature line and will create an elevation point. The Insert PVI dialog will open, allowing you to fine-tune the station and elevation values.

Delete Elevation Point   The Delete Elevation Point will delete a point or points that are highlighted in the Grading Elevations Editor. Note that this tool will allow you to delete only elevation points.

Elevations From Surface   Clicking the Elevations From Surface tool will open the Select Surface dialog if there are multiple surfaces from which to choose. If you have selected a station point or points, it will assign elevations to only those points. If no station points are selected, the entire feature line will be draped over the surface, assigning elevations to all station points.

Reverse The Direction The Reverse The Direction tool will do exactly as it says; it will reverse the direction of the feature line, thereby changing the direction of the stationing and the grade-ahead/grade-back directions.

Show Grade Breaks Only The Show Grade Breaks Only tool is a toggle (click, it's on, and click, it's off) that will display only the rows where the grade breaks on the feature line. Therefore, if two adjacent segments share the same grade value, the station point that they share will be hidden because the grade doesn't break on that point.

Unselect All Rows The Unselect All Rows tool does exactly as it says; it will deselect any rows that have been highlighted for editing.

5. Click the green check mark in the upper-right corner to dismiss Panorama.

Using the Grading Elevation Editor is the most basic way to manipulate elevation information. Keep this drawing open for use in the next exercise.

USING OTHER FEATURE-LINE ELEVATION EDITING TOOLS

To access the commands for editing feature-line elevation information, select a feature line to access the Feature Line contextual tab and toggle on the Edit Elevations panel, as shown in Figure 14.21. Many of the tools in the Elevation Editor may seem redundant from the Grading Elevation Editor tools discussed earlier, but they are placed here for ease of use.

FIGURE 14.21
The Edit Elevations panel on the Feature Line contextual tab

Moving across the panel beyond the Elevation Editor tool, which was just discussed, you find the following tools for modifying or assigning elevations to feature lines:

Insert Elevation Point The Insert Elevation Point tool inserts an elevation point at the point selected or multiple elevation points at a specified increment. The elevation occurring on the feature line at the location inserted will be assigned to the elevation point. This elevation can be edited later. Note that elevation points can control only elevation information; an elevation point cannot be moved to alter the original orientation of the feature line.

Delete Elevation Point The Delete Elevation Point tool deletes the selected elevation point; the points on either side then become connected linearly on the basis of their current elevations. You can also delete all elevation points on a feature line with this command. When deleting an elevation point, the one that will be deleted is highlighted in green.

Quick Elevation Edit The Quick Elevation Edit tool allows you to use onscreen cues to set elevations and slopes quickly between PIs on any feature lines.

◆ Hover over a PI or an elevation point and a triangular glyph appears showing the elevation of that station point at the cursor. Click to trigger the prompt at the command line and type in a new elevation.

♦ Hover over a segment on the feature line and an arrowhead glyph appears showing the direction and grade of the segment. Click to trigger the prompt at the command line and type in a new grade. The elevation of the PI in which the arrow is pointing to will adjust.

Edit Elevations   The Edit Elevations tool steps through the selected feature line, much like working through a polyline edit at the command line, allowing you to change elevations and grades or insert, move, and delete elevation points. A triangular glyph shows up at the current vertex. To skip editing the vertex and move on to the next, press the Enter key to accept the current value.

Set Grade/Slope Between Points   The Set Grade/Slope Between Points tool sets a continuous slope along the feature line between selected points. As you select the points, you will be asked to specify or verify the elevation at each point.

Insert High/Low Elevation Point   The Insert High/Low Elevation Point tool places a new elevation point on the basis of two picked points: the grade ahead of the first point and the grade behind the second point. This calculated point is placed at the intersection of two vertical slopes.

Raise/Lower By Reference   The Raise/Lower By Reference tool allows you to adjust a feature-line station point vertically based on a grade, slope, or elevation difference in relation to a point on another 3D object or point. This relationship isn't dynamic!

Set Elevation By Reference   The Set Elevation By Reference tool at first looks like the same command as the Raise/Lower By Reference tool. The differences are that you can execute this tool on multiple points on the feature line without leaving the command, and you can insert new elevation points. This relationship isn't dynamic!

Adjacent Elevations By Reference   The Adjacent Elevations By Reference tool allows you to adjust the elevation of multiple vertices on a feature line by specifying grade, slope, or elevation difference from another 3D object. If the 3D object has length, elevations are projected to the feature-line station points perpendicularly from the 3D object. This relationship isn't dynamic!

Grade Extension By Reference   The Grade Extension By Reference tool allows you to set the grade, slope, or elevation difference between feature-line segments across a gap. For example, you might use this tool along the back of curbs at locations such as driveways or intersections. This relationship isn't dynamic!

Elevations From Surface   The Elevations From Surface tool sets the elevation at each PI and elevation point on the basis of the selected surface. It will optionally add elevation points at any point where the feature line crosses a surface TIN line.

Raise/Lower   The Raise/Lower tool simply moves the entire feature line in the z direction by an amount entered at the command line. A positive number raises and a negative number lowers.

Some of the tools can be difficult to understand, so you'll look at them in the next exercise and see how they function in some basic scenarios:

1. If not opened for the previous exercise, open the `1403_EditingFeatureLineElevations` `.dwg` or `1403_EditingFeatureLineElevations_METRIC.dwg` file. You do not need to have completed the previous exercise to proceed.

2. Zoom into the entrance to the parking lot of the site.

   Notice that the corridor has been cleaned up at the entrance. A region was inserted and an assembly was used that omitted the curb, gutter, and sidewalk in the entrance area. To review regions and the use of multiple assemblies in a corridor, see Chapter 10, "Advanced Corridors, Intersections, and Roundabouts."

   Also, two feature lines were extracted from the corridor representing the flowline at the curb and gutter on both sides of the region. They are dynamically linked to the corridor so they will update if the corridor is modified. To review the Feature Lines From Corridor command, see Chapter 9.

3. On the Prospector tab, expand the Sites ➤ Parking Lot collection.

4. Right-click Feature Lines and select Properties from the context menu.

5. In the Feature Line Site Properties dialog on the Options tab, do the following:

   a. Fill in the Filter Unused Styles check box.

   Only the styles in use will display.

   b. Highlight the Corridor Grading style.

   c. Click the up arrow button a number of times to move the Corridor Grading feature line style to the top of the list, as shown in Figure 14.22.

FIGURE 14.22
Assigning priority
in the Feature Line
Site Properties
dialog

This will set the initial priority by style when feature lines cross where no PIs exist. This means that the feature line style that is higher on the list will set the elevation where it intersects another. If the feature lines have the same style applied, the one modified last will win.

   d. Click OK to close the dialog.

6. Select the white polyline representing the edge of pavement of the parking lot.

7. On the Home tab ➢ Create Design panel ➢ Feature Line drop-down, select Create Feature Lines From Objects.

8. In the Create Feature Lines dialog, do the following:

   a. Set the Site to Parking Lot.

   b. In the Style area, use the drop-down to set the Style to Grading Edge Of Pavement.

   c. Under Conversion Options, clear the check box for Assign Elevations And Weed Points. The Erase Existing Entities check box should remain checked.

   d. Click OK to close.

9. Select the newly created feature line.

10. On the contextual tab ➢ Edit Elevations panel, select the Elevation Editor tool.

11. Scroll through the Grading Elevation Editor to review it.

   Notice that the elevations of the feature line at stations 0+00 and 9+21.75 (0+000 and 0+280.97 if metric) are already set because these stations were touching the extracted corridor feature lines when the polyline was converted. The feature line is matching grade with the road at the flowline on both sides of the entrance.

12. Leave the Grading Elevation Editor open. Either push it to the side or minimize it.

13. With the feature line still selected, on the contextual ribbon ➢ Edit Elevations panel, click Quick Elevation Edit.

   a. Hover over the middle of the left curb return. Use your scroll button to zoom in or out if necessary.

   Notice the triangular glyph that appears on the segment, which changes directions depending on which end of the segment your cursor is nearest. The direction in which the triangle is pointing is the direction in which you will be applying the grade. Notice that the triangular glyph turns gray when it points to where the edge of pavement feature line touches the corridor's dynamically linked feature line. This glyph indicates that this elevation is being influenced by another feature line.

   b. Position the cursor so that the triangular glyph is pointing toward the parking lot, as shown in Figure 14.23, and left-click.

FIGURE 14.23
Editing the grade
of a feature
line with Quick
Elevation Edit

c. At the Specify grade or [Slope]: prompt, type 3 ↵ to specify a 3 percent grade.

d. Go to the Grading Elevation Editor and scroll to the bottom of the list to look at the elevation assigned at station 8+90.59 (0+271.46 if metric).

e. With the Quick Elevation Edit tool still running, hover over the PT of the right curb return of the entrance.

A tooltip showing elevation will appear with an equilateral triangular glyph, as shown in Figure 14.24. With the Quick Elevation Edit tool, not only can you edit the grade or slope of a feature line segment, but you can also edit the elevation of a PI.

FIGURE 14.24
Editing the eleva-
tion of a feature
line with Quick
Elevation Edit

    f. Click over the PI.

    g. At the `Specify elevation or [Surface]:` prompt, type **7.07** (**2.151** if metric).

    h. Check the Grading Elevation Editor at station 0+31.70 (0+009.67 if metric), and notice that the elevation you just typed in has been assigned to the second station on the list.

    i. Leave the Grading Elevation Editor open.

    j. Press Esc twice to end the command and deselect.

14. Pan over to the Building feature line and select.

Previously, you used the Elevations From Surface tool to assign elevations to the feature line. You also had the Insert Intermediate Grade Break Points check box filled. Figure 14.25 displays how the Set Elevations From Surface dialog was configured in the previous exercise.

FIGURE 14.25
Set Elevations
From Surface
dialog

The circular grips called elevation points on the feature line are there because TIN lines from the surface crossed the feature lines at those locations. You will remove the elevation points from the feature line so you can set elevations at just the four corners of the building for now.

15. With the feature line still selected, on the contextual tab ➤ Edit Elevation panel, select Delete Elevation Point.

As the cursor nears the feature line, circular glyphs appear where the circular grips are located, and triangular glyphs appear at the four corners. This tool will remove only the circular glyphs (elevation points).

    a. At the `Specify point or [All]:` prompt, type **A** ↵.

    b. Press Esc to end the command.

If you take a look at the Grading Elevation Editor on Panorama, you may notice that it is still displaying the numerous stations associated with the parking lot feature line. The Grading Elevation Editor will not automatically change its contents based on the current selection.

16. In the Grading Elevation Editor tab on Panorama, do the following:

a. Click the Select A Feature Line, Parcel Line, or Survey Figure tool, which is the green button in the upper-left corner of Panorama.

Since the feature line was still selected when you clicked the tool, the Grading Elevation Editor instantly updated.

b. Select all the PIs by selecting the first line, then holding the Shift key down, and selecting the last line.

c. Click into one of the elevation fields and enter **8** (**2.5** for metric) to set the initial elevation of each PI outside the building.

17. In the Grading Elevation Editor tab on Panorama, click the Select A Feature Line, Parcel Line, or Survey Figure tool.

18. Using the pick box, select the magenta feature line representing the edge of the concrete around the pool area.

Notice that an elevation has been assigned to the beginning station of the feature line at point 1. Since the edge of concrete feature line intersects the building feature line, they are sharing the same elevation. The final station near the northeast corner of the building at point 8 should be set by the building feature line, but it is still at elevation 0. Zooming in closer to this area will reveal that the feature line doesn't quite intersect the building. Since you need the PI of the building and the PI of the edge of concrete to match elevations at this location, you will connect them.

19. Click the magenta feature line, click the grip of the PI near point 8, and Endpoint Osnap it to the northeast building corner.

The Grading Elevation Editor will update, as shown in Figure 14.26. Notice the + sign near the bottom-right corner of the green triangle in the first and last rows? That shows that the feature lines touch.

FIGURE 14.26
Updated Grading Elevation Editor after grip-editing the edge of concrete feature line

Station	Elevation	Length	Grade Ahead	Grade Back
0+00.00	8.00'	6.22'	-128.65%	128.65%
0+06.22	0.00'	42.59'	0.00%	0.00%
0+48.81	0.00'	102.00'	0.00%	0.00%
1+50.81	0.00'	12.00'	0.00%	0.00%
1+62.81	0.00'	113.94'	0.00%	0.00%
2+76.75	0.00'	54.44'	0.00%	0.00%
3+31.19	0.00'	51.92'	0.00%	0.00%
3+83.10	0.00'	37.70'	0.00%	0.00%
4+20.80	0.00'	153.36'	0.00%	0.00%
5+74.16	0.00'	194.14'	0.00%	0.00%
7+68.30	0.00'	110.94'	7.21%	-7.21%
8+79.24	8.00'			

20. Close Panorama by clicking the green check mark in the upper-right corner.

Next, you'll set the grades on the edge of concrete feature line. The object is to get the runoff to flow away from the building toward the southern end of the site.

21. Select the magenta feature line, and on the contextual ribbon ➤ Edit Elevation tab, select Set Elevation By Reference.

    a. At the `Specify the reference point:` prompt, Endpoint Osnap to the northeast corner of the building at point 8.

    b. At the `Specify point or [Insert]:` prompt, hover over the northeast corner of the edge of concrete near point 7 and left-click (there is no need to use Osnaps), as shown in Figure 14.27.

FIGURE 14.27
Using Set Elevation By Reference to grade the edge of concrete

    c. At the `Specify grade or [Slope Difference]:` prompt, type **−0.5** ↵ for grade.

The command will repeat itself so you can select another point to be graded relative to the reference point selected when the command launched.

22. On the contextual ribbon ➤ Edit Elevation tab, select Set Elevation By Reference to reset the command.

    a. At the `Specify reference point:` prompt, Endpoint Osnap on the northeast corner of the edge of concrete at point 7 (the point you just assigned an elevation to).

    b. At the `Specify point or [Insert]:` prompt, click the southeast corner of the edge of concrete at point 6.

    c. At the `Specify grade or [Slope Difference]:` prompt, type **−0.5** ↵ for grade.

23. On the contextual ribbon ➤ Edit Elevation tab, select Set Elevation By Reference to reset the command.

    a. At the `Specify reference point:` prompt, Endpoint Osnap on the first PI of the magenta feature line at point 1 on the south side of the building, as shown in Figure 14.28.

FIGURE 14.28
Using Set Elevation By Reference on the south side of the building

    b. At the `Specify point or [Insert]:` prompt, click the next PI on the magenta feature line at point 2.

    c. At the `Specify grade or [Slope Difference]:` prompt, type **–1** ↵ for grade.

    d. At the `Specify point or [Insert]:` prompt, click the PI on the magenta feature line at point 3.

    e. At the `Specify grade or [Slope Difference]:` prompt, type **–1** ↵ for grade.

    f. At the `Specify point or [Insert]:` prompt, click the PC on the magenta feature line at point 4.

    g. At the `Specify grade or [Slope Difference]:` prompt, type **–1** ↵ for grade.

    h. Press Esc to end the command.

24. On the contextual ribbon ➤ Edit Elevation tab, select Elevation Editor.

In the Grading Elevation Editor, note that stations 0+48.81 through 2+76.75 (0+015.48 through 0+084.96 if metric) are still at elevation 0. These PIs occur in the sidewalk area and you'll grade them later. Station 4+20.80 (0+129.26 if metric) occurs at the PT at point 5. You'll apply a continuous grade between points 4 and 6.

    a. Select stations 3+83.10 through 5+74.16 (0+116.69 through 0+175.32 if metric) in the Grading Elevation Editor.

    b. Select the Flatten Grade Or Elevations tool at the top of the Grading Elevation Editor.

    c. In the Flatten dialog, select Constant Grade and click OK to assign.

According to the Grading Elevation Editor, a grade of –0.43 has been assigned. Now you'll set a low point at the midpoint of the segment between points 5 and 6.

    d. Close the Grading Elevation Editor. The magenta feature line should still be selected.

25. On the contextual ribbon ➤ Edit Elevation tab, select Insert High/Low Elevation Point.

    a. At the `Specify the start point:` prompt, select the PI at point 6.

    b. At the `Specify the end point:` prompt, select the next PI at point 5.

A triangular directional glyph appears near the last point picked, indicating the direction the grade will be applied.

    c. At the `Specify grade ahead or [Slope]:` prompt, type **–1** ↵.

A triangular directional glyph appears now near the first point picked indicating the direction the next grade will be applied.

    d. At the `Specify grade back or [Slope]:` prompt, type **–0.5** ↵.

The location of the low point is calculated with the grades provided, and a circular elevation point is inserted at that location, as shown in Figure 14.29.

FIGURE 14.29
Location of elevation point calculated with the Insert High/Low Elevation Point tool

    e. Press Esc twice to end the command and deselect.

To set the grades on the sidewalk, you will get a little crafty. You'll create a temporary surface that defines a grade of 2 percent away from the building. Then you'll assign elevations to the sidewalk area with this surface. You will do something similar later in the next section using grading groups.

26. Select the building feature line and on the contextual ribbon ➤ Edit Geometry tab, select Stepped Offset.

    a. At the `Specify offset distance or [Through Layer]:` prompt, type **25** (**8** if metric) ↵.

    b. At the `Specify side to offset or [Multiple]:` prompt, pick a point outside the building area.

    c. At the `Specify elevation difference or [Grade Slope Elevation Variable]:` prompt, type **G** ↵ to specify grade.

    d. At the `Specify grade or [Slope Elevation Difference Variable]:` prompt, type **–2** ↵. Press Esc twice.

27. Select the new feature line, and on the contextual tab, expand the Modify panel to select Move To Site.

    a. In the Move To Site dialog under Destination Site, select Temp.

    b. Click OK to close.

Leaving the new feature line in the same site as the edge of concrete and building feature line would have caused an elevation point to have been inserted wherever it crossed over these feature lines. Moving it to another site keeps that from occurring.

28. Select the building feature line and the new offset feature line.

29. On the contextual tab ➤ Modify panel, click the Add To Surface As Breakline tool.

a. In the Select Surface dialog, click the plus sign button to create a new surface.

    b. In the Create Surface dialog, type **Temp** for the surface name.

    c. For Style, click into the Style value field. Then click the ellipsis button to open the Select Surface Style dialog.

    d. In the Select Surface Style dialog, select the style called Border Only and click OK to close.

    e. Click OK to close the Create Surface dialog.

    f. Click OK to close the Select Surface dialog, and the Add Breaklines dialog opens.

    g. Under Supplementing Factor, fill in the Distance check box.

    h. In the Distance field, type **25** (**8** if metric).

       Creating surface points at this frequency will produce a set of uniform triangles across the sidewalk area, which makes for a more accurate surface.

    i. Click OK to close, and press Esc to deselect the feature lines.

30. Select the magenta feature line, and on the contextual tab ➤ Edit Elevations panel, click Elevation Editor.

    a. In the Grading Elevation Editor, select the four PIs with an elevation value of 0 by holding down the Shift key during the selection.

    b. At the top of the Grading Elevation Editor, click the Elevations From Surface tool.

    c. In the Select Surface dialog, select the Temp surface using the drop-down and click OK.

    d. Click the green check mark in the Grading Elevation Editor to close it, and press Esc to deselect the feature line.

Last, you will make an adjustment to the red feature line on the west side of the site representing the tennis court. As you may recall, the northwest corner was set by acquiring its elevation from the existing surface, and then from that corner typical cross slopes were applied. You will now raise the tennis court to ensure that it will be higher than the surrounding ground.

31. Select the red feature line representing the tennis court, and on the contextual tab ➤ Edit Elevations panel, click the Raise/Lower tool.

    a. At the Specify Elevation Difference: prompt, type **0.5** (**0.15** for metric) ↵.

    b. Press Esc to deselect.

When this exercise is complete, you can close the drawing. A saved copy of this drawing (1403_Editing FeatureLineElevations_FINISHED.dwg or 1403_ Editing FeatureLineElevations_METRIC_FINISHED.dwg) is available from the book's web page.

You are halfway to completing the construction of your grading model. In an upcoming section, you will use another grading tool called Grading Groups to assign elevations in the parking lot. By using all the tools in the Feature Lines toolbar, you can quickly grade elements of your design and pull them together in a surface.

Labeling Feature Lines

Feature lines can be labeled with their overall length, segment length, vertex elevation, and segment grade or slope. This is helpful to the designer because as you change your design, you can monitor geometry values, grades, and elevations since the labels update as you go. In the next couple of exercises, you'll label a few critical points on your site design to help you better understand the drainage patterns.

Feature lines do not have their own unique label styles, but they do use Line and Curve labels under General styles. You can learn more about label styles in Chapter 18, "Label Styles." The templates that ship with Civil 3D contain styles for labeling segment slopes, so you'll label the grades of feature line segments in the following exercise:

1. Open the 1404_LabelingFeatureLines.dwg or 1404_LabelingFeatureLines_METRIC .dwg file.

2. From the Annotate tab ➤ Labels & Tables panel, click the Add Labels icon to display the Add Labels dialog.

3. In the Add Labels dialog, do the following:

    a. Set the Feature drop-down to Line And Curve.

    b. Set Label Type to Single Segment.

    c. Set Line Label Style to Feature Line Info.

    d. Set Curve Label Style to Feature Line Info.

    When complete, the dialog should look like Figure 14.30.

FIGURE 14.30
Adding feature
line grade labels

4. Click the Add button.

5. At the Select point on entity: prompt, pick several segments on the magenta feature line, as shown in Figure 14.31.

FIGURE 14.31
Feature line grade labels in the Imperial drawing

You can also try to change the slopes of some of the segments in Elevation Editor to see what happens to the labels.

When this exercise is complete, you can close the drawing. A saved copy of this drawing (1404_LabelingFeatureLines_FINISHED.dwg or 1404_LabelingFeatureLines_METRIC_ FINISHED.dwg) is available from the book's web page.

Grading Objects

Once a feature line is created for site grading, there are two main uses. One is to incorporate the feature line itself directly into a surface object as a breakline; the other is to create a grading object (referred to hereafter as simply a *grading* or *gradings*) using the feature line as a baseline. A grading consists of a baseline and grading criteria, which describes how a slope projects from the baseline feature line. This slope can be defined by using a certain combination of the following criteria: distance, slope or grade, relative elevation, or actual elevation. Surfaces can also be part of the criteria. Grading criteria can be defined and stored in grading criteria sets for ease of management. Styles can be applied to gradings for visual preferences or to convey information such as cut or fill.

Gradings are stored on Prospector within Sites in a branch called *Grading Groups*. They must be created in the same site as their originating feature lines. Gradings produce feature lines along the limits of each projected slope. These feature lines, like corridor feature lines, cannot be edited. They can be added to surfaces and also used to create other gradings. When these grading-dependent feature lines are used to create other gradings, the additional gradings become part of the grading group. These gradings are joined and will change when the baseline feature line or a parent grading is modified.

In this section, you'll use a number of methods to create gradings, edit those gradings, and finally convert the grading group into a surface.

Creating Gradings

Certification
Objective

Let's look at grading a pond. In this section, you'll look at grading groups and then create the individual gradings within the group. Grading groups act as a collection mechanism for dependent gradings, and they let Civil 3D keep track of which gradings are to act in sync with each other.

One thing to be careful of when you're working with gradings is that they are part of a site. Any feature line within that same site will react with the feature lines created by the grading. For that reason, the exercise drawing has another site called Pond Grading to be used for just pond grading.

1. Open the `1405_GradingThePond.dwg` or `1405_GradingThePond_METRIC.dwg` file.

2. Select the feature line representing the edge of pond to activate the Feature Line contextual tab.

3. From the Feature line contextual tab, expand the Modify panel, and choose Move To Site to display the Move To Site dialog.

4. Set the Destination Site drop-down to the site named Pond Grading and click OK.

   This will avoid interaction between the pond gradings and any other feature lines in the drawing.

 With the feature line still selected, on the Feature Line contextual tab ➤ Launch Pad panel, choose Grading Creation Tools.

   The Grading Creation Tools toolbar, shown in Figure 14.32, appears. The left section is focused on settings, the middle on creation, and the right on editing.

FIGURE 14.32
The Grading
Creation Tools
toolbar

 6. On the Grading Creation Tools toolbar, click the Set The Grading Group tool to the far left of the toolbar to display the Site dialog.

7. Choose the Pond Grading site from the drop-down list and click OK.

   The Create Grading Group dialog is displayed.

8. Enter **Pond Grading** in the Name text box, as shown in Figure 14.33, and click OK.

FIGURE 14.33
Assign the name
Pond Grading in
the Create Grading
Group dialog

You'll revisit the surface creation options in a bit.

9. On the Grading Creation Tools toolbar, click the Select The Target Surface tool located next to the Select The Grading Group tool to display the Select Surface dialog.

10. Select Existing Surface in the drop-down list and click OK.

11. On the Grading Creation Tools toolbar, verify that Grading Criteria is set to Grade To Distance and click the Create Grading tool, or click the down arrow next to the Create Grading tool and select Create Grading, as shown in Figure 14.34.

FIGURE 14.34
Creating a grading
using the Grade To
Distance criteria

12. At the Select the feature: prompt, select the pond feature line. If you get a dialog asking you to weed the feature line, select the Continue Grading Without Feature Line Weeding option.

13. At the Select the grading side: prompt, pick a point on the inside of the pond basin to indicate the direction of the grading projections.

14. At the `Apply to entire length? [Yes No]:` prompt, enter **Y** ↵ to apply the grading to the entire length of the pond outline.

15. At the `Specify distance:` prompt, enter **5** ↵ (or **1.5** ↵ for metric users) at the command line as the distance.

16. At the `Format [Grade Slope]:` prompt, enter **S** ↵.

17. At the `Slope:` prompt, enter **–10** ↵ for a 10 horizontal to 1 vertical slope.

The first grading has been created. The lines onscreen are part of the Grading style.

18. Press Esc to end the command.

Gradings can be modified with the Grading Editor. In the Grading Editor, you can edit any of the criteria you used to apply the grading slopes.

19. Click the diamond-shaped glyph located inside the grading you just created.

20. On the contextual tab ➤ Modify panel, click Grading Editor.

Panorama opens displaying the Grading Editor.

21. On the Grading Editor tab under the Grading Method parameter group, click in the Distance Value field and type in a new distance value of **10** (or **3** for metric users). If you watch the grading group, you can see it update after you enter the new value.

22. Click the green check mark to dismiss the vista.

Now you will attach more gradings to complete the pond design.

23. On the Grading Creation Tools toolbar, set Grading Criteria to Grade To Elevation, and click the Create Grading tool.

24. At the `Select the feature:` prompt, select the inner boundary of the grading made in step 17.

25. At the `Apply to entire length? [Yes/No]:` prompt, enter **Y** ↵ to apply to the whole length. Notice that you did not have to select a side, because there is already a grading object on one side of the selected feature line.

26. At the `Elevation:` prompt, enter **1** ↵ (**0.3** ↵ for metric users) for the target distance to build the safety ledge.

27. At the `Cut Format [Grade Slope]:` prompt, enter **S** ↵.

28. At the `Slope:` prompt, enter **3** ↵.

29. At the `Fill Format [Grade Slope]:` prompt, enter **S** ↵.

30. At the `Slope:` prompt, enter **3** ↵.

31. Press Esc to end the command. Your pond should look like Figure 14.35.

FIGURE 14.35
Creating a grading
group

32. On the Grading Creation Tools toolbar, set Grading Criteria to Grade To Surface, and click the Create Grading tool.

33. At the `Select the feature:` prompt, select the edge of pond feature line.

34. At the `Select the grading side:` prompt, click outside the feature line.

35. At the `Apply to entire length [Yes No]?` prompt, enter **Y** ↵.

36. At the `Cut Format [Grade Slope]:` prompt, enter **S** ↵.

37. At the `Cut Slope:` prompt, enter **3** ↵ for a 3 horizontal to 1 vertical slope.

38. At the `Fill Format [Grade Slope]:` prompt, enter **S** ↵.

39. At the `Fill Slope:` prompt, enter **3** ↵ for a 3 horizontal to 1 vertical slope.

40. Press Esc to end the command.

Your drawing should look similar to Figure 14.36.

FIGURE 14.36
Feature-line grad-
ing for the pond

41. On the Grading Creation Tools toolbar, click the down arrow next to the Create Grading tool and select Create Infill.

    An infill is a grading that is used to fill in holes.

42. Click in the open area in the middle of the pond.

43. Press Esc to end the command. Next, you will check the pond volume to make sure it meets the capacity needed.

44. On Prospector, expand the Sites ➤ Pond Grading ➤ Grading Groups branches, select Pond Grading, right-click, and choose Properties.

45. In the Grading Group Properties dialog, fill in the check box for Automatic Surface Creation.

    The Create Surface dialog opens.

46. Click OK to accept the defaults in the Create Surface dialog.

47. Back in the Grading Group Properties dialog, fill in the check box under Volume Base Surface and verify that Existing Surface is selected.

    A surface was previously created using the edge of pond feature line for the purpose of running this analysis. The Grading Group Properties dialog should be set as shown in Figure 14.37.

FIGURE 14.37
Configure the
Grading Group
Properties

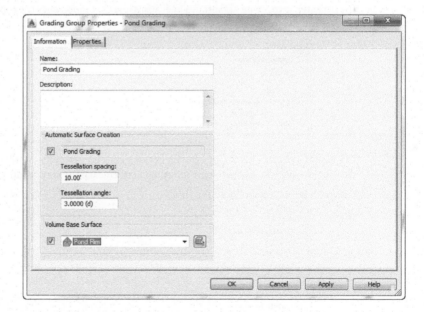

48. Click OK to close the dialog.

49. Up on the ribbon on the Analyze tab ➤ Volumes And Materials panel, choose Grading Volume Tools.

The Grading Volume Tools toolbar opens. Note the value for Cut: 2657.30 cubic yards (1932.91 cubic meters). This represents the total volume that this pond can hold.

50. Click the Lower The Grading Group button in the Grading Volume Tools toolbar.

This action just lowered the pond by the amount that is entered in the white field on the right side of the box. Notice that the Cut value has increased, which means the pond's capacity has increased: 3079.79 cubic yards (3037.36 cubic meters).

When this exercise is complete, you can close the drawing. A saved copy of this drawing (1405_GradingThePond_FINISHED.dwg or 1405_GradingThePond_METRIC_FINISHED.dwg) is available from the book's web page.

Each piece of this pond is tied to the next, creating a dynamic model of your pond design on the basis of the designer's intent. Next, you will learn how to use grading groups to help grade the parking lot.

BUILDING CURB AND GUTTER

Gradings are great for modeling curbs and gutters. For a standard curb and gutter, you would need two types of criteria:

◆ Criteria defining the gutter pan

◆ Criteria defining the face of the curb

The first step is to create and grade the feature line that represents the top of the curb. Apply criteria that define the face of the curb.

Parameter	Value	Lock
⊟ **Grading Method**		
Target	Distance	
Distance	0.10'	🔒
Projection	Relative Elevation	
⊟ **Relative Elevation Projection**		
Relative Elevation	-0.50'	🔒
⊟ **Conflict Resolution**		
Interior Corner Overlap	Use Average Slope	🔒

Then apply criteria that represent the gutter pan. You can apply a mix of catch and spill criteria. Just make sure you leave enough space in between each for transition.

The catch criteria could look like this:

Parameter	Value	Lock
⊟ **Grading Method**		
Target	Distance	
Distance	2.00'	🔒
Projection	Slope	
⊟ **Slope Projection**		
Format	Slope	🔒
Slope	12.00:1	🔒
⊟ **Conflict Resolution**		
Interior Corner Overlap	Use Average Slope	🔒

The spill criteria could look like this:

Parameter	Value	Lock
⊟ **Grading Method**		
Target	Distance	
Distance	2.00'	🔓
Projection	Slope	
⊟ **Slope Projection**		
Format	Slope	🔓
Slope	-12.00:1	🔓
⊟ **Conflict Resolution**		
Interior Corner Overlap	Use Average Slope	🔓

In the following example, catch criteria were applied to the left, and spill criteria were applied to the right.

Next, a transition was applied in between the gradings by expanding the Create Grading drop-down and selecting Create Transition from the Grading Creation Tools toolbar.

The result is a transitional slope in between the two oppositely sloped gutter pans.

Using Gradings for Interim Surfaces

An interim surface is like a temporary surface in a way. It's a surface that is built for the purpose of extracting elevations. It's a stepping-stone to getting to the final solution. The Temp surface you built around the building a few exercises ago was an interim surface.

In this exercise, you will take a feature line and add a grading to both sides that projects outward at an upward slope of 1 percent. Then you will use the Elevations From Surface command to assign the elevations to portions of the parking lot feature line.

1. Open the `1406_GradingsAndInterimSurfaces.dwg` or `1406_GradingsAndInterimSurfaces_METRIC.dwg` file.

   A bio-retention area will be placed between the two parking areas. The grading concept is to direct the flow toward the green feature line between the parking areas.

2. Select the green feature line between the parking areas.

3. On the contextual tab ➤ Launch Pad panel, select Grading Creation Tools.

4. On the Grading Creation Tools toolbar, click Set The Grading Group.

   a. Set Site Name to Temp2.

   b. Click the Create A Grading Group button, and in the Create Grading Group dialog under Name, enter **Temp2**.

   c. Fill the check box next to Automatic Surface Creation.

   d. Set Surface Style to _No Display.

   e. Click OK to close.

   f. Click OK to accept the defaults in the Create Surface dialog.

   g. Click OK to close the Select Grading Group dialog.

5. On the Grading Creation Tools toolbar, set Grading Criteria to Grade To Distance.

6. On the Grading Creation Tools toolbar, click the Create Grading button.

7. At the `Select the feature:` prompt, click the green feature line between the parking areas.

8. At the `Select the grading side:` prompt, click to the north side of the feature line.

9. At the `Apply to entire length? [Yes No]:` prompt, enter **Y** ↵.

10. At the `Specify distance:` prompt, enter **80** (**25** if metric) ↵.

11. At the `Format [Grade Slope]:` prompt, enter **G** ↵.

12. At the `Grade:` prompt, enter **1** ↵.

13. Repeat steps 7 through 11 for the south side of the feature line.

14. Press Esc to end the command and close the Grading Creation Tools.

   You now have an interim grading group surface built over the parking area, as shown in Figure 14.38.

FIGURE 14.38
A grading group
used as an interim
surface built over
the parking lot

15. Select the red feature line representing the edge of the parking lot.

16. On the contextual tab ➤ Edit Elevations panel, select Elevation Editor.

17. Using the Shift key, select stations 0+59.82 through 3+67.24 (0+018.24 through 0+111.94 if metric).

18. At the top of the Grading Elevation Editor, click the Elevations From Surface tool.

19. In the Select Surface dialog, choose Temp2.

20. Click OK to close.

21. Repeat steps 17 through 20 for stations 4+38.36 through 7+45.78 (0+133.62 through 0+227.32 if metric).

22. In the Grading Elevation Editor, select stations 0+31.70 through 0+59.82 (0+009.67 through 0+018.24 if metric).

23. Click the Flatten Grades Or Elevations button.

24. In the Flatten dialog, select Constant Grade.

25. Click OK to close.

26. Repeat steps 22 through 25 for the following station ranges:

    a.   3+67.24 through 4+38.36 (0+111.94 through 0+133.62 if metric)

    b.   7+45.78 through 8+90.59 (0+227.32 through 0+271.46 if metric)

The Grading Elevation Editor should look something like Figure 14.39.

FIGURE 14.39
Grading Elevation Editor after applying elevations from interim surface

Station	Elevation	Length	Grade Ahead	Grade Back
0+00.00	6.71'	31.70'	1.14%	-1.14%
0+31.70	7.07'	4.56'	1.56%	-1.56%
0+36.26	7.14'	23.56'	1.56%	-1.56%
0+59.82	7.51'	7.85'	0.64%	-0.64%
0+67.68	7.56'	13.00'	1.00%	-1.00%
0+80.68	7.69'	100.00'	-0.00%	0.00%
1+80.68	7.69'	13.00'	-1.00%	1.00%
1+93.68	7.56'	7.85'	-0.64%	0.64%
2+01.53	7.51'	24.00'	-1.00%	1.00%
2+25.53	7.27'	7.85'	-0.64%	0.64%
2+33.38	7.22'	13.00'	-1.00%	1.00%
2+46.38	7.09'	100.00'	0.00%	-0.00%
3+46.38	7.09'	13.00'	1.00%	-1.00%
3+59.38	7.22'	7.85'	0.64%	-0.64%
3+67.24	7.27'	23.56'	0.00%	-0.00%
3+90.80	7.27'	24.00'	0.00%	-0.00%
4+14.80	7.27'	23.56'	0.00%	-0.00%
4+38.36	7.27'	7.85'	-0.64%	0.64%
4+46.22	7.22'	13.00'	-1.00%	1.00%
4+59.22	7.09'	100.00'	0.00%	-0.00%
5+59.22	7.09'	13.00'	1.00%	-1.00%
5+72.22	7.22'	7.85'	0.64%	-0.64%
5+80.07	7.27'	24.00'	1.00%	-1.00%
6+04.07	7.51'	7.85'	0.64%	-0.64%
6+11.92	7.56'	13.00'	1.00%	-1.00%
6+24.92	7.69'	100.00'	-0.00%	0.00%
7+24.92	7.69'	13.00'	-1.00%	1.00%
7+37.92	7.56'	7.85'	-0.64%	0.64%
7+45.78	7.51'	61.27'	-0.30%	0.30%
8+07.04	7.33'	83.55'	-0.30%	0.30%
8+90.59	7.07'	31.16'	-3.06%	3.06%
9+21.75	6.12'			

When this exercise is complete, you can close the drawing. A saved copy of this drawing (1406_GradingsAndInterimSurfaces_FINISHED.dwg or 1406_GradingsAndInterimSurfaces_METRIC_FINISHED.dwg) is available from the book's web page.

Finishing Touches

You've just completed some basic grading tasks focusing on the tennis courts, building and pool area, pond, and parking area as separate components. Now it is time to bring the components together in a finished grade surface model. Once the surface model is created, you'll be able to see which areas will need further attention.

1. Open the 1407_FinishingTouches.dwg or 1407_FinishingTouches_METRIC.dwg file.

   The sidewalk grades were set from a surface (Temp) that was created by projecting a slope of 2 percent downward and away from the building. The parking lot elevations at the four PIs that coincide with the edge of sidewalk were set by another method. You want these elevations to match. So you will apply the elevations from the surface called Temp to these PIs.

2. Select the parking lot feature line.

3. On the contextual tab ➤ Edit Elevations panel, select Elevation Editor.

4. With the Shift key, select stations 2+01.53 through 2+25.53 (0+061.43 through 0+068.75 if metric).

5. At the top of the Grading Elevation Editor, click the Elevations From Surface tool.

6. In the Select Surface dialog, choose Temp.

7. Click OK to close.

8. Repeat steps 4 through 7 for stations 5+80.07 through 6+04.07 (0+176.81 through 0+184.13 if metric).

9. Use the green check mark to close the Grading Elevation Editor.

10. Select the feature lines representing the tennis court (red), the parking lot (red), the edge of concrete (magenta), the building (blue), and the pool (green).

11. On the contextual tab ➤ Modify panel, select Add To Surface As Breakline.

12. In the Select Surface dialog, click the plus sign to add a surface.

13. In the Create Surface dialog, enter **Finished Grade** for the surface name.

14. Click OK to close the Create Surface dialog.

15. Click OK to close the Select Surface dialog.

16. In the Add Breaklines dialog, do the following:

    a. Enter **Site Features** for Description.

    b. Under Supplementing Factors, fill the Distance check box and configure a supplementing distance of **25′** (**8** m if metric).

    c. Under Mid-ordinate Distance, enter **0.1′** (**0.03** m if metric).

    d. Click OK to close the Add Breaklines dialog; then click the green check mark to close the Panorama's Event Viewer.

17. Press Esc to deselect.

OVERCOMING CROOKED CONTOURS

Sometimes, no matter how hard you try, the finished grade contours generated from your grading will not be picture-perfect. Here is a trick to overcome that when other methods of smoothing are not working in your favor:

1. Draw a polyline in the shape of the contour you want. Be sure to assign it the correct elevation.

2. Add it to the surface as a contour.

Before:

After:

You have just set up your finished grade surface model. To make it even more user friendly, add some surface labels.

18. Select the surface by clicking the green surface border.

19. On the contextual tab ➤ Labels & Tables panel, select Add Labels ➤ Spot Elevations.

20. Click the building corners, pavement corners, sidewalk corners, and any other location where you'd like a reading on the elevation value. Press Esc twice when you have finished placing spot elevations.

Your drawing should look something like Figure 14.40.

Now that the model is built, you can see how the different feature lines are contributing to the surface grades and can make some adjustments.

FIGURE 14.40
Finished grade surface model with dynamic elevation labels

21. On Prospector, expand the Surfaces branch.

22. Right-click Finished Grade and select Rebuild – Automatic.

It appears that the grade for the tennis courts was set too low.

23. Select the red feature line representing the tennis courts.

24. On the contextual tab ➤ Edit Elevations tab, select Raise/Lower.

25. At the Specify elevation difference: prompt, enter **1.5 (0.5** if metric) ↵. Click the green check mark to close Panorama.

The surface updates, as shown in Figure 14.41.

FIGURE 14.41
Updated surface after raising the tennis courts feature line

You can use any of the tools that were introduced to you in the chapter on the feature lines for this site to add high/low points or adjust elevations and grades. Feel free to experiment further with this file.

When this exercise is complete, you can close the drawing. A saved copy of this drawing (1407_GradingFinishingTouches_FINISHED.dwg or 1407_GradingFinishingTouches_METRIC_FINISHED.dwg) is available from the book's web page.

The Bottom Line

Convert existing linework into feature lines.   Many site features are drawn initially as simple linework for the 2D plan. By converting this linework to feature-line information, you avoid a large amount of rework. Additionally, the conversion process offers the ability to drape feature lines along a surface, making further grading use easier.

> **Master It**   Open the MasterIt.dwg or MasterIt_METRIC.dwg file from the book's web page. Convert the magenta polyline, describing a proposed temporary swale, into a feature line and drape it across the EG surface to set elevations; then set intermediate grade break points.

Model a simple breakline with a feature line.   Feature lines define linear slope connections or, in other words, breaklines. This can be the flow of a drainage channel, the outline of a building pad, or the back of a street curb. These linear relationships can help define grading in a model or simply enhance understanding of design intent.

Master It Edit the radius of the curve on the feature line you just created to be 100′ (30 m). Set the grade from the west end of the feature line to the PC of the edited curve to 4 percent, and set the remainder to a constant slope. Draw a temporary profile view to verify that the channel is below grade for most of its length.

Model planar site features with grading groups. Once a feature line defines a linear feature, gradings collected in grading groups model the slope projections from that line to other points in space. These projections can be combined to model a site much like a TIN surface, producing a dynamic design tool.

Master It Use grading criteria to define the pilot channel, with grading on both sides of the sketched centerline. Define the channel using a Grading To Distance value of 5′ (1.5 m) with a slope of 3:1, and connect the channel to the EG surface using a grading with slopes that are 4:1. Generate a surface from the grading group. If prompted, do not weed the feature line.

Chapter 15

Plan Production

So, you've toiled for days, weeks, or maybe months creating your design in the Autodesk®
AutoCAD® Civil 3D® program, and now it's time to share it with the world—or at least your
corner of it. Even in this digital age, paper plan sets still play an important role. You generate these
sheets in Civil 3D using the Plan Production feature. This chapter takes you through the steps
necessary to create a sheet set, including viewport planning, generating sheets, data management,
and publishing.

In this chapter, you will learn to:

- ◆ Create view frames.

- ◆ Edit view frames.

- ◆ Generate sheets and review Sheet Set Manager.

- ◆ Create section views.

Preparing for Plan Sets

Plan Production tools enable you to quickly create sheet files by automating a process you have
been doing manually for years. Creating layouts, creating and orienting your viewports, inserting
and filling in title blocks, establishing external and data references, creating match lines, inserting north arrows, and setting up Sheet Set Manager are all menial but necessary tasks you must
undergo in order to publish your design to paper. Before you can put Plan Production tools into
action, you need to address some prerequisites. Let's examine those components first.

Prerequisite Components

The Plan Production feature uses several components to create a sheet set. This chapter will
explore these elements in detail, but for now, we'll take a brief look at what the components are.

Drawing Template   Plan Production creates new layouts for each sheet in a plan set. To
do this, the feature uses drawing templates with predefined layout tabs. These layout tabs
contain a suitable border and up to two scaled viewports with configured types of plan,
profile, or section.

For the exercises in this chapter, the default location for the final sheets will be `C:\`
`Mastering\Ch15\FinishedSheets`. It is recommended that you download all of the
files (www.sybex.com/go/masteringcivil3d2016) and place them in the `C:\Mastering\`
`Ch15` folder.

Object and Display Styles Plan Production generates the following objects: view frames, view frame groups, match lines, and section sheets. Before creating plan sheets, you'll want to make sure you have styles set up for each of these objects. Section view group plot styles are associated with section sheet objects.

Alignments and Profiles The Plan Production feature is used primarily for creating plan and profile views. For this to happen, your drawing must contain (or data reference) at least one alignment and profile. You must also have a sheet template ready with associated plan and profile viewports. You can produce plan-only or profile-only sheets if desired as long as you prepare a sheet template layout that supports single-plan or single-profile viewports. Plan Production tools cannot produce sheet files with two or more viewports of the same type.

Sample Lines and Sections Creating section sheets requires an alignment, a sample line group, cross sections, a group plot style, and a sheet template with associated section viewports.

With these elements in place, you're ready to dive in and create some sheets. The general steps in creating a plan set are as follows:

1. Meet the prerequisites listed previously.

2. Create view frames.

3. Create plan or plan-profile sheets.

4. (Optional) Create section view groups.

5. (Optional) Create section sheets.

6. Manage the sheets using Sheet Set Manager.

7. Plot or publish (hard copy or digitally).

The next sections describe this process in detail and the tools used in Plan Production. Sheet Set Manager, which is found in basic AutoCAD, is an integral part of this process.

Using View Frames and Match Lines

When you create sheets using the Plan Production tools, Civil 3D first automatically helps you divide your alignment into areas that will fit on your plotted sheet and display at the desired scale. To do this, Civil 3D creates a series of rectangular frames placed end to end (or slightly overlapping) along the length of alignment, like those in Figure 15.1. These rectangles are referred to as *view frames* and are automatically sized and positioned to meet your plan sheet requirements. This collection of view frames is referred to as a *view frame group*. Where the view frames overlap one another, Civil 3D creates *match lines* that establish continuity from frame to frame by referring to the previous or next sheet in the completed plan set. View frames and match lines are created in Model Space, using the prerequisite elements described in the previous section.

FIGURE 15.1
View frames and
match lines

The Create View Frames Wizard

The first step in the process of creating plan sets is to generate view frames. Civil 3D provides an intuitive wizard that walks you through each step of the view frame creation process. Let's look at the Create View Frames Wizard and the various page options. After you've seen each page, you'll have a chance to put what you've learned into practice in an example.

From the Output tab ➤ Plan Production panel, choose Create View Frames to launch the Create View Frames Wizard (Figure 15.2). The wizard consists of several pages. A list of these pages is shown along the left sidebar of the wizard, and an arrow indicates which page you're currently viewing. You move among the pages using the Next and Back navigation buttons along the bottom of each page. Alternatively, as with all wizards, you can jump directly to any page by clicking its name in the list on the left. The following sections walk you through the pages of the wizard and explain their features.

FIGURE 15.2
The Create
View Frames –
Alignment wizard
page

CREATE VIEW FRAMES – ALIGNMENT PAGE

You use the first page of the Create View Frames Wizard (shown previously in Figure 15.2) to select the alignment and station range along which the view frames will be created.

Alignment   In the top area of this page, you select the alignment along which you want to create view frames. You can either select it from the drop-down list or click the Select From The Drawing button to select the alignment onscreen.

Station Range   In the Station Range area of the page, you define the station range over which the frames will be created. Selecting Automatic creates frames from the alignment start to the alignment end. Selecting User Specified lets you define a custom range, either by keying start and end station values in the appropriate box or by clicking the button to the right of the station value fields and graphically selecting the station from the drawing.

An example of when you would want to select specific stations is if you have a subdivision that will be constructed in phases. You have designed an entire roadway but need to only create specific sheets for a specific phase.

CREATE VIEW FRAMES – SHEETS PAGE

You use the second page of the Create View Frames Wizard (Figure 15.3) to establish the sheet type and the orientation of the view frames along the alignment. A plan production *sheet* is a layout tab in a drawing file. To create the sheets, Civil 3D references a predefined drawing template (with the filename extension .dwt). As mentioned earlier, the template must contain layout tabs, and in each layout tab the viewport's Viewport Properties options must be set to either Plan or Profile. Each viewport must have an appropriate scale assigned. Later in this chapter, you'll learn about editing and modifying templates for use in Plan Production.

FIGURE 15.3
Create View
Frames – Sheets
wizard page

Sheet Settings

The Plan Production feature provides options for creating three types of sheets:

Plan And Profile This option generates a sheet with two viewports; one viewport shows a plan view, and the other shows a profile view of the section of the selected alignment segment.

Plan Only As the name implies, this option creates a sheet with a single viewport showing only the plan view of the selected alignment segment.

Profile Only Similar to Plan Only, this option creates a sheet with a single viewport, showing only the profile view of the selected alignment segment.

INFORMATIONAL GRAPHICS

Did you notice the nifty graphic to the right of the sheet-type options in Figure 15.3? This image changes depending on the type of sheet you've selected. It provides a schematic representation of the sheet layout to further assist you in selecting the appropriate sheet type. You'll see this type of graphic image throughout the Create View Frame Wizard and in other wizards used in Civil 3D.

After choosing the sheet type, you must define the template file and the layout tab within the selected template that Civil 3D will use to generate your sheets. Several predefined templates ship with Civil 3D and are part of the default installation. Be sure to choose the sheet type before selecting the template so that layouts associated with that sheet type will be displayed and selectable. Follow these steps:

1. Click the ellipsis button on this page to display the Select Layout As Sheet Template dialog, shown in Figure 15.4.

FIGURE 15.4
Use the Select Layout As Sheet Template dialog to choose which layout you would like to apply to your newly created sheets.

This dialog provides the option to select the DWT file and the layout tab within the template.

2. Click the ellipsis button in the Select Layout As Sheet Template dialog to browse to the desired template location.

Typically the default template location is:

```
C:\Users\<username>\AppData\Local\Autodesk\C3D 2016\enu\Template\Plan Production\
```

Alternatively, if you are working in a network environment, your templates can be kept in a common folder on the network.

After you select the template you want to use, a list of the layouts that contain the appropriate viewports contained in the DWT file appears in the Select Layout As Sheet Template dialog.

3. Choose the appropriate layout.

Notice that in the template selected (see Figure 15.4) there are layouts for various sheet sizes as well as various scales that are included in the Plan Production templates that ship with Civil 3D.

View Frame Placement

Your view frames can be placed in one of two ways: either along the alignment or rotated to north. Use the bottom area of the Sheets page of the wizard to establish the placement.

Along Alignment   This option aligns the long axes of the view frames parallel to the alignment. Refer to the graphic to the right of the radio buttons in the dialog for a visual representation. This graphic is shown at the left in Figure 15.5.

FIGURE 15.5
View Frame
Placement shown
using the Along
Alignment option
(left) and the
Rotate To North
option (right)

Rotate To North   As the name implies, this option aligns the view frames so they're all rotated to the north direction, regardless of the changing rotation of the alignment centerline. *North* here is synonymous with the True North according to the world coordinate system. This graphic is shown at the right in Figure 15.5.

TWISTED NORTH

If you want the north arrow to rotate according to the view twist of the viewports that are created, the block that is being used for the north arrow must be included in the template and must be located in the layout. You will have a place to select this block within the creation of sheets.

Set The First View Frame Before The Start Of The Alignment By

Regardless of the view frame placement you choose, you have the option to place the first view frame some distance before the start of the alignment. The Set The First View Frame Before The Start Of The Alignment By option is useful if you want to show a portion of the site, such as an existing offsite road, in the plan view. When this option is selected, the text box becomes active, letting you enter the desired distance.

CREATE VIEW FRAMES – VIEW FRAME GROUP PAGE

You use the third page of the Create View Frames Wizard (Figure 15.6) to define creation parameters for your view frames and the view frame group to which they'll belong. The page is divided into two areas: the top for the view frame group and the bottom for the view frames themselves.

FIGURE 15.6
Create View
Frames – View
Frame Group
wizard page

View Frame Group   Use this area of the View Frame Group page to set the name and an optional description for the view frame group. The name can consist of manually entered text, text automatically generated based on the Name template settings, or a combination of both.

NAME TEMPLATE

To adjust the Name template settings, in the Create View Frames – View Frame Group dialog, click the Edit View Frame Group Name button to open the Name Template dialog, shown here.

Continues

Continued

With the settings shown previously in Figure 15.6, the name will include manually defined prefix text (VFG –) followed by automatically generated text, which inserts the view frame group alignment name and a sequential counter number. This will result in a view frame group name of, for example, VFG – Frontenac Drive – 1.

The Name Template dialog box isn't unique to the Plan Production feature. However, the property fields available vary depending on the features to be named. If you need to reset the incremental number counter, use the text box in the lower area of the Name Template dialog box. You can change the increment value in the Name Template dialog box as well.

View Frame   Use this area of the View Frame Group page to set various parameters for the view frames, including the layer for the frames, view frame names, view frame object and label styles, and label location. Each view frame can have a unique name (using an incremental counter), but the other parameters are the same for all view frames. Note that it is a good practice to modify these in the feature and command settings of your template so they are the default values used every time you run the command.

Layer   This option defines the layer on which the view frames are created. This layer is defined in the Drawing Settings dialog, but you can override it by clicking the Layer button and selecting a different layer. Setting the view frame layer to No-Plot will ensure that your drawing does not end up plotting with unwanted rectangles.

Name   The Name setting is nearly identical in function to that of the View Frame Group Name setting discussed earlier. With the settings shown previously in Figure 15.6, the default naming results would be VF – (1), VF – (2), and so on.

Style   Like nearly all objects in Civil 3D, view frames have styles associated with them. The view frame style is simple, with only one component: the view frame border. You use the drop-down list to select a predefined style.

Label Style   Also like most other Civil 3D objects, view frames have label styles associated with them. And like other label styles, the view frame labels are created using the Label Style Composer and can contain a variety of components.

Label Location   The last option on this page lets you set the label location. The default feature setting places the label at the top left of the view frame.

For view frame labels placed at the top of the frame, the term *top* is relative to the frame's orientation. For alignments that run left to right across the page, the top of the frame points toward the top of the screen. For alignments that run right to left, the top of the frame points toward the bottom of the screen.

CREATE VIEW FRAMES – MATCH LINES PAGE

You use the fourth page of the Create View Frames Wizard (Figure 15.7) to establish settings for match lines. Match lines are used to maintain continuity from one sheet to the next. They're typically placed at or near the edge of a sheet, with instructions like "See Sheet XX" for continuation.

FIGURE 15.7
Create View
Frames – Match
Lines: page

Insert Match Lines You have the option to automatically insert match lines. Match lines are used only for plan views, so if you're creating Plan And Profile or Plan Only sheets, the option is automatically selected and can't be deselected.

Positioning Use this area of the Match Lines page to define the initial location of the match lines and provide the ability to later move or reposition the match lines.

> **Snap Station Value Down To The Nearest** By selecting this option, you override the drawing station settings and define a rounding value specific to match line placement. With the settings shown previously in Figure 15.7, a value of 1 is entered, resulting in the match lines being placed at the nearest whole station. For example, if the station was 8+14.83 and the value was 1, it would round down to 8+14, but for the same station, if the value was set to either 50 or 100, it would round down to 8+00.
>
> This feature always rounds down (snap station down as opposed to snap station up). The exception to this is that if the rounding would put the match line at an undesirable location (such as before the previous match line or before the beginning of the alignment), then no rounding would be performed and the calculated station would be used.
>
> **Allow Additional Distance For Repositioning (Increases View Overlap)** Selecting this option activates the text box, allowing you to enter a distance by which the views on adjacent sheets will overlap and the maximum distance that you can move a match line from its original position within the overlap area. While the match line locations are originally created automatically, there are going to be instances when you will want to move the match line if it bisects a critical location. Any value entered will decrease the station range between match lines.

Match Line Use this area of the Match Lines page to provide the settings for the match line. This area is similar to those for view frames on the previous page of the wizard. You can define the layer, the name, and the style.

With the settings shown previously in Figure 15.7, the match lines will be named using a predefined text (ML –) and a next counter: ML – (1), ML – (2), ML – (3), and so on.

Labels   The options in this area of the Match Line page are also similar to those for view frames. Different label styles are used to annotate match lines located at the left and right sides of a frame. This lets you define match-line label styles that reference either the previous or next station adjacent to the current frame. You can also set the location of each label independently using the Left and Right Label Location drop-down lists. You have options for placing the labels at the start, end, or middle of the match line or at the point where the match line intersects the alignment.

With the settings shown previously in Figure 15.7, the label style for use at the left match line is shown in Figure 15.8. This Basic Left label style uses the Match Line Number, Match Line Station value, and Previous Sheet Number.

FIGURE 15.8
An example match
line label style

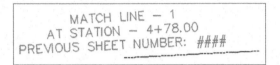

MATCH LINE — 1
AT STATION — 4+78.00
PREVIOUS SHEET NUMBER: ####

CREATE VIEW FRAMES – PROFILE VIEWS PAGE

The final page of the Create View Frames Wizard (Figure 15.9) is optional and will be disabled and skipped if you chose to create Plan Only sheets on the Sheets page of the wizard. Use the drop-down lists to select both the profile view style and the band set style. These styles will be discussed in Chapter 19, "Object Styles."

FIGURE 15.9
Create View
Frames – Profile
Views wizard page

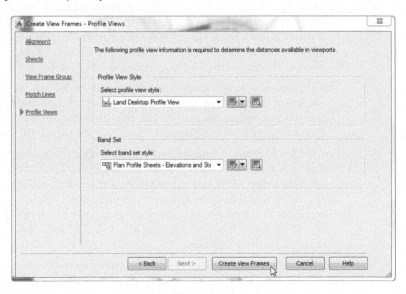

Civil 3D Plan Production tools use the settings in the profile view style and band styles to determine placement of the profile view in the viewport, sometimes disregarding station labels below the profiles. For that reason often it is necessary to force the program to boost the profile view higher in the viewport by adding a "white space" band. This would be an invisible band of a certain height. Even though you can't see the band, Civil 3D provides space for it in the viewport.

This last page of the wizard has no active Next button since this is the last page. Complete the creation of the view frames by clicking the Create View Frames button.

Creating View Frames

Now that you understand the wizard pages and available options, you'll try them in this exercise:

1. Open the `1501_ViewFrameWizard.dwg` (`1501_ViewFrameWizard_METRIC` `.dwg`) file. (Remember, all data can be downloaded from `www.sybex.com/go/` `masteringcivil3d2016`.)

   This drawing contains several alignments and profiles as well as styles for view frames, view frame groups, and match lines.

2. To launch the Create View Frames Wizard, from the Output tab ➤ Plan Production panel, choose Create View Frames.

3. On the Alignment page, do the following:

   a. Select Frontenac Drive from the Alignment drop-down list.

   b. For Station Range, verify that Automatic is selected.

   c. Click Next to advance to the next page.

4. On the Sheets page, do the following:

   a. In the Sheet Settings area, select the Plan And Profile option.

   b. Under Template For Plan And Profile Sheet, click the ellipsis button to display the Select Layout As Sheet Template dialog.

   c. In the Select Layout As Sheet Template dialog, click the ellipsis button and browse to the templates in the chapter folder: `C:\Mastering\Ch15\`.

   d. Select the template named `MasteringPandPTemplate.dwt` (or `MasteringPandPTemplate_Metric.dwt`) and click Open.

   A list of the layouts in the DWT file appears in the Select Layout As Sheet Template dialog.

   e. Select the layout named ARCH D Plan And Profile 20 Scale (or ISO A1 Plan and Profile 1 to 500 for metric users) and click OK to dismiss the Select Layout As Sheet Template dialog.

   f. In the View Frame Placement area, select the Along Alignment option.

   g. Select the Set The First View Frame Before The Start Of The Alignment By option.

   Note that the default value for this particular drawing is 30′ (or 10 m for metric users).

   h. Click Next to advance to the next page.

5. On the View Frame Group page, confirm that all settings are as follows (these are the same settings shown previously in Figure 15.6) and then click Next to advance to the next page:

SETTING	VALUE
View Frame Group Name	VFG – <[View Frame Group Alignment Name(CP)]> – (<[Next Counter(CP)]>)
View Frame Name	VF – (<[Next Counter(CP)]>)
Style	Basic
Label Style	Basic
Label Location	Top Left

6. On the Match Lines page, confirm that all settings are as follows (these are the same settings shown previously in Figure 15.7) and then click Next to advance to the next page:

SETTING	VALUE
Snap Station Value Down To The Nearest	1
Layer	C-ANNO-MTCH
Name	ML – (<[Next Counter(CP)]>)
Style	Basic
Left Label Style	Basic Left
Left Label Location	End
Right Label Style	Basic Right
Right Label Location	Start

7. On the Profile Views page, confirm that the settings are as follows (these are the same settings shown previously in Figure 15.9) and then click Create View Frames:

SETTING	VALUE
Select Profile View Style	Land Desktop Profile View
Select Band Set Style	Plan Profile Sheets – Elevations And Stations

The view frames and match lines are created, as shown in Figure 15.10.

FIGURE 15.10
Finished view
frames and
match lines in the
drawing

Because of the sheet sizes and scales, the Imperial drawing in this example generates four view frames, while the metric drawing generates only two view frames.

THE EFFECTS OF INCREMENTAL COUNTING

The numbering for your view frames, view frame groups, and match lines may not identically match that shown in the images. This is because of the incremental counting Civil 3D performs in the background. As previously mentioned, each time you create one of these objects, the counter increments. You can reset the counter by modifying the Name template.

When this exercise is complete, you can close the drawing. A saved copy of this drawing is available from the book's web page with the filename 1501_ViewFrameWizard_FINISHED.dwg (1501_ViewFrameWizard_METRIC_FINISHED.dwg).

Editing View Frames and Match Lines

After you've created view frames and match lines, you may need to edit them. Edits to some view frame and match line properties can be made via the Prospector tab in the Toolspace palette by expanding the View Frame Groups branch, as shown in Figure 15.11.

FIGURE 15.11
View Frame
Groups in
Prospector

You can change some information in the Preview area of Prospector when you highlight either the View Frames branch or the Match Lines branch. Alternatively, you can make further edits from the View Frame Properties dialog or the Match Line Properties dialog. One way of accessing these dialogs is through the View Frame contextual tab or the Match Line contextual tab. Another method is by right-clicking the desired object in Prospector and selecting Properties. For both view frames and match lines, you can change the object's name or style only via the Information tab in their Properties dialog. All other information displayed on the other tabs is read-only.

You make changes to geometry and location graphically using special grip edits (Figure 15.12). Like many other Civil 3D objects with special editing grips (such as profiles and pipe network objects), view frames and match lines have editing grips you use to modify the objects' location, rotation, and geometry. Let's look at each separately.

FIGURE 15.12
View frame and
match line grips

View frames can be graphically edited in three ways. Once you select a view frame object (the rectangular object selected at the top portion of the image in Figure 15.12), you can move it, slide it along the alignment, and rotate it as follows:

To Move a View Frame   The standard square grip is used for most typical edits, including moving the object.

To Slide a View Frame   The diamond-shaped grip along the alignment at the center of the frame lets you move the view frame in either direction along the alignment while maintaining the orientation (Along Alignment or Rotated North) you originally established for the view frame when it was created.

To Rotate a View Frame   The circular handle grip works like the one on pipe-network structures. Using this grip, you can rotate the frame around its center.

DON'T FORGET YOUR AutoCAD FUNCTIONS!

While you're getting wrapped up in learning all about Civil 3D and its great design tools, it can be easy to forget it's built upon on an incredibly powerful AutoCAD application.

AutoCAD features add functionality beyond what you can do with Civil 3D commands alone. First, make sure the Dynamic Input option is enabled either by clicking the button at the bottom left of your screen as shown here or by pressing F12. By default, the button is not available, but it can be added by clicking the customization button at the right end of the taskbar and checking Dynamic Input from the list.

This gives you additional functionality when you're moving a view frame. With Dynamic Input enabled, you can enter an exact station value to precisely locate the frame where you want it. Similar to moving a view frame, with Dynamic Input active you can enter an exact rotation angle. Note that this rotation angle is relative to your drawing settings (for example, 0 degrees is to the left, 90 degrees is straight up, and so on).

Also, selecting multiple objects and then selecting their grips while holding Shift makes each grip "hot" (usually a red color). This allows you to grip-edit one object and all of the "hot" objects will also experience the same grip edit, like sliding a group of view frames along the alignment.

You can edit a match line's location and length using special grips. As with view frames, you can slide them along the alignment and rotate them. They can also be lengthened or shortened. Unlike view frames, they can't be moved to an arbitrary location. Once you select a match line object (the object selected on the lower side of Figure 15.12), you can edit it as follows:

To Slide a Match Line   The diamond-shaped grip at the center of the match line lets you move the match line in either direction along the alignment while maintaining the orientation (Along Alignment or Rotated North) that you originally established for the view frame.

Note that the match line can be moved in either direction only a distance equal to or less than that entered on the Match Line page of the wizard at the time the view frames were created. For example, if you entered a value of 50′ (15 m) for the Allow Additional Distance For Repositioning option, your view frames are overlapped 50′ (15 m) to each side of the match line, and you can slide the match line only 25′ (15 m) in either direction from its original location. Unless you move the view frame, then those extents will be the new maximum move distance.

To Rotate a Match Line   The circular handle grip enables you to rotate the match line just as you can with the circular handle grip on a view frame.

To Change a Match Line's Length   When you select a match line, a triangular grip is displayed at each end. You can use these grips to increase or decrease the length of each half of the match line. For example, moving the grip on the top end of the match line changes the length of only the top half of the match line; the other half of the match line remains unchanged. See the sidebar "Don't Forget Your AutoCAD Functions!" for tips on using AutoCAD features. If you select a match line, click one of the triangular grips, and then hold Shift and select the other triangular grip, the match line will shorten on one end as you lengthen the other end, and vice versa.

The following exercise lets you put what you've learned into practice as you change the location and rotation of a view frame and change the location and length of a match line:

1. Open the 1502_EditViewFramesAndMatchLines.dwg (1502_ EditViewFramesAndMatchLines_METRIC.dwg) file from this book's web page. This drawing contains view frames and match lines already created.

2. Confirm that Dynamic Input is enabled; if it is not, press F12.

3. Select the view frame, which consists of stations 9+56 to 14+34 (or 0+267 to the end for metric users), and select its diamond-shaped sliding grip.

4. Slide this diamond grip so the overlap with the lower view frame isn't so large. Either graphically slide it to station 11+00 (or 0+360 for metric users) or enter **1100** ↵ (**360** ↵ for metric users) in the Dynamic Input text box.

5. Press Esc to clear your selection.

6. Select the view frame, which consists of stations 14+34 to the end (or 0+267 to the end for metric users), and select the circular rotation grip.

7. Rotate the view frame slightly to better encompass the road. Enter **8** ↵ (**268** ↵ for metric users).

8. Press Esc to clear your selection of the view frame.

   Next, you will adjust the match line's location.

9. Select the match line, which is currently at station 14+34 (or 0+267 for metric users), and then select its diamond sliding grip.

10. Either graphically slide it to station 13+25 (or 0+250 for metric users) or enter **1325** ↵ (**250** ↵ for metric users) in the Dynamic Input text box.

    Notice that the match line label is updated with the revised station.

    Next, you'll adjust the length of the match line to fit within the view frame extents.

11. Select the triangular lengthen grip at the west end of the match line, and either graphically shorten it to 75′ (or 50 m for metric users) or enter **75** ↵ (or **50** ↵ for metric users) in the Dynamic Input text box.

12. Select the triangular lengthen grip at the east end of the same match line, and either graphically shorten it to 75′ (or 50 m for metric users) or enter **75** ↵ (or **50** ↵ for metric users) in the Dynamic Input text box.

13. Press Esc to clear your selection.

When this exercise is complete, you can close the drawing. A saved copy of this drawing is available from the book's web page with the filename 1502_EditViewFramesAndMatchLines_FINISHED.dwg (1502_EditViewFramesAndMatchLines_METRIC_FINISHED.dwg).

Now that you have generated the view frames and match lines in the drawing and you have placed them where you want them, let's look at using these objects to generate sheets.

Creating Plan and Profile Sheets

The Plan Production feature uses the concept of *sheets* to generate the pages that make up a set of plans. Simply put, *sheets* are layout tabs with viewports showing a given portion of your design model, based on the view frames previously created. The viewports have special viewport properties set that define them as either plan or profile viewports. These viewports must be predefined in a drawing template (DWT) file to be used with the Plan Production feature. You manage the sheets using the standard AutoCAD Sheet Set Manager feature.

The Create Sheets Wizard

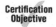

Certification Objective

After you've created view frames and match lines, you can proceed to the next step of creating sheets. Like view frames, sheets are created using a wizard. Let's look at the Create Sheets Wizard and the various page options. After you've seen each page, you'll have a chance to put what you've learned into practice in an example.

From the Output tab ➤ Plan Production panel, you launch the Create Sheets Wizard by choosing Create Sheets. As with the Create View Frames Wizard, a list of the Create Sheets Wizard's pages is shown along the left sidebar, and an arrow indicates which page you're currently viewing. You move among the pages using the Next and Back navigation buttons along the bottom of each page. Alternatively, you can jump directly to any page by clicking its name in the list on the left. The following sections walk you through the pages of the wizard and explain their features.

CREATE SHEETS – VIEW FRAME GROUP AND LAYOUTS PAGE

You will use the first page of the Create Sheets Wizard (Figure 15.13) to select the view frame group for which the sheets will be created. It's also used to define how the layouts for these sheets will be generated and which sheets will be created (all or a range).

FIGURE 15.13
Create Sheets –
View Frame Group
And Layouts wiz-
ard page

View Frame Group In the top area of this page, you select the view frame group. You can either select it from the drop-down list or click the Select From The Drawing button to select the view frame group onscreen. After you've selected the group, you use the View Frame Range option to create sheets for all frames in the group or only for specific frames of your choosing.

All Select this option when you want sheets to be created for all view frames in the view frame group.

Selection Select this option to activate the Choose View Frames button. Click this button to display the Select View Frames dialog, where you can select specific view frames from a list. You can select a range of view frames by using the standard Windows selection technique of clicking the first view frame in the range and then holding Shift while you select the last view frame in the range. You can also select individual view frames in nonsequential order by holding Ctrl while you make your view frame selections. Figure 15.14 shows two of the four view frames selected in the Select View Frames dialog.

FIGURE 15.14
Select view frames
by using standard
Windows selection
techniques.

Layout Creation   In this area, you define where and how the new layouts for each sheet are created as well as the name format for these sheets and information about the alignment of the north arrow block.

There are three options for creating layout sheets: The layouts are created in multiple new drawing files (with a limit to the maximum number of layout sheets created in each file), all the new layouts are created in a new drawing file, or all the layout tabs are created in the current drawing (the drawing you're in while executing the Create Sheets Wizard).

Number Of Layouts Per New Drawing   This option creates layouts in new drawing files and limits the maximum number of layouts per drawing file to the value you enter in the text box. For best performance, Autodesk recommends that a drawing file contain no more than 10 layouts. On the last page of this wizard you're given the option to select the objects for which data references will be made. These data references are then created in the new drawings.

All Layouts In One New Drawing   As the name implies, this option creates all layouts for each view frame in a single new drawing. Use this option if you have fewer than 10 view frames, to ensure best performance. If you have more than 10 view frames, the previous option is recommended. On the last page of this wizard you're given the option to select the objects for which data references will be made. These data references are then created in the new drawing.

All Layouts In The Current Drawing   When you choose this option, all layouts are created in the current drawing. You need to be aware of two scenarios when working with this option. (As explained later in Chapter 16, "Advanced Workflows," you can share a view frame group via data shortcuts and link it to other drawings as a data reference.)

◆ When creating sheets, it's possible that your drawing references the view frame group from another drawing (rather than having the original view frame group in your current drawing). In this case, you're given the option to select the additional objects for which data references will be made (such as alignments, profiles, pipes, and so on). These data references are then created in the current drawing. You select these objects on the last page of the wizard.

◆ If you're working in a drawing where the view frames were created (therefore, you're in the drawing in which the view frame group exists), the last page of this wizard is disabled. This is because in order for you to create view frames (and view frame groups), the alignment (and possibly the profile) must either exist in the current drawing or be referenced as a data reference (recall the prerequisites for creating view frames, mentioned earlier).

Layout Name   Use this text box to enter a name for each new layout. As with other named objects in Civil 3D, you can use the Name template to create a name format that includes information about the object being named. With the settings shown previously in Figure 15.13, the layouts will be named using a predefined text (Sheet –) and the next counter: Sheet – (1), Sheet – (2), Sheet – (3), and so on. Using the Name template, you could alternatively use the Parent Drawing Name, View Frame Start/End Raw Station, View Frame Start/End Station Value, View Frame Group Alignment Name, and View Frame Group Name options.

Real World Scenario

WHERE AM I?

We strongly recommend that you set up the Name template for the layouts so that it includes the View Frame Group Alignment Name option and the station range (View Frame Start Station Value and View Frame End Station Value). This conforms to the way many organizations create sheets, helps automate the creation of a sheet index, and generally makes it easier to navigate a DWG file with several layout tabs.

This would result in a name that is listed as follows:

```
<[View Frame Group Alignment Name]> <[View Frame Start Station Value]>
to <[View Frame End Station Value]>
```

This will generate a layout named similar to Frontenac Drive 0 + 00.00 to 4 + 78.00.

Choose The North Arrow Block To Align In Layouts   If the template file you've selected contains a north arrow block, it can be aligned so that it points north on each layout sheet. The block must exist in the template and be located in the layout. If there are multiple blocks, select the one you want to use from the drop-down list.

CREATE SHEETS – SHEET SET PAGE

You use the second page of the Create Sheets Wizard (Figure 15.15) to determine whether a new or existing sheet set (with the filename extension .dst) is used and the location of the DST file. The sheet file storage location and sheet file name are also defined here. Additionally, on this page you decide whether to add the sheet set file (with the filename extension .dst) and the sheet files (with the filename extension .dwg) to the Autodesk® Vault project if this platform is used for data management.

FIGURE 15.15
Create Sheets –
Sheet Set wizard
page

Sheet Set   In the Sheet Set area of the page, you select whether to create a new DST file or add the sheets created by this wizard to an existing DST file.

New Sheet Set   Selecting this option allows you to generate a new sheet set. In the text box, you can enter a name for the sheet set or accept the name that is generated for you.

Add To Existing Sheet Set   Selecting this option enables you to add to a sheet set that has already been generated. Click the ellipsis button to browse to the location of the DST file. If you are working in a Vault project, you can click the Vault button to browse to the file in the vault project. If Autodesk Vault is not installed, the Vault button will be inactive.

Sheet Set Storage Location   This text box is active only if you have selected New Sheet Set. When it's active, you can type the path to the folder where the DST file will be created or you can use the ellipsis to browse to the storage location. If you are working in a vault project, you can click the Vault button to browse to the storage location in the vault project. If Autodesk Vault is not installed, the Vault button will be inactive.

Sheets   This area is active only if you are creating layouts in new drawings. If you choose to create layouts in the current drawing, the area will be inactive.

Sheet Files Storage Location   Type the path to the folder where the sheet files will be created, or you can use the ellipsis to browse to the storage location. If you are working in a vault project, you can click the Vault button to browse to the storage location in the vault project. If Autodesk Vault is not installed, the Vault button will be inactive.

Sheet File Name   As with many of the previous names, you can use a Name template to specify how the name for the sheet file is generated. With the settings shown previously in Figure 15.15, the sheet files will be named using the View Frame Group Name entry and the next counter in parentheses. Using the Name template, you could alternatively use the Parent Drawing Name, View Frame Start/End Raw Station, View Frame Start/End Station Value, and View Frame Group Alignment Name options.

WHAT IS A SHEET?

The Create Sheets – Sheet Set page can be a little confusing because of the way the word *sheets* is used. In some places, *sheets* refers to layout tabs in a given drawing (DWG) file. On this page, the word *sheet* is being paired with the word *file(s)* and refers to DWG files that contain a collection of *sheet* layouts.

CREATE SHEETS – PROFILE VIEWS PAGE

The third page of the Create Sheets Wizard (Figure 15.16) lists the profile view style and the band set selected in the Create View Frames Wizard. You can't change these selections. You can, however, make adjustments to other profile settings.

FIGURE 15.16
Create Sheets –
Profile Views page

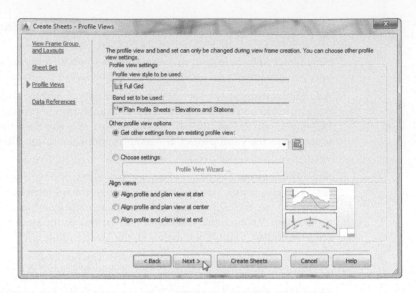

Other Profile View Options   The Other Profile View Options area lets you modify certain profile view options either by using an existing profile view in your drawing as an example or by running the Profile View Wizard. Regardless of what option you choose, the "other options" you can change are limited to the following in the Profile View Wizard:

- Profile View Datum By Minimum Elevation or Mean Elevation on the Profile View Height page

- Split Profile View options from the Profile View Height page

- All options on the Profile Display Options page

- If available, all options on the Pipe/Pressure Network Display page

- Most of the settings on the Data Bands page

- All options on the Profile Hatch Options page

- All settings on the Multiple Plot Options page

See Chapter 7, "Profiles and Profile Views," for details on each of these settings. The inactive settings are ones that were previously set when you were going through the settings of the Create View Frames Wizard. If you need to change these settings, you will have to delete your current view frame group and regenerate the view frames with the desired settings.

Align Views   In the Align Views area of the page, you can choose Align Profile And Plan View At Start, Align Profile And Plan View At Center, or Align Profile And Plan View At End.

CREATE SHEETS – DATA REFERENCES PAGE

The final page of the Create Sheets Wizard (Figure 15.17) is used to create data references in the drawing files that contain your layout sheets.

FIGURE 15.17
Create Sheets –
Data References
wizard page

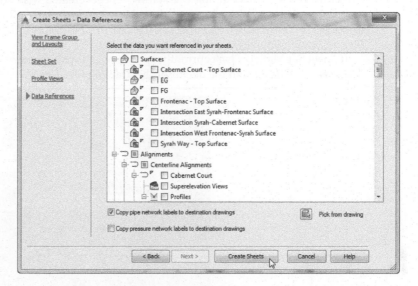

Select The Data You Want Referenced In Your Sheets   This area contains a list of objects in the current drawing that can be data referenced into the sheet files. Depending on the way sheet settings were configured in the Create View Frames Wizard (Plan And Profile, Plan Only, or Profile Only), certain objects will be selected for you. If there are other data references you want referenced into the drawing, you may use the check boxes here to select them.

Pick From Drawing   Use the Pick From Drawing button to select those objects you want to data reference from the drawing area.

Copy Pipe Network Labels To Destination Drawings   It's common to create references to pipe networks that are to be shown in plan and/or profile views. If you choose to create references for pipe network objects, you can also copy the labels for those network objects into the sheet file. This saves you from having to relabel your pipe networks.

Copy Pressure Network Labels To Destination Drawings   When this check box is selected, pressure network labels will be copied to the sheet file.

Managing Sheets

After you've completed all pages of the Create Sheets Wizard, you create the sheets by clicking the Create Sheets button. Doing so completes the wizard and starts the creation process. You can also click the Create Sheets button on any pages in this wizard. If you're creating sheets with profile views, you're prompted to select a profile view origin. Civil 3D then displays several dialogs, indicating the process status for the various tasks, such as creating the new sheet drawings and creating the DST file. Once that's complete, the Panorama Event Viewer vista will list two new events, in this example one stating "Sheets created were added to the sheet set file `C:\Mastering\Ch15\FinishedSheets\VFG - Frontenac Drive - (1).dst`" and one stating "4 layout(s) created in path `C:\Mastering\Ch15\FinishedSheets`." For the case of the metric data files, the statement will refer only to two layouts.

If Sheet Set Manager isn't currently open, it opens with the newly created DST file loaded. The sheets are listed, and the details of the drawing files for each sheet appear (Figure 15.18).

FIGURE 15.18
New sheets in
Sheet Set Manager

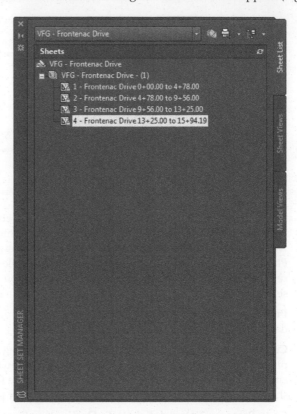

If you double-click to open the new drawing file that contains the newly created sheets, you'll see layout sheet tabs created for each of the view frames as selected in the Create Sheets Wizard. The sheets are named using the Name template as defined in the Create Sheets Wizard. Figure 15.19 shows the names that result from the following template:

```
<[View Frame Group Alignment Name]> <[View Frame Start Station Value]>
to <[View Frame End Station Value]>
```

FIGURE 15.19
The template produces the Frontenac Drive tab names shown here assigned to each sheet

To create the final sheets in this new drawing, Civil 3D creates external references (XRefs) to the drawing containing the view frames; creates direct data references (DRefs) for the alignments, profiles, and any additional objects you selected in the Create Sheets Wizard; and, if profile sheet types were selected in the Create View Frames Wizard, creates profile views in the final sheet drawing.

The following exercise pulls all these concepts together:

1. Open the 1503_SheetsWizard.dwg (1503_SheetsWizard_METRIC.dwg) file.

   This drawing contains the view frame group, alignment, and profile for Frontenac Drive. Note that the drawing doesn't have profile views.

2. To launch the Create Sheets Wizard, from the Output tab ➤ Plan Production panel, choose Create Sheets.

   For some users, the Panorama might appear, stating that the template was not found in the original location. Dismiss the notification.

3. On the View Frame Group And Layouts page, do the following:

   a. Verify that View Frame Range is set to All.

   b. Verify that Number Of Layouts Per New Drawing is set to 10.

      Since this view frame group has fewer than 10 view frames, only one drawing will be generated, but it is good practice to set this value to 10 nonetheless.

   c. Set Layout Name to **<[View Frame Group Alignment Name]> <[View Frame Start Station Value]> to <[View Frame End Station Value]>**.

   d. From the Choose The North Arrow Block To Align In Layouts drop-down list, select North.

   e. Click Next to advance to the next page.

USE A NAME TEMPLATE

To set the layout name in step 3 or any of the other steps that require the use of the Name template, don't type all that text into the text box. Instead, follow these simple steps:

1. Click the Edit Layout Name button to the right of the Layout Name text box to display the Name Template dialog.

2. Delete all the text in the Name text box that you do not want.

3. Using the Property Fields drop-down list, select the first piece of text that you want. In this example, it will be View Frame Group Alignment Name.

4. Click Insert.

5. Repeat steps 3 and 4 for each of the property fields you want to use. If using start or end stations, use Start Station Value or End Station Value properties instead of their raw station counterparts. Also don't forget to fill in the right words between the property fields.

6. Once complete, click OK to dismiss the Name Template dialog.

The Layout Name option is now filled in based on the Name template.

4. On the Sheet Set page, do the following:

   a. Select the New Sheet Set option and set Name to **VFG - Frontenac Drive** (or **VFG - Frontenac Drive_METRIC** for metric users).

   b. For the Sheet Set File Storage Location option, use the ellipsis to browse to `C:\Mastering\Ch15\FinishedSheets`, and click Open to dismiss the Browse For Sheet Set Folder dialog.

      Notice that by changing this location, the Sheet Files Storage Location entry automatically changes to match.

   c. Verify that Sheet File Name is set to the following for metric users:

      ```
      <[View Frame Group Name]> - (<[Next Counter]>)
      for Imperial users or
      <[View Frame Group Name]> - (<[Next Counter]>)_METRIC
      ```

   d. Click Next to advance to the next page.

5. On the Profile Views page, do the following:

   a. For Other Profile View Options, select Choose Settings and then click the Profile View Wizard button.

      The Create Multiple Profile Views dialog opens.

   b. On the left side of the Create Multiple Profile Views dialog, click Profile Display Options to jump to that page.

    c. On the Create Multiple Profile Views – Profile Display Options page, verify that the Draw option is selected for only the EG – Frontenac Drive profile and the Frontenac Drive FG profile.

    d. Scroll to the right and verify that the Labels setting for the EG – Frontenac Drive profile is set to No Labels and that the Frontenac Drive FG Profile is set to Complete Label Set.

    e. On the left side of the Create Multiple Profile Views dialog, click Data Bands to jump to that page.

    f. On the Create Multiple Profile Views – Data Bands page, change Profile2 to Frontenac Drive FG for both bands.

    g. Click Finish to dismiss the Create Multiple Profile Views Wizard and return to the Create Sheets Wizard.

    h. Verify that Align Views is set to Align Profile And Plan View At Start.

    i. Click Next to advance to the next page.

6. On the Data References page, confirm that at minimum the Frontenac Drive alignment and both the EG – Frontenac Drive and Frontenac Drive FG profiles are selected; then click Create Sheets to complete the wizard.

    Before creating the sheets, Civil 3D must save your current drawing.

7. Click OK when prompted to save.

    The drawing is saved, and you're prompted for an insertion point for the profile view. The location you pick represents the lower-left corner of the profile view grid.

8. Select an open area in the drawing, above the right side of the site plan.

    Civil 3D displays a progress dialog box, and then the Panorama palette is displayed with information about the results of the sheet-creation process.

9. Close the Panorama palette.

INVISIBLE PROFILE VIEWS

Note that the profile views are created in the current drawing only if you selected the option to create all layouts in the current drawing. Because you didn't do that in this exercise, the profile views aren't created in the current drawing. Rather, they're created in the sheet files in modelspace in a location relative to the point you selected in this step.

After the sheet-creation process is complete, the Sheet Set Manager window opens.

10. Click the first sheet of the sheet set shown in Figure 15.20, named Frontenac Drive 0+00.00 to 4+78.00 (or Frontenac Drive 0+000.00 to 0+250.00 for metric users).

FIGURE 15.20
Sheet Set Manager
once the sheet-
creation process is
complete

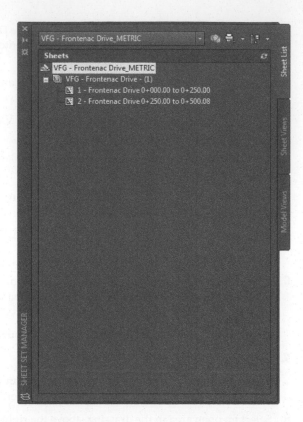

Notice that the name conforms to the Name template and includes the alignment name and the station range for the sheet.

11. Review the details listed for the sheet by hovering over the sheet on the Sheet List tab of Sheet Set Manager or by right-clicking in the white space of the dialog and selecting Preview/Details Pane. In particular, note the filename and storage location.

12. Double-click this sheet to open the new sheets drawing and display the layout tab for Frontenac Drive 0+00.00 to 4+78.00 (or Frontenac Drive 0+000.00 to 0+250.00 for metric users). Dismiss the Panorama of any warnings.

13. Review the multiple tabs created in this drawing file as previously shown in Figure 15.19. If layout tabs are not displayed, then you may turn them on in the Options dialog by going to the Display tab ➤ Layout Elements area, filling the Display Layout And Model Tabs check box, and then clicking OK.

The template used also takes advantage of AutoCAD fields, some of which don't currently have values assigned.

When this exercise is complete, you can close the drawing. A saved copy of this drawing is available from the book's web page with the filename `1503_SheetsWizard_FINISHED.dwg` (`1503_SheetsWizard_METRIC_FINISHED.dwg`). You can find the finished folder under the `FinishedSheetsAuthor` folder for reference.

Now that you have the plan and profile sheets generated, let's look at generating some section sheets using the Plan Production feature.

Creating Section Sheets

Creating section sheets is a two-step process; it's just like creating plan and profile sheets but with one difference: There are no view frames to tweak. Instead, you will have section sheets, which are objects. Section sheets have group plot styles assigned to them that control the arrangement of section arrays per sheet. These section sheets are created when you run the Create Multiple Section Views command using the Production option. If you have already created multiple section views using the Draft option, you will have to re-create your section views using the Production option. This is a prerequisite for running the Create Section Sheets command. Here is the two-step process:

1. Generate multiple section views with the Placement option set to Production. You will have the opportunity to select styles to use for section view, section, and group plot styles as you work through the wizard. All section views created with this command become part of a section view group that can be managed from Prospector.

2. Generate section sheets, which will create your layouts and your sheet set. Section sheet layouts are created in the same drawing as your production section views; there is no option to create them in new drawings.

Creating Multiple Section Views

Before creating multiple section views for the purpose of sheet creation, be sure you have section, section view, and group plot styles in place. If you have any questions about these styles, refer to Chapter 19.

In this exercise, you'll walk through creating multiple section views for the main road of the sample set:

1. Open the `1504_MultipleSectionViews.dwg` (`1504_MultipleSectionViews_METRIC.dwg`) file from the provided dataset.

   In this drawing, sample lines have been added along the Frontenac Drive alignment. These lines are sampling the existing and proposed surfaces.

2. From the Home tab ➤ Profile & Section Views panel, choose Section Views ➤ Create Multiple Views to display the Create Multiple Section Views Wizard, shown in Figure 15.21.

FIGURE 15.21
Create Multiple
Section Views –
General wizard
page

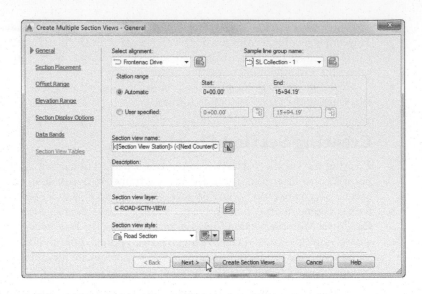

3. On the General page, do the following:

   a. Verify that Section View Style is set to Road Section.

   b. Click Next to advance to the next page.

   The Section Placement page (Figure 15.22) is where you configure your placement options. If you select Production, you must use the ellipsis to browse to the DWT file containing your section layouts and choose the layout desired based on sheet border and viewport scale. If you select Draft, section views will be laid out in a single grid format.

FIGURE 15.22
Create Multiple
Section Views –
Section Placement
page and Select
Layout As Sheet
Template dialog

4. On the Section Placement page, do the following:

   a. In the Placement Options area, verify that Production is selected.

   b. For Template For Cross Section Sheet, use the ellipsis to browse to `C:\Mastering\CH15` and select `MasteringSectionTemplate.dwt` (or `MasteringSectionTemplate_METRIC.dwt` for metric users). Click Open, and under Select A Layout To Create New Sheets, choose ARCH D Section 50 Scale (or ISO A1 Section 1 to 500 for metric users). Click OK.

   c. Verify that Group Plot Style is set to Basic.

   d. Click Next to advance to the next page.

The Offset Range page (Figure 15.23) determines the width of the section views.

FIGURE 15.23
Create Multiple Section Views – Offset Range page

5. On the Offset Range page, do the following:

   a. Using the User Specified option, set the left offset range to **-50'** (or **-20** m for metric users).

   b. Set the right offset range to **50'** (or **20** m for metric users).

   c. Click Next to advance to the next page.

The Elevation Range page (Figure 15.24) determines the height of the section views. The options on the Elevation Range page help if you have extra-tall sections, allowing you to set some limits manually.

FIGURE 15.24
Create Multiple
Section Views –
Elevation Range
page

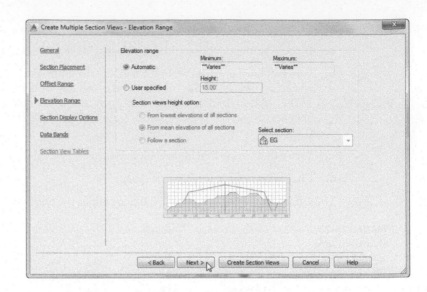

6. On the Elevation Range page, click Next to advance to the next page.

7. On the Section Display Options page, do the following:

   a. Verify that the Label Set column for all the items is set to _No Labels. Leave all the other settings as default.

   b. Verify that in the Style column the style for EG is set to Existing Ground, the style for FG is set to Finished Ground, and each of the corridor surface styles is set to Basic, as shown in Figure 15.25.

FIGURE 15.25
Changing styles
in the Create
Multiple Section
Views – Section
Display Options
wizard page

    c. Click Next to advance to the next page.

  8. On the Data Bands page, do the following:

    a. Verify that the Select Band Set drop-down list is set to Offsets Only.

    b. Under Set Band Properties, verify that Surface1 is set to EG and Surface2 is set to FG, as shown in Figure 15.26.

FIGURE 15.26
Create Multiple
Section Views –
Data Bands wizard
page

    c. Click Create Section Views to dismiss the wizard and place your section views in the drawing.

  9. Click a point to the east of the plan view to draw the section views and sheet outlines.

Your drawing should look something like Figure 15.27.

FIGURE 15.27
The finished mul-
tiple section views
operation

When this exercise is complete, you can close the drawing. A saved copy of this drawing is available from the book's web page with the filename `1504_MultipleSectionViews_FINISHED.dwg` (`1504_MultipleSectionViews_METRIC_FINISHED.dwg`).

Now that you have your production section views, you can begin the process of creating section sheets for plotting.

Creating Section Sheets

Many long transportation projects such as highways, light-rail, or canals require the production of many section sheets. In this exercise, you'll convert a section view group into a collection of sheets and place them in a new sheet set.

1. Open the 1505_CreatingSectionSheets.dwg (1505_CreatingSectionSheets_METRIC .dwg) file.

   This file contains the section view group for the Frontenac Drive alignment.

2. From the Output tab ➢ Plan Production panel, choose Create Section Sheets to display the Create Section Sheets dialog.

3. In the Create Section Sheets dialog, do the following:

   a. Verify that New Sheet Set name is set to FrontenacSections (FrontenacSections_METRIC).

   b. Click the ellipsis to set Sheet Set Storage Location to C:\Mastering\Ch15\ FinishedSheets.

   The Create Section Sheets dialog should now look similar to Figure 15.28.

FIGURE 15.28
The Create Section
Sheets dialog

Note that when you are creating section sheets in a drawing where there is more than one section view group, you will have to repeat this command for each section view group.

4. Click Create Sheets to dismiss the dialog and generate sheets.

   Before creating the sheets, Civil 3D must save your current drawing.

5. Click OK when prompted to save.

The drawing is saved, and Civil 3D will generate new layouts in the drawing and sheets in a sheet set. Sheet Set Manager will appear.

6. Switch to the Section Sheet – (2) layout tab.

Your layout should look something like Figure 15.29.

FIGURE 15.29
A completed section sheet

7. Close the Sheet Set Manager palette.

When this exercise is complete, you can close the drawing. A saved copy of this drawing is available from the book's web page with the filename 1505_CreatingSectionSheets_FINISHED.dwg (1505_CreatingSectionSheets_METRIC_FINISHED.dwg). For this exercise you can find the finished version of the sheet set file of the author under the FinishedSheetsAuthor folder.

While there are still some tweaks to be made to any sheet, large portions of the mundane details are handled by the wizards and tools. There are some elements that you can modify to customize these details for your organization, and you'll look at those in the next section.

Drawing Templates

The beginning of this chapter mentioned that there are several prerequisites to using the Plan Production tools in Civil 3D. The list includes drawing templates (DWT) set up to work with the Plan Production feature and styles for the objects generated by this feature. In this section of the chapter, you'll learn how to prepare drawing templates for use in creating your finished sheets.

Civil 3D ships with several predefined template files for various types of sheets that Plan Production can create. By default, these templates are installed in a subfolder called Plan Production, which is located in the standard Template folder. You can see the Template folder location by opening the Files tab of the Options dialog, as shown in Figure 15.30.

FIGURE 15.30
Template files
location

Figure 15.31 shows the default contents of the Plan Production subfolder. Notice the templates for Plan, Profile, and Plan And Profile sheet types. There are Imperial and metric versions of each.

FIGURE 15.31
Plan Production
DWT files

As previously discussed, each template contains layout tabs with pages set to various sheet sizes and plan scales. For example, the Civil 3D (Imperial) Plan and Profile.dwt template has layouts created at various ANSI and ARCH sheet sizes and scales, as shown in Figure 15.32.

FIGURE 15.32
Various predefined layouts in standard DWT

If you decide to make your own Plan Production templates, it is good practice to provide multiple drawing sizes and scales so that you have them available when you go to make your sheets. But beyond just having them available, make sure that the layout names that you provide in your Plan Production template are descriptive enough that you know which one to select. You may also insert a border on each layout tab or opt to externally reference the border later, after sheets are created.

The viewports in these templates must be rectangular in shape and must have Viewport Type set to Plan, Profile, or Section, depending on the intended use. You set Viewport Type on the Design tab of the Properties dialog, as shown in Figure 15.33.

FIGURE 15.33
Viewport Properties – Viewport Type

> **IRREGULAR VIEWPORT SHAPES**
>
> Just because the viewports must start out rectangular doesn't mean they have to stay that way. Experiment with creating viewports from rectangular polylines that have vertices at the midpoint of each side of the viewport (not just at the corners). After you've created your sheets using the Plan Production tool, you can stretch your viewport into irregular shapes. You can also convert a rectangular viewport into an irregular viewport by selecting the viewport, right-clicking, selecting Viewport Clip, and following the prompts (you could also type **vpclip** at the command prompt and follow the prompts).

The Bottom Line

Create view frames.   When you create view frames, you must select the template file that contains the layout tabs that will be used as the basis for your sheets. This template must contain predefined viewports. You can define these viewports with extra vertices so you can change their shape after the sheets have been created.

Master It   Open the MasterIt_1501.dwg (MasterIt_1501_METRIC.dwg) file. Run the Create View Frames Wizard to create view frames for Alignment A in the current drawing. (Accept the defaults for all other values.) These view frames will be used to generate Plan and Profile sheets on ARCH D (ISO A1 for metric users) sheets at 20 scale (1:200 scale for metric users) using the plan and profile template MasteringPandPTemplate.dwt or MasteringPandPTemplate_METRIC.dwt. All files should be saved in C:\Mastering\Ch15\.

Edit view frames.   The grips available to edit view frames allow the user some freedom on how the frames will appear.

Master It   Continue working in the previous exercise file or open the MasterIt_1501_FINISHED.dwg (MasterIt_1501_METRIC_FINISHED.dwg) file, and move the VF– (1) view frame to Sta. 2+20 (or Sta. 0+050 for metric users) to lessen the overlap. Then adjust Match Line 1 (or Match Line 2 for metric users) so that it is now at Sta. 4+25 (or Sta. 0+200 for metric users) and shorten it so that the labels are completely within the view frames.

Generate sheets and review Sheet Set Manager.   You can create sheets in new drawing files or in the current drawing. The resulting sheets are based on the template you chose when you created the view frames. If the template contains customized viewports, you can modify the shape of the viewport to better fit your sheet needs.

Master It   Open the MasterIt_1503.dwg (MasterIt_1503_METRIC.dwg) file. Run the Create Sheets Wizard to create plan and profile sheets in the current drawing for Alignment A using the plan and profile template MasteringPandPTemplate.dwt or MasteringPandPTemplate_METRIC.dwt. Make sure to choose a north arrow and add the sheets to a new sheet set named Alignment A (Alignment A_METRIC for metric users). (Accept the defaults for all other values.)

Create section views. More and more municipalities are requiring section views. Whether this is a mile-long road or a meandering stream, Civil 3D can handle it nicely via Plan Production.

Master It Open the `MasterIt_1504.dwg` (`MasterIt_1504_METRIC.dwg`) file. Create section views and Plan Production section sheets in a new sheet set for Alignment A using the Road Section section view style and the section sheet template `MasteringSectionTemplate.dwt` or `MasteringSectionTemplate_METRIC.dwt`. Make sure the sections are set to be generated on ARCH D (ISO A1 for metric users) sheets at 20-scale (1:200 scale for metric users). Also, make sure to provide as Sheet Set name Alignment A_XC (Alignment A_XC_METRIC for metric users). (Accept the defaults for all other values.) All files should be saved in `C:\Mastering\Ch15\FinishedSheets`.

Chapter 16

Advanced Workflows

The Autodesk® AutoCAD® Civil 3D® program is unique in that, with a few exceptions, the data you create is stored in the DWG file. Using data shortcuts will allow you to divide the work among your co-workers and keep your drawing size down. Using data shortcuts will also enable you to keep your existing surface in your topographic survey file and reference it into your design files.

In this chapter you will also look at LandXML as a tool to share data. Using this file format, you can transfer "intelligent" data without a DWG file.

In this chapter, you will learn to:

◆ Create a data shortcut folder.

◆ Create data shortcuts.

◆ Export to earlier releases of AutoCAD.

◆ Export to LandXML.

Data Shortcuts

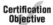
Certification Objective

A *data shortcut* is a link between drawings that allows specific types of Civil 3D data to be shared. The shortcut itself does not contain data, but it is a pointer, directing Civil 3D to read information from a common pool of data. A *data shortcut* is created in the source drawing, and a *data reference* is the manifestation of the data in a recipient drawing.

There are many situations in which you need data or information to link between drawings. Connections between drawings can be in the form of external references (XRefs), data references, or a combination of the two. These two options are similar but not the same. Table 16.1 compares them.

TABLE 16.1:   XRef vs. data reference

EXTERNAL REFERENCE (XREF)	DATA REFERENCE
For most objects, an XRef is a graphic-only representation of objects created in another drawing.	A data reference is an information/graphic-only link to Civil 3D data created in another DWG file.
Any objects (base AutoCAD or Civil 3D) can be displayed in XRefs.	Only specific types of Civil 3D data can be used as data references.
Visibility of objects is controlled by original drawing styles and layers.	Visibility of data is controlled by host drawing styles and layers.
With the exception of Catchment and Intersection objects, you can use the Civil 3D Add Labels commands on items in an XRef. All other objects (e.g., Surfaces, Alignments, Pipes, Profile Views, etc.) can be labeled through an XRef.	To use Civil 3D object data in design (i.e., using a surface to create an existing ground profile or using an alignment as a corridor baseline), the object must be data referenced.
A drawing containing a Civil 3D corridor can be XRef'ed into a host drawing. Sample lines can pull corridor data from the XRef.	A data reference to an alignment in conjunction with an XRef to the corridor enables sample lines to be created in a separate drawing.

A feature introduced in Civil 3D 2014 brought another important exception to the general rule that external references are "graphics only." Users now have the ability to use figures, lines, polylines, and feature lines as corridor targets through an external reference.

As noted, only Civil 3D objects can be used with data shortcuts. Not all object types are available through shortcuts. The following objects are available for use through data shortcuts:

◆ Alignments

◆ Surfaces

◆ Profiles

◆ Pipe networks

◆ Pressure networks

◆ View frame groups

A NOTE ABOUT THE EXERCISES IN THIS CHAPTER

This chapter is about workflow; therefore, it is difficult to jump in partway through the chapter. To get the most out of the exercises, you should work from the beginning to end because all of the exercises build on the previous ones. If you skip any exercises (including "Creating Cross-Section Sheets in Their Own Drawing"), the subsequent steps will not work.

Use the recommended names for objects and drawings you create on your own. Doing so will make things go much smoother for you.

Remember that you can always get the original files from the chapter folder that you can download from www.sybex.com/go/masteringcivil3d2016.

Getting Started

When you first create a data shortcut project, you have the option of using a *project template*. A project template is simply a set of folders, subfolders, and files created to help you keep your file store organized.

In the following exercise, you will create folders for use when creating a data shortcut project:

1. Open Windows Explorer and navigate to C:\Civil 3D Project Templates.

2. Create a new folder titled **MasteringCivil3D**.

3. Inside MasteringCivil3D, create subfolders called **Design**, **Documents**, **Sheets**, and **Survey**, as shown in Figure 16.1.

FIGURE 16.1
Folder structure and standard project files should be included in the project template.

4. Locate the file 1601_Project Checklist.doc from this chapter's files that you downloaded from www.sybex.com/go/masteringcivil3d2016.

5. Place the file in the Documents folder you created in step 3.

6. Locate the file 1601_SheetSetTemplate.dst from within this chapter's files.

7. Place the file in the Sheets folder you created in step 3.

This directory structure will appear when a data shortcut project is created. A Documents folder is included as an example of other folders not related to Civil 3D that you might need in your project. The 1601_Project Checklist.docx and 1601_SheetSetTemplate.dst files will be copied automatically to each project you create from this template.

A completed version of this set of folders is in the dataset for your reference and is called 1601_MasteringC3D_FINISHED.

Setting a Working Folder and Data Shortcut Folder

You can think of the working folder as a project drive. The working folder can contain a number of projects, each with a data shortcut folder where the shortcut files reside.

In this exercise, you'll set the working folder and create a new project:

1. Create a new blank drawing using the template of your choice.

   You won't save this file, but you do need to have a file open to see the Prospector tab of Toolspace. You need to complete the previous exercise before beginning this one.

2. From the Manage tab ➤ Data Shortcuts panel, click Set Working Folder to display the Browse For Folder dialog, as shown in Figure 16.2.

FIGURE 16.2
Creating a new
working folder.

3. In the Browse For Folder dialog, on Local Disk (C:), browse to the Mastering folder you created for your course files.

4. With the Mastering folder highlighted (as shown in Figure 16.2), click OK.

5. From the Manage tab ➤ Data Shortcuts panel, click New Shortcuts Folder to display the New Data Shortcut Folder dialog, shown in Figure 16.3.

FIGURE 16.3
Creating a new
shortcut folder.

6. In the New Data Shortcut Folder dialog, type _**North River Crossing** for the Name field and click the Use Project Template check box.

7. Select the MasteringCivil3D2016 folder from the list, as shown in Figure 16.3, and click OK to dismiss the dialog.

Notice that the Data Shortcuts branch in Prospector now reflects the path of the project you just created, as shown in Figure 16.4.

FIGURE 16.4
The Data Shortcuts area listed in Prospector.

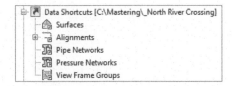

If you open Windows Explorer and navigate to C:\Mastering_North River Crossing, you'll see the folders from the MasteringCivil3D project template plus a special folder named _Shortcuts, as shown in Figure 16.5. This folder is created for the data shortcut XML files. When a data shortcut is defined, an XML file containing the path, drawing name, and originating object name is placed in this folder.

FIGURE 16.5
Your new project shown in Windows Explorer. Mastering is the working folder; _North River Crossing is the data shortcut folder.

In business, your working folder and data shortcuts folder should be on a network drive. If you have an established workflow for creating project folders and don't really need to use the Civil 3D project template, you can do the following:

1. Manually create a folder named **_Shortcuts** in your preferred location in your project folder structure.

This folder must be at least two levels deep in your directory structure.

2. On the Manage tab ➤ Data Shortcuts panel, click Set Working Folder and select a folder two levels above the _Shortcuts folder.

3. On the Manage tab ➤ Data Shortcuts panel, click Set Shortcuts Folder and select the folder that is displayed in the Set Data Shortcut Folder dialog, as shown in Figure 16.6.

FIGURE 16.6
Select the folder that contains your manually created _Shortcuts folder in the Set Data Shortcut Folder dialog.

This dialog will display only folders that contain a _Shortcuts subfolder.

Creating Data Shortcuts

With a shortcut folder in place, it's time to use it. In this exercise, you'll publish data shortcuts for the alignments and layout profiles in your project:

1. Open the 1602_ExistingSurface.dwg (1602_ExistingSurface_METRIC.dwg) file, which you can download from this book's web page.

    This drawing contains points and an existing ground surface. You need to have completed the previous exercise before continuing.

2. From the Application menu, click Save As, and save a copy of this drawing to C:\Mastering_North River Crossing\Survey.

LOCATING YOUR DRAWING FILES

When you're working with data shortcuts, the location of your drawing files containing your data is important. If you create a data shortcut to a surface and then later move the drawing file containing the surface, you will cause a broken reference in every file containing a reference to the surface. Plus, the data shortcut to the surface in the Prospector will no longer work. Later in this chapter, the "Fixing Broken References and Drawing Associations" section will explain what to do if relocating or renaming a project is unavoidable.

Create Data
Shortcuts

3. From the Manage tab ➤ Data Shortcuts panel, click Create Data Shortcuts.

Because the drawing was previously associated to another project, you are presented with a Create Data Shortcuts – Current Project dialog notifying you of this. To continue, you must associate this drawing to the _North River Crossing project.

4. Click Close to dismiss the dialog.

5. Right-click the Data Shortcuts branch of the Prospector and click Associate Project To Current Drawing.

6. Click OK to accept the defaults in the Associate Project To Current Drawing dialog.

7. Again, from the Manage tab ➤ Data Shortcuts panel, click Create Data Shortcuts.

8. In the Create Data Shortcuts dialog, place a check mark next to Existing Surface, as shown in Figure 16.7, and click OK.

FIGURE 16.7
Adding surface data to data shortcuts.

9. Save and close the current drawing file.

10. Open the `1602_Alignments-Profiles.dwg` (`1602_Alignments-Profiles_METRIC.dwg`) file from your class data.

    This file contains five alignments that you will add to the data shortcut project.

11. From the Application menu, click Save As, and save a copy of this file to `C:\Mastering\_North River Crossing\Design`.

12. Repeat steps 5 and 6 to reassociate the drawing to the _North River Crossing project.

13. From the Manage tab ➤ Data Shortcuts panel, click Create Data Shortcuts.

14. In the Create Data Shortcuts dialog, place a check mark next to the Alignments collection, which will select all the alignments and profiles if any exist (as shown in Figure 16.8), and click OK.

FIGURE 16.8
Adding alignment
data to the pool of
data shortcuts.

You should now have surfaces and alignments available for use in the data shortcuts list in Prospector, as shown in Figure 16.9. Notice in Figure 16.9 how highlighting the data shortcut in the list reveals the source location at the bottom of Toolspace.

FIGURE 16.9
List of Civil 3D
data shortcuts
available to the
current project.

Keep 1602_Alignments-Profiles.dwg (1602_Alignments-Profiles_METRIC.dwg) open for the next exercise.

Creating a Data Reference

Now that you've created the shortcut files to act as pointers back to the original drawing, you'll use them in other drawings. In this section, you will create and use data references.

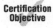
**Certification
Objective**

Data references are made using the Data Shortcuts branch within Prospector. In this exercise, you'll create a reference to the surface you previously shared to the project.

You need to have completed the previous exercises to continue.

1. Keep working in `1602_Alignments-Profiles.dwg` (`1602_Alignments-Profiles_METRIC.dwg`).

2. In Toolspace, expand the Prospector ➢ Data Shortcuts ➢ Surfaces collection, right-click Existing Surface, and select Create Reference, as shown in Figure 16.10.

FIGURE 16.10
The Create Surface
Reference dialog.

3. In the Create Surface Reference dialog, leave all surface options at their defaults and click OK. Zoom extents to view the surface.

4. Save the current drawing and keep it open for the next exercise.

You should now see the surface in the drawing. At first glance, it does not look different from other surfaces you've worked with within Civil 3D. If you examine the Surfaces branch of Prospector, however, you'll see that there is no Definition collection (as shown in Figure 16.11). You cannot edit a surface or any other object that is data referenced. If a change needs to be made to Existing Surface, you would need to open the drawing file where it was originally created.

FIGURE 16.11
You can see and
use the surface,
but you cannot
add to or edit the
surface definition.

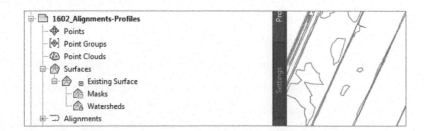

Any changes to the surface will be communicated through the data shortcut to the drawings where it is referenced. If the drawing is open when a data-referenced source file has been changed, a bubble message will pop up to inform the user that the item must be synchronized to view the most up-to-date information. If a recipient drawing is closed at the time the change takes place, all data references will automatically be synchronized as the file opens.

RENAMING OBJECTS AFTER REFERENCE CREATION

If the objects in the source drawing are renamed, the new name is communicated through the data shortcut upon synchronization. The Object Name Change dialog will open to inform you of the change and give you the choice of accepting the new name or keeping the old.

> **Object Name Change**
>
> The name of the source object for this reference has changed.
> Old name:
> AeccDbSurfaceTin name: Existing Surface (2)
> C:\Civil 3D Projects\2015\Project
> ABC-123\Survey\1602_ExistingConditions.dwg
>
> Current name:
> AeccDbSurfaceTin name: EG
> C:\Civil 3D Projects\2015\Project
> ABC-123\Survey\1602_ExistingConditions.dwg
>
> Please choose an action:
>
> ⇨ Update the reference name
>
> ⇨ Keep the old reference name
>
> [Close]

In the next part of the exercise, you will use the skills you learned in Chapter 7, "Profiles and Profile Views," to create an existing ground profile and a design profile. After you have all the information, you will use skills from Chapter 9, "Basic Corridors," to put the information together. You need to have completed the previous exercises to continue.

5. Keep working in `1602_Alignments-Profiles.dwg` (`1602_Alignments-Profiles_METRIC.dwg`).

6. Select the ROAD A alignment.

7. In the Alignment contextual tab ➢ Launch Pad panel, click Surface Profile.

8. In the Create Profile From Surface dialog, do the following:

  a. Click Add.

  b. Click Draw In Profile View.

9. In the Create Profile View dialog, click Create Profile View, and click to place the profile view anywhere in the drawing to the right of the surface.

10. Select the profile view. From the Profile View contextual tab ➤ Launch Pad panel, click Profile Creation Tools.

11. In the Create Profile – Draw New dialog, name the new profile **FG-ROAD A**.

12. Set Profile Style to Design Profile and click OK.

13. From the Profile Layout Tools, click Insert PVIs Tabular.

14. Enter the data for your unit system, as shown in Figure 16.12; then click OK.

FIGURE 16.12
Profile data
Imperial (left) and
Metric (right).

You can close the Profile Layout Tools toolbar when finished.

15. Save the drawing.

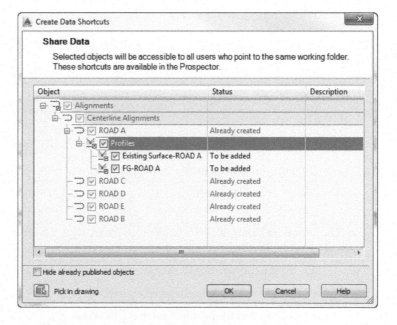

16. From the Manage tab ➤ Data Shortcuts panel, click Create Data Shortcuts.

17. Place a check mark next to Profiles, as shown in Figure 16.13, and click OK.

FIGURE 16.13
Adding additional
drawing data to
the data shortcut
project.

The alignments that you added earlier are listed but are grayed out. Once you add an item to the Data Shortcut list, you do not need to add it again. Only new data will be added to the list of data shortcuts. Shown in gray will be the list of items that are already published as data shortcuts. If you find the list of already published items distracting, you can hide all of the published items by clicking the Hide Already Published Objects check box at the bottom of the dialog.

18. Save and close 1602_Alignments-Profiles.dwg (1602_Alignments-Profiles_METRIC.dwg).

19. From your class files, open 1603_Corridor.dwg (1603_Corridor_Metric.dwg).

20. From the Application menu, click Save As, and save the drawing to C:\Mastering_North River Crossing\Design.

21. From the Prospector tab of Toolspace, expand the Data Shortcuts branch and then expand Surfaces.

22. Right-click Existing Surface and click Create Reference.

23. In the Create Surface Reference dialog, leave all default settings and click OK.

24. From the Prospector tab of the toolbar, expand the Data Shortcuts branch and then expand Alignments ➤ Centerline Alignments ➤ ROAD A ➤ Profiles.

25. Right-click FG-ROAD A and select Create Reference, as shown in Figure 16.14.

FIGURE 16.14
Creating a data reference to a profile will automatically create a data reference for its alignment.

26. In the Create Profile Reference dialog, change Profile Style to Design Profile and click OK.

If you zoom extents in the drawing, you should see the alignment and existing surface.

The profile data is referenced but is not currently visible. If you wanted to, you could create a profile view. However, you do not need the profile to be visible to create a corridor.

27. From the Home tab ➤ Create Design panel, click Corridor. In the Create Corridor dialog, do the following:

a. Name the corridor **ROAD A**.

b. Verify that the alignment is set to ROAD A.

c. Verify that the profile is set to FG-ROAD A.

    d. Set the assembly to Basic Assembly.

    e. Set Target Surface to Existing Surface.

    f. Clear the check box for Set Baseline And Region Parameters.

    g. Click OK.

    h. Close the Panorama before proceeding.

28. After the corridor builds successfully, save and close the drawing; you will come back to it later.

 Real World Scenario

CREATING CROSS-SECTION SHEETS IN THEIR OWN DRAWING

Unlike plan and profile sheets, cross-section sheets do not give you any options for automatically creating layouts in new sheets.

It is a great idea to create section views in their own drawing for the following reasons:

◆ The scale used for plotting sections is usually different from what is used for other parts of the design. You can set your annotation scale to match your plot scale in your section view drawing.

◆ Corridor drawings already contain lots of data; create section views in their own drawing to keep file size down.

The following exercise builds from what you have already created in this chapter. You will step through the procedure of creating cross-section sheets using a combination of external reference and data shortcut functionality. You may want to review Chapter 12, "Cross Sections and Mass Haul," if you have trouble completing the steps in this exercise.

1. Start a new drawing with the Civil 3D template of your choice.

2. Verify that the correct data shortcut project folder is selected and then save the drawing to the folder C:\Mastering_North River Crossing\Sheets as **1604_Sections.dwg** or, if metric, **1604_Section_METRIC.dwg**.

3. From the Prospector tab of Toolspace, expand Data Shortcuts ➢ Alignments ➢ Centerline Alignments, right-click ROAD A, and click Create Reference.

4. In the Create Alignment Reference dialog, leave all the defaults and click OK.

5. From the Insert tab ➢ Reference panel, click Attach.

6. At the bottom of the Select Reference File dialog, set Files Of Type to Drawing (*.dwg).

7. Browse to C:\Mastering_North River Crossing\Design, select 1603_Corridor.dwg (1603_Corridor_METRIC.dwg), and click Open. In the Attach Reference dialog, do the following:

    a. Set Reference Type to Overlay.

    b. Set Path Type to Relative Path.

    c. Clear any check boxes under Specify On Screen for Insertion Point, Rotation, or Scale.

    d. Click OK.

You may receive an Unreconciled New Layers message, which you can dismiss by clicking the X. Also, dismiss Panorama if opened.

Continues

Continued

Zoom extents to get a look at your drawing so far. You now have everything you need to create sample lines in this new drawing, the alignment, and the externally referenced corridor.

8. From the Home tab ➤ Profile & Section Views panel, click Sample Lines.

9. At the `Select an alignment <or press enter key to select from list>`: prompt, press Enter to pick ROAD A from a list in the Select Alignment dialog and click OK.

10. In the Create Sample Line Group dialog, keep all default options and styles.

Pause here and take note of a few interesting things. Existing Surface is appearing even though it is not data referenced. Additionally, you should see the corridor listed. You cannot data reference a corridor, but you can use sample lines to reach through an external reference to sample your corridor model. If you had created corridor surfaces, those too would appear in this dialog.

11. Click OK.

12. From the Sample Line Tools toolbar ➤ Sample Line Creation Methods drop-down, click the By Range Of Stations tool.

13. Set the left and right swath widths to **100'(30** m).

14. Keep the default sampling increments and click OK.

15. Press Esc to complete the command.

16. From the Home tab ➤ Profile & Section Views panel ➤ Section Views, click Create Multiple Views.

17. In the Create Multiple Section Views dialog, leave all the defaults and click Create Section Views.

18. Click to place the sheets to the right of the existing objects in the drawing.

19. Save the drawing and keep it open for the next exercise.

After you have successfully created sample lines, the procedure for creating section sheets is the same as you learned in previous chapters.

Updating References

When you need to make a change, you can use the tools in the Data Shortcut menu to jump back to that file, make the changes, and refresh the reference.

1. If it is not open from the exercise in "Creating Cross-Section Sheets in Their Own Drawing," open the file 1604_Sections.dwg.

   Ideally, you saved it to C:\Mastering_North River Crossing\Sheets.

2. Keep this drawing open and also open the file 1603_Corridor.dwg.

3. In Prospector, expand Data Shortcuts ➤ Surfaces.

4. Right-click Existing Surface and select Open Source Drawing, as shown in Figure 16.15.

FIGURE 16.15
Open Source
Drawing is a fast
way to jump to the
drawing you want.

At this point, you should have three drawings open (1602_ExistingSurface, 1603_Corridor, and 1604_Sections; or, 1602_ExistingSurface_METRIC, 1603_Corridor_METRIC, and 1604_Sections_METRIC if metric). You can use the tabs across the top of the screen to switch drawings. You can also use the Quick View Drawings button at the bottom of the AutoCAD window to switch between open drawings.

The 1602_ExistingSurface.dwg (1602_ExistingSurface_METRIC.dwg) file should be active and ready to make updates. Remember that the surface is read-only in all other project files; this is the only drawing in which changes can be made to the surface.

In this drawing, you will add polyline contours to the surface definition. The change to the surface will affect all drawings where the surface is used as a data reference. The dynamic communication between drawings shows the power of the Data Shortcut tool.

5. Select the surface in the drawing window.

6. On the contextual ribbon ➤ Modify panel ➤ Add Data tool, select Contours.

   a. In the Add Contour Data dialog, under Description, enter **Mound** and click OK.

   b. In the drawing window, select the green polyline contours with a crossing selection box.

   c. Press Enter when finished.

7. Save and close 1602_ExistingSurface.dwg (or 1602_ExistingSurface_METRIC.dwg).

8. Switch drawings so that 1603_Corridor.dwg (1603_Corridor_METRIC.dwg) is the active drawing.

Shortly after bringing this drawing to the forefront, you should see an alert symbol appear on the external reference icon on the status bar indicating that data shortcut definitions may have changed, as shown in Figure 16.16.

FIGURE 16.16
Civil 3D will send the user a message when a data-referenced object has changed.

9. Right-click and click Synchronize.

In some situations, you see a warning symbol in the Prospector. In that case, you can always synchronize directly from the right-click menu of the referenced object, as shown in Figure 16.17.

FIGURE 16.17
Synchronizing from the object's right-click menu.

You may receive a message in Panorama indicating that the item was synchronized.

10. Dismiss this message by clicking the green check box.

The surface that changed is used as a target in the corridor; therefore, the corridor needs to be rebuilt.

11. Expand Prospector ➤ Corridors, right-click the ROAD A corridor and select Rebuild.

12. Save and close 1603_Corridor.dwg (1603_Corridor_METRIC.dwg).

13. Switch to 1604_Sections.dwg if it is not already current.

This time, you will receive a message that your external reference file has changed, as shown in Figure 16.18. If you accidentally dismiss this message without updating, a warning symbol will remain in the tray area at the bottom of your screen. You can always right-click to reload the reference from this icon.

FIGURE 16.18
Reload the external reference to ensure your cross sections reflect the design update.

14. Zoom to the section view at station 16+00 (0+300 if metric) and take a look at the section line representing Existing Surface.

15. Click Reload 1603_Corridor or 1603_Corridor_METRIC if metric in the External References dialog.

Your sections should now reflect all the design changes. If you receive a message regarding unreconciled layers, click the X to dismiss it.

16. Save and close all drawings.

You can find a completed version of the project folder with updates with this chapter's dataset. The folder is called _North River Crossing.

BEST PRACTICES FOR EMPLOYING DATA SHORTCUTS

When people first add data shortcuts into their workflow, they often have the following questions:

I work on only small sites by myself. Do I need to use data shortcuts?   Even if you work on small projects, you should use data shortcuts for cross-section sheets.

How should I break up my project?   Every project is different, of course, but use these guidelines:

Existing Survey and Surface   The first drawing you create is usually the existing conditions. Keep survey points, figures, and the existing surface together in the first drawing. Create a data shortcut to the existing surface. Points can't be shared via data shortcuts, but you can always use a point query to pull specific points between drawings if you have access to the survey database.

Alignments and Profiles   While the existing surface is being fine-tuned, you can get to work on developing the alignments and profiles right away. Alignments and profiles are fairly lightweight in terms of how much data they consume. You can usually store all of your project's alignment and profile data in the same DWG file.

Corridors   If you're working with intersections, alignments and profiles must live in the corridor drawing since the intersection tool needs to override elevations on secondary profiles.

Continues

Continued

Use multiple corridor drawings when dealing with a large network of roads. This way several designers can work on different segments of the project at the same time. Be mindful not to put too much data in one file—you may want to keep interchanges and roundabouts in their own drawings. At the end of the process, data shortcuts will allow you to piece in the proposed surface.

Pipe Networks and Pressure Networks   Pipe networks and pressure pipe networks can be used with data shortcuts. It is okay to put a large network in one file, but you may want to split the type of pipe network (storm versus sanitary, for example) if different designers are working on portions concurrently. Interference checks work between gravity pipe networks even if they are data references.

Site Grading   Surfaces made from grading groups like ponds are good candidates for data shortcuts. So are any other site components that can be represented by a surface like a building pad, a berm, or even a parking lot.

Where is the data stored?   The data for a data shortcut is stored in the source DWG file. The data shortcut file itself is simply a pointer that keeps track of filenames and paths. No object data is stored with the data shortcut.

Can I store my working folder and data shortcut folder on a network?   Yes! This is an excellent way to work. You can keep your working folder, data shortcut folder, and project drawings on a network drive.

What if I need to share the project data with another office?   This question is where data shortcuts get a little tricky. How to handle multiple offices depends on the scenario:

Example 1   Your Houston office is working on the road design while the Chicago office is working on grading. You want a live, remote workflow with frequent syncing between offices. For this type of scenario, you would be better served by Autodesk® Vault Collaboration: www.autodesk.com/products/vault-family/overview.

Example 2   Your Houston office has completed this stage of the road design, and the next phase will be done in the Chicago office. In other words, no live data exchange needs to take place. You can move the entirety of the project's data shortcut folder to the new location. You can also use eTransmit (discussed later in this chapter) to ensure that all drawings and attached images are included.

FIXING BROKEN REFERENCES AND DRAWING ASSOCIATIONS

A broken reference is fairly easy to fix, but you will not be able to continue working in your design until broken references are resolved.

Actions that will cause broken references include the following:

◆   Renaming a source file

◆   Moving a source file

◆ Missing a source file

◆ Renaming project folders

In the following exercise, you will associate drawings that have been renamed to a project that has been renamed and fix the broken data references that you find. You *do not* need to have completed the previous exercises to continue.

1. Using Windows Explorer, locate the folder called _Broken Reference.

   This is part of the download for this chapter at the book's web page.

2. Copy this folder and its contents to C:\Mastering.

3. Open the 1605_Corridors.dwg file, located in C:\Mastering_Broken Reference\ Design.

   This file contains a number of references pointing to files that have been renamed. Panorama may appear with the messages regarding the problems that it found.

4. If it's open, close the Panorama window by clicking the green check mark.

5. On the Manage tab ➢ Data Shortcuts panel, click Set Working Folder:

   a. Set the working folder to C:\Mastering. Even if this is already the current working folder, the data shortcuts list will update by selecting the folder again.

   b. Click OK to close.

6. On the Manage tab ➢ Data Shortcuts panel, click Set Shortcuts Folder:

   a. Select _Broken Reference.

   b. Click OK to close.

7. In Prospector, locate the Data Shortcuts branch and expand Surfaces.

   Because the Shortcuts project folder was renamed, the shortcuts in the project need repairing.

8. Under the Data Shortcuts branch in the Prospector, right-click Existing Surface and click Repair Broken Shortcut.

9. In the Choose The File Containing The Referenced Object dialog, browse to the 1605_ ExistingSurface.dwg file in the C:\Mastering_Broken Reference\Survey folder and click Open.

10. In Prospector, expand Data Shortcuts branch ➢ Alignments ➢ Centerline Alignments.

11. For ROAD A, right-click and click Repair Broken Shortcut.

12. In the Choose The File Containing The Referenced Object dialog, browse to the 1605_ Alignments-Profiles.dwg file in the C:\Mastering_Broken Reference\Design folder and click Open.

13. In the Additional Broken Shortcuts dialog, click Repair All Broken Shortcuts.

14. Back up in the drawing collection in Prospector, expand Alignments ➤ Centerline Alignments. You will see that next to ROAD A is a warning chevron.

15. Right-click ROAD A and select Repair Broken References, as shown in Figure 16.19.

FIGURE 16.19
Choosing
Repair Broken
References.

After fixing the first broken reference, if more broken references exist, you will be prompted to fix them in the Additional Broken References dialog, shown in Figure 16.20.

FIGURE 16.20
The Additional
Broken References
message.

16. Click Repair All Broken References.

17. Close the current drawing. You may save it, but you will not need it for additional exercises.

The ability to repair broken links helps make file management a bit easier, but there will be times when you need to completely change the path of a shortcut to point to the correct file. To do so, you must use the Data Shortcuts Editor.

eTransmit + Data Shortcuts

If you need to pass a project on to another designer with all the information they need, use the eTransmit command.

To find the eTransmit command, select the Application menu ➤ Publish ➤ eTransmit. If a file contains a data shortcut, the eTransmit command will recognize the link and include the necessary drawings. You can even include non-AutoCAD files such as Word or Excel documents by clicking the Add File button.

AutoCAD will generate a zip file that contains any external reference files (including DWF, DGN, PDF, or TIF references), plot configurations, images, and templates used in sheet creation. When your recipient unzips the file, the connections between drawings are maintained.

Be warned that the data shortcut source files may not be placed in their original location!

THE DATA SHORTCUTS EDITOR

A Civil 3D drawing stores links to the information it uses in its database. The Data Shortcuts Editor is used to update or change the file to which a shortcut points. You may want to do this when preparing a deliverable.

In the following exercise, you'll copy the current chapter project to another folder and update the data shortcut paths with the Data Shortcuts Editor (the procedure is the same for both metric and Imperial units):

1. Using Windows Explorer, locate the folder called `_Deliverable`.

   This is part of the download for this chapter at the book's web page.

2. Copy this folder and its contents to `C:\Mastering`, as shown in Figure 16.21.

FIGURE 16.21
Simulating a new project phase by copying the example project to a new folder.

Next, you will open the Data Shortcuts Editor to correct the file paths in the `_Deliverable` version.

3. In Windows, choose Start ➤ All Programs ➤ Autodesk ➤ Autodesk AutoCAD Civil 3D 2016 – English and click the Data Shortcuts Editor to load it.

4. Select File ➤ Open Data Shortcuts Folder to display the Browse For Folder dialog.

5. Browse to `C:\Mastering` and, with the `_Deliverable` folder highlighted, click OK.

   Your Data Shortcuts Editor should resemble Figure 16.22.

FIGURE 16.22
Inside the Data Shortcuts Editor.

Several things need to be changed before the new phase of the project can begin. Some of the data references are looking for the incorrect file.

Notice that the Path column of the table still refers to the old path. To make a clean break from the old project to move forward into the Submitted version, you need to change all these.

6. Click to set your cursor into the Path field for Existing Surface.

7. Choose Find And Replace.

   Unfortunately, there is no browse option here, but you can use the basic Windows Copy and Paste tools to make this a little easier.

8. Delete **\Survey** from the Find field and then copy the path to the clipboard.

9. Paste the path into the Replace With field.

10. In the Replace With field, replace the text _Another Project with **_Deliverable**, as shown in Figure 16.23.

FIGURE 16.23
Updating the paths to the new project.

11. Click Replace All.

    Your data shortcut paths are now correct (as shown in Figure 16.24) and ready for more action. Click Cancel to close the Find And Replace tool.

FIGURE 16.24
Updated paths.

Object Name	Path
Existing Surface	C:\Mastering_Deliverable\Survey
ROAD A	C:\Mastering_Deliverable\Design
ROAD B	C:\Mastering_Deliverable\Design
ROAD C	C:\Mastering_Deliverable\Design
ROAD D	C:\Mastering_Deliverable\Design
ROAD E	C:\Mastering_Deliverable\Design
Existing Surface (1)-ROAD A	C:\Mastering_Deliverable\Design
FG-ROAD	C:\Mastering_Deliverable\Design

12. Click Cancel to close the dialog.

13. Click the Save icon to commit your changes.

14. You can now close the Data Shortcuts Editor and return to Civil 3D.

INTRODUCING THE NEW MANAGE DATA SHORTCUTS TOOL

A new feature in Civil 3D 2016 is the ability to map broken data references or remap drawing objects in a drawing to data shortcuts within a shortcuts project folder.

On the Manage tab ➤ Data Shortcuts panel, the Manage Data Shortcuts icon will open the Link To A Data Shortcut dialog when clicked.

Data references in the drawing are shown in the pane on the left side of the dialog. Data shortcuts from the current project folder are displayed in the pane on the right side of the dialog. Drawing objects can be mapped to project shortcuts by selecting the object in the left pane and the shortcut in the right pane and then clicking the Click To Link The Selected Object To The Selected Shortcut icon.

Resolved or unresolved data references are immediately remapped to the selected shortcut in the project as indicated by the information reported in the Item View below each pane.

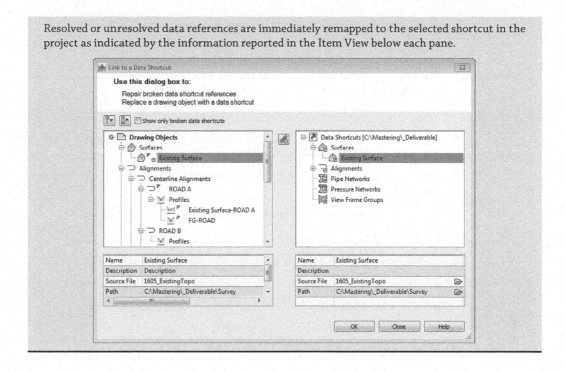

Sharing Data with a Non–Civil 3D World

Not everybody uses Civil 3D 2016, so you need to know how to convert your drawing files and extract your design data for those people who are using previous versions of AutoCAD or different land development software.

Delivering DWG Formats

Files created in Civil 3D 2016 are backward compatible to Civil 3D 2014. Currently, these are the only two versions that will work together without losing significant amounts of data. Even though Civil 3D 2014 was said to be backward compatible with Civil 3D 2013, it is not advisable to use them together.

The Save As command can be misleading for Civil 3D users. Keep in mind that the Save As command works only on AutoCAD objects such as lines, arcs, and circles—*not* Civil 3D objects. To save to a version of Civil 3D 2012 or prior, you will need to use the Application menu ➤ Export ➤ Export Civil 3D Drawing. This is a new command in Civil 3D 2016. The result will be exploded Civil 3D objects.

In the following exercise, you will export a Civil 3D 2016 corridor model to an AutoCAD 2010 file format:

1. Open C:\Mastering_North River Crossing\Design\1603_Corridor.DWG.

   For this exercise, you need to have completed the _Deliverable data shortcut project earlier in the chapter.

2. From the Application menu, click Export ➤ Export Civil 3D Drawing.

3. In the Export AutoCAD Civil 3D Drawing dialog, click the Export Settings button.

   a. Under DWG File Version, select 2010 from drop-down menu.

   b. Click OK to close.

   Note the settings for the treatment of external references.

4. Under Files To Export, click Selected Drawings In Source Folder and select the check box next to Include Drawings In Subfolders.

5. On the right side of the dialog under Source Folder, click the ellipsis button next to the field.

   a. In the Browse For Folder dialog, select the _Deliverable folder.

   b. Click OK to close the dialog.

6. Under Destination Folder, click the ellipsis button next to the field.

   a. In the Browse For Folder dialog, select the _Deliverable folder.

   b. Click the Make New Folder button at the bottom of the dialog.

   c. For the new folder name, type **2010 DWG Files**.

   d. Click OK to close the dialog.

7. Uncheck the check box next to Include Sheets. Leaving it filled will export the layouts as separate drawing files.

   The Export AutoCAD Civil 3D Drawing dialog should look like Figure 16.25.

FIGURE 16.25
Export AutoCAD Civil 3D Drawing dialog, a new feature in Civil 3D 2016.

8. Click Export.

   The export may take a few minutes.

9. When the Export Status dialog reads 4 Of 4 Files Exported, click OK to close even though the green progress bar is still animated.

10. Click Cancel to close the Export AutoCAD Civil 3D Drawing dialog.

11. Open C:\Mastering_Deliverable\2010 DWG Files\survey\ACAD-1602_ ExistingSurface-Model.dwg (ACAD-1602_ExistingSurface_METRIC.dwg if metric).

    As the file opens, the command line will echo Opening An AutoCAD 2010/ LT 2010 Format File.

12. Click a contour.

    This export command will explode all objects to AutoCAD entities. The contour is now a polyline and has taken on the layer assigned to it through the style once assigned to it. It also forces color, linestyle, lineweight, and any properties overrides in the styles to the resulting entities.

13. Press Esc to deselect the contour.

14. Close the drawing without saving. You don't want to upgrade the file format.

15. Close all the drawings.

Compare the content of your 2010 DWG Files folder with the contents of the 2010 DWG Files_FINISHED folder, which can be downloaded from the book's website.

Using LandXML

LandXML is not specific to Civil 3D. It is a file format that allows users to share data in a non-proprietary format. You can use LandXML to archive projects and to send information to non–Civil 3D users or users of Civil 3D using 2012 or earlier.

A drop-down in the Import LandXML dialog lets you select the version of LandXML. This is a result of that consortium. The latest, as of this writing, is the 1.2 schema. Most CAD programs have methods of importing and exporting LandXML files, and this is one way to tackle that barrier.

Alas, the need to send data to older versions of Civil 3D is not always avoidable. In the following exercise, you will step through an example of what needs to happen to force Civil 3D to previous versions:

1. Open 1606_LandXML-OUT.dwg (1606_LandXML-OUT_METRIC.dwg), which can be found at this book's web page.

2. From the Output tab ➤ Export panel, select Export To LandXML.

   The Export To LandXML dialog, shown in Figure 16.26, opens.

FIGURE 16.26
The Export To
LandXML dialog.

3. Click OK.

4. In the Export To LandXML dialog, browse to the same folder as the source drawing.

5. Keep the default name (the dialog will pick up the name of the drawing you are exporting from) and click Save.

   You now have as much Civil 3D as possible packed up into the LandXML file. This file contains the following:

   ◆ Alignments

   ◆ Point groups and points

   ◆ Surfaces

   ◆ Profiles

   ◆ Pipe data

   If you are ever sent a LandXML file, you will need to import the contents into a file created from your Civil 3D template.

6. Create a new drawing using the template of your choice.

7. On the Insert tab ➢ Import panel, click LandXML.

8. In the Import LandXML dialog, browse for and select the XML file you created in steps 4 and 5; click Open.

   Figure 16.27 shows the Import LandXML dialog.

FIGURE 16.27
Importing
LandXML data.

9. Click OK.

10. Dismiss Panorama if it's open.

11. Browse Prospector for the data that was imported.

    At this point you could change styles and apply label styles to certain objects.

12. Save and close the drawing.

You can find completed versions of the resulting file after LandXML import with this book's dataset. Compare your work with 1606_LandXML-IN_FINISHED.dwg or 1606_LandXML-IN_METRIC_FINISHED.dwg.

The Bottom Line

Create a data shortcut folder. The ability to load design information into a project environment is an important part of creating an efficient team. The main design elements of the project are available to the data shortcut mechanism via the working folder and data shortcut folder.

Master It Using the MasterIt1601.dwg (MasterIt1601_METRIC.dwg) drawing, create a new data shortcut folder called MasterIt. Use the _Sample Project project template.

Create data shortcuts. To allow sharing of the data, shortcuts must be made before the information can be used in other drawings.

Master It Continue working in the drawing from the previous "Master It" exercise. Save the drawing to the Source Drawings folder in the Master Data Shortcuts project you created in the previous exercise. Create data shortcuts to all the available data in the MasterIt1601.dwg (MasterIt1601_METRIC.dwg) file.

Export to earlier releases of AutoCAD.   Being able to export to earlier base AutoCAD versions is sometimes necessary.

> **Master It**   Using `MasterIt1601.dwg` (`MasterIt1601_METRIC.dwg`), export the Civil 3D file so it can be used by a user working in base AutoCAD 2010.

Export to LandXML.   Being able to work with outside clients or even other departments within your firm that do not have Civil 3D is an important part of collaboration.

> **Master It**   Using `MasterIt1601.dwg` (`MasterIt1601_METRIC.dwg`), create a LandXML file with all of the exportable information.

Chapter 17

Quantity Takeoff

The goal of every project is eventually construction. Before the first bulldozer can be fired up and the first pile of dirt moved, the owner, city, or developer has to know how much all of this paving, pipe, and dirt are going to cost. Although contractors and construction managers are typically responsible for creating their own estimates for contracts, the engineers often perform an estimate of cost to help judge and award the eventual contract. To that end, many firms have entire departments that spend their days counting manholes, running planimeters around paving areas, and measuring street lengths to figure out how much striping will be required.

The Autodesk® AutoCAD® Civil 3D® software includes a Quantity Takeoff (QTO) feature to help relieve that tedious burden. You can use the model you've built as part of your design to measure and quantify the pieces needed to turn your project from paper to reality. You can export this data to a number of formats and even to other applications for further analysis.

In this chapter, you will learn to:

◆ Open and add to a list of pay items.

◆ Assign pay items to AutoCAD objects and pipe networks.

◆ Use QTO tools to review what items have been tagged for analysis.

◆ Generate QTO output to a variety of formats for review or analysis.

Employing Pay Item Files

Before you can begin running any sort of analysis or quantity, you have to know what items you are trying to quantify. Various municipalities, states, and review agencies have their own lists of items and methods of breaking down the quantities involved in a typical development project.

There are three main files associated with quantity takeoff in Civil 3D: the pay item list, the pay item categorization file, and the formula file. Each file serves a different purpose and is stored externally to the project. Once a file has been associated to a drawing file (DWG), the path to these files is stored with the DWG.

Pay Item List When preparing quantities, different types of measurements are used based on the items being counted. Some are simple individual objects such as light posts, fire hydrants, and manholes. Only slightly more complicated are linear objects such as road striping and area items such as grass cover. These measurements are also part of the pay item list.

At minimum, the pay item list will provide you with three main pieces of information for each item:

◆ The pay item number

◆ The pay item description

◆ The pay item unit of measure

There are three file types allowable for the pay item list file:

◆ CSV (Comma Delimited)

◆ AASHTO TransXML

◆ Florida DOT

Pay Item Categorization File In any project, there can be thousands of items to tabulate. To make this process easier, most organizations have built pay categories, and Civil 3D makes use of this system in a categorization file. Civil 3D includes an option to create favorite items that are used most frequently. This file, which is always formatted as an XML file, is optional.

Formula File The formula file is used when the unit of measure for the pay item needs to be converted or calculated based on another value. For example, bituminous concrete for a parking lot is usually paid for by the ton, but you will generally be obtaining an area from CAD. You can set up a formula that converts square feet into tons, taking into account an assumed depth and density. Later in this chapter, you will create a formula that relates length to light poles along the road.

A command is available if you need to disconnect your pay item and formula files from the drawing. At the command line you can type **DETACHQTOFILES**. The Undo command will not reconnect them if you type this in accidentally.

In the next section, you will learn how to connect the needed pay item files and create favorites.

Pay Item Favorites

Your Civil 3D file will "remember" which files it needs to correctly assess quantities. The Favorites list is a separate category that can be populated for quick access to commonly used pay items. This list is saved inside the DWG.

In this exercise, you'll look at how to open a pay item and categorization files and add a few items to the Favorites list for later use:

1. Create a new drawing using the _AutoCAD Civil 3D (Imperial) NCS template. Metric users should use the _AutoCAD Civil 3D (Metric) NCS template.

2. From the Analyze tab ➤ QTO panel, choose QTO Manager (see Figure 17.1) to display the QTO Manager.

FIGURE 17.1
The QTO tools on
the Analyze tab

3. Click the Open button at the top left of the QTO Manager to display the Open Pay Item File dialog.

4. In the Open Pay Item File dialog, verify that the Pay Item File Format drop-down list is set to CSV (Comma Delimited).

5. Click the Open button next to the Pay Item File text box to browse for the file.

    In Windows 7 and Windows 8, you can find this file in C:\ProgramData\Autodesk\ C3D 2016\enu\Data\Pay Item Data\Getting Started\.

C:\PROGRAMDATA

If you do not see the ProgramData folder listed in C:\, follow these simple steps:

1. Open Windows Explorer.

2. Click the Organize button at the upper left.

3. Select Folder And Search Options to display the Folder Options dialog.

4. On the View tab, in Advanced Settings, select the radio button Show Hidden Files, Folders, And Drives.

5. Click OK to accept the settings in the Folder Options dialog.

Metric users should copy the Getting Started_METRIC.csv file to C:\ProgramData\ Autodesk\C3D 2016\enu\Data\Pay Item Data\Getting Started\, downloadable from the book's web page (www.sybex.com/go/masteringcivil3d2016).

6. Select the Getting Started.CSV file or Getting Started_METRIC.csv.

7. Click Open to select this CSV pay item file.

8. Click the Open button next to the Pay Item Categorization File text box to browse for the file.

9. Navigate back to the Getting Started folder and select the Getting Started Categories.xml file.

    This file can be used by both Imperial and metric users.

10. Click Open to select the file.

    Your display should look similar to Figure 17.2.

FIGURE 17.2
Open Pay Item File
dialog

11. Click OK to accept the settings in the Open Pay Item File dialog.

The QTO Manager will now be populated with a collection of divisions, as shown in Figure 17.3. These divisions came from the `Getting Started Categories.xml` file.

FIGURE 17.3
The QTO Manager in Panorama populated within categories (Divisions and Groups)

12. Expand the Division 200 ➤ Group 201 ➤ Section 20101 branches, and select the item 20101-0000 CLEARING AND GRUBBING. You may need to widen the Pay Item ID column.

13. Right-click and select Add To Favorites List, as shown in Figure 17.4.

FIGURE 17.4
Selecting a pay item to add as a favorite

14. Expand a few other branches to familiarize yourself with these pay items.

15. Add the following to your Favorites list in preparation for the next exercise:

◆ 60404-2000 CATCH BASIN, TYPE 2

◆ 61106-0000 FIRE HYDRANT

◆ 61203-0000 MANHOLE, SANITARY SEWER

◆ 63401-0600 PAVEMENT MARKINGS, TYPE C, BROKEN

16. Save the drawing as **1701_QTOPractice.dwg** or **1701_QTOPractice_METRIC.dwg** and keep it open for the next exercise.

When finished, scroll to the top of the Pay Item ID list and expand the Favorites category. Your QTO Manager should look similar to Figure 17.5.

FIGURE 17.5
A list of favorites within the QTO Manager

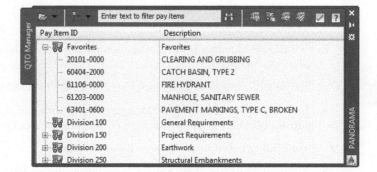

Civil 3D ships with a number of pay item list categorization files but only one actual pay item list. This avoids any issue with out-of-date data. One commonly used categorization type found in the C:\ProgramData\Autodesk\C3D 2016\enu\Data\Pay Item Data\CSI\ folder is MasterFormat2004. In the United States folder, you can also find categorization files for AASHTO and Federal Highway Administration. The pay item files that install with the software are intended to be examples. Contact your reviewing agency for access to its pay item list and categorization files if they're not already part of the Civil 3D product.

Once you have pay items to choose from, it's time to assign them to your model for analysis.

Searching for Pay Items

In the top of the QTO Manager is an extremely handy filter tool. If you don't know what category an item is listed under, you can type it in the field to the left of the binoculars icon.

When you first click the binoculars icon to execute the filter, it will appear as if nothing happened. That's because the category headings are in the way of the listing. To see an uncategorized version of the list your filter produced, select Turn Off Categorization from the drop-down to the left of the filter field, as shown in Figure 17.6.

FIGURE 17.6
Choose Turn Off
Categorization to
see the results of
your filter.

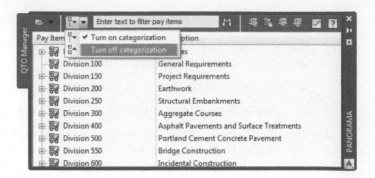

In the following exercise, you will use the filter functionality to add items to your Favorites list:

1. If it's not still open from the previous exercise, open the `1701_QTOPractice.dwg` or `1701_QTOPractice_METRIC.dwg` file. You must complete the previous exercise before proceeding.

2. If the QTO Manager is not already open, from the Analyze tab ➤ QTO panel, choose QTO Manager to open it.

3. To the left of the filter field, click the drop-down to select Turn Off Categorization.

4. In the filter field of the QTO Manager, type **grandi** and then click the binoculars icon. You can alternatively press ↵ instead of clicking the binoculars icon.

   Your filter should result in three types of trees.

5. Right-click the first item, Fagus Grandifloria, and select Add To Favorites List.

6. In the filter field of the QTO Manager, type **Washington** and then click the binoculars icon.

7. Add 63620-0500 Pole, Type Washington Globe No. 16 Light Standard to the Favorites List.

You will find that by adding your most frequently used items to the Favorites list, they will be at your fingertips instead of you having to dig through branch after branch of pay items.

When this exercise is complete, you may close the drawing. A saved copy of this drawing is available from the book's web page with the filename `QTOPractice_FINISHED.dwg` or `QTOPractice_METRIC_FINISHED.dwg`.

🌐 Real World Scenario

CREATING YOUR OWN CATEGORIZATION FILE

One of the challenges in automating any quantity takeoff analysis is getting the pay item list and categories to match up with your local requirements. Getting a pay item list is pretty straightforward—many reviewing agencies provide their own list for public use to keep all bidding on an equal footing.

Creating the category file can be slightly more difficult, and it will probably require experimentation to get it just right. In this example, you'll walk through creating a couple of categories to be used with a provided pay item list.

Note that modifying the QTO Manager affects all open drawings. You might want to finish the other exercises and come back to this when you need to make your own file in the real world.

1. Create a new drawing using the `_AutoCAD Civil 3D (Imperial) NCS` or `_AutoCAD Civil 3D (Metric) NCS` template.

2. From the Analyze tab ➤ QTO panel, choose QTO Manager to display the QTO Manager.

3. Click the Open button at the top left of the QTO Manager to display the Open Pay Item File dialog.

4. Verify that Pay Item File Format is set to CSV (Comma Delimited).

5. Click the Open button next to the Pay Item File text box and navigate to open the `Mastering.csv` or `Mastering_METRIC.csv` file.

   Remember, all files can be downloaded from www.sybex.com/go/masteringcivil3d2016.

6. Click the Open button next to the Pay Item Categorization File text box to display the Open Pay Item Categorization File dialog.

7. Browse to open the `MasteringCategories.xml` file (the same file is acceptable for both Imperial and metric users) and then click OK to accept the settings in the Open Pay Item File dialog.

   Your QTO Manager should look like this after expanding the 100 Series category:

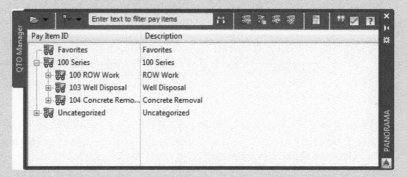

8. Launch XML Notepad. (This is a simple XML editor that you can download for free from Microsoft.)

9. Browse to and open the `MasteringCategories.xml` file from within XML Notepad.

10. Expand the PayItemCategorizationRules ➤ Categories branch, right-click the Category branch, and select Duplicate, as shown here.

Continues

Continued

Note that the duplicated category branch is made current.

11. Expand the new category branch; then modify the values on the right side of the dialog for the duplicate category to match the following graphic:

12. Delete the extra category branches under the new branch by right-clicking the two extra category listings and choosing Delete.

13. Save and close the modified `MasteringCategories.xml` file.

14. Switch back to the Civil 3D QTO Manager.

Next, you will need to reload the categorization file to view the changes.

15. Click the Open drop-down menu in the top left of the QTO Manager and select Open ➤ Categorization File.

16. Browse to the `MasteringCategories.xml` file again and open it.

Once Civil 3D processes your XML file, your QTO Manager should look similar to this:

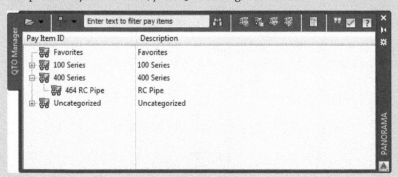

When this exercise is complete, you may close the drawing. A saved copy of this drawing is available from the book's web page with the filename `1702_QTOCategories_FINISHED.dwg` or `1702_`

QTOCategories_METRIC_FINISHED.dwg. In addition, a saved copy of the modified XML file is available with the filename MasteringCategories_modified.xml.

Creating a fully developed category list is a bit time-consuming, but once it's done, the list can be shared with your entire office so everyone has the same data to use.

Keeping Tabs on the Model

Once you have a list of pay items that must be quantified in your project, you have to assign these pay items to items in your drawing file. You can do so in any of the following ways:

- Assign pay items to simple AutoCAD objects such as blocks and lines.

- Assign pay items to corridor components.

- Assign pay items to pipes and structures in pipe networks.

- Assign pay items to pressure network pipes, fittings, and appurtenances.

In the next few sections, you'll explore each of these methods, along with some formula tools that can be used to convert things such as linear items to individual quantity counts.

AutoCAD Objects as Pay Items

The most basic use of the QTO tools is to assign pay items to things like blocks and linework within your drawing file. The QTO tools can be used to quantify any number of things, including tree plantings, signposts, and area items such as clearing and grubbing. In the following exercise, you'll assign pay items to blocks as well as to some closed polylines. Be sure the Getting Started.csv (or Getting Started_METRIC.csv) and Getting Started Categories.xml files are loaded as described in the first exercise.

1. Open the 1703_AcadObjectsInQTO.dwg or 1703_AcadObjectsInQTO_METRIC.dwg file.

2. From the Analyze tab ➢ QTO panel, choose QTO Manager to display the QTO Manager.

3. Expand the Favorites branch, right-click CLEARING AND GRUBBING, and select Assign Pay Item To Area, as shown in Figure 17.7.

FIGURE 17.7
Assigning an area-based pay item

4. At the `select Point or [select Object]:` prompt, type **O** ↵ to activate the Object option for assignment.

5. Click the closed polyline around the outer edge of the site, as shown in Figure 17.8.

FIGURE 17.8
Selecting a closed
polyline for
an area-based
quantity

Notice that the closed polyline fills with a solid hatch pattern indicating what area is being used. The command line should also echo `Pay item 20101-0000 assigned to area` when you pick the polyline.

6. Press ↵ to end the command.

7. Select the hatch to activate the Hatch Editor contextual tab.

8. From the Hatch Editor contextual tab ➤ Properties panel, change Hatch Transparency to **90**.

9. Right-click the hatch and select Display Order ➤ Send To Back.

10. Move the QTO Manager to the side and zoom in to the intersection of ROAD A and ROAD B where you can see one or more of the blocks representing trees.

11. Select one of the tree blocks and then right-click and choose Select Similar. All of the tree blocks are selected.

12. Back in the QTO Manager, under the Favorites branch, select 62606-0150 Fagus Grandifloria, American Beech.

13. Near the top of the panel, click the Assign The Selected Pay Items To Object(s) In The Drawing button.

Notice the great tooltips on these buttons.

14. Move your cursor over the graphics area of the drawing and press ↵ to end the assigning command.

15. Repeat steps 11 through 14 to assign the pay item 61106-0000 Fire Hydrant to all of the fire hydrant blocks on the site.

When this exercise is complete, you may close the drawing. A saved copy of this drawing is available from the book's web page with the filename AcadObjectsInQTO_FINISHED.dwg or AcadObjectsInQTO_METRIC_FINISHED.dwg.

ASSIGNING PAY ITEMS

The two assignment methods described in this section, by object or by area, are essentially inter-changeable. Pay items can be assigned to any number of AutoCAD objects, meaning you don't have to redraw the planners' or landscape architects' work in Civil 3D to use the QTO tools.

Keep in mind that the pay item tag is saved with the block. This is a good thing if you assign a pay item to a block and copy the block because the copies will be automatically tagged. If you assign a pay item to an object and use the **WBLOCK** command to copy that object out of your current drawing and into another, the pay item assignment goes along as well.

You'll find out how to unassign pay items after learning about all the ways to assign them.

Pricing Your Corridor

The corridor functionality of Civil 3D is invaluable. You can use it to model everything from roads to streams to parking lots. With the QTO tools, you can also use the corridor object to quantify much of the project construction costs.

ASSEMBLIES AND QTO ARE RELATED

Be mindful of what parts of an assembly are available when creating quantity takeoff assignments in the code set style.

If you plan to price an item based on the centerline of your road, make sure you have set a crown point code in your assembly properties. If you used the LaneSuperelevationAOR subassembly, this is defined by the Inside Point Code value if your slope direction is set to Away From Crown.

Continues

Continued

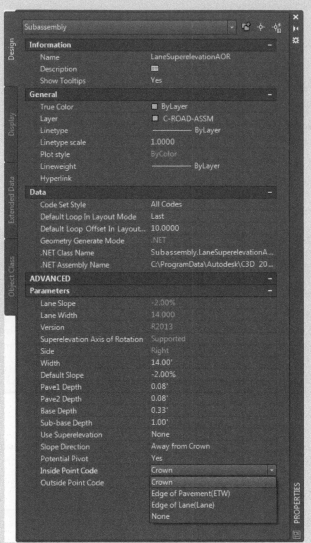

Changes to QTO information will not cause your corridor to flag itself as out of date. Before you run a takeoff report, it is a good idea to rebuild your corridors to ensure that the most up-to-date information is accounted for.

In this example, you'll use the pay item list along with a formula to convert the linear curb measurement to an incremental count of light poles required for the project:

1. Open the `1704_QTOCorridors.dwg` or `1704_QTOCorridors_METRIC.dwg` file.

2. From the Analyze tab ➢ QTO panel, choose QTO Manager.

3. Expand the Open button in the top-left corner of the QTO Manager and select Open ➤ Formula File.

4. In the Open dialog, browse to the C:\Mastering\Ch17 folder and select Getting Started Formulas.for file. Click Open to continue.

5. Expand the Favorites branch to display your 63620-0500 light standard pay item.

6. Widen Panorama to reveal the Formula column, and click in the Formula cell in the 63620-0500 light standard row, as shown in Figure 17.9.

FIGURE 17.9
Click in the Formula cell to display this warning dialog

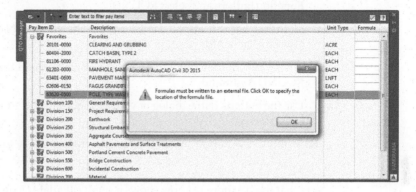

Civil 3D will display the Pay Item Formula: 63620-0500 dialog, as shown in Figure 17.10. (The Expression box will be empty when you first open it, but you'll take care of that in the next steps.)

FIGURE 17.10
The completed pay item expression

Assume that you need a street light every 300 feet (or 100 m for metric) but only on one side of the street. To do this, you add up all the lengths of curb and then divide by 2 because you want only one half of the street to have lights. You then divide by 300 (or 100 for metric) because you are running lights in an interval. Finally, you round to the nearest integer and add 1 to make the number conservative.

7. Enter the formula using the following steps:

a. Click the Property button and select Item Length from the drop-down list.

b. Use the buttons in the dialog or your keyboard to divide this value by 2 to get half of the curb length.

c. Use the buttons in the dialog or your keyboard to divide this value by 300 (or 100), which is the spacing of the light standards.

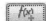

d. To round this value, move your cursor to the beginning of the expression, click the Function button, and select ROUND.

Note that there are also ROUNDUP and ROUNDDOWN expressions available if these are better suited for your calculations.

e. Move your cursor to the end of the expression and add the closing parenthesis for the ROUND command.

f. Use the buttons in the dialog or your keyboard to add 1 to the calculation to be conservative.

The formula should now match the one shown previously in Figure 17.10.

8. Click OK.

Note that the pay item list now shows a small calculator icon on that row to indicate a formula is in use.

Now that you've modified the way the light poles will be quantified from your model, you can assign the pay items for light poles and road striping to your corridor object. This is done by modifying the code set, as you'll see in the next steps.

9. In the Toolspace Settings tab, expand General ➤ Multipurpose Styles ➤ Code Set Styles, right-click All Codes, and select Edit to display the Code Set Style – All Codes dialog.

10. On the Codes tab, expand the Point branch and find the row for Crown, as shown in Figure 17.11.

As always, you may need to widen some of the columns to view the necessary text.

11. Click the truck icon in the Pay Item column, shown in Figure 17.11, to open the Pay Item List dialog.

12. Expand the Favorites branch, and select Pavement Markings, Type C, Broken.

13. Click OK to return to the Code Set Style – All Codes dialog.

You should see the pay item number of 63401-0600 in the Pay Item column of your dialog.

FIGURE 17.11
Select the Crown row in the Point branch in the Code Set Style – All Codes dialog.

14. Again in the Point branch, find the row for Back_Curb, and repeat steps 11 through 13 to assign 63620-0500 to the Back_Curb code.

    Remember, this is your light-standard pay item with the formula from the previous steps. Your Code Set Style – All Codes dialog should look like Figure 17.12, which lists a pay item for both of these point codes.

FIGURE 17.12
Completed code set editing for pay items

15. Click OK to accept the settings in this dialog.

16. Switch to Prospector and expand the Corridor branch.

17. Right-click North River Crossing and select Properties to open the Corridor Properties dialog.

18. On the Codes tab, expand the Point branch.

Notice that the Back_Curb and Crown codes reflect pay items in the far-right column.

19. Click Cancel to exit the dialog.

When this exercise is complete, you can close the drawing. A saved copy of this drawing is available from the book's web page with the filename 1704_QTOCorridors_FINISHED.dwg or 1704_QTOCorridors_METRIC_FINISHED.dwg.

BEST PRACTICE: STORING A FORMULA FILE WITH THE PROJECT FILES

Every drawing in which you utilize QTO tools is intended to have its own, unique formula file. We recommend that when you create a new formula file, you store it in the same folder as the rest of the project.

If you need to send a drawing to another firm and you want them to have your quantity takeoff formulas, use eTransmit to export everything they need to work with the drawing. You can access the eTransmit command by clicking the Application menu in the upper-left corner and selecting Publish ➤ eTransmit. In the Transmittal Setup, fill in the Include Files from Data Links check box and the eTransmit command will attach the pay item file, the categorization file, and the formula file as part of the transmission.

Corridors can be used to measure a large number of items. You've always been able to manage pure quantities of material, but now you can add to that the ability to measure linear and incremental items as well. Although we didn't explore every option, you can also use link codes to assign pay items to your corridor models. Point codes measure the length of the associated feature line. Link codes measure cumulative area between assemblies.

Now that you've looked at AutoCAD objects and corridors, it's time to examine the pipe network objects in Civil 3D as they relate to pay items.

Pipes and Structures as Pay Items

One of the easiest items to quantify in Civil 3D is the pipe network. There are numerous reports that will generate pipe and structure quantities. This part of the model has always been fairly easy to account for; however, with the ability to include it in the overall QTO reports, it's important to understand how parts get pay items assigned. There are two methods: via the parts lists and via the part properties. These methods can also be applied to pressure network pipes, fittings, and appurtenances.

ASSIGNING PAY ITEMS IN THE PARTS LIST

Ideally, you'll build your model using standard Civil 3D parts lists that you've set up as part of your template. These parts lists contain information about pipe sizes, structure thicknesses, and so on. They can also contain pay item assignments. This means that the pay item property will be assigned as each part is created in the model, skipping the assignment step later.

In this exercise, you'll see how easy it is to modify parts lists to include pay items:

1. Open the `1705_QTOPipeNetworks.dwg` or `1705_QTOPipeNetworks_METRIC.dwg` file.

2. On the Settings tab of Toolspace, expand the Pipe Network ➤ Parts Lists branch.

3. Highlight and right-click Sanitary Sewer and select Edit to display the Network Parts List – Sanitary Sewer dialog.

4. On the Pipes tab, expand the Sanitary Sewer ➤ PVC Pipe (PVC Pipe SI for metric) part family.

   Notice that the far-right column is the Pay Item assignment column.

5. Click the truck icon in the 8-inch PVC (or 200 mm PVC Pipe) row to display the Pay Item List dialog.

6. Turn off categorization and enter **PVC** in the text box, as shown in Figure 17.13, and press ↵ to filter the dialog.

FIGURE 17.13
Filtering and selecting the 8-inch PVC conduit as a pay item

7. Select the CONDUIT, 8-INCH, PVC item (CONDUIT, 200 MM PVC) as shown and click OK to assign this pay item to the applicable pipe part.

8. Repeat steps 4 through 7 to assign pay items to 10- and 12-inch (250 mm and 300 mm) PVC conduits.

   Your dialog should look like Figure 17.14.

FIGURE 17.14
Completed pipe
parts pay item
assignments

9. On the Structures tab of the Networks Parts List dialog, expand the Sanitary Sewer ≻ Concentric Cylindrical Structure branch (or Concentric Cylindrical Structure SI if metric).

10. Click the truck icon on the Concentric Structure row to display the Pay Item List dialog.

11. In the Pay Item List dialog under Favorites, select MANHOLE, SANITARY SEWER, and click OK.

The Network Parts List should now look similar to Figure 17.15.

FIGURE 17.15
Completed struc-
ture parts pay
item assignments

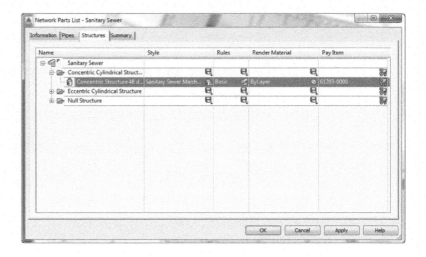

12. Click OK to accept the settings in the Network Parts List.

When this exercise is complete, you can save the drawing and keep it open to continue on to the next exercise. Or you can use the saved copy of this drawing available from the book's web page (1705_QTOPipeNetworks_FINISHED.dwg or 1705_QTOPipeNetworks_METRIC_FINISHED.dwg).

PAY ITEMS AS PART PROPERTIES

If you have existing Civil 3D pipe networks that were built before your parts list had pay items assigned or if you change out a part during your design, you need a way to review and modify the pay items associated with your network. Unfortunately, doing so isn't as simple as just telling Civil 3D to reprocess some data, but it's not too complicated either. You simply remove the pay item associations and then add new ones.

In this exercise, you'll add pay item assignments to a number of parts already in place in the drawing:

1. Continue working in your file, or open the 1705_PipeNetworks_FINISHED.dwg or 1705_QTOPipeNetworks_METRIC_FINISHED.dwg file.

2. If the QTO Manager is not already open, from the Analyze tab ➤ QTO panel choose QTO Manager to open it.

3. Slide the QTO Manager to one side, and then select one of the manholes in the Sanitary Network (they have an S symbol on them).

4. Right-click and choose Select Similar. Fourteen manholes should highlight, as shown in Figure 17.16.

FIGURE 17.16
Use Select Similar to find all sanitary manhole structures.

5. In the QTO Manager, expand Favorites and select MANHOLE, SANITARY SEWER.

6. Click the Assign The Selected Pay Items To Object(s) In The Drawing button.

7. At the command line, press ↵ to complete the assignment.

You can pause your cursor over one of the manholes, and the tooltip will reflect a pay item now, in addition to the typical information found on a manhole.

When this exercise is complete, you may save the drawing and keep it open to continue on to the next exercise. Or you may use the saved copy of this drawing available from the book's web page (1706_QTOPipeNetworks_FINISHED.dwg or 1706_QTOPipeNetworks_METRIC_FINISHED.dwg).

HEADS UP ON PIPE NETWORK AND PRESSURE NETWORK QTO ASSIGNMENTS

Pay items change when network parts change if the new part has a pay item assigned in the parts list. However, if you swap to a part that does not have a pay item assigned, Civil 3D drops the QTO tag.

The best way to keep a proper count of your pipe network or pressure network parts is to make sure every part in your network parts list has an appropriate pay item.

If you graphically change a pipe property (such as its diameter), this will not cause a change in the pay item assignment. You should always use Swap Part to change sizes, as you learned in Chapter 13, "Pipe Networks."

This is something you definitely want to keep an eye on. So, if you do need to change a pay item assignment to a part that's already in the network, how do you do it? You'll find that out in the next section.

Assigning pay items to existing structures and pipes is similar to adding data to standard AutoCAD objects. As mentioned before, the pay item assignments sometimes get confused in the process of changing parts and pipe properties, and they should be manually updated. To do so, you'll need to remove pay item data and then add it back in, as demonstrated in this exercise:

1. Continue working with your file or open the `1706_QTOPipeNetworks_FINISHED.dwg` or `1706_QTOPipeNetworks_METRIC_FINISHED.dwg` file.

2. Pan to the west end of ROAD A where the sanitary sewer network terminates.

3. Pause your cursor over the pipe connected to the structure at the termination of the sewer network.

   The tooltip will appear indicating the pipe information but no pay item, as shown in Figure 17.17.

FIGURE 17.17
Tooltip for a pipe without an assigned pay item

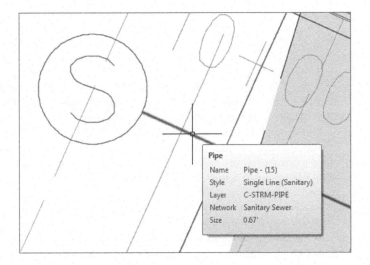

4. Select the pipe, and from the contextual tab ➤ Modify panel, select Swap Part.

   This will display the Swap Part Size dialog.

5. Select 12 Inch PVC (or 300 mm PVC Pipe) from the list of sizes (the original size of pipe—you are not changing the diameter) and then click OK.

6. Pause near the newly sized pipe and notice that the tooltip now shows the pay item, as shown in Figure 17.18.

FIGURE 17.18
Tooltip after the pipe part has been swapped to a part with an assigned pay item

When this exercise is complete, you may close the drawing. A saved copy of this drawing is available from the book's web page with the filename 1707_QTOPipeNetworks_FINISHED.dwg or 1707_QTOPipeNetworks_METRIC_FINISHED.dwg.

You might wonder why Civil 3D allows you to have multiple pay items on a single object. For example, linear feet of striping and tree counts can both be derived from street lengths; bedding and pipe material can both be calculated from pipe objects. You can also add related tasks to an item. For instance, a tree is usually a pay item by itself, but the labor to install the tree may be treated as a separate pay item.

You've now built up a list of pay items, tagged your drawing a number of ways, updated and modified pay item data, and looked at formulas in pay items. In the next section, you'll make a final check of your assignments before running reports.

Highlighting Pay Items

Before you run any reports, it's a good idea to make a cursory pass through your drawing and look at what items have had pay items assigned and what items have not. This review will allow you to ideally catch missing items (such as hydrants added after the pay item assignment was done) as well as see any items that perhaps were blocked in with unnecessary pay items already assigned. In this exercise, you'll look at tools for highlighting objects with and without pay item assignments:

1. Open the 1708_QTOHighlighting.dwg or 1708_QTOHighlighting_METRIC.dwg file.

2. From the Analyze tab ➢ QTO panel, choose QTO Manager to display the QTO Manager.

3. In the QTO Manager, select Highlight Objects With Pay Items, as shown in Figure 17.19.

FIGURE 17.19
Turning on high-
lighting for objects
with pay items
assigned

Notice that from this same drop-down menu you can also choose Highlight Objects Without Pay Items, Highlight Objects With Selected Pay Items, or Clear Highlight.

4. Pan around the drawing and zoom in on the trees at the intersection of ROAD A and ROAD B.

5. In the QTO Manager, select Highlight Objects Without Pay Items.

Notice that the trees turn from green to muted gray. This means they have a pay item assigned.

6. In the QTO Manager, switch back to Highlight Objects With Pay Items.

Next, you will change the pay item assignment for the trees at the intersection of ROAD A and ROAD B since the planner has decided to use a different tree type.

7. In the QTO Manager, click the Remove Pay Item(s) From Specified Objects button.

8. At the Select object(s): prompt, select five of the trees near the intersection and press ↵ to end the command.

Notice that the trees go from green to a muted gray, indicating that they no longer have a pay item associated since the highlighting is enabled.

9. In the QTO Manager, enter **Maple** in the text box to filter.

10. Turn the categorization option off to more easily see the filtered results.

11. Select item 62601-0100.

12. Click the Assign The Selected Pay Items To Objects In The Drawing button.

13. At the Select pay item(s) from master pay item list or [Enter]: prompt, press ↵.

14. At the Select object(s): prompt, select the same five trees that you just unassigned pay items from and press ↵ to end the command.

Notice that the trees go from a muted gray to green, indicating that they once again have pay items associated with them since the highlighting is enabled.

Unassigning and then reassigning a pay item may seem cumbersome. Instead, you may find it simpler to edit the pay item.

15. In the QTO Manager, click the Edit Pay Items On Specified Object button.

16. At the Select object(s): prompt, select the remaining tree near the intersection to display the Edit Pay Items dialog.

17. Select the FAGUS GRANDIFLORIA row and then click the red X in the upper right to remove this pay item from the tree, as shown in Figure 17.20.

FIGURE 17.20
Editing pay item assignments: deleting the tree pay item

18. Click the plus sign in the upper right to display the Pay Item List dialog in order to add a new pay item to the tree.

19. Enter **Maple** in the text box to filter.

20. Select item 62601-0100 and click OK.

21. Click OK to accept the new pay item designation shown in the Edit Pay Items dialog.

22. In the QTO Manager, select Highlight Objects Without Pay Items from the drop-down menu shown previously in Figure 17.19.

    This switches the highlighting from objects that do have pay items to objects that do not have pay items.

23. In the QTO Manager, select Clear Highlight to return the drawing view to normal.

When this exercise is complete, you may close the drawing. A saved copy of this drawing is available from the book's web page with the filename 1708_QTOHighlighting_FINISHED.dwg or 1708_QTOHighlighting_METRIC_FINISHED.dwg.

While highlighting objects with QTO Manager, you can add, remove, or edit pay items using the tools at the top of the QTO Manager. You can leave the objects highlighted while performing any other AutoCAD command. This makes it easier to correct any mistakes made during the assignment phase of the process. Finally, always be sure to clear highlighting before exiting the drawing or your peers might wind up awfully confused when they open the file!

Inventorying Your Pay Items

At the end of the process, you need to generate some sort of report that shows the pay items in the model, the quantities of each item, and the units of measurement. This data can be used as part of the plan set in some cases, but it's often requested in other formats to make further analysis possible. In this exercise, you'll look at the Quantity Takeoff tool that works in conjunction with the QTO Manager to create reports:

1. Open the `1709_QTOReporting.dwg` or `1709_QTOReporting_METRIC.dwg` file.

2. From the Analyze tab ➢ QTO panel, choose Takeoff to display the Compute Quantity Takeoff dialog, shown in Figure 17.21.

FIGURE 17.21
The Compute
Quantity Takeoff
dialog with default
settings

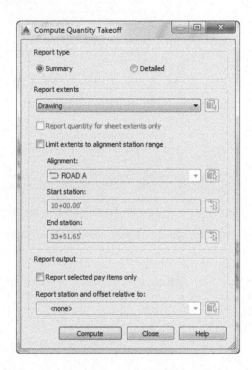

LIMITING THE REPORT EXTENTS

Note that you can limit the report extents by drawing, by sheets if done from paperspace, by selection set, or by alignment station ranges. Most of the time, you'll want to run the full drawing. You can set the report output for only selected pay items if, for instance, you just want a table of pipe and structures.

---

3. Click Compute to open the Quantity Takeoff Report dialog, as shown in Figure 17.22.

FIGURE 17.22
Quantity Takeoff
Report in the
default XSL format

The report is shown in the default Extensible Stylesheet Language (XSL) format.

4. From the drop-down menu on the lower left of the dialog, select Summary (TXT).xsl to change the format to something more understandable, as shown in Figure 17.23.

FIGURE 17.23
Quantity Takeoff
Report in the
Summary TXT
format

At this point, you can export this data as a text file, but for the purpose of this exercise, you'll simply insert it into the drawing.

5. Click the Draw button at the bottom of the dialog.

6. At the `Select report table origin:` prompt, click near some clear space, and you'll be returned to the Quantity Takeoff Report dialog.

7. Click Close to dismiss this dialog and then click Close again to dismiss the Compute Quantity Takeoff dialog.

8. The program zooms into where you clicked in step 6, and you should see something like Figure 17.24.

FIGURE 17.24

Summary takeoff data inserted into the drawing

```
                              Summary Takeoff Report
                              ----------------------
Pay Item ID    Description                                                  Quantity    Unit
-----------------------------------------------------------------------------------------------
20101-0000     CLEARING AND GRUBBING                                        60.50       ACRE
61106-0000     FIRE HYDRANT                                                 4           EACH
61203-0000     MANHOLE, SANITARY SEWER                                      14          EACH
62601-0100     ACER RUBRUM, RED MAPLE, 1 1/2-INCH TO 2-INCH CALIPER, BALLED AND BURLAPPED  6      EACH
62606-0150     FAGUS GRANDIFLORIA, AMERICAN BEECH, 1 1/2-INCH TO 2-INCH CALIPER, BALLED AND BURLAPPED  58   EACH
63610-3500     CONDUIT, 8-INCH, PVC                                         544.09      LNFT
```

When this exercise is complete, you may close the drawing. A saved copy of this drawing is available from the book's web page with the filename `1709_QTOReporting_FINISHED.dwg` or `1709_QTOReporting_METRIC_FINISHED.dwg`.

That's it! The hard work in preparing QTO data is in assigning the pay items. The reports can be saved to HTML, TXT, or XLS format for use in almost any analysis program.

The Bottom Line

Open and add to a list of pay items. The pay item list is the cornerstone of quantity take-offs. You should download and review your pay item list and compare it against the current reviewing agency list regularly to avoid any missed items.

Master It Using the template of your choice, open the `Getting Started.csv` (or `Getting Started_Metric.csv`) pay item file that you have been working with in the previous exercises and add the 12-, 18-, and 24-Inch Pipe Culvert (or 300 mm, 450 mm, and 600 mm Pipe Culvert) pay items to your Favorites list in the QTO Manager.

Assign pay items to AutoCAD objects and pipe networks. The majority of the work in preparing quantity takeoffs is in assigning pay items accurately. By using the linework, blocks, and Civil 3D objects in your drawing as part of the process, you reduce the effort involved in generating accurate quantities.

Master It Open the `MasteringQTO.dwg` or `MasteringQTO_Metric.dwg` file and assign the CLEARING AND GRUBBING pay item to the polyline that was originally extracted from the border of the corridor. Change the hatch to have a transparency of 80.

Use QTO tools to review what items have been tagged for analysis. By using the built-in highlighting tools to verify pay item assignments, you can avoid costly errors when running your QTO reports.

Master It Verify that the area in the previous exercise has been assigned a pay item.

Generate QTO output to a variety of formats for review or analysis. The quantity takeoff reports give you a quick understanding of what items have been tagged in the drawing, and they can generate text in the drawing or external reports for uses in other applications.

Master It Display the length of Type C Broken markings in a Quantity Takeoff Report with the Summary (TXT) report style using the `MasteringQTOReporting.dwg` or `MasteringQTOReporting_Metric.dwg` file.

Chapter 18

Label Styles

The creation of proper styles and settings can make or break your experience with Autodesk® AutoCAD® Civil 3D® software. Styles control the display properties of Civil 3D objects and labels. Understanding and applying styles correctly can mean the difference between getting a job out in several hours and fighting with your project drawing for days.

This chapter is organized by style type. First, read the chapter to be introduced to the style concepts in a logical manner. Later, when you use this chapter as a reference to build styles, you will likely jump around to the examples that meet your needs.

In this chapter, you will learn to:

◆ Override individual labels with other styles.

◆ Create a new label set for alignments.

◆ Create and use expressions.

◆ Apply a standard label set to profiles.

Label Styles

The best design in the universe is not worth anything unless it is labeled properly. Civil 3D labels are smart objects that are dynamically linked to the object they are labeling. Civil 3D labeling is customizable to fit your design needs and local requirements.

When talking about labels in Civil 3D, keep in mind that you are not just dealing with text. Labels can contain lines and blocks if desired. Label styles control the plotted height, contents, and precision of text. They also control how leaders are applied when the label is dragged away from its initial position. You will even work with some labels that contain no text at all!

General Labels

Certification Objective

On the Settings tab, you'll see a complete list of objects that Civil 3D uses to build its design model. Each of them has special features unique to the object being described, but there are some common features as well. The General collection contains settings and styles that are applied to various objects across the entire product.

The General collection serves as the catchall for styles that apply to multiple objects and for settings that apply to *no* objects. For instance, the Civil 3D General Note object doesn't really belong with the Surface or Pipe collection. It can be used to relate information about those objects, but because it can also relate to something like "Don't Dig Here!" or a northing-easting of an arbitrary location, it falls into the General category.

The Label Styles collection allows Civil 3D users to place general text notes or label single entities while still taking advantage of the flexibility and scaling properties. The various label styles shown in Figure 18.1 can give you some idea of their uses.

FIGURE 18.1
Line label styles

Label styles are a critical part of producing plans with Civil 3D. In this chapter, you'll learn how to build a new basic label and explore some of the common components that appear in every label style throughout the product.

Frequently Seen Tabs

To get into a label style, find the appropriate label type in the Settings tab of Toolspace. The Settings tab is organized into object collections. For each of the objects that can be labeled, the Label Styles branch will organize its labels based on their function, which makes it easy to find the label style you need to edit. When you locate the desired label style, right-click the style to display Label Style menu options:

Edit Opens the label style for modification

New Copies the label style as a child style, a style that inherits its settings from a parent

Copy Creates a duplicate label style

Delete Erases the label style. Visible only if the style is not is use.

Find References Visible only if label style is in use. Searches settings and objects and lists where label styles are in use. The result of the search is displayed in a References dialog box.

Replace With Visible only if label style is in use. Finds a label style in use in the drawing and replaces it with another.

All styles, regardless of type, have a few things in common:

Information Tab The Information tab, shown in Figure 18.2, controls the name of the style.

FIGURE 18.2
The Information
tab exists for all
object and label
styles.

If desired, you can create a description. This information will appear as a tooltip as you browse through the Settings tab.

On the right side of the dialog, you will see the name of the person who originally created the style, the date when it was created, and the last person who modified the style. These names are initially pulled from the Windows login information, and only the Created By field can be edited.

General Tab   The General tab (Figure 18.3) contains basic settings for the label style and consists of the following:

Text Style   This option refers to the AutoCAD text style used in the label. Text styles must already be created in the drawing.

Label Visibility   This option allows the label to be not shown even if applied.

Display Mode   This option allows a label to be displayed in either a Label mode or a Tag mode. This setting is available only for label styles of specific object types including lines, curves, parcels, and alignments.

Layer   In Chapter 1, "The Basics," you learned that the Object Layer tab in the Drawing Settings dialog is where you configure insertion layers for object types, labels, and tables. Freezing an object layer will, of course, make any object contained on that layer disappear. The Layer setting here on the General tab allows you to specify a layer that will override the layer properties of the object layer and also add another layer for controlling visibility of specific label types. For example, the object layer for alignment labels could be set to C-ALIGN-LABL. However, Major Station label styles could be configured to place the label on C-ROAD-STAN-MAJR. When C-ALIGN-LABL is frozen, all alignment labels disappear. When C-ROAD-STAN-MAJR is frozen, only Major Station labels disappear. If this setting is left set to layer 0, then the label using this style will default to the object layer display properties.

FIGURE 18.3
The General tab

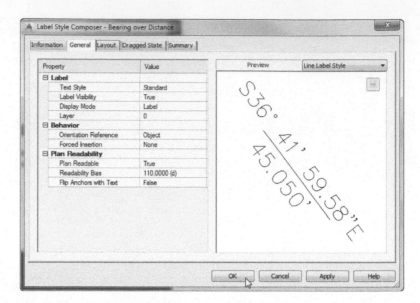

Orientation Reference This option controls how text rotation is controlled. Figure 18.4a shows the label aligned with the object. Figure 18.4b shows the text rotated to the view. Even though the view has been rotated, the text still appears parallel with the bottom of the screen. The last, and least used, option for orientation reference is the World Coordinate System option, which is shown in Figure 18.4c. The view is rotated, and the direction of the text rotates with the World Coordinate System.

FIGURE 18.4
Orientation reference options set to Object (a), View (b), and World Coordinate System (c)

(a)

(b)

(c)

Forced Insertion   This option makes more sense in other objects and will be explored further. The Forced Insertion feature allows you to dictate the insertion point of a label on the basis of the object being labeled. Figure 18.5 shows the effects of the various options on a bearing and distance label.

FIGURE 18.5
Forced Insertion options for parcel segments

Plan Readable   When this option is enabled, text maintains the up direction in spite of view rotation. Rotating 100 labels is a tedious, thankless task, and this option handles it automatically.

Readability Bias   This option specifies the angle at which readability kicks in. This angle is measured from the 0 degree of the x-axis that is common to AutoCAD angle measurements. When a piece of text goes past the readable bias angle, the text flips 180 degrees to maintain vertical orientation, as shown in Figure 18.6. The default Readability angle is 110. A common desired default is 90.1, which would flip any text just after passing a vertical direction.

FIGURE 18.6
Plan-readable text shown on contours; note the difference in direction for the true and false settings (PR = Plan Readable).

Flip Anchors With Text Most users leave this setting at its default, False, and never give it another thought. Figure 18.7a shows what happens to the text insertion points when this option is set to False and readability kicks in. The SW bearing is followed by its distance as originally configured. Readability has been applied to the NW bearing because it was configured to be oriented to the object it is labeling.

FIGURE 18.7
Flip Anchors With
Text when read-
ability kicks in
set to False (a); set
to True (b)

(a)

(b)

Without readability, the label would be upside down. Distance and bearing have been flipped individually so it appears the two values are out of order. When this setting is set to True, the distance text flips to the other side of the bearing, as shown in Figure 18.7b. You'll have the opportunity to work with this setting in a later exercise.

Layout Tab Each label can be made up of several components. A Label component can be text, a block, or a line. Depending on the type of label style, other options can include Reference Text, Ticks (station labels), Direction Arrow (line labels), or Text For Each (structure styles only). The top row of buttons controls the selection, creation, and deletion of these components, as shown in Figure 18.8.

Component Name From the Component Name drop-down, choose the component you want to modify. The components are listed in the order in which they were created. When you make changes to properties on the Layout tab, pay attention to which component is active. Any changes you make to the properties will apply only to the active component. It is important to note that in the label's dragged state the displayed order reflects the order in which the components were created.

FIGURE 18.8
The Layout tab

Create Component   The Create Component button lets you add new components to enhance your labels. A component can be Text, Line, Block, Tick, Direction Arrow, Reference Text, or Text For Each. The options will vary depending on the object you are labeling. Not every option is available in every label. For example, Text For Each is available only in structure labels.

The ability to label one object while referencing another (reference text) is one of the most powerful labeling features of Civil 3D. This is what allows you to label a spot elevation for both an existing and a proposed surface at the same time, using the same label. Alignments, COGO points, parcels, profiles, surfaces, and survey figures can all be used as reference text. Text For Each is a type of component that can label properties of connected pipes in a structure label. Note that not all label styles include reference text.

Copy Component   The Copy Component button copies the component currently selected in the Component Name drop-down. This will be helpful when you're creating label styles that contain multiple pieces of similar information.

Delete Component   The Delete Component button deletes components. Components that are configured as anchors for other components can be deleted, but you will receive a warning. Table tag components, found in curve, line, alignment segment, and parcel segment labels, cannot be deleted.

Component Draw Order The Component Draw Order button lets you shuffle components up and down within the label. This feature is especially important when you're using masks or borders as part of the label.

Once a component is added, the component properties can be addressed one by one by starting at the top and working your way down to the bottom of the dialog. There are three groups of property types: General, Text, and Border.

The General properties consist of the following:

Name This option defines the name used in the Component Name drop-down and when selecting other components for anchor components. Once a component is configured as an anchor component, the name cannot be changed until the reference is removed. When you're building complicated labels, a descriptive name goes a long way.

Visibility When this option is set to True, the component can be seen onscreen. When a component can't be seen, you can do some cool tricks with styles, as you'll see in the "Pipe Labels" section later in this chapter.

Used In This is available for labels of specific elements such as lines, curves, parcels, and alignments. The component can be assigned to be displayed in either Label or Tag mode.

Anchor Component This setting allows you to position the component relative to the feature being labeled or to another component.

Anchor Point The options here may vary depending on the Anchor Component setting. When the feature is being used as an Anchor component, the anchor point can be a location relative to the feature offering combinations of middle, top, and bottom vertical positions with left, right, and center horizontal positions. Line components offer start, middle, and end anchor points. Also note that for specific elements such as points, pipes, and structures, there is an option to set the anchor point to the element's dimension (see the Attachment property on the Layout tab for more on anchor points).

The settings available for text objects as components are found under the Layout tab of the Label Style Composer dialog, as displayed in Figure 18.9.

FIGURE 18.9
The circle and square indicate the places where the anchor point and attachment point are defined.

Property	Value
☐ **General**	
Name	Distance
Visibility	True
Used in	Label Mode
Anchor Component	Bearing
Anchor Point	Top Left ⃝
☐ **Text**	
Contents	<[General Segment Le…
Text Height	0.1500"
Rotation Angle	0.0000 (d)
Attachment	Top center ☐
X Offset	0.0000"
Y Offset	-0.0250"
■ Color	■ BYLAYER
Lineweight	ByLayer
Maximum Width	0.0000"
☐ **Border**	
Visibility	False
Type	Rectangular
Background Mask	True
Gap	0.0250"
■ Color	■ BYLAYER
Linetype	ByBlock
Lineweight	ByLayer

The Text properties consist of the following:

Contents   This is where the information contained in the label is composed. Click the Value field to reveal an ellipsis. If the ellipsis is clicked, the Text Component Editor dialog opens to where property fields and text can be configured. Also under the Text Component Editor you can find a Format tab that allows you to apply text justification and override the font used in the style.

Text Height   This option determines the plotted height of the label. This setting overrides the height configured in the text style. Regardless of how the text style is configured in the label, text placed by Civil 3D is always annotative. The two viewports in Figure 18.10 show some COGO points along a road. Even when the viewport scales differ, the text is the same size. For a block component this setting will be called Block Height, while for a line component this will be the Line Length.

FIGURE 18.10
Annotative text shown at multiple scales

Rotation Angle, X Offset, and Y Offset   These options give you the ability to adjust the placement of the component by rotating or displacing the text in an x or y direction. Set your text as close as possible using the anchors and attachments, and use the offsets as additional spacing. If border gap is used, this will affect spacing as well.

Allow Curved Text   This option is available for labeling of curved components (alignment curves) where, if desired, the text can align to the outside or inside of the curve.

Attachment   This option determines which of the nine points on the Label Components bounding box are attached to the anchor point. Figure 18.9 defines the place where this setting can be changed, while Figure 18.11 illustrates the relationship between the anchor points and attachments.

FIGURE 18.11
Schematic show-
ing the relation-
ship between
anchor points
(circles) and attach-
ments (squares)

Color and Lineweight   These options allow you to override the color and lineweight assigned by the layer configured on the General tab.

Maximum Width   Some labels can be rather lengthy. Instead of letting the Label component continue indefinitely across the page, you can use Maximum Width to force word wrap after a specified plotted length. The default setting of 0.00 will not force word wrap.

Note that lines and blocks have different components such as length type, fixed length, and so on.

The Border properties consist of the following:

Visibility   Use this option to turn the border on and off for the component. Remember that component borders shrink to the individual component; if you're using multiple components in a label, each will have its own Border component.

Type   This option allows you to select a rectangle, a rounded rectangle (slot), or a circle border. Figure 18.12 shows examples of the three types of borders.

FIGURE 18.12
Border types
shown on vari-
ous surface label
styles.

Background Mask   This option lets you determine whether linework and text behind this component are masked. This option can be handy for construction notes in place of the usual wipeout tools. The surface labels in Figure 18.12 show the background mask in action.

Gap   This option determines the offset from the Component bounding box to the outer points on the border. Setting this to half of the text size usually creates a visually pleasing border.

Color, Linetype, and Lineweight   These options allow you to override the display properties assigned by the layer configured on the General tab.

Dragged State Tab   Typically, dragging a label in Civil 3D creates a leader and rearranges the text. The settings that control these two actions appear on this tab (see Figure 18.13).

FIGURE 18.13
The Dragged State tab

Many of the property types found on this tab appeared on the Layout tab, so they don't need to be defined again. There are two groups of property types: Leader and Dragged State Components.

Settings found in the Leader properties sections include the following:

Arrow Head Style   This allows you to set the appearance of the leader. The same Arrow Head styles that appear in Dimension styles are available in Dragged State.

Arrow Head Size   This setting controls the length of the arrow head as well as the length of the landing leading to the text object.

Type   This option specifies the leader type. The options are Straight Leader and Spline Leader. Civil 3D labels can have only one leader.

Settings for Color, Linetype, Lineweight, and Visibility that are found in the Leader section apply only to the leader, not the component itself.

Settings found in the Dragged State Component properties include the following:

Display   In this option, you can choose Stacked Text or As Composed. The Stacked Text option will remove any blocks, ticks, lines, dimensions, or borders that are components of the label, and it will stack the Text components as a list in the order in which they were created, realign the text to horizontal, and justify based on the direction you drag. The As Composed option leaves blocks, ticks, lines, text, dimensions, or borders intact, and it adds a leader next to the attached component that is anchored to the feature.

Text Height Text Height was mentioned for the previous setting. However, there is a separate setting for Text Height when in dragged state and the label style Display property is configured to Stacked Text.

Leader Attachment When the label style Display property is configured to Stacked Text, this property sets the location of the landing relative to the top line, bottom line, or middle of the stacked text.

Leader Justification When the label style Display property is configured to Stacked Text, this property determines if and how text is justified. When set to True and the leader is to the left of the text, the text will be left justified; when set to True and the leader is to the right of the text, the text will be right justified. When set to False, the leader is always left justified.

Maximum Text Width This property works in the same way as Maximum Width on the Layout tab.

Figure 18.14a shows an alignment label as it was originally placed. Figure 18.14b shows the same label in a dragged state with the Stacked Text option set. Figure 18.14c shows the label in a dragged state with the As Composed option set.

FIGURE 18.14
An alignment label
as originally placed
(a); dragged state,
Stacked Text (b);
and dragged state,
As Composed (c)

```
ALIGNMENT=BOURBON STREET
STATION=2+70.18
OFFSET=90.68L
NORTHING=2006.37
EASTING=889.94
```

(a)

```
ALIGNMENT=BOURBON STREET
STATION=2+70.18
OFFSET=90.68L
NORTHING=2006.37
EASTING=889.94
```

(b)

```
ALIGNMENT=BOURBON STREET
STATION=2+70.18
OFFSET=90.68L
NORTHING=2006.37
EASTING=889.94
```

(c)

Summary Tab   The Summary tab is exactly what it sounds like—that is, a summary of all other settings that exist in the style. Figure 18.15 shows the information from other tabs in list form, as well as their override status.

FIGURE 18.15
The Summary tab
of a label style

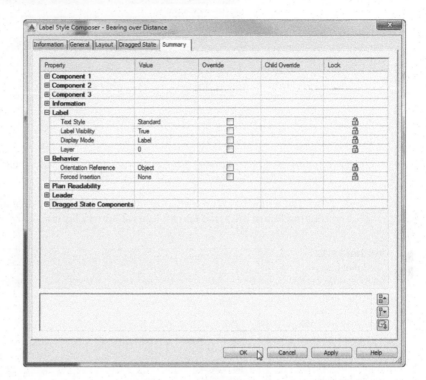

As with other settings in Civil 3D, a hierarchy helps determine which styles take precedence over other styles. There are also defaults that can be set or changed at a drawing-wide level and overridden at an object level. Make sure to put some thought into using these hierarchical settings and relationships. By using them efficiently, you can save a lot of time because you won't need to tweak every setting in each label you create—and you will be creating many labels.

In this first exercise, you will set all the labels to use the same initial text style:

1. Open the drawing `1801_LabelBasics.dwg` (`1801_LabelBasics_METRIC.dwg`), which you can download from this book's web page at `www.sybex.com/go/masteringcivil3d2016`.

2. From the Settings tab of Toolspace, right-click the name of the drawing and select Edit Label Style Defaults, as shown in Figure 18.16.

FIGURE 18.16
Accessing the global label settings

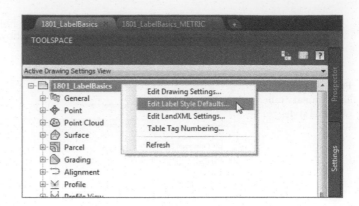

3. Expand the Label category and, clicking within the Value cell and clicking the ellipsis button, change Text Style to Arial. Click OK.

4. Click the white arrow in the Child Override column to force all the label styles in this drawing to use the same text style, as shown in Figure 18.17.

FIGURE 18.17
The label placement options at the drawing level. Note the Child Override arrow with a red X, which means that this change will be applied to all existing styles in the drawing

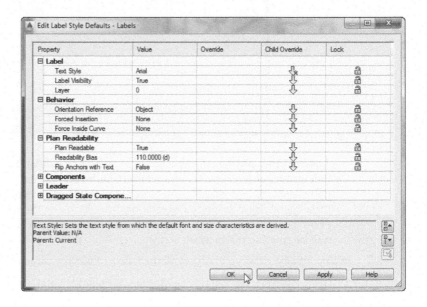

5. Do not make any more changes to this dialog. Examine the various options and settings and click OK.

6. Keep the drawing open for the next exercise.

GETTING TO KNOW THE TEXT COMPONENT EDITOR

The Text Component Editor dialog is where you can combine property fields from objects with static text to create dynamic object labels. The interface is logical and will do exactly what you tell it to do—but not necessarily what you *want* it to do. However, after you see the reasoning behind its behavior, you will soon master it!

To enter the Text Component Editor dialog, from the Layout tab of any text style, click the ellipsis that pops up when you click the Value column of the Text Contents area.

Within the Text Component Editor dialog, the Properties tab has two main areas:

◆ The left side is where you select the Property field of the Civil 3D object you want to pull into your label.

◆ The right side indicates the fields and static text already in the label.

To modify an existing Property field, highlight the field on the right side of the dialog. Property values will always highlight as a unit. Each code in the label represents a setting for units, precision, or other format the text can display. What appears on the left is a decoded list of what is currently highlighted on the right. After you make any changes, don't forget to click the white arrow to update the information on the right.

Before adding new text to a label, make sure that no existing text is highlighted on the right, so you won't overwrite it.

Continues

Continued

The Properties list shows everything that can be included in the label; therefore, depending on the object and label type you are working with, the contents of the list will vary. Here you see some of the available properties for an alignment major station label.

Once you select a Property field, you can configure the units, precision, and any other special rounding or formatting you would like to see.

When everything is set, click the white arrow next to the Properties list.

The Format tab is used to add special symbols or override the color, justification, or font.

Inevitably, you will forget to click the white arrow that adds or updates the text. You may even click it twice and end up with duplicates! Now that you've been given the heads-up, you'll be able to laugh it off, knowing that it happens to even the most seasoned users.

General Note Labels

General Note labels are versatile, non-object-specific labels that can be placed anywhere in the drawing. There are several advantages to using these instead of base AutoCAD Mtext. Notes will leader and scale the same as the rest of your Civil 3D labels—and best of all, they can contain reference text.

Continuing with the previous exercise, you'll create an alternative parcel label that contains reference text.

1. Continue working in 1801_LabelBasics.dwg (1801_LabelBasics_METRIC.dwg). You need to have completed the previous exercise before continuing with this one.

2. From the Settings tab of Toolspace, expand General ➤ Label Styles ➤ Note.

3. Right-click Note and select New (as shown in Figure 18.18).

FIGURE 18.18
Creating your first new label style from the Settings tab

4. On the Information tab, name the style **Easement Parcel Text**.

5. On the General tab, set Layer to C-PROP-TEXT and set Orientation Reference to View.

6. On the Layout tab, click the Value field next to Contents under the Text category.

   Clicking this will cause an ellipsis button to appear.

7. Click the ellipsis button to enter the Text Component Editor dialog.

8. On the right side of the Text Component Editor dialog, delete the existing text and replace it with **Drainage Easement**, as shown in Figure 18.19. Click OK.

FIGURE 18.19
Entering the Text Component Editor dialog for basic text

9. Back in the Layout tab, set Border Visibility to False.

10. Click the flyout next to Create Text Component and select Reference Text.

   You will be prompted to select the type of reference text, as shown in Figure 18.20.

FIGURE 18.20
Picking the refer-
ence type

11. In the Select Type dialog, select Parcel and click OK.

12. Click in the Value field next to Name under the General category, rename Reference Text.1 to **Parcel Area**, and make the following changes:

   a. Set Anchor Component to Text.

   b. Set Anchor Point to Bottom Center.

   c. Set Attachment to Top Center.

   d. To enter the Text Component Editor dialog, click the Value field next to Contents and click the ellipsis.

13. In the Text Component Editor dialog, delete the default label text.

14. On the left side of the Text Component Editor dialog, do the following:

   a. Set the Properties drop-down to Parcel Area.

   b. Set Unit to Acre (Hectare for metric users).

   c. Set Precision to 0.01.

15. When you have set the properties, click the white arrow to place the text in the right side of the editor.

16. Click to place your cursor after the previously inserted text and add a space. Type **ACRES** (or **HECTARES** for metric users) after the coding.

   The Text Component Editor dialog will resemble Figure 18.21. If the text is not centered, you can select the data, and by switching to the Format tab, you can align it to center.

FIGURE 18.21
Adding "smart"
text to the Text
Component Editor
dialog

17. Click OK.

    You will still have question marks in the preview, but this is completely as expected.

18. Set the gap under the border to **0.05"** (**2.00** mm for metric users). Click OK to complete the command.

19. On the Annotate tab ➤ Labels & Tables panel, click the top half of the Add Labels button.

20. With Feature and Label Type both set to Note, change Note Label Style to Easement Parcel Text, and click Add.

21. At the `Pick Label Location:` prompt, click anywhere in the example parcel.

22. At the `Select parcel for label style component Parcel Area:` prompt, click the label on Property : 1.

23. Press Esc to finish placing the labels.

    Your completed and placed label should resemble Figure 18.22.

FIGURE 18.22
Your first label!
Referencing a parcel area.

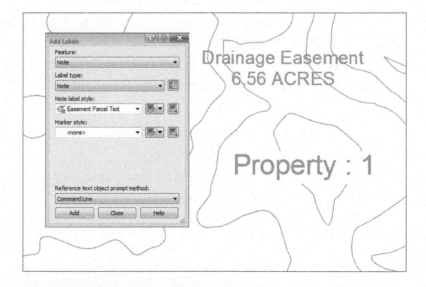

Save and close the drawing. A saved copy of this drawing, with the filename 1801_ LabelBasics_FINISHED.dwg (1801_LabelBasics_METRIC_FINISHED.dwg), is available from the book's web page.

Point Label Styles

Certification
Objective

If you have used other software packages for surveying work, odds are that you controlled the display of point label text with layers, but Civil 3D is different. In Civil 3D, you can control what information is showing next to a point by swapping the label style applied to a group of points.

In the following exercise, you will create a new point label style. Your first point label style will show only Point Number and Description, so you will need to delete the default Elevation component.

1. Open the drawing 1802_PointLabels.dwg (1802_PointLabels_METRIC.dwg), which you can download from this book's web page.

2. From the Settings tab of Toolspace, expand Point ➢ Label Styles.

3. Right-click Label Styles and select New.

4. On the Information tab, name the style **Point Number & Description**.

5. On the General tab, set the layer to V-NODE-TEXT, and leave all other General tab options at their defaults.

6. On the Layout tab, do the following:

    a. Set the Active Component to Point Number.

    b. Change the Anchor Component to <Feature>.

    c. Set Anchor Point to Middle Right.

    d. Set Attachment to Middle Left.

    e. Change the Active Component to Point Elevation.

    f. Click the red X to delete this component.

    You will receive a warning that reads "This label component is used as an anchor in this style or in a child style. Do you want to delete it?"

    g. Click Yes.

    h. Change Active Component to Point Description.

    i. Change Anchor Component to Point Number.

    j. Change Anchor Point to Middle Right.

    k. Change Attachment to Middle Left.

    l. Change X Offset to **0.05"** (1 mm for metric users).

7. Click OK to complete the label style.

8. On the Prospector tab of Toolspace, expand Point Groups branch and locate the point group named TOPO; right-click TOPO and select Properties.

9. On the Information tab, set Point Label Style to **Point Number & Description**.

10. Click OK to close the Point Group.

   All the points in the group will change to resemble Figure 18.23.

FIGURE 18.23
Completed point
label style.

In the previous exercise, you created a simple new label style and made some modifications to the default components. In the following exercise, you will remove all the default components and add Northing and Easting values to the label using the Text Component Editor dialog.

1. Continue working in the drawing 1802_PointLabels.dwg (1802_PointLabels_METRIC .dwg). You need to have completed the previous exercise.

2. From the Settings tab of Toolspace, choose Point ➤ Label Styles.

3. Right-click Label Styles and select New.

4. On the Information tab, name the style **Northing & Easting**.

5. On the General tab, set the layer to V-NODE-TEXT, set Orientation Reference to View, and leave all other General tab options at their defaults.

6. On the Layout tab, do the following:

   a. Click the red X until all three default components are gone.

      For the second component being deleted, you will receive a warning that reads "This label component is used as an anchor in this style or in a child style. Do you want to delete it?"

   b. Click Yes and then delete the last component.

   c. Click the Create Text Component button to create a new Text component and rename the component to **N-E**.

   d. Set Anchor Point to Bottom Center.

   e. Set Attachment to Top Center.

   f. Click the Value field next to Contents and click the ellipsis to enter the Text Component Editor dialog.

7. In the Text Component Editor dialog, do the following:

   a. Highlight the default label text and delete it by pressing the Delete key.

   b. From the Properties list, select Northing.

    c. Set Precision to **0.01** (two decimal places).

    d. Click the white arrow to place the text to the right.

    e. Before the label text, place an **N:** as a static text. Move to the end of the line. Press the Enter key to move to the next line.

    f. From the Properties list, select Easting and set Precision to **0.01** (two decimal places).

    g. Click the white arrow to place the text to the right.

    h. Before the label text, place an **E:** as static text.

The Text Component Editor dialog will now resemble Figure 18.24. If the components are not centered, select the data and from the Format tab align them to center.

FIGURE 18.24
The Northing &
Easting label in
progress

    i. Click OK to dismiss the Text Component Editor dialog, and click OK to complete the style.

8. On the Prospector tab of Toolspace, expand Point Groups branch, locate the point group named Group2; right-click it and select Properties.

9. Set the Point Label Style to **Northing & Easting**, and then click OK.

The labels will resemble Figure 18.25.

FIGURE 18.25
Northing &
Easting in the completed exercise

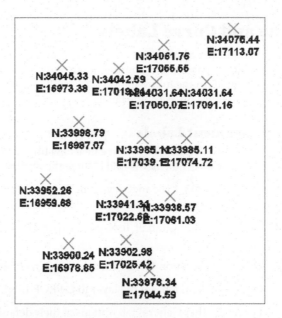

FIGURE 18.25
Northing &
Easting in the completed exercise

Save and close the drawing. A saved copy of this drawing, `1802_PointLabels_FINISHED` `.dwg` (`1802_PointLabels_METRIC_FINISHED.dwg`), is available from the book's web page.

SANITY-SAVING SETTINGS

The Civil 3D template has AutoCAD styles, linetypes, layers, Civil 3D styles, and a plethora of helpful goodies that make doing your job easier. There are a few drawing-specific AutoCAD variables you may not have thought of that will improve your relationship with Civil 3D:

MSLTSCALE   This variable stands for modelspace linetype scale. We strongly recommend you have this set to 1 in your template. This setting makes linetypes react to your annotation scale. All your other Civil 3D objects are doing it, so having your linetypes follow suit will help! A general rule of thumb is that MSLTSCALE, PSLTSCALE, and LTSCALE should be set to 1. For more information on what these control, check out the Help system.

LAYEREVALCTL   Set this to 0 to avoid the annoying pop-up that flags users when there are new layers in a drawing. Civil drafters are constantly using XRefs and inserting blocks, both of which cause the pop-up to occur.

AUNITS   This variable defines the angular units for the base AutoCAD part of the world. Keep this set at 0 (decimal degrees) to help differentiate base AutoCAD angular entry from Civil 3D angular entry.

Line and Curve Labels

You can add bearing and distance labels to many Civil 3D objects. Anything from plain lines and polylines to parcels and alignment tangent segments can use nearly identical label types.

The examples in the following exercises will use parcels for labeling, but the tools can be applied to all other types of line labels.

Single Segment Labels

In the following exercise, you will create a new line label style that uses default components. You will remove the direction arrow and change the display precision of the direction component.

1. Open the 1803_LineandCurveLabels.dwg (1803_LineandCurveLabels_METRIC.dwg) drawing file, which you can download from this book's web page.

2. From the Settings tab of Toolspace, expand Parcel ➤ Label Styles ➤ Line; right-click Line and select New.

3. On the Information tab, name the style **Parcel Segment**.

4. On the General tab, set the layer to C-PROP-LINE-TEXT.

   Leave all other General tab options at their defaults.

5. On the Layout tab, do the following:

   a. Change Active Component to Direction Arrow and click the red X to delete this component.

   b. Change Active Component to Distance.

   c. Click the Value field next to Contents and click the ellipsis to enter the Text Component Editor dialog.

6. In the Text Component Editor dialog, do the following:

   a. Click the text to highlight the Segment Length contents on the right.

      All of the text should highlight as a unit.

   b. On the left side of the Text Component Editor dialog, change the Precision value to **0.01**.

   c. Click the white arrow to update the text.

   d. Click OK to dismiss the Text Component Editor dialog and click OK to complete the style.

7. Select the Annotate tab ➤ Labels & Tables panel and click the top of the Add Labels button to add labels to the parcels. In the Add Labels dialog, do the following:

   a. Set Feature to Parcel.

   b. Set Label Type to Single Segment.

   c. Set Line Label Style to Parcel Segment.

d. Click Add and select for labeling the segments from Parcels 2 and 3.

e. Close the Add Labels dialog and press Esc.

The completed labels will resemble Figure 18.26.

FIGURE 18.26
Your new bearing
and distance line
label style in action
on parcel segments

Compare your drawing at this point against 1803_LineandCurveLabels_A.dwg (1803_LineandCurveLabels_A_METRIC.dwg) if needed.

Spanning Segment Labels

When you look at the labels you created in the previous exercise, you may notice that they stop at each parcel vertex. If there is a series of back lot lines that share the same bearing, most plats show this using a single label outside the overall property line displaying the bearing and the combined distance of these lot lines. To label this in Civil 3D, a separate label style is needed.

Spanning labels can be used in both line and curve parcel labels. In the following exercise, you will create line labels that span multiple parcel segments:

1. Continue working in the finished drawing from the previous exercise or open 1803_LineandCurveLabels_A.dwg (1803_LineandCurveLabels_A_METRIC.dwg).

2. From the Settings tab of Toolspace, expand Parcel ➤ Label Styles ➤ Line, right-click Parcel Segment, and select Copy.

3. On the Information tab, name the style **Parcel Spanning Segment**.

4. On the General tab, under Plan Readability, change Readability Bias to **90.1** and change Flip Anchors With Text to True.

5. On the Layout tab, do the following:

   a. Change Active Component to Table Tag.

   b. Change the Span Outside Segments setting to True.

   c. Change Active Component to Bearing.

  d. Change the Span Outside Segments setting to True.

  e. Change the Active Component name to Distance.

  f. Change Anchor Component to Bearing.

  g. Change Anchor Point to Bottom Right.

  h. Change the Span Outside Segments setting to True.

  i. Change Attachment Point to Bottom Left.

  j. Change the X Offset to **0.2"** (**3 mm** for metric users) and make sure that the Y Offset is set to 0.

 6. Click OK to complete the style.

 7. Using a technique similar to the one you used in the previous exercise, add a spanning label to the parcels along the east side of the right-of-way just north of Parcel 3. This time use Spanning Segment as the line label style. Your completed label will resemble Figure 18.27.

FIGURE 18.27
Spanning label shown on the outside of parcel segments

Compare your drawing at this point against 1803_LineandCurveLabels_B.dwg (1803_LineandCurveLabels_B_METRIC.dwg) if needed.

When you place spanning labels on segments, the Distance component must be forced to the outside of the parcel line. You may need to use the Flip Label command on occasion to move the Distance component to the right location. To access the Flip Label command, select the label and then click the contextual tab ➢ Modify panel.

Curve Labels

In base AutoCAD, creating curve labels is a chore. If you want text to align to curved objects, you won't be able to use it as traditional Mtext. Luckily, Civil 3D gives you the ability to add curved text without compromising its usability.

In the following exercise, you will create a curve label style with a delta symbol (Δ) and text that curves with the parcel segment:

1. Continue working in the finished drawing from the previous exercise or open 1803_ LineandCurveLabels_B.dwg (1803_LineandCurveLabels_B_METRIC.dwg). You need to have completed the previous exercise to continue.

2. From the Settings tab of Toolspace, expand Parcels ➤ Label Styles ➤ Curve, right-click Curve, and select New.

3. On the Information tab, rename the style to **Delta Length & Radius**.

4. On the General tab, set Layer to C-PROP-LINE-TEXT.

5. On the Layout tab, do the following:

    a. Change Active Component to Distance And Radius.

    b. Click the Value field next to Contents and click the ellipsis to enter the Text Component Editor dialog.

    c. Highlight the segment length property on the right and change the precision to **0.01**.

    d. Click the white arrow to update the style.

    e. Highlight the Segment Radius property and change the precision to **0.01**.

    f. Click the white arrow to update the text.

    g. Delete the comma that appears as static text in the Text Component Editor dialog and click OK.

6. Click the Create Text Component button and do the following:

    a. Rename the new text component to **Delta**.

    b. Change Attachment to Bottom Center.

    c. Change the Y Offset to **0.025"** (**1** mm for metric users).

    d. Set Allow Curved Text to True.

7. In the Contents field, click the ellipsis button to bring up the Text Component Editor dialog and do the following:

    a. Remove the default label text.

    b. Switch to the Format tab, click the Symbol button, and select Other.

       You should now see the Character Map dialog (Figure 18.28).

FIGURE 18.28
Browse for special symbols using the Windows character map.

c. Browse through the symbols of the dialog to find the delta symbol; when you locate it, click the symbol, click the Select button, and then click Copy. Click the red X to close the Character Map dialog.

d. Back in the Text Component Editor dialog, click the right side of the dialog, right-click, and select Paste.

e. Press the Backspace key if the cursor jumps to the next line of text.

   You should see the delta symbol appear in the Text Component Editor dialog.

f. Enter the equals sign (=) as static text after the delta.

g. Switch back to the Properties tab.

h. From the Properties drop-down, select Segment Delta Angle, and do the following:

   ◆ Set Format to DD°MM'SS.SS".

   ◆ Set the Precision value to **1 Second.**

   ◆ Click the white arrow to place the text in the right side.

   ◆ Click OK to exit the Text Component Editor dialog.

8. Click OK to complete the style.

9. Add labels to Parcel 1 using the same technique you used in the previous exercise.

   Remember to make sure that your style selection is set correctly for both the curve and line before adding labels.

10. Set the active curve label style to Delta Length & Radius and add labels to some curves. If labels overlap, drag one of the labels by selecting it and then pick the square-shaped grip and drag it to a new location.

When it is applied to the design, your completed label should resemble Figure 18.29.

FIGURE 18.29
Completed curve
labels with delta
symbol and curved
text

Save and close the drawing. A saved copy of this drawing, 1803_LineandCurveLabels_
FINISHED.dwg (1803_LineandCurveLabels_METRIC_FINISHED.dwg), is available from the
book's web page.

Pipe and Structure Labels

No two municipalities seem to label their pipes and sewer structures exactly the same way.
Fortunately, Civil 3D offers a lot of flexibility in how you label these items.

Pipe Labels

Pipe labels have three separate label types: Plan Profile, Crossing Section, and the recently introduced Crossing Profile. All these label types have many of the same options, but those options
are used in different view directions for some of them.

In the following exercise, you will use a common trick. When a nonvisible component acts as
an anchor to visible objects, you can use the flow direction arrow to force text to be placed at the
ends and middle of the pipe regardless of the pipe length.

1. Open the 1804_PipeandStructureLabels.dwg (1804_PipeandStructureLabels_
METRIC.dwg) drawing file, which you can download from this book's web page.

2. From the Settings tab of Toolspace, expand Pipe ➢ Label Styles ➢ Plan Profile; then
right-click Plan Profile and select New.

3. On the Information tab, name the style **Length Diameter Slope**.

4. On the General tab, set the layer to C-STRM-TEXT.

5. On the Layout tab, delete the existing Pipe Text component by clicking the red X.

6. Expand the Create Component drop-down and select Flow Direction Arrow; then adjust
these settings:

   a. Set Visibility to False.

   b. Set Anchor Point to Top Outer Diameter.

    c. Set a Y offset of **0.1″** (**0.3** mm).

7. Expand the Create Component drop-down and select Text. Change these settings:

    a. Rename Text Component to **Length**.

    b. Set Anchor Component to Flow Direction Arrow.1.

    c. Set Anchor Point to Start.

    d. Set Attachment to Bottom Left.

8. In the Contents field, click the ellipsis button to bring up the Text Component Editor dialog and do the following:

    a. Delete the default label text.

    b. From the Properties drop-down list, set 2D Length – Center to Center current.

    c. Set Precision to **1** and Rounding to round up. This causes the pipe length value to round to the next-highest whole unit.

    d. Click the white arrow to place the text in the editor.

    e. Add a foot symbol (or **m** for meters) after the text component.

    f. Click OK.

9. With Length as the current component, click Copy Component. Then change these settings:

    a. Rename the text component to **Diameter**.

    b. Change Anchor Point to Middle.

    c. Change Attachment to Bottom Center.

10. Enter the Text Component Editor dialog and do the following:

    a. Delete all of the text.

    b. From the Properties drop-down list, select Inner Pipe Diameter.

    c. Set the Precision to **1** and click the white arrow to add the text.

    d. Add the inch symbol (or **mm** for millimeters) after the text component.

    e. Click OK to exit the Text Component Editor dialog.

11. With Diameter as the current component, click Copy Component. Then change these settings:

    a. Rename the text component to **Slope**.

    b. Set Anchor Point to End.

    c. Set Attachment to Bottom Right.

12. Enter the Text Component Editor dialog and do the following:

    a. Delete all of the text.

    b. Set Pipe Slope as the current property in the drop-down list.

    c. Click the white arrow to add the text.

    d. Click OK to exit the Text Component Editor dialog.

13. Click OK to complete the style.

14. Add the label to the pipe by doing the following:

    a. On the Annotate tab ➢ Labels & Tables panel, click the top half of the Add Labels button.

    b. Set the Feature option drop-down to Pipe Network and Label Type to Single Part Plan.

    c. Set Pipe Label Style to Length Diameter Slope.

    d. Click Add. Select any pipe in plan view.

Your labeled pipe will resemble Figure 18.30.

FIGURE 18.30
Use the invisible arrow trick to label pipe

Compare your drawing at this point against 1804_PipeandStructureLabels_A.dwg (1804_PipeandStructureLabels_A_METRIC.dwg) if needed.

Structure Labels

Structure labels are unique because they possess a special component that references information from each connected pipe, allowing you to place pipe properties in structure labels. Examples would be pipe invert, pipe direction (NE, SW, and so on), and flow direction (in or out).

🌐 Real World Scenario

ADDING EXISTING GROUND ELEVATION TO STRUCTURE LABELS

In design situations, it's often desirable to track not only the structure rim elevation at finished grade but also the elevation at existing ground. This gives the designer an additional tool for optimizing the earthwork balance.

This exercise will lead you through creating a structure label that includes surface-reference text. It assumes you're familiar with Civil 3D label composition in general:

1. Continue working in the finished drawing from the previous exercise since you need to have it completed for this exercise or open `1804_PipeandStructureLabels_A.dwg` (`1804_PipeandStructureLabels_A_METRIC.dwg`).

2. From the Settings tab of Toolspace, expand Structure ➤ Label Styles; then right-click Label Styles and select New.

3. In the Label Style Composer dialog, do the following:

   a. On the Information tab, name the label **Structure w Surface**.

   b. On the General tab, set the layer to C-STRM-TEXT.

   c. On the Layout tab is a default Text component called Structure Text. Set the Y offset to **-0.25"** (**-1** mm).

4. Click in the Contents value box; then click the ellipsis to bring up the Text Component Editor dialog and do the following:

   a. Delete the `<[Description(CP)]>` text string.

   b. Set the Properties drop-down to Name and click the white arrow.

   c. Place the cursor after the new Property field. Press the Enter key to move to the next line and then type **RIM** with a space after it.

   d. Set the Properties drop-down to Insertion Rim Elevation, set Precision to two decimal places, and click the white arrow.

   e. Click OK to dismiss the Text Component Editor dialog.

5. In the Label Style Composer, choose Reference Text from the Create Component drop-down.

6. In the Select Type dialog, choose Surface and then click OK.

7. Rename the component from Reference Text.1 to **Existing Ground**.

8. Enter the Text Component Editor dialog and do the following:

   a. Delete the Label Text string.

   b. Type **EG** and a space in the text window.

   c. Use the Properties drop-down to select Surface Elevation.

   d. Set Precision to **0.01**.

   e. Click the white arrow.

   f. Click OK to dismiss the Text Component Editor dialog.

9. In the Label Style Composer, do the following:

   a. Change Anchor Component For Existing Ground to Structure Text.

   b. Change Anchor Point to Bottom Center.

   c. Change Attachment to Top Center.

10. Choose the Text For Each option from the Create Component drop-down.

11. In the Select Type dialog, choose Structure All Pipes and then click OK.

12. Enter the Text Component Editor dialog and do the following:

   a. Delete the default Label Text string.

   b. Type **INV** and a space in the text window.

   c. Use the Properties drop-down to select Connected Pipe Invert Elevation.

   d. Set Precision to **0.01**.

   e. Click the white arrow.

   f. Click OK to dismiss the Text Component Editor dialog.

13. In the Label Style Composer, do the following:

   a. Change Anchor Component For Text for Each.1 to Existing Ground.

Continues

Continued

    b. Change Anchor Point to Bottom Center.

    c. Change Attachment to Top Center.

14. Click OK to dismiss the Label Style Composer.

15. Select the Annotate tab ➢ Labels & Tables panel and click the top half of the Add Labels button.

    a. In the Add Labels dialog, set the Feature option to Pipe Network.

    b. Set Label Type to Single Part Plan.

    c. Set Structure Label Style to Structure w Surface.

    d. Verify that Reference Text Object Prompt Method at the bottom of the Add Labels dialog is set to Command Line.

    e. Click Add.

16. At the `Select structure or pipe:` prompt, click the structure you want to label.

You will immediately see a prompt at the command line that reads `Select surface for label style component Existing Ground:`.

17. Press the Enter key to select EG from the surface listing and then click OK. Press the Enter key to end the labeling and close the Add Labels dialog.

Your label is now complete. Close the Add Labels dialog and press Esc to clear any object selection.

Save and close the drawing. A saved copy of this drawing, 1804_PipeandStructureLabels_FINISHED.dwg (1804_PipeandStructureLabels_METRIC_FINISHED.dwg), is available from the book's web page.

Profile and Alignment Labels

Profile and alignment labels can take on many forms. On an alignment you may want to show station labels every 100′ (25 m) in addition to PC, PT, and PI information. On a profile, you will want tangent grades, curve information, and grade breaks.

Many types of label styles can be applied to an alignment and profile. Each type has a unique set of properties. Fortunately, these styles can be applied in sets to expedite labeling.

Label Sets

A *label set* is a grouping of labels that apply to the same object. In lieu of having one big style that accounts for multiple aspects of an object, the labels are broken out into specific types to allow you more control.

Label sets come into play with alignments and design profiles. When you look at an alignment or profile and see labels, you are usually seeing multiple label styles in action.

Consider the alignment shown in Figure 18.31. How many labels are on this alignment? The geometry points, the major stations, the minor ticks, superelevation critical points, and design speed are all different label types.

FIGURE 18.31
One alignment, five label styles in play

How did those labels get there? When you first created the alignment or profile, one of the options was to specify a label set (as shown in Figure 18.32a). All label types included in the label set by default are placed on the alignment at all locations where they can be applied with their associated style. Also after the creation you can select the alignment, and from the contextual tab you can add specific labels, as shown in Figure 18.32b.

To edit which labels are applied to an alignment or profile, click one of the alignment labels, and from the Labels – Alignment Geometry Point Label Group contextual tab ➢ Modify panel, select Edit Label Group. Note that the contextual tab name will be different depending on which alignment label you choose.

Label sets also control some aspects of the location of the annotation. An alignment label set controls the major and minor station labeling increment and the type of geometry points that are labeled. A profile label set can control whether labels are positioned with respect to the graph top or bottom edge or to the profile. Figure 18.33 shows the two columns, Dim Anchor Opt and Dim Anchor Val, where this positioning is configured.

FIGURE 18.32
Specifying an alignment label set upon creation (a) and adding specific labels after alignment creation (b)

(a)   (b)

FIGURE 18.33
Profile labels and placement options

Alignment Labels

You'll create individual label styles over the next couple of exercises and then pull them together with a label set. At the end of this section, you'll apply your new label set to the alignments.

MAJOR STATION

Major station labels typically include a tick mark and a station callout. In this exercise, you'll build a style to show only the station increment and run it parallel to the alignment:

1. Open the 1805_Alignment&ProfileLabels.dwg (1805_Alignment&ProfileLabels_METRIC.dwg) file, which you can download from this book's web page.

2. Switch to the Settings tab, and expand the Alignment ➤ Label Styles ➤ Station ➤ Major Station branch.

3. Right-click Parallel With Tick and select Copy.

   The Label Style Composer dialog appears.

4. On the Information tab, type **Index Station** in the Name field.

5. Switch to the Layout tab.

6. Click in the Value field next to Contents, and click the ellipsis button to enter the Text Component Editor dialog.

7. Click in the preview area, and delete the text that's already there.

8. With Station Value as the active property, click the Output Value field to select it; then click again to open the drop-down.

   You will need to scroll down to see the Output option.

9. Select the Left Of Station Character option, as shown in Figure 18.34, and click the white arrow. (For metric users, the resulting label will be more interesting if you use the Right Of Station Character option instead. Because this alignment is less than 300 m, the left option will give you all 0s!).

FIGURE 18.34
Modifying the Station Value Output value in the Text Component Editor dialog

10. Click OK to close the Text Component Editor dialog.

11. Click OK to close the Label Style Composer dialog.

12. Keep the drawing open for the next part of the exercise.

The label style now shows in your label styles, but it hasn't been applied to any alignments yet.

GEOMETRY POINTS

Geometry points reflect the PC, PT, and other points along the alignment that define the geometric properties. The existing label style was not configured to be plan-readable, so you'll copy it and make a minor change in this exercise. You need to have completed the previous exercise to begin working on the following exercise:

1. Continue working in the 1805_Alignment&ProfileLabels.dwg (1805_Alignment&ProfileLabels_METRIC.dwg) file. You need to have had completed the previous exercise in order to continue.

2. Expand the Alignment ➤ Label Styles ➤ Station ➤ Geometry Point branch.

3. Right-click Perpendicular With Tick and select Copy to open the Label Style Composer.

4. On the Information tab, change the name to **Perpendicular with Line**.

5. Switch to the General tab.

6. Change the Readability Bias setting to **90**.

This value will force the labels to flip at a much earlier point.

7. Switch to the Layout tab and make these changes:

    a. Change the active component selection to the one named Tick.

    b. Click the Delete Component button (the red X).

    c. Choose Line from the Create Component drop-down.

    d. Change Angle to **90**.

    e. Change back to the Geometry Point & Station component.

    f. Change Anchor Component to Line.1.

    g. Change Anchor Point to End.

    h. Change Rotation Angle to **0**.

8. Click OK to close the Label Style Composer dialog.

This new style flips the plan-readable labels sooner and includes a line with the label. Next, you will put the styles together in a set.

ALIGNMENT LABEL SET

Once you have several labels you want to use on an alignment, it is time to save them as an alignment label set. You need to have completed the previous exercise in order to begin working on the following exercise:

1. Continue working in 1805_Alignment&ProfileLabels.dwg (1805_ Alignment&ProfileLabels_METRIC.dwg). You must have completed the previous exercises to continue. On the Settings tab of Toolspace, expand the Alignment ➤ Label Styles ➤ Label Sets branch.

2. Right-click Label Sets and select New to open the Alignment Label Set dialog.

3. On the Information tab, change the name to **Paving**.

4. Switch to the Labels tab.

5. Set the Type drop-down to the Major Stations option and the Major Station Label Style drop-down to the Index Station style you just created; then click the Add button.

6. Set the Type drop-down to the Minor Stations option and the Minor Station Label Style drop-down to the Tick option; then click the Add button.

7. Set the Type drop-down to Geometry Points and the Geometry Point Label Style drop-down to Perpendicular With Line. Then click the Add button to open the Geometry Points dialog, as shown Figure 18.35.

FIGURE 18.35
Deselecting
the Alignment
Beginning and
Alignment End
geometry point
check boxes

8. Deselect the Alignment Beginning and Alignment End check boxes as shown and then click OK to dismiss the dialog.

   Three label types will appear in the Alignment Label Set dialog.

9. Click OK to dismiss this dialog.

In the next exercise, you'll apply your label set to the example alignment and then see how an individual label can be changed from the set. You need to have completed the previous exercise to begin working on the following exercise:

1. Continue working in the 1805_Alignment&ProfileLabels.dwg (1805_Alignment&ProfileLabels_METRIC.dwg) file. Select the Example alignment onscreen.

2. On the alignment's contextual tab, click to expand the Add Labels button under the Labels & Tables panel and choose Add/Edit Station Labels to display the Alignment Labels dialog.

   This dialog shows which labels are currently applied to the alignment. Initially, it will be empty.

3. Click the Import Label Set button near the bottom of this dialog.

   Any labels appearing in this listing will be replaced by the labels in the set that is imported.

4. In the Select Label Set dialog, use the drop-down to select the Paving label set and click OK.

   The Alignment Labels list populates with the option you selected.

5. Click OK to dismiss the dialog.

6. When you finish, press Esc to be sure you have deselected your alignment, and zoom in on any of the major station labels.

7. Hold down the Ctrl key, and select one of the major station labels.

   Notice that a single label is selected, not the label set group.

8. Now that the single label is selected, drag the grip to place it into dragged state. Then click the circular grip to reset the label to its original position.

9. While the label is still selected, access the AutoCAD properties palette by pressing the Ctrl+1 key combination. You can access the same tool palette by using the button in the General Tools panel of the contextual tab.

   The Properties palette appears, allowing you to pick another label style from the Major Station Label Style drop-down.

10. Change the Label Style value to Parallel With Tick and change the Flipped value to True, as shown in Figure 18.36.

FIGURE 18.36
Modifying a single label's properties through the base AutoCAD properties palette

11. Press Esc to deselect the label item.

If you add labels to an alignment and like the look of the set, use the Save Label Set option. By using alignment label sets, you'll find it easy to standardize the appearance of labeling and stationing across alignments. Building label sets can take some time, but it's an easy, effective way to enforce standards.

Compare your drawing at this point against the 1805_Alignment&ProfileLabels_A.dwg (1805_Alignment&ProfileLabels_A_METRIC.dwg) file if needed.

STATION OFFSET LABELING

Beyond labeling an alignment's basic stationing and geometry points, you may want to label points of interest in reference to the alignment. Station offset labeling is designed to do just that. In addition to labeling the alignment's properties, you can include references to other object types in your station-offset labels. The objects available for referencing are as follows:

◆ Other alignments

◆ COGO points

◆ Parcels

◆ Profiles

◆ Surfaces

◆ Survey figures

In Chapter 10, "Advanced Corridors, Intersections, and Roundabouts," you used special alignment labels that referenced other alignments to make adjusting your design easier. In this exercise, you will make a similar type of label. The label you create in the following exercise finds the intersection of two alignments. You need to have completed the previous exercise in order to begin working on the following exercise:

1. Continue working with the finished version of your previous exercise; otherwise, use the 1805_Alignment&ProfileLabels_A.dwg (1805_Alignment&ProfileLabels_A_METRIC .dwg) drawing file.

2. On the Settings tab, expand Alignment ➤ Label Styles ➤ Station Offset.

3. Right-click the Station And Offset style and select Copy to open the Label Style Composer dialog.

4. On the Information tab, change the name of your new style to **Alignment Intersection**.

Make it a habit to update the description of the new label to reflect the intent of that label every time you copy or define a new label style.

5. Switch to the Layout tab. In the Component Name drop-down, select Marker, and click the red X to delete the component.

6. Change the name of the Station Offset component to **Main Alignment**.

7. In the Contents field, click the ellipsis button to bring up the Text Component Editor dialog.

8. Select the text in the preview area and delete it all.

9. Type **Sta.** in the preview area; be sure to leave a space after the period.

10. In the Properties drop-down field, select Station Value, and set Precision to **0.01**.

11. Click the white arrow in the Text Component Editor dialog; add a space after the inserted text.

12. In the Properties drop-down field, select Alignment Name.

13. Click the white arrow to add this bit of code to the preview.

Your Text Component Editor dialog should look like Figure 18.37.

FIGURE 18.37
The start of the alignment label style

14. Click OK to return to the Label Style Composer dialog.

15. Under the Border property, set the Visibility field to False.

16. Click the Create Component drop-down and select Reference Text.

17. In the Select Type dialog that appears, select Alignment and click OK.

18. Change the name to **Intersecting Alignment**.

19. In the Anchor Component field, select Main Alignment.

20. In the Anchor Point field, select Bottom Left.

21. In the Attachment field, select Top Left.

When you choose the anchor point and attachment point in this fashion, the bottom left of the Main Alignment text is linked to the top left of the Intersection Alignment text.

22. Click in the Contents field, and click the ellipsis button to open the Text Component Editor dialog.

23. Delete the default label text that currently appears in the preview area.

24. Type **Sta.** in the preview area; be sure to leave a space after the period.

25. In the Properties drop-down, select Station Value, and set Precision to **0.01**.

26. Click the white arrow in the Text Component Editor dialog and add a space after the inserted text.

27. In the Properties drop-down, select Alignment Name.

28. Click the white arrow.

29. Click OK to exit the Text Component Editor dialog, and click OK again to exit the Label Style Composer dialog.

30. Add the label to the drawing by selecting the Annotate tab ➢ Labels & Tables panel and clicking the top half of the Add Labels button.

31. Change the label settings to match those shown in Figure 18.38, and click Add.

FIGURE 18.38
Adding the new
alignment label

The same label could have been added using the Station Offset – Fixed Point option. This option is more likely to be used if the point of intersection between the alignments does not change. Therefore, consider your intent when using either of the labeling options.

32. Watch the command line for placement instructions.

You will be prompted to select the alignment, the station along the alignment (which is the intersection point of both alignments), and the offset. You will then be prompted to select the intersecting alignment.

33. Press Esc to complete the labeling command.

34. Click the label to select it and reveal the grips. Select the square grip and drag it away from the current location to form a leader.

Your completed label should look like Figure 18.39.

FIGURE 18.39
The completed
alignment label
with reference text

Compare your drawing at this point against the file 1805_Alignment&ProfileLabels_B.dwg
(1805_Alignment&ProfileLabels_B_METRIC.dwg) if needed.

PROFILE LABELS

It's important to remember that the profile and the profile view aren't the same thing. The labels
discussed in this section are those that relate directly to the profile. This usually means station-
based labels, individual tangent and curve labels, or grade breaks. You'll look at individual label
styles for these components and then at the concept of the label set.

HORIZONTAL ALIGNMENT PROFILE LABELS

As with alignments, you apply labels to profiles in the form of profile label sets. For now,
though, in this exercise you'll learn how to add alignment labels that describe the horizontal
data along a profile object. You will need to have completed the previous exercise in order to
begin working on the following exercise:

1. Continue working with the finished version of your previous exercise; otherwise, use the
   1805_Alignment&ProfileLabels_B.dwg (1805_Alignment&ProfileLabels_B_METRIC
   .dwg) file.

2. Pick the blue layout profile (the profile with two vertical curves) to activate the profile
   contextual tab.

3. From the Profile contextual tab ➤ Labels panel, select Edit Profile Labels to display the
   Profile Labels dialog (see Figure 18.40).

   Selecting the type of label from the Type drop-down changes the Style drop-down to
   include styles that are available for that label type. Next to the Style drop-down are the
   usual Style Edit/Copy button and a preview button. Once you've selected a style from
   the Style drop-down, clicking the Add button places it on the profile. The middle portion
   of this dialog displays information about the labels that are being applied to the profile
   selected; you'll look at that in a moment.

FIGURE 18.40
An empty Profile
Labels dialog

4. Choose the Major Stations option from the Type drop-down.

The name of the second drop-down changes to Profile Major Station Label Style to reflect this option.

5. Set the style to Perpendicular With Tick in this drop-down.

6. Click Add to apply this label to the profile.

7. Choose Horizontal Geometry Points from the Type drop-down.

The name of the Style drop-down changes to Profile Horizontal Geometry Point.

8. Select the Horizontal Geometry Station style, and click Add again to display the Geometry Points dialog shown in Figure 18.41.

FIGURE 18.41
The Geometry
Points dialog
appears when you
add labels to hori-
zontal geometry
points.

This dialog lets you apply different label styles to different geometry points if necessary.

9. Deselect the Alignment Beginning and Alignment End rows, as shown in Figure 18.41, and click OK to close the dialog.

10. Click the Apply button and then drag the dialog out of the way to view the changes to the profile (see Figure 18.42).

FIGURE 18.42
Labels applied to major stations and alignment geometry points

11. In the middle of the Profile Labels dialog, change the Increment value in the Major Stations row to **50′** (**10** m), as shown in Figure 18.43.

FIGURE 18.43
Modifying the Major Stations labeling increment

This modifies the labeling increment only, not the grid or other values.

12. Click OK to close the Profile Labels dialog.

13. Press Esc to deselect the layout profile.

As you can see, applying labels one at a time could turn into a tedious task. After you learn about the types of labels available, you'll revisit this dialog and look at the two buttons at the bottom for dealing with label sets.

LINE LABELS

Line labels in profiles are typically used to convey the slope or length of a tangent segment. In this exercise, you'll add a length and slope to the layout profile. You will need to have completed the previous exercise to begin working on the following exercise:

1. Continue working in the 1805_Alignment&ProfileLabels.dwg (1805_Alignment&ProfileLabels_METRIC.dwg) file.

2. Switch to the Settings tab of Toolspace.

3. Expand the Profile ➤ Label Styles ➤ Line branch.

4. Right-click Percent Grade and select the Copy option to open the Label Style Composer dialog and create a duplicate style.

5. On the Information tab, change the name to **Length and Percent Grade**.

6. Switch to the Layout tab and make these changes:

    a. Change Attachment to Top Center.

    b. Set the Y-offset to **-0.025"** (**-1 mm**).

    c. Set Background Mask to True and Border Visibility to False.

7. Click the Value field next to Contents and click the ellipsis to enter the Text Component Editor dialog.

8. Put the cursor to the beginning of existing text and change the Properties drop-down to the Tangent Slope Length option and the Precision value to **0.01**, as shown in Figure 18.44.

FIGURE 18.44
The Text Component Editor dialog with the values for the Tangent Slope Length entered

9. Click the white arrow, and then in between the two properties add a foot symbol (or **m** for meter), a space, and an @ symbol so that it looks like Figure 18.44.

10. Click OK to close the Text Component Editor dialog, and click OK again to close the Label Style Composer.

11. Pick the layout profile. From the Profile contextual tab ➤ Labels panel, select Edit Profile Labels to display the Profile Labels dialog.

12. Change the Type drop-down to the Lines option. The name of the Style drop-down changes to Profile Tangent Label Style. Select the Length And Percent Grade option.

13. Click the Add button and then click OK to exit the dialog.

14. Press Esc to deselect the layout profile.

The profile view should look like Figure 18.45.

FIGURE 18.45
A new line label applied to the layout profile

WHERE IS THAT DISTANCE BEING MEASURED?

The *tangent slope length* is the distance along the vertical geometry between vertical curves. This value doesn't include the tangent extensions. There are a number of ways to label this length; be sure to look in the Text Component Editor if you want a different measurement.

CURVE LABELS

Vertical curve labels are one of the most confusing aspects of profile labeling. Many people become overwhelmed rapidly because there's so much that can be labeled, and there are so many ways to get all the right information in the right place. In this quick exercise, you'll look at some of the special label anchor points that are unique to curve labels and how they can be helpful. You will need to have completed the previous exercise in order to begin working on the following exercise:

1. Continue working in the `1805_Alignment&ProfileLabels.dwg` (`1805_Alignment&ProfileLabels_METRIC.dwg`) file.

2. Pick the layout profile. From the Profile contextual tab ➤ Labels panel, select Edit Profile Labels to display the Profile Labels dialog.

3. Choose the Crest Curves option from the Type drop-down.

   The name of the Style drop-down changes to Profile Crest Curve Label Style.

4. Select the Crest Only option.

5. Click the Add button to apply the label to the list.

6. Choose the Sag Curves option from the Type drop-down.

   The name of the Style drop-down changes to Profile Sag Curve Label Style.

7. Select the Sag Only label style. Click the Add button to apply the label.

8. Click OK to close the dialog.

9. Press Esc to deselect the layout profile.

   Your profile should look like Figure 18.46.

FIGURE 18.46
Curve labels applied with default Dim Anchor values

Most labels are applied directly on top of the object being referenced. Because typical curve labels contain a large amount of information, putting the label right on the object can yield undesired results. In the following exercise, you'll modify the label settings to review the options available for curve labels. You will need to have completed the previous exercise in order to begin working on the following exercise:

1. Continue working in the `1805_Alignment&ProfileLabels.dwg` (`1805_Alignment&ProfileLabels_METRIC.dwg`) file.

2. Pick the layout profile. From the Profile contextual tab ➤ Labels panel, select Edit Profile Labels to display the Profile Labels dialog.

3. Scroll to the right and change both Dim Anchor Opt values for Crest Curves and Sag Curves to Graph View Top.

   You may need to make the columns wider to view the names.

4. Change the Dim Anchor Val for both curves to **-2.25"** (**-40** mm), and click OK to close the dialog.

5. Press Esc to deselect the layout profile.

   Your drawing should look like Figure 18.47.

FIGURE 18.47
Curve labels anchored to the top of the profile view

The labels can also be grip-modified to move higher or lower as needed. By using the top or bottom of the graph as the anchor point, you can apply consistent and easy labeling to the curve, regardless of the curve location or size.

THOSE CRAZY CURVE LABELS!

A profile curve label can be as intricate or simple as you desire. Civil 3D gives you many options for where along the curve feature you want your Label component to appear. The following illustration shows where some of the commonly used curve locations are in a label:

GRADE BREAKS

The last label style typically involved in a profile is a grade-break label at PVI points that don't fall inside a vertical curve, such as the beginning or end of the layout profile. Additional uses include things like water-level profiling, where vertical curves aren't part of the profile information or existing surface labeling. In this exercise, you'll add a grade-break label and look at another option for controlling how often labels are applied to profile data. You will need to have completed the previous exercise in order to begin working on the following exercise:

1. Continue working in the 1805_Alignment&ProfileLabels.dwg (1805_Alignment&ProfileLabels_METRIC.dwg) file.

2. Pick the green surface profile (the irregular profile). From the Profile contextual tab ➢ Labels panel, select Edit Profile Labels to display the Profile Labels dialog.

3. Choose Grade Breaks from the Type drop-down.

   The name of the Style drop-down changes to Grade Breaks.

4. Select the Station Over Elevation style from the Profile Grade Break Label Style option and click the Add button.

5. Click Apply and drag the dialog out of the way to review the change.

   A sampled surface profile has grade breaks everywhere the alignment crosses a surface TIN line. Why wasn't your view coated with labels?

6. Back in the Profile Labels dialog, scroll to the right and change the Weeding value to **150′** (**45 m**). Click OK.

7. Select one of the new grade-break labels. Use the square grip at the location where the label touches the profile to form a leader and clean up any labels that overlap.

   The profile labels should appear as shown in Figure 18.48.

FIGURE 18.48
The grade-break labels on a sampled surface are starting to get crowded, so weeding combined with dragged labels can bring some clarity to the profile view.

8. Click OK to dismiss the dialog.

9. Press Esc to deselect the layout profile.

Weeding lets you control how frequently grade-break labels are applied. This makes it possible to label profiles with frequent grade breaks, such as a surface profile, at even increments instead of at every PVI.

As you've seen, there are many ways to apply labeling to profiles, and applying these labels to each profile individually could be tedious. In the next section, you'll build a label set to make this process more efficient.

PROFILE LABEL SETS

Applying labels to both crest and sag curves, tangents, grade breaks, and geometry with the label style selection and various options can be monotonous. Thankfully, Civil 3D gives you the ability to use label sets, as in alignments, to make the process quick and easy. In this exercise, you'll apply a label set, make a few changes, and export a new label set that can be shared with team members or imported to the Civil 3D template. You will need to have completed the previous exercise to begin working on the following exercise:

1. Continue working in the 1805_Alignment&ProfileLabels.dwg (1805_Alignment&ProfileLabels_METRIC.dwg) file.

2. To tidy things up, you can select one of the grade-break labels from the previous exercise. Press Delete on your keyboard to remove the label.

3. Pick the layout profile. From the Profile contextual tab ➤ Labels panel, select Edit Profile Labels to display the Profile Labels dialog.

4. Click the Import Label Set button near the bottom of the dialog to display the Select Label Style Set dialog.

5. Select the Complete Label Set option from the drop-down and click OK.

6. Click OK again to close the Profile Labels dialog and see the profile view. Press Esc to clear any selection.

   The label set you chose contains curve labels, grade-break labels, and line labels.

7. Pick the layout profile. From the Profile contextual tab ➤ Labels panel, select Edit Profile Labels to display the Profile Labels dialog.

8. Click Import Label Set to display the Select Label Style Set dialog.

9. Select the No_Labels option from the drop-down and click OK.

   All the labels from the listing will be removed.

   In the next steps, you will add labels to the listing and save the listing as its own label set for future use.

10. Set Active Type to Lines. Set Profile Tangent Label Style to Length And Percent Grade, and click Add.

11. Set Active Type to Grade Breaks. Set Profile Grade Break Label Style to Station Over Elevation, and click Add.

12. Set Type to Crest Curves. Set Profile Crest Curve Label Style to Crest Only, and click Add.

13. Set Type to Sag Curves. Set Profile Sag Curve Label Style to Sag Only, and click Add.

14. Set the Crest Curves and Sag Curves label types to use Graph View Top as the Dim Anchor Opt.

15. Set both Dim Anchor Val fields to **-1.5″** (**-40** mm), as shown in Figure 18.49.

FIGURE 18.49
Four label types and dimension anchor settings in the label set to be saved

16. Click the Save Label Set button to open the Profile Label Set dialog and create a new profile label set.

17. On the Information tab, change the name to **Road Profile Labels**.

18. Click OK to close the Profile Label Set dialog.

19. Click OK to close the Profile Labels dialog.

20. Press Esc to deselect the layout profile if it's still selected.

21. On the Settings tab of Toolspace, expand Profile ➤ Label Styles ➤ Label Sets.

    Note that the Road Profile Labels set is now available for sharing or importing to other profile label dialogs.

Save and close the drawing. A saved copy of this drawing, 1805_ Alignment&ProfileLabels_FINISHED.dwg (1805_Alignment&ProfileLabels_METRIC_ FINISHED.dwg), is available from the book's web page.

Label sets are the only way to apply profile labeling uniformly. When you're working with a well-developed set of styles and label sets, going from sketched profile layout to plan-ready output is quick and easy.

Advanced Style Types

Now that you are familiar with the basics of label styles, you are ready to take your skills to the next level. The styles in the following section combine aspects of label styles and object styles. You will cover object styles more in depth in Chapter 19, "Object Styles."

You have a great deal of control over every detail, even ones that may seem trivial. Instead of being bogged down trying to understand every option, don't be afraid to try a "trial and error" approach. If you make a change you don't like, you can always edit the style until you get it right.

Table Styles

Civil 3D does a beautiful job of placing dynamically linked data tables that relate to your objects. The tables use the Text Component Editor to grab dynamic information from your data. You also have control over fill colors, table headings, and how the data is sorted.

For the table style, the Data Properties tab contains all the column information. You can add columns by clicking the plus sign. You can remove columns by highlighting the column you want to remove and clicking the Delete button. You change column order by dragging them around and dropping them where you want them to go, as shown in Figure 18.50.

FIGURE 18.50
Modifying table column positions. Selecting one column and dragging it to change its position in the list.

In the following exercise, you will see the basic steps of modifying a table style. Now that you understand the ins and outs of the Label Style Composer, this procedure should be a breeze:

1. Open the 1806_Tables.dwg (1806_Tables_METRIC.dwg) file, which you can download from this book's web page.

   This file contains a parcel line table whose style you will modify.

2. Zoom into the parcel line table.

   Notice that there are several things you will want to change:

   ◆ The line numbers are out of order.

◆ The directions have far too much precision.

◆ The length does not display units.

All that is about to change.

3. Click the table to select it. From the Table contextual tab ➤ Modify panel, select the Table Properties drop-down and choose Edit Table Style.

4. Switch to the Data Properties tab.

The Data Properties tab (Figure 18.51) is the main control area for all table styles. This is where you set behavior, text styles, and sizes for fields.

FIGURE 18.51
The Data Properties tab for table styles. Sorting of the data can be enabled with a simple toggle.

5. Place a check mark next to Sort Data, and set the Sorting column to **1**.

Column 1 corresponds to the Column Value containing the Parcel Line Number. Set the Order option to Ascending. The Ascending option will ensure that the parcel numbers are listed in the table from the lowest to highest value.

6. Double-click the column heading field for Length.

Doing so opens a stripped-down version of the Text Component Editor dialog. Headings and table titles are static text only; therefore, only the text formatting tools are shown.

7. Add **(feet)** or **(meters)** after the column heading to add a proper units heading to the column, as shown in Figure 18.52, and click OK.

FIGURE 18.52
Adding static text
to a table column
heading

8. Double-click the Direction Column Value field below the column heading.

   Doing so opens the Text Component Editor dialog, similar to what you've used in earlier exercises.

9. Click the text in the preview area so that it becomes highlighted.

10. Change Precision to **1 Second**.

11. Click the white arrow to update the text. Click OK.

12. Click OK to complete the table style modifications.

   Save and close the drawing. A saved copy of this drawing, 1806_Tables_FINISHED.dwg (1806_Tables_METRIC_FINISHED.dwg), is available from the book's web page.

Code Set Styles

Code set styles determine how your assembly design will appear, and they are used in many places. A code set style is in play when you first create your assembly. One is used in corridor creation and in the Section Editor. The most apparent use of a code set style is in section views.

   A code set style is a collection of many other styles. In a code set style, you will find the following:

◆ Link styles and link label styles

◆ Points styles, point label styles, and feature line styles

◆ Shapes styles and shape label styles

◆ Quantity takeoff pay items

◆ Render materials for visualization tasks

When naming your code set style, you'll find it helpful to have the name of the set reflect its use. Multiple code set styles are needed because of different applications of their use. When you are designing an assembly, you may want to see more labels than when you are getting ready to plot the assembly in a cross-section sheet. Labeling that is useful in a cross-section sheet but may obstruct your view of the design when working with it in the corridor cross-section editor.

The hardest part of working with code set styles is figuring out the name of the link or point you want to label. Luckily, it is unusual for users to label shapes, so you won't need to worry about those. The names of each point or link can be found in the subassembly properties. Most of the links and points are logically named, but there's no harm in a little trial and error if you are not sure.

SHAPES

Shapes are the areas that define materials. Because people don't usually label these materials in a section view, you won't be experiencing these in an exercise.

One heads-up, however: Resist the temptation to use a hatch pattern on shapes where multiple cross-section views will be created. Solid fills and no patterns are your best bet to avoid performance issues and the annoying "Hatch pattern is too dense" warning.

LINKS AND LINK LABELS

You learned in Chapter 8, "Assemblies and Subassemblies," that a link is the linear part of a subassembly. The object style for the link itself is simple—just a single linear component. The label for a link is usually expressed as a percent grade or as a slope ratio.

In the following exercise, you will modify a code set style to apply link labels to an assembly:

1. Open the 1807_CodeSetStyles.dwg (1807_CodeSetStyles_METRIC.dwg) file, which you can download from this book's web page.

   This file contains corridor and cross-section views. Zoom into one of the cross-section views so you can observe the changes as you apply them to the code set style.

2. From the Settings tab of Toolspace, expand General ➢ Multipurpose Styles ➢ Code Set Styles; right-click All Codes and select Edit.

   If you edit an object or label style by selecting the style in the Settings tab of Toolspace, you can typically see the changes as soon as you click Apply. This is not always the case when you access the edit style tool from within other dialogs such as the Alignment Label Set dialog.

3. On the Codes tab under the Link category, select Pave, and click the Label Tag icon in the Label Style column, as shown in Figure 18.53.

FIGURE 18.53
Adding labels to the link codes in the code set style

4. In the Pick Style dialog, select the Flat Grades label style and click OK; then click Apply to examine the change on the cross sections.

   You should see that the lanes now have slope information labeled.

5. Under the Link category, locate Daylight; click the Label Tag icon in the Label Style column, and in the Pick Style dialog select Steep Grades as the label style.

6. Click OK and then click OK to dismiss the All Codes label style and see what is happening with the cross section.

   The cross sections should resemble Figure 18.54.

FIGURE 18.54
Cross section with link labels applied to pave and daylight links

POINTS AND POINT LABELS

A common frustration for new users of Civil 3D is the marker styles and their labels. For cross-section views, you may not want points to display at all. In the following exercise, you will create a new code set style, modify point codes, and add more labels to the sections. You need to have completed the previous exercise in order to begin working on the following exercise:

1. Continue working in 1807_CodeSetStyles.dwg (1807_CodeSetStyles_METRIC.dwg).

2. From the Settings tab of Toolspace, expand General ➤ Multipurpose Styles ➤ Code Set Styles. Right-click All Codes and select Copy.

3. On the Information tab, rename the style to **All Codes-Plotting**.

4. On the Codes tab, locate and expand the Point category. Locate the Back_Curb point and click the Label Tag icon in the Label Style column. In the Pick Style dialog, set the style to Offset Elevation. Click OK.

5. Repeat step 4 to set the label style for Sidewalk_Out to Offset Elevation. You may need to make the Name column wider for selection.

6. Click the first point name, <default>. While holding down the Shift key on your keyboard, scroll down to the last point listing, Top_Curb, and click it. With all of the points selected, click the Tag icon in the Style column and change the style to _No Markers. Click OK.

   The Code Set Style dialog should resemble Figure 18.55.

7. Click OK.

FIGURE 18.55
Points set to _No Markers and labels set to Offset Elevation

You can't see any changes to your cross sections yet because the style is not active.

8. Select a section view by selecting its corresponding section view station label. From the Section Views contextual tab ➤ Modify View panel, select the top half of the View Group Properties icon.

9. On the Sections tab, change the style of Example Corridor to the All Codes-Plotting style you created, as shown in Figure 18.56, and click OK.

FIGURE 18.56
Setting the code set style current on the section views

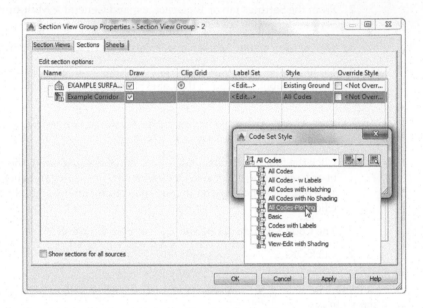

10. Click OK again to complete the changes to the Section View Group Properties dialog.

Your section view should resemble Figure 18.57.

FIGURE 18.57
New code set style applied to the section view

The created section views use the legacy labeling for points. We will now use the feature of labeling corridor sections using section labels for corridor points, instead of code sets.

11. From the Settings tab of Toolspace, expand Section ➤ Label Styles ➤ Corridor Points. Right-click the branch and choose New.

12. In the Information tab, name this new style **Corridor Points**.

13. In the Layout tab, for the Line component set Fixed Length to **2** (**40** mm for metric users).

14. Still in the Layout tab, change the active Component Name to the one named Point Code. Then set the following:

   ◆ Anchor Component to Line

   ◆ Anchor Point to End

   ◆ Attachment to Bottom Right

   ◆ Y Offset to **0.025** (**0.50** mm for metric users)

15. Still in the Layout tab, change the active Component Name to the one named Offset And Elevation. Then set the following:

   ◆ Anchor Component to Point Code

   ◆ Anchor Point to Bottom Right

   ◆ Attachment to Top Right

   ◆ Y offset to **-0.05** (**-1.00** mm for metric users)

16. In the Contents Text Component Editor, set the precision for both the Subassembly Point Offset and the Subassembly Point Elevation coding to **0.01** using the same steps that you followed throughout this chapter.

17. In the right pane of the Contents Text Component Editor editor, modify the text before the Subassembly Point Offset to show **OS:** and a space and the text before the Subassembly Point Elevation to **EL:** and a space. Also eliminate the comma in between the two components. (See Figure 18.58 for the layout of items needed in the contents.)

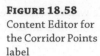

FIGURE 18.58
Content Editor for
the Corridor Points
label

18. Click OK to close the Text Component Editor and click OK again to finish creating
the style.

19. Hit Esc to deselect any selected item. At the command line, type
CORRIDORSECTIONLABELSCONV and press Enter; then, at the `Select Section view you
want to convert:` prompt, select one of the section views by picking the section view
label. Press Enter, and from the next prompt select Corridor Points Style Labels.

You will not notice any labels assigned yet.

20. Select the corridor section, and from the contextual tab, within the Labels panel, choose
Edit Section Labels for the Section Labels dialog to show up.

21. In the Section Labels dialog, change Type to Corridor Points, and from the Section
Corridor Points Label Style drop-down, select Corridor Points and click the Add button.
Click OK to dismiss the dialog box.

Now you will notice the new labels applied to the section view. You can convert the labels
back and forth by issuing the same command and picking the desired output. Your converted section view will look like Figure 18.59.

FIGURE 18.59
Section view using the newly introduced Corridor Points Labels feature

Save and close the drawing. A saved copy of this drawing, 1807_CodeSetStyles_FINISHED .dwg (1807_CodeSetStyles_METRIC_FINISHED.dwg), is available from the book's web page.

IT'S JUST AN EXPRESSION

Expressions allow you to use properties available in a label and to perform calculations. The resulting expression can be used as part of a displayed label or as any of the numerical text settings such as text height, rotation angle, or width.

A frequently seen use of expressions is with surface spot elevations for the display of cut and fill volumes across a volume surface. Beginning with the 2015 version, it is now possible to reassign created labels to a different surface than the original labeled surface.

1. Open the 1808_Expressions.dwg (1808_Expressions_METRIC.dwg) drawing.

   Within the drawing you will notice the outline of a surface that represents the volume comparison in between an existing ground surface and a design surface. You will build the expressions and label style to represent the cut and fill values.

2. From the Settings tab of Toolspace, expand Surface ➤ Label Styles ➤ Spot Elevations. Right-click the Expressions branch and choose New.

3. In the New Expression dialog, enter **Surface Negative Value** under Name.

Continues

Continued

4. In the Expression area, click the left button on the right side of the window. From the drop-down list, select Surface Elevation. The value is added to the Expression field. Next, complete the expression to match the following: `{Surface Elevation}*-1`.

5. Click OK to complete the creation of the expression once you verified that the format result is set to Double.

   This expression converts a negative surface value to a positive one.

6. Create a new expression with the name **Surface Block Plus Scale.** Use the same workflow to complete an expression that matches the following (metric users use 0.002): `IF({Surface Elevation}>0,0.006,.0001^10)`. Click OK.

This expression represents a logical IF statement that checks whether the Surface Elevation value is larger than 0, and for the true value it assigns a value of 0.006 (0.002 for metric users); otherwise, it assigns a large micro value not visible to the eye. This statement will be used in the definition of the fill values for the label.

7. Create a new expression and name it **Surface Block Minus Scale**. Use the same workflow to complete an expression to match the following (metric users use 0.002): `IF({Surface Negative Value}>0,0.006,.0001^10)`. Click OK.

This expression represents a logical IF statement that checks whether the Surface Negative value is larger than 0, and for the true value it assigns a value of 0.006 (0.002 for metric users); otherwise, it assigns a low value not visible to the eye. This statement will be used in the definition of the cut values for the label.

8. From the Settings tab of Toolspace, expand Surface ➤ Label Styles, right-click Spot Elevation, and choose New.

9. In the Information tab, enter the name **Spot Cut Fill**. Switch to the Layout tab.

10. Delete all components in the list and click the Create Component button to create the following components: a text component with a name of **Cut Value**, a text component with a name of **Fill Value**, a block component with a name of **Cut_Block**, and a block component with a name of **Fill_Block**.

11. For the Fill_Block component, set the following:

 ◆ Set Anchor Component to Feature.

 ◆ Set Anchor Point to Middle Center.

 ◆ Set Block Name to Fill_Block. (Browse to find it by clicking within the cell and then select it from the Select Block dialog.)

Continues

Continued

- ◆ Set Block Height to Surface Block Plus Scale. (Click in the cell and from the drop-down arrow select the expression value mentioned previously.)
- ◆ Set Color to Green.

12. For the Cut_Block component, set the following:

- ◆ Set Anchor Component to Feature.
- ◆ Set Anchor Point to Middle Center.
- ◆ Set Block Name to Cut_Block. (Browse to find it by clicking within the cell and then select it from the Select Block dialog.)
- ◆ Set Block Height to Surface Block Minus Scale. (Click in the cell and from the drop-down arrow select the expression value mentioned previously.)
- ◆ Set Color to Red.

13. For the Fill Value component, set the following:

- ◆ Set Anchor Component to Fill_Block.
- ◆ Set Anchor Point to Middle Right.
- ◆ Set Contents to Surface Elevation with two decimals.
- ◆ Set Text Height to Surface Block Plus Scale. (Click in the cell and from the drop-down arrow select the expression value mentioned previously.)
- ◆ Set Attachment to Middle Left.
- ◆ Set Color to Green.

14. For the Cut Value component, set the following:

- ◆ Set Anchor Component to Cut_Block.
- ◆ Set Anchor Point to Middle Right.
- ◆ Set Contents to Surface Negative Value with two decimals.
- ◆ Set Text Height to Surface Block Minus Scale. (Click in the cell and from the drop-down arrow select the expression value mentioned previously.)
- ◆ Set Attachment to Middle Left.
- ◆ Set Color to Red.

Click OK to complete the definition of the style.

15. Select the surface by selecting the boundary, and from the contextual tab ➢ Labels & Tables panel, expand the Add Labels button and choose Add Surface Labels to bring up the Add Labels dialog.

16. In the Add Labels dialog, Feature will be set to Surface. Set the label type to Spot Elevations On Grid, and from the Spot Elevation Label Style list, choose Spot Cut Fill label and set the marker style to _No Markers. Click the Add button.

17. At the `Select a surface <or press enter key to select from the list>:` prompt, click the green outline of the displayed surface. Otherwise, press Enter, and from the Select A Surface dialog, select EGvsFG surface and click OK.

18. At the Specify a grid basepoint: prompt, using your Endpoint Osnap (F3 key enables Osnaps), select the lower-left corner of the displayed rectangle.

19. At the Grid Rotation prompt, press Enter to accept the default value of 0.

20. At Grid X spacing, enter **10** (**3** for metric users) and press the Enter key.

21. At Grid Y spacing, enter **10** (**3** for metric users) and press the Enter key.

22. At the Specify the upper right location of the grid: prompt, using again the Endpoint Osnap, select the top-right corner of the displayed rectangle.

23. At the Change the size or rotation of the grid/grid squares [Yes No] <No>: prompt, accept the default No entry by pressing the Enter key.

The following figure shows a portion of the result of the surface labeling:

12	−2.46	−0.78	+0.93	+2.81	+4.25	+5.18	+6.12	+7.05	+6.60	+4.48	+2.02	+
68	−1.00	+0.60	+1.20	+1.96	+3.07	+4.00	+4.94	+5.59	+4.15	+1.71	+0.82	+
36	−0.30	+0.29	+0.73	+0.98	+1.89	+2.82	+2.84	+2.21	+1.45	+1.54	+2.08	+
23	−0.74	−0.40	−0.32	−0.23	−0.27	−0.22	−0.55	−0.40	+1.87	+2.80	+3.33	+
78	−1.70	−1.62	−1.53	−2.24	−3.66	−5.09	−3.03	+0.29	+2.56	+4.06	+4.07	+
90	−2.85	−2.93	−4.32	−5.71	−6.61	−5.22	−3.84	−0.89	+2.59	+4.22	+2.94	+
90	−4.75	−6.14	−7.54	−7.02	−5.71	−4.38	−3.02	−1.38	+0.97	+2.88	+1.72	+
75	−8.05	−8.64	−7.36	−6.06	−4.74	−3.43	−3.02	−2.38	−0.07	+1.35	+1.48	−
97	−9.04	−7.69	−6.37	−5.09	−4.04	−4.15	−4.31	−3.42	−1.26	+0.05	+1.26	−

The following happens in the background: for each of the spot elevations in the drawing, for the positive (fill) values, the fill block and label are displayed, while the cut block and label are resized by a scale that makes them "invisible." At the same time, for a negative value, the opposite happens. Expressions made this possible.

Save and close the drawing. A saved copy of this drawing, 1808_Expressions_FINISHED .dwg (1808_Expressions_METRIC_FINISHED.dwg), is available from the book's web page.

The Bottom Line

Override individual labels with other styles. In spite of the desire to have uniform labeling styles and appearances between alignments within a single drawing, project, or firm, there are always exceptions. Using the Ctrl+click method for element selection, you can access commands that let you modify labels and even change their styles.

Master It Open the drawing `MasterIt_1801.dwg` (`MasterIt_1801_METRIC.dwg`). Create a copy of the Perpendicular With Tick Major Station style called **Major With Marker**. Change Tick Block Name to **Marker Pnt**. Replace some (but not all) of your major station labels with this new style.

Create a new label set for alignments. Label sets let you determine the appearance of an alignment's labels and quickly standardize that appearance across all objects of the same nature. By creating sets that reflect their intended use, you can make it easy for a designer to quickly label alignments according to specifications with little understanding of the requirement.

Master It Continue working in the `MasterIt_1801.dwg` (`MasterIt_1801_METRIC.dwg`) file if you completed the previous exercise, or open the `MasterIt_1801_FINISHED.dwg` (`MasterIt_1801_METRIC_FINISHED.dwg`) file, and create a new label set named Major Only containing only the new major station label defined in the previous exercise and apply it to all the alignments in that drawing.

Create and use expressions. Expressions give you the ability to add calculated information to labels or add logic to label creation.

Master It Continue working in the `MasterIt_1801.dwg` (`MasterIt_1801_METRIC.dwg`) file, or open the `MasterIt_1802_FINISHED.dwg` (`MasterIt_1802_METRIC_FINISHED.dwg`) file, and create an expression called Top of Curb that adds 0.5' (0.15 m) to a surface elevation. Use the expression in a spot elevation label that shows both the surface elevation and the expression-based elevation to a two decimal precision.

Apply a standard label set to profiles. Standardization of appearance is one of the major benefits of using Civil 3D styles in labeling. By applying label sets, you can quickly create plot-ready profile views that have the required information for review.

Master It Continue working in the `MasterIt_1801.dwg` (`MasterIt_1801_METRIC.dwg`) file or open the `MasterIt_1803_FINISHED.dwg` (`MasterIt_1803_METRIC_FINISHED.dwg`) file, and apply the Road Profile Labels label set to all layout profiles.

Chapter 19

Object Styles

As you learned in the previous chapter, styles control the display properties of labels, but they also control the display properties of Autodesk® AutoCAD® Civil 3D® objects such as points, surfaces, alignments, profile views, pipes, sections, and so on.

Alignments are composed of components such as lines, curves, and spirals. Surfaces contain contours, triangles, boundaries, and points. A point has an important marker component.

Object styles enable you to control which components are displayed and how they are displayed. Traditionally, you control the display of such items with layers and AutoCAD properties. Styles offer a quick way to change an object's display state for the purpose of plotting, editing, or analysis.

In this chapter, you will learn to:

◆ Override object styles with other styles.

◆ Create a new surface style.

◆ Create a new profile view style.

Getting Started with Object Styles

Before you get your hands on specific object styles and begin working with them, you should understand some general things all styles have in common.

Certification Objective There are several ways to enter the various dialogs used for editing styles. The easiest, most direct way to access any Style dialog is from the Settings tab. Right-click any style you see listed and select Edit, as shown in Figure 19.1.

FIGURE 19.1
Every style can be edited by right-clicking the style name from the Settings tab of Toolspace.

You can also enter a Style dialog from the Information tab of the Object Properties dialog of any object by clicking the Edit button. Figure 19.2 shows the active style on a surface, with the Edit button to the right. Editing at this level affects all objects that use the style, the same as it would if you had entered the style from the Settings tab. The downside to editing a style in this manner is that you will not immediately be able to click Apply to see your change because the Object Properties dialog is open beneath it. You'll need to exit the Style dialog and click Apply at the object level before you'll see your style update.

FIGURE 19.2
An object's properties reveal the current style, which can be edited, as in this Alignment Properties dialog.

🌐 **Real World Scenario**

MAKING SENSE OF CHILD STYLES AND OVERRIDES

Civil 3D styles are configurable at several levels. In Chapter 1, "The Basics," you learned that the Drawing Settings dialog is where you make adjustments to the overall settings that affect all styles, such as setting precision values and object layers. On the object level in the Settings tab, you will find Feature Settings, which you can use to override any settings being applied by Drawing Settings. The Feature Settings dialog is also used to assign default styles. Finally, inside the object level you will find Command Settings, where you can override settings applied by Drawing or Feature Settings at the command level. For example, when using the CreateProfileFromSurface command, you are usually creating an existing profile so you could configure the settings of that command to use an existing surface style. These layers of parent-child settings are often referred to as hierarchical settings.

Styles themselves can be used to override other styles. These other styles are referred to as child styles. For example, a precision of two decimal places (0.00) may be adequate for station labels. However, when creating corridors, you may find it advantageous to see more decimal places of precision. Set the station precision to 0.00 in Drawing Settings. Then farther down on the Settings tab, right-click Corridor and select Edit Feature Settings.

Inside the Edit Feature Settings – Corridor dialog, you might experience déjà vu from when you edited the Ambient Settings tab in the Drawing Settings dialog. All the same settings (and a few more object-specific ones) are here. The difference is that changing the setting here will affect only corridors.

The check mark in the Override column indicates that this setting differs from settings higher up in Drawing Settings. At the bottom of the dialog further information is provided regarding the parent setting and its value.

An arrow in the Child Override column indicates that farther down the chain of command a style or setting differs. To force these subordinate styles or Command Settings to match the style of the parent, click the arrow so that a red X appears. The red X indicates that the change you make, in the dialog you are looking at, will be pushed to its child styles or Command Settings.

The Lock column allows you to lock a setting, which prevents it from being changed from Command Settings.

As you are designing the styles for use in your office, be sure to keep an eye on the overrides that are set. Any override styles applied can be removed by unchecking the Override column in the Edit Feature Settings dialog.

Frequently Seen Tabs

When creating or editing an object style, you will be opening a Style dialog containing several tabs. Some of the tabs contain settings that are unique to the object. Some tabs are common to all or several types of objects. In this section, you will learn about those tabs.

INFORMATION TAB

The Information tab (Figure 19.3) contains the field where the name of the style is entered or changed.

FIGURE 19.3
The Information tab exists for all object styles.

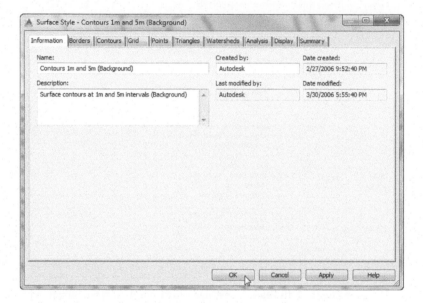

The description is optional. However, a description may be helpful to others who will be using your template. If you do use descriptions, be sure to revise them when you copy your styles for other purposes to avoid confusing your users. The description can be seen in tooltip form as you search through the Settings tab, as shown in Figure 19.4.

FIGURE 19.4
Tooltip showing style informa-tion, including the description

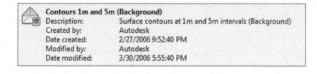

On the right side of the dialog, you will see the name of the user who created the style, the date when it was created, the last person who modified the style, and the date it was modified. These names are initially pulled from the Windows login information and only the Created By field can be edited.

DISPLAY TAB

On the Display tab, you will find a list of components available for display within the object. You will see this tab in every Object Style dialog. The Display tab controls the look of the object in Plan, Model, Profile, and Section view directions. Not every style type will have all of these view directions available. In Figure 19.5, you can see that a surface style has Plan, Model, and Section view directions with multiple components, a point style has an extra view direction for Profile but with only two components, while a view frame style has only one view direction and one component.

FIGURE 19.5
The View Direction options and their components for a surface style, a point style, and a view frame style

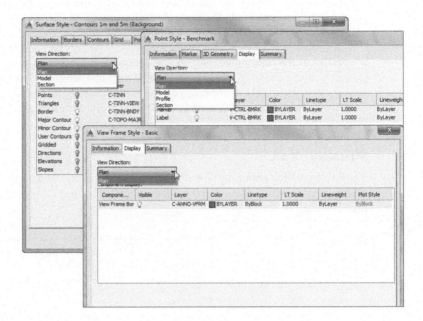

This is 3D software, so objects exist in three dimensions. View Direction controls the display of an object depending on how you are looking at it. Certain items, such as a profile view, are intended to be seen only in plan, so they do not have multiple view directions listed. Alignments can be seen in plan, model, and section views. Profiles can be seen in profile, model, and section views, as shown in Figure 19.6.

FIGURE 19.6
The View Direction options for a profile style

While other tabs in an object style control the specifics of *how* certain components look or behave, the Display tab controls *if* the component displays at all. The Visibility lightbulb indicates whether the component will be displayed when the style is applied to the object. In the Surface Style dialog shown in Figure 19.5, you can see that borders, major contours, and minor contours will all display for the surface object style, but the other components will not be displayed in plan view. In the Profile Style dialog shown in Figure 19.6, all components will be displayed, except the Arrow component.

Each component can have a layer designation. The component layer will override the display properties of the object layer, which was set initially in the Drawing Settings ➢ Object Layer tab. When the component is set to layer 0, it will display using the display properties of the object layer as long as all other properties on the style's Display tab are set to ByLayer. This is another example of the parent-child settings. A setting of ByBlock will allow you to manage its display settings through the AutoCAD object Properties palette.

SUMMARY TAB

The Summary tab contains a list of all the settings configured on the other tabs of the style's dialog. Settings are editable on the Summary tab. Figure 19.7 shows the Summary tab of a profile style.

FIGURE 19.7
The Summary tab of a profile style

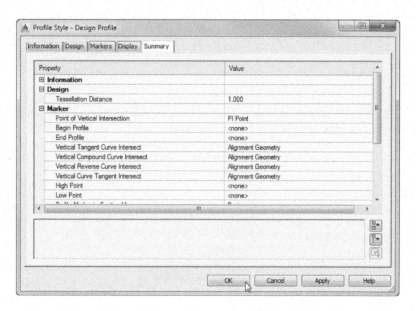

You can click the plus (+) or minus (–) button next to each category branch to expand to see further settings. At the bottom-right corner of the dialog are three buttons. The top button collapses all of the category branches, and the middle button expands all of the category branches. The bottom Override All Dependencies button can also be found on a Label Style Summary tab, but it is inactive for object styles. At the bottom of this dialog, additional information will be shown for the property selected.

General Settings

On the Settings tab of Toolspace, the General collection (or branch) contains settings and styles that can be applied to multiple object types in various scenarios. The General branch has three collections:

◆ Multipurpose Styles

◆ Label Styles

◆ Commands

You learned about the Label Styles collection in Chapter 18, "Label Styles," and now you will look at the Multipurpose Styles and Commands collections.

MULTIPURPOSE STYLES

If you expand the Multipurpose Styles collection, you will see seven folders, as shown in Figure 19.8.

FIGURE 19.8
General ➤
Multipurpose
Styles

These style types are used to control the display of components in various objects. For example, Marker Styles, Link Styles, and Shape Styles are typically used in section views containing corridors and assemblies, whereas Feature Line Styles, shown in Figure 19.9, are used when grading linear features and displaying corridors in plan.

FIGURE 19.9
The Feature Line
Styles collection

TOGGLE TOOLSPACE ORIENTATION

Toolspace is shown horizontally in Figure 19.9 and in other figures throughout this chapter for illustration purposes. If you like the way this looks, you can set your Toolspace like this by clicking the Orientation toggle at the top of Toolspace when it is floating (not docked). This will bring the item view to the right side of Toolspace instead of the default location at the bottom.

COMMANDS

A Commands folder will reside in almost every object branch of the Settings tree. Each item listed in this folder represents a command in that object category and is named after the keystrokes necessary to execute that command at the command line, as shown in Figure 19.10.

FIGURE 19.10
The Commands
folder

```
⊟ 🗁 Commands
    📴 AddLineBetweenPoints
    📴 AddNoteLabel
    📴 AddSegmentLabel
    📴 AddSegmentLabels
    📴 CreateArcByBestFit
    📴 CreateLineByBestFit
    📴 CreateParabolaByBestFit
    📴 ImportGISData
    📴 MapCheck
```

Point and Marker Object Styles

Markers are used in many places throughout Civil 3D. They are called from other styles to show vertices on Civil 3D objects such as feature lines, alignments, profiles, and figures. They can also be attached to the origination point on labels such as alignment station offset labels or surface spot elevations. Markers can even be used to indicate the start of a flow path.

MARKER TAB

Marker styles and point styles both contain a Marker tab (Figure 19.11). The Marker tab controls what symbol or block is used, its rotation, and how it should be sized when it is placed in the drawing.

FIGURE 19.11
The Marker tab
for the PI Point
Marker style

Three symbol types can be used. Use Custom Marker and Use AutoCAD BLOCK Symbol For Marker are the most popular options. Use AutoCAD POINT For Marker doesn't actually produce an AutoCAD point but uses the AutoCAD point style and size specified by the DDPTYPE dialog. When you choose the Use Custom Marker option, you can produce a marker similar in appearance to an AutoCAD point, but it will use the size options on the right side of this tab instead of the DDPTYPE dialog.

When you choose the Use AutoCAD BLOCK Symbol For Marker option, you will be able to access a list of blocks in your drawing. If the block you want to use does not yet exist in the drawing, you can right-click the block list and choose Browse, as shown in Figure 19.12.

FIGURE 19.12
Right-click to browse for a block if it is not already defined in your drawing.

The Size options control how the marker is scaled when inserted in the drawing (Figure 9.13).

FIGURE 19.13
The Size options for marker display

Use Drawing Scale   Use Drawing Scale allows you to specify the plotted size of the symbol. The model space size of the symbol will be the size specified in the style multiplied by your annotation scale.

Use Fixed Scale   Use Fixed Scale will scale the symbol based on the X, Y, and Z scale entered in the Fixed Scale area, just like a block. This option will also apply the Fixed Scale factor in the description key set when configured to a point.

Use Size In Absolute Units   Use Size In Absolute Units is the option you will use to specify a real-world size for the symbol regardless of scale. For example, if you want a manhole to always show as 5 feet in diameter, you could use this option. In the case of survey points used with description keys, if this option is set to .0833 (1 inch) and a size parameter is included in the point description, the symbol will be scaled to the value measured in the field.

Use Size Relative To Screen   Use Size Relative To Screen allows you to specify the size of the symbol as a percentage of your screen. The marker will change size as you zoom in or out similar to how points resize in GIS applications.

Two orientation buttons (as shown on the right side of the dialog in Figure 19.11) control whether the symbol stays rotated to the world coordinate system or the view.

CREATE A MARKER STYLE

Now it's time to get your hands on some object styles. You will start with simple styles and work your way up in complexity as this chapter progresses. In this first exercise, you will create a marker style:

1. Start a new blank drawing from the _AutoCAD Civil 3D (Imperial) NCS template that ships with Civil 3D. For metric users, use the _AutoCAD Civil 3D (Metric) NCS template.

2. From the Settings tab of Toolspace, expand General ➢ Multipurpose Styles ➢ Marker Styles.

3. Right-click Marker Styles and select New.

4. On the Information tab, do the following:

   a. Set Name to **PI Marker**.

   b. Add the description **Use to indicate PI in alignments**.

   Your login name will be listed in the Created By and Last Modified By fields.

5. On the Marker tab, do the following:

   a. Click the Use AutoCAD BLOCK Symbol For Marker radio button.

   b. In the block listing, highlight STA by clicking it.

   c. Verify that Size Options is set to Use Drawing Scale.

   d. Set the size to **0.2"** (or **5** mm).

   e. Leave all other Marker settings at their defaults.

6. On the Display tab with View Direction set to Plan, do the following:

   a. Click in the Layer column for the Marker component to display the Layer Selection dialog.

   b. In the Layer Selection dialog, set the layer to C-ROAD-STAN and click OK.

   Note that you may need to widen the column to view the full layer name.

   c. Click in the Color column for the Marker component to display the Select Color dialog.

   d. In the Select Color dialog, click the ByLayer button and click OK.

7. Repeat step 6 for View Direction set to Model, Profile, and Section.

8. Click OK to complete the creation of a new marker style.

9. From the Application menu, select Save As ➢ Drawing Template.

10. Set File Name to **1901_PointObject.dwg** (**1901_PointObject_METRIC.dwg**) and click Save.

Your PI marker will now be listed in the General ➤ Multipurpose Styles ➤ Marker Styles branch. Remember that you can import this style into any other drawing by using the Import Styles button found in the Styles panel of the Manage tab, and if you create this marker in a drawing template, it is accessible for any future projects that start with this template. Keep this drawing file open for the next portion of the exercise.

CREATE A SURVEY POINT STYLE

Survey point styles contain many of the same options as marker styles. As you work through the following example, you will perform many of the same steps as you did in the previous exercise:

1. Continue working in the drawing file from the previous exercise. You need to have completed the previous exercise.

2. From the Settings tab of Toolspace, expand Point ➤ Point Styles.

3. Right-click Point Styles and select New.

4. On the Information tab, do the following:

   a. Set Name to **TRUNK**.

   b. Add the description **Simple circle representing trunk diameter in inches** (or **Simple circle representing trunk diameter in mm**).

5. On the Marker tab, do the following:

   a. Click the Use Custom Marker radio button.

   b. Click the Blank Marker option from the group of symbols on the left.

   c. Click to add the Circle option on the right.

   d. Verify that Size Options is set to Use Size In Absolute Units, and set the size to **0.0833** (or **0.001** for metric).

   This value will scale down the symbol so the trunk diameter represents inches (or millimeters). Leave all other Marker settings at their defaults.

6. On the Display tab with View Direction set to Plan, do the following:

   a. Click in the Layer column for the Marker component to display the Layer Selection dialog.

   b. In the Layer Selection dialog, set the Marker layer to V-NODE-TREE and click OK.

   c. Repeat steps a and b to set the layer for the Label component to V-NODE-TREE. Leave the other settings at their defaults.

Hint! To save time in this step, you could alternatively use the Shift key to multiselect the Marker and Label components, as shown in Figure 19.14. By selecting both first, when you select the layer for one component, it will apply to both components.

FIGURE 19.14

Use the Shift key on your keyboard as you click the components to multiselect.

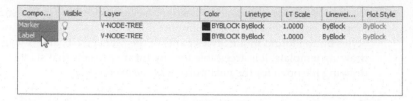

Compo...	Visible	Layer	Color	Linetype	LT Scale	Linewei...	Plot Style
Marker	💡	V-NODE-TREE	■ BYBLOCK ByBlock		1.0000	ByBlock	ByBlock
Label	💡	V-NODE-TREE	■ BYBLOCK ByBlock		1.0000	ByBlock	ByBlock

7. Repeat step 6 for View Direction set to Model, Profile, and Section, at the same time turning on the Visibility lightbulb for all components.

8. Click OK to complete the creation of a new point style.

You can save and keep this drawing file open to continue to the next exercise, or you can use the saved copy of this drawing file, 1901_PointObject_FINISHED.dwg (1901_PointObject_METRIC_FINISHED.dwg), available from the book's web page at www.sybex.com/go/masteringcivil3d2016.

Creating Linear Object Styles

In this section, you will see some linear styles such as alignments, profiles, and parcels. Ideally, you are already seeing that concepts from one type of style often apply to other types of styles. For alignment styles and profile styles, this is especially true.

Both alignment styles and profile styles have a Design tab, as shown in Figure 19.15. In the case of alignment styles, the Enable Radius Snap option restricts the grip-edit behavior of alignment curves. If you enable this option and set a value of 0.5′, the resulting radius value of curves will be rounded to the nearest 0.5′. In the case of profiles, the curve tessellation distance is a little more abstract. *Curve tessellation* refers to the smoothing factor applied to the profile when viewing it in 3D. Most users leave these settings at their default values.

FIGURE 19.15

Design tabs exist in both alignment and profile object styles.

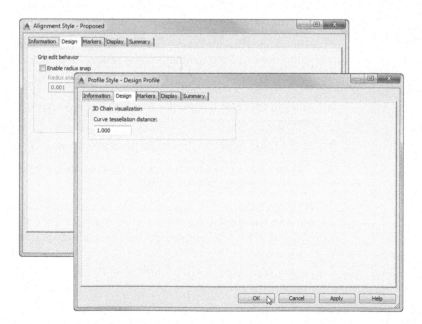

Alignment styles and profile styles have similar Markers tabs. This tab is where you can place markers (like the one you created in the first exercise of the chapter) at specific geometry points. Figure 19.16 shows the markers assigned to various locations along an alignment.

FIGURE 19.16
Markers for an alignment style

At the bottom of Figure 19.16, you see Arrowhead information. Both alignment styles and profile styles have the option of showing a direction arrow on each segment. You can omit this by turning the Arrow component off in the Display tab or by setting the component to a layer that is set to No Plot. When designing roundabouts, consider the latter because knowing the direction of an alignment comes in handy, as you saw in Chapter 10, "Advanced Corridors, Intersections, and Roundabouts."

Figure 19.17 shows some commonly highlighted horizontal geometry points and components in an alignment.

FIGURE 19.17
Example alignment with alignment marker points labeled

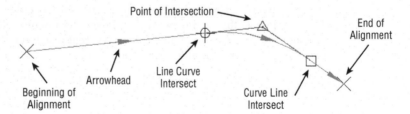

Figure 19.18 shows the Markers tab for the profile style. It looks pretty similar to the alignment Markers tab.

FIGURE 19.18
Markers for a profile style

Figure 19.19 shows some commonly highlighted vertical geometry points in a profile.

FIGURE 19.19
Example profile with profile marker points labeled

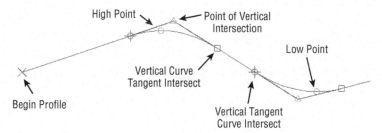

Alignment Styles

Alignment styles can be helpful in identifying key design components, as well as showing the stationing direction. Use multiple alignment styles to visually differentiate centerline alignments from supplemental alignments such as offset alignments and curb return alignments.

In the following exercise, you will create a style that restricts radius grip edits to 5-foot increments and displays basic alignment components:

1. Open the 1901_PointObject_FINISHED.dwg (1901_PointObject_METRIC_FINISHED .dwg) file.

   You can download either file from this book's web page.

2. From the Settings tab of Toolspace, expand Alignment ➢ Alignment Styles.

3. Right-click Alignment Styles and select New.

4. On the Information tab, set Name to **Centerline**.

5. On the Design tab, do the following:

    a. Verify that Enable Radius Snap is selected.

    b. Verify that Radius Snap is set to **5** (or **1** for metric).

    To see the Help document about any dialog, press F1 on your keyboard to be taken directly to the help section for that topic or click the Help button on the tab when you have a question regarding a specific tab on a dialog.

6. On the Markers tab, do the following:

    a. Set the Point Of Intersection marker by double-clicking the current value of <None>.

    b. In the Pick Marker Style dialog, select PI Marker from the marker listing and click OK.

    c. Using the same procedure, set the Through Points marker and the Station Reference Point marker both to <None>.

    Note that <None> is located near the top of the list.

7. On the Display tab with the View Direction set to Plan, do the following:

    a. Using the Shift key to select Arrow, Line Extensions, and Curve Extensions together, click one of their lightbulb icons to turn off the display of these three components.

    b. Using the Shift key to select Line, Curve, and Spiral, click in the Layer column to display the Layer Selection dialog.

    c. In the Layer Selection dialog, set the layer to C-ROAD-CNTR and click OK. This will set the layer for all three of the selected components.

    The Warning Symbol displays when design criteria or design checks are violated only if its display is turned on in this dialog. Design criteria and design checks were covered in Chapter 6, "Alignments." Leave its default display setting at On.

    Leave the Model and Section view directions at their defaults.

8. Click OK to finish creating a new alignment style.

This alignment will display the line, curve, and spiral on layer C-ROAD-CNTR, and a marker will be shown at the Point Of Intersection, as shown in Figure 19.20.

FIGURE 19.20
Centerline align-
ment style

When this exercise is complete, you can save and close the drawing. A saved copy of this drawing file, `1902_AlignmentObject_FINISHED.dwg` (`1902_AlignmentObject_METRIC_FINISHED.dwg`), is available from the book's web page.

Parcel Styles

The parcel styles have several unique features that make them different from other styles.

In the Design tab of a parcel (shown in Figure 19.21), you see parcel-specific options. A fill distance can be specified to place a hatch pattern along the perimeter of the parcel. This setting is used to help differentiate special parcels such as parks, limits of disturbance, or environmentally sensitive areas.

FIGURE 19.21
Parcel style options and the resulting parcel graphic

The *fill distance* indicates the width of the hatch pattern. The Component Hatch Display characteristics, including the pattern, angle, and scale, are specified at the bottom of the Display tab. Be sure to turn on Parcel Area Fill and configure a layer for it so it can be turned off independently from the parcel itself, since hatches tend to slow down the graphics. Figure 19.21 also shows the parcel graphic resulting from the design settings shown.

Feature Line Styles

Feature lines are found in quite a few different places. They are created automatically as part of corridors, are created as a result of generating a grading group, or can be created independently by the user. Because their scope crosses functionality, you will find feature line styles in the General ➤ Multipurpose Styles collection in the Settings tab.

By definition, a feature line is a 3D object; therefore, its style can be controlled in plan, model, profile, and section views. As shown in Figure 19.22, a feature line can use markers at geometry points.

FIGURE 19.22
Feature-line
profile marker
options (left) and
section marker
option (right)

Creating Surface Styles

Surface styles are the most widely used styles in any Civil 3D project. Depending on what objects are visible in the style that is active, certain editing options may be restricted. For example, points need to be visible before the Civil 3D software will let you use the Delete Point command on a surface.

There are seven tabs in the Surface Style dialog. Each tab corresponds to components listed in the Display tab. However, the Analysis tab covers the following components: Directions, Elevations, Slope, and Slope Arrows. Note that while some display components of these analyses are covered under this tab, they are also controlled by settings in the surface properties. While the Display tab is where the basic AutoCAD properties of each component are set, these other tabs allow you to configure in detail how each component is displayed. Some of these settings include applying marker styles to watersheds, setting 3D parameter borders, configuring contour intervals and depression ticks, and configuring color ranges for the different analysis tools.

Once a surface is created, you can display information in many ways. The most common so far have been contours and triangles, but these are the basics. By using varying styles, you can show a large amount of data with one single surface. Not only can you do simple things such as adjust the contour interval, but the Civil 3D program can apply a number of analysis tools to any surface:

Contours   Allows the user to apply to multiple ranges a color scheme or linetype as opposed to the typical minor-major scheme. This is commonly used in cut-fill maps to color negative contours one way, positive contours another, and the balance or zero contours yet another.

Directions   Draws arrows showing the normal direction of the surface face. This tool is typically used for aspect analysis, helping site planners review the way a site slopes with regard to cardinal directions and the sun.

Elevations   Creates bands of color to differentiate various ranges of elevations. You can use this tool to create a simple weighted distribution to help create marketing materials, hard-coded elevations to differentiate a floodplain and other elevation-driven site concerns, or ranges to help a designer understand the earthwork involved in creating a finished surface.

Slopes   Colors the face of each triangle on the basis of the assigned slope values. While a distributed method is the normal setup, a common use is to check site slopes for compliance with the Americans with Disabilities Act (ADA) of 1990 requirements or other site slope limitations, including vertical faces (where slopes are abnormally high).

Slope Arrows   Displays the same information as a slope analysis, but instead of coloring the entire face of the TIN, this option places an arrow pointing in the downhill direction and colors that arrow on the basis of the specified slope ranges. This is useful in confirming surface flow direction for site drainage.

User-Defined Contours   Refers to contours that typically fall outside the normal intervals. These user-defined contours are useful for drawing lines on a surface that are especially relevant but don't fall on one of the standard levels. A typical use is to show the normal water surface elevation on a site containing a pond or lake.

Watersheds   Used for watershed analysis, this style allows you to examine how water flows along and off of a surface. Using the surface TIN, the drain targets and watersheds are defined. An example of creating a watersheds surface style is provided later in this section.

In the following exercises, you will walk through the steps of creating and modifying surface styles.

Contour Styles

Contouring is the standard surface representation on which land development plans are built. In this example, you'll create a new surface contouring style and modify the interval to a setting more suitable for commercial site design review:

1. Open the `1903_SurfaceStylesContours.dwg` (`1903_SurfaceStylesContours_METRIC.dwg`) file, which you can download from this book's web page.

2. From the Settings tab of Toolspace, expand Surface ➢ Surface Styles.

3. Right-click Surface Styles and select New.

4. On the Information tab, do the following:

   a. Set Name to **Exaggerated Existing Contours**.

   b. Add the description **2′ minor contours with a 5× exaggeration when viewed in 3D** (or **1m minor contours with a 5× exaggeration when viewed in 3D** for metric).

5. On the Contours tab, do the following:

   a. Expand the Contour Intervals category.

   b. Set Minor Interval to **2′** (or **1 m**).

Notice that the Major Interval automatically adjusts to **10′** (or **5** m) or to whatever the minor interval is set times five.

c. Expand the Contour Smoothing category (you may have to scroll down).

d. Set Smooth Contours to True, which activates the Contour Smoothing slider bar near the bottom.

Don't change this Smoothing value, but keep in mind that this gives you a level of control over how much Civil 3D modifies the contours it draws.

SURFACE VS. CONTOUR SMOOTHING

Remember, contour smoothing is not surface smoothing. *Contour smoothing* applies smoothing at the individual contour level but not at the surface level. If you want to make your surface contouring look fluid, you should be smoothing the surface.

The Contours tab will now look similar to Figure 19.23.

FIGURE 19.23
The Contours tab in the Surface Style dialog

6. On the Triangles tab, do the following:

a. Change Triangle Display Mode to Exaggerate Elevation.

b. Set Exaggerate Triangles By Scale Factor to **5** (see Figure 19.24).

FIGURE 19.24
Exaggerate the
elevations shown
in the Object
Viewer.

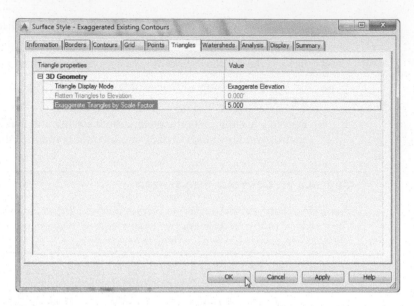

7. On the Display tab with View Direction set to Plan, do the following:

   a. Shift+click to highlight all the components.

   b. Click in the Color column of one of the components to display the Select Color dialog.

   c. In the Select Color dialog, click the ByLayer button and then click OK.

   d. While all the components are still highlighted, set Linetype to ByLayer using a similar procedure to steps b and c.

BYLAYER OR BYSTYLE

If you are a true CAD stickler, you will try to set as many items as possible to ByLayer. This approach greatly simplifies things if you need to change color or linetype using the Layer Manager. Alternatively, you can define the color and linetype independently through the style. Don't forget that you can also set the items to ByBlock, where their display will be controlled by the properties assigned to the object through the AutoCAD Properties palette.

You will be using only Minor Contour in this style, but later you will copy this style, and your efforts will be carried forward.

   e. With all the components still selected, click one of the lightbulbs that is on to turn off all components. Then select only the Minor Contour component and turn on its lightbulb.

f. Set the Minor Contour layer to C-TOPO-MINR.

Your Display tab should now resemble Figure 19.25.

FIGURE 19.25
Setting Minor Contour component to be the only one displayed for this surface style in plan

8. On the Display tab, change View Direction to Model and do the following:

a. Shift+click to highlight all the components.

b. Using the same procedure previously used, set all the colors and linetypes to ByLayer.

c. Verify that Triangles is the only component displayed.

d. Set only the Triangles layer to C-TINN-VIEW.

To see the surface in the Object Viewer or in any other 3D view, you must have triangles set to display in the Model View Direction.

9. Click OK to complete the style. Save the drawing.

10. From the Prospector tab of Toolspace, expand Surfaces, right-click the EG surface, and select Surface Properties.

11. On the Information tab, set Surface Style to Exaggerated Existing Contours, and click OK.

The surface should be rendered faster than you can read this sentence, even with the contour interval you've selected with only the minor contours displayed. After the style is applied to the surface model, you should see simple contours in plan view (the left image in Figure 19.26) and an exaggerated surface model in the Object Viewer (the right image in Figure 19.26).

FIGURE 19.26
The surface show-
ing your new style
in plan (left) and
in model (right), as
shown in a custom
3D isometric view
using the 3D wire-
frame visual style

You skipped over one portion of the surface contours that many people consider a great benefit of using Civil 3D: depression contours. If this option is turned on via the Contours tab, ticks
will be added to the downhill side of any closed contours leading to a low point. This is a stylis-
tic option, and usage varies widely.

You can save and keep this drawing open to continue to the next exercise or use the
finished version of this drawing, 1903_SurfaceStylesContours_FINISHED.dwg (1903_
SurfaceStylesContours_METRIC_FINISHED.dwg), available from the book's web page.

Triangles and Points Surface Styles

The next style you create will help facilitate surface editing. To work with the Swap Edge and
Delete Line Surface edits, you must be able to see triangles. To work with the Delete Point,
Modify Point, and Move Point commands, you must be able to see surface points.

It is important to note that the points you see in the surface style do not refer to survey
points. The points you are working with in this exercise are *triangle vertices*. The triangle vertices and survey points will initially be in the same locations for a surface built from points.
However, as breaklines are added or edits are made to the triangle vertices, the surface model
will differ from the original survey.

1. Open 1903_SurfaceStylesContours_FINISHED.dwg (1903_SurfaceStylesContours_
   METRIC_FINISHED.dwg).

   You can download either file from this book's web page.

2. From the Settings tab of Toolspace, expand Surface ➤ Surface Styles.

3. Right-click the Exaggerated Existing Contours style and select Copy, as shown in
   Figure 19.27.

FIGURE 19.27
Access Copy by
right-clicking the
style name.

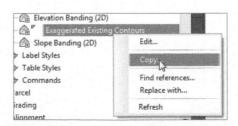

4. On the Information tab, do the following:

    a. Rename the surface style to **Surface Editing**.

    b. Remove the text in the description file and type the description **Points and triangles**.

5. On the Points tab, do the following:

    a. Expand Point Size and set the Point Units to **3'** (or **1** m), if not already set.

    b. Expand Point Display and click the ellipsis for Data Point Symbol, if not already set.

    c. Set the point type to the X symbol, as shown in Figure 19.28, if not already set.

FIGURE 19.28
Change the Point Display symbol so the points stand out within the style.

6. On the Triangles tab, remove the exaggeration by setting the Triangle display mode back to Use Surface Elevation.

7. On the Display tab with View Direction set to Plan, do the following:

    a. Use the lightbulb icons to turn off visibility for Minor Contour and turn it on for Points and Triangles.

    b. Click in the Layer column for the Points component to display the Layer Selection dialog.

    c. In the Layer Selection dialog, with layer 0 selected, click the New button to create a new layer for the Points component.

    d. In the Create Layer dialog, set Layer Name to **C-TINN-PNTS**, set Color to Red, and click OK to finish creating the layer.

    e. In the Layer Selection dialog, select the layer as C-TINN-PNTS and click OK.

    f. Click in the Layer column for the Triangles component to display the Layer Selection dialog.

g. In the Layer Selection dialog, select the Triangles layer as C-TINN-VIEW and click OK.

Your Display tab will resemble Figure 19.29.

FIGURE 19.29
Change the Points and Triangles visibility and layers in the Display tab.

8. Click OK to complete the style.

9. Use the same procedure from the previous exercise to apply the Surface Editing style to the surface.

Your surface will resemble Figure 19.30.

FIGURE 19.30
Triangles and points shown using the new surface style

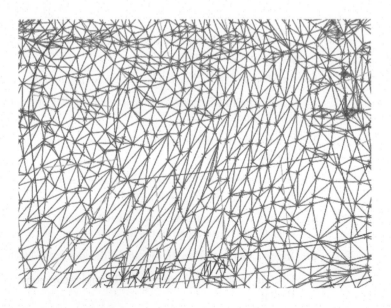

With the points and triangles displayed, you can edit the surface, such as deleting points or swapping edges.

You can save and keep this drawing open to continue to the next exercise or use the saved copy of this drawing, 1903_SurfaceStyleTriangles_FINISHED.dwg (1903_SurfaceStyleTriangles_METRIC_FINISHED.dwg), available from the book's web page.

Analysis Styles

Analysis styles are unique in several ways. To see the style applied to your design, you must run the analysis in the surface properties in addition to applying the style to the surface. Although layers can now be configured to these styles, colors and behavior are configured on the Analysis tab. Visibility can be controlled by turning off the layer assigned on the Display tab of the style, by turning off the Analysis component in the style, or by assigning another style that doesn't display that component.

You can choose distribution methods to apply to your analysis on the Analysis tab of the surface style. The distribution method is selected by configuring the Group By option under each analysis type. Here's what they mean:

Equal Interval   This method uses a stepped scale, created by taking the minimum and maximum values and then dividing the delta into the number of selected ranges. For example, if the surface has elevations from 0 to 10, with four ranges they will be 0 to 2.5, 2.5 to 5.0, 5.0 to 7.5, and 7.5 to 10. This method can create real anomalies when extremely large or small values skew the total range so that much of the data falls into one or two intervals, with almost no sampled data in the other ranges.

Quantile   This method is often referred to as an *equal count distribution* and will create ranges that are equal in sample size. These ranges will not be equal in linear size but in distribution across a surface. For example, if the surface has elevations from 0 to 10 with most of the surface at the higher elevations, with four ranges they may be 0 to 4.78 (25 percent of the surface), 4.78 to 6.25 (25 percent of the surface), 6.25 to 7.95 (25 percent of the surface), and 7.95 to 10 (25 percent of the surface).

This method is best used when the values are relatively equally spaced throughout the total range, with no extremes to throw off the group sizing.

Standard Deviation   Standard Deviation is the bell curve that most engineers are familiar with, suited for when the data follows the bell distribution pattern. It generally works well for slope analysis, where very flat and very steep slopes are common, and would make another distribution setting unwieldy.

You looked at an elevations, slopes, and slope arrows analysis earlier in Chapter 4, "Surfaces." In the following exercise, you will create a surface style for watershed analysis. To apply the new style to the surface, you must also run the analysis.

1. Open 1903_SurfaceStylesTriangles_FINISHED.dwg (1903_SurfaceStylesTriangles_METRIC_FINISHED.dwg).

    You can download either file from this book's web page.

2. From the Settings tab of Toolspace, expand Surface ➤ Surface Styles.

3. Right-click the Exaggerated Existing Contours style and select Copy.

4. On the Information tab, do the following:

   a. Rename the surface style to **Watershed Analysis**.

   b. Remove the current description and type **Display watersheds and slope arrows.**

5. On the Triangles tab, change Triangle Display Mode to Use Surface Elevation.

6. On the Watersheds tab, do the following:

   a. Expand the Boundary Segment Watershed category.

   b. Set Use Hatching to False.

   c. Expand the Multi-Drain Watershed category.

   d. Set Use Hatching to False.

   Your Watersheds tab will look like Figure 19.31.

FIGURE 19.31
Changing the hatch options for watershed areas

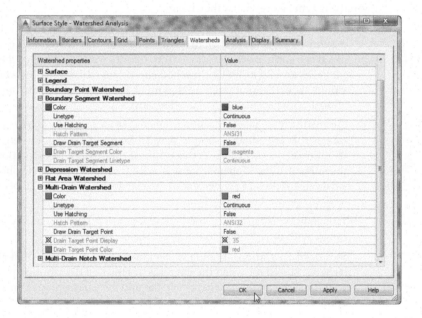

7. On the Analysis tab, do the following:

   a. Expand the Slope Arrows category.

   b. Change Scheme to Hydro.

   c. Change Arrow Length to **2′** (or **1** m).

   The Analysis tab will resemble Figure 19.32.

FIGURE 19.32
Set the color scheme and arrow length on the Analysis tab.

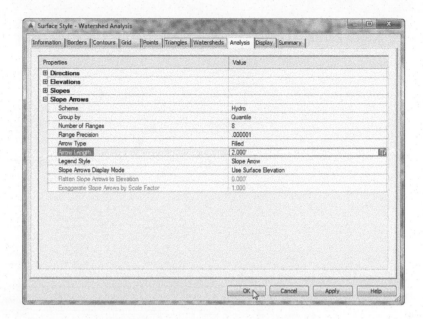

8. On the Display tab with View Direction set to Plan, do the following:

   a. Turn off visibility for the Minor Contour component, and turn it on for Slope Arrows and Watersheds—you may have to scroll.

   b. Set the Watershed component layer to C-TOPO-WSHD.

9. Click OK to complete the surface style.

10. Select the surface, and from the contextual tab in the Modify panel, click Surface Properties.

11. On the Information tab, set Surface Style to Watershed Analysis and click Apply.

12. On the Analysis tab, do the following:

    a. Set Analysis Type to Watershed.

    b. Set Merge Depressions to **0.4′** (or **0.1** m).

    c. Place a check mark next to Merge Adjacent Boundary Watersheds.

    d. Click the Run Analysis arrow in the middle of the dialog to populate the Range Details area.

    Your Surface Properties Analysis tab should resemble Figure 19.33.

FIGURE 19.33
You must run the analysis in Surface Properties before the Watershed style kicks in.

13. Click OK to close the Surface Properties dialog.

Your surface model should resemble Figure 19.34.

Now that the watershed analysis has been run, you could provide further information by generating a dynamic Watershed table similar to how you generated a table showing other surface information in Chapter 4.

FIGURE 19.34
The surface set to use the Watershed Analysis style

When this exercise is complete, you can close the drawing. A saved copy of this drawing, 1903_SurfaceStylesWatershed_FINISHED.dwg (1903_SurfaceStylesWatershed_METRIC_FINISHED.dwg), is available from the book's web page.

Creating Pipe and Structure Styles

In Chapter 13, "Pipe Networks," you learned that the first step to managing pipes and structures was to build a parts list. One of the functions of a parts list is to associate styles to pipes and structures. In this section, you will learn how to create the pipe and structure styles that are used by a parts list.

In your template, you will have many styles assigned to the various parts lists. You will want to have separate styles for water parts, storm sewer parts, and waste water parts. Additionally, you may want to have separate styles for existing and proposed systems. The main difference between the styles for the different systems will be the layers you set in the Display tab.

Pipe Styles

It seems like no two municipalities want pipes displayed the same way on construction documents. Fortunately, Civil 3D offers many variations for pipe display that will satisfy miscellaneous submittal requirements. With one pipe style, you can control how a pipe is displayed in plan, profile, and section views. You can use multiple pipe styles to graphically differentiate larger pipes from smaller ones. This section explores all the options.

Information Tab This tab allows you to define the name for the style and its description.

Plan Tab The tab you see in Figure 19.35 controls how your pipe is represented when you're working in plan view.

FIGURE 19.35
The Plan tab in the Pipe Style dialog

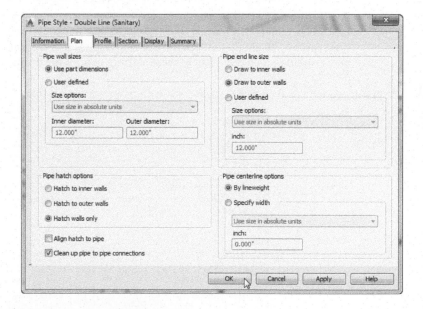

Options on the Plan tab include the following:

Pipe Wall Sizes You can choose between having the program apply the part size directly from the part catalog (that is, the literal pipe dimensions as defined in the catalog) and specifying your own constant or scaled dimensions.

Pipe Hatch Options   If you choose to show pipe hatching, this part of the tab gives you options to control that hatch. You can hatch the entire pipe to the inner or outer walls, or you can hatch the space between the inner and outer walls only, as shown in Figure 19.36. There are also options to align the hatch to the pipe and to clean up pipe-to-pipe connections.

FIGURE 19.36
Pipe hatch to
inner walls (a),
outer walls (b),
and hatch walls
only (c)

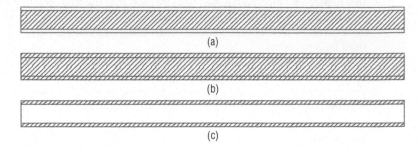

Pipe End Line Size   If you choose to show an end line, you can control its length with these options. An end line can be drawn connecting the outer walls or the inner walls, or you can specify your own constant or scaled dimensions. The pipes from Figure 19.36 are all shown with pipe end lines drawn to outer walls.

Pipe Centerline Options   If you choose to show a centerline, you can display it by the lineweight established in the Display tab, or you can specify centerline widths based on the pipe inner or outer wall dimension, a scaled dimension, or a constant dimension. You could use this option for your waste water pipes in places where the width of the centerline widens or narrows on the basis of the pipe diameter.

Profile Tab   The Profile tab (see Figure 19.37) is almost identical to the Plan tab, except the controls here determine what your pipe looks like in profile view. The only additional settings on this tab are the ones in the Crossing Pipe Hatch Options area. If you choose to display crossing pipe with a hatch, these settings control the location of that hatch.

FIGURE 19.37
The Profile tab
in the Pipe Style
dialog

Section Tab   If you choose to show a hatch on your pipes in section, you control the hatch location on this tab (see Figure 19.38). There is also the option to display the pipe as sliced pipe, where its display in section view uses the actual position of where the sample line crosses the pipe.

FIGURE 19.38
The Section tab in the Pipe Style dialog

PRESSURE PIPE STYLES

The Pressure Pipe Style dialog looks similar to the Pipe Style dialog, with Plan and Profile tabs that have similar behavior to that discussed for regular pipes.

Continues

Continued

The two biggest differences are that there is no Section tab and there is no Crossing Pipe Hatch Options area on the Plan tab. Also, the Pipe Centerline Options and Clean Up Pipe To Pipe Connections options are not available. There are a few other minor changes to how the user can define sizes.

In the examples that follow, you will create various types of pipe styles.

The first style is for a situation where the pipe must be shown in plan view with a single line, the thickness of which matches the pipe's inner diameter. In profile view, the pipe will show the inner diameter lines, and in section view, it will show as a hatch-filled ellipse.

1. Open the `1904_PipeStyle.dwg` (`1904_PipeStyle_METRIC.dwg`) file, which you can download from this book's web page.

2. From the Settings tab of Toolspace, expand Pipe ➤ Pipe Styles.

3. Right-click Pipe Styles and select New.

4. On the Information tab, set Name to **Proposed Sanitary CL**.

5. On the Plan tab, do the following:

   a. Verify that Pipe Centerline Options is set to Specify Width.

   b. Set Specify Width to Draw To Inner Walls.

6. On the Profile tab, no changes are needed.

7. On the Section tab, verify that Display as Hatched Pipe is set to Hatch To Inner Walls.

8. On the Display tab with View Direction set to Plan, do the following:

   a. Turn off the display for all components except Pipe Centerline. You may need to change the column width in order to read the component names.

   b. Set the Pipe Centerline layer to C-SSWR-PIPE.

9. On the Display tab, change View Direction to Profile and do the following:

   a. Turn off the display for all components except Inside Pipe Walls.

   b. Set the layer to C-SSWR-PROF.

10. On the Display tab, change View Direction to Section and do the following:

    a. Set Crossing Pipe Inside Wall to the C-SSWR-PIPE layer and make it visible.

b. Set Crossing Pipe Hatch to the C-SSWR-PIPE-PATT layer and make it visible.

c. Turn the display off for Crossing Pipe Outside Wall and Sliced Solid Pipe Walls.

d. At the bottom of the dialog, click in the Pattern column for the Crossing Pipe Hatch component type to display the Hatch Pattern dialog.

e. Set Type to Solid Fill, as shown in Figure 19.39, and click OK.

FIGURE 19.39
Setting the Hatch Pattern display for the Section view direction

11. Click OK to finish creating the new pipe style.

12. From the Prospector tab of Toolspace, expand Pipe Networks ➤ Networks ➤ Sanitary Network and select Pipes.

13. Using the Shift key, select all of the pipes in the item list.

14. Right-click the heading of the Style column and select Edit.

15. In the Select Pipe Style dialog, select Proposed Sanitary CL and click OK.

16. Examine the pipe in the plan, profile, and section views, as shown in Figure 19.40.

FIGURE 19.40
Proposed Sanitary
CL pipe style
shown in plan (a),
profile (b), and
section (c)

(a)

(b)

(c)

You can save and keep this drawing open to continue to the next exercise or use the finished copy of this drawing, 1904_PipeStyle_FINISHED.dwg (1904_PipeStyle_METRIC_FINISHED .dwg), available from the book's web page.

HEY! WHY DOES MY PIPE LOOK LIKE AN OCTAGON?

The Civil 3D program helps itself perform better on large drawings by knocking down the resolution of 3D curved objects, such as the pipe in the cross-section view in the previous steps.

FACETDEV=0.5   FACETDEV=0.001

The system variable you can use to make these pipes look nicer is Facet Deviation, or FACETDEV. The default FACETDEV value for any Imperial unit drawing is 0.5 inches. In metric drawings, the default is 10 millimeters. The lower the FACETDEV value, the smoother the 3D curve.

Note that another variable, FACETMAX, controls the maximum number of facets on any curved object. The Civil 3D default of 500 facets is usually more than enough to display a Civil 3D pipe smoothly.

In the next pipe style example, you will create a style that uses several options for hatching pipe walls for a pipe:

1. Open 1904_PipeStyle_FINISHED.dwg (1904_PipeStyle_METRIC_FINISHED.dwg).

2. From the Settings tab of Toolspace, expand Pipe ➢ Pipe Styles.

3. Right-click Pipe Styles and select New.

4. On the Information tab, set Name to **Proposed Hatch Wall**.

5. On the Plan tab, do the following:

   a. Verify that Pipe Hatch Options is set to Hatch Walls Only.

   b. Verify that Align Hatch To Pipe is selected.

6. On the Profile tab, do the following:

   a. Verify that Pipe Hatch Options is set to Hatch Walls Only.

   b. Verify that Align Hatch To Pipe is selected.

7. On the Display tab with View Direction set to Plan, do the following:

   a. Verify that the only components turned on are Inside Pipe Walls, Outside Pipe Walls, Pipe End Line, and Pipe Hatch.

   b. Set all four layers to C-SSWR-PIPE.

   c. Click the Component Hatch Display Scale field and type in a new value of **0.1**.

8. On the Display tab, change View Direction to Profile and do the following:

   a. Verify that the only components turned on are Inside Pipe Walls, Outside Pipe Walls, Pipe End Line, and Pipe Hatch.

   b. Set all four of these layers to C-SSWR-PROF.

9. Click OK to complete the creation of the new pipe style.

10. From the Prospector tab of Toolspace, expand Pipe Networks ➤ Networks ➤ Sanitary Network and select Pipes.

11. Select all of the pipes in the Item list using the Shift key.

12. Right-click the heading of the Style column and select Edit.

13. In the Select Pipe Style dialog, select Proposed Hatch Wall and click OK.

14. Examine the pipe in plan and profile, as shown in Figure 19.41. It looks similar in both views.

FIGURE 19.41
Proposed Hatch
Wall pipe style
shown in plan

Depending on your drawing's scale, it may or may not be worth it to you to add a pipe wall hatch because with thin walls it may be hard to see, as shown in Figure 19.41.

When this exercise is complete, you can save and close the drawing. A saved copy of this drawing, `1904_PipeStyleHatch_FINISHED.dwg` (`1904_PipeStyleHatch_METRIC_FINISHED.dwg`), is available from the book's web page.

You could do this same exercise for a Pressure Pipe style. The only difference would be setting the layers to C-WATR-PIPE instead of C-SSWR-PIPE or to C-WATR-PROF instead of C-SSWR-PROF.

Structure Styles

The following tour through the structure-style interface can be used for reference as you create company-standard styles:

Information Tab This tab allows you to define the name for the style and its description.

Model Tab The Model tab (Figure 19.42) controls what represents your structure when you're working in 3D. Typically, you want to leave the Use Catalog Defined 3D Part radio button selected so that when you look at your structure, it looks like your flared end section or whatever you've chosen in the parts list.

FIGURE 19.42
The Model tab in the Structure Style dialog

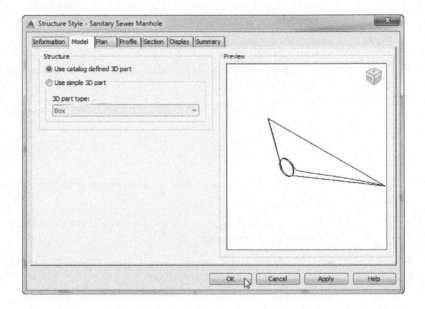

Plan Tab The Plan tab (Figure 19.43) enables you to compose your object style to match any particular standard.

FIGURE 19.43
The Plan tab in the Structure Style dialog

Options on the Plan tab include the following:

Use Outer Part Boundary   This option uses the limits of your structure from the parts list and shows you an outline of the structure as it would appear in the plan.

User Defined Part   This option uses any block you specify. In the case of your flared end section, you can chose a symbol to match the CAD standard of your company. When using User Defined Part, you also must provide Size Options. The options in this drop-down are similar to what you see in other styles, such as point or marker styles in Civil 3D.

♦   Use Drawing Scale will display and scale the block based on the annotative scale assigned to the drawing.

♦   Use Fixed Scale allows you to enter X, Y, and Z scale factors as you would do when inserting a block.

♦   Use Size In Absolute Units is a common way to represent a manhole at a specified size.

♦   Use Size As Percentage Of Screen keeps the part the same size whether you zoom in close or are far away.

♦   Use Fixed Scale From Part Size will stretch the block around the part even if the dimensions of both don't match.

Enable Part Masking   This option creates a wipeout or mask inside the limits of the structure. Any pipes that connect to the center of the pipe appear trimmed at the limits of the structure. This will mask the pipes entering and exiting the structure based on where they intersect the actual walls of the structure as modeled. Keep in mind that when using a block, these locations may not match the extents of the block.

Profile Tab   The Profile tab (Figure 19.44) is where you configure what your structure will look like in profile view.

FIGURE 19.44
The Profile tab in the Structure Style dialog

Options on the Profile tab include the following:

Display As Solid   This option uses the limits of your structure from the parts list and shows you the mesh of the structure as it would appear in profile view.

Display As Boundary   This option uses the limits of your structure from the parts list and shows you an outline of the structure as it would appear in profile view. You'll use this option for the sanitary manhole.

Display As Block   This option uses any block you specify. When using a structure displayed as a block, you also must provide Size Options. The Size Options are the same as the ones described for the Plan tab.

Enable Part Masking   This option creates a wipeout or mask inside the limits of the structure. Any pipes that connect to the center of the pipe appear trimmed at the limits of the structure.

Section Tab   The Section tab (Figure 19.45) is where you configure what your structure will look like in section view.

FIGURE 19.45
The Section tab in the Structure Style dialog

These options look (and behave) very much like the Profile tab options listed earlier with the following exception: beginning with the 2015 release it gives you the option to display the sliced section of the structure.

In the following exercise, you'll create a new structure style that uses a block in plan view to represent a sanitary manhole. Because the block is drawn at actual size, you will use the size option Use Fixed Scale.

1. Open the 1905_StructureStyle.dwg (1905_StructureStyle_METRIC.dwg) file, which you can download from this book's web page.

2. From the Settings tab of Toolspace, expand Structure ➤ Structure Styles.

3. Right-click Structure Styles and select New.

4. On the Information tab, rename the style to **Simple Sanitary Manhole**.

5. On the Plan tab, do the following:

   a. Verify that User Defined Part is selected.

   b. Set Block Name to **_Wipeout_Circle** using the list box.

   c. Set Size to Use Fixed Scale.

   d. Set the X and Y scale factors to **3** (**1** for metric).

6. On the Display tab with View Direction set to Plan, set the Structure layer to C-SSWR-STRC.

7. Repeat step 6 with View Direction set to Profile and then repeat with View Direction set to Section.

8. Click OK to complete the style.

9. From the Prospector tab of Toolspace, expand Pipe Networks ➢ Networks ➢ Sanitary Network and select Structures.

10. Using the Shift key, select all of the structures in the Item list.

11. Right-click the heading of the Style column and select Edit.

12. In the Select Structure style dialog, select Simple Sanitary Manhole and click OK.

13. To observe the style change in plan, select any one of the structures, right-click and click Zoom To. Run a regen command to refresh the representation of the data in the file.

When this exercise is complete, you can save and close the drawing. A saved copy of this drawing, 1905_StructureStyle_FINISHED.dwg (1905_StructureStyle_METRIC_FINISHED .dwg), is available from the book's web page.

While this example discussed creating object styles for a structure, you will find that the same procedure is applicable to the Appurtenances and Fittings styles used in pressure pipe networks.

Creating Profile View Styles

Certification
Objective

When you are looking at a profile view that contains data, you are seeing many styles displayed. The profiles themselves (existing and proposed) have a profile object style applied to them. The labels consist of many types of styles, as you learned in Chapter 18. Additionally, there are profile view styles and band styles to consider.

This section focuses on the profile view. A profile view controls many aspects of the display. The profile view style consists of some of the following properties:

◆ Vertical exaggeration

◆ Grid spacing

◆ Elevation and station annotation

◆ Title annotation

Figure 19.46 shows a profile view with some of its basic components labeled. There are many more components in a profile view style.

FIGURE 19.46

Profile view style with some of its basic components labeled

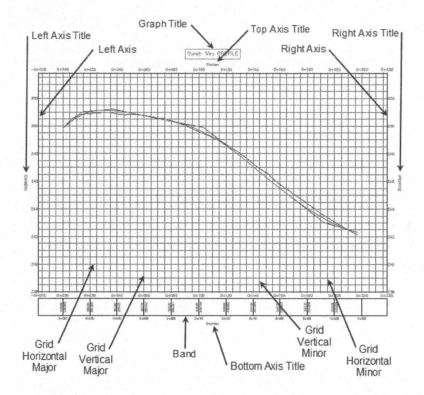

In the example that follows, you will be making major modifications to a profile view style. The profile view you will be practicing with does not contain any bands. Later in this section, you will learn the ins and outs of band creation and modification.

1. Open the `1906_ProfileViewStyles.dwg` (`1906_ProfileViewStyles_METRIC.dwg`) file.

   This file contains a profile view of Cabernet Court with an ugly style applied to it. You will perform a complete makeover on this style.

2. Zoom in as close as possible so you can see the entire profile view and select the profile view by clicking anywhere on a grid line or axis.

3. From the Profile View contextual tab, select Profile View Properties ➤ Edit Profile View Style, as shown in Figure 19.47.

FIGURE 19.47
Accessing the profile view style

4. Position the dialog on your screen so you can make changes to the style and observe the changes in the profile view behind it.

5. On the Graph tab, change the Vertical Exaggeration value to **10**, as shown in Figure 19.48, and click Apply.

FIGURE 19.48
Change Vertical Exaggeration on the Graph tab of the Profile View Style dialog.

When you do, you will notice that the Vertical Scale listed in the dialog automatically changes from 1″ = 50′ to 1″ = 5′ (or from 1:500 to 1:50 for metric users). In addition, if you can see your profile view in the background, you should notice that it has expanded vertically by a factor of 10.

6. On the Grid tab, do the following:

a. Verify that both the Clip Vertical Grid and Clip Horizontal Grid options are unchecked.

If you need additional information on any of the controls on this tab, click the Help button at the bottom of the dialog.

b. Set Grid Padding (Major Grids) to **0.5** for Above Maximum Elevation and **0.5** for Below Datum.

This setting will create additional space above and below the design data at 0.5 times the vertical major tick interval (you will set the major tick interval later).

c. Set all values for Axis Offset (Plotted Units) to **0**.

d. Click Apply to review changes on the profile view.

This will ensure that the axes and the grid lines coincide around the edges of the view. The settings on the Grid tab should match those shown in Figure 19.49.

FIGURE 19.49
The Grid tab of the Profile View Style dialog

7. On the Title Annotation tab, do the following:

a. In the Graph View Title area, change Text Height to **0.4"** (or **10** mm).

b. In the Graph View Title area, click the Edit Mtext button.

c. In the Text Component Editor dialog, remove all the text in the Text Component Editor window.

You will be starting over with a blank Text Component Editor dialog.

d. From the Properties drop-down, select Parent Alignment and make these changes:

◆ Set Capitalization to Upper Case.

◆ Click the white arrow button to add the Property field to the Text Component Editor window.

◆ Click in the Text Component Editor window behind the Property field, add a space, and type **PROFILE VIEW**.

e. Click OK to accept the entry in the Text Component Editor dialog.

f. Change the Y Offset for the Title Position to **2"** (or **10** mm).

8. Click Apply and examine your changes in the background.

The Title Annotation tab should match the settings shown in Figure 19.50.

FIGURE 19.50
Working with the
Graph View Title
size and placement

Do not bother to adjust any settings for Axis Title Text on the right side of Figure 19.50 because the display will be turned off for all four of these possible elements.

9. On the Horizontal Axes tab, do the following:

a. Verify that the Select Axis To Control radio button is set to Bottom.

b. In the Major Tick Details area, set Interval to **100'** (or **20** m).

c. In the Major Tick Details area, click the Edit Mtext button.

d. In the Text Component Editor dialog, do the following:

◆ Remove all the text in the Text Component Editor window.

◆ From the Properties drop-down, select Station Value.

◆ Change Precision to **1**.

◆ Click the white arrow button to add the Property field to the Text Component Editor window.

e. Click OK to accept the entry in the Text Component Editor dialog.

f. In the Major Tick Details area, change Rotation to **90**.

g. In the Major Tick Details area, change the X offset to **0″ (0 mm)** and the Y offset to **−0.25″ (−10 mm)**.

h. In the Minor Tick Details area, set Interval to **50′ (10 m)**.

No other changes are needed in the Minor Tick Details area. Click Apply to see the changes.

The Horizontal Axes tab should match the settings shown in Figure 19.51.

FIGURE 19.51
The bottom axis controls grid spacing

10. On the Vertical Axes tab, do the following:

a. Verify that the Select Axis To Control radio button is set to Left.

b. In the Major Tick Details area, click the Edit Mtext button.

c. In the Text Component Editor dialog, do the following:

♦ Remove all the text in the Text Component Editor window.

♦ From the Properties drop-down, select Profile View Point Elevation.

♦ Change Precision to **1**.

♦ Click the white arrow button to add the Property field to the Text Component Editor window.

d. Click OK to exit the Text Component Editor dialog.

e. In the Major Tick Details area, change the X offset to **−0.25"** (**−5** mm) and the Y offset to **0"** (0 mm).

All the changes made up to this point on the Vertical Axes tab apply to the Left axis. You will now do similar modifications to the Right axis.

f. Change the Select Axis To Control radio button to Right.

g. In the Major Tick Details area, click the Edit Mtext button.

h. In the Text Component Editor dialog, do the following:

◆ Remove all the text in the Text Component Editor window.

◆ From the Properties drop-down, select Profile View Point Elevation.

◆ Change Precision to **1**.

◆ Click the white arrow button to add the property value to the Text Component Editor window.

i. Click OK to exit the Text Component Editor.

j. In the Major Tick Details area, change the X offset to **0.25"** (**5** mm) and the Y offset to **0"** (0 mm).

11. Click Apply and examine your changes.

Figure 19.52 shows what your Vertical Axes tab should look like at this point in the exercise.

FIGURE 19.52
Don't forget to change the settings for both the Left and Right axes on this tab

12. On the Display tab, do the following:

    a. Select all of the components and use the lightbulb icon to turn off visibility for all the components.

    b. Turn back on the visibility for the following components:

- Graph Title
- Left Axis
- Left Axis Annotation Major
- Right Axis
- Right Axis Annotation Major
- Top Axis
- Bottom Axis
- Bottom Axis Annotation Major
- Grid Horizontal Major
- Grid Horizontal Minor
- Grid Vertical Major
- Grid Vertical Minor

13. Click OK to complete the profile view style.

Your profile view should resemble Figure 19.53.

FIGURE 19.53
The profile view style updated to reflect the changes

CABERNET COURT PROFILE VIEW

When this exercise is complete, you can save and close the drawing. A saved copy of this drawing, `1906_ProfileViewStyles_FINISHED.dwg` (`1906_ProfileViewStyles_METRIC_FINISHED.dwg`), is available from the book's web page.

WHAT DRIVES PROFILE VIEW GRID SPACING?

On the Horizontal Axes tab and Vertical Axes tab of the Profile View Style dialog, you may notice that you can control opposing axes separately. Each tab has a toggle for Select Axis To Control: Top or Bottom and Left or Right.

The Bottom and Left options in the respective tabs control grid spacing. For both axes, you will find options for Major Tick Details. The Interval values for the major ticks are the key to getting the grid spacing to look the way you want. Changes to either horizontal or vertical major tick intervals will affect the height and length of the profile view, as well as grid spacing. Changing the Interval value on Minor Tick Details will affect the grid spacing but will not affect the aspect ratio of the profile view.

Here is a common practice for setting major tick interval values for your horizontal and vertical axes:

Vertical Exaggeration value (Grid tab) × Major Tick Interval value (Vertical Axes tab – right or left) = Major Tick Interval value (Horizontal Axes tab – top or bottom).

Therefore, a profile view style with Vertical Exaggeration set to 10 and Vertical Major Tick Intervals set to 5′ would yield horizontal major tick intervals set to 50′.

Even if you don't turn on the ticks or grid lines on these axes, the spacing increment will be reflected in the profile view.

Profile View Bands

Data bands are strips of labels and/or schematics that display additional information about the profile or alignment that is referenced in a profile view. The most common band type is the profile data band.

Bands can be applied to both the top and bottom of a profile view, and there are six band types: Profile Data Bands, Vertical Geometry Bands, Horizontal Geometry Bands, Superelevation Data Bands, Sectional Data Bands, and Pipe Network Bands. These band types were discussed in Chapter 7, "Profiles and Profile Views," but graphic reminders of the various band types are shown in Figures 19.54 through 19.59.

FIGURE 19.54
Profile Data Band showing existing and proposed elevation in addition to major stations

FIGURE 19.55
Vertical Geometry Band

FIGURE 19.56
Horizontal Geometry Band

FIGURE 19.57
Superelevation Data Band

FIGURE 19.58
Section Data Band

FIGURE 19.59
Pipe Data Band
showing invert
elevations and
slope schematic

Bands can be assigned to band sets. Like alignment label sets and profile label sets, a band set determines which bands are applied to a profile view and how they are positioned. The most common use for a band set is to create a single, viewable band and an additional nonvisible band for spacing purposes in plan and profile sheet generation. However, depending on your jurisdictional requirements, you may have to put together a more extensive band set.

In the following exercise, you will create a band that contains existing and proposed profile elevations:

1. Open the 1906_ProfileViewBand.dwg (1906_ProfileViewBand_METRIC.dwg) file.

   This file contains a profile view and an empty band on the bottom of the view. You will be adding information to the Profile Data Band.

2. From the Settings tab of Toolspace, expand Profile View ➤ Band Styles ➤ Profile Data.

3. Right-click the style called Mastering EG & FG and select Edit.

4. On the Band Details tab, do the following:

   a. Change Band Height to **1.0"** (or **25** mm).

   b. On the right side of the Band Details tab, highlight Major Station, and click the Compose Label button, as shown in Figure 19.60.

FIGURE 19.60
The Band Details
tab

c. On the Layout tab of the Label Style Composer – Major Station dialog, click the Create Text Component button and make these changes:

- Set Name to **Station**.

- Use the drop-down to change Anchor Point to Band Bottom.

- Use the drop-down to change Attachment to Top Center.

- Change the Y offset to **–0.1"** (or **–0.5** mm).

- Click the Contents value, which currently reads Label Text, and click the ellipsis to display the Text Component Editor dialog.

- In the Text Component Editor, remove all text in the Text Component Editor window and select Station Value from the Properties drop-down list.

- Set Precision to **1**.

- Click the white arrow button to add the Property field to the Text Component Editor window.

    d. Click OK to exit the Text Component Editor.

    e. Click the Create Text Component button again, and make these changes:

- Set Name to **Existing El**.

- Use the drop-down to change Anchor Point to Band Middle.

- Set Rotation Angle to **90**.

- Use the drop-down to change Attachment to Bottom Center.

- Change the X offset to **–0.02"** (or **–0.5** mm).

- Click the Contents value, which currently reads Label Text, and click the ellipsis to display the Text Component Editor dialog.

- In the Text Component Editor window, remove all the text and select Profile1 Elevation from the Properties drop-down list.

- Set Precision to **0.01** (or **0.001** for metric).

- Click the white arrow button to add the Property field to the Text Component Editor window.

    f. Click OK to exit the Text Component Editor.

    g. Click the Copy Component button and make these changes:

- Change Name to **Proposed El**.

- Verify that Anchor Point is set to Band Middle.

- Verify that Rotation Angle is set to 90.

- Use the drop-down to change Attachment to Top Center.

- Change the X offset to **0.02"** (or **0.5** mm).

- ◆ Click the Contents value and click the ellipsis to display the Text Component Editor dialog.

- ◆ In the Text Component Editor window, click the existing Property field and select Profile2 Elevation from the Properties drop-down list.

- ◆ Verify that Precision is 0.01 (or 0.001 for metric).

- ◆ Click the white arrow button to add the Property field to the Text Component Editor window.

   h. Click OK to exit the Text Component Editor.

   i. Click OK to finish working with the Major Stations Label Composer and return to the Band Details tab.

5. On the Display tab, use the lightbulb icon to turn off visibility for Minor Ticks. Click OK.

6. In the profile view properties, make sure that on the Bands tab for the selected profile view Profile1 is set to EG – Cabernet Court and Profile2 is set to Cabernet Court FG. Click OK.

The completed band should resemble Figure 19.61.

FIGURE 19.61
Text along the bottom of your profile view in the form of a band

As you can see, profile bands can provide a lot of information in a compact manner. In this example, you provided information only at the major stations, but you could also provide information at minor stations, horizontal geometry points, vertical geometry points, station equations, and incremental distances.

When this exercise is complete, you can save and close the drawing. A saved copy of this drawing, `1906_ProfileViewBand_FINISHED.dwg` (`1906_ProfileViewBand_METRIC_FINISHED.dwg`), is available from the book's web page.

Creating Section View Styles

Section view styles share many of the same concepts as creating profile view styles. In fact, the Section View Style dialog has all the same tabs and looks nearly identical to the Profile View Style dialog. A new introduced feature this year is the capability to define for a style the section view direction in a similar way as the profile view styles.

In this section, you will walk through the creation of a section view style suitable for creating a section sheet:

1. Open the 1907_SectionStyles.dwg (1907_SectionStyles_METRIC.dwg) file.

   This file contains section views created with the default settings for section views.

2. From the Settings tab of Toolspace, expand Section View ➢ Section View Styles and select Road Section.

3. Right-click Road Section and select Edit.

4. On the Grid tab, set Grid Padding (Major Grids) to **0** for the Above Maximum Elevation and Below Datum options.

5. On the Display tab, turn off the visibility for all components except the following:

   ◆ Graph Title

   ◆ Left Axis Annotation Major

   ◆ Right Axis Annotation Major

   ◆ Bottom Axis Annotation Major

6. Click OK.

   Your section views should resemble Figure 19.62.

FIGURE 19.62
Yes, this is correct! It is a very stripped-down section view.

7. Select one of the views by clicking the station label.

8. From the Section View contextual tab ➢ Modify View panel, select Update Group Layout.

   The section views will rearrange to fit more sections per page.

The section view is so bare bones because the section view grid will come from the group plot style, so the only information you really need is in this simple style.

To continue to the next exercise, you can save and keep this drawing open or use the finished copy of this drawing, 1907_SectionStyles_FINISHED.dwg (1907_SectionStyles_METRIC_FINISHED.dwg), available from the book's web page.

Group Plot Styles

Group plot styles determine how sections are arranged on a sheet. When multiple section views are created, the group plot style uses the `Section` template file discussed in Chapter 15, "Plan Production," and places sections inside the paperspace viewport.

1. If your file isn't still open from the previous exercise, open `1907_SectionStyles_FINISHED.dwg` (`1907_SectionStyles_METRIC_FINISHED.dwg`).

   You can download either file from this book's web page. This file contains section views already created.

2. From the Settings tab of Toolspace, expand Section View ➤ Group Plot Styles.

3. Right-click Basic and select Edit.

4. On the Array tab, change the column spacing to **4"** (or **100** mm). Change the row spacing to **2"** (or **50** mm), as shown in Figure 19.63.

FIGURE 19.63
The Array tab controls section view spacing.

These spacing changes should allow a more aesthetic arrangement of cross sections per page and ample room for moving the views up and right to fit on the page better in the upcoming steps.

5. On the Plot Area tab, leave all the default settings. Figure 19.64 shows the default settings for the imperial version of the exercise.

FIGURE 19.64
Grid spacing on
sheets is specified
on the Plot Area
tab.

This is where you configure grid spacing per sheet.

6. On the Display tab, do the following:

   a. Verify that the visibility is turned on for Major Horizontal Grid and Major Vertical Grid.

   b. Verify that the visibility is turned off for Minor Horizontal Grid and Minor Vertical Grid.

   c. Verify that the layers for all of the grid components are set to C-ROAD-SCTN-GRID.

   d. Verify that the layers for Print Area and Sheet Border are set to C-ROAD-SCTN-TTLB.

   e. Set Color for Major Horizontal Grid and Major Vertical Grid to **9**.

   f. Set Color for Print Area to Cyan and Sheet Border to Green. Your Display tab will look like Figure 19.65.

FIGURE 19.65
The Display com-
ponents for the
group plot style

7. Click OK to complete the group plot style edits.

   Your section view sheets should be shaping up to the point where you could almost generate sheets. There may be instances when some text is placed outside the cyan line that represents the viewport border. In the next steps, you will use a nonvisible section band to prevent this from happening and push the views onto the page.

8. From the Settings tab of Toolspace, expand Section View ➤ Band Styles ➤ Section Data.

9. Right-click Section Data and select New.

10. On the Information tab, set Name to **_NO DISPLAY**.

    Prefixing the style name with the underscore ensures it will appear at the top of the Style list.

11. On the Band Details tab, do the following:

    a. Set Band Height to **0.2"** (or **5** mm).

    b. Set Text Box Width to **0.2"** (or **10** mm).

    c. Set Offset From Band to **0"** (or **0** mm).

    Even though the band will not be visible, the Civil 3D program still accounts for this spacing when placing the views on the sheet. In this step, you are using this to your advantage.

12. On the Display tab, verify that the visibility is turned off for all components.

13. Click OK to finish creating the new section data band style.

14. Select any section view by clicking the station label or the elevation label.

15. From the Section View contextual tab ➤ Modify View panel, choose View Group Properties to display the Section View Group Properties dialog.

16. On the Section Views tab, do the following:

    a. Click the ellipsis in the Change Band Set column, as shown in Figure 19.66. You may need to widen the column to view the full titles.

FIGURE 19.66
Changing the band set in use for all section views

The Section View Group Bands dialog will appear.

b. Verify that Band Type is set to Section Data.

c. Set the band style as _NO DISPLAY and click Add.

d. Set the Gap distance to **0**, as shown in Figure 19.67, and click OK to dismiss the Section View Group Bands dialog.

FIGURE 19.67
Set the band style as _NO DISPLAY and set the gap to 0.

e. Click OK to exit the Section View Group Properties dialog.

17. From the Section View contextual tab ➤ Modify View panel, select Update Group Layout.

The cross-section sheets should look similar to Figure 19.68.

FIGURE 19.68
The completed exercise

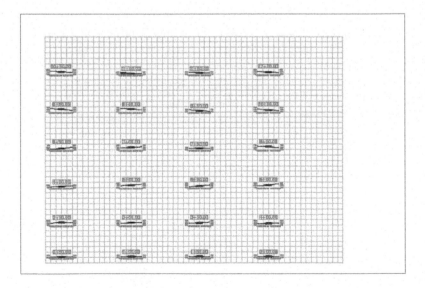

When this exercise is complete, you can save and close the drawing. A saved copy of this drawing is available from the book's web page with the filename 1907_GroupPlotStyles_ FINISHED.dwg (1907_GroupPlotStyles_METRIC_FINISHED.dwg).

With all of the object styles, you have a great deal of control over every detail, even ones that may seem trivial. Instead of being bogged down trying to understand every option, don't be afraid to use a "trial and error" approach. If you make a change you don't like, you can always edit the style until you get it right.

The Bottom Line

Override object styles with other styles. In spite of the desire to have uniform styles and appearances between objects within a single drawing, project, or firm, there are always going to be changes that need to be made.

Master It Open the MasterIt_1901.dwg (MasterIt_1901_METRIC.dwg) file and change the alignment style associated with Alignment B to Layout. In addition, change the surface style used for the EG surface to Contours And Triangles, but change the contour interval to **1'** and **5'** (or **0.5** m and **2.5** m) and the color of the triangles to yellow.

Create a new surface style. Almost every set of plans that you send out of the office is going to include a surface, so it is important to be able to generate multiple surface styles that match your company standards. In addition to surface styles for production, you may find it helpful to have styles to use when you are designing that show a tighter contour spacing as well as the points and triangles needed to make some edits.

Master It Open the MasterIt_1902.dwg (MasterIt_1902_METRIC.dwg) file and create a new surface style named **Micro Editing**. Set this style to display contours at **0.5'** and **1.0'** (or **0.1** m and **0.2** m), as well as triangles and points. Set the EG surface to use this new surface style.

Create a new profile view style. Everyone has their preferred look for a profile view. These styles can provide a lot of information in a small space, so it is important to be able to create a profile view that will meet your needs.

Master It Open the MasterIt_1903.dwg (MasterIt_1903_METRIC.dwg) file and create a new profile view style named **Mastering Profile View.** Set this style to not clip the vertical or horizontal grid. Set the bottom horizontal ticks at **50'** and **10'** intervals (**25** m and **5** m). Set the left and right vertical ticks at **10'** and **2'** intervals (**5** m and **1** m). In addition, turn off the visibility of Graph Title, Bottom Axis Annotation Major, and Bottom Axis Annotation Horizontal Geometry Point. Set the profile view in the drawing to use this new profile view style.

Appendix A

The Bottom Line

Each of The Bottom Line sections in the chapters suggests exercises to deepen skills and understanding. Sometimes there is only one possible solution, but often you are encouraged to use your skills and creativity to create something that builds on what you know and lets you explore one of many possibilities.

Chapter 1: The Basics

Find any Civil 3D object with just a few clicks. By using Prospector to view object data collections, you can minimize the panning and zooming that are part of working in a CAD program. When common subdivisions can have hundreds of parcels or a complex corridor can have dozens of alignments, jumping to the desired one nearly instantly shaves time off everyday tasks.

Master It Open 0103_Example.dwg (0103_Example_METRIC.dwg) from www.sybex .com/go/masteringcivil3d2016 and find parcel number 6 without using any AutoCAD commands or scrolling around on the drawing screen.

Solution

1. In Toolspace, go to the Prospector tab and expand Sites ➢ ROW ➢ Parcels.

2. Right-click Special ROW: 6 and select Zoom To.

Modify the drawing scale and default object layers. Civil 3D understands that the end goal of most drawings is to create hard-copy construction documents. When you set a drawing scale, Civil 3D removes a lot of the mental gymnastics that other programs require when you're sizing text and symbols. When you set object layers for the entire drawing, Civil 3D makes uniformity of drawing files easier than ever to accomplish.

Master It Continue working in the file 0103_Example.dwg (0103_Example_METRIC .dwg). It is not necessary to have completed the previous exercise to continue. Zoom to extents and change the Annotation scale in the Model tab from the 50-scale drawing to a 100-scale drawing. (For metric users, change the scale from 1:250 to 1:1000.)

Solution In the lower-right corner of the application window, select 1″ = 100′ (1:1000) from the Annotation Scale list. Notice the change in size of the annotation to reflect the new scale.

Navigate the ribbon's contextual tabs. As with AutoCAD, the ribbon is the primary interface for accessing Civil 3D commands and features. When you select an AutoCAD Civil 3D object, the ribbon displays commands and features related to that object. If several object types are selected, the Multiple contextual tab is displayed.

Master It Continue working in the file 0103_Example.dwg (0103_Example_METRIC .dwg). It is not necessary to have completed the previous exercise to continue. Using the ribbon interface, access the Alignment Properties for QuickStart Alignment and rename it Existing CL.

Solution

1. Select QuickStart Alignment to display the contextual Alignment tab of the ribbon.

2. From the Alignment contextual tab ➤ Modify panel, click Alignment Properties.

3. In the Alignment Properties menu, select the Information tab.

4. Rename the alignment to **Existing CL** in the Name Section of the tab and click OK.

Create a curve tangent to the end of a line. It's rare that a property stands alone. Often, you must create adjacent properties, easements, or alignments from their legal descriptions.

Master It Open the drawing MasterIt_0101.dwg (MasterIt_0101_METRIC.dwg). Create a curve tangent to the east end of the line labeled in the drawing. The curve should meet the following specifications:

- Radius: 200.00′ (60 m)
- Arc Length: 66.58′ (20 m)

Solution

1. On the Home tab ➤ Draw panel ➤ Curves Creation drop-down, select Create Curve From End Of Object.

2. Select the east side of the line that is labeled Create A Curve Tangent To This Line.

3. On the command line, press ↵ to confirm that you will enter a radius value.

4. On the command line, type **200.00 (60)** and then press ↵.

5. Type **L** to specify the length and then press ↵.

6. Type **66.58 (20)** and then press ↵.

Label lines and curves. Although converting linework to parcels or alignments offers you the most robust labeling and analysis options, basic line- and curve-labeling tools are available when conversion isn't appropriate.

Master It Add line and curve labels to each entity created in MasterIt_0101.dwg or MasterIt_0101_METRIC.dwg. It is recommended that you complete the previous exercise so you will have a curve to work with. Choose a label that specifies the bearing and distance for your lines and length, radius, and delta of your curve. Check your final result against the completed file found on the book's web page named MasterIt_0101_FINISHED.dwg (MasterIt_0101_METRIC_FINISHED.dwg).

Solution

1. Go to the Annotate tab of the ribbon ➤ Labels & Tables panel and click the Add Labels button. Then do the following:

    ◆ Set Feature to Line And Curve.

    ◆ Set Label Type to Multiple Segment.

    ◆ Set Line Label Style to Bearing Over Distance.

    ◆ Set Curve Label Style to Distance – Radius And Delta.

2. Click Add and then select each line and curve by clicking it in the drawing.

The default label should be acceptable. If not, perform the following steps:

1. Select one of the newly placed labels.

2. On the Labels: General Segment Label contextual tab ➤ Modify panel, click Label Properties.

3. In the resulting AutoCAD Properties palette, select an alternative label in the General section.

Chapter 2: Survey

Properly collect field data and import it into Civil 3D. Once survey data has been collected, you will want to pull it into Civil 3D via the survey database. This will enable you to create lines and points that correctly reflect your field measurements.

Master It Open `MasterIt_0201.dwg`, create a new survey database, and import the `MasterIt_0201.txt` (or `MasterIt_0201_METRIC.txt`) point file into the drawing. The format of this specific file is PENZD (comma-delimited).

Solution

1. Open `MasterIt_0201.dwg` (or `MasterIt_0201_METRIC.dwg`).

2. On the Survey tab, create a new local survey database.

3. Right-click Import Events and click Import Survey Data.

4. On the Specify Database page of the wizard, select your new database and click Next.

5. On the Specify Data Source page, configure Data Source Type as Point File, click the plus sign to browse to the `MasterIt_0201.txt` (or `MasterIt_0201_METRIC.txt`) file, select and open the point file format as PENZD (comma-delimited), and click Next.

6. On the Specify Network page, click Create New Network, give the new network a name, and click OK. Select the Network and click Next.

7. On the Import Options page, select Mastering Civil 3D as the current figure prefix database (if the previous exercise wasn't performed, this figure prefix database is

available from the book's website), and edit the options to insert both the figures and the survey points. Click Finish.

Your drawing should look like `MasterIt_0201_FINISHED.dwg` (`MasterIt_0201_METRIC_FINISHED.dwg`), which you can download from this book's web page, `www.sybex.com/go/masteringcivil3d2016`.

Set up description key and figure databases.   Proper setup is key to working successfully with the Civil 3D survey functionality.

Master It   Create a new description key set and the following description keys using the default styles. Make sure all description keys are going to layer V-NODE:

♦ CL*

♦ EOP*

♦ TREE*

♦ BM*

Change the description key search order so that the new description key set takes precedence over the default.

Create a figure prefix database called MasterIt containing the following codes:

♦ CL

♦ EOP

♦ BC

Test the new description key set and figure prefix database by importing the point file `MasterIt_CodeTest_0202.txt` (use the same file for both US and metric units). Note that this file is a comma-delimited PNEZD file.

Solution

1. Create a new drawing based on a Civil 3D template.

2. On the Settings tab, locate the Description Key Sets branch. Right-click Description Key Sets and select New. Give the description key set the name of your choice and click OK.

3. Right-click the new description key set and select Edit Keys. Add the description keys, including the asterisk, as shown in the list.

4. Set the layer for each item in the table to V-NODE.

5. Close the Description Key Editor and save the drawing.

6. Right-click Description Key Sets and select Properties.

7. Move your new description key set to the top of the listing using the arrows. Click OK.

8. In the Toolspace ➢ Survey tab, right-click Figure Prefix Databases and select New.

9. Create a new figure prefix database called **MasterIt**.

10. Expand the Figure Prefix Database branch, right-click the new figure prefix database, and select Manage Figure Prefix Database.

11. Add the required codes to the list. Leave all options as default and click OK.

12. On the Survey tab, right-click Survey Databases, select New Local Survey Database, and give it a name of your choice. Click OK.

13. Right-click Import Events and select Import Survey Data. Import the file `MasterIt_CodeTest_0202.txt`. Select the survey database you just created. When importing, verify that the point file format is set to PNEZD (comma delimited) and the current figure prefix database is set to MasterIt. Be sure that Process Linework During Import, Insert Figure Objects, and Insert Survey Points are each set to Yes.

Your file should now contain linework that reflects your efforts. Compare your work with `MasterIt_0202_FINISHED.dwg` (`MasterIt_0202_METRIC_FINISHED.dwg`), which you can download from this book's web page, `www.sybex.com/go/masteringcivil3d2016`.

Translate surveys from assumed coordinates to known coordinates.   Understanding how to manipulate data once it is brought into Civil 3D is important to making your field measurements match your project's coordinate system.

Master It   Create a new drawing based on the template of your choice and start a new survey database. Import `MasterIt_0203.fbk` (or `MasterIt_0203_METRIC.fbk`). When you import the file, turn on the Insert Network Object option. Translate the database based on the following settings:

◆ Base Point 1

◆ Rotation Angle of 10.3053°

Solution

1. Create a new drawing and a new survey database.

2. Create a new Import Event and import the `MasterIt_0203.fbk` (or `MasterIt_0203_METRIC.fbk`) file into a new network. Turn on the Insert Network Object option.

3. Right-click the survey database, click Translate Survey Database Network, and rotate the network based on the point number and rotation you were given.

4. Save the drawing and leave it open.

Your drawing should look like `MasterIt_0203_FINISHED.dwg` (`MasterIt_0203_METRIC_FINISHED.dwg`), which you can download from this book's web page, `www.sybex.com/go/masteringcivil3d2016`.

Perform traverse analysis.   Traverse analysis is needed for boundary surveys to check for angular accuracy and closure. Civil 3D will generate the reports that you need to capture these results.

Master It   Use the survey database and network from the previous "Master It" exercise. Analyze and adjust the traverse using the following criteria:

- ◆ Use an Initial Station value of 2 and an Initial Backsight value of 1.
- ◆ Use the Compass Rule option for Horizontal Adjustment.
- ◆ Use Length Weighted Distribution Method for Vertical Adjustment.
- ◆ Use a Horizontal Closure Limit value of 1:20,000.
- ◆ Use a Vertical Closure Limit value of 1:20,000.

Solution

1. Continue working in the drawing from the previous "Master It" exercise.

2. From the Survey tab of Toolspace, right-click Networks ➤ Traverses and create a new traverse from the four points using the initial station and backsight point numbers given.

3. Right-click the new traverse, perform a traverse analysis using the method and closure limits given, and apply the changes to the survey database. Click OK to close the Traverse Analysis dialog.

You compare your analysis to `MasterIt_0204 Balanced Angles.trv`, `MasterIt_0204 Raw Closure.trv`, `MasterIt_0204 Vertical Adjustment.trv`, and `MasterIt_0204.lso` (`MasterIt_0204_METRIC Balanced Angles.trv`, `MasterIt_0204_METRIC Raw Closure.trv`, `MasterIt_0204_METRIC Vertical Adjustment.trv`, and `MasterIt_0204_METRIC.lso`), which you can download from this book's web page, `www.sybex.com/go/masteringcivil3d2016`.

Chapter 3: Points

Import points from a text file using description key matching. Most engineering offices receive text files containing point data at some time during a project. Description keys provide a way to automatically assign the appropriate styles, layers, and labels to newly imported points.

Master It Open `Masterit_0301.dwg` (`Masterit_0301_METRIC.dwg`), which you can download from the book's web page. Revise the Civil 3D description key set to contain only the parameters listed next.

CODE	POINT STYLE	POINT LABEL STYLE	FORMAT	LAYER
GS*	Basic	Elevation Only	Ground Shot	V-NODE
EP*	Basic	Elevation and Description	Road Edge	V-NODE
HYD*	Hydrant (existing)	Elevation and Description	Hydrant	V-NODE-WATR
SW*	Basic	Elevation and Description	Sidewalk	V-NODE
TREE*	Tree	Elevation and Description	Tree	V-NODE-TREE

Import the PENZD (space delimited) file `MasterIt_0301.txt` (`MasterIt_0301_METRIC .txt`). Confirm that the description keys made the appropriate matches by looking at a handful of points of each type. Do the trees look like trees? Do the hydrants look like hydrants?

Save the resulting file for use in the remaining exercises.

Solution

1. Open `Masterit_0301.dwg` (`Masterit_0301_METRIC.dwg`).

2. Switch to the Settings tab of Toolspace, and under the Point Collection locate the description key set called Civil 3D.

3. Right-click this set and choose Edit Keys.

4. Revise the three keys to match the GS, EP, and HYD specifications listed under the "Master It" instructions.

5. Right-click the EP key and choose Copy.

6. Edit the copied key to match the SW specifications listed in the "Master It" instructions. Repeat steps 5–6 for TREE code and exit Panorama.

7. On the Home tab of the ribbon ➤ Create Ground Data panel, select Points ➤ Point Creation Tools and then click the Import Points icon on the toolbar.

8. Click the plus white icon to add a file to import and navigate to the `MasterIt_0301 .txt` (`MasterIt_0301_METRIC.txt`) file. If necessary, change Files Of Type to Text/ Template/Extract File (*.txt). Click Open to continue.

9. Select PENZD (Space Delimited) from the listing, check Add Points To Point Group, and create a point group with the name of your choosing. Verify that everything in the Advanced Options area is unchecked. Click OK. Click OK again to complete the command.

10. Use Zoom Extents to see the points.

11. Save the file and keep it open for use in the next "Master It" exercise.

Note that each description key parameter (style, label, format, and layer) has been respected. Your hydrants should appear as hydrants on the correct layer, your trees should appear as trees on the correct layer, and so on. Compare your work to `MasterIt_0301_ FINISHED.dwg` (`MasterIt_0301_METRIC_FINISHED.dwg`).

Create a point group. Building a surface using a point group is a common task. Among other criteria, you may want to filter out any points that tend to have erroneous elevations such as utilities or vegetation.

Master It Create a new point group called Topo that includes all points *except* those with a descriptor code of TREE and HYD. Use the DWG created in the previous "Master It" exercise or start with `MasterIt_0301_FINISHED.dwg` (`MasterIt_0301_METRIC_ FINISHED.dwg`).

Solution

1. In Prospector, right-click Point Groups and choose New.

2. On the Information tab, enter **Topo** as the name of the new point group.

3. On the Include tab, fill the check box for Include All Points.

4. On the Exclude tab, click the With Raw Descriptions Matching check box to turn it on, and enter **TREE*, HYD*** in the field.

5. Click OK to close the box.

6. Save the file.

7. Compare your work to the file `MasterIt_0302_FINISHED.dwg` (`MasterIt_0302_METRIC_FINISHED.dwg`).

Export points to LandXML and ASCII format. It's often necessary to export a LandXML or ASCII file of points for stakeout or data-sharing purposes. Unless you want to export every point from your drawing, it's best to create a point group that isolates the desired point collection.

Master It Create a new point group that includes all the points with a raw description of SW. Export this point group via LandXML and a PENZD comma-delimited text file.

Use the DWG created in the previous "Master It" exercise or start with `MasterIt_0302_FINISHED.dwg` (`MasterIt_0302_METRIC_FINISHED.dwg`).

Solution

1. In Prospector, right-click Point Groups and choose New.

2. On the Information tab, enter **Sidewalk** as the name of the new point group.

3. Switch to the Include tab.

4. Select the With Raw Descriptions Matching check box and enter **SW*** in the field.

5. Confirm in Prospector that all the points have the description SW and click OK.

6. Right-click the Sidewalk point group and choose Export LandXML.

7. Click OK in the Export To LandXML dialog.

8. Choose a location to save your LandXML file and then click Save.

9. Navigate to the LandXML file to confirm it was created.

10. Right-click the **Sidewalk** point group and choose Export Points.

11. Choose the PENZD (comma-delimited) format and a destination file, and confirm that the Limit To Points In Point Group check box is selected for the Sidewalk point group. Also, confirm that all Advanced Options are unchecked. Click OK.

12. Navigate to the ASCII file to confirm it was created.

13. Save the file.

14. Compare your work to the file `MasterIt_0303_FINISHED.dwg` (`MasterIt_0303_METRIC_FINISHED.dwg`).

Create a point table. Point tables provide an opportunity to list and study point properties. In addition to basic point tables that list number, elevation, description, and similar options, you can customize point table formats to include user-defined property fields.

Master It   Use the DWG created in the previous "Master It" exercise or start with `MasterIt_0303_FINISHED.dwg` (`MasterIt_0303_METRIC_FINISHED.dwg`). Create a Centerline point group to include all the centerline points and create a point table for this point group using the PNEZD format table style.

Solution

1. In Prospector, right-click Point Groups and choose New.

2. On the Information tab, enter **Centerline** as the name of the new point group.

3. Switch to the Include tab.

4. Select the With Raw Descriptions Matching check box and type **CL*** in the field.

5. Confirm on the Point List tab that all the points have the description CL and click OK.

6. Change to the Annotate tab ➤ Labels ➤ Tables panel and select Add Tables ➤ Add Point Table.

7. Choose the PNEZD format for the table style.

8. Click the Point Groups icon, choose the Centerline point group, and click OK. Click OK to insert the table. Leave the defaults as they are.

    The command line prompts you to choose a location for the upper-left corner of the point table.

9. Choose a location on your screen somewhere to the right of the project.

10. Zoom in and confirm your point table.

11. Compare your work to the file `MasterIt_0304_FINISHED.dwg` (`MasterIt_0304_METRIC_FINISHED.dwg`).

Chapter 4: Surfaces

Create an existing ground surface using points.   The most common way to create a surface model is by adding point data to the definition of a surface.

Master It   Open the `MasterIt0401.dwg` or the `MasterIt0401_METRIC.dwg` file. Create a new surface called **Existing**. Add the point group Topo to its definition. Leave the default styles.

Solution

1. On the Home tab ➤ Create Ground data panel of the ribbon, click Surfaces ➤ Create Surface.

2. Name the surface **Existing** and click OK.

3. In Prospector, expand the Surfaces ➤ Existing ➤ Definition branches.

4. Right-click Point Groups and select Add.

5. Select the point group Topo and click OK.

Modify and update a TIN surface. TIN surface creation is mathematically precise, but sometimes the assumptions behind the equations leave something to be desired. By using the editing tools built into Civil 3D, you can create a more realistic surface model.

Master It Continue working in the file from the previous exercise or open the `MasterIt0402.dwg` or the `MasterIt0402_METRIC.dwg` file. Use the irregular-shaped polyline and apply it to the surface as an outer boundary of the surface. Make the boundary a destructive breakline.

Solution

1. Expand the Surfaces ➤ Existing ➤ Definition branches.

2. Right-click Boundaries and select the Add option.

3. Verify that the check box by Non-Destructive Breakline is unchecked and click OK. Select the magenta-colored polyline to complete the boundary addition.

Prepare a slope analysis. Surface analysis tools allow users to view more than contours and triangles in Civil 3D. Engineers working with nontechnical team members can create strong, meaningful, analysis displays to convey important site information using the built-in analysis methods in Civil 3D.

Master It Open the `MasterIt0403.dwg` or the `MasterIt0403_METRIC.dwg` file. Create a slope banding analysis showing slopes under and over 10 percent and insert a dynamic slope legend to help clarify the result of the analysis.

Solution

1. Select the surface. From the TIN Surface contextual tab ➤ Modify panel, click the Surface Properties icon.

2. On the Information tab, set the Surface Style field to Slope Banding (2D).

3. Switch to the Analysis tab for the Slopes analysis type.

4. Set Ranges Number to 2 and then click the Run Analysis arrow.

5. Change both the maximum slope for ID 1 and the minimum slope for ID 2 to 10 percent.

6. Click OK to close the Surface Properties dialog.

7. Select the surface to display the TIN Surface contextual tab.

8. From the TIN Surface contextual tab ➤ Labels & Tables panel, choose Add Legend Table.

9. Enter **S** ↵ and then **D** ↵ at the command line and pick a placement point on the screen to create a dynamic elevations legend.

Label surface contours and spot elevations. Showing a stack of contours is useless without context. Using the automated labeling tools in Civil 3D, you can create dynamic labels that update and reflect changes to your surface as your design evolves.

Master It Open the `MasterIt0404.dwg` or the `MasterIt0404_METRIC.dwg` file. Label the major contours on the surface at 2′ and 10′ (Background) or 1 m and 5 m (Background).

Solution

1. Select the surface. From the TIN Surface contextual tab ➤ Modify panel, click the Surface Properties icon.

2. On the Information tab, change the style to Contours 2′ and 10′ (Background) or Contours 1 m and 5 m (Background).

3. Click OK to close the dialog and press Esc to deselect.

4. From the Annotate tab ➤ Labels & Tables panel, click the Add Labels button.

5. Set Feature to Surface and Label Type to Contour – Multiple.

6. Set Major Contour Label Style to Existing Major Labels and Minor Contour Label Style to <none>.

7. Click Add.

8. Pick a point on one side of the site and draw a contour label line across the entire site. Press Esc to exit the command.

Import a point cloud into a drawing and create a surface model. As laser scan data collection becomes more common and replaces other large-scale data-collection methods, the ability to use point clouds in Civil 3D is critical. Intensity helps postprocessing software determine the ground cover type. While Civil 3D can't do postprocessing, you can see the intensity as part of the point cloud style.

Master It Import an LAS format point cloud file (`MasterIt0405_Denver.las`) into the Civil 3D template of your choice. As you create the point cloud file, set the style to Elevation Ranges. Use a portion of the file to create a Civil 3D surface model. No coordinate system needs to be set for this example.

Solution

1. Start a new file by using the default Civil 3D template of your choice. Save the file before proceeding as **MasterIt0405_DenverUSA.dwg**.

2. In Prospector, right-click Point Clouds and select the Create Point Cloud option to display the Create Point Cloud Wizard.

3. Set the name of the point cloud to **Denver**.

4. Set the point cloud style to Elevation Ranges, and click the Next button.

5. Use the white plus sign to browse to the LAS file.

6. Select `MasterIt0405_Denver.las` and select click Open. Click Finish. The New Point Cloud Processing In Background dialog will open. Click Close to dismiss.

This file contains 4.7 million data points, so be patient while the file imports.

7. When the point cloud has completed processing, zoom extents. Select the bounding box representing the point cloud to display the Point Cloud contextual tab.

8. Select the Add Points To Surface command.

9. Name the surface, set a surface style, and click the Next button.

10. Choose the Window radio button and click Define Region In Drawing.

11. Define the region by creating a window around the western half of the point cloud.

12. Click Next to see the Summary page and click the Finish button. Close Panorama. Because of the large size of point cloud files, no finished drawing is available on the web page.

Chapter 5: Parcels

Create parcels from objects. The first step in any parceling project is to create an outer boundary for the site together with all the known linework.

Master It Open the Masterit_0501.dwg (Masterit_0501_METRIC.dwg) file, which you can download from www.sybex.com/go/masteringcivil3d2016. Convert the polyline segments to parcels and place them in a new site named Subdivision Lots.

Solution

1. From the Home tab ➤ Create Design panel, select Parcel ➤ Create Parcel From Objects.

2. At the Select lines, arcs, or polylines to convert into parcels or [Xref]: prompt, pick all polylines in the drawing either by picking one by one or by using a selection window and pressing ↵.

   The Create Parcels – From Objects dialog appears.

3. Create a new site by using the drop-down menu options within the dialog and name it **Subdivision Lots**. Click OK to dismiss the Site Properties dialog. From the drop-down menus, select Subdivision Lots, Property, and Parcel Name in the Site, Parcel Style, and Area Label Style selection boxes, respectively.

   Keep the default values for the remaining options.

4. Click OK to dismiss the dialog.

5. Save the drawing, but keep it open for the next exercise. If you want to see what the drawing should look like at this point, you can open Masterit_0501_FINISHED.dwg (Masterit_0501_METRIC_FINISHED.dwg), available from the book's website.

Create a right-of-way parcel using the right-of-way tool. For many projects, the ROW parcel serves as frontage for subdivision parcels. For straightforward sites, the automatic Create ROW tool provides a quick way to create this parcel.

Master It   Continue working in the Masterit_0501.dwg (Masterit_0501_METRIC.dwg) file or you can open Masterit_0501_FINISHED.dwg (Masterit_0501_METRIC_FINISHED .dwg), available from the book's website. Create a ROW parcel that is offset by 30′ (10 m) on either side of the road centerline with no fillets at boundary ends. Then clean up the ROW parcel area on each side of the alignment at the ends. Note: The south side parcel represents the existing main road ROW.

Solution

1. Since the alignment is not part of the Subdivision Lots site, it will need to be moved from siteless mode to the desired site. Therefore, move it to Subdivision Lots by selecting in the drawing, right-clicking and choosing the Move To Site option, and selecting the previously mentioned site. Or you can use the Prospector options for the alignment.

2. From the Home tab ➢ Create Design panel, select Parcel ➢ Create Right Of Way.

3. At the Select parcels: prompt, pick the area labels of your newly created parcels.

4. Press ↵ to stop picking parcels.

   The Create Right Of Way dialog appears.

5. Expand the Create Parcel Right Of Way branch and enter **30′ (10 m)** in the Offset From Alignment text Value field.

6. Expand the Cleanup At Parcel Boundaries branch.

7. Select None from the drop-down menu in the Cleanup Method selection box.

8. Expand the Cleanup At Alignment Intersections branch. Verify that Cleanup Method is set to None.

9. Click OK to dismiss the dialog and create the ROW parcels.

10. From the Home tab ➢ Create Design panel, select Parcel Creation Tools. Click the Delete Sub-Entity tool and pick to delete on the North side the two segments inside the ROW and on the south side the parcel segments representing the extension of the alignment ROW inside the existing ROW.

11. Save the drawing, but keep it open for the next exercise. If you want to see what the drawing should look like at this point, you can open Masterit_0502_FINISHED.dwg (Masterit_0502_METRIC_FINISHED.dwg), available from the book's website.

Create subdivision lots automatically by layout.   The biggest challenge when creating a subdivision plan is optimizing the number of lots. The precise sizing parcel tools provide a means to automate this process.

Master It   Continue working in the previous drawing or open Masterit_0502_ FINISHED.dwg (Masterit_0502_METRIC_FINISHED.dwg), available from the book's website. Create a series of lots with a minimum of 10,890 sq. ft. (1,012 m^2) and 90′ (30 m) frontage on each side of the ROW beginning at the existing ROW and ending at the ROW intersection with the southeast segments of the two north parcels. Set the Use Minimum Frontage At Offset option to No and redistribute the remainder; then set the Minimum Depth and Width values to 50′ (15 m). Leave all other options at their defaults.

Solution

1. From the Home tab's Create Design panel, select Parcel ➤ Parcel Creation Tools.

2. Expand the Parcel Layout Tools toolbar.

3. Change the value of the following parameters by clicking in the Value column and entering the new values:

    ◆ Minimum Area: **10,890** sq. ft. (**1,012** square meters)

    ◆ Minimum Frontage: **90′ (30 m)**

4. Change the following parameters by clicking in the Value column and selecting the appropriate option from the drop-down menu:

    ◆ Minimum Frontage at Offset: No

    ◆ Minimum Width: **50′ (15m)**

    ◆ Minimum Depth: **50′ (15m)**

    ◆ Automatic Mode: On

    ◆ Remainder Distribution: Redistribute Remainder

5. Click the Slide Line – Create tool.

    The Create Parcels – Layout dialog appears.

6. Select Subdivision, Property, and Parcel Name from the drop-down menus in the Site, Parcel Style, and Area Label Style selection boxes, respectively.

    Keep the default values for the rest of the options.

7. Click OK to dismiss the dialog.

8. At the `Select Parcel to be subdivided or [Pick]:` prompt, pick the West Parcel neighboring the ROW by selecting its area label.

9. At the `Select start point on frontage:` prompt, use your Endpoint Osnap to pick the point on the existing ROW where the west proposed ROW begins.

    The parcel jig appears.

10. Move your cursor slowly along the ROW parcel segment and notice that the parcel jig follows the segment.

11. At the `Select end point on frontage:` prompt, select the point on the proposed ROW where this ROW parcel meets the southeast line of the north parcel.

12. At the `Specify angle or [Bearing aZimuth]:` prompt, type **90** and press ↵. If you receive the message `No Solution Found` on your command line, try again. This may mean you snapped to the wrong spot.

13. At the `Accept Result?` prompt, press ↵ to accept the lot layout. Press Esc twice to exit the command.

14. Repeat steps 8 to 13 for the east side parcel, with the start point at the point on the existing ROW where the east-side ROW begins and the end point at the point where the east-side ROW meets the southeast segment of the north parcel on this side.

15. Save the drawing, but keep it open for the next exercise. If you want to see what the drawing should look like at this point, you can open `Masterit_0503_FINISHED.dwg` (`Masterit_0503_METRIC_FINISHED.dwg`), available from the book's website.

Add multiple-parcel segment labels.   Every subdivision plat must be appropriately labeled. You can quickly label parcels with their bearings, distances, direction, and more using the segment labeling tools.

Master It   Continue working in the previous drawing or open `Masterit_0503_FINISHED.dwg` (`Masterit_0503_METRIC_FINISHED.dwg`), available from the book's website. Place Bearing Over Distance labels on every parcel line segment and Delta Over Length And Radius labels on every parcel curve segment using the Multiple Segment Labeling tool.

Solution

1. From the Annotate tab ➤ Labels & Tables panel, select Add Labels ➤ Parcel ➤ Add Parcel Labels.

2. From the drop-down menus, in the Add Labels dialog, select Multiple Segment, Bearing Over Distance, and Delta Over Length And Radius in the Label Type, Line Label Style, and Curve Label Style selection boxes, respectively.

3. Click Add.

4. At the `Select parcel to be labeled by clicking on area label:` prompt, pick the area label for each of your single-family parcels. After each pick, press ↵ to accept Clockwise as the default.

5. Save the drawing. If you want to see what the drawing should look like at this point, you can open `Masterit_0504_FINISHED.dwg` (`Masterit_0504_METRIC_FINISHED.dwg`), available from the book's website.

Chapter 6: Alignments

Create an alignment from an object.   Creating alignments based on polylines is a traditional method of building engineering models. With built-in tools for conversion, correction, and alignment reversal, it's easy to use the linework prepared by others to start your design model. These alignments lack the intelligence of crafted alignments, however, and you should use them sparingly.

Master It   Open the `Masterit_0601.dwg` (`Masterit_0601_METRIC.dwg`) file and create alignments from the linework found there, having as alignment style the Layout style, using the All Labels label set, and making sure that the source objects are erased.

Solution

1. From the Home tab ➤ Create Design panel, choose Alignment ➤ Create Alignment From Objects.

2. When prompted to select objects, pick the lines and arc; then press Enter twice to complete the selection process and accept the alignment direction. Make sure that the alignment direction follows the direction of the arrow next to the Start Here annotation.

3. In the Create Alignment From Objects dialog, verify that Alignment Label Set is set to All Labels and Alignment Style is set to Layout.

4. Uncheck the Add Curves Between Tangents option, but make sure that the Erase Existing Entities option is checked and click OK.

Create a reverse curve that never loses tangency. Using the alignment layout tools, you can build intelligence into the objects you design. One of the most common errors introduced into engineering designs is curves and lines that aren't tangent, requiring expensive revisions and resubmittals. The free, floating, and fixed components can make smart alignments in a large number of combinations available to solve almost any design problem.

Master It Open the `Masterit_0602.dwg` (`Masterit_0602_METRIC.dwg`) file and create an alignment using the linework on the right as a guide. Create a reverse curve with both radii equal to 200 (or 60 for metric users) and with a pass-through point at the intersection of the two arcs.

Solution

1. From the Home tab ➤ Create Design panel, choose Alignment ➤ Alignment Creation Tools.

2. In the Create Alignment – Layout dialog, accept the defaults and click OK to display the Alignment Layout Tools toolbar.

3. Use the Fixed Line (Two Points) tool to trace both lines and press ↵ when complete to end the command.

4. Use the Floating Curve (From Entity, Radius, Through Point) tool to draw an arc from the endpoint of the west line with a radius of **200** (or **60** for metric users). Set the Curve Solution Angle to be **Lessthan180**. The pass-through point will be at the intersection of the two sketched arcs.

5. Press ↵ when complete to end the command.

6. Use the Free Curve Fillet (Between Two Entities, Radius) tool to create a reverse curve from the floating curve created in the previous step to the last fixed segment with a radius of **200** (or **60** for metric users) and Curve Solution Angle of **Lessthan180.** When prompted, be sure to indicate that this is a reverse curb.

7. Close the Alignment Layout Tools toolbar.

Replace a component of an alignment with another component type. One of the goals in using a dynamic modeling solution is to find better solutions, not just the first solution. In the layout of alignments, this can mean changing components along the design path or changing the way they're defined. The ability of Civil 3D to modify alignments' geometric construction without destroying the object or forcing a new definition lets you experiment without destroying the data already based on an alignment.

Master It Convert the first curve along the alignment in the `Masterit_0603.dwg` (`Masterit_0603_METRIC.dwg`) file to a floating arc that is constrained by the next segment. Then change the radius of the curves to 150 (or 45 for metric users). Make sure that the tangency is maintained all across the alignment.

Solution

1. Select the alignment to activate the Alignment contextual tab.

2. From the Alignment contextual tab ➤ Modify panel, choose Geometry Editor to display the Alignment Layout Tools toolbar.

3. Select the Alignment Grid View tool.

4. Starting with the first segment, click in the Tangency Constraint field and change it to **Constrained By Next (Floating)**.

5. Repeat for the other segments except the last one, which cannot be modified because it is dependent on the previous constraint.

6. Change the radii of the two curves to **150** (or **45** for metric users). Close Panorama and toolbar when finished.

Create alignment tables. Sometimes there is just too much information displayed on a drawing, and to make it clearer, tables are used to show bearings and distances for lines, curves, and segments. With their dynamic nature, these tables are kept up-to-date with any changes.

Master It Open the `Masterit_0604.dwg` (`Masterit_0604_METRIC.dwg`) file and generate a line table, a curve table, and a segment table. Use whichever style you want to accomplish this.

Solution

For lines:

1. Select the alignment to activate the Alignment contextual tab.

2. From the Alignment contextual tab ➤ Labels & Tables panel, choose Add Labels ➤ Multiple Segment and select the alignment. Press Enter to end the selection process.

3. On the Alignment contextual tab ➤ Labels & Tables panel, choose Add Tables ➤ Add Line.

4. Using the Pick On-Screen button at the bottom of the dialog, select the line segment labels of the alignment. Press Enter to end the selection process.

    If a warning comes up regarding child styles, select the Convert All Selected Label Styles To Tag mode.

5. Click OK to accept the settings in the dialog.

6. Place the table anywhere on your drawing. The bearings and distances are now replaced by tag labels.

For curves:

1. If not done during the lines portion of the exercise, select the alignment, and on the Alignment contextual tab ➤ Labels & Tables panel, choose Add Labels Multiple Segments and select the alignment. Press Enter to end the selection process.

2. From the Alignment contextual tab ➤ Labels & Tables panel, select Add Tables ➤ Add Curve.

3. Using the Pick On-Screen button at the bottom of the dialog, select the curve segment labels of the alignment. Press Enter to end the selection process.

   If a warning comes up regarding child styles, select the Convert All Selected Label Styles To Tag mode.

4. Click OK to accept the settings in the dialog.

5. Place the table anywhere on your drawing. The bearings and distances are now replaced by tag labels.

For segments:

1. If not done during the lines portion of the exercise, select the alignment, and on the Alignment contextual tab ➤ Labels & Tables panel, choose Add Labels Multiple Segments and select the alignment.

2. From the Alignment contextual tab ➤ Labels & Tables panel, choose Add Tables ➤ Add Segment.

3. In the By Alignment section, select the alignment you want to label and click OK.

4. Place the table anywhere on your drawing. The bearings and distances are now replaced by tag labels.

   If a warning comes up regarding child styles, select the Convert All Selected Label Styles To Tag mode.

Chapter 7: Profiles and Profile Views

Sample a surface profile with offset samples. Using surface data to create dynamic sampled profiles is an important advantage of working with a three-dimensional model. Quick viewing of various surface centerlines and grip-editing alignments makes for an effective preliminary planning tool. Combined with offset data to meet review agency requirements, profiles are robust design tools in Civil 3D.

Master It Open the MasterIt_0701.dwg (MasterIt_0701_METRIC.dwg) file and sample the ground surface along Alignment A, along with offset values at 15' left and 15' right (or 4.5 m left and 4.5 m right) of the alignment. Generate a profile view showing this information using the Major Grids profile view style with no data band sets.

Solution

1. From the Home tab ➤ Create Design panel, choose Profile ➤ Create Surface Profile.

2. Verify that Alignment A and the EG surface are selected and then click the Add button to add the EG surface.

3. Check the Sample Offsets check box and enter **15, -15** (or **4.5, -4.5** for metric users) in the box below the sample offsets and then click the Add button.

4. Click the Draw In Profile View button to open the Create Profile View Wizard.

5. On the General page of the wizard, verify that the profile view style is set to Major Grids.

6. On the Data Bands wizard page, verify that Select Band Set is set to _No Bands.

7. Click the Create Profile View button.

8. Place the profile anywhere on the drawing.

9. Save the drawing, but keep it open for the next exercise. If you would like to see what the drawing should look like at this point, you can open `MasterIt_0701_FINISHED.dwg` (`MasterIt_0701_METRIC_FINISHED.dwg`), available from the book's website.

Lay out a design profile on the basis of a table of data. Many programs and designers work by creating pairs of station and elevation data. The tools built into Civil 3D let you input this data precisely and quickly.

Master It Continue in the previous file or open `MasterIt_0701_FINISHED.dwg` (`MasterIt_0701_METRIC_FINISHED.dwg`). Create a layout profile on Alignment A using the Layout profile style and the Complete Label Set with the following information for Imperial users:

STATION	PVI ELEVATION	CURVE LENGTH
0+00	822.00	
1+80	825.60	300'
6+50	800.80	

Or use the following information for metric users:

STATION	PVI ELEVATION	CURVE LENGTH
.0+000	250.400	
0+062	251.640	100 m
0+250	244.840	

Solution

1. Create a surface profile for Alignment A and generate a profile view (if not done in the previous example) or use the `MasterIt_0701_FINISHED.dwg` (`MasterIt_0701_METRIC_FINISHED.dwg`) file.

2. From the Home tab ≻ Create Design panel, choose Profile ≻ Profile Creation Tools.

3. Select a grid line on the profile view that shows the surface profile. The Create Profile – Draw New dialog will open.

4. Verify that Profile Style is set to Layout and Profile Label Set is set to Complete Label Set.

5. Click OK to dismiss the Create Profile – Draw New dialog.

6. In the Profile Layout Tools toolbar, set the Length value of the Curve settings to the specified curve length.

7. Use the Draw Tangents With Curves button and the Transparent Commands toolbar to enter station elevation data.

8. Once finished, close the toolbar, and if needed, move the labels to be legible.

9. Save the drawing, but keep it open for the next exercise. If you would like to see what the drawing should look like at this point, you can open `MasterIt_0702_FINISHED.dwg` (`MasterIt_0702_METRIC_FINISHED.dwg`), available from the book's website.

Add and modify individual entities in a design profile. The ability to delete, modify, and edit the individual components of a design profile while maintaining the relationships is an important concept in the 3D modeling world. Tweaking the design allows you to pursue a better solution, not just a working solution.

Master It Continue in the previous file or open `MasterIt_0702_FINISHED.dwg` (`MasterIt_0702_METRIC_FINISHED.dwg`). For the layout profile created in the previous exercise, modify the curve so that it is 200' (or 60 m for metric users). Then insert a PVI at Station 4+90, Elevation 794.60 (or at Station 0+150, Elevation 242.840, for metric users), and add a 300' (or 96 m for metric users) parabolic vertical curve at the newly created PVI.

Solution

1. Continue in the drawing you have open from the previous exercise or open the `MasterIt_0702_FINISHED.dwg` (`MasterIt_0702_METRIC_FINISHED.dwg`) file. Pick the Design profile, and from the Profile contextual tab ≻ Modify Profile panel, click the Geometry Editor button.

2. In the Profile Layout Tools toolbar, select the Profile Grid View button.

3. In the Profile Entities tab of Panorama, change the Profile Curve Length field to **200** (or **60** for metric users).

4. In the Profile Layout Tools toolbar, select the Insert PVI button.

5. Using the Profile Station Elevation transparent command, select the profile grid, and enter **490** for the station and **794.60** for the elevation (or **150** for the station and **242.840** for the elevation for metric users). Press Esc twice.

6. Back in the Profile Layout Tools toolbar, click the drop-down arrow next to the Vertical Curve Creation button and select More Free Vertical Curves ➤ Free Vertical Parabola (PVI Based).

7. Pick the newly created PVI and enter **300** (or **96** for metric users) for Curve Length. Press ↵ twice.

8. Close the Profile Grid View and the toolbar and save the drawing, but keep it open for the next exercise. If you would like to see what the drawing should look like at this point, you can open `MasterIt_0703_FINISHED.dwg` (`MasterIt_0703_METRIC_FINISHED.dwg`), available from the book's website.

Apply a standard band set. Standardization of appearance is one of the major benefits of using styles in labeling. By applying band sets, you can quickly create plot-ready profile views that have the required information for review.

Master It Continue in the previous file or open `MasterIt_0703_FINISHED.dwg` (`MasterIt_0703_METRIC_FINISHED.dwg`). Apply the Cut And Fill band set to the layout profile created in the previous exercise with the appropriate profiles referenced in each of the bands.

Solution

1. Continue in the drawing you have open from the previous exercise or open the `MasterIt_0703_FINISHED.dwg` (`MasterIt_0703_METRIC_FINISHED.dwg`) file, pick a grid line in the profile view, and from the Profile View contextual tab ➤ Modify View panel, choose Profile View Properties to display the Profile View Properties dialog.

2. On the Bands tab, click Import Band Set, and select the Cut And Fill band set. Click OK.

3. Select Bottom Of Profile View from the Location drop-down list.

4. Scroll over and change Profile2 to Layout (1) for both rows.

5. Select Top Of Profile View from the Location drop-down list.

6. Scroll over and change Profile2 to Layout (1).

7. Click OK to apply the settings.

8. Save the drawing. If you would like to see what the drawing should look like at this point, you can open `MasterIt_0704_FINISHED.dwg` (`MasterIt_0704_METRIC_FINISHED.dwg`), available from the book's website.

Chapter 8: Assemblies and Subassemblies

Create a typical road assembly with lanes, curbs, gutters, and sidewalks.   Most corridors are built to model roads. The most common assembly used in these road corridors is some variation of a typical road section consisting of lanes, curbs, gutters, and sidewalks.

Master It   Create a new drawing from either the Civil 3D metric or Imperial template. Build a symmetric assembly using LaneSuperelevationAOR, UrbanCurbGutterValley2, and LinkWidthAndSlope for terrace and buffer strips adjacent to the UrbanSidewalk. Use widths and slopes of your choosing.

Solution

1. Create a new drawing from the DWT of your choice.

2. From the Home tab ➤ Create Design panel, choose Assembly ➤ Create Assembly.

3. Name your assembly and set styles as appropriate. Click OK.

4. Pick a location in your drawing for the assembly.

5. Locate the Lanes tab on the Tool Palettes window.

6. Click the LaneSuperelevationAOR button on the Lanes tab.

7. Use the AutoCAD Properties palette to edit the subassembly parameters, and follow the command-line prompts to set the LaneSuperelevationAOR on the left and right sides of your assembly.

8. Repeat the process with UrbanCurbGutterValley2, LinkWidthAndSlope, and UrbanSidewalk.

9. Complete this portion of the exercise by placing a final LinkWidthAndSlope on the outside of the UrbanSidewalk.

10. Save the drawing for use in the next "Master It" exercise.

Edit an assembly.   Once an assembly has been created, it can be easily edited to reflect a design change. Often, at the beginning of a project you won't know the final lane width. You can build your assembly and corridor model with one lane width and then change the width and rebuild the model immediately.

Master It   Working in the drawing from the preceding exercise, edit the width of each LaneSuperelevationAOR to **14′ (4.3** m), and change the cross slope of each LaneSuperelevationAOR to −**3.00**%.

Solution

1. Select the right lane subassembly. Be sure this is the only element selected.

2. From the Subassemblies contextual tab ➤ Modify Subassembly panel, choose Subassembly Properties.

3. On the Parameters tab, change the width to **14′ (4.3** m). Note that width will be listed twice.

4. Change the Default Slope to −3.00%. Then click OK.

5. Repeat for the left lane subassembly. Save the drawing for use in the next "Master It" exercise.

Add daylighting to a typical road assembly. Often, the most difficult part of a designer's job is figuring out how to grade the area between the last engineered structure point in the cross section (such as the back of a sidewalk) and the existing ground. An extensive catalog of daylighting subassemblies can assist you with this task.

Master It Working in the drawing from the preceding exercise, add the DaylightMinWidth subassembly to both sides of your typical road assembly. Establish a minimum width between the outermost subassembly and the daylight offset of 10′ (3 m).

Solution

1. Locate the Daylight tab on the tool palette.

2. Click the DaylightMinWidth button on the tool palette.

3. Use the AutoCAD Properties palette to verify that Min Width is set to **10′ (3 m)**.

4. Follow the command-line prompts to set the DaylightMinWidth on the right and left sides of your assembly.

5. Press Esc on your keyboard to complete the command.

You should now have daylighting subassemblies visible on both sides of your assembly. To see what the drawing should look like at this point, you can open `0807_MasteringAssemblies_FINISHED.dwg` or `0807_MasteringAssemblies_METRIC_FINISHED.dwg`.

Chapter 9: Basic Corridors

Build a single baseline corridor from an alignment, profile, and assembly. Corridors are created from the combination of alignments, profiles, and assemblies. Although corridors can be used to model many things, most corridors are used for road design.

Master It Open the `MasterIt_0909.dwg` or `MasteringIt_0909_METRIC.dwg` file. Build a corridor named Corridor A on the basis of the Alignment A alignment, the FG profile, and the Basic Assembly. Set EG as the target surface. Set all frequencies to 10′ (or 3 m for metric users).

Solution

1. From the Home tab ➢ Create Design panel, choose Corridor.

2. In the Name text box, name your corridor **Corridor A**.

   Keep the default values for Corridor Style and Corridor Layer.

3. Verify that Alignment is set to Alignment A and Profile is set to FG.

4. Verify that Assembly is set to Basic Assembly.

5. Verify that Target Surface is set to EG.

6. Verify that Set Baseline And Region Parameters is checked.

7. Click OK to accept the settings in the Create Corridor dialog and to display the Baseline And Region Parameters dialog.

8. Click the Set All Frequencies button to display the Frequency To Apply Assemblies dialog.

9. Change the value for all the frequencies to **10′** (or **3 m** for metric users).

10. Click OK to accept the settings in the Frequency To Apply Assemblies dialog.

11. Click OK to accept the settings in the Baseline And Region Parameters dialog.

12. You may receive a dialog warning that the corridor definition has been modified. If you do, select the Rebuild The Corridor option.

A finished copy of this drawing is available from the book's web page with the filename `MasterIt_0909_FINISHED.dwg` or `MasterIt_0909_METRIC_FINISHED.dwg`.

Use targets to add lane widening.   Targets are an essential design tool used to manipulate the geometry of the road.

> **Master It**   Open the `MasterIt_0910.dwg` or `MasterIt_0910_METRIC.dwg` file. Set Right Lane to target Alignment A-Right.

Solution

1. Select the corridor, and from the Corridor contextual tab ➢ Modify Corridor panel choose Corridor Properties icon.

2. On the Parameters tab, in the Targets column in the baseline row, click the ellipsis button to display the Target Mapping dialog.

3. In the Target Mapping dialog, click <None> in the Width Alignment row for Right Assembly Group to display the Set Width Or Offset Target dialog.

4. Select Alignment A-Right and click Add.

5. Click OK to dismiss the Set Width Or Offset Target dialog.

6. Click OK to accept the settings in the Target Mapping dialog.

7. Click OK to accept the settings in the Corridor Properties dialog and allow the corridor to rebuild.

A finished copy of this drawing is available from the book's web page with the filename `MasterIt_0910_FINISHED.dwg` or `MasterIt_0910_METRIC_FINISHED.dwg`.

Create a corridor surface.   The corridor model can be used to build a surface. This corridor surface can then be analyzed and annotated to produce finished road plans.

Master It   Open the `MasterIt_0911.dwg` or `MasterIt_0911_METRIC.dwg` file. Create a corridor surface for the Alignment A corridor from Top links. Name the surface Corridor A-Top.

Solution

1. Select the corridor and from the Corridor contextual tab ➤ Modify Corridor panel, choose Corridor Properties icon.

2. On the Surfaces tab, click the Create A Corridor Surface button in the upper-left corner of the dialog.

3. Click the surface item under the Name column and change the default name of your surface to **Corridor A-Top**.

4. Verify that Links has been selected from the drop-down list in the Data Type selection box.

5. Verify that Top has been selected from the drop-down list in the Specify Code selection box.

6. Click the Add Surface Item button to add Top Links to the surface definition.

7. Click OK to accept the settings in the dialog; then choose Rebuild The Corridor when prompted.

    The corridor and surface will build.

A finished copy of this drawing is available from the book's web page with the filename `MasterIt_0911_FINISHED.dwg` or `MasterIt_0911_METRIC_FINISHED.dwg`.

Add an automatic boundary to a corridor surface.   A surface can be improved with the addition of a boundary. Single-baseline corridors can take advantage of automatic boundary creation.

Master It   Open the `MasterIt_0912.dwg` or `MasterIt_0912_METRIC.dwg` file. Use the Automatic Boundary Creation tool to add a boundary using the Daylight code.

Solution

1. Select the corridor, and from the Corridor contextual tab ➤ Modify Corridor panel choose the Corridor Properties icon and switch to the Boundaries tab.

2. Right-click the surface entry and choose Add Automatically ➤ Daylight. Click Daylight to continue.

3. Click OK to accept the settings in the dialog; then choose Rebuild The Corridor when prompted.

The corridor and surface will rebuild.

A finished copy of this drawing is available from the book's web page with the filename `MasterIt_0912_FINISHED.dwg` or `MasterIt_0912_METRIC_FINISHED.dwg`.

Chapter 10: Advanced Corridors, Intersections, and Roundabouts

Create corridors with non-centerline baselines. Although for simple corridors you may think of a baseline as a road centerline, other elements of a road design can be used as a baseline. In the case of a cul-de-sac, the EOP, the top of curb, or any other appropriate feature can be converted to an alignment and profile and used as a baseline.

Master It Open the `MasterIt1001.dwg` (`MasterIt1001_METRIC.dwg`) file, which you can download from `www.sybex.com/go/masteringcivil3d2016`. Add the cul-de-sac alignment and profile to the corridor as a baseline. Create a region under this baseline that applies the Intersection Typical assembly.

Solution

1. Select the corridor. From the Corridor contextual tab ➢ Modify Corridor panel, click Corridor Properties.

2. Switch to the Parameters tab.

3. Click Add Baseline, choose Cul de Sac EOP in the Create Corridor Baseline dialog, and click OK.

4. In the Profile column, click inside the <Click here. . .> box, choose Cul de Sac EOP FG in the Select A Profile dialog, and click OK.

5. Right-click the new baseline and choose Add Region.

6. Select Intersection Typical in the Create Corridor Region dialog and click OK.

7. Click OK to leave the Corridor Properties dialog and rebuild the corridor.

You can find an example of the finished exercise in `MasterIt1001_SolutionA.dwg` (`MasterIt1001_SolutionA_METRIC.dwg`) on the book's web page.

Add alignment and profile targets to a region for a cul-de-sac. Adding a baseline isn't always enough. Some corridor models require the use of targets. In the case of a cul-de-sac, the lane elevations are often driven by the cul-de-sac centerline alignment and profile.

Master It Continue working in the `MasterIt1001.dwg` (`MasterIt1001_METRIC.dwg`) file. You need to have completed the previous exercise before continuing. Add the Second Road alignment and Second Road FG profile as targets to the cul-de-sac region. Adjust Assembly Application Frequency to 5′ (1 m) for tangents and curves.

Solution

1. Select the corridor. From the Corridor contextual tab ➢ Modify Corridor panel, click Corridor Properties.

2. In the Corridor Properties dialog, switch to the Parameters tab.

3. Click the Target Mapping button in the RG – Intersection Typical region.

4. In the Target Mapping dialog, do the following:

    a. Assign Second Road as Width Alignment for Lane – L.

    b. Assign Second Road FG profile as Outside Elevation Profile.

5. Click OK to leave the Target Mapping dialog.

6. Click the Frequency button in the same region.

7. Change the Curve Increment value to **5′ (1 m)**.

8. Click OK to exit the Frequency To Apply Assemblies dialog.

9. Click OK to leave the Corridor Properties dialog and rebuild the corridor.

An example of the finished exercise can be found in `MasterIt1001_SolutionB.dwg` (`MasterIt1001_SolutionB_METRIC.dwg`) on the book's web page.

Create a surface from a corridor and add a boundary.   Every good surface needs a boundary to prevent bad triangulation. Bad triangulation creates inaccurate contours and can throw off volume calculations later in the process. Civil 3D provides several tools for creating corridor surface boundaries, including an Interactive Boundary tool.

Master It   You need to have completed the previous exercise before continuing. Keep working in the `MasterIt1001.dwg` (`MasterIt1001_METRIC.dwg`) file. Create an interactive corridor surface boundary for the entire corridor model.

Solution

1. Select the corridor. From the Corridor contextual tab ➤ Modify Corridor panel, click Corridor Properties.

2. In the Corridor Properties dialog, switch to the Boundaries tab.

3. Select the corridor surface, right-click, and choose Add Interactively.

4. Follow the command-line prompts to add a boundary based on feature lines all the way around the entire corridor.

5. Type **C** ↵ to close the boundary and end the command.

6. Click OK to leave the Corridor Properties dialog and rebuild the corridor.

You can find an example of the finished exercise in `MasterIt1001_SolutionC.dwg` (`MasterIt1001_SolutionC_METRIC.dwg`) on the book's web page.

Chapter 11: Superelevation

Add superelevation to an alignment.   Civil 3D has convenient and flexible tools that will apply superelevation to an alignment curve using AASHTO standards.

Master It   Open the `MasterIt1101.dwg` (`MasterIt1101_METRIC.dwg`) file, which you can download from www.sybex.com/go/masteringcivil3d2016. Verify that the design speed of the road is 20 miles per hour (35 km per hour) and apply superelevation to the entire length of the alignment. Use AASHTO 2011 design criteria with an eMax of 6 percent for a two-lane, crowned roadway. Use the option to automatically resolve overlap.

Solution

1. Select the alignment. From the Alignment contextual tab ➢ Modify panel, choose Alignment Properties.

2. On the Design Criteria tab, verify that there is a check mark next to Use Criteria-Based Design.

3. Set the design criteria file to _Autodesk Civil 3D Imperial (2011) Roadway Design Standards using the ellipsis and set the Minimum Radius Table branch to use AASHTO 2011 US Customary eMax 6% on the right side of the dialog.

4. Verify that the design speed is set to 20 mph (35 km/h) on the left side, and click OK.

5. From the Alignment contextual tab, click Superelevation ➢ Calculate/Edit Superelevation.

6. Click Calculate Superelevation Now.

7. Step through the Superelevation Wizard, taking all the defaults for Roadway Type, Lanes, and Shoulder Control.

8. On the Attainment page, place a check mark next to Automatically Resolve Overlap. Click Finish.

You should now have superelevation applied to the design with no overlap.

Create a superelevation assembly.   For superelevation to happen, you need to have an assembly that is capable of superelevation.

Master It   Continue working in `MasterIt1101.dwg` (`MasterIt1101_METRIC.dwg`). You must have completed the previous exercise before starting this one. Create an undivided crowned road assembly named AOR similar to the one in the top image shown earlier in the chapter in Figure 11.10. Set each lane to be **14′ (4.5** m) wide and each shoulder to be **6′ (2** m) wide. Set the Use Superelevation parameter to Right Lane Outside and Left Lane Outside. Leave all other options at their defaults. If time permits, build a corridor based on the alignment and assembly.

Solution

1. From the Home tab ➢ Create Design panel, choose Assembly ➢ Create Assembly.

2. Name the assembly **AOR** and set the assembly type to Undivided Crowned Road. Click OK.

3. Click to place the assembly in the graphic.

4. From the Lanes subassembly palette, click the LaneSuperelevationAOR subassembly and set the lane width to **14′ (4.5** m) in the Properties palette.

5. Click the assembly to place one lane on the right; click again to place the assembly to the left. Press Esc when complete.

6. Select the right subassembly and set its Use Superelevation parameter to Right Lane Outside. Press Esc to clear the selection.

7. Select the left subassembly and set its Use Superelevation parameter to Left Lane Outside. Press Esc to clear the selection.

8. Place the shoulders on each side using ShoulderExtendAll and setting the shoulder width to **6′ (2 m)**; then press Esc when finished.

9. If time permits, create a corridor based on the alignment and assembly you just created.

10. Save the drawing.

Create a rail corridor with cant. Cant tools allow users to create corridors that meet design criteria specific to rail needs.

Master It In the drawing `MasterIt1102.dwg` (`MasterIt1102_METRIC.dwg`), create a Railway assembly named Rail with the RailSingle subassembly using the default parameters for width and depth. Add a LinkSlopeToSurface generic link with 50 percent slope to each side. Add cant to the alignment in the drawing using the default settings for attainment. Create a corridor named Rail from these pieces using the design profile and daylighting to the existing intersection.

Solution

1. From the Home tab ➢ Create Design panel, choose Assembly ➢ Create Assembly.

2. Name the assembly **Rail** and set the assembly type to Railway. Click OK and place the assembly in the graphic.

3. From the Bridge And Rail subassembly palette, click the RailSingle subassembly.

4. Click the assembly in the drawing to place the rail design.

5. From the Generic palette, click LinkSlopeToSurface.

6. Set the slope to **−50%** and configure a side parameter to place on the right and then the left sides of the assembly.

7. Press Esc to complete the process.

8. Select the alignment. From the Alignment contextual tab ➢ Modify panel, choose Cant ➢ Calculate/Edit Cant.

9. Click Calculate Cant Now, and click Finish.

10. Build a corridor from the alignment, the assembly, and the proposed profile (which has been designed for you ahead of time).

11. Set the target surface to Existing Intersection, and clear the check box for Set Baseline And Region Parameters.

12. Click OK.

If you need assistance building your corridor, review Chapters 9 and 10. But ideally you've figured it out by this point!

Create a superelevation view. Superelevation views are a great place to get a handle on what is going on in your roadway design. You can visually check the geometry as well as make changes to the design.

Master It Open the drawing `MasterIt1103.dwg` (`MasterIt1103_METRIC.dwg`). Create a superelevation view for the alignment. Show only the left and right outside lanes as blue and red, respectively.

Solution

1. Select the alignment and choose Superelevation ➤ Create Superelevation View.

2. In the Create Superelevation View dialog, toggle off Left Outside Shoulder and Right Outside Shoulder. The remaining check boxes are for the lane views.

3. Set Left Outside Lane Color to Blue, set Right Outside Lane Color to Red, and click OK.

4. Place the view in the graphic.

Chapter 12: Cross Sections and Mass Haul

Create sample lines. Before any section views can be displayed, sections must be created from sample lines.

Master It Open `MasterIt_1201.dwg` (`MasterIt_1201_METRIC.dwg`) and create sample lines along the USH 10 alignment every 50 feet (20 meters for metric users). Sample all data, and set the left and right swath widths to 50 (20 for metric users).

Solution

1. From the Home tab ➤ Profile & Section Views panel, choose Sample Lines.

2. Select the USH 10 alignment and sample all data; then click OK.

3. In the Sample Line toolbar, click the By Range Of Stations option.

4. Create sample lines by station range and set your sampling increments and swaths for both left and right to **50** (**20** for metric users); then click OK and press ↵ to complete the command.

5. Save the drawing and keep it open for use in the next exercise. (See `MasterIt_1201_FINISHED.dwg` or `MasterIt_1201_METRIC_FINISHED.dwg` for finished versions of this exercise.)

Create section views. Just as profiles can be shown only in profile views, sections require section views to be displayed. Section views can be plotted individually or all at once. You can break them up into groups for plotting into sheets.

Master It In the previous exercise, you created sample lines. In that same drawing, create section views for all the sample lines. For U.S. units, use a cross-section scale of 1″ = 20′ on an Arch D size layout sheet. For metric units, use a cross-section scale of 1:500 on an ISO A0 size sheet. For all other options, use the default settings and styles.

Solution

1. Continue working in `MasterIt_1201.dwg` (`MasterIt_1201_METRIC.dwg`) if you finished the previous exercise, or open `MasterIt_1201_FINISHED.dwg` (`MasterIt_1201_METRIC_FINISHED.dwg`).

2. For U.S. users, change the annotation scale to **1″ = 20′**. For metric users, make sure the annotation scale is **1:500**.

3. Select one of the sample lines.

4. From the Sample Line contextual tab ➤ Launch Pad panel, click Create Section View ➤ Create Multiple Section Views.

5. On the section placement page, click the ellipsis to set the Arch D Section 20 Scale option (ISO A0 Section 1 to 500 for metric users). Click OK.

6. Leave all options at their defaults and click Create Section Views.

7. Click in the graphic to place the views. Save the drawing and keep it open for use in the next exercise. (See `MasterIt_1202_FINISHED.dwg` or `MasterIt_1202_METRIC_FINISHED.dwg` for finished versions of this exercise.)

Define and compute materials. Materials are required to be defined before any quantities can be displayed. You learned that materials can be defined from surfaces or from corridor shapes. Corridors must exist for shape selection, and surfaces must already be created for comparison in materials lists.

Master It Continuing using `MasterIt_1201.dwg` (`Master It_1201_METRIC.dwg`), create a materials list that compares Existing Intersection with HWY 10 DATUM Surface. Use the Earthworks Quantity takeoff criteria. Be sure you have completed all the previous "Master It" exercises before continuing.

Solution

1. Continue working in `MasterIt_1201.dwg` (`MasterIt_1201_METRIC.dwg`) if you finished the previous exercise, or open `MasterIt_1202_FINISHED.dwg` (`MasterIt_1202_METRIC_FINISHED.dwg`).

2. Select one of the sample lines.

3. From the Sample Line contextual tab ➤ Launch Pad panel, click Compute Materials. Select the alignment and sample line group and then click OK.

4. In the upper-right corner of the Compute Materials dialog, set the quantity takeoff criteria to Earthworks.

5. Set the Existing Ground surface to Existing Intersection by clicking the <Click Here...> field.

6. Set Datum Object Name to HWY 10 DATUM and click OK. Save the drawing and keep it open for use in the next exercise. (See `MasterIt_1203_FINISHED.dwg` or `MasterIt_1203_METRIC_FINISHED.dwg` for finished versions of this exercise.)

Graphically, nothing will appear. Continue to the next exercise to see the results of your work.

Generate volume reports. Volume reports give you numbers that can be used for cost estimating on any given project. Typically, construction companies calculate their own quantities, but developers often want to know approximate volumes for budgeting purposes.

Master It   Continue using `MasterIt_1201.dwg` (`MasterIt_1201_METRIC.dwg`). Be sure you have completed all the previous "Master It" exercises before continuing. Use the materials list created earlier to generate a volume report. Create a web browser–based report and a total volume table that can be displayed on the drawing.

Solution

1. Continue working in `MasterIt_1201.dwg` (`MasterIt_1201_METRIC.dwg`) if you finished the previous exercise, or open `MasterIt_1203_FINISHED.dwg` (`MasterIt_1203_METRIC_FINISHED.dwg`).

2. Without any object selected, go to the Analyze tab ➢ Volumes And Materials panel and click Volume Report.

3. Leave all options at their defaults and click OK.

4. If asked "Do you want to allow scripts to run?" click Yes.

   Your report will be displayed.

5. Close the browser window.

6. In Civil 3D, from the Analyze tab ➢ Volumes And Materials panel, click Total Volume Table.

7. Leave all options at their defaults and click OK. Place the table anywhere on the screen.

8. Save the drawing. (See `MasterIt_1204_FINISHED.dwg` or `MasterIt_1204_METRIC_FINISHED.dwg` for finished versions of this exercise.)

Chapter 13: Pipe Networks

Create a pipe network by layout. After you've created a parts list for your pipe network, the first step toward finalizing the design is to use Pipe Network By Layout.

Master It   Open the `MasterIt_1301.dwg` or `MasterIt_1301_METRIC.dwg` file. Use Network Creation Tools to create a waste water pipe network named Mastering. Use the Composite surface, and name only structure and pipe label styles. Don't choose an alignment at this time. Create 8' (200 mm) PVC pipes and a manhole called SMH. There are blocks in the drawing to assist you in placing manholes. Begin at the START HERE marker, and place a manhole at each marker location. You can erase the markers when you've finished.

Solution

1. From the Home tab ➢ Create Design panel, select Pipe Network ➢ Pipe Network Creation Tools.

2. In the Create Pipe Network dialog, set the following parameters:

- Network Name: **Mastering**
- Network Parts List: Waste Water
- Surface Name: **Composite**
- Alignment Name: <none>
- Structure Label Style: Name Only (Sanitary)
- Pipe Label Style: Name Only

3. Click OK. The Network Layout Tools toolbar will appear.

4. Set the structure to Concentric Cylindrical Structure NF (Concentric Cylindrical Structure SI) ➢ SMH and the pipe to PVC Pipe (PVC Pipe SI) ➢ 8.0 inch PVC Pipe (200 mm PVC Pipe).

5. Click Draw Pipes And Structures, and use your Insertion Osnap to place a structure at each marker location.

6. Press ↵ to exit the command. Close the toolbar.

7. Move the structure labels as desired.

8. Select a marker, right-click, choose Select Similar, and click Delete.

See `MasterIt_1301_FINISHED.dwg` or `MasterIt_1301_METRIC_FINISHED.dwg` for the result.

Create an alignment from network parts and draw parts in profile view.   Once your pipe network has been created in plan view, you'll typically add the parts to a profile view based on either the road centerline or the pipe centerline.

Master It   Continue working in the `MasterIt_1301.dwg` or `MasterIt_1301_METRIC` `.dwg` file. You need to have completed the previous exercise before beginning this one. Create an alignment named Mastering from your pipes so that station zero is located at the START HERE structure. Create a profile view from this alignment and show the pipes and profiles for the EG and Corridor FG surfaces on the profile view. Use defaults for everything, except change the Corridor FG profile style to FG Profile on the profile view.

Solution

1. Select the structure labeled START HERE to display the Pipe Networks contextual tab and select Alignment From Network on the Launch Pad panel.

2. Select the last structure in the pipe run and press ↵ to accept the selection.

3. In the Create Alignment dialog, name the alignment **Mastering** and make sure the Create Profile And Profile View check box is selected.

4. Accept the other defaults and click OK.

5. In the Create Profile From Surface dialog, sample both the EG and Corridor FG surfaces for the profile. Select the surfaces and click Add. Change the Corridor FG profile style to **FG Profile**.

6. Click Draw In Profile View.

7. In the Create Profile View dialog, click Create Profile View and choose a location in the drawing for the profile view.

A profile view showing your pipes appears. See `MasterIt_1302_FINISHED.dwg` or `MasterIt_1302_METRIC_FINISHED.dwg` for the result.

Label a pipe network in plan and profile.   Designing your pipe network is only half the process. Engineering plans must be properly annotated.

Master It   Continue working in the `MasterIt_1301.dwg` or `MasterIt_1301_METRIC` `.dwg` file. You need to have completed the previous exercise before beginning this one. Add the Length Description And Slope pipe label style to profile pipes and the Data With Connected Pipes (Sanitary) structure label style to profile structures. Assign the alignment created in the previous "Master It" exercise to all pipes and structures.

Solution

1. Select one of the pipe or structure objects. From the Pipe Networks contextual tab ➢ Labels & Tables panel, select Add Labels ➢ Add Pipe Network Labels.

2. In the Add Labels dialog, change Feature to Pipe Network and then change Label Type to Entire Network Profile.

   ◆ For pipe labels, choose Length Description And Slope.

   ◆ For structure labels, choose Data With Connected Pipes (Sanitary).

3. Click Add and choose any pipe or structure in your profile view.

4. Drag or adjust any profile labels as desired.

5. In the Prospector tab of Toolspace, expand Pipe Networks ➢ Networks ➢ Mastering and select Pipes.

6. Select all pipes in Prospector, right-click the Reference Alignment column header and select Edit.

7. Choose the Mastering alignment and then click OK.

8. Repeat steps 5 through 7 but choose Structures.

See `MasterIt_1303_FINISHED.dwg` or `MasterIt_1303_METRIC_FINISHED.dwg` for the result.

Create a dynamic pipe table.   It's common for municipalities and contractors to request a pipe or structure table for cost estimates or to make it easier to understand a busy plan.

Master It   Continue working in the `MasterIt_1301.dwg` or `MasterIt_1301_METRIC.dwg` file. You need to have completed the previous exercise before beginning this one. Create a pipe table for all pipes in your network. Use the default table style.

Solution

1. Select one of the pipe or structure objects. From the Pipe Networks contextual tab ➢ Labels and Tables panel, select Add Tables ➢ Add Pipe.

2. In the Pipe Table Creation dialog, make sure your pipe network is selected.

3. Accept the other defaults and click OK.

4. Place the table in your drawing.

See `MasterIt_1304_FINISHED.dwg` or `MasterIt1304_METRIC_FINISHED.dwg` for the result.

Chapter 14: Grading

Convert existing linework into feature lines.   Many site features are drawn initially as simple linework for the 2D plan. By converting this linework to feature-line information, you avoid a large amount of rework. Additionally, the conversion process offers the ability to drape feature lines along a surface, making further grading use easier.

Master It   Open the `MasterIt.dwg` or `MasterIt_METRIC.dwg` file from the book's web page. Convert the magenta polyline, describing a proposed temporary swale, into a feature line and drape it across the EG surface to set elevations; then set intermediate grade break points.

Solution

1. From the Home tab ➢ Create Design panel, choose Feature Lines ➢ Create Feature Lines From Objects.

2. Select the magenta polyline. Press the Enter key.

3. Fill in the Assign Elevations check box and then click OK.

4. Select the EG surface in the Assign Elevations dialog.

5. Verify that Insert Intermediate Grade Break Points is checked.

6. Click OK to close the dialog and return to your model.

You can find an example of the finished exercise in `MasterIt_SolutionA.dwg` (`MasterIt MasterIt_SolutionA METRIC.dwg`) on the book's web page.

Model a simple breakline with a feature line.   Feature lines define linear slope connections or, in other words, breaklines. This can be the flow of a drainage channel, the outline of a building pad, or the back of a street curb. These linear relationships can help define grading in a model or simply enhance understanding of design intent.

Master It   Edit the radius of the curve on the feature line you just created to be 100′ (30 m). Set the grade from the west end of the feature line to the PC of the edited curve to 4 percent, and set the remainder to a constant slope. Draw a temporary profile view to verify that the channel is below grade for most of its length.

Solution

1. Select the feature line to activate the Feature Line contextual tab.

2. From the Feature Line contextual tab ➤ Modify panel, toggle on the Edit Geometry panel if not already visible.

3. From the Feature Line contextual tab ➤ Edit Geometry panel, choose the Edit Curve tool.

4. Select the feature line curve.

5. In the Edit Feature Line Curve dialog, change the radius to **100′ (30 m)** and click OK.

6. Press the Enter key to end the command.

7. From the Feature Line contextual tab ➤ Modify panel, toggle on the Edit Elevations panel if not already visible.

8. From the Feature Line contextual tab ➤ Edit Elevations panel, select Elevation Editor.

9. Press Esc once so you can view the feature line glyphs.

10. Select station 0+00, which will show the triangular glyph on the western end of the feature.

11. Hold down the Shift key and select station 0+86.66 (0+027.76 if metric).

12. Click in one of the Grade Ahead fields and enter a value of **4**.

13. Select the PI at station 0+86.66 (0+027.76 if metric).

14. Hold down the Shift key and select station 2+29.01 (0+069.54 if metric).

15. Click the Flatten Grade Or Elevations tool to open the Flatten dialog.

16. Select Constant Grade and click OK to close the Flatten dialog.

17. Select the feature line, and from the Feature Line contextual tab ➤ Launch Pad panel, choose Quick Profile.

18. Change the profile view style to Land Desktop Profile View, click OK to accept the rest of the defaults, and pick a point on the screen to draw the quick profile view.

19. Dismiss Panorama to view the Quick Profile.

You can find an example of the finished exercise in `MasterIt_SolutionA.dwg` (`MasterIt MasterIt_SolutionA METRIC.dwg`) on the book's web page.

Model planar site features with grading groups. Once a feature line defines a linear feature, gradings collected in grading groups model the slope projections from that line to other points in space. These projections can be combined to model a site much like a TIN surface, producing a dynamic design tool.

Master It Use grading criteria to define the pilot channel, with grading on both sides of the sketched centerline. Define the channel using a Grading To Distance value of 5′ (1.5 m) with a slope of 3:1, and connect the channel to the EG surface using a grading with slopes that are 4:1. Generate a surface from the grading group. If prompted, do not weed the feature line.

Solution

1. From the Home tab ➤ Create Design panel, choose Grading ➤ Grading Creation Tools to activate the Grading Creation Tools toolbar.

2. Click the Create A Grading Group tool to create a grading group and name the group.

3. Verify that the Automatic Surface Creation option is checked, and click OK.

4. Click OK to accept the surface creation options.

5. Click the Set The Target Surface tool to set the target surface to EG, and click OK.

6. Change Grading Criteria to Grade To Distance.

7. Click the Create Grading tool, and pick the feature line.

8. If the Weed Feature Line dialog appears, select Continue Grading Without Feature Line Weeding.

9. Pick the left or right side, and enter **Y**↵.

10. Enter **5** ↵ **(1.5)** for the distance.

11. Enter **S** ↵ to enter slope.

12. Enter **3** ↵ for the slope value.

13. Pick the main feature line again, and grade the other side using the same steps.

14. Change Grading Criteria to Grade To Surface.

15. Click the Create Grading tool.

16. Select either outer feature line (right or left), and enter **Y** ↵.

17. Enter **S** ↵ to enter cut format.

18. Enter **4** ↵ for the cut slope value.

19. Enter **S** ↵ to enter fill format.

20. Enter **4** ↵ for the fill slope value.

21. Repeat for the remaining outer feature line.

22. Press Esc to complete the gradings.

23. Close the Grading Creation Tools toolbar.

You can find an example of the finished exercise in `MasterIt_SolutionC.dwg` (`MasterIt MasterIt_SolutionC METRIC.dwg`) on the book's web page.

Chapter 15: Plan Production

Create view frames. When you create view frames, you must select the template file that contains the layout tabs that will be used as the basis for your sheets. This template must contain predefined viewports. You can define these viewports with extra vertices so you can change their shape after the sheets have been created.

Master It Open the MasterIt_1501.dwg (MasterIt_1501_METRIC.dwg) file. Run the Create View Frames Wizard to create view frames for Alignment A in the current drawing. (Accept the defaults for all other values.) These view frames will be used to generate Plan and Profile sheets on ARCH D (ISO A1 for metric users) sheets at 20 scale (1:200 scale for metric users) using the plan and profile template MasteringPandPTemplate.dwt or MasteringPandPTemplate_METRIC.dwt. All files should be saved in C:\Mastering\ Ch15\.

Solution

1. From the Output tab ➢ Plan Production panel, choose Create View Frames.

2. On the Alignment page, select Alignment A from the Alignment drop-down list and click Next.

3. On the Sheets page, select the Plan And Profile option.

4. Click the ellipsis button to display the Select Layout As Sheet Template dialog.

5. In the Select Layout As Sheet Template dialog, click the ellipsis button, browse to C:\ Mastering\Ch15\, select the template named MasteringPandPTemplate .dwt (or MasteringPandPTemplate_METRIC.dwt for metric users), and click Open.

6. Select the layout named ARCH D Plan And Profile 20 Scale (or ISO A1 Plan And Profile 1 to 200 for metric users), and click OK.

7. Click Create View Frames.

8. Save and leave the drawing open for the next part of this "Master It" series.

You can check your result against the finished drawing as found within the dataset for this chapter under the name of MasterIt_1501_FINISHED.dwg (MasterIt_1501_METRIC_ FINISHED.dwg).

Edit view frames. The grips available to edit view frames allow the user some freedom on how the frames will appear.

Master It Continue working in the previous exercise file or open the MasterIt_1501_ FINISHED.dwg (MasterIt_1501_METRIC_FINISHED.dwg) file, and move the VF– (1) view frame to Sta. 2+20 (or Sta. 0+050 for metric users) to lessen the overlap. Then adjust Match Line 1 (or Match Line 2 for metric users) so that it is now at Sta. 4+25 (or Sta. 0+200 for metric users) and shorten it so that the labels are completely within the view frames.

Solution

1. Click the VF– (1) view frame.

2. Make sure you have Dynamic Input on.

3. Click the diamond grip and type **220** ↵ (or **50** ↵ for metric users).

4. Press Esc to clear the selection.

5. Click Match Line 1 (or Match Line 2 for metric users) to show its grips.

6. Click the diamond grip and type **425** ↵ (or **200** ↵ for metric users).

7. Click the triangular grip on one end of the match line and shorten it so that the label is completely within the view frames.

8. Repeat step 7 for the triangular grip on the opposite end of the match line.

   The match line is now centered better between the two view frames.

9. Save the drawing.

You can check your result against the finished drawing as found within the dataset for this chapter under the name of `MasterIt_1502_FINISHED.dwg` (`MasterIt_1502_METRIC_FINISHED.dwg`).

Generate sheets and review Sheet Set Manager. You can create sheets in new drawing files or in the current drawing. The resulting sheets are based on the template you chose when you created the view frames. If the template contains customized viewports, you can modify the shape of the viewport to better fit your sheet needs.

Master It Open the `MasterIt_1503.dwg` (`MasterIt_1503_METRIC.dwg`) file. Run the Create Sheets Wizard to create plan and profile sheets in the current drawing for Alignment A using the plan and profile template `MasteringPandPTemplate.dwt` or `MasteringPandPTemplate_METRIC.dwt`. Make sure to choose a north arrow and add the sheets to a new sheet set named Alignment A (Alignment A_METRIC for metric users). (Accept the defaults for all other values.)

Solution

1. From the Output tab ➤ Plan Production panel, choose Create Sheets.

2. On the View Frame Group And Layouts page, in the Layout Creation area, select All Layouts In The Current Drawing.

3. Verify that the north arrow is selected from the drop-down list.

4. In the Sheet Set section of the wizard under New Sheet Set, enter **Alignment A** (**Alignment A_METRIC** for metric users).

5. Set Sheet Set Storage Location to `C:\Mastering\Ch15\FinishedSheets\`.

6. Click Create Sheets.

7. Click OK to save the drawing.

8. Click a location as the profile origin.

9. Dismiss the Panorama Event Viewer.

10. Save the drawing.

You can check your result against the finished drawing as found within the dataset for this chapter under the name of `MasterIt_1503_FINISHED.dwg` (`MasterIt_1503_METRIC_FINISHED.dwg`).

Create section views. More and more municipalities are requiring section views. Whether this is a mile-long road or a meandering stream, Civil 3D can handle it nicely via Plan Production.

Master It Open the `MasterIt_1504.dwg` (`MasterIt_1504_METRIC.dwg`) file. Create section views and Plan Production section sheets in a new sheet set for Alignment A using the Road Section section view style and the section sheet template `MasteringSectionTemplate.dwt` or `MasteringSectionTemplate_METRIC.dwt`. Make sure the sections are set to be generated on ARCH D (ISO A1 for metric users) sheets at 20-scale (1:200 scale for metric users). Also, make sure to provide as Sheet Set name Alignment A_XC (Alignment A_XC_METRIC for metric users). (Accept the defaults for all other values.) All files should be saved in `C:\Mastering\Ch15\FinishedSheets`.

Solution

1. From the Home tab ➤ Profile & Section Views panel, choose Section Views ➤ Create Multiple Views.

2. On the General page, verify that Section View Style is set to Road Section and click Next.

3. On the Section Placement page, select the Production option.

4. Click the ellipsis button to display the Select Layout As Sheet Template dialog.

5. In this dialog, click the ellipsis button, browse to `C:\Mastering\Ch15\`, select the template named `MasteringSectionTemplate.dwt` (or `MasteringSectionTemplate_METRIC.dwt` for metric users), and click Open.

6. Select the layout named ARCH D Section 20 Scale (or ISO A1 Section 1 to 200 for metric users), and click OK.

7. Click Create Section Views.

8. Click a location as the section origin. The multiple section views are created.

9. From the Output tab ➤ Plan Production panel, choose Create Section Sheets.

10. In the Create Section Sheets dialog, verify that New Sheet Set is selected and named Alignment A_XC (Alignment A_XC_METRIC for metric users), and set Sheet Set Storage Location to `C:\Mastering\Ch15\FinishedSheets`.

11. Click Create Sheets.

12. Click OK to save the drawing.

You can check your result against the finished drawing as found within the dataset for this chapter under the name of `MasterIt_1504_FINISHED.dwg` (`MasterIt_1504_METRIC_FINISHED.dwg`).

Chapter 16: Advanced Workflows

Create a data shortcut folder.   The ability to load design information into a project environment is an important part of creating an efficient team. The main design elements of the project are available to the data shortcut mechanism via the working folder and data shortcut folder.

Master It   Using the `MasterIt1601.dwg` (`MasterIt1601_METRIC.dwg`) drawing, create a new data shortcut folder called `MasterIt`. Use the `_Sample Project` project template.

Solution

1. Open the `MasterIt1601.dwg` (`MasterIt1601_METRIC.dwg`) drawing.

2. On the Manage tab ➤ Data Shortcuts panel, click New Shortcuts Folder.

3. Give the project a name of your choosing, such as **MasterIt**, and place a check mark next to Use Project Template.

4. With `_Sample Project` highlighted, click OK.

The data shortcut folder is now complete.

Create data shortcuts.   To allow sharing of the data, shortcuts must be made before the information can be used in other drawings.

Master It   Continue working in the drawing from the previous "Master It" exercise. Save the drawing to the `Source Drawings` folder in the Master Data Shortcuts project you created in the previous exercise. Create data shortcuts to all the available data in the `MasterIt1601.dwg` (`MasterIt1601_METRIC.dwg`) file.

Solution

1. Continue working in the drawing from the previous "Master It" exercise.

2. From the Application menu, use Save As to save the drawing to `C:\Mastering\ MasterIt\Source Drawings`.

3. On the Manage tab ➤ Data Shortcuts panel, click Create Data Shortcuts.

4. Place a check mark next to all items that appear in the data listing, and click OK.

Export to earlier releases of AutoCAD.   Being able to export to earlier base AutoCAD versions is sometimes necessary.

Master It   Using `MasterIt1601.dwg` (`MasterIt1601_METRIC.dwg`), export the Civil 3D file so it can be used by a user working in base AutoCAD 2010.

Solution

1. Continue working in the drawing from the previous "Master It" exercise.

2. From the Application menu, select Export ➤ Export Civil 3D Drawing.

3. Do not include drawings in subfolders and do not include sheets.

4. Set Export Settings to use the 2010 file version.

5. Set Source Folder and Destination Folder to `C:\Mastering\MasterIt\Source Drawings`.

6. Click Export.

7. Click OK and then Cancel to close dialogs when the export is finished.

Export to LandXML.   Being able to work with outside clients or even other departments within your firm that do not have Civil 3D is an important part of collaboration.

Master It   Using `MasterIt1601.dwg` (`MasterIt1601_METRIC.dwg`), create a LandXML file with all of the exportable information.

Solution

1. Continue working in the drawing from the previous "Master It" exercise.

2. From the Output tab ➢ Export panel, click Export To LandXML. Use all the default settings and click OK.

3. Save the file with the default name in the same directory as `MasterIt1601.dwg` (`MasterIt1601_METRIC.dwg`).

Chapter 17: Quantity Takeoff

Open and add to a list of pay items.   The pay item list is the cornerstone of quantity takeoffs. You should download and review your pay item list and compare it against the current reviewing agency list regularly to avoid any missed items.

Master It   Using the template of your choice, open the `Getting Started.csv` (or `Getting Started_Metric.csv`) pay item file that you have been working with in the previous exercises and add the 12-, 18-, and 24-Inch Pipe Culvert (or 300 mm, 450 mm, and 600 mm Pipe Culvert) pay items to your Favorites list in the QTO Manager.

Solution

1. Start a new file by using the default Civil 3D template of your choice.

2. On the Analyze tab ➢ QTO panel, open the QTO Manager.

3. Click the Open button at the top left of the QTO Manager.

4. Verify that the Pay Item File Format drop-down list is set to CSV (Comma Delimited).

5. Click the Open button next to the Pay Item File text box.

6. Navigate to the `Getting Started` folder and select the `Getting Started.csv` file. Metric users should use the `Getting Started_METRIC.csv` file, which is downloadable from the book's web page.

7. Click Open to select this CSV pay item file.

8. Click OK.

9. Enter **12-Inch Pipe** (or **300 mm Pipe**) in the text box to filter.

10. Right-click the 12-INCH PIPE CULVERT item (or the 300 MM PIPE CULVERT item) and select Add To Favorites List.

11. Repeat steps 9–10 for the other sizes.

A saved copy of this drawing is available from the book's web page with the filename `MasteringPayItemList_FINISHED.dwg` or `MasteringPayItemList_METRIC_FINISHED.dwg`.

Assign pay items to AutoCAD objects and pipe networks. The majority of the work in preparing quantity takeoffs is in assigning pay items accurately. By using the linework, blocks, and Civil 3D objects in your drawing as part of the process, you reduce the effort involved in generating accurate quantities.

Master It Open the `MasteringQTO.dwg` or `MasteringQTO_Metric.dwg` file and assign the CLEARING AND GRUBBING pay item to the polyline that was originally extracted from the border of the corridor. Change the hatch to have a transparency of 80.

Solution

1. Open the drawing first and then the QTO Manager from the Analyze tab ➤ QTO panel.

2. Expand the Favorites branch and select the CLEARING AND GRUBBING item.

3. Right-click and select Assign Pay Item To Area.

4. Switch to the Object option by entering **O** ↵ at the command line.

5. Select the polyline representing the limits of corridor surface.

6. Press ↵ again to end the command.

7. Select the hatch to activate the Hatch Editor contextual tab.

8. From the Hatch Editor contextual tab ➤ Properties panel, change Hatch Transparency to **80**. Using Display Order, send the hatch to the back.

9. On the Settings tab, expand the Pipe Networks ➤ Parts Lists branches, right-click Storm Sewer, and select Edit.

10. In the Network Parts List – Storm Sewer dialog, expand the Storm Sewer ➤ Concrete Pipe (or Concrete Pipe SI) branches.

11. For 12-inch Concrete Pipe (or 300 mm Concrete Pipe), click the icon in the Pay Item column.

12. Turn off Categorization and search for the 12-INCH PIPE CULVERT item (or the 300 MM PIPE CULVERT item).

13. Select the item and click OK.

14. Click OK to close the parts list.

Use QTO tools to review what items have been tagged for analysis. By using the built-in highlighting tools to verify pay item assignments, you can avoid costly errors when running your QTO reports.

Master It   Verify that the area in the previous exercise has been assigned a pay item.

Solution

1. Turn on Highlight Objects With Pay Items in the QTO Manager.

2. Pan and hover over the hatch to confirm that the tooltip indicates a pay item assignment.

A saved copy of this drawing is available from the book's web page with the filename `MasteringQTO_FINISHED.dwg` or `MasteringQTO_METRIC_FINISHED.dwg`.

Generate QTO output to a variety of formats for review or analysis.   The quantity takeoff reports give you a quick understanding of what items have been tagged in the drawing, and they can generate text in the drawing or external reports for uses in other applications.

Master It   Display the length of Type C Broken markings in a Quantity Takeoff Report with the Summary (TXT) report style using the `MasteringQTOReporting.dwg` or `MasteringQTOReporting_Metric.dwg` file.

Solution

1. Open the drawing and from the Analyze tab ➢ QTO panel, select Takeoff and click Compute to run the report with default settings.

2. In the lower-left corner of the Quantity Takeoff Report dialog, change the report style to Summary(TXT).xsl.

3. Click the Draw button at the bottom of the dialog.

4. Click near some clean space, and you'll be returned to the Quantity Takeoff Report dialog.

5. Click Close to dismiss this dialog and then click Close again to dismiss the Compute Quantity Takeoff dialog.

6. The calculated amount for Type C Broken Pavement Markings should be 3,163.30′ (or 1,000.528 m).

A saved copy of this drawing is available from the book's web page with the filename `MasteringQTOReporting _FINISHED.dwg` or `MasteringQTOReporting_METRIC_FINISHED.dwg`.

Chapter 18: Label Styles

Override individual labels with other styles.   In spite of the desire to have uniform labeling styles and appearances between alignments within a single drawing, project, or firm, there are always exceptions. Using the Ctrl+click method for element selection, you can access commands that let you modify labels and even change their styles.

Master It   Open the drawing `MasterIt_1801.dwg` (`MasterIt_1801_METRIC.dwg`). Create a copy of the Perpendicular With Tick Major Station style called **Major With Marker**. Change Tick Block Name to **Marker Pnt**. Replace some (but not all) of your major station labels with this new style.

Solution

1. On the Settings tab, expand the Alignment ➢ Label Styles ➢ Station ➢ Major Station branch.

2. Right-click Perpendicular With Tick and select Copy.

3. On the Information tab, change the name to **Major with Marker**.

4. Change to the Layout tab.

5. Select Tick from the Component drop-down.

6. Click in the Value field next to Block name and click the ellipsis.

7. In the Select a Block dialog, select Marker Pnt and click OK.

8. Click OK to close the Label Style Composer dialog.

9. Open the AutoCAD Properties palette.

10. Ctrl+click one or more major station labels.

11. In the AutoCAD Properties palette, change the major station label style to **Major with Marker**.

A saved copy of this drawing (`MasterIt_1801_FINISHED.dwg` (`MasterIt_1801_METRIC_FINISHED.dwg`) is available from the book's web page.

Create a new label set for alignments.   Label sets let you determine the appearance of an alignment's labels and quickly standardize that appearance across all objects of the same nature. By creating sets that reflect their intended use, you can make it easy for a designer to quickly label alignments according to specifications with little understanding of the requirement.

> **Master It**   Continue working in the `MasterIt_1801.dwg` (`MasterIt_1801_METRIC`
> `.dwg`) file if you completed the previous exercise, or open `MasterIt_1801_FINISHED.dwg`
> (`MasterIt_1801_METRIC_FINISHED.dwg`) file, and create a new label set named Major
> Only containing only the new major station label defined in the previous exercise and
> apply it to all the alignments in that drawing.

Solution

1. On the Settings tab, expand the Alignments ➢ Label Styles ➢ Label Sets branch.

2. Right-click Label Sets Branch and select New.

3. In the Alignment Label Set dialog, change the name to **Major Only** on the Information tab.

4. Switch to the Labels tab and then select Major Stations in Type and Major With Marker in Major Station Label Style. Click the Add button.

5. Click OK to close the Alignment Label Set dialog.

6. Select an alignment label and on the contextual tab ➢ Modify panel, click Edit Label Group.

7. In the Alignment Labels dialog, click Import Label Set.

8. In the Select Label Set dialog, use the drop-down to select the Major Only label set. Click OK to close the dialog. Click OK again to close the Alignment Labels dialog.

9. Repeat for each alignment.

   A saved copy of this drawing (`MasterIt_1802_FINISHED.dwg` (`MasterIt_1802_METRIC_FINISHED.dwg`) is available from the book's web page.

Create and use expressions. Expressions give you the ability to add calculated information to labels or add logic to label creation.

Master It Continue working in the `MasterIt_1801.dwg` (`MasterIt_1801_METRIC.dwg`) file, or open the `MasterIt_1802_FINISHED.dwg` (`MasterIt_1802_METRIC_FINISHED.dwg`) file, and create an expression called Top of Curb that adds 0.5′ (0.15 m) to a surface elevation. Use the expression in a spot elevation label that shows both the surface elevation and the expression-based elevation to a decimal precision of two.

Solution

1. In the Settings tab of Toolspace, expand Surface Label Styles ➢ Spot Elevation, right-click Expressions, and click New.

2. In the New Expression dialog, name the expression **Top of Curb**.

   The Expression will read `{Surface Elevation}+0.5` (for metric `{Surface Elevation}+0.15`).

3. Use the Properties button to select the Surface Elevation Property field and type **+0.5** (**+0.15** for metric) behind it.

4. Set Format as Double.

5. Click OK.

6. In the same branch of Settings, right-click Spot Elevation and select New.

7. In the Label Style Composer dialog, name the label **Top of Curb** on the Information tab.

8. On the Layout tab of the Label Style Composer, click the Value field next to Contents and click the ellipses to open the Text Component Editor dialog.

9. Select the existing component and, from the left side, change the precision to 0.01. Click the white arrow to update the expression on the right. Add the new expression after the surface elevation text. Place your mouse cursor in between the existing elevation text and the new expression, and press the Enter key to ensure the text appears on two lines with the expression-based label on the bottom.

10. Click OK twice to exit both dialogs.

11. Place the new label in the drawing to check your work by using the surface labeling tools.

A saved copy of this drawing (`MasterIt_1803_FINISHED.dwg` (`MasterIt_1803_METRIC_FINISHED.dwg`) is available from the book's web page.

Apply a standard label set to profiles.   Standardization of appearance is one of the major benefits of using Civil 3D styles in labeling. By applying label sets, you can quickly create plot-ready profile views that have the required information for review.

Master It   Continue working in the `MasterIt_1801.dwg` (`MasterIt_1801_METRIC.dwg`) file or open the `MasterIt_1803_FINISHED.dwg` (`MasterIt_1803_METRIC_FINISHED.dwg`) file, and apply the Road Profile Labels label set to all layout profiles.

Solution

1. Pick one of the layout profiles, and on the contextual tab ➤ Label panel, select Edit Profile Labels.

2. In the Profile Labels dialog, click Import Label Set.

3. In the Select Label Set dialog, use the drop-down to select the Road Profile Labels label set.

4. Click OK twice to exit both dialogs.

5. Repeat this procedure for all layout profiles.

A saved copy of this drawing (`MasterIt_1804_FINISHED.dwg` (`MasterIt_1804_METRIC_FINISHED.dwg`) is available from the book's web page.

Chapter 19: Object Styles

Override object styles with other styles.   In spite of the desire to have uniform styles and appearances between objects within a single drawing, project, or firm, there are always going to be changes that need to be made.

Master It   Open the `MasterIt_1901.dwg` (`MasterIt_1901_METRIC.dwg`) file and change the alignment style associated with Alignment B to Layout. In addition, change the surface style used for the EG surface to Contours And Triangles, but change the contour interval to 1′ and 5′ (or **0.5** m and **2.5** m) and the color of the triangles to yellow.

Solution

1. Select Alignment B, and from the Alignment contextual tab, go to Modify tab ➤ Alignment Properties.

2. On the Information tab, set Alignment Object Style to Layout and click OK. Click Esc to deselect.

3. Select the EG surface, and on the Surface contextual tab, go to Modify tab ➤ Surface Properties.

4. On the Information tab, set Surface Style to Contours And Triangles, and click OK.

5. From the Settings tab of Toolspace, expand Surface ➤ Surface Styles.

6. Right-click Contours And Triangles and select Edit.

7. On the Contours tab, do the following:

   a. Expand the Contour Intervals category.

   b. Set the Minor Interval to **1'** (or **0.5 m**).

   Notice that the Major Interval automatically adjusts to 5' (or 2.5 m).

8. On the Display tab with View Direction set to Plan, set the color of the Triangles component to yellow.

9. Click OK to complete the revisions to the style. Click Esc to deselect.

Create a new surface style. Almost every set of plans that you send out of the office is going to include a surface, so it is important to be able to generate multiple surface styles that match your company standards. In addition to surface styles for production, you may find it helpful to have styles to use when you are designing that show a tighter contour spacing as well as the points and triangles needed to make some edits.

Master It Open the `MasterIt_1902.dwg` (`MasterIt_1902_METRIC.dwg`) file and create a new surface style named **Micro Editing**. Set this style to display contours at 0.5' and 1.0' (or 0.1 m and 0.2 m), as well as triangles and points. Set the EG surface to use this new surface style.

Solution

1. From the Settings tab of Toolspace, expand Surface ➤ Surface Styles.

2. Right-click Surface Styles and select New.

3. On the Information tab, set Name to **Micro Editing**.

4. On the Contours tab, do the following:

   a. Expand the Contour Intervals category.

   b. Set the Minor Interval to **0.5'** (or **0.1 m**). Notice that the Major Interval automatically adjusts to 2.5' (or 0.5 m).

   c. Override the Major Interval to **1.0'** (or **0.2 m**).

5. On the Display tab with View Direction set to Plan, verify that the only components turned on are Points, Triangles, Minor Contours, and Major Contours.

6. Click OK to complete creation of a new surface style.

7. Select the EG surface, and from the contextual tab ➤ Modify panel, select Surface Properties.

8. On the Information tab, set Surface Style to Micro Editing, and click OK.

Create a new profile view style. Everyone has their preferred look for a profile view. These styles can provide a lot of information in a small space, so it is important to be able to create a profile view that will meet your needs.

Master It   Open the `MasterIt_1903.dwg` (`MasterIt_1903_METRIC.dwg`) file and create a new profile view style named **Mastering Profile View.** Set this style to not clip the vertical or horizontal grid. Set the bottom horizontal ticks at 50′ and 10′ intervals (25 m and 5 m). Set the left and right vertical ticks at 10′ and 2′ intervals (5 m and 1 m). In addition, turn off the visibility of Graph Title, Bottom Axis Annotation Major, and Bottom Axis Annotation Horizontal Geometry Point. Set the profile view in the drawing to use this new profile view style.

Solution

1. From the Settings tab of Toolspace, expand Profile View ➢ Profile View Styles.

2. Right-click Profile View Styles and select New.

3. On the Information tab, set Name to **Mastering Profile View**.

4. On the Grid tab, verify that Clip Vertical Grid and Clip Horizontal Grid are not selected.

5. On the Horizontal Axes tab, do the following:

   a. Verify that the Axis To Control radio button is set to Bottom.

   b. In the Major Tick Details area, set Interval to **50′** (or **25** m).

   c. In the Minor Tick Details area, set Interval to **10′** (or **5** m).

6. On the Vertical Axes tab, do the following:

   a. Verify that the Axis To Control radio button is set to Left.

   b. In the Major Tick Details area, set Interval to **10′** (or **5** m).

   c. In the Minor Tick Details area, set Interval to **2′** (or **1** m).

   d. Change the Axis To Control radio button to Right.

   e. In the Major Tick Details area, set Interval to **10′** (or **5** m).

   f. In the Minor Tick Details area, set Interval to **2′** (or **1** m).

7. On the Display tab with View Direction set to Plan, turn off the visibility of Graph Title, Bottom Axis Annotation Major, and Bottom Axis Annotation Horizontal Geometry Point.

8. Click OK to complete creation of a new Profile View style.

9. Select the profile view in the drawing, and on the Profile View contextual tab, go to Modify View panel and select Profile View Properties.

10. On the Information tab, set Object Style to Mastering Profile View, and click OK.

Appendix B

Certification

Autodesk certifications are industry-recognized credentials that can help you succeed in your design career, providing benefits to both you and your employer. Getting certified is a reliable validation of skills and knowledge, and it can lead to accelerated professional development, improved productivity, and enhanced credibility.

This Autodesk Official Training Guide can be an effective component of your exam preparation. Autodesk highly recommends (and we agree!) that you schedule regular time to prepare, review the most current exam preparation roadmap and objectives available at www.autodesk.com/certification, use Autodesk Official Training Guides, take a class at an Authorized Training Center (find ATCs near you here: www.autodesk.com/atc), and use a variety of resources to prepare for your certification—including plenty of actual hands-on experience.

Certification Objective

To help you focus your studies on the skills you'll need for these exams, Table B.1 shows the objectives that could potentially appear on an exam and in what chapter you can find information on that topic—and when you go to that chapter, you'll find certification icons like the one in the margin here. The topics and exam objectives listed in the table are from the Autodesk Certification Exam Guide.

TABLE B.1: Certified Professional Exam sections and objectives

TOPIC	LEARNING OBJECTIVE	CHAPTER
User Interface	Navigate the user interface.	1
	Use the functions on the Prospector tab.	1
	Use the functions on the Settings tab.	1
Styles	Create and use object styles.	19
	Create and use label styles.	18
Lines and Curves	Use the Line and Curve commands.	1
	Use the Transparent command.	1
Points	Create points using the Point Creation command.	3
	Create points by importing point data.	3
	Use point groups to control the display of points.	3

TABLE B.1:   Certified Professional Exam sections and objectives   *(continued)*

TOPIC	LEARNING OBJECTIVE	CHAPTER
Surfaces	Create and edit surfaces.	4
	Use styles and settings to display surface information.	4 and 14
	Create a surface by assembling fundamental data.	4
	Use styles to analyze surface display results.	4
Parcels	Create parcels using the parcel layout tools.	5
	Design a parcel layout.	5
	Select parcel styles to change the display of parcels.	5
	Select styles to annotate parcels.	5
Alignments	Create alignments.	6
	Design a geometric layout.	6
Profiles and Profile Views	Create a surface profile.	7
	Design a profile.	7
	Create a layout profile.	7
	Create a profile view style.	19
	Create a profile view.	7
Corridors	Design and create a corridor.	9
	Derive information and data from a corridor.	9
	Design and create an intersection.	10
Sections and Section Views	Create and analyze sections and section views.	12
Pipe Networks	Design and create a pipe network.	13
Grading	Design and create a grading model.	14
	Create a grading model feature line.	14
Managing and Sharing Data	Use data shortcuts to share/manage data.	16

TOPIC	LEARNING OBJECTIVE	CHAPTER
	Create a data sharing setup.	16
Plan Production	Generate a sheet set using plan production.	15
	Create a sheet set.	15
Survey	Use description keys to control the display of points created from survey data.	2
	Use figure prefixes to control the display of linework generated from survey data.	2
	Create a boundary drawing from field data.	2

These Autodesk certification exam objectives were accurate at press time; to find the latest information about the exam and what is covered, go to www.autodesk.com/certification. Good luck preparing for your certification!

Index